LEGAL REASONING, WRITING, AND OTHER LAWYERING SKILLS

LEGAL REASONING, WRITING, AND OTHER LAWYERING SKILLS

FOURTH EDITION

Robin Wellford Slocum

Chapman University
Fowler School of Law (retired)

Gina Nerger

Director of Legal Writing
Professor of Legal Writing
University of Tulsa College of Law

CAROLINA ACADEMIC PRESS
Durham, North Carolina

Library of Congress Cataloging-in-Publication Data

Names: Slocum, Robin Wellford, author. | Nerger, Gina, author.
Title: Legal Reasoning, Writing, and Other Lawyering Skills / Robin Wellford Slocum,
    Gina Nerger.
Description: Fourth edition. | Durham, North Carolina : Carolina Academic
    Press, LLC, 2022. | Includes index.
Identifiers: LCCN 2021059844 (print) | LCCN 2021059845 (ebook) | ISBN
    9781531024048 (paperback) | ISBN 9781531024055 (ebook)
Subjects: LCSH: Legal composition. | Law--United States--Methodology.
Classification: LCC KF250 .S568 2022 (print) | LCC KF250 (ebook) | DDC
    808/.06634--dc23/eng/20220202
LC record available at https://lccn.loc.gov/2021059844
LC ebook record available at https://lccn.loc.gov/2021059845

Carolina Academic Press
700 Kent Street
Durham, North Carolina 27701
(919) 489-7486
www.cap-press.com

CONTENTS

PREFACE

Evaluating a client's legal problem and communicating that analysis to the client is the cornerstone of any lawyer's practice. However, this fundamental role requires that you be proficient in a number of different roles—that of investigator (eliciting the relevant facts that give rise to a legal issue and researching the relevant law), advisor (assessing how the law impacts your clients, and advising them of their legal rights and obligations), and advocate (advocating for your clients' interests). Day in and day out, in every field of law, you will have the opportunity to practice and master these skills. *Legal Reasoning, Writing, and Other Lawyering Skills* is designed to help you develop these fundamental lawyering skills.

Legal writing is challenging, in part, because the clarity and effectiveness of the final product depends on the clarity of the underlying legal reasoning. Thus, this book teaches and illustrates the underlying skills of legal reasoning and analysis that are integral components of effective legal writing. The forms of written communication in legal writing are also new and challenging. In fact, even though you have been writing most of your life, the legal writing terrain is deceptively challenging for that very reason. To become a skilled legal writer, you must be willing to abandon writing techniques that have worked well in other disciplines, and be open to learning new ways of expressing yourself. Therefore, this book is also designed to help you become a skilled writer by teaching and illustrating effective templates for written legal analysis and argument. It is our hope that you will not only find this book to be a valuable learning guide during law school, but that it will also serve as a useful resource to you as you begin practicing law.

Like learning to play a musical instrument, you will become expert at legal writing by practicing—the more you practice, the more accomplished you will become. To help you learn and then master the skills of legal reasoning and writing, this book emphasizes the process of legal reasoning and writing, from the reading and thinking stages, through the outlining and drafting stages, to the final written product itself. Taking the musical analogy a step further, no one would expect a novice musician to master Beethoven's Ninth Symphony without first having practiced and mastered more basic musical scores. Similarly, law students learn legal writing most easily by first mastering basic skills, and then building gradually towards mastery of more complex skills. Therefore, the chapters incorporate a building block approach, demonstrating how to evaluate a single case before evaluating how to synthesize a group of cases, and how to draft a simple memo based on one case before drafting a more complex memo based on multiple cases.

Because illustrations are a critically important component of the learning process, this book liberally illustrates every step of the process, from reading a case, to evaluating how a case affects a client's problem, to synthesizing a group of cases, to outlining a template for your written product, to the drafting process itself. Comments are inserted alongside each illustration to help you understand the reasoning, logic, and drafting decisions that underlie each part of the illustration. To help you evaluate the illustrations at a deeply comprehensive level, the book uses several repeating hypothetical problems to illustrate each pre-drafting and drafting step. These illustrations are also linked to the sample office memos and court briefs illustrated in the Appendices. Thus, you will have the opportunity not just to review sample documents, but to study the underlying analysis, logic, and choices that influence drafting decisions in the final products.

ACKNOWLEDGMENTS

Robin Wellford Slocum:

I would like to thank my students at both Washington University and Chapman University, the Fowler School of Law, without whom this book would not have been possible. Their questions, challenges, and breakthroughs inspired me to try new approaches, and pushed me to grow as a teacher. I am also grateful to so many colleagues at both schools who were the source of ideas and who provided me with support, suggestions, and helpful feedback throughout my time at both schools. I am grateful, as well, to have been part of the national legal writing community for many years—a community of creative, inspiring teachers who so generously shared their innovative ideas and expertise, as well as their support and friendship. Ideas from this collective community of educators have inspired teaching approaches, exercises, and ideas that appear in this book. Finally, I am so grateful to Gina Nerger, co-author of this fourth edition, who came to this project with such vision and ideas for making this book better, and whose positive energy and tireless work ethic made this new edition even better than I could have imagined. It has been a rich, exciting collaboration.

Gina Nerger:

I would like to thank my family for their support and encouragement through the drafting and editing of this book. Their support and love have meant the world. I would also like to thank my supportive colleagues at The University of Tulsa College of Law. They have always believed in me and never set limits on what they believed I could achieve. Thank you, also, to my students. It is through working with you, and learning from you, that I was able to contribute to this text. The relationships formed, and watching you grow and succeed, are what have kept me inspired and excited as an educator.

I would like to thank my mentor, colleague, and friend, the late Professor Evelyn Hutchison, for all she taught me while we worked together at TU Law. Not only did she guide the way in the foundations of legal writing teaching, but she showed me the grace and patience required for success in this field. Without her, my contributions to this text would not have been possible. She continually built me up with her words of affirmation and encouraged me to reach for more. Finally, thank you to my mom, the late Nancy Gates, for being my cheerleader and setting me up for success. I owe it all to you.

LEGAL REASONING, WRITING, AND OTHER LAWYERING SKILLS

INTRODUCTION TO LEGAL WRITING & OTHER LAWYERING SKILLS

The skills of evaluating and solving client legal problems, and communicating that analysis in writing, are the cornerstones of a lawyer's practice. This book describes and illustrates the basic lawyering skills that will help you advise prospective clients of their legal rights and duties and advocate your clients' interests.

I. THE LAWYER'S DIFFERENT ROLES

A. The Role of an Investigator

Before you can begin to advise a client or persuade another lawyer or a judge, you first have to discover why the client is seeking your advice, and then conduct some research to help you understand how the law affects the client's factual situation. Discovering the relevant facts and arriving at a solid understanding of the law is challenging, and, as a novice learning new skills, you will undoubtedly make mistakes and may at times even be frustrated by how challenging it can be to master these skills. Although there are no easy shortcuts, be assured that mistakes are a normal part of the learning process; you will have plenty of opportunities to learn from your mistakes and to hone these skills, not simply in this course but throughout your law school career. Chapter 5 discusses your role as an investigator interviewing clients and discovering "what happened." More generally, Chapters 4 through 8 and Chapter 12 discuss the basic skills involved in evaluating the law and determining how the law affects your clients' legal problems.

B. The Role of an Advisor

1. Nature of This Role

Lawyers are often depicted in the media as modern-day gladiators who fight in the contemporary battlefield of the courtroom. It might surprise you to know, however, that litigation is only one of many specialty areas in which lawyers practice. Many lawyers never become litigators and never enter a courtroom, and even those lawyers who choose to be courtroom advocates also wear a different hat altogether—that of an advisor to their clients.

What does it mean to be a legal advisor? Think back to a time in which you asked someone for an important piece of advice—advice that had serious consequences, with advantages and disadvantages related to each of the different directions you might take (perhaps the decision to attend law school was such a time). When you have brought a scenario to mind, ask yourself what you really wanted from your trusted friend or family member. Did you want that person to persuade you to select a particular choice by emphasizing all of the reasons he or she thought it would be such a great choice, while ignoring the risks and downsides to that choice? Or did you want that person to ask probing questions that would help you clarify your thinking, and to offer a candid assessment of the risks and the attendant benefits of each possible course of action?

Most people facing significant decisions want the latter. They don't want to be sold a sanitized version of the truth, but would rather know going into a situation what risks they face so that they can carefully decide whether the benefits outweigh the risks. As a lawyer, this is perhaps your most significant role—to serve as a wise advisor to your clients. In your role as an advisor, you will not only advise your clients about what the law permits them to do, but you will also help them weigh the legal risks involved in pursuing various courses of actions and help your clients come to a decision that will ultimately serve their best interests.

As you might imagine, your role as an advisor will often require diplomacy and tact. On the one hand, you have a responsibility to be candid with your clients. On the other hand, you must also maintain your client morale and the rapport that is a necessary component of the attorney-client relationship. When clients hire you to represent them, their concerns may range from questions about embarking on a corporate merger to requests to represent them in what might be an emotionally difficult lawsuit. Whatever the nature of their request and however much they would like for you to give them your blessing to embark on a proposed course of action, your role as an advisor requires that you be honest with them, even if your response isn't something they necessarily want to hear.[1] That means that you must use your best judgment in

---

[1]. The Model Rules of Professional Conduct, adopted in many states, require lawyers to "render candid advice" to their clients. Model R. Prof. Conduct 2.1 (ABA 2002). In a comment describing the meaning of this rule, the drafters of the rule state: "a lawyer shall not be deterred from giving candid advice by the prospect that the advice will be unpalatable to the client." *Id.* at 2.1, cmt. 1.

interpreting what the law means and how it affects a client's situation, considering not only how the law might favor your client's position, but also how ambiguities in the law might present risks for your client.

2. Types of Communication

As a lawyer, you will often advise your clients of the results of your research verbally, in a telephone call or meeting. You will also put much of your analysis into written form, either in addition to or in lieu of such meetings. By reducing your analysis to written form, you will not only be able to clarify for your colleagues and clients the results of your research and analysis, but you will also be able to preserve your thinking and research results for future reference. In your role as an advisor, you can expect to draft documents that include (1) somewhat formal, relatively lengthy legal memoranda that are viewed only by other members of your legal team; (2) short legal memoranda that provide a succinct summary of your legal analysis; (3) e-mail communications; and (4) client letters.

In recent years, due to rising legal costs and the economy, short memos, letters, and e-mail communications have become the norm, while longer, more formal memoranda tend to be used more infrequently. As a lawyer, you might expect to draft relatively lengthy, more formal memos for clients in which there is a significant amount of money at stake, while using a more succinct written form of communication for more simplistic legal issues. You might also be asked to draft more formal legal memoranda as a summer law clerk—this is one way in which some law firms evaluate the legal skills of their summer law clerks and determine whether to hire them as lawyers after graduation.

Given the norm for short memos and e-mail communications, it would be reasonable to assume that this course might focus to a greater degree on short documents and only cover the longer, more formal memoranda peripherally, if at all. However, perhaps counter-intuitively, drafting a succinct, short memo requires greater expertise than drafting a longer, more formal legal memorandum. This is because short memos must not only be succinct, but also thorough, covering all of the important bases. To illustrate the difference between a "short" memo and a "succinct" memo, consider the following hypothetical law school class. If I were to offer a *short* lecture to my class, I might say "Good morning class. Have a great day. Goodbye." In contrast, if I were to offer a *succinct* lecture, I might cover five or six different principles, with examples, within a half hour time period—thorough, but concise.[2]

The succinct but thorough analysis requires a level of expertise that, as a novice legal writer, you will not possess when you begin this course. This ability to "thin-

---

2. Analogy borrowed from Anthony G. Volini, Legal Writing Instructor, DePaul University College of Law.

slice"[3] your analysis by assessing what it is most important and what can be omitted is an ability that you will develop and hone throughout law school. Paradoxically, as you learn to draft a more formal, longer office memorandum, the fundamental skills you develop in the process will serve as essential stepping-stones for you to write shorter, more succinct memos. Because the more formal office memorandum serves as a foundation upon which so many legal skills can build, it is discussed in depth in Chapters 9–18 of this book.

This book also describes and illustrates the other common forms of written communication you will routinely draft as a lawyer. Chapter 19 describes short memos, Chapter 20 discusses professional e-mail communications, and Chapter 21 discusses client letters. In this course, you may or may not be asked to draft these common types of documents. Whether or not you draft short documents in this course, the basic skills you will learn while drafting a longer office memorandum will provide you with skills for drafting shorter memos as well. In other words, the skills you will learn are transferable to shorter memo-writing.

C. The Role of an Advocate

The other role you will assume when you practice law is the role of an advocate. You might be surprised to learn that you will assume the role of an advocate for your future clients even if you never step foot in a courtroom. For example, assume you choose to specialize in the field of real estate law. As a real estate lawyer negotiating the terms of a favorable lease agreement for a client, you will assume the role of an advocate as you argue why your client is entitled to favorable terms. As a tax lawyer, you might advocate for your clients' interests when seeking a favorable outcome from the Internal Revenue Service. Or, as a copyright lawyer, you would undoubtedly not only help your clients gain the protection of a copyright, but assume an advocacy role should a competitor attempt to infringe on your client's copyright.

In your role as an advisor to your clients, you will also reduce your persuasive arguments into written form. These written arguments are often included in letters to opposing counsel, and in documents submitted to judges and to other adjudicators. Chapters 23–30 describe the basic persuasive argument strategies and constructs that are commonly used in all arguments, irrespective of the forum. Because lawyers commonly submit arguments to courts, and because such arguments are an effective vehicle for you to learn basic persuasive skills, Chapters 31–35 describe the particular nuances of drafting arguments to trial and appellate courts. Chapter 36 discusses how to engage in an oral argument before a court. Not surprisingly, lawyers also communicate with opposing counsel in writing. Chapter 37 discusses the special considerations involved in drafting demand and settlement letters to opposing counsel.

---

3. "Thin-slice" is a term used by Malcolm Gladwell in the book *Blink*, in which he uses psychology and behavioral economics to explain how experts solve problems. Malcolm Gladwell, *Blink* (Little, Brown & Co. 2005).

D. A Suggestion

As you may have guessed by now, the process of analyzing a legal problem and conveying that analysis to a client or colleague likely differs from anything you have ever experienced before. Legal analysis and writing differ from the writing you performed as an undergraduate and differs from the narrative writing to which you are exposed when reading a novel or the newspaper. If you try to cling to the writing practices that have worked so well for you in other disciplines, you will likely experience some difficulty and frustration when learning these new skills. Instead, this book invites you to suspend all judgment of what has worked for you in the past, and stay open to learning new analytical skills and new ways of communicating information.

II. THE CLIENT

After just the first week or two of law school, you might understandably begin to think that your professional career has everything to do with "thinking like a lawyer," and very little to do with human interaction. In reality, for most of you, much of your legal career will be spent counseling clients and helping them negotiate deals and resolve legal disputes. As you consider your role as a lawyer, it's important to consider your future clients—who they are and their expectations of you as their lawyer.

As you read cases in law school and consider hypothetical client problems, it is all too easy to begin to think of clients as "uni-dimensional"—abstract people who exist only on paper and whose real lives have nothing to do with the legal issues you are evaluating. In reality, life just isn't that neat. Your working relationship with your clients, and the legal advice you give them, will unquestionably impact other aspects of their lives as well. Whatever their reasons for seeking your legal counsel, and however successful you might be in achieving your clients' goals, your clients' legal questions also have non-legal consequences. The legal course of action your clients ultimately decide to take might affect the quality of their business or personal relationships, their emotional and psychological well-being, and even raise morality issues for them (or you). Even the money they spend to pay your legal fees may affect the quality of their lives—perhaps their ability to purchase a home, or send a child to college, or take a desired vacation. For better or worse, you will impact real human beings in your capacity as a lawyer, and your impact will extend beyond the quality of the legal advice you give them.

You might be wondering why you are being asked to think about future clients who are, for now at least, only hypothetical characters. There are a number of reasons why it would be valuable for you to flesh out the uni-dimensional characters in your fact patterns into multi-dimensional people. Appreciating your "clients" and the other "people" in your fact patterns as multi-dimensional people will help you overcome the tendency to evaluate legal problems in polarities of good/bad, right/wrong, and yes/no. Thinking in polarities is a common problem most students experience when they enter law school—they tend to see the law either as entirely favoring the client's interests or entirely disfavoring the client's interests. Usually, however, such an analysis of the law is myopic and unrealistic, limiting students in their ability to be effective legal advisors to their clients. By learning to appreciate that people (and their behavior) are more complex than your first impression might lead you to believe, you will begin to develop perspective and an awareness of the many shades of gray that color many legal problems. Developing perspective is a quintessential lawyering skill that is an important part of your legal education.

Your ability to understand your clients and what they want from you will help you in other ways as well. Understanding your clients, including the underlying dynamics of why your clients are motivated to pursue certain legal strategies, will help you establish rapport and trust, making it easier for you to elicit the relevant facts from your clients, and to advise and counsel them. Equally as important, paying attention to the underlying motivations, interests, and needs of the people in your fact patterns will help you develop emotional intelligence — an intelligence that will help you distinguish between legal options and arguments that are legitimate and persuasive, and those that just aren't very viable or realistic.[4] This course provides an excellent forum for you to develop these skills that will later become important for you as a practicing lawyer.

Exercise 1-1: Your Role with Future Clients

Before you begin to consider hypothetical fact patterns and provide written advice to "clients" in this course, this exercise provides you with a starting point to help you develop judgment and perspective. This exercise asks you to consider the emotional reactions your clients might have to specific legal situations, as well as possible emotional, psychological, and monetary concerns your clients might have. Although you may find it challenging to think in these terms, it is well worth your time and effort to develop this ability. The ability to understand what might be happening beneath the surface of your clients' legal concerns will help you become a more effective advisor to your clients (and a more effective advocate as well, because this skill will also help you predict how your arguments might impact others).

These exercises also ask you to consider the emotional responses and judgments that *you* might have that might impair your ability to be an effective advisor or advocate for a client. As Chapter 4 explores in greater detail, whether you are consciously aware of them or not, your emotions, judgments, and biases affect your perspec-

---

4. "Emotional intelligence" has been defined as a cluster of traits that not only help us communicate and work effectively with other people, but also help us foresee how others might respond to persuasive arguments. In a number of studies, emotional intelligence has been found to be the most important factor in measuring effectiveness in the workplace—more important than either I.Q. or expertise. *See* Daniel Goleman, *Working with Emotional Intelligence* 31 (2006).

tive—they can sabotage both your efforts to elicit an accurate portrayal of "what happened" and your efforts to be an effective advocate for your client. However, knowledge is power. By becoming more explicitly aware of your own emotions, judgments, and biases you can overcome some of the insidious ways in which they can hijack your efforts to be logical and realistic in your assessment of a legal situation.

Finally, these exercises ask you to think about your own values and moral code and how that might affect your representation of some clients. As you begin your law school career, this is a good time to consider the kind of lawyer you aspire to be—not necessarily in the sense of the area of law in which you might specialize, but the person you would like to be as you advise and counsel your future clients, and advocate for their interests. There will almost certainly be times when the course of action a client wants to take will violate your own ethical or moral code, whether or not that conduct is actually illegal. This exercise asks you to begin to appreciate the challenge of such dilemmas and to think about possible ways in which you can be both an effective lawyer for your clients and in alignment with your own values and moral code.

1. You are a public defender who has been asked to represent a 19-year-old man who has been charged with homicide. Your client was driving a car while intoxicated and ran a red light, killing a 5-year-old girl who was lawfully walking across the crosswalk at the time. Your client has previously been convicted of driving while intoxicated, and at the time of the accident was driving with a suspended license.
   a. What emotional response do you have to the accident itself? To your new client?
   b. What emotions might your client be experiencing as a result of this incident and his impending trial?
   c. What might your client want and need from you during this representation? (Consider possible psychological, emotional, and monetary concerns as well as his legal concerns.)
   d. What biases, judgments, or concerns do you have that might affect your ability to represent this client as effectively and fairly as you might like?
   e. What steps could you take to minimize the negative effects of any biases, judgments, or concerns you might have?

2. You represent a college friend who is going through a bitter divorce. You suspect that your client is hiding assets from his wife, but you are not 100% certain that he is doing so. Your client wants you to negotiate a favorable settlement agreement on his behalf.
   a. What emotional response do you have about your suspicions and your continuing representation of your friend? About your client?
   b. How might the dual-nature of your relationship with this client (client as well as friend) affect your judgment as his lawyer?
   c. What emotions might your client be experiencing about this legal situation?

    d. What might your client want and need from you during this representation? (Consider possible psychological, emotional, and monetary concerns as well as his legal concerns.)

    e. What biases, judgments, or concerns do you have that might affect your ability to represent this client as effectively and/or fairly as you might like?

    f. Given the possibility that your client is hiding money, what do you think you *should* do in this situation? If different, what do you think you *would* do?

3. You represent two illegal immigrants who were apprehended by members of a private paramilitary organization as they were trying to enter the country illegally. The mission of the paramilitary group is to prevent immigrants from illegally crossing the border from Mexico, using whatever means necessary. Members of this group pistol-whipped and threatened your clients as they attempted to enter the United States, and your clients feared they would be killed. Your clients want you to file a lawsuit on their behalf, stating that they suffer from post-traumatic stress resulting from the ordeal.

    a. What emotional response do you have to the depiction of what happened? To your clients?

    b. What emotions might your clients be experiencing about this situation?

    c. What might your clients want and need from you during this representation? (Consider possible psychological, emotional, and monetary concerns as well as their legal concerns.)

    d. What biases, judgments, or concerns do you have that might affect your ability to represent these clients as effectively and/or fairly as you might like?

    e. What steps could you take to minimize the negative effects of any biases, judgments, or concerns you might have?

4. You represent a privately-held corporation and are performing the legal work necessary to transition the company to go public. The CEO is a hard-driving workaholic who routinely works 80-hour workweeks; she accepts no excuses for work that does not satisfy her exacting standards. The CEO has expressed to you that the public stock offering you are working on is the most important challenge of her 30-year career with the company.

    a. What emotional response do you have to working with this client?

    b. What emotions might the CEO be experiencing about offering her company to the public?

    c. What might your client want and need from you during this representation? (Consider possible psychological, emotional, and monetary concerns as well as legal concerns.)

    d. What biases, judgments, or concerns do you have that might affect your ability to represent this client as effectively and/or fairly as you might like?

    e. What steps could you take to minimize the negative effects of any biases, judgments, or concerns you might have?

III. EMPLOYERS' EXPECTATIONS

You will soon be swept up in the law school experience and all of the attendant excitement and anxiety. Burdened with seemingly limitless demands on your time and faced with the prospect of final exams, it is easy to lose perspective of why you decided to go to law school. However, the following survey conducted by the American Bar Foundation does provide some perspective.

In a survey conducted by the American Bar Foundation, over 100 hiring attorneys were interviewed in the Chicago, Illinois legal market.[5] The hiring partners were asked to identify the skills they demanded that new lawyers bring with them to their firms and/or corporations, and those skills they expected new lawyers to develop "on the job." The survey reflects the reality in today's legal market that most employers expect new law school graduates to begin their new careers already possessing a certain level of competence in the basic legal skills you will learn in this course. As you review the following excerpts from that survey, you may be surprised to see that the fundamental skills you will learn in this course are the top five ranked skills that employers will expect you to know when you walk in the door.

SKILLS	BRING	DEVELOP
Oral communication	91%	9%
Written communication	90	10
Library legal research	92	9
Computer legal research	84	16
Ability in legal analysis and legal reasoning	81	19
Instilling others' confidence in you	52	48
Knowledge of procedural law	28	72
Understanding and conducting litigation	6	94
Negotiation	4	96
Counseling	9	91
Organization and management of legal work	33	67
Sensitivity to professional ethical concerns	74	25
Ability to diagnose and plan solutions for legal problems	41	59
Ability to obtain and keep clients	8	92
Fact gathering	47	53

---

5. Bryant B. Garth & Joanne Martin, *Law Schools and the Construction of Competence*, 43 J. Leg. Educ. 469, 490 (1993).

IV. TIMELINE OF DOCUMENTS LAWYERS ROUTINELY PREPARE

As a lawyer, you will draft office memos, client letters, and letters to other lawyers throughout the entire time you represent a particular client, whether or not any lawsuit has been filed. Even when you represent a client in a lawsuit, you will continue to memorialize the results of your research and analysis by drafting office memos and letters. To help give you some perspective, the flowchart below reflects the documents you can expect to draft on a regular basis while advising clients, beginning with the first meeting with a client and continuing throughout the stages of a lawsuit (if, in fact, a lawsuit ensues). The arrow to the right indicates the documents you will continue to draft throughout your representation of a client, irrespective of the stage or type of representation. You may find the flowchart useful because it will provide you with an underlying context as you are asked to draft documents in this course. In addition, because most of the cases in your casebooks arise from a lawsuit, the flowchart can also provide you with a framework for understanding the procedural context of the cases in your casebooks as well.

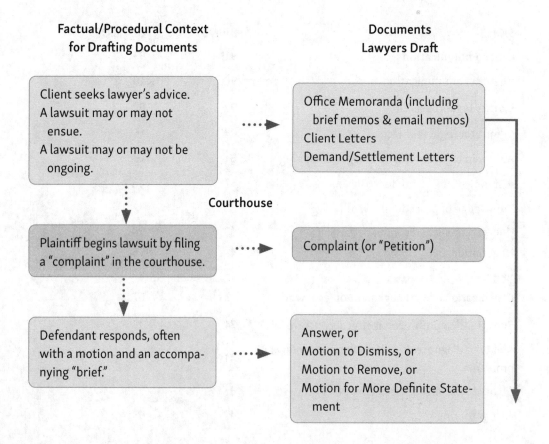

Factual/Procedural Context for Drafting Documents	Documents Lawyers Draft
Client seeks lawyer's advice. A lawsuit may or may not ensue. A lawsuit may or may not be ongoing.	Office Memoranda (including brief memos & email memos) Client Letters Demand/Settlement Letters

Courthouse

Plaintiff begins lawsuit by filing a "complaint" in the courthouse.	Complaint (or "Petition")
Defendant responds, often with a motion and an accompanying "brief."	Answer, or Motion to Dismiss, or Motion to Remove, or Motion for More Definite Statement

**Factual/Procedural Context
for Drafting Documents**

**Documents
Lawyers Draft**

If the lawsuit survives the defendant's motions, the parties engage in "discovery" to obtain information about each other.

$\cdots\blacktriangleright$

Interrogatories
Request for Documents
Request for Admissions
Motion to Compel
Motion for Sanctions

Either party may ask the judge to enter judgment in its favor without going to trial.

$\cdots\blacktriangleright$

Motion for Summary Judgment

During the trial, parties may ask the judge to grant a variety of different requests, or "motions."

$\cdots\blacktriangleright$

Motion to Suppress
Motion in Limine
Motion for Directed Verdict
Bench Briefs
Jury Instructions

After the trial, the losing party may ask the trial court to reverse the verdict and then may file an appeal to a higher court. The winning party responds to the appeal.

$\cdots\blacktriangleright$

Post-Trial Brief
Motion for New Trial
Motion for J.N.O.V.
Appellant's Brief
Appellee's Brief

INTRODUCTION TO
AMERICAN LEGAL SYSTEM

I. INTRODUCTION

You likely have a basic understanding of how our legal system works from current events reported in the news, and perhaps even from a civics course you took in high school or college. At the risk of revisiting material with which you are already familiar, this chapter begins by summarizing some core points about our legal system that will serve as a foundation for your work as a lawyer. The importance of this background information will become clearer to you as the chapter and exercises unfold, when you will be asked to apply your knowledge of our legal system to better understand its specific relevance to you as a lawyer.

A. Two Basic Court Systems

Before you begin reading about the sources of law in our court system, you might find it helpful to have some context that directly applies to your life as a law student. Consider for a moment your decision to attend orientation classes at your new law school. The first decision you had to make when you arrived for orientation (assuming this was your first visit to your new law school) was to make sure you found the right building in your university. Knowing that you were to appear for an orientation meeting in Room 201, for example, wouldn't help you at all if you ended up in the school of arts and sciences instead of the law school building. The law school and school of arts and sciences are two very different schools in two very different buildings—while classes are taught in each building and some of the room numbers might be the same, the classes themselves are different and are centered around two different disciplines.

Similarly, as a law student and ultimately as a lawyer, you will likewise need to identify "where you are" in terms of the legal issues you will be researching and evaluating. There are two basic court systems in our country—federal and state. The federal court system has its own set of laws and courts, and each state also has its own unique set of laws and courts. Like your law school and the school of arts and sciences, both federal and state legal systems operate simultaneously and pretty much independently.

When a client asks you for legal advice, one of the first things you will need to do is figure out which court system and set of laws controls your client's actions. Some conduct is governed solely by the state court legal system, while other conduct is governed solely by the federal court legal system. And there are also some instances in which *both* federal and state laws apply. So, for example, if your client lived in Chicago, Illinois and had a legal issue that arose there, you would first need to consider whether federal laws or Illinois state laws governed the client's conduct—or both. Assuming the legal matter happened to involve litigation, that information would also denote the type of court (Illinois state court or federal court) in which you would file a lawsuit on behalf of the client. As a general rule, federal courts and agencies interpret legal issues that arise from federal law, while state courts resolve legal disputes that arise from state laws.[1]

B. Sources of Law

The laws from both the federal and state legal systems stem from three primary sources: constitutions, statutes, and case law.

1. Constitutions

Both the federal and state governments operate under a set of rules enumerated in a constitution. Constitutions lay out various rights of citizens, and they describe the relationship between the government and its citizens. Although constitutional laws are relatively small in number, they are important because they protect rights that we as a society have found to be of fundamental importance. The right to be free from "unreasonable searches and seizures" is one such important right. As a law student, you will have the opportunity to study cases interpreting the important rights that are embodied in the United States Constitution in a specific class focused on constitutional law. You may also study state constitutional laws within your coursework.

2. Statutes & Administrative Regulations

In both the federal and state legal systems, the legislative branch of government also creates law by enacting statutes that govern the rights and duties of the people who have the requisite minimum contacts within that jurisdiction. Although legislators enact statutes, they also authorize agencies to issue regulations that help interpret

---

1. As you will learn in your civil procedure class, there are a few exceptions. Even though the federal and state court systems are separate legal systems, federal courts, in limited circumstances, sometimes hear disputes that arise from state laws. Similarly, state courts sometimes consider federal laws, assuming certain jurisdictional issues are satisfied.

and clarify what a statute means. For example, you might be familiar with Title VII, a statute that makes it illegal for employers to discriminate against their employees on the basis of their race, color, religion, gender, or place of birth. Congress also gave a federal agency the authority to implement regulations and guidelines that help interpret Title VII and give it practical effect—the Equal Employment Opportunity Commission (EEOC).

3. Case Law

Some laws are derived from court decisions, and we call this "case law." There are two types of case law: (1) interpretive law and (2) common law. Interpretive case law is formed when judges interpret enacted law, such as statutes. For example, you read above that Title VII is a statute that prohibits workplace discrimination on the basis of protected classifications, including religion. Congress did not define the word "religion" or provide any specific guidance within its statutory language on the types of beliefs that qualify as religious. Thus, courts have interpreted the term "religion" within case law, providing more specific instruction on what Congress *intended* the word to mean. For example, the United States Court of Appeals for the Fifth Circuit has held that "religion," as it pertains to Title VII, encompasses a belief that is "'sincere and meaningful ... which occupies in the life of its possessor a place parallel to that filled by ... God.'"[2] This definition provides a clear example of interpretive case law.

In addition, case law may take the form of "common law," which is law derived completely from court decisions. It is created when a controversy arises and there is an absence of statutory or other law on the matter. In that situation, the court itself must create a set of rules to fairly resolve the dispute.

The common law originated in England, and it is interesting to think of how it has evolved over time. In earlier times, judges started from a few basic ideas that seemed to be universally accepted in medieval society. As new factual controversies arose, the judges expanded on and refined their interpretations of the common law by focusing on the similarities to and distinctions from previous cases. Although the common law emerged from England, it was brought to the United States by British colonists, eventually becoming each state's original body of law.[3] Today, although statutes have replaced a fair amount of the common law, the common law still exists. As importantly, the common law method of reasoning by analogy is still the primary means by which lawyers evaluate cases and predict what the law might say about their clients' conduct.

---

2. *Davis v. Fort Bend Cnty.*, 765 F.3d 480, 485 (5th Cir. 2014) (quoting *United States v. Seeger*, 380 U.S. 163, 176 (1965)).

3. Richard K. Neumann, Jr., *Legal Reasoning and Legal Writing: Structure, Strategy, and Style* 5 (4th ed. Aspen L. & Bus. 2001).

Exercise 2-1: Nature of the Law

Now that you have read about the sources of law, review the following exercise and consider what the "law" is and whether the absence of a written law necessarily means that a law does not exist.

Sometime in the future, as a result of a major catastrophe, life as we know it no longer exists.[4] A group of survivors congregated and formed a new society, Gilligan's Island. During one of the many social gatherings on the island, the Skipper became enamored with Ginger, an attractive young woman who had captured the interest of a number of men, including the Professor. In fact, Ginger and the Professor had been romantically involved for a period of months, and the Professor was hopelessly in love with her. However, Ginger encouraged the attention of both the Skipper and the Professor. During one particularly heated confrontation over which man was more deserving of Ginger's affection, the Professor became enraged and struck the Skipper over the head with a shovel, killing him.

The group of survivors quickly elected you as judge and directed you to empanel a group of citizens to try the Professor for killing the Skipper. During his trial, the Professor admitted that he killed the Skipper, but claimed that he had broken no law because the island does not have a law that forbids killing.

As the judge in the *Professor's* case, you clearly have been delegated the power to hear the case, i.e., you have jurisdiction. However, before you can proceed with the Professor's trial, you must decide if killing someone is against the law on the island. Deciding whether killing is against the law on the island requires you to think about the question of what "law" is.

Does law consist only of positive, affirmative declarations? That is, must someone with recognized authority enact a rule in order for there to be a law that can be enforced? If that definition of law is too narrow, from where else might "law" be derived? From religious doctrine? From societal values? From natural law?

In our legal system, the judge typically decides what the "law" is. As judge, what is your decision in the *Professor's* case? What value judgments does your decision embody?

If you believe that you should penalize the Professor for killing the Skipper, what are the limits of this approach? Would you reach the same result if the Professor had only injured the Skipper rather than killed him? What if the injury was merely a bruised rib cage from which the Skipper fully recovered? If you would rule differently under these facts, why?

---

4. The ideas for Exercises 2-1, 2-2, and 2-3 were inspired by James E. Moliterno & Fredric I. Lederer, *An Introduction to Law, Law Study, and the Lawyer's Role*, Ch. 3 (1991).

C. How the Branches of Government Work Together

Although each source of law stands on its own, there is also significant interplay between the three branches of government. Because constitutions and statutes are generally future-oriented, they are written in broad, general terms that embrace a wide range of future conduct that might fall within their ambit. Inevitably, when the broad language of a statute or constitution is applied to a specific factual situation, questions arise. Does this specific conduct fall within the ambit of that law? Is this particular individual the type of person the legislature intended to cover? As these questions arise in individual cases, judges are required to interpret the meaning of specific statutes and constitutions. By giving texture and additional substance to the law, judges play an active role in the evolving interpretation of what a law means, even when the law itself is based on a statute or constitution. This is embodied within interpretive case law, as discussed earlier in the chapter.

Sometimes when a judge interprets a statute, the legislature disagrees with how the court interpreted the statute's language. When that happens, the legislature might amend the statutory language to clarify its meaning. In the process, the new legislation invalidates earlier court decisions that interpreted the statute in a different manner. For example, in 1991, Congress amended the Civil Rights Act of 1964 so as to nullify a series of Supreme Court cases that interpreted the Civil Rights Act in a manner with which Congress disagreed.

The process sometimes works the other way as well. When the legislature passes a statute, it must pass constitutional muster—a judge can invalidate a statute if the judge concludes that it violates either the relevant state's or United States constitution. For example, in the landmark civil rights case of *Brown v. Board of Education*, the United States Supreme Court invalidated a Kansas statute that permitted the segregation of public schools, holding that the state-sanctioned segregation violated the 14th Amendment to the Constitution. Thus, the judiciary's role in deciding whether a statute is unconstitutional provides another important interplay between the branches of government.

Exercise 2-2: Nature of the Law

Consider again the Gilligan's Island scenario. Assume that, following your ruling in the *Professor's* case, the new society realized that it should enact some laws that embody the values of the people. The citizens elected a twenty-person legislative body and authorized that representative group to adopt any laws they believe to be fair and just. The legislative body quickly and without debate enacted the following statute:

> Any person who kills another person shall be guilty of murder and shall be sentenced to death or life in prison.

Some months later, Mr. Thurston Howell, III injured his back while helping to build a new community center. To help relieve the pain, Mr. Howell took a powerful herbal pain reliever before going to sleep. The herbs not only help relieve Mr. Howell's pain and allow him to sleep, but make his dreams unusually vivid. During that particular night, Mr. Howell dreamt that he was being attacked by a lion. While still asleep, Mr. Howell believed that he was subduing the lion that was attacking him. In reality, Mr. Howell suffocated Mrs. Howell with a pillow, killing her.

You are the duly elected judge on the island. The island constable arrested Mr. Howell and brought him before you for trial on murder charges. Mr. Howell admitted he killed Mrs. Howell, but claimed that the killing was not against the law because it was an accident and he certainly did not intend to kill his wife.

As the judge, you must decide what the statute means. When interpreting a statute, judges typically begin by reading the statutory language to identify its plain meaning. When the language is ambiguous or when the plain meaning would lead to an absurd or unreasonable result, judges sometimes go beyond the literal language of the statute and look for legislative intent by examining the statute's legislative history. Here, however, there is no legislative history, as the legislative body passed the statute quickly and without debate.

What is your decision in *Howell's* case? Should you apply the plain meaning of the statute and find Mr. Howell guilty of murder? Or should you go beyond the plain meaning and conclude that the legislatively body surely would have exempted killing under these circumstances had they thought of it? What arguments support your decision?

Before reading any further, take a moment and consider the potential problems with the decision you just reached—what undesirable consequences could result from that decision?

D. Our System of Stare Decisis

By now, you have identified a conundrum that judges sometimes face when interpreting the law. On the one hand, judges want to impose rulings that are fair and seem to further the legislative intent or policy concerns underlying the law. On the other hand, our legal system is premised on the idea that there be predictability and consistency in how our laws are interpreted. It would be difficult for us, as citizens, to know what behavior is lawful unless we know what the law means and can trust that it will be interpreted consistently in the future. Therefore, judges look to the decisions of prior courts for guidance in interpreting the law. This process of judicial interpretation is known as *stare decisis*—a Latin phrase meaning that courts should stand by earlier legal decisions ("precedent") and interpret the law in the same way as earlier courts have done.

Exercise 2-3: Nature of the Law

Consider again the Gilligan's Island scenario. Whatever your actual decision in Exercise 2-2, assume for present purposes that the judge in *Howell's* case decided to apply probable legislative intent rather than the plain meaning of the statute. Therefore, the judge instructed the jury, in the form of a written decision, that "*the crime of murder requires the intent to kill.*" After deliberating, the jury acquitted Mr. Howell, finding that he did not possess the intent to kill Mrs. Howell. Some members of the legislative body vocally criticized the judge for "creating" law in this manner, arguing that only the legislative body should have the ability to create law. Despite such criticism, the legislative body did not change the statute. Now assume that the judge retired, and the legislative body selected you as the new judge.

Six months later, another killing occurred. After drinking seven margaritas and becoming drunk, Marianne got into a heated argument with Ginger. Although the two women were friends, they had a contentious history between them and were known to quarrel. In the heat of the argument, Marianne became so enraged that she pulled out a small, snub-nosed pistol and began waving it around. During her drunken rambling, Marianne pulled the trigger and shot Ginger in the chest, killing her. Marianne was so intoxicated that she could not walk and had to be carried away to the local jailhouse. The next morning when Marianne awoke, she experienced a blackout from the previous evening. Marianne didn't recall anything about her argument with Ginger, nor did she recall shooting Ginger or killing her. Marianne has expressed horror that she could have done such a thing, and claims that she would never knowingly have shot her dear friend.

The constable arrested Marianne and, because you are the new judge, the constable brought her before you for trial on murder charges. Marianne claims that the killing was not against the law. Marianne argues that she was so intoxicated that she didn't know what she was doing and could not therefore have possessed the "intent" to kill Ginger.

As the new judge, you must first decide whether to recognize the former judge's decision that the "crime of murder requires the intent to kill." Assume that the Anglo-American system of *stare decisis* applies. As the new judge, would you, or should you, follow the retired judge's interpretation of the statute?

Assume you decide that your decision should be consistent with *Howell* and that you therefore adopt the same interpretation of the law as the judge in the *Howell* case—that the crime of murder requires the intent to kill. You are now faced with an additional question as you apply the legal definition of murder to the facts of *Marianne's* case. Are the facts in *Marianne's* case close enough to the facts of *Howell* as to require the same result (to acquit Marianne of the charge of murder)? Or are the facts different enough to reach a different decision than the judge in *Howell's* case? What is your decision in *Marianne's* case?

II. *STARE DECISIS*—MANDATORY & PERSUASIVE PRECEDENT

In evaluating cases under our system of *stare decisis*, judges consider two different kinds of precedent: *mandatory* and *persuasive* precedent. As you might guess from what the names imply, courts are *required* to follow only earlier cases that qualify as mandatory precedent. In contrast, courts may or may not be persuaded to follow earlier cases that are only persuasive precedent. As a future lawyer who will advise clients of their legal rights, it is critical that you know how to tell the difference between mandatory and persuasive precedent.

Whether a case is mandatory or persuasive precedent depends on two questions—the jurisdiction within which the case arose and the hierarchal level of that court within the jurisdiction. If you remember the following two-part test, you can resolve nearly any jurisdictional question. Case law derived from a previous court decision is binding for a new dispute only if: (1) the previous case arose within the *same jurisdiction* as the dispute presently before the court; and (2) the earlier case was decided by a *higher-level court* within the same jurisdiction.

As will be discussed shortly, this two-part test works seamlessly when the court deciding the new dispute is interpreting its own laws. In other words, if a federal court is deciding a matter involving a federal law, this two-part test will clearly showcase which federal cases are binding on that court. Similarly, when a state court is deciding a matter of state law, the two-part test will showcase which court opinions within that state are binding on the case.[5]

A. The *Jurisdictional* Part of the Test

The jurisdictional part of the test can be deceptively challenging if you are unfamiliar with the way in which the federal and state court systems are organized. You can't begin to answer the question of whether a legal precedent is mandatory or persuasive precedent unless you have a very clear understanding of (a) the jurisdiction in which your new legal problem is based, and (b) the jurisdiction in which the earlier case

---

5. The question becomes more challenging when there is a cross-over, and a state court, for example, is tasked with applying a federal law. In a cross-over case, a state court interpreting federal law is generally bound by federal case law within the federal circuit in which the state court resides. A federal court interpreting state law is bound by case law from the highest court in that state and, potentially, by court decisions of that state's intermediate court. You will learn these rules in more depth in your civil procedure course.

arose. This is a fundamentally important question that merits some review, even if you are already somewhat familiar with the federal and state court jurisdictions.

1. Federal Courts

Federal courts have jurisdiction to resolve disputes that involve the United States Constitution, federal statutes, and federal regulations. In addition, federal courts have jurisdiction to resolve disputes that involve state laws if the parties satisfy other jurisdictional requirements (i.e., diversity of citizenship; pendent jurisdiction). Unlike the differing state laws, federal laws are, by definition, national in scope and apply irrespective of whether conduct covered by the law arises within the state of New York, the state of Florida, or the state of Illinois.

Because our nation is so vast and the volume of lawsuits so expansive, for practical reasons Congress has divided the country into thirteen federal judicial circuits. There are eleven numbered circuits, such as the United States Court of Appeals for the First Circuit, the Second Circuit, and so on. In addition to the eleven numbered circuits, there is also the United States Court of Appeals for the District of Columbia and the United States Court of Appeals for the Federal Circuit. The Federal Circuit resolves disputes involving patents, certain international trade disputes, and some cases involving damage claims against the United States government. Take a look at the accompanying map of the thirteen judicial circuits to gain a sense of how the country is divided into separate regions. Note that each numbered federal judicial circuit encompasses a number of different states. As you review the map, recall, however, that the jurisdiction of a federal judicial circuit extends to acts within those states that affect a *federal* law.[6] In what federal circuit do you reside?

How do the different federal judicial circuits affect the doctrine of *stare decisis*? An earlier case is mandatory, or binding, precedent only with respect to new federal court cases that arise within the same judicial circuit. For example, a decision issued by the United States Court of Appeals for the First Circuit is binding only on future cases that arise within the First Circuit. That decision does not carry any binding weight within any other circuit. A judge or panel of judges within the Second Circuit is free to agree or disagree with the manner in which the First Circuit Court of Appeals interprets a federal law.

2. State Courts

Each individual state has its own laws and court system. State court judges have sole jurisdiction to resolve controversies involving their state's constitution, statutes, and common law. Therefore, earlier cases have binding effect only on future disputes that arise within that same state. In fact, a case from one state may have very little

---

6. In addition, as you will learn in your civil procedure course, federal courts also have the power to hear a limited set of state law claims when the jurisdictional requirements of the federal court are satisfied.

persuasive impact on a judge in another state. As an example, a judge in the state of Illinois interpreting Illinois' burglary statute would not be required to follow a Wisconsin judge's interpretation of a similar Wisconsin statute and may not even find the Wisconsin case persuasive. Unlike the sources of federal law, which apply nationwide, each state's laws are different from the laws in other states and result from a unique balancing of interests and public policy within that state.

B. The Court *Hierarchy* Part of the Test

In order for an earlier case to have mandatory precedential effect, the earlier case must not only arise from within the same jurisdiction as the problem you are researching, but the earlier case must be decided by a *higher-level court* within that jurisdiction. The federal government, the District of Columbia, and each individual state have their own hierarchy of courts within their court systems. However, irrespective of the jurisdiction in which you practice law, an overriding principle applies: higher-level courts are binding on lower-level courts. Lower-level courts are never binding on higher-level courts.

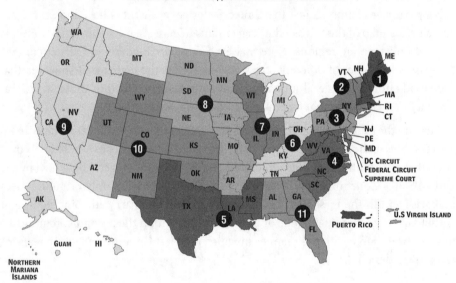

Geographic Boundaries
of United States Courts of Appeals and United States District Courts

1. Federal Court System

The federal court system has three levels of courts: (1) the trial court level (*District Courts*); (2) the intermediate appellate court level (*United States Courts of Appeals*); and (3) and the highest appellate court level (the *United States Supreme Court*). As the highest level court in the federal system, decisions of the United States Supreme Court are binding on all other federal courts. Decisions of each United States Court of Appeals are binding only on the lower federal courts within their jurisdiction. Federal district court decisions are not binding on other courts—even other court decisions within the same jurisdiction.

Graphically, the federal court system is organized like this:[7]

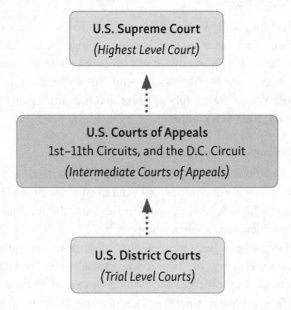

a. Federal District Courts

If you were to file a lawsuit that involved a federal law, you would likely[8] file the lawsuit in a federal district court, which is the name of the trial level court within the federal judiciary system.[9] Each of the twelve federal circuits (the eleven numbered circuits and the District of Columbia), has a number of district courts within its jurisdiction. The size and number of federal district courts within a particular circuit depends upon the size and caseload of that district. Additionally, each federal district court is typically comprised of more than one judge, again depending upon the size and caseload of the district.

b. United States Courts of Appeal

If you were to try a case in federal district court but then wish to appeal that court's decision, you would appeal to the next highest level court in the federal system—one of the United States courts of appeals. If your case were tried in a New York district

---

7. In addition, there are also federal courts that have special subject matter jurisdiction, such as federal claims courts; bankruptcy and tax courts; and veterans, armed forces, and international trade courts.

8. Litigants are also *permitted* to file federal law claims in state court, unless the federal courts have exclusive jurisdiction over the issue.

9. For present purposes, assume that the legal matter you are handling does not involve a specialized issue that would be addressed by the United States Tax Court, the Court of Federal Claims, or the Court of International Trade.

court, you would appeal the decision to the Second Circuit Court of Appeals, the circuit that encompasses New York. On the other hand, if your case were tried in a Texas district court, you would appeal to the Fifth Circuit Court of Appeals, the circuit that encompasses Texas.

All active judges on a federal court of appeals do not hear every case that comes before that court. Instead, cases are heard by three-judge panels during one week of the month. Sometimes, for unusually significant cases, all active judges on a federal court of appeals hear a case together, as a group. These decisions are called *en banc* decisions—a French term that simply signifies that the entire panel of judges heard the arguments and rendered an opinion.

c. United States Supreme Court

Assuming that you were in the position of appealing a decision from one of the United States courts of appeals, your appeal would be filed with the United States Supreme Court. As the highest level of court in the land, the nine-member Supreme Court consents to review only a select few appeals each year. Out of thousands of petitions for appeal every year, the Supreme Court consents to hear only 100 to 200 per year. Generally, it agrees to hear only those cases that are of exceptional constitutional or statutory magnitude, or those cases upon which lower courts have disagreed in their interpretation of federal law, i.e., where two or more federal circuit courts of appeal are split in their interpretation of an important law. When the Supreme Court declines to hear an appeal, the technical term is that it has *denied certiorari*. This term is abbreviated for citation purposes. Thus, when you see the phrase "*cert. denied*" following the citation of a case, that means that the lawyers in that case appealed the case to the United States Supreme Court and that the Supreme Court declined to hear the appeal.

2. State Court Systems

Like the federal court system, many, but not all, states have three levels of courts—trial level courts, intermediate appellate level courts, and a final appellate level court. (Most states have courts of limited jurisdiction as well, such as small claims courts or municipal courts.) However, some states have only two levels of courts. To complicate matters even further, some states call their final appeals court the "Supreme Court," while other states call their final appeals court the "Appellate Court." Thankfully, you are likely to practice law only in a few different jurisdictions and will become familiar with your jurisdictions' court systems during summer clerkships or externships, or as you begin practicing law. As law students, however, the *Bluebook* and the *ALWD Manual* can be helpful in unraveling a particular state's court system. Appendix 1 of the ALWD Citation Manual, and Table 1 of the Bluebook, list each state alphabetically and designate each state's court structure.[10] Ignoring the

---

10. The ALWD Citation Manual and the Bluebook only list those state courts from which decisions are actually published. In most states, intermediate appellate court and final appellate court decisions are

courts of very limited jurisdiction, such as small claims and municipal courts, a typical state court system such as Missouri would look like this:

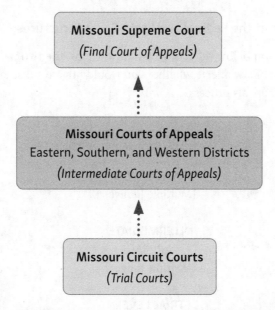

Like the federal court system, in a state system, the highest level of appellate court binds all lower level courts. In most states, intermediate level appellate courts bind all trial level courts within all districts within the state.[11] For example, an earlier case decided by the Court of Appeals for the Western District of Missouri would bind all state trial courts within the state, even those trial courts that sit within the Eastern District of Missouri.

However, there is a caveat of which you should be aware: because court decisions are not binding on other courts that operate at the same level, it is possible for different intermediate appellate courts within a state to conflict. For example, suppose the Court of Appeals for the Western District of Missouri disagreed with a decision of the Court of Appeals for the Eastern District of Missouri. As a lawyer trying to sift through the conflicting opinions, you would need to consider the district under which your case falls. If, for instance, you were involved in a lawsuit in a trial court that happens to fall within the Western District of Missouri, the earlier decision of the Court of Appeals for the Western District of Missouri would be mandatory, binding authority for your case. The trial judge in your case would be required to follow the interpretation of the law rendered by the Court of Appeals for the Western District of

---

published and are therefore denoted in the ALWD Citation Manual and the Bluebook. However, most states do not publish their trial court opinions. For example, the state of Missouri does not publish trial court opinions. Thus, the citation manuals do not list Missouri's trial level courts.

11. Some states, such as Oklahoma, are unique. Their intermediate appellate court opinions are not deemed binding upon lower courts unless the highest appellate level court has given its stamp of approval for publication.

Missouri—even if the trial court judge happened to personally agree with the legal interpretation rendered by the Eastern District.

C. Illustration of the Federal and State Court Structures

The illustration below reflects, in practical terms, the two parallel court systems, how the source of law affects whether you would litigate a dispute in federal or state court, and the appeals process.

TRIAL COURT STRUCTURE

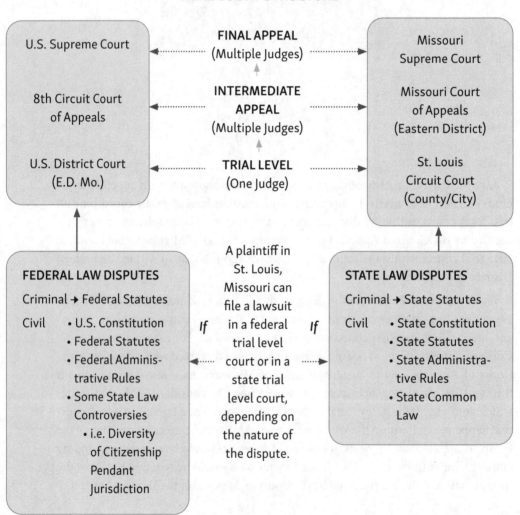

U.S. Supreme Court	**FINAL APPEAL** (Multiple Judges)	Missouri Supreme Court
8th Circuit Court of Appeals	**INTERMEDIATE APPEAL** (Multiple Judges)	Missouri Court of Appeals (Eastern District)
U.S. District Court (E.D. Mo.)	**TRIAL LEVEL** (One Judge)	St. Louis Circuit Court (County/City)

FEDERAL LAW DISPUTES

Criminal → Federal Statutes

Civil
- U.S. Constitution
- Federal Statutes
- Federal Administrative Rules
- Some State Law Controversies
  - i.e. Diversity of Citizenship Pendant Jurisdiction

A plaintiff in St. Louis, Missouri can file a lawsuit *If* in a federal trial level court or in a *If* state trial level court, depending on the nature of the dispute.

STATE LAW DISPUTES

Criminal → State Statutes

Civil
- State Constitution
- State Statutes
- State Administrative Rules
- State Common Law

Exercise 2-4: Mandatory and Persuasive Precedent

Factual Situation: Assume that you are practicing law in Los Angeles, California. California falls within the Ninth Circuit Court of Appeals. You represent Tim Jones, who has asked for your advice concerning a potential lawsuit against his former employer, Rainmaid. After a lengthy discussion, you discovered the following facts. Jones is a member of a religious sect that worships the sun. When the sun shines, the religion requires its followers to dance in the sun on Wednesday afternoons and worship the sun god. The religious doctrine strictly forbids its members from engaging in any kind of work on such afternoons. Rainmaid recently fired Jones for refusing to work on one such Wednesday afternoon. Jones has informed you that he told Rainmaid at the time he was hired that his religion would require him to miss work on certain Wednesday afternoons. Jones claims that he and his employer verbally agreed that Jones would compensate for the lost time by working Wednesday evenings instead. Jones has given you a copy of his employment contract, which states that Rainmaid would not fire Jones except "for good cause." Jones is a data processor. His job duties included inputting data about Rainmaid's customers into a computer and then generating invoices for the customers.

Jones is worried about the expenses of a lawsuit and the time involved. Depending upon the results of your research, you agreed that you might be willing to accept the case on a contingency fee basis (i.e., if you win the lawsuit, you take 1/3 of the judgment as your legal fees; if you lose, you take nothing). Jones was also amenable to the idea of at least considering paying you on an hourly basis. You and he agreed that, before you actually filed any lawsuit on his behalf, you would let him know the likelihood of success of such a lawsuit. You agreed to forward to him a legal memorandum that would educate him about the relevant law and the likelihood of success.

Possible Legal Claims: After talking to your client, you have pursued the possibility of filing a lawsuit on Jones' behalf, alleging two separate claims for relief. One such claim would allege that Rainmaid breached the employment contract by firing Jones without good cause.

The second claim would seek damages against Rainmaid for religious discrimination in violation of Title VII, a federal statute. Title VII makes it an unlawful employment practice for an employer "to discharge any individual... because of such individual's... religion...." 42 U.S.C. § 2000(e)-2.

Consider the following questions concerning the Title VII claim:

1. Is this claim based on constitutional, statutory, or common law?
2. Is this a civil or a criminal lawsuit?
3. In what court would you file this lawsuit?

4. You conducted some initial research to investigate the viability of your client's claims. You found a July 2020 case in which a federal appeals court in the Tenth Circuit held that another member of this same religious sect had a Title VII cause of action against her employer when her employer fired her for missing work on Wednesday afternoons.
   a. Is this case mandatory precedent or persuasive precedent?
   b. Based on this case, should you go ahead and file a lawsuit against Tim's employer under the Title VII claim?
   c. What additional information would you want to know before filing a Title VII lawsuit?
      i.   About the case itself?
      ii. About other cases?

5. After more exhaustive research, you were able to find only one other case in the country that involved a claim by a member of this sect against a former employer. In this second case, a 2015 case, the Ninth Circuit Court of Appeals, in a case originating from an Oregon federal district court, held that the plaintiff did not state a valid claim under Title VII because the employer had a legitimate business reason for firing the plaintiff for failing to work on Wednesday afternoons.
   a. Is the federal appellate court case that originated in an Oregon district court mandatory precedent or persuasive precedent?

6. Which of the two cases is more important, the Tenth Circuit case decided in 2020, or the 2015 case?

7. Are either of the two cases unimportant to your client's Title VII claim?

8. In light of the Oregon case, should you forget about filing a Title VII claim against Rainmaid?

9. What other facts would you want to know about the cases in order to assess the value of your client's Title VII claim?
   a. What additional facts might help your client?
   b. What additional facts might hurt your client?

10. Should you tell your client about both cases, or just the case that has the favorable holding?

Consider the following questions concerning the breach of contract claim:

1. Is this claim based on constitutional, statutory, or common law?

2. Is this a civil or a criminal lawsuit?

The 2015 federal appellate court case that held the plaintiff did not have a cause of action under Title VII also considered the plaintiff's claim that the employer breached the employment contract by firing him. In this Ninth Circuit case, the court held that the plaintiff did not state a valid claim for breach of an employment contract because the employer had "good cause" to fire the employee.

3. Is the Ninth Circuit case that originated in an Oregon district court mandatory or persuasive authority?

4. In light of this Ninth Circuit case, should you forget about filing a breach of contract claim against Jones' employer?

5. Assume there are no other cases in the country that have addressed these issues with respect to this religious sect. What other kinds of cases might prove to be helpful as you investigate your client's potential claims? Consider:
   a. the legal issue involved in the cases;
   b. the nature of the relationship between the plaintiff and the defendant; and
   c. the nature of the dispute between the plaintiff and the defendant.

6. As you research the issue further, in what jurisdiction would you focus your research efforts?

CHAPTER IN REVIEW

Core Concepts

1. There are two parallel legal systems: federal and state.
   a. Federal system has 13 judicial circuits.
   b. Each state system is also subdivided into different jurisdictions (*e.g.*, southern, northern).
2. Both legal systems have three sources of law. What are they?
3. Each legal system has different levels of courts, with appeals that can be taken from trial-level courts to higher-level courts.
4. The persuasive appeal of a case depends on whether the case is mandatory or persuasive precedent.
   • What is the two-part test that determines whether legal precedent is mandatory or merely persuasive?

READING AND BRIEFING CASES

The Basics

I. DEVELOPING THE SKILL OF READING CASES

You might have entered law school with the expectation that reading cases would be like reading textbooks in high school and college. Most law students quickly discover, however, that reading cases is challenging, and even frustrating at times. How can you decipher from the often obscure language within a case what the professor wants you to learn? And in this course in particular, how can you use a case as a useful guide to help you advise a client? Finding the answers to these questions can be particularly challenging because you are simultaneously struggling to understand new terminology, the structure of our legal system, and even the structure of a court opinion itself.

Although every new law student faces these challenges, the findings from a number of studies may surprise you. These studies reveal that students who end up towards the bottom of their law school class rely on the "default" reading strategies that novices typically use.[1] These default reading strategies consist of highlighting information in the case, taking some notes, and paraphrasing what they think the court said. These are all useful reading strategies, but they are not enough in and of themselves.

In contrast, those students who end up at the top of their law school class employ reading strategies that are similar to the strategies that experts use when they read cases. Fortunately, these reading strategies can be learned. There are three basic strategies that will help you read cases more efficiently and with greater understanding and retention. First, rather than relying solely on the default reading strategies de-

---

1. *See* Leah M. Christensen, *Legal Reading and Success in Law School: An Empirical Study*, 30 Seattle U. L. Rev. 603 (2007); James F. Stratman, *When Law Students Read Cases: Exploring Relations Between Professional Legal Reasoning Roles and Problem Detection*, 34 Discourse Processes 57 (2002); Laurel C. Oates, *Beating the Odds: Reading Strategies of Law Students Admitted Through Alternative Admissions Programs*, 83 Iowa L Rev. 139 (1997); Dorothy H. Deegan, *Exploring Individual Differences Among Novices Reading in a Specific Domain: The Case of Law*, 30 Reading Res. Q. 154 (1995); Mary A. Lundeberg, *Metacogntive Aspects of Reading Comprehension: Studying Understanding in Legal Case Analysis*, 22 Reading Res. Q. 407 (1987).

scribed above, high-performing students use a variety of different reading strategies to *actively resolve the confusion* they experience when reading cases. Second, rather than reading cases in the role of a "student" preparing for class, high-performing law students *assume the role of a lawyer* advising a client about the law. Finally, high-performing law students establish the *context* of the case before they begin to read it.[2]

A. Actively Resolve Confusion

Almost no law student enters law school without experiencing a certain degree of confusion when s/he first begins to read legal cases. However, the manner in which students resolve the questions that inevitably come to mind differs dramatically. Empirical studies reflect that when high-performing students become confused, *they stop and find answers to their questions before moving on.* They answer their questions either by re-reading portions of the case again, or by referring to a legal dictionary or other secondary source for help in understanding the court's vocabulary. In contrast, when low-performing students have questions, they tend to make tentative assumptions about what the court likely meant, and hope that it will become clear as they continue reading. Unfortunately, many times their assumptions prove to be incorrect and they miss the significance of an important part of the court's opinion, or even become misled as they build one incorrect assumption on top of another one.

One reason students fail to take enough time to resolve the questions that come up when they read cases is because of time constraints—it takes time and patience to understand what it is a court is really saying. The reality is that, as a novice legal reader, you will spend inordinate amounts of time reading and understanding cases because you are, in a sense, having to learn a foreign language. It is natural to have to read and re-read certain paragraphs and to refer to other sources to clarify the meaning of some of the words with which you are unfamiliar. Particularly at the beginning of your law school career you will spend a great deal of time trying to decipher the underlying meaning and import of the cases you have been assigned to study. However, if you spend the time in the beginning of this process to resolve the questions that occur to you as you read cases, your hard work will pay dividends later on when the reading process inevitably becomes easier and more natural as you "learn the language."

B. Assume the Role of a Lawyer Solving a Problem

If you read cases with the mind-set that you are a student preparing for class, you will likely miss aspects of the cases that are important for you to know. With that purpose in mind, it is all too easy, for example, to skim over important facets of a case because their importance might not seem apparent to you in your role as a student preparing for class.

---

2. These strategies are discussed at greater length in: Legal M. Christensen, *Legal Reading and Success in Law School: An Empirical Study*, 30 Seattle U. L. Rev. 603 (2007).

In contrast, if you assume the role of a lawyer attempting to understand the law so that you can advise a hypothetical "client," you will naturally pay greater attention to the important aspects of each case—not only because the cases will seem more interesting to you, but because your brain will automatically look for answers to the questions it will naturally be posing. In your role as a lawyer advising a client, for example, the facts of a case would become very important because you would be simultaneously comparing them to your client's situation to determine whether they are more or less favorable than your client's facts. Similarly, the punishment that was meted out in a precedent case would naturally become important to you in your role as a lawyer because it would affect your assessment of the punishment your own client might receive. In effect, the goal of problem-solving enhances your ability to attend to details that might otherwise escape your attention.

Reading cases in the role of a lawyer also requires that you be an "active critic" rather than a passive reader. As active critics, good lawyers constantly assess the accuracy and reasonableness of their initial assumptions about what a case means. Are they reading the court's holding too narrowly, or too broadly? Is there a more favorable way to interpret the case, or a more unfavorable way to construe it? If the opposing lawyer were to read the same case, how might the opposing lawyer interpret the case?

As active critics, good lawyers (and high-performing students) are also critical of the cases they read. They ask themselves whether or not they agree with a court's holding and whether they think the court was misguided (or, alternatively, whether they think the court's reasoning was brilliant). They also consider the implications of the court's holding, and whether there are unfavorable policy ramifications the court may not have considered. This role not only helps lawyers formulate arguments in their own cases, but also helps them move beyond a superficial understanding to a more profound understanding of the case.

In short, experienced lawyers and high-performing law students share the characteristic of being actively engaged in the reading process rather than passive readers. As a new law student, it will take some time for you to become adept at assuming this role. However, you can accelerate your development as an active critic by consciously assuming the role of a lawyer solving a problem for a hypothetical client. Chapter 7 of this book describes in greater detail how to read and evaluate cases in the role of a lawyer advising clients.

C. Establish Context

High-performing law students also become familiar with the context of each case before they begin reading it. This strategy mimics that of experienced lawyers as they research the law to resolve legal questions for their clients. The context of a particular case will provide you with the necessary perspective to understand why a particular case is relevant. And, as you understand in a more concrete way the bigger picture of what is happening in the case, you will find it easier to absorb (and to remember) the important details.

This reading strategy requires you to ask yourself a series of questions as you begin to read a case. One of the more basic questions you should resolve before reading a case concerns the *subject matter* of the case—*e.g.,* does the case involve the breach of a contract or does it involve an intentional tort? As you research cases for some of the assignments in this course, you will find many, many cases that might be superficial-ly interesting. However, some cases may well be irrelevant because they don't address the exact issue you are attempting to resolve on behalf of your hypothetical client. Chapter 18 provides some time-saving strategies you can adopt to help you weed out irrelevant cases when you are researching cases for assignments in this course.

In your other classes, you may find it useful to take a look at the table of contents in your casebooks to locate the cases you are reviewing. Where do the cases fall with-in the table of contents? For example, a typical contracts course covers such basic legal concepts as how parties form contracts, how parties might break ("breach") a con-tract, and the types of damages or other relief a party might recover when a contract has been breached. Knowing that a case falls within the contract formation part of the casebook would signal to you that the case will contain important information about how parties form, or fail to form, valid contracts.

You should also identify the parties in the lawsuit—is this a criminal case, or a civil case between two private parties? This question not only helps you understand the "bigger picture" of what is happening in the case, but will also impact your assess-ment of how relevant it is to the hypothetical client situation you are researching.

Other basic questions that provide context concern the type of court that decided the case (federal/state, trial/appellate, my jurisdiction/other jurisdiction) and the date the case was decided. Is this a case that is controlling (mandatory) precedent, or is it persuasive only? Is this a recent case or an older one? Was it decided before or after the other cases you are reading? What may have been going on in history at the time of a particular case that might explain a sudden change in the case law? Why might these questions be important to you as a lawyer? For example, if you practiced law in California and found an interesting case interpreting New York law, would you rely on the New York case in giving your California client legal advice?

It is also important to understand the "procedural" context of the case. First take a look at the type of court that decided the case. Is this an appellate court opinion or a trial court opinion? Most of the cases you will read in your casebooks are appellate court opinions. In an appellate court case, one basic procedural context is that the losing party has appealed the trial court's decision and is arguing that the trial court was wrong in the way that it interpreted or applied the law.

There is, however, another important layer to the procedural context of a case. Although one of the parties has appealed the lower court's decision, what exactly is the losing party appealing? Consider the timeline of a lawsuit and clarify where along that timeline the court decided the issues you are reading. Has a jury already heard the case and reached a verdict, or did the trial court dismiss the plaintiff's complaint as a matter of law because the facts just didn't create a legal cause of action? How might this distinction be important to you in your role as a lawyer? Suppose your client wanted to file a lawsuit to recover money from a former business partner and your client's factual situation was similar to the precedent case. Would the distinction be meaningful to you in assessing the relative strength of your client's legal case?

Consider another example of how the procedural context of a case would be relevant to you in your role as a lawyer. Assume that you have evaluated two appellate court cases and that, in both cases, the courts interpreted the law in a manner that is favorable to your client. In the first case, assume that the appellate court agreed with the jury's verdict and *affirmed* the trial court's decision; in the second case, an appellate court reversed the trial court's decision and *remanded* the case back to the trial court so that a jury could consider new evidence and reach a new verdict. As a lawyer who would like to make favorable factual comparisons to these cases, how might this distinction be important to you? Would you be more comfortable relying on a case in which a jury actually reached a verdict, or on a case in which the jury did not actually reach a verdict because of the procedural context of the case (the appellate court reversed and remanded the case for a new trial)?[3]

II. COMPONENTS OF A COURT OPINION

A. An Overview

Whether reading a case for one of your other classes or for this course, understanding the general characteristics, or components, of a case will help you grasp and retain what you are reading. Court opinions typically include most of the following components:

1. The *facts* of the case, including:
   a. "procedural" facts (how the court system processes the dispute), and
   b. "evidentiary" facts (the underlying dispute itself);

2. The original *rule or rules of law* the court evaluates, which might arise from:
   a. a statute,
   b. a constitution, or
   c. the common law;

3. The *issue or issues* presented to the court to resolve, which may include:

---

3. It often happens that, after an appellate court has reversed and remanded a case for a new trial, the parties settle the case in a settlement that is never made public.

a. "law-centered" issues (what the law *means*), and

b. "fact-centered" issues (how the law was applied to the dispute itself);

4. A summary of the various *arguments* raised by the attorneys in the case;

5. The court's *holding* on each issue (how it resolved the dispute);

6. The court's *rationale* (the reasons it resolved the dispute in the way that it did), which may include:

   a. interpretations and definitions of the law (*explanatory reasoning*),

   b. application of the legal requirements to the facts of the case (*application reasoning*),

   c. public policy implications, and

   d. gratuitous dicta suggesting how different facts might compel a different outcome;

7. The court's *judgment* (the formal action it ordered).

B. Individual Components of a Case

1. Case Facts

a. Procedural Facts

Procedural facts might best be viewed as the events that happened in the lawsuit itself, *after* a lawsuit has been filed. They include such facts as who is being sued? by whom? for what? and in which court? On appeal, the procedural facts include such information as who lost in the trial court and why. Often, you will find the procedural facts at the beginning of a court opinion because they set the context for the issues the judge will address in the opinion. The time line of a lawsuit depicted in Chapter 1 describes the various procedural contexts from which legal issues arise.

b. Evidentiary Facts

Evidentiary facts are the factual story of the parties' dispute itself. Therefore, they describe what happened *before* the parties ended up in court and explain why the parties are in court. These facts can have profound legal significance, because court holdings hinge on the factual story of the dispute itself. However, not all evidentiary facts are legally significant to a court's holding. Some facts merely provide helpful background, or context, so that you can better understand the factual story of the case.

As you read cases in law school, one skill you will develop is the ability to distinguish between legally important facts (also known as "legally significant facts" or "critical facts") and those facts that only provide background context. However, you usually will not be able to make this determination until *after* you have read the court's holding and rationale. (That means that you will have to read a case more than one time in order to fully understand it.)

As you begin to consider the weight and importance of case facts, it might be useful to categorize different types of facts. The most critically important facts in a case are often called *outcome determinative* facts; in other words, had these facts not existed, the court would have reached a different decision. Courts often explicitly signal that certain facts are outcome determinative by clearly linking their holding to the existence of specific facts when discussing those facts within the rationale section of the court opinion.

Other facts, although perhaps not outcome determinative, are nonetheless *legally significant*. Legally significant facts are those facts that are important enough to have contributed, at least in part, to a court's ultimate decision. Sometimes courts make it very clear which facts were important to them, and sometimes you will have to deduce what facts were important simply by reading and re-reading a case and using logical inferences to arrive at your analysis.

Finally, some facts included within court opinions have little to no legal significance. These facts simply provide factual context for the other more important facts so that you, the reader, can more easily understand what happened in the case.

2. Issues

Issues are the legal questions a court must answer to resolve the dispute between the parties in a particular case. Courts address and resolve two kinds of issues: (a) *law-centered issues*, when the court must interpret what a particular law means; and (b) *fact-centered issues*, when the court must apply a rule of law to the factual dispute between the parties. In a particular case, the court may be asked to resolve a law-centered issue, a fact-centered issue, or both.

a. Law-Centered Issues

Sometimes judges are asked to decide the *meaning* of a particular rule of law, separate and apart from the specific factual controversy before the judge. Such issues are law-centered because the judge's determination is not dependent on the facts in the case before it. The *Nelson v. Lewis*[4] case illustrated later in this chapter contains a law-centered issue. In Illinois, a state statute protects dog owners from liability if the dog had "provocation" to attack a person.[5] Courts had interpreted the term "provocation" to include any intentional act that incites a dog's attack. However, the *Nelson* court was asked to resolve a new question—whether the statutory term "provocation" includes even *unintentional* acts that might incite a dog to attack. This issue is law-centered because the court's interpretation of the statute does not depend on the specific facts in the *Nelson* case itself.

---

4. 344 N.E.2d 268 (Ill. App. Ct. 1976).
5. 510 Ill. Comp. Stat. § 55/1 (2004).

b. Fact-Centered Issues

Courts are also asked to decide how a settled rule of law should be *applied* to a particular factual controversy. In *Nelson v. Lewis*, the appellate court was also asked to resolve a fact-centered issue—whether, in the particular situation before the court, a child's unintentional act of stepping on a dog's tail was an unintentional act that provoked the dog to bite within the meaning of the statute. Notice that, in contrast to the law-centered question, here the court was asked to apply the rule of law to the very specific facts of the case before it: the child's unintentional act of stepping on a dog's tail.

3. Holdings

A holding is the court's answer to an issue. Accordingly, the number of holdings in a case is dictated by the number of issues the attorneys raised before the court. You may find only a single holding in a case, or numerous holdings. The issues before the court also dictate whether the holding is law-centered or fact-centered. In *Nelson v. Lewis*, the court responded to the law-centered issue by holding that even unintentional acts of children can constitute legal "provocation" under Illinois' dog-bite statute. The court responded to the fact-centered issue by holding that, under the specific facts of the case before it, the child's act of stepping on the dog's tail "provoked" the dog within the legal meaning of Illinois' dog-bite statute.

It is tempting as a new law student to search for clear, concrete, immovable answers to questions. However, what makes law so fascinating, and challenging, are the ambiguities and questions that courts leave unresolved. Holdings are not static, rigid rules of law. Rather, they are fluid and capable of being interpreted narrowly or broadly. As a law student, your professors will ask you hypothetical questions in class designed, in part, to help stimulate you to consider just how narrowly or broadly you might construe a court's holding.

As an advocate, you will face the same challenge. For example, assume for a moment that you represent a client in the state of Illinois who was attacked and bitten by a dog after she screamed in fright upon seeing the dog.

The dog's owner has claimed that, under *Nelson v. Lewis*, your client's unintentional act of screaming "provoked" the dog's attack within the meaning of the statute. This argument rests upon a broad interpretation of the *Nelson* court's holding—in order for this argument to succeed, the dog owner's lawyer must argue that the *Nelson* holding broadly encompasses *any* unintentional act that ultimately provokes a dog to attack.

In contrast, as a lawyer representing the injured woman who was attacked by the dog, you would interpret the *Nelson* court's holding more narrowly. You would argue that the *Nelson* court's holding was narrowly limited to unintentional acts that involved actual *physical contact* with a dog. You would build your case from a narrow interpretation of the *Nelson* court's holding, arguing that, unlike the act of stepping on a dog's tail when the dog is chewing on a bone, your client's act of screaming in fright did not involve any physical contact with the dog itself. You would then argue that this factual distinction is important enough to be *legally significant*. In other words, the factual distinction means that the result for your client should be different than the result in *Nelson*—your client did not legally "provoke" the dog's attack within the meaning of the statute.

If the trial court judge were to agree with your opponent's broad interpretation of the *Nelson* court's holding, your client would not be able to recover damages against the dog owner under the Dog Bite Statute. On the other hand, if the trial court judge were to adopt your narrow interpretation of the *Nelson* court's holding, your client would be in a position to recover damages for her injuries. Chapter 7 discusses this process in greater detail.

4. Rationale

Courts usually state the reasoning, or *rationale*, that justifies their holdings. The rationale section is important for you, as a legal reader, to understand because it provides the information you will use when engaging in legal analysis and interpreting rules of law. Unfortunately, sometimes courts don't clearly explain why they held the way they did, and you must try to identify the unstated, or implied, reasons that support the holding. However, many times courts do provide thorough and precise reasoning for their holdings, and this information will be instructive for you as you work with the case opinion and analyze it in conjunction with your own client problem.

Although a court's rationale often appears directly after its statement of the holding, it can also be scattered throughout the opinion; therefore, you will need to re-read relevant cases a number of times to ensure that you accurately understand why each court held as it did. To identify the court's rationale, consider the legal issues before the court and note how the court explained the relevant legal standards to support its holding on these issues (explanatory reasoning). In a case that involves fact-centered issues, the court will also explain how it applied the legal standards to a set of facts in order to justify its holding (application reasoning). Thus, a well-crafted opinion of that type contains two types of reasoning—explanatory reasoning and application reasoning.

Explanatory reasoning is just as its name suggests—it is reasoning that explains the required legal components of the issue at hand. For example, in the *Nelson v. Lewis* case excerpt given later in this chapter, the court begins its rationale section by quoting the Dog Bite Statute. It then notes that "[u]nder this statute[,] there are four elements that must be proved: injury caused by a dog owned or harbored by the defendant; lack of provocation; peaceable conduct of the person injured; and the presence of the person injured in a place where he has a legal right to be."[6] Later, the court explains that the element of "[p]rovocation is defined as an act or process of provoking,

---

6. *Id.* at 270.

stimulation[,] or incitement," and that "an unintentional act can constitute provocation within the plain meaning of the statute."[7]

Upon reading this section of explanatory reasoning, you now understand that lack of provocation is a required component of the Dog Bite Statute, and that unintentional acts can suffice as provocation. This explanatory reasoning is instructive for you in understanding the legal components the court used to reach its decision, and it will also prove valuable to your reader once you engage in analysis and draft legal documents such as memoranda and briefs.

In a fact-centered case, after the court explains the legal components with explanatory reasoning, it applies those components to the facts of the case to support its holding. This is known as application reasoning, and you can often spot it with lead-in language such as "in the present case." In the dog bite example, we can identify the following statements as application reasoning: "In the present case, it was admitted that the plaintiff jumped or fell on the dog's tail; that the dog was of a peaceful and quiet temperament; and that the dog was gnawing on a bone when the incident occurred."[8] The court then notes that "[u]nder these circumstances, we believe that the Dalmatian was provoked, although the provocation was not intentional."[9]

The application reasoning is what brings the legal requirements and the case facts together to support the court's holding. This reasoning tells you precisely why *in this case* the legal components were or were not met. Again, this reasoning aids in your understanding of the basis for the holding, and it will be beneficial as you use your legal analytical skills to draft legal documents.

A court's rationale sometimes also includes "dicta." Dicta is simply gratuitous rationale; in other words, the additional language doesn't really directly support the court's holding. For example, often dicta takes this form: *If x, y, z facts were present here, which they are not, the result would have been different.* Notice how such language, although it doesn't directly support the holding, could be useful to you as a lawyer if the factual situation you're later investigating happens to include "x, y, or z" facts. The dicta would provide you with valuable information as to how the court might apply the law under the new factual situation that you are researching.

As an example, in the *Nelson v. Lewis* case, the court stated: "the present appeal does not involve a vicious attack which was out of all proportion to the unintentional acts involved." By that statement, the court implied that a different fact pattern might merit a different result—an unintentional act may not constitute "provocation" under the statute if the dog's attack is out of proportion to the unintentional act. Importantly, although dicta can be persuasive evidence of what a court actually meant or in-

---

7. *Id.* at 270-71.
8. *Id.* at 271.
9. *Id.*

tended, it is not actually controlling, or binding, on later courts. Therefore, a later court might, or might not, choose to adopt an earlier court's dicta.

5. Judgment

The court's judgment is that part of the opinion in which the court indicates the formal action, if any, that is to be taken now that the court has resolved (the "holding") the legal "issues" before it. The court may affirm, reverse, remand, or vacate a lower court's decision. The court may award damages, or equitable relief, or it may order that something be done (*e.g.*, declaratory relief).

III. ILLUSTRATION OF A COURT OPINION

The *Nelson v. Lewis* case illustrated below contains all seven components of a court opinion.[10] The annotations on the right-hand column signal each component of the opinion and how a lawyer might interpret the opinion. While reading *Nelson v. Lewis*, keep in mind that the court resolved both a law-centered issue (can unintentional acts provoke a dog?) and a fact-centered issue (did this particular act of falling on the dog's tail provoke the dog?). The court jumped back and forth between the two issues and its rationale for each issue, making the opinion a bit difficult to follow.

While reading the case, consider the following questions. What three reasons did the court give to justify its law-centered holding (that unintentional acts can "provoke" a dog under the statute)? What key facts did the court emphasize to justify its fact-centered holding (that the act of stepping on the dog's tail "provoked" the dog under the statute)?

JO ANN NELSON, a Minor, by Eric D. Nelson, her
Father and Next Friend, Plaintiff-Appellant,
v. GEORGE N. LEWIS,
Defendant-Appellee

No. 75-432

Appellate Court of Illinois, Fifth District

36 Ill. App. 3d 130; 344 N.E.2d 268

March 3, 1976, Filed

MR. PRESIDING JUSTICE KARNS delivered the opinion of the court. JONES and G.J. MORAN, JJ., concur. Plaintiff, by her father and next friend, brought an action under the Illinois "dog-bite" statute (Ill. Rev. Stat. 1973, ch. 8, par.

> This paragraph describes the **procedural** facts—what happened procedurally after the plaintiff filed the lawsuit.

---

10. *Nelson v. Lewis*, 344 N.E.2d 268 (Ill. Appt. Ct. 1976). The idea of using the Dog Bite Statute and *Nelson v. Lewis* was inspired by Diana V. Pratt, *Legal Writing: A Systematic Approach* (West 1989).

366)] for injuries inflicted upon her by defendant's dog. From judgment entered on a jury verdict for the defendant, she appeals.

On the date of her injury, plaintiff Jo Ann Nelson, a 2½-year-old, was playing "crack-the-whip" in defendant's backyard with his daughter and other children. Jo Ann was on the end of the "whip." The testimony shows that after she had been thrown off the whip, Jo Ann fell or stepped on the dog's tail while the dog was chewing a bone. The dog, a large Dalmatian, reacted by scratching the plaintiff in her left eye. There was no evidence that plaintiff or anyone else had teased or aggravated the dog before the incident, nor was there evidence that the dog had ever scratched, bitten, or attacked anyone else. According to its owner, the dog had not appeared agitated either before or after the incident. As a result of her injuries, Jo Ann incurred permanent damage to a tear duct in her left eye. It was established that Jo Ann's left eye will overflow with tears more frequently and as a result of less irritation than normal, but that her vision in the eye was not affected.

Our statute pertaining to liability of an owner of a dog attacking or injuring persons provides:

> "If a dog or other animal, without provocation, attacks or injures any person who is peacefully conducting himself in any place where he may lawfully be, the owner of such dog or other animal is liable in damages to such person for the full amount of the injury sustained." (Ill. Rev. Stat. 1973, ch. 8, par. 366.)

Under this statute there are four elements that must be proved: injury caused by a dog owned or harbored by the defendant; lack of provocation; peaceable conduct of the person injured; and the presence of the person injured in a place where he has a legal right to be.

(*Siewerth v. Charleston*, 89 Ill. App. 2d 64, 231 N.E.2d 644 (1967); *Messa v. Sullivan*, 61 Ill. App. 2d 386, 209 N.E.2d 872 (1965); *Beckert v. Risberg*, 50 Ill. App. 2d 100, 199 N.E.2d 811 (1964) *rev'd on other grounds*, 33 Ill. 2d 44, 210 N.E.2d 207 (1965).) There is no dispute but that the dog caused the plaintiff's injury; the defendant owned the dog; the plaintiff's conduct was peaceable; and she was injured

---

*This paragraph describes the **evidentiary** facts—those facts that tell the story of the incident that triggered the lawsuit. As a lawyer representing a client who was attacked by a dog, you would pay careful attention to these facts because you would want to know how similar (or different) your client's facts were from the Nelson case facts.*

Here, the court quotes the statute…

and then analyzes the statute, finding that the statute has four elements.

Here, the court provides a useful roadmap for you by:
(1) eliminating the statutory elements that do not present a genuine issue for the court; and
(2) identifying the issue the court will resolve.

in a place where she had a legal right to be. The issue presented is whether plaintiff's unintentional act constitutes "provocation" within the meaning of the statute.

It appears that this issue has not been passed upon by an Illinois court. The statute does not distinguish between intentional and unintentional acts of provocation and thus, defendant argues, an unintentional act, so long as it provokes an animal or dog, may constitute provocation. Defendant's position, that the mental state of the actor who provokes a dog is irrelevant, is consistent with the commonly understood meaning of provocation. Provocation is defined as an act or process of provoking, stimulation or incitement. (Webster's Third New International Dictionary 1827 (1961).) Thus it would appear that an unintentional act can constitute provocation within the plain meaning of the statute.

> Because no earlier Illinois cases have addressed the issue, the court cannot rely on statutory interpretations, or rules of law, established by earlier courts.

> **Rationale #1:**
> *What is the 1st reason the court gives to support its law-centered holding?*

In the present case, it was admitted that the plaintiff jumped or fell on the dog's tail; that the dog was of a peaceful and quiet temperament; and that the dog was gnawing on a bone when the incident occurred.

> **Rationale** for fact-centered issue: *what facts were critically important to the court here?*

Under these circumstances, we believe that the Dalmatian was provoked, although the provocation was not intentional.

> **Holding** for fact-centered issue.

Plaintiff argues that since her act was unintentional, or that because she was of an age at which she could not be charged with scienter, she did not provoke the dog within the meaning of the act. Although her counsel presents a strong argument for interpreting the instant statute to impose essentially strict liability upon a dog owner for injuries caused to a child of tender years, we cannot agree that the public policy of this State compels the adoption of such a standard.

> This paragraph describes the **plaintiff's lawyer's argument** for the law-centered issue.

> **Holding** for law-centered issue.

[T]his act was apparently drawn to eliminate as much as possible any inquiry into subjective considerations. Whether the injured person was attacked or injured while conducting himself in a peaceful manner in a place where he could lawfully be are all matters which require no inquiry into a person's intent. We believe that the determination of "provocation" should also be made independently of such considerations. A determination of provocation does not require consideration of the degree of willfulness which motivates the provoking cause.

> **Rationale #2:**
> *What is the 2nd reason the court gives to support its law-centered holding?*

Rationale #3:
What is the 3rd reason the court gives to support its law-centered holding?

Dicta: court implies result might be different under different set of facts.

Can you identify both the **law-centered** and the **fact-centered** holdings here?

The court's **judgment.**

Had the legislature intended only intentional provocation to be a bar to recovery we think it would have so specified. Its conclusion apparently was that an owner or keeper of a dog who would attack or injure someone without provocation should be liable. This implies that the intent of the plaintiff is immaterial.

Although we believe that the instant statute does not impose liability upon a dog owner whose animal merely reacts to an unintentionally provocative act, the present appeal does not involve a vicious attack which was out of all proportion to the unintentional acts involved. *E.g., Messa v. Sullivan, supra.* The Dalmatian here apparently only struck and scratched plaintiff with a forepaw in response to the plaintiff's stepping or falling on its tail while it was gnawing on a bone, an act which scarcely can be described as vicious.

Therefore we hold that "provocation" within the meaning of the instant statute means either intentional or unintentional provocation; that the defendant's dog was provoked by the plaintiff's unintentional acts and did not viciously react to these acts; and that no reversible error was committed in the trial court.

For the foregoing reasons, the judgment of the Circuit Court of St. Clair County is affirmed.

Affirmed.

IV. BRIEFING A CASE

A. What Is a Case Brief?

The word "brief" has two different meanings in the law. The written arguments attorneys submit to courts and other adjudicators are generically referred to as briefs. Later in this book, when you learn how to draft persuasive arguments, you will read more about the types of briefs attorneys file with courts. However, for present purposes, the term "case brief" simply refers to your own written notes about a case. Although a case brief is simply your personal notes about a case, most briefs follow a fairly structured format that is different from the type of notes you may have taken in the past.

There are three good reasons to brief cases. First, briefing a case will help you prepare for class. Taking written notes about a case allows you to sharpen your thinking about a case. It is all too easy when passively reading a case to presume you understand it, when in fact there may be gaps in your understanding or ambiguities in the case that merit further thought. The process of writing will help you identify any gaps in your understanding and will reduce the risk that you might inadvertently miss a key component of the case.

Second, case briefs will serve as an important resource tool for you during class discussion. Most law students find law school classes to be rigorous and challenging, and they can also be intimidating. Having a case brief laid out in front of you can boost your confidence when a professor calls on you to discuss the case. A written case brief also serves as an important anchor, or framework, during class discussion to help you make sense of why the professor might be asking a seemingly endless stream of questions about a case.

Third, case briefs will help you prepare for final examinations. You will study an enormous number of cases throughout the semester. Imagine yourself at the end of the term looking back at the hundreds of cases you studied during the semester. Without written case briefs, it would be almost impossible to recall all of the myriad details and important rules of law you gleaned from the wide range of cases you studied. Your case briefs will help you organize each course into a study outline as you prepare for exams.

The case briefs you will prepare for doctrinal classes will differ somewhat from the case briefs you will draft for this course. This chapter discusses the basic components of the case briefs you will prepare for your doctrinal classes. Chapter 7 discusses in depth the more detailed notes you will take in your role as a lawyer representing a client.

B. The Components of a Case Brief for a Doctrinal Class

There are a variety of ways in which you can brief cases. Because you will draft case briefs for your personal benefit, think about your learning style and what is most useful for you. The goal in briefing cases is to produce a brief that will not only be helpful to you in preparing for class and participating in class discussion, but will also be helpful to you months later when you study for final exams. With that said, some professors have strong style preferences about case briefing and provide their students with detailed instructions for briefing cases in their courses. In those courses, you should follow your professors' instructions when briefing cases. Generally, however, case briefs describe, on a separate sheet of paper (or on a separate document on your computer): (1) the name of the case; (2) the relevant facts of the case; (3) the issues involved; (4) the holdings in the case; (5) the court's rationale; (6) the court's dicta, if any; and (7) the court's judgment.

◎ ILLUSTRATION: *Nelson v. Lewis*

Nelson v. Lewis, 344 N.E.2d 268 (Ill. App. Ct. 1976)

FACTS: **Evidentiary**—Plaintiff is a minor child who was injured when a dog bit her while she was playing "crack the whip" in a friend's yard. While playing, the plaintiff either fell or stepped on the dog's tail while the dog was chewing a bone. The dog reacted by scratching the plaintiff in her eye. The dog had not appeared agitated before the incident and had never attacked anyone before.

Procedural—Plaintiff sued the dog's owner for damages under the Illinois Dog Bite Statute. Plaintiff appealed a jury verdict for defendant.

ISSUE I **(Law-Centered Issue):** Can a person's unintentional act constitute "provocation" within the meaning of the Dog Bite Statute when the act triggers a response from a dog that is in proportion to the unintentional act?

HOLDING: Yes, unintentional acts directed towards a dog can "provoke" the dog within the meaning of the Dog Bite Statute when the resulting attack is in proportion to the unintentional act.

RATIONALE:
   (1) Webster's Dictionary definition of provocation, a commonly understand definition, does not require intent.
   (2) The other statutory elements also ignore the plaintiff's state of mind or intent; therefore, the legislature must have not been concerned with intent.
   (3) The plain language of the statute does not contain any restrictive language modifying the statutory term "provocation." Had the legislature intended unintentional provocation to bar recovery, it would have modified the term "provocation."

ISSUE II **(Fact-Centered Issue):** Does the act of unintentionally falling on a dog's tail constitute "provocation" within the meaning of the Dog Bite Statute when the dog's response is in proportion to the inciting act?

HOLDING: Yes, the unintentional act of stepping on a dog's tail while the dog is chewing on a bone constitutes "provocation" within the meaning of the Dog Bite Statute, when the dog's response is in proportion to the inciting act.

RATIONALE:
   (1) Explanatory reasoning: Provocation may involve stimulation or incitement, and unintentional acts suffice.
   (2) Application reasoning: The child unintentionally stepped on the dog's tail while the dog was chewing a bone, and the dog was of a peaceable

temperament with no violent past; the dog responded by merely swiping its paw at the plaintiff.

DICTA: Court emphasized that the dog's response was proportional to the plaintiff's act of provocation; court implied that a vicious attack that is out of proportion to the child's unintentional act may not be protected under the statute.

JUDGMENT: Affirmed.

C. Suggestions for Drafting Case Briefs

1. Case Facts: Evidentiary Facts

When describing "what happened" in the case, the goal is to include only those facts that you believe are legally significant, and the basic background facts that will help provide context for the factual story. Legally significant facts are those facts the court expressly found to be significant, as well as those facts you think were probably relevant to the court, even though the court did not expressly so state. Because you will not know what facts are legally significant until after you have studied the court's holding and rationale, you will need to wait until after you have read a case in its entirety before describing the case facts. In the *Nelson* sample case brief, the factual statement contains not just the specific facts the court expressly found relevant, but also the facts that the dog had not previously been violent and did not appear agitated before the incident. Common sense would suggest that these latter facts may also have been relevant to the court—if the dog had a known violent temperament and was already visibly agitated just prior to the incident, the defendant would probably have had more difficulty convincing the court that the child's act of stepping on its tail was the inciting cause of the attack.

2. Issues

Clearly identifying the issues a court addresses is one of the more challenging aspects of writing a case brief and takes time and practice to master. Don't become discouraged if the issues you draft as a new law student are not perfect models of clarity. Most law students begin drafting issues by either framing the issue too broadly or too narrowly. If you draft a statement of an issue that is too broad and general, you will have difficulty later when you use the case brief to study for final exams. Months later, when you go back and review your case briefs, it will seem as if a group of cases each cover the same general idea, and you won't be able to recall why a specific case in particular was unique and therefore important.

Using the *Nelson* case as an example, consider the following broad description of the fact-centered issue:

> **Example 1:**
>
> *Issue:* Did plaintiff provoke defendant's dog under the statute?

Fast-forward three months and picture yourself trying to use this case brief as a study guide for final exams. This issue-statement is so broad and general that you would likely not recall what it was specifically about the *Nelson* case that was important, nor would you know where the *Nelson* case fits within the broader scheme of the course.

On the other hand, if you draft issues that are too narrow and detailed, you will not capture the "bigger picture" of why the case is relevant. As an example, consider the following very detailed description of the issue:

> **Example 2:**
>
> *Issue:* Did Jo Ann Nelson, a 2 ½ -year-old child, provoke a dog to swipe her with its paw, scratching her eye, when she fell on the dog's tail while playing the game of crack-the-whip in her backyard while the dog was peacefully chewing on a bone, and the dog had not previously been violent?

This example contains all of the relevant facts but is so detailed that the reason the case is important would likely get lost within the numerous factual details. In addition, as you use your case briefs as study guides later in the semester, the detailed facts would make it more difficult for you to distill what was essential about this case and to determine how the case fits into the larger scheme of the course.

As you draft briefs, the goal is to find a balance between being too broad and too specific. This rule of thumb might help: For fact-centered issues, include within your statement of the issue both (1) the element of the rule of law that is in dispute; and (2) a summary of only the most critically important facts the court relied on to justify its holding.

The following illustration strikes the appropriate balance between being too broad and too narrow. As you review Example 3, take a moment and identify the parts of the question that make it valuable. Where does the relevant element of the rule of law appear in the following statement of the Issue? What two critically important facts are included, or summarized, in this statement?

> **Example 3:**
>
> *Issue:* Does the act of unintentionally falling on a dog's tail constitute "provocation" within the meaning of the Dog Bite Statute when the dog's response is in proportion to the inciting act?

3. Holdings

The term "holding" is a somewhat ambiguous term of art. In a broad sense, a court's holding is how the court "processes" (interprets and/or applies) the rule of law. In the *Nelson* case, there are two rules of law that the court processes: the court held that (1) unintentional acts can provoke dogs under the dog bite statute; and (2) the unintentional act of falling on a dog's tail provoked a dog's response under the statute, because the response was proportional to the inciting act.

The term "holding" can also be more narrowly defined as the court's "yes" or "no" answer to the "issue." In the *Nelson* case, the court responded "yes" to both legal issues. Of course, without a well-crafted statement of the issue, a simple "yes" or "no" in a case brief would not be useful to you later when you tried to recall why a case was important. Because you read cases to learn how courts interpret and apply various rules of law, the relevant rules of law should appear somewhere in your case brief—either within your statement of the "issue" or within your statement of the "holding," or both.

If you craft your statement of an issue carefully, so that the issue itself contains the important rule of law the case illustrates, you may wish to state your holding as a simple yes or no answer. In the *Nelson* case, the following statement of the issue and holding would be effective:

> **ISSUE:** Does the act of unintentionally falling on a dog's tail when the dog is chewing on a bone constitute "provocation" within the meaning of the Dog Bite Statute when the dog's response is in proportion to the inciting act?
>
> **HOLDING:** Yes.

In the above example, you can identify the important rule of law the case illustrates by reading your statement of the issue. Many students prefer, however, to broaden the holding so that it restates the important rule of law in a clear, declarative statement. Framing the rule of law in a declarative statement may make it easier for you to absorb at a glance why a case is important. The following example illustrates this method of drafting holdings.

> **ISSUE:**   Does the act of unintentionally falling on a dog's tail constitute "provocation" within the meaning of the Dog Bite Statute when the dog's response is in proportion to the inciting act?
>
> **HOLDING:** Yes, the unintentional act of stepping on a dog's tail while the dog is chewing on a bone constitutes "provocation" under the Dog Bite Statute, when the dog's response is in proportion to the inciting act.

4. Rationale

When stating the court's rationale, the goal is to capture the key reasons the court held as it did. Avoid simply rewriting large portions of the court's opinion; that would not only be tedious, but your brief would not be a very effective summary of the case. At the same time, an effective case brief should not omit any of the key reasons that support the court's holding. The court's rationale may be scattered throughout the opinion, requiring you to read the case very carefully. For example, in the *Nelson* case, the court's rationale not only appeared in various places throughout the opinion, but the opinion also jumped back and forth between the reasons that supported its law-centered holding and the reasons that supported its fact-centered holding.

Earlier in this chapter we discussed the two types of reasoning that often appear for fact-centered issues—explanatory reasoning and application reasoning. When briefing the case, the reasoning order is important. A well-crafted opinion will begin with explanatory reasoning, laying the foundation for the legal requirements, and will then engage in application reasoning to apply those requirements to the case facts. Your case brief should follow that same order, and only after laying out the legal requirements with explanatory reasoning should you bring in the factual basis for the result with application reasoning.

Although dicta can also be considered part of the court's rationale, you may wish to summarize the dicta under a separate heading in your case brief. Dicta differs from other rationale because it is gratuitous—or not actually necessary to support the court's holding. However, dicta can be important because it may indicate how the court might resolve the same issue under slightly different factual circumstances.

5. Judgment

Conclude your case brief with a description of how the court disposed of the case as a result of its holding. For example, a court might affirm the lower court's decision, reverse the lower court's decision, reverse and remand the case, or deny a motion.

Exercise 3-1: Briefing a Case

....

Brief the following case:

State v. Haley
Court of Appeals, 1983.
64 Or. App. 209, 667 P.2d 560.

GILLETTE, Presiding Judge.

Defendant seeks reversal of his convictions for driving while suspended (ORS 487.560(1)) and driving under the influence of intoxicants (ORS 487.540), contending that the trial court erred by withdrawing his affirmative defense of necessity from the jury. Because defendant offered no evidence to support one of the two elements of that defense, the trial court's ruling was not reversible error. We therefore affirm.

Prior to trial, defendant stipulated that he was driving a motor vehicle on the night of his arrest, that his driver's license was suspended and that he was under the influence of intoxicants. Despite these stipulations, defendant pleaded not guilty to the charge of driving while suspended and raised a "necessity" defense under ORS 487.560(2)(a). That statute states:

"(2) In a prosecution [for the crime of 'driving while suspended'] ˙˙˙ it is an affirmative defense that:

"(a) An injury or immediate threat of injury to human or animal life and the urgency of the circumstances made it necessary for the defendant to drive a motor vehicle at the time and place in question; ˙˙˙"

In support of his defense, defendant introduced evidence that his father had fallen from a bar stool and broken his ankle and that he, defendant, was driving his father to the hospital when the police officer stopped their car. The state asked the court to withdraw the necessity defense from the jury; the court granted the motion. This appeal followed.

. . . .

Defendant next contends that the trial court erroneously interpreted ORS 487.560(2)(a) by requiring defendant to show that his father's injury was "life-threatening." The trial court's oral ruling on the state's withdrawal motion demonstrates that the court interpreted the statutory phrase "injury or threat of injury to human or animal life" to mean "life-threatening injury" and granted the motion in part because defendant had failed to produce evidence of a life-threatening injury.[11] The state agrees with the trial

---

11. The State, arguing its motion for withdrawal, said:

"* * * [W]hat I am saying is [that defendant had] not shown that there was an *immediate life threatening situation.* * * * Neither [has defendant] shown that it was necessary for [defendant] to drive rather than calling an ambulance; rather than seeking aid from other people in the bar;

court's interpretation. Defendant, on the other hand, contends that the statute does not require such evidence. We are thus called on to decide for the first time whether ORS 487.560(2)(a) requires proof of an injury of "life-threatening" severity.[12]

As noted, the statute requires a defendant to show "an injury or threat of injury to human or animal life." This phrase could mean either: (1) actual or threatened harm to a human being or an animal, as opposed to other, inanimate property, or (2) actual or threatened harm severe enough to cause the death of a human being or an animal. Neither the remainder of the statute nor its commentary resolves this ambiguity. We are convinced, however, that the legislature intended the statute to have the former meaning.

First, a comparison of the "necessity" defense at issue here and the more general "choice of evils" defense in ORS 161.200 suggests that the reference to "human or animal life" in ORS 487.560(2)(a) is simply intended to make the "necessity" defense unavailable when the "injury or threat of injury" is to real or personal *property* rather than a living creature. By contrast, the "choice of evils" statute provides:

"(1) Unless inconsistent with*** some other provision of law, conduct which would otherwise constitute an offense is justifiable and not criminal when:

"(a) That conduct is necessary as an emergency measure to avoid an imminent public or private injury; and

"(b) The threatened injury is of such gravity that, according to ordinary standards of intelligence and morality, the desirability and urgency of avoiding the injury clear-

---

rather than calling the police; rather than having two people who were examined by another police officer who were found not to be under the influence of intoxicants. Have them drive. * * *"

The trial judge then made the following findings and statements in his oral ruling:

* * * "Certainly there is no evidence at all that there was a *life threatening situation* here. * * *

" * * * [T]here is no evidence in the case that there was *a threat of injury to life,* and so I will withdraw the emergency defense.

" * * * I find that there was no *threat of injury to* the defendant's father's *life* and that there was no urgency or [of] circumstances that made it necessary for the defendant to drive a vehicle at the time and place in question * * *.

" * * * There was no evidence in the case at all that it appeared to the defendant that there was a *life threatening* situation. * * *

" * * * [The] injury had already taken place [and] there is nothing to indicate that the defendant's father's injury would have been worsened or that he could have been further injured had the defendant not driven him to the hospital. * * * " (Emphasis supplied.)

12. The State contends that we answered this question in the affirmative in *State v. Peters, supra.* The defendant in *Peters* alleged that his mother's illness required him to drive her to the hospital. The severity of the defendant's mother's illness was not in issue, but we noted in passing that "the jury could have found [from the evidence] that the situation appeared to defendant to be life-threatening." The state argues that this language establishes a requirement that defendants prove "life-threatening" injury in order to establish a necessity defense. The state is mistaken. As noted above, a defendant asserting a necessity defense must prove two elements: (1) actual or threatened injury and (2) urgent circumstances. The issue in *Peters* involved the second element. Our brief discussion of the "injury" element was therefore dictum rather than a considered interpretation of the pertinent statutory language.

ly outweigh the desirability of avoiding the injury sought to be prevented by the statute defining the offense in issue.

"* * * *"

This language and the Official Commentary to the 1971 Oregon Criminal Code, at
20, demonstrate that the choice of evils defense may be invoked by a defendant who
has acted unlawfully in order to prevent the destruction of inanimate property. The
necessity defense is similar in nature to the choice of evils defense but narrower: it will
only shelter a defendant whose illegal action was intended to remedy or prevent injury to human or animal *life*. This difference in the scope of the two defenses was
achieved by the legislature's use of the phrase "human or animal life" in ORS 487.560(2)
(a). We think it is fair to assume that the creation of that distinction was the only
purpose of the phrase "human or animal life."

Second, the imposition of a "life-threatening" standard could have unreasonably
harsh effects in certain circumstances. For example, suppose that a suspended driver
and another person travel 30 miles by motor vehicle to a remote area in order to camp
and hike. In the course of a hike, the suspended driver's companion breaks his leg. It is
clear to the suspended driver that his companion is not in danger of dying, although
he is in pain. The driver is faced with a choice: he can violate ORS 487.560(1) and drive
30 miles for help, or he can *hike* that distance. The state's construction of subsection (2)
(a) would compel the latter decision, but we think it unlikely that the legislature intended such a harsh result. We have often held that we "presume the legislature did not
intend harsh results that literal application of statutory terms would cause." *State ex rel
Juv. Dept. v. Gates*, 56 Or.App. 694, 699, 642 P.2d 1200 (1982); *Mallon v. Emp. Div.*, 41
Or.App. 479, 484, 599 P.2d 1164 (1979). *A fortiori*, we are not inclined to read into
ambiguous language a meaning with the potential to produce such results.

Third, there is no harm in omitting a "life-threatening" requirement from the defense. If the state is concerned that, absent such a requirement, suspended drivers will
use passengers' minor cuts and pulled muscles to establish the defense, the state's fear
is unfounded. In addition to proving the existence or threat of an injury, a defendant
must demonstrate that the "urgency of the circumstances" compelled him to drive.
The circumstances attending most minor injuries will not be "urgent" enough to aid
in the establishment of a necessity defense.

Our refusal to apply a "life-threatening" standard does not, however, require reversal. As the findings quoted, *supra*, n. 4, demonstrate, the trial court found no evidence
that "the urgency [of] the circumstances made it necessary" for defendant to drive his
father to the hospital. This finding was based on evidence that defendant made no
attempt to telephone an ambulance, the police or other emergency services, although
he knew such services existed in the vicinity, and did not request the driving assistance of other individuals at the bar who were both sober and licensed. Defendant
offered no explanation for his failure to secure an alternative form of transportation
for his father, and he points to no other evidence which could support an inference

that the "urgency of the circumstances" compelled *him* to drive his injured parent to the hospital. The language of ORS 487.560(2)(a) makes it clear that a defendant seeking to establish a necessity defense must prove *both* injury and urgent circumstances. Defendant's failure to offer evidence to establish the latter element justified the trial court's decision to withdraw the necessity defense from the jury. *State v. Peters, supra.*

Affirmed.

Exercise 3-2: Briefing a Case

Review the chart below.[13] The left-hand boxes describe each of the component parts of a case brief. The right-hand boxes depict how each of the component parts are illustrated in a case brief of the *Haley* case. Draw a line matching each component in the left-hand column of the chart below with the corresponding appropriate text in the right-hand column.

FACT-CENTERED (NARROW) HOLDING
How does the court answer the narrow legal question? What statement of the law can you glean from the case that compels how the court answers the specific factual question before the court?

Although Def. knew that alternative means of transportation existed, he did not try to call emergency services or seek assistance from a sober and licensed driver before driving his father to the hospital.

RATIONALE: FACTUAL ISSUE
What reasons did the court give for answering the factual issue the way that it did?

Does an "injury... to human or animal life" within the meaning of Oregon's necessity defense statute require that the harm be "life-threatening"?

LAW-CENTERED (BROAD) ISSUE
Is there a broad legal question not dependent on the facts of this case that the court considers in this case?

No. The Defendant's father's injury did not rise to the level of "urgent" circumstances under the necessity defense statute when there were other options Def. could have taken to transport his father to the hospital.

---

13. This exercise is adapted from a presentation and materials by Rory Bahadur, Associate Professor of Law, Washburn University School of Law, at the following conference: *Implementing Best Practices and Educating Lawyers: Teaching Skills and Professionalism Across the Curriculum*, Institute for Law Teaching & Learning, Gonzaga University School of Law, June 24, 2009.

PROCEDURAL FACTS/ POSTURE

Who are the parties or litigants? What were they seeking when the suit was filed? What was the legal basis of the suit? How did the case reach the appellate court from the trial court?

The Defendant was charged and convicted of: (1) driving while under the influence of intoxicants; and (2) driving under a suspended license. Def. raised the affirmative defense of "necessity" under Oregon statute, claiming that it was necessary for him to drive. Def. appeals the trial court's refusal to submit the necessity defense to the jury.

JUDGMENT

What did the appellate court do with the case?

The appellate court affirmed the trial court's conviction.

EVIDENTIARY FACTS

What are the important "what happened" facts of this case? What happened here that is necessary to repeat in the analysis so that you have a good idea of what happened relative to the decision of the court?

The Defendant and his father were in a bar, and the father fell and broke his ankle. Although Def. was intoxicated and had a suspended license, he drove his father to the hospital. While driving to the hospital, he was stopped by police and arrested. Def. didn't try to call an ambulance or ask anyone else at the bar to drive.

LAW-CENTERED (BROAD) HOLDING

If there is a law-centered issue, how does the court answer the broad legal question? Look for a broad legal rule that can be applied outside the factual parameters of this case to other cases involving the same issue. You should be able to lift this rule and apply it in a different case dealing with the same issue.

No. The necessity defense statute encompasses any injury to human life, whether life threatening or not.

Under the "necessity" defense statute, did the "urgency of the circumstances" make it necessary for an intoxicated person with a suspended license to drive a person with an ankle injury to the hospital, when other means of transportation existed?

RATIONALE: LAW-CENTERED ISSUE

If there is a law-centered issue, what reasons did the court give for answering the broad legal question the way that it did? Are there policy reasons? Statutory interpretation reasons?

FACT-CENTERED (NARROW) ISSUE

What is the specific question the appellate court is trying to answer as it applies the law to the specific evidentiary facts of the case before the court?

(1) An "injury to human life" does not mean that the injury has to be life-threatening. The word "life" merely clarifies that the injury doesn't include property interests (distinguishing the broader "choice of evils" statute, which includes the destruction of property). (2) Imposing a "life-threatening" requirement could have unreasonably harsh results—the legislature presumably did not intend for a literal interpretation that could lead to such harsh results. (3) No harm would result by omitting a requirement that an injury be "life threatening" because Def. is still required to show that the "urgency of the circumstances" compelled him to drive. **DICTUM**: "Urgent" circumstances could be: hiker with a broken ankle facing a 30-mile hike vs driving.

CHAPTER IN REVIEW

···

Core Concepts

COMPONENTS OF A COURT OPINION:

a. Case Facts, including:
   i. *Procedural* facts → what happened in court; and
   ii. *Evidentiary* facts → the "story" of the dispute between the parties;
b. Issue(s), including:
   i. *Law-centered* issues → deciding the *meaning* of a rule of law, and/or
   ii. *Fact-centered* issue(s) → deciding how the rule of law affects the factual situation before the court;
c. Holding(s) → the court's answer to the legal question before it;
d. Rationale → the reasons that justify the court's holding;
e. Judgment → the court's formal action that is to be taken because of the court's holding (*e.g.*, affirm, reverse, remand, or vacate).

COMPONENTS OF A CASE BRIEF (FOR A DOCTRINAL CLASS):

a. Describe the procedural and evidentiary case facts.
   - *Tip*: Wait until after reading the opinion to draft the facts so that you know which facts are legally significant.
b. Describe the issue(s), including:
   i. The key element of the rule of law that is at issue; and
   ii. A summary of the critical client facts that illustrates the factual dilemma the court faces when interpreting the rule of law (if a fact-centered issue).
c. Describe the court's holding(s) → how the court answered the issue.
d. Describe the court's rationale, including each of the key reasons why the court held as it did.
   - Identify any dicta within the court's rationale → gratuitous rationale that does not directly support the holding (often a statement implying that the result might be different under a hypothetical set of facts).
e. Describe how the court disposed of the case as a result of its holding.

The case notes that you take for this course should include the information described in this chapter. However, as a lawyer representing a client, your notes for this course will need to be even more detailed than for a case brief for a doctrinal class. Chapter 7 discusses in depth the more detailed notes you will take in your role as a lawyer representing a client.

THE LAWYER AS ADVISOR

"Human" Factors That Complicate Your Role

One of the quintessential lawyering skills you will learn in law school is how to "think like a lawyer." This is a broad term that embraces many different analytical skills. However, a basic component of this skill is the ability to evaluate the law fairly and objectively so that you can candidly advise your clients about the law's impact on them. As an advisor to your clients, you will need to use your best judgment in considering not only how the law might favor your clients' legal positions, but also how ambiguities in the law might present risks for your clients as well. Unfortunately, there are some "human" factors that will impede your efforts to attain the broad perspective that is a necessary foundation from which you can accurately assess your clients' legal situations. Empirical studies from neuroscientists and psychologists suggest that you cannot effectively overcome the hidden biases that undermine clarity and logic unless you first understand the nature of the problem, and then employ strategies that have proven to be effective in overcoming them.

A. The Problem: Hidden Biases that Undermine Perspective

1. Leaping to Premature (and Inaccurate) Conclusions

When most people think of the brain, they think of that part of the brain that engages in complex thinking and problem-solving—the "neo-cortex" region of the brain. For purposes of simplicity, the neo-cortex region of the brain will be referred to here as the "thinking" brain. Most people believe that the thinking brain drives all of their thinking and ensures that their decisions are based on a logical and rational processing of information. However, in reality, the thinking brain does not operate alone; instead, it operates in tandem with the emotional center of the brain—an area in the mid-section of the brain referred to as the "limbic" system (referred to here as the "emotional" brain). The "thinking" and the "emotional" brains not only operate in tandem, but the two regions themselves are connected by a veritable messy soup of circuits.[1]

Although the thinking and the emotional brains work in tandem, the emotional brain reacts more quickly than the thinking brain. The snap judgments and instincts drawn from the emotional brain can serve as important radars for danger; at the same time, these instincts are often mistaken and misguided. The emotional brain is crude and sloppy in the way that it processes information, drawing connections between things that share only surface similarities and leaping to premature conclusions based on biases and emotions that are largely unconscious. Unfortunately, the emotional part of the brain often leaps to these conclusions before the thinking brain has even registered what is happening and had an opportunity to mull over the implications of the incoming data.[2]

Even more problematic, the emotional part of the brain is simplistic and childlike in the way that it evaluates the world. The emotional brain doesn't grasp the subtle shades of gray in a situation, but instead categorizes behavior into polarities of good/bad, black/white, and right/wrong. However, many legal problems that require your expertise are not that simplistic; rather, they require that you identify the complexities and myriad shades of gray within the legal situation and use your best judgment to counsel your clients about how best to proceed. Unfortunately, the emotional brain's simplistic way of viewing the world can easily undermine your efforts to grasp complexities and nuances.

2. Stubbornly Clinging to Premature (and Biased) Conclusions

The emotional brain's tendency to leap to quick and often inaccurate conclusions would not be so problematic if the thinking brain would ultimately take over and logically evaluate the information you are attempting to analyze. Unfortunately, that doesn't always happen. Instead, the two regions of the brain continue to work in tandem, with the thinking brain trying its best to be dispassionate and logical, and the emotional brain seeking to prove that its first impression was "right." In other words, the emotional brain is *self-confirming*. As the two regions of the brain work together to evaluate a problem, the emotional brain can be insidious, offering tainted justifications and biased rationalizations to appease the thinking brain's need for logic. And, because the emotional brain wants to be "right," it actively looks for evidence that proves it was right, and ignores or discounts evidence that would tend to disprove its first impression.[3]

---

1. Louis Cozolino, *The Neuroscience of Psychotherapy: Building and Rebuilding the Human Brain* 8–9, 16–21 (2002).

2. Daniel Goleman, *Emotional Intelligence: Why it Can Matter More Than IQ* 294–95 (2006).

3. *See, e.g.*, Richard E. Redding & N. Dickon Reppucci, *Effects of Lawyers' Socio-Political Attitudes on Their Judgments of Social Science in Legal Decision Making*, 23 Law & Human Behavior 31 (1999).

The way in which our brains process information exacerbates this problem. The vast majority of the information we observe and acquire never actually reaches our conscious awareness. In the split second before we become consciously aware of what is "happening" in any given moment, neural pathways in our brains process and organize all of the bits of data and determine what to "upload" to our conscious awareness. This might not be too problematic if our brains simply uploaded a neutral, abbreviated version of what is actually happening, like the CliffsNotes to a novel. However, this isn't what happens. Instead, our brains *highlight* those aspects of the experience that reinforce our pre-existing beliefs while diminishing and even *completely blocking* from our conscious awareness those aspects of an experience that conflict with our beliefs. Because we are unaware that this is happening, we believe that the world as we see it is the one and only "objective reality," rather than only a single biased and very narrow version of "reality."[4]

3. The Implications for You as a Law Student and Lawyer

As a law student and a future lawyer, the implications of how your brain processes information are significant. Inevitably you will find that you like and have an affinity for certain clients and/or their causes, and that you dislike other clients or have negative judgments about their behavior or beliefs. These biases are at work *even as you read cases and client fact patterns;* you will find yourself naturally sympathetic to some behavior and critical of other behavior. These biases can subvert your ability to rationally and dispassionately evaluate cases and assess their impact on a client's situation. Because the emotional brain is self-confirming and wants to be right, your brain will tend to "upload" and highlight all of the information in a case or client fact pattern that supports your initial inclination, and ignore or minimize information that would tend to disprove or conflict with your initial inclination. A number of empirical studies reveal that we are highly critical of evidence suggesting that our initial inclination was wrong, and accept at face value all of the inferences that suggest we're right.[5] As a lawyer, this universal human phenomenon places you in danger of failing to understand the "other side" of a legal position, and of either over- or under-estimating the strength of a client's case.

As an example, assume that you just received an e-mail from a partner in your law firm. You have not worked with the partner before, but the partner has a reputation of being a workaholic, demanding, and "difficult." In the e-mail, the partner informs you that the firm will be interviewing a new client in an hour, and that your presence is requested at the interview. The e-mail message relays only the bare facts that the client is an old college friend of the partner's who was just fired from her position as

---

4. *See* Louis J. Cozolino, *The Neuroscience of Psychotherapy: Building and Rebuilding the Human Brain* 160–61 (2d ed. 2000).

5. *See, e.g.,* Ross et al., *Perseverance in Self-Perception and Social Perception: Biased Attributional Processes in the Debriefing Paradigm*, 32 J. of Person. & Soc. Psych. 880 (1975).

a firefighter. The e-mail message states that the client wants to sue the fire department because the client believes her termination was a direct result of sexual discrimination.

Before reading any further, take a moment and mentally place yourself in this situation, as if you really did receive the e-mail. What is your first instinct about this situation? Do you have any concerns about working with this partner? Do you have concerns about the partner's ability to remain objective? Do you have any concerns about your ability to provide a balanced, objective assessment of the strength of the client's case given the partner's friendship with the potential client?

Now think about the "story" you tentatively sketched out in your mind to flesh out the brief summary of facts in the e-mail message. What story did you hypothesize to round out the facts about the new client's situation? Did you hypothesize facts that would tend to illustrate the new client may have been a victim of sexual discrimination, or did you have a sense instead that she may have been fired for justifiable reasons? Why or why not?

Your first instincts about the situation can reflect underlying (and often unconscious) biases and judgments, and these biases and judgments have the potential to undermine your best efforts to be fair and impartial. If your first instinct was to conclude that the client was likely the victim of unlawful discrimination, you might have found her claims to be credible because you have an underlying bias, or belief, that women are often the victims of sexual discrimination. Or perhaps your instinct would be to trust the client's version of what happened simply because she is your client and on "your side." Or perhaps concerns about job security and a fear of "rocking the boat" with the partner who asked for your assistance might have subtly led you to find the client's claims more credible. In a real life situation, you might genuinely like your client and find yourself wanting to "take her side," accepting at face value everything she relays to you.

Now assume instead that your first instinct was to be skeptical about the client's claim that she was the victim of sexual discrimination. If this was your first instinct, you might have been skeptical because of an underlying bias, or belief, that people in this situation are often thin-skinned and prone to exaggeration and/or that women are typically not the victims of sexual discrimination. Or perhaps a personal dislike of the partner might have influenced you—you might have thought that if this client is an old friend of the difficult partner, perhaps the client also has a difficult personality, which could be the "real" cause of her termination from employment. Or perhaps you dislike the idea of filing suit against a fire department, or believe that women aren't physically strong enough to handle the job duties required of a firefighter.

Any of these concerns or biases has the potential to affect both your assessment of the various cases you read during your research, and the types of questions you might ask (or fail to ask) your potential client in a client interview. While researching case law to evaluate the strengths and weaknesses of your client's case, your tendency would be to focus on language in the cases and factual analogies that would support your initial instinct, and to minimize or even ignore language or factual analogies that would undercut your initial assumption. In an actual client interview, your biases or concerns could even lead you to ask questions designed to confirm your initial instinct about the client and to fail to ask questions that might actually reveal your initial instinct was incorrect. In other words, the emotional brain will have undermined your efforts to be objective and rational—and the stronger the bias, the greater the danger.

B. The Solution: Prosecute Your Thinking

1. Look for Red-Flags

a. Your Reactions

None of us are immune from biased thinking and from leaping to premature conclusions. However, there are steps you can take to unbind yourself from the problems associated with your biases and judgments. First, knowledge is power. An important first step is simply to be aware that this problem exists in the first place and to pay attention to red-flags that can serve as warning signals that biases are sabotaging your capacity to reason clearly and dispassionately. One such red-flag is a strong response to a client or fact pattern; a strong response is an indication that the emotional brain is invested in how you evaluate the situation. A strong reaction is particularly notable when you find yourself resisting thinking about how the "other side" might have merit because you are possessed of absolute certainty that you are "right" about your response. This stubborn insistence on being "right" is a hallmark of the emotional brain—a staunch certainty in the "rightness" of a position and a childlike categorizing of conduct into polarities of good/bad, black/white, and right/wrong.

As an example, consider the ill-advised, and widely publicized prosecution of three Duke Lacrosse players who were wrongly accused of raping a woman at a party. Mike Nifong, the district attorney who decided to prosecute the Duke Lacrosse players, ignored evidence that suggested the students were innocent and focused his attention on "evidence" that could suggest their guilt. The prosecutor clung to his belief in the students' guilt despite a mountain of evidence that suggested his belief was wrong. In hindsight, it is easy to identify this as a situation in which the emotional brain likely blindsided the prosecutor's thinking brain (recall that the emotional brain offers seductive justifications and rationalizations to appease the thinking brain's need for logic).[6]

---

6. It is, of course, within the realm of possibility that a prosecutor, for career or personal reasons, might choose to willfully violate his ethical duties as a lawyer and prosecute a defendant he believes is innocent. This possibility might explain at least some of the accounts of prosecutors who have prosecuted people who were ultimately exonerated. However, for most prosecutors who have chosen to contribute to the public good by serving as a prosecutor, the answer is likely more complex than that. For present purposes, we'll

However, there were red flags at the time that could have alerted the prosecutor to the fact that his emotional brain was interfering with his judgment. For example, in numerous interviews, Mike Nifong stated that that there was "no doubt in [his] mind" that the Duke Lacrosse players raped the victim.[7] Nifong's absolute certainty that he was prosecuting the right men was compounded by his *acceptance at face value* of inferences that would suggest his initial instincts were sound and his *discounting* of evidence that would suggest the students were innocent. For example, six months after Nifong filed indictments against the Lacrosse players, Nifong publicly admitted that neither he, nor anyone in his entire office, had ever interviewed the victim herself.[8] If this statement is in fact true, it means that he accepted at face value the victim's testimony even though he never spoke to her (and even though her story changed as time went on).[9]

At the same time, Nifong minimized and discounted evidence indicating that his initial conclusion might be wrong. For example, although Nifong initially stated that DNA evidence would be the crux of his case, no DNA from any member of the Lacrosse team was found on the victim or her clothing. Nifong minimized this important evidence by concluding that the Lacrosse players must have used condoms.[10] Although this could possibly explain the lack of DNA evidence, interestingly enough, the victim never stated that any of her attackers used a condom.[11] Moreover, the DNA of four unknown men was found on the victim's person and underwear.[12] Nifong apparently ignored these important inconsistencies by *accepting at face value* an explanation that would be consistent with his initial belief that the defendants were guilty.

As another example, mere days after the party at which the alleged rape occurred, the victim was shown photo lineups of the thirty-six (36) Duke Lacrosse players and was not able to pick out a single player as one of her attackers. Rather than question the veracity of the victim, Nifong appeared to dismiss this fact as irrelevant. Nifong chose to find more persuasive the victim's later ability to pick out her alleged rapists from the same photo line-up several weeks later. Nifong apparently dismissed as irrelevant the fact that one of the players the alleged victim finally identified had no

assume that Mike Nifong is not simply an amoral person with no conscience, but a prosecutor who was attempting to perform his job responsibly and ethically.

7. Daniel Schorn, *Duke Rape Suspects Speak Out*, 60 Minutes (Oct. 11, 2006), https://www.cbsnews.com/news/duke-rape-suspects-speak-out/.

8. Lloyd Vries, *No Excuses Now for Nifong in Duke Case*, CBS News (Apr. 11, 2007), https://www.cbsnews.com/news/no-excuses-now-for-nifong-in-duke-case/.

9. Aaron Beard, *Duke Prosecutor Is Under Heavier Fire*, Associated Press (Dec. 28, 2006), https://www.washingtonpost.com/wp-dyn/content/article/2006/12/28/AR2006122800714_pf.html.

10. Stuart Taylor Jr., *An Outrageous Rush to Judgment*, CBS News (April 2006), https://www.theatlantic.com/magazine/archive/2006/04/an-outrageous-rush-to-judgment/304904/.

11. *Duke Lacrosse Prosecutor Faces Ethical Complaint*, CNN Law Center (Dec. 28, 2006), http://www.cnn.com/2006/LAW/12/28/duke.lacrosse/index.html.

12. *Nifong Pleads Not Guilty to Contempt*, CBS News (Aug. 30, 2007), https://www.cbsnews.com/news/nifong-pleads-not-guilty-to-contempt/.

moustache, while she claimed the assailant had a moustache. When the player's lawyer offered to show Nifong photographs that would have revealed that his client had
no mustache the night of the party, Nifong declined to view the photographs.[13] Again,
Nifong's acceptance at face value of evidence proving he was "right," and dismissal of
evidence suggesting he was "wrong," is a classic example of how the emotional brain
can hijack the thinking brain's ability to logically and rationally evaluate information.

b. Your Judgments & Biases

We each judge the world and others constantly; indeed, judgments help us differen-
tiate between conduct and goals that might be beneficial for us to pursue and those that
might not ultimately be in our best interests. In fact, your biases helped you choose
which law school to attend. Your decision to attend the law school you are now attending likely included such factors as geographic location, the existence of specialty programs or clinics that appealed to you, your "sense" of the school's educational mission,
and/or its national ranking. In short, you literally would not be able to make decisions
without the input of the judgments and biases that stem from the emotional brain.

At the same time, judgments and biases about *other* people and their conduct can
thwart your efforts to gain the necessary perspective to logically evaluate a client's legal
situation. Judgments (particularly strongly held judgments) that someone else's conduct is "good" or "bad" or "right" or "wrong" are hallmarks of the emotional brain, and
can skew your perspective and ability to logically and rationally evaluate the situation.

The acronym "MOANS" can be a useful means of identifying some of the underlying negative judgments that can undermine your efforts to be objective. The
"MOANS" acronym stands for: *M*ust; *O*ught to; *A*lways; *N*ever; and *S*hould. The acronym represents value judgments that other people "*must*" "*ought to*" or "*should*"
behave in a certain way (and your belief that if they fail to do so, they are somehow
"wrong" or even "bad" people). They also represent the emotional brain's tendency to
over-exaggerate and catastrophize behavior, by believing that someone you are negatively judging "*always*" behaves inappropriately or "*never*" behaves appropriately. A
strong judgment about a behavior or person is a signal that the emotional brain is
hijacking your efforts to be objective.

You might be experiencing some resistance to the idea that judgments can be a
"bad" thing. After all, isn't this what the law purports to do—to promote justice by
punishing "bad" people and vindicating the rights of the innocent? This discussion
does not purport to engage in a moral debate, or to convince you that there is no such
thing as "good" or "evil" in the world. We can leave such discussions for philosophy
courses. Instead, the purpose of this chapter is simply to alert you to the reality that
your own values and judgments can, at times, undermine your efforts to attain the
necessary perspective from which you can logically and fairly evaluate a legal problem.

---

13. *Duke Lacrosse Case of False Rape Allegations*, http://www.ejfi.org/Courts/Courts-26.htm.

As an example, consider again the wrongful prosecution of the Duke Lacrosse players. Besides the prosecutor's stubborn refusal to consider that his initial instinct might have been wrong, there were other red flags at the time that could have alerted Nifong to the fact that his emotional brain was interfering with his judgment. In public interviews, Nifong described the Duke Lacrosse players as "a bunch of hooligans."[14] These word choices reveal both that he had a strong *emotional reaction* to the case, and that he had *strong negative judgments* about the players. His characterizations of the defendants reflected that he considered the players to be "bad" people—a hallmark of the simplistic thinking of the emotional brain. This language, and the prosecutor's apparently strong emotional response to the case, were red-flags that the emotional brain was interfering with the thinking brain's efforts to weigh the evidence dispassionately and critically.

What underlying biases might these judgments reveal? Only Nifong can know for sure. However, his public statements, taken together with his background, suggest some possible biases. The prosecutor was a social worker for several years before attending law school, and his wife worked for an advocacy program for abused and neglected children. This background, in conjunction with his responsibilities as a district attorney, might have predisposed him to prematurely accept the story of an alleged victim over the alleged perpetrators' claims that they were innocent. Moreover, the alleged rape occurred during a party replete with alcohol in which the victim was hired to perform as a stripper. It is not too much of a stretch to surmise that Nifong held some negative judgments about students who participated in the "revelry."

There may have been more personal biases that affected Nifong's judgment, as well. The Duke Lacrosse players were white, and the alleged victim was black; at the time, Nifong was in the midst of a hotly contested re-election campaign in a city with a large black population. In public interviews, Nifong referred to the Lacrosse players as "a bunch of hooligans" whose "daddies could buy them expensive lawyers."[15] He was accused by some of playing up the racial aspects of the case to help him win re-election. Again, we can only speculate as to Nifong's motives. However, self-interest can be a quite unconscious and insidious bias that can undermine your efforts to evaluate a legal situation logically and dispassionately.

Although you may never run for public office, consider a more common self-interest that has the potential to create bias. Unless you have agreed to represent a client *pro bono* (free of charge), the client's payment of legal fees will help you earn a living. Think back to the situation with the hypothetical client who was just terminated from her position as a firefighter. If you were to accept the case, your law firm would be paid by the hour to represent the client, taking in potentially hefty legal

---

14. *Committee Disbars Nifong for Using Duke Case to Boost Political Aspirations* (June 16, 2007), https://www.espn.com/college-sports/news/story?id=2906338.

15. K.C. Johnson, *Disgrace in Durham* (June 13, 2006), http://academic.brooklyn.cuny.edu/history/johnson/nas.htm.

fees. However, if you were to decide the case didn't have legal merit, your law firm would necessarily forego the legal fees that would accompany your legal representation. Although you would not want to represent a client whose claim was frivolous (and it would be unethical to do so),[16] consider the subtle influence money could potentially have on your assessment of the merits of a client's case. Do you think it is possible that your desire to earn a living (or to keep the partner happy) might subtly influence you to accept at face value certain aspects of the client's story that, under other circumstances, you might not accept? Or perhaps to interpret the case law as being more favorable than it actually is? This is a subtle bias that every practicing lawyer faces. The best lawyers are aware of this potential bias and keep it in mind as they evaluate their clients' legal cases.

2. "Complexify" Your Understanding

Assume that, after prosecuting your thinking, you have identified some underlying judgments or biases against the other party (or your client) that could undermine your efforts to evaluate the legal situation dispassionately and logically. Your underlying biases will have been revealed by your strong reactions to a party's conduct, your absolute certainty in your position, and/or the simplistic "good/bad," "right/wrong" judgments you are using to describe the situation.

One fundamental problem with the emotional brain's simplification of behavior into categories of "good" and "bad" is that people are more complex than these labels would suggest. People are generally not entirely "good" or entirely "bad." Good people sometimes are inconsiderate, selfish, or even cruel. Smart people sometimes do stupid things. For every version of "what happened" in any conflict, there is another version, and the "truth" usually lies somewhere in between. The emotional brain, however, strives for simplicity, and it does so by ignoring mitigating circumstances and the shades of gray that would provide you with a more accurate perspective. Left to its own devices, the emotional brain resists examining evidence that would suggest that it might have leapt to an inaccurate conclusion, and focuses instead on accumulating "evidence" that proves you were right all along. You might envision this reduced ability to think clearly and logically as "view[ing] situations through a narrow-angle lens."[17] From the vantage point of the narrow-angle lens, you will not have the broad perspective necessary to fairly and dispassionately evaluate a legal problem.

To avoid viewing the legal situation through a biased, "narrow-angle lens," you need to "prosecute" the emotional brain's simplistic characterizations of the behavior that has generated a negative judgment in you. Although you may not ever approve

---

16. The Model Rules of Professional Conduct expressly prohibit lawyers from pursuing legal actions and defenses that are "frivolous." *See* Model R. Prof. Conduct 3.1 (ABA 2002).

17. Robin Wellford Slocum, *The Dilemma of the Vengeful Client: A Prescriptive Framework for Cooling the Flames of Anger*, 92 Marquette L. Rev. 481, 490 (2009).

of a person or behavior you have judged, the goal is to "complexify" your understanding of the underlying behavior. When you begin to appreciate that the person or situation may be more complex than you initially believed, your emotional brain's hold over your thinking brain can begin to soften and relax its need to be "right." Once the emotional brain has softened its grip, your thinking brain has a better chance of gaining control over your ability to fairly evaluate the legal problem.

The first step in "complexifying" your understanding is to consider your judgment and identify specifically what it is about the person's behavior that you are judging. Does the behavior suggest to you that the person is "disrespectful"? Is the other person "stupid"? Is the other person "immoral" or "bad"? Next, make a good faith effort to look within yourself. Can you find a piece of yourself within your critical judgments about the other person? If you judge the other person as being stupid, can you think of a time in which you made a stupid mistake that you later came to regret? If you believe the other person is "immoral," can you think of a time when you may have acted in a way that is inconsistent with your own ideals? The goal here is not necessarily to make excuses for someone's "bad" behavior or to condone it. Instead, the goal is to loosen the grip of the emotional brain's tendency to over-simplify the issue so that you can gain a more objective perspective of the legal problem.

Another way to loosen the grip of the emotional brain is to consider what might have *prompted* the person to engage in the "bad" behavior. Your emotional brain summarily concludes that the "bad" behavior suggests the person is evil, or that a legal cause of action associated with the behavior has absolutely no merit. Again, these simplistic assumptions can undermine your efforts to evaluate the strengths and weaknesses of a client's legal case.

If you have difficulty coming up with ideas, sometimes it is easier to figuratively put yourself in the other person's shoes—even if you have never been provoked to do something as extreme as the party you are judging. For example, assume a client or another party tried to kill someone in a fit of rage. Although you have never tried to kill anyone, think back to a time when you were very angry and reacted in a manner that you later regretted. What provoked you to lash out in anger? Did you feel the other person was being disrespectful? Unkind? Selfish? Or were you particularly reactive and sensitive at the time because you had just received bad news? Were you under pressure to finalize a project, or to measure up to someone's expectations? Are you particularly reactive when you are under stress? Are you provoked to anger when someone else attempts to "control" you? To impose on your time or freedom to do what you want to do? This type of mental exploration can help the emotional brain soften its initial assumptions and make way for the thinking brain to prosecute your initial instinct.

Consider again the example of Mike Nifong, whose biases and premature judgments about the "guilt" of four innocent Duke Lacrosse players resulted in their wrongful prosecution. Although we can only speculate about Nifong's biases, assume that Nifong had been able to identify that he held a bias against "immature rich kids" who organized a "jock" party replete with alcohol and strippers. Nifong could have challenged the emotional brain's simplistic dismissal of the Lacrosse players as "irresponsible hooligans" by complexifying his understanding of his own judgments. If Nifong had openly prosecuted his own thinking, he would presumably have been able to find at least one instance in which he behaved in a way that could be characterized as "immature" or "irresponsible." In fact, Nifong's ill-advised prosecution of the Lacrosse players could serve as a prime example of irresponsible behavior.

3. Assume Your Initial Conclusion Is Inaccurate

From your awareness that you have underlying biases related to the case, the next step in prosecuting your thinking is to take a long, hard look at your initial tentative assessment of the relative merits of the case. Remind yourself that your initial conclusion was premature and reflects only one way of looking at the events. Then, to free up your mind and disengage from your initial biases, assume that your initial conclusion was not only premature, but also *inaccurate*. In other words, pretend for a moment that the *opposite* of what you actually believe is in fact true.

Thus, in the hypothetical case involving the female firefighter who was just fired from her job, if you initially concluded that the client was likely the victim of unlawful sexual discrimination, you would assume for a moment that the client was *not* the victim of unlawful discrimination (and vice versa). This can be a challenge because the emotional brain wants to be "right." You may need to remind yourself that the "reality" you see is only one small slice of what is actually happening "out there." Like the prosecutor in the Duke Lacrosse players' case, your emotional brain might well be seducing you down a slippery slope into the bottom of a deep well from which you literally lose all perspective.

4. Actively Search for Evidence that Supports the Opposite Conclusion

The next step is also critically important. Assuming just for the moment that your initial inference might be wrong, actively search for evidence that could support the *opposite* conclusion. Had Nifong done so, he might well have saved three innocent young men the strain and heartache of having to defend themselves from baseless charges, and ultimately saved his own career.

In the example of the hypothetical client who was fired from her position as a firefighter, assume that, after researching the law on sexual discrimination, you concluded that the case law supports your premise that your client was the victim of unlawful sexual discrimination. To prosecute your thinking, you would read through each "favorable" case again. This time, you would read each case with the assumption that the case actually supports the *other lawyer's* position. You would figuratively place yourself in the shoes of the lawyer and actively look for factual analogies that are favorable to the other party. You would then look for language in the case that you, in the shoes of the other lawyer, could use to support the other position.

You might ultimately decide that your initial conclusion was correct and that the case law really does support your initial position. That can happen—the law is sometimes that clear-cut. However, the law is often *not* that clear-cut, particularly in law school fact patterns. With the exception of those instances in which the law really is that clear-cut, if you take a good look at a case from the opposite perspective, you will usually be able to find language and/or facts in the case that support the opposite position. Therefore, be very suspicious about your own ability to impartially read the case law if you have not shifted your analysis at all after actively looking for language and factual analogies that would support the "other side." Before concluding that you have gleaned everything there is to grasp from a case, give the case a third or a fourth look until you are absolutely certain that you have evaluated the law from every perspective and are in a position to give the client a balanced assessment of the strengths and weaknesses of the client's case.

THE LAWYER AS INVESTIGATOR

The Client Interview

I. THE "HUMAN" FACTORS THAT COMPLICATE YOUR ROLE AS INVESTIGATOR

You might think that obtaining the relevant facts from a client would be relatively straightforward. After all, you and your client both share the common goal of ensuring that you obtain all of the important facts about the client's legal problem. Nonetheless, as Chapter 4 described in some detail, there are "human" factors that can cause you to leap to premature and sometimes inaccurate conclusions about your clients or their legal problems. Because the "emotional brain" is self-confirming and seeks to make its first impression "right," your biases and assumptions can lead you to ask questions of your clients that confirm your initial assumptions, and to fail to ask questions that might expose the flaws in your initial assumptions. Part II of this chapter describes an interview process that can help you avoid this problem.

There are also, however, "human" factors that can interfere with your *clients'* ability to provide you with all of the relevant information about their legal cases. Like you, your clients also suffer from biases and assumptions that can skew the accuracy of their factual stories. And, like you, your clients have a self-image they want to maintain. Your clients' shame about their own behavior, for example, can create an internal tug-of-war between their desire to educate you about all of the relevant details of their situation and their resistance to disclose details that might make them appear foolish. This internal tug-of-war can be conscious or unconscious. There are also some clients who intentionally withhold information from their lawyers out of a misguided sense that "what their lawyers don't know can't hurt them." For other clients, their reluctance to tell you what happened might stem from a resistance to re-live a traumatic event. Other impediments are more mundane—because many of your clients will not have had legal training, they simply won't be able to distinguish between the parts of their stories that have legal significance and those details that are irrelevant. Therefore, they might not disclose important details to you simply because they don't know the details are important.

There is an art and a strategy to encouraging clients to be candid with you, and to knowing how to ask the right kinds of questions and in the right order. Part II of this chapter describes an interview process, and a question-and-answer format, that will help you overcome some of the problems that can undermine your efforts to ask the right questions, as well as the problems that can interfere with your clients' ability to share with you all of the important details of their stories. First, however, it's important to understand in greater detail the "human" factors your clients will bring with them to your legal office.[1]

A. The Client's Biases Create Inaccurate, One-Sided Stories

Recall from Chapter 4 that the "emotional brain" works in tandem with the "thinking brain," and can undermine the thinking brain's efforts to evaluate a situation rationally and dispassionately—both because it often leaps to premature (and inaccurate) conclusions, and because it wants to be "right." Therefore, at a subconscious level, neural pathways in our brains "upload" to our conscious awareness those aspects of an experience that support our biases, and minimize or ignore those aspects of an experience that would suggest the situation is not quite as clear-cut as we would like to believe. Now imagine a client who comes to you for advice about a conflict the client has been unable to resolve. Your client will inevitably have a biased view of the facts relating to the legal problem; the more extreme the client's emotional reaction to the legal situation, the more dangerous the potential for bias. In fact, one certainty on which you can rely is that the client's version of "what happened" will be one-sided. If you naively accept the client's biased version of events as the "true" version of events, you as a lawyer might well overestimate the strength of your client's legal position, and underestimate the other party's position. There are two sides to every story, and your goal as a lawyer is to understand *both* sides so that you can attain an accurate perspective of "what happened." Only from that place of understanding can you accurately assess the legal issues and properly advise your client.

Eliciting the "other side" of the story can be a delicate balancing act because you have a relationship with the client that you don't want to jeopardize. Therefore, you can't simply tell the client that you know the client is biased and want to hear the other side to the story. As well, many clients are so invested in their side of the story that they aren't even consciously aware of facts that don't support their version of the

---

1. Many of the ideas in this chapter have been developed from materials in the following textbooks: David A. Binder *et al., Lawyers as Counselors: A Client-Centered Approach* (2d ed., West 2004); Robert F. Cochran, Jr., John M.A. DiPippa & Martha M. Peters, *The Counselor-at-Law: A Collaborative Approach to Client Interviewing & Counseling* (2d ed., LexisNexis 2006); Robert M. Bastress & Joseph Harbaugh, *Interviewing, Counseling and Negotiation: Skills for Effective Representation* (LexisNexis 1990).

events; their emotional brain has minimized the details that don't corroborate their own version of events. Fortunately, there are questioning techniques you can use that will help you elicit the "other side" of the story while also maintaining a positive relationship with your clients. Part II of this chapter describes in greater detail a questioning strategy that can help you achieve these goals.

B. Fear of Judgment

Each of us has a self-image that we strive to foster and convey to others. Whatever those desirable qualities might be that we value in ourselves (to be smart, competent, good, loving, etc.), most of us would like others to see those qualities within us as well. Yet one of the challenges of being human is that we don't always live up to our internal standards. For example, if it is important to you to be smart and competent, there will undoubtedly be times in which you disappoint yourself—none of us can be 100% competent all of the time. A common reaction is not only to be disappointed in ourselves, but also to fear that others will judge us just as harshly as we have judged ourselves. Another common reaction is to blame someone else when we fail to live up to our own idealized version of ourselves; the tendency is to blame someone else for causing us to fail and to minimize our own role in creating the "failure." In either event, and to varying degrees, most of us tend to conceal our ineptitude and foibles from others—particularly from people we don't know and trust.

This effort to "look good" can create a real dilemma for a client who is in legal trouble. Assume, for example, that your client is involved in a legal dispute. On the one hand, your client would want you to have all of the information you need in order to represent her as effectively as you can. At the same time, in every dispute there are two sides to the story, and your client is likely not an entirely blameless victim in the dispute. Therefore, your client faces a dilemma—although the client knows that you really should be aware of all the facts in order to deliver the best possible legal representation, the client is also invested in "looking good." If the client engaged in behavior that she does not view as worthy of her highest ideal of herself, then she will experience some degree of reluctance to share with you the myriad pieces of the story that might make her look bad in your eyes—even though you need to know these facts in order to evaluate the legal problem. Even more problematic, her own judgments and biases about her "bad" behavior may well have caused her to forget, or to minimize, her own role in contributing to the conflict.

These dilemmas do not just exist for clients who are involved in litigation. Clients experience these dilemmas in a variety of different legal settings, from concerns about their competence and intellectual acuity, to concerns about their ethics and morality. Because most people are reluctant to expose their vulnerabilities to relative strangers, it is important that you develop the requisite level of trust and respect that will help your clients feel comfortable enough to expose their vulnerabilities to you.

1. Think back to a time when you made a mistake and were concerned that others might judge you. Now think about a person who you felt comfortable talking to about the problem. What was it that this person did or conveyed to you that helped encourage you to open up and talk about what happened?

2. What ideas do you have that might encourage such a client to open up to you?

3. As you read Part II of this chapter, consider which active listening skills you could use to help such a client feel more comfortable with you.

C. Fear of Bad News

Some clients consciously decide to withhold information from their lawyers; they fear that if their lawyer knew the entire unvarnished truth, the lawyer would either decline to represent them, or perhaps tell them news they don't want to hear. Such clients cling to an unrealistic hope that if they succeed in withholding the information from their lawyer, the "bad news" will never come out. Unfortunately, bad news usually has a way of leaking out at some point—often from another party in the legal dispute. This can impact your ability to represent the client effectively, particularly when you have developed a legal strategy that fails to take into account the unfavorable information the client has been concealing from you.

1. How might you appeal to the client's self-interest to encourage the client to disclose unfavorable information?

2. If you were to tell the client you suspect she is lying, what might be some possible negative repercussions to your future working relationship with the client?

3. Would it ever be appropriate to tell a client that you suspect she is concealing information from you? Or that you suspect her of being untruthful?

D. Emotional Trauma

At times, you may represent a client who has undergone a traumatic event. Here, too, your client faces a dilemma. On the one hand, the client wants you to learn all of the important factual details that would help you best represent him. On the other hand, recounting those factual details would require the client to effectively re-live the traumatic event. The fact that you, as his lawyer, are a virtual stranger would only increase the client's anxiety about re-telling the story.

1. What ideas do you have that might encourage such clients to tell their stories in a manner that would be respectful of the clients' need for safety and emotional control?

2. Assume there are details about the story that are not sensitive, while other details are more traumatic. Which part of the story might you ask the client to talk about first?

3. As you read Part II of this chapter, consider which active listening skills you could use to help such a client feel more comfortable with you.

E. Failure to Identify Information as "Relevant"

One of the more common challenges lawyers face when they interview clients is that clients often don't realize that certain aspects of their story might be important. Most clients are not legally trained and just don't know which facts are relevant and which facts are not. Or they simply might not remember some of the important details of what happened. Without skillful questioning, a client might neglect to tell you important information that would affect the quality of the legal advice you give the client. Your failure to elicit all of the relevant facts could lead to your giving inaccurate legal advice that might have serious consequences for the client. Therefore, it's important to use a combination of both broad ("open") questions and more narrowly tailored ("closed") questions to elicit all of the important facts.

Part II of this chapter describes a strategy for asking questions that encourages full disclosure and minimizes the likelihood of your missing important information. However, the strategy is based on a commonsense approach to eliciting information that has the greatest potential to be both complete *and* accurate. Before you read further, consider the following questions and what strategies make the most sense to you. By thinking about the logic underlying the questioning strategy, the strategies are more likely to resonate with you on a deeper level, and you will be more likely to remember them later.

1. What type of questions do you think would be more likely to give you perspective about the scope and parameters of a client's legal situation: (i) broad open questions about what is on the client's mind ("*tell me more about why you're here today and what you hope to accomplish*") or (ii) more narrowly tailored, closed questions about specific details concerning the situation ("*do you have concerns about the fact that he was angry when he said you were being fired*")?

2. Given your response to the question posed above, do you think it makes more sense to begin a client interview with open questions or narrowly tailored, closed questions?

3. Which type of questions do you think would be more successful in triggering a client's memory about specific factual details of an event she has forgotten: (i) broad open questions about the event in general ("*tell me more about the event*"), or (ii) more narrowly tailored questions about specific details about the event ("*do you recall whether he responded to your statement that….*")?

II. THE PHASES OF THE CLIENT INTERVIEW

A. Setting the Stage—Building Rapport and Trust

Consider for a moment a time in which you had a problem that you really couldn't handle on your own—a problem in which you needed advice and help from someone more knowledgeable than you. Perhaps you had a medical problem and needed medical advice, or perhaps you had a financial problem that required the services of a financial advisor or accountant. Now think about your first impression of the expert whose advice and counsel you sought. Did that person make you feel comfortable, or uncomfortable? What was it about that person's behavior that made you feel that way? If you were uncomfortable, what could that person have done differently to make you feel more comfortable, or to make you feel that you and your problems were important to him or her? If you were comfortable and had the sense that you were important to the advisor, what was it specifically that the person did that put you at ease?

1. Genuine Regard for the Client

There are a number of strategies good listeners use to encourage people to open up and share their stories with them, and it's certainly important to be aware of those strategies. However, by far the most important thing you can do as a lawyer interviewing a client is to actually care about the client as a person. As one successful salesperson observed: "*Nobody cares how much you know until they know how much you care.*"[2] As a lawyer, it is tempting to figuratively put your clients into legal boxes, referring to them as "the client with the messy divorce," or "the client with the tax problems." With this mindset, it's all too easy to dismiss the importance of the "human" factors and to think that you have to begin client meetings by immediately getting down to the business of ferreting out the legal issues.

Unfortunately, such an approach is likely to prove unsuccessful with many clients—most people want to know that you have a genuine interest and regard for them before trusting you with the specifics of their legal problems. In fact, a number of studies suggest that what clients really want from their lawyers, in addition to expertise, is "loyalty, respect, warmth, advice, and understanding." These qualities all "speak to the inescapable personal needs at play in any human encounter, however goal-directed it may be."[3]

2. Active Listening Techniques

a. Encouragers

One of your goals as a lawyer is to help put your clients at ease and encourage them to share their stories with you. However, many clients, particularly clients who

---

2. Origin unknown.

3. Kristin B. Gerdy, *Clients, Empathy, and Compassion: Introducing First-Year Students to the "Heart" of Lawyering*, 87 Neb. L. Rev. 1, 11 (2008), *citing* Stephen Ellmann, *Empathy and Approval*, 43 Hastings L.J. 991, 994 (1992).

have not had much experience dealing with lawyers, are understandably a bit anxious and nervous about going to a lawyer's office and meeting their new lawyer. They may also have an expectation that, as the lawyer, *you* will be doing most of the talking and they will be doing most of the listening. It may not occur to them that, as the client, they actually possess a wealth of information that only they can convey to you—and they will have to open up and talk to you in order for you to obtain that information.

There are some common non-verbal and verbal cues that subtly let people know that we are interested in listening to what they have to say, and that encourage people to continue talking. These cues are sometimes referred to as "encouragers." Encouragers are surprisingly effective at putting clients at ease and conveying the message that it is not only okay, but also highly desirable, that they continue to talk and to share with you their stories.

Nodding our head while listening to someone is a common non-verbal cue signaling that we are interested listeners. We also use such common verbal cues as "uh huh," "ummm," "I see," and "yes" to indicate that we are interested listeners. Each of these encouragers sends a subtle signal to the speaker that "Yes, I'm listening, and what you're telling me is important. Please go on." As you talk with your friends and family members and watch people in conversation, begin to notice and pick up on these encouragers. Watch what happens to the person telling a story when she is the recipient of such encouragers. For some of you, these encouragers may feel natural and easy because you unconsciously use them already in your conversations with others. For some of you, these cues might feel unnatural, contrived, and awkward. However, as with anything in life, if you begin to practice using these encouragers in your conversations with friends and family members, they will begin to feel more natural to you, and you may be surprised at the results you receive. In time, the ease with which you use such encouragers in everyday conversations will transfer to your communications with clients as well.

b. Client Recognition and Validation

Although we all differ in the degree to which we would like to be validated or recognized for what we do well, each of us has a basic need for approval and validation. For most people, this need is particularly important when we are in a situation in which we feel some degree of discomfort and uncertainty about our "performance." Particularly for clients who are relatively inexperienced with lawyers, there is likely to be some anxiety about whether they are talking too much (or too little), or conveying information that might (or might not) be irrelevant. This anxiety is likely to be magnified if they have done something they believe was stupid or perhaps even criminal.

There are a few fairly straightforward ways in which you can help put clients at ease. One way is to recognize and validate their efforts when they share something that you see as a "positive." For example, you might say something like: "*This is good stuff, and exactly the kind of thing I need to know about. Tell me more.*" Or, if the client shares something that she did well, you might validate that behavior with a remark such as: "*That was a smart thing to do,*" or, "*Very savvy.*" In short, by recognizing and validating behavior that puts the client in a positive light, you subtly encourage the client to relax and to "tell you more."

c. Normalizing Client Discomfort

Some clients may seem to you to be particularly uncomfortable and anxious when you meet with them. Their anxiety and discomfort could stem from any number of reasons. They may simply be uncomfortable meeting with a lawyer; they may have been through a traumatic experience; or they might be embarrassed about something they have done. One way to help clients become more comfortable is to "normalize" their anxiety. For example, in the case of a client who appears visibly anxious and ill-at-ease meeting with you, you might normalize the client's anxiety by sharing that it is normal for people who come to see a lawyer to experience some degree of anxiety or unease. In the case of a client who has been through a traumatic experience, you might share your understanding of how difficult it must be to have to re-live the experience by sharing the details of the story with you. Or consider a client who has ended up in your law office as a result of a contentious dispute, one in which your client may have said or done things in anger that he later regrets. How might you normalize that behavior? Would it help the client to know that you understand that sometimes people say and do things in anger that they wouldn't otherwise do?

d. Open Questions & Broad Invitations

Open questions are another effective way of establishing rapport and trust. By their very nature, they signal that you are interested in the other person and learning more about them. Open questions are typically "who, what, when, and where" questions. For example, you might ask the client: "*What brings you here today?*" Or you might signal your interest in learning more about the client's story by extending a broad invitation to continue the story, by saying, "*Tell me more,*" perhaps accompanied by a head nod.

B. The Overview Phase

After you have engaged in small talk and set the client at ease, you will need to get an overview of why the client has come to see you. This phase of the client interview is important in two respects. First, you will need to find out the reason your client has come to see you and obtain an overview of the client's concerns and questions. Second, this gives you an opportunity to educate the client about what to expect in the meeting, as well.

1. Asking the Client for an Overview of the "Problem"

Recall how the "emotional" brain leaps to premature and often incorrect conclusions and assumptions. This phase of the interview helps you guard against this tendency because it requires that you ask the client questions that can help you keep an open mind as to the nature of your client's problems, goals, and concerns. The client obviously has a reason for making the appointment to see you, although the typical client often doesn't have a clear idea of the precise legal issues involved. At this point, the goal is simply to get a sense of the over-all problem. In this phase of the interview, elicit the following information from the client: (1) why the client has come to see you; (2) the client's ultimate goals; and (3) the client's concerns, both legal and non-legal.

A mistake some lawyers make when questioning clients about their goals and concerns is to focus exclusively on their clients' legal and economic goals while neglecting to consider non-legal and non-economic implications. The legal choices clients consider almost always have non-legal implications as well; in fact, the non-legal consequences of a client's legal decision can be more significant to the client than the legal options themselves. Therefore, it's also wise to ask the client about the client's non-legal and even non-economic goals.

For example, suppose your client has been sued for copyright infringement; however, the client is also in the midst of negotiating an important business deal on an unrelated matter. How might the impact of the lawsuit affect the unrelated business deal the client is attempting to negotiate? Would the time and energy required to defend the lawsuit affect the client's ability to attend to the myriad details required to negotiate a successful business deal? Could the resulting publicity from the lawsuit sour the business deal in any way? Or could the legal fees the client would be required to spend in a protracted court battle drain the company's resources at a time when the client needs the capital for the unrelated business deal? How important is it to the client to be vindicated by a favorable jury verdict? Or, alternatively, how might a protracted legal battle impair the client's quality of life? Perhaps the client wants to engage in a protracted legal battle, or perhaps a quick resolution facilitated by a mediator might best serve your client's interests. The point is that you won't know the answer to these questions until you ask your clients about their ultimate goals.

When questioning clients about their ultimate goals, it's also important to resist the tendency to assume that the client's values and goals are similar to your own. For example, assume you are someone who would definitely want to pursue justice in court if you were the victim of an unlawful act. You might be surprised to learn that your client does not share your values or beliefs. Perhaps your client wants only an apology and is not interested in pursuing a court action, or perhaps your client wants to see whether there is a way to repair a bad business relationship and is not interested in pursuing damages in court.

Finally, it's important to find out from the client what concerns the client might have about pursuing legal action. Initiating or defending a lawsuit is time consuming and can be emotionally exhausting and frustrating. As well, your client could end up spending a significant amount of money in legal fees to achieve the desired outcome. Given the importance of the client's overall goals, it may or may not be worth it to the client to spend the time and money to pursue a legal action. It's best if you know upfront your client's concerns and ultimate goals. Only then can you be in a position to help the client figure out what kind of legal representation, if any, can best meet the client's needs.

2. Giving the Client an Overview of What to Expect

Many clients walk into lawyers' offices having had little exposure to lawyers and unrealistic expectations about what to expect from you. After you get an overview of why the client has come to see you, this is the perfect opportunity for you, in turn, to educate the client about what to expect from *you*. Educating the client about what to expect from the meeting serves two purposes. It helps put the client at ease by alleviating some of the client's anxiety about the unknown, and it helps educate the client about the role you want the client to assume in the meeting.

You might tell the client that you will ask her to give you a detailed account of "what happened" and that you will likely interrupt the client from time to time with questions because it is important that you understand all of the important details—you want to make sure that you "get it right." Particularly as a new lawyer, you might not be in a position by the end of the meeting to advise the client about the legalities of a proposed course of action. Instead, you might need to engage in some follow-up research to evaluate the strength of the client's case. By alerting your client to this likelihood at the beginning of the meeting, you will have forewarned the client that a follow-up meeting will likely be necessary; this helps avoid the prospect of the client receiving an unfavorable surprise at the end of the meeting.

C. Eliciting Detailed Facts—The Timeline Approach

1. Ask Open Questions

For many kinds of legal issues, the most effective strategy to elicit the relevant facts is to "begin at the beginning." If the client is experiencing a legal problem, you might ask the client to identify the logical beginning point. For example, you might say: "*Tell me when you first became aware of this problem.*" From that starting point, ask open-ended questions that help the client move through the timeline, such as: "*What happened next?*" and "*Then what happened?*"

Keeping a client moving through a timeline is deceptively challenging because you will be tempted to become sidetracked by issues that come up during the timeline discussion that seem to be just as important as the original topic. For example, assume you are investigating the possibility that a client was the victim of unlawful discrimination when she was terminated from employment. While telling you about an important meeting, suppose the client mentioned that her most recent employee performance review was one of the topics of discussion at the meeting. Upon hearing this information, you might immediately begin to wonder when the performance review was actually conducted, whether there are any written records of the client's performance review, and whether the topic of the performance review was raised in any other meetings. Unfortunately, if you begin questioning the client about each of these side-topics as they occur to you, it becomes all too easy to pursue the side-topics and forget to finish up with the *original* topic—the meeting itself. There might be other important details of the meeting you need to know about and won't discover if you become side-tracked with other issues.

One way to avoid this problem is to keep a separate notepad handy so that you can mentally "park" possible new and relevant topics by jotting them down when they occur to you. That way, you can continue to ask your client about all of the relevant details of a meeting, knowing that you are maintaining a written list of "parked" topics that you will pursue with the client *after* you have finished discussing the original topic. After the client finishes going through the timeline of events, you can go back to each "parked" topic and ask a series of questions designed to flesh out the details of each parked topic.

2. Follow-Up with Closed Questions

Leading with open questions is the most time-efficient, and accurate, way to get a sense of the bigger picture of "what happened." Open questions also help you avoid focusing your attention on one event or idea too soon and thereby failing to identify all of the potential legal theories that might be relevant to your client's situation. Asking open questions also helps you from making premature assumptions about where you assume the client is probably going with a story (only to find out later that your assumption was wrong and that you just spent precious time asking questions that ultimately turned out to be irrelevant).

Although it is most time-efficient to lead with broad, open questions, there is a time and a place for closed questions, which are more pointed and narrow in scope than open questions. Closed questions are those questions that ask the client to supply more detailed information about a specific topic that you believe may be relevant. They can not only trigger the client's memory, but can also give you detailed information that will help you evaluate the strengths and weaknesses in your client's legal position.

For example, consider the hypothetical situation in which a client believes she was the victim of sexual discrimination when she was fired from her position as a firefighter. Suppose you asked your client to start from the beginning by telling you when she first became aware there was a problem. Assume your client responded by telling you that she was caught by surprise by the announcement that she was being fired, and that the first time she was aware of any problem was in a meeting that occurred that day. You might ask your client a series of open questions about the meeting, such as, "*Who was present at the meeting?*" and "*What was said?*" Although your client's responses are likely to be helpful as she draws upon her memory to recall exactly what happened at the meeting, there will be lapses in her memory as well. This is the ideal time to follow your open questions with closed questions that can help jog the client's memory and help you obtain a more precise picture of what happened during the meeting.

Thus, you might ask the client such closed questions as: "*What did you say when he told you that you were being terminated from employment?*" A more pointed and narrower version of a closed question would be: "*Did he seem angry when he told you...?*" Questions that ask for a clear-cut yes-or-no response are even narrower versions of closed questions. Thus, you might ask: "*Was the battalion chief at the meeting?*" As these questions indicate, the strategic use of closed questions is essential to your ability to obtain detailed information about potentially important legally significant facts.

3. Probe for the "Other" Side of the Story

a. Look for Inconsistencies and Illogical or One-Sided Explanations

At this point in the client interview, you will likely have heard a version of events that portrays the client in the best possible light and minimizes or ignores potential problems or holes in the client's story. As the client's lawyer, it's important that you know "the good, the bad, and the ugly" in order to properly advise your client about the strengths and weaknesses of the client's case. The first step in eliciting a more accurate and complete picture of what happened is to make note of any inconsistencies in the client's story and of any facts or events that just don't make sense to you. These are likely areas in which the client's own biases have impaired the client's perspective and perhaps even blinded the client to seeing the bigger picture.

b. Ask Probing Questions about Each Inconsistent or Illogical Aspect of the Story

After identifying specific aspects of the client's story that seem internally inconsistent, illogical, or particularly one-sided, the next step is to probe each of the troublesome parts of the story in greater detail. This can be a sensitive area to explore because your goal is not simply to elicit the "other" side of the story, but to do so without jeopardizing the relationship you are building with the client. A way in which you can accomplish this goal without jeopardizing the lawyer-client relationship is figuratively to include a third-party in the conversation who can assume the role of the "bad cop."

For example, in the hypothetical situation with the client who believes she was the victim of sexual discrimination, you might pose questions from the perspective of the employer. Assume that, after hearing the client's version of the events, you believe there *may* have been a discriminatory motive; at the same time, you are not convinced that you have heard the entire story because the events just seem too one-sided and extreme. Perhaps you found it illogical that the client would not have had any idea that there was a problem with her work prior to the day she was fired. Or, perhaps the client portrayed the fire chief as being such an idiot that you just find her depiction of the fire chief to be implausible. You might say something like:

> *You know, it certainly sounds like there may have been a discriminatory motive here. But I also want to make sure I understand how the fire chief is likely to re-spond. So putting yourself in the role of the fire chief for a moment, what reasons do you think he would give for why he fired you?*

Assume the client angrily responded: "He told me he just felt I was insubordinate, but that's a <u>crock</u>! I wasn't insubordinate, and that's just an excuse to cover-up the fact that he's a misogynist!"

The client's emotional response to the question, combined with language that re-flects negative biases, are an indication that the client's emotional brain is likely inter-fering with her ability to be a fair and accurate observer of "what happened." It may or may not be true that the fire chief is a misogynist, or that the reason for her termi-nation from employment was a mere cover-up for discrimination. However, the cli-ent's response is a red-flag of your client's bias and serves as a warning to you that you should be particularly careful in following through with detailed questions to uncov-er the "other side" of the story.

Although your client's version of events might be one-sided, your client's response has also provided you with at least one defense the other party might have—that your client was insubordinate. You would then follow-up with questions designed to flesh out the details of the other party's defense. For example, you might ask: "*So he said you were 'insubordinate.' Tell me more about that. What else did he say about your being insubordinate?*".... "*What incidents did he base this conclusion on?*".... "*Were there any other meetings during which the topic of insubordination was raised?*" And so forth.

c. Ask About Potential Evidence Concerning Each Possible Defense

It's also important to ask the client about potential evidence upon which the other party might rely. Obviously, if the other party has evidence to support his/her defense, this would weaken your client's legal claim. Evidence can take the form of written documents or of witnesses. In the hypothetical situation of the terminated firefighter, you would ask the client questions about possible written documentation: "*Is there anything in writing that could support his claim that you were insubordinate?*" And, because witnesses are another form of evidence, you would also ask: "*Does anyone else at the fire station have any knowledge about your alleged insubordination?"* And: *"Who do you think the fire chief might call as witnesses to defend his conduct?"*

d. Use a Combination of Open and Closed Questions to Explore Every Possible Hole in Your Client's Story

Before moving on to other topics, it's important to keep asking the client questions about weaknesses or holes in the client's version of events until you have run out of possible ideas. In the hypothetical example of the client who was terminated from employment, the client identified one possible defense the fire chief might employ—that the client was insubordinate. After probing for detailed information, and evidence, about a possible "insubordination" defense, you would also ask the client: *"Other than insubordination, can you think of any other possible reasons the fire chief might give for firing you?"*

If the client responds with a "no" to your open question, recall that the client is not a neutral observer but a biased participant in the events. Therefore, your client's version of what happened can't be wholly trusted at this point. Instead, you should follow through with more pointed, narrowly focused questions to test the client's memory and to see whether there might be other possible problems with the client's case that the client has either minimized or "forgotten."

It is at this point, when the trail of finding possible holes in the client's version of events seems to have grown cold, that you must be both creative and logical. To avoid simply trusting your client's biased version of what happened, assume for a moment that your client is simply wrong in her assessment. In this hypothetical, you would assume, for example, that your client was fired for *legitimate* reasons. If that premise were true, then your assumption would be that the employer had a valid reason for firing your client—your job as an investigator is to find out what that reason might be. Therefore, step back and ask yourself why employees are typically fired. What kinds of behaviors cause them to be fired? One behavior that might come to mind is that employees are sometimes fired because they have absenteeism problems. Employees are also sometimes fired because they are incompetent. Think for a moment—what are some other reasons why employers sometimes fire their employees?

At this point, you will have no idea whether any of your ideas may uncover relevant facts or evidence. You might think of this part of the client interview as throwing darts at a dartboard. Some of the darts may hit the target, while others might fall harmlessly off the wall. You won't know whether any of your ideas might hit the target unless you take the initiative to consider the other side's version of the story and ask your client about them.

Therefore, after thinking about possible defenses the other party might have, turn each of your ideas into a closed question to ask the client. To avoid harming the relationship you are developing with the client, you might appeal to the client's self-interest by saying something like this:

Before we decide what legal strategy might be in your best interest, it's important that we think through each of the possible reasons the fire chief might give for why he fired you. The last thing we want is to be surprised later with new information we hadn't considered. So I'm going to ask you a series of questions that might or might not be relevant, but they're worth asking because one or more of the questions might possibly jog your memory about another possible argument the fire chief might raise.

You would then ask the client a series of closed questions designed to test whether any of your ideas might hit a target. For example, you might ask: *"Is it possible the fire chief might claim that you had an absenteeism problem?"*. . . . *"How about competency—might the fire chief claim that you weren't able to perform the job duties competently?"*. . . . And so on, until you have explored every reasonable avenue of defense.

D. Eliciting Detailed Facts—Verifying Possible Legal Theories

After you have elicited from the client a detailed version of "what happened," you may have some ideas about possible legal theories that could be relevant to your client's situation. For example, in the hypothetical situation of the client who believes she was the victim of sexual discrimination, one element you would need to prove is that there was a discriminatory motive for her termination from employment. The questions described above are an example of a questioning technique designed to verify whether you have a legitimate legal basis to prove discriminatory motive—they pointedly probe for holes in the client's version of events to determine whether there might be a *non*-discriminatory motive for her termination from employment.

The process of eliciting facts to verify possible legal theories should not be haphazard. Instead, it's important to write down each element of each legal claim you think might be relevant, and then proceed from there to ask questions designed to flesh out the factual validity of each and every element. As a new lawyer, you may not know enough about the law at this point in the client interview to ask follow-up questions designed to test the viability of possible different legal theories. If that were the case, you would schedule a follow-up meeting with the client, or perhaps a telephone conference call, after you have had an opportunity to research the law. Nonetheless, sometimes you will know in advance of the first meeting with a client that the client has a possible "discrimination" claim, or "breach of contract" claim. In that event, it is helpful to conduct some preliminary research *before* the meeting so that you can be prepared to ask the client questions that can help you assess the viability of possible legal claims.

For example, in the hypothetical situation of the client who believes she was the victim of sexual discrimination, if you had engaged in some preliminary research before the meeting you would have discovered that there is a federal statute (Title VII), as well as a state statute that prohibits employers from engaging in sexual discrimination in their employment practices. Assume you discovered that, in order to prevail, you would need to prove: (1) that your client is a member of a protected class (in this case the protected class is her gender); (2) that she was subject to an adverse employment decision; (3) that the adverse employment decision was motivated by her gender; and (4) that she was otherwise qualified for the position.

Knowing that these are the criteria you must prove, this would be the appropriate time in the interview to go back over your notes and fill in the details to ensure that you have a complete and accurate understanding of all of the facts that relate to each of the elements you would need to prove should you elect to file a lawsuit. Before reading further, pause for a moment and consider: If these were the four elements you would need to prove, which elements do you think would be easiest to prove? Which elements would you likely need to flesh out further by asking follow-up questions of the client?

Assume you decided that you should ask additional questions about the requirement that the client must be "otherwise qualified" for the position. To set up the pointed questions you will be asking the client, first give your client an explanation of why you're going to ask the additional questions. For example, you might say:

> *Should we elect to pursue a legal claim, one of the legal elements the law requires us to prove is that you were "otherwise qualified" for the position. I'd like to explore that idea further by asking you some questions so that we can assess where we stand with that, and evaluate possible arguments the fire chief might make.*

After laying the groundwork for additional follow-up questions, you would again follow the strategy of beginning this new topic with open questions, followed by more narrowly-tailored closed questions that can jog the client's memory and give you additional details. An example of an open question would be: "*If you were the fire chief, what possible arguments might you make that you weren't qualified, or competent, to handle the job?*" Again, notice here that you have preserved the lawyer-client relationship by making the other party the "bad cop." What other open questions might you ask in this situation?

After you have elicited whatever information you can from open questions about a specific topic (here, the legal element you must prove), it is again time to shift to more narrowly-tailored closed questions. What might be some reasons that the client would not be "otherwise qualified" for the job? How might you ask such questions without jeopardizing the relationship you are establishing with the client?

E. Concluding the Interview

After you have elicited the relevant facts from the client, it's time to conclude the interview and for you and the client to determine whether you each wish to pursue the matter further. After speaking with the client, you might conclude that this is not the type of case you would like to pursue, or that the case just doesn't have legal merit. On the other hand, the client might decide that she doesn't want to pursue any legal action at this time, or that she wants to think about it before deciding whether to pursue a legal relationship with you.

Assuming, however, that you and the client decide to proceed further, you will need to agree on the terms of your representation, including the fee structure and the scope of the legal services you are agreeing to provide. Has the client asked you to represent her in litigation, or has the client asked you only to conduct additional legal research and provide her with an opinion letter before she decides whether to continue to pursue legal action? It's important to ensure that both you and the client clearly understand the exact nature and scope of the legal services you will be providing to the client.

You will also need to identify clearly the "next steps" required of both you *and* the client. Are there steps the client must take, such as providing relevant documents to you? For example, in the case of an employee who has been terminated from employment, you would ask the client to provide you with copies of her annual performance reviews. You should also clarify the specific and concrete steps that *you* have agreed to take. Are you engaging in legal research and then calling the client to discuss the results, or are you also preparing a written legal memorandum and/or an opinion letter?

Timing is another important detail that can be easy to overlook. To a client involved in a legal problem, a "reasonable" amount of time for you to research the law and get back in touch with her might seem like three or four days. However, to you as a busy lawyer with many other clients also making demands on your time, a "reasonable" amount of time might seem more like two to three weeks. Assume that you neglected to identify a specific time frame during which you would report back to the client. Now place yourself in the shoes of the client who had expectations that she would hear back from you by the end of the week but instead doesn't hear back from you for three weeks. As the client, what impression would you have formed of your lawyer? Is this a lawyer you would like to continue to work with in the future? You can avoid such misunderstandings and resulting client frustration by agreeing upon a time frame for completing the next steps that is both reasonable and specific—and then adhering to your agreement.

EVALUATING RULES OF LAW

I. WHAT ARE RULES OF LAW?

Rules of law are not that different from the rules we encounter on a daily basis—from the "12 item limit" in the express checkout lane of the grocery store to a required attendance policy in class. Like rules imposed by private individuals and businesses, legislatures and courts also impose rules of law that regulate the conduct of the government and its citizens. As most commonly understood, a rule of law is a broad legal rule that grants rights, prohibits conduct, or mandates compliance with its provisions. However, the term "rule of law" is a relatively generic term that can refer both to the broad legal rules set forth in statutes and constitutions, and to judicial interpretations of such rules of law. To avoid confusion as you develop your understanding of rules of law, this coursebook refers to the former type of rules as "original" rules of law because they are the original source of a law you might be evaluating. In contrast, because courts interpret and refine original sources of law, this book separately refers to the courts' interpretations of the law as "interpretive" rules of law. Because original rules of law are the starting point for every legal inquiry, the remainder of this chapter discusses original rules of law. Chapter 2 introduced the concept of "interpretive" case law, and in Chapter 7, you will learn more about interpretive rules of law, and how courts interpret and refine original rules of law through their decision-making process.

A. Original Rules of Law

Original rules of law stem from the original three sources of law—constitutions, statutes, and common law—and are intended to govern behavior following their enactment or creation.[1] In other words, they are forward-directed. Because original rules of

---

1. A few statutes are applied retroactively. However, these statutes are the exception and not the general rule.

law are intended to apply prospectively to a large number of people, they are usually written in fairly broad, general language.

Today, statutes are the most common source for original rules of law. Both federal and state legislatures have enacted countless statutes that govern our behavior. Although statutes are the most common source of original rules of law, constitutions and the common law are also sources. For example, we learned in Chapter 2 that a federal statute known as Title VII prohibits employers from discriminating against their employees on the basis of race, color, religion, gender, or place of birth. The law found within Title VII is an original rule of law. It is considered "original" because it is law passed directly from Congress that has later been interpreted and applied by courts. In other words, it comes directly from the law-maker and is not an "interpretive" rule of law. As an example of an original source of law emanating from a *constitutional* source, the First Amendment to the United States Constitution prohibits Congress, among other things, from enacting any law "abridging the freedom of speech."[2] The First Amendment, a law prohibiting Congress from engaging in certain conduct that abridges the freedom of speech, is an original rule of law.

The common law elements of a contract illustrate an original rule of law that arises from the *common law*. To create a valid contract, there must be an "offer," an "acceptance," and "consideration" for the contract. This statement of the law, setting out in general terms the required elements of a common law contract, is also an original rule of law. It comes directly from the law-maker (the judiciary), and isn't simply an interpretive rule of law.

B. The Structure of Original Rules of Law

Whenever you begin evaluating a client's legal question, your work will always begin at the same place—determining which law applies and what the law actually means. However, laws are often vague, poorly written, and susceptible to different meanings. Therefore, it's easy to misinterpret what the law means and/or fail to identify an element that might be important to your client.

Best Practices Tip: An effective strategy to minimize the potential for mistakes is not only to read the language of the rule carefully, but also to outline, in your own writing, the separate components of the rule.

These are the components to look for when you read rules of law:[3]

---

2. U.S. Const. amend. I.

3. Adapted from Richard K. Neumann, Jr., *Legal Reasoning and Legal Writing* 16 (4th ed. Aspen L. & Bus. 2001).

1. a. An element or set of elements or
    b. Guidelines or factors; *and*

2. A word or phrase that indicates whether the rule is mandatory, prohibitory, or discretionary; *and*

3. A result that occurs after evaluating the elements or factors.

   In addition, some rules of law also contain:

4. An exception or group of exceptions.

1. More About Elements, Factors, and Guidelines

a. Elements

Elements are simply a set of standards or requirements that, if proven, compel a particular result. What makes an element test unique, compared to other types of tests that utilize factors or guidelines, is that an element test requires that *all* required elements be satisfied in order to compel the particular result. This type of rule is by far the most common type of original rule of law. Although some legal rules have only a single element, original rules of law more typically have two or more elements.

To illustrate, suppose you represent a major league athlete who claims that he was hired by a sportswear company to endorse its footwear. Your client claims that the sportswear company has now tried to walk away from the business deal. Before advising your client about possible legal remedies, you would first need to research the law in your jurisdiction to learn more about the law of contracts. As you researched the law, you would discover that there are three basic common law elements of a contract: (1) an "offer"; (2) an "acceptance"; and (3) "valid consideration" for the offer. Leaving aside for the moment the possible defenses the sportswear company might have to invalidate an otherwise binding contract, the structure of this common law rule of law would signal to you that you must prove all three elements in order to be successful in claiming that your client had a valid contract.

b. Factors and Guidelines

Although the most common rule structure is a rule with elements, legislatures and courts have also created laws that provide judges with guidelines and factors to consider when interpreting legal rules. Legal rules that contain factors or guidelines typically list a series of factors or criteria to guide judges in their decision-making process. Unlike the set-of-elements rule structure, statutes or case law with guidelines or factors provide judges with discretion to arrive at a result that seems fair and equitable.

You might be wondering why this distinction is important. Consider the practicalities of representing a client in a legal dispute. As you evaluate the merit of your client's position, it would be of utmost importance to you to know whether you would have to prove each and every element of a rule of law in order to prevail, or whether, instead, the language suggests only factors or guidelines for a court to consider. As an example, say you are representing a client in a divorce and will seek spousal support for the client. You research case law in your jurisdiction and find that courts are to consider the following factors in awarding spousal support: (1) earning capacity and needs, (2) obligations and assets, (3) age and health, (4) standard of living, and (5) other factors the court deems just and equitable. This factor test alerts you as to what kinds of evidence the court expects to hear about in deciding the spousal support issue and, therefore, guides you on how to make a case that spousal support for your client is warranted.

2. Some Commonly Used, Important Terms

a. The Importance of "And" and "Or"

It is easy to dismiss the importance of such seemingly innocuous terms as "and" and "or." However, these small words can have significant impact in terms of what a law means or requires. When elements are separated by the conjunctive term "and," each element must be satisfied. Using the earlier illustration of the sports figure as an example, the common law definition of a contract requires that you prove each of three elements—offer, acceptance, *and* consideration. Suppose you were to conclude that you could prove there was an "offer" and "consideration" for the endorsement deal, but that no valid "acceptance" was given. Because you couldn't actually prove that each of the required three elements was satisfied, you would not have a viable legal claim. Accordingly, you would have to advise your client that the law, unfortunately, doesn't support his efforts to compel the sportswear company to honor the agreement, even though he thought it was a legally binding "contract."

In contrast, the term "or" signals that either one of two or more elements may satisfy the legal rule. To illustrate, assume you represent a teenager who is being prosecuted in the state of Texas for causing a fire that damaged part of a teacher's desk at her high school. When you interviewed your client, she told you that she never intended to damage the desk. Instead, she claims that she attempted to light a paper towel on fire only as a prank. When the fire burned more quickly than she had anticipated, your client accidentally dropped the burning paper towel on the teacher's desk, burning the desk in the process.

As you research Texas law on arson, assume you found a statute that states: "a person commits [arson] if the person starts a fire . . . or causes an explosion with intent to destroy or damage" certain defined properties.[4] Re-read the statutory language—how many times does the term "or" appear in this statute? Consider the legal

---

4. Tex. Penal Code § 28.02 (2009).

significance of each of the "or" terms that are used in the statute. Does the term "or" expand the scope of the statute, or does it limit its application?

Under this Texas statute, could you defend your client by arguing that she never actually *destroyed* the teacher's desk, but only *damaged* it? Why or why not? Now consider another possible, and more ambiguous argument. Under this statute, could you defend your client by arguing that she never actually *intended* to damage the desk, but that the damage was caused by accident? Does it matter whether the "intent to destroy or damage" language modifies only "damage caused by explosions," or whether the "intent to destroy or damage" phrase embraces damage caused both by fires *and* explosions? Take a moment and mull it over, considering what you think the legislators probably intended when they drafted this language. Reading a statute and considering how and why it makes sense is a good starting point for deciphering a statute. The next step would be to verify your common sense assumption by researching how courts in Texas have interpreted this specific language (in other words, locating "interpretive" case law).

b. The Importance of "Shall" and "May"

The terms "shall" and "may" are two other important terms that are often used in rules of law. As the terms imply, the words "shall" and "shall not" are terms commonly used to indicate that a rule *requires* or *prohibits* a specific result. For example, the federal tax code mandates that all tax returns based on the calendar year "*shall* be filed on or before the 15th day of April."[5]

Although "shall" and "shall not" are the most commonly used terms to indicate that a rule requires or prohibits a certain result, it is important to read the language of a rule carefully to determine whether the language is mandatory or merely permissive. Even the phrase "may not" can signal a mandatory rule if the phrase is linked to other language that suggests that result. Consider a state statute that declares: "A married person, not lawfully separated from the person's spouse, *may not* adopt a child *without* the consent of the spouse...."[6] Taken in its entirety, do you think a married person can adopt a child without the consent of the spouse?

In contrast, the term "may" is commonly used to indicate that a rule is discretionary. For example, assume you have successfully won a lawsuit in which your client sued his former employer for age discrimination. You want the former employer to pay your attorney's fees. The statute provides that "the court... *may* allow the prevailing party... a reasonable attorney's fee."[7] Can you force the employer to pay your attorney's fees, or is it up to the court's discretion?

---

5. 26 U.S.C. § 6072 (emphasis added).
6. Cal. Fam. Code § 8603 (2010) (emphasis added).
7. 42 U.S.C. § 2000e-5(l) (emphasis added).

Best Practices Tip: Create a template for evaluating (and outlining) rules of law that includes these two ideas: (1) are the separate components alternatives (*or*), or are they each required (*and*); and (2) is the rule of law requiring or prohibiting certain conduct, or is it instead permissive or discretionary?

II. OUTLINING RULES OF LAW

A. Outlining Rules of Law with Elements

1. Elements

You should have a sense by now of just how important it is to begin any legal analysis with a clear and thorough understanding of each component of the rule of law on which you will be building your legal analysis. Like a house of cards, your legal analysis can collapse if you begin with an inaccurate or superficial understanding of the rule of law. To avoid that outcome, outlining the separate components of a rule of law is an essential starting point for any legal inquiry.

As you outline a rule of law, it's important to isolate and number each separate element of the rule of law. If you inadvertently characterize several distinct elements as a single element, you might well miss an opportunity to create an argument or fail to advise your client of an important requirement that you just didn't identify as being important.

For purposes of illustration, assume you are a state prosecutor and that you are evaluating whether you can charge a thief with burglary under Illinois' residential burglary statute.[8] Illinois' residential burglary statute is a typical example of a rule in which the elements are not separately and clearly delineated. That Statute states:

> A person commits residential burglary when he or she knowingly and without authority enters … the dwelling place of another … with the intent to commit therein a felony or theft.

It would be almost impossible to evaluate the meaning of this rule of law and to determine whether you could prosecute the thief under this Statute without first outlining the law itself. Before reading any further, take a moment and identify each of the elements of this Statute. How many elements did you identify?

An outline of the residential burglary statute would look like this:

---

8. 720 Ill. Comp. Stat. § 5/19-3 (2013).

A person commits residential burglary who:

1. knowingly *and*
2. without authority
3. enters
4. the dwelling place
5. of another
6. with the intent to commit therein a:
   a. felony, *or*
   b. theft.

As a practical matter, the above outline serves an important purpose. As a prosecutor evaluating whether you could successfully prosecute the defendant for residential burglary, you have a clear foundation on which you could build your analysis—you now know that you would have to prove six different elements of the Statute. This outline would not only be an important reference tool for you as you researched the law and created a legal strategy, but would also help you identify what questions you would need to ask the victims and possible witnesses so that you could determine whether you have enough evidence to prove each element.

There is no exact science to creating workable, clear outlines, but there are outlining errors that are harmless, and other errors that can sabotage your success. As an example of the former, you might have concluded that the residential burglary statute contained more than six elements. For instance, you might have decided to identify the terms "person," "commits" and "residential burglary" as separate elements under the Statute. It wasn't necessary to break down this particular phrase because this language in the Statute simply identifies the nature of the crime itself (residential burglary) and is the legal *result* of applying the elements test. It is only the remainder of the statutory language that describes the separate elements you would need to prove if you were to prosecute the defendant for this crime. At the same time, although breaking down these words into separate elements wouldn't prove to be useful to you as a lawyer, doing so is relatively harmless, albeit misleading.[9]

However, problems sometimes arise when lawyers over-simplify a statute by grouping two or more elements of the rule of law as a single element. For example, in the residential burglary case, consider the potential problems you might experience if you didn't break down the words of the residential burglary statute into at least six

---

9. While doing so is relatively harmless, it may prove confusing, however. Because "residential burglary" is the name of the crime itself and thus the end result of applying the element test, it would prove confusing and ultimately misleading to attempt to evaluate the legal end result as an "element."

elements. Suppose you identified as a single element the following phrase: "*enters the dwelling place of another.*" Although the phrase superficially seems to embody a single idea, it would be dangerous to clump the three elements embodied in this language into a single element.

As an example, suppose the defendant you are prosecuting opened an unlocked door to the homeowner's garage but was stopped by a guard dog before he actually crossed the threshold of the doorway. How many possible issues do you see here—one, two, three, more? If you had framed the above language as a single element, it would be easy to overlook the significance of other potential issues as you focused instead only on the legal issue that you first noticed. You might, for example, have focused on the "enters" language and researched whether a thief actually "enters" someone's home if he only opens an unlocked door and fails to cross the threshold. By framing the statutory phrase as a single element, you might become so focused on the "enters" question that you would fail to consider other potential issues presented by this "element," such as whether a garage is a "dwelling place" under the Statute.

Worse yet, without an outline that isolates each separate element of the rule of law, you might fail to ask your client the right kinds of questions that would alert you to possible problems in your legal case. For example, if you were focused only on the question of whether the thief actually "entered" the dwelling, you might neglect to ask the homeowners questions about their use of the garage (i.e., is it used as a typical garage, or as a dwelling?). By failing to ask the right questions up front, you can be blindsided later when you learn of harmful facts for the first time from the opposing counsel.

A thorough outline can minimize this risk. When you separately identify each of the rule's elements in your outline, you can use the outline itself as a checklist for the factual evidence you will need to develop. In contrast, with an overly simplistic outline, you would have to rely on a combination of luck and skill to ensure that you asked the right questions.

You can also minimize the potential for making these kinds of mistakes by treating your initial outline as only a *preliminary* one. After you have created an initial outline, take a few more moments and actively question the accuracy of your initial choices. A good question to ask is: Is it possible for the client or other party to fulfill or satisfy some word or group of words within the proposed element but not fulfill or satisfy another word or phrase within the element? If so, then break down the element even further, until you are confident that each element expresses only a single idea.

For example, consider again the phrase "enters the dwelling place of another." Suppose you tentatively concluded that this phrase was a single element. As you actively questioned this initial assumption, you would consider the first three words of the phrase—the "enter" and "dwelling place" terms. Then you would ask yourself whether it would be possible for an alleged thief to have "entered" a building that is not in fact a "dwelling place." Your response would alert you to a mistake in your tentative outline—because it is possible for a thief to enter a building that is not a residence, these terms constitute two separate elements, not one.

Next you would take a look at your new proposed element "dwelling place of another" and ask yourself the same type of question—is it possible for a person to be apprehended trying to break into a "dwelling place" he claims is his own? You might conclude that "this just isn't likely to happen. I can't really see that happening." But think again: is it *possible* for someone to be apprehended entering his own dwelling? Suppose the alleged thief is an estranged spouse who claims that he is co-owner of the home? Again, because there are two separate ideas contained within this phrase, it's safer, and therefore far better practice, to break the words down into their smallest components. Because your outline will be the starting point for your legal analysis, the goal is to isolate and separately identify each separate idea raised by the language in the rule of law.

2. Result

Of course it is also important to make sure that you understand the context for the rule of law you are evaluating. What happens if you can prove that each of the elements has been satisfied? Or, alternatively, what happens should you *not* be able to prove each of the elements of the rule of law? Is your client *required* to do something (e.g., file documents with a governmental agency or pay their taxes)? *Prohibited* from doing something (e.g., firing someone on the basis of gender discrimination)? *Allowed* to do something (e.g., merge with another corporation or file a lawsuit)?

In the residential burglary example, the Statute clearly states the result that occurs when each of the six elements are proven—a person commits residential burglary. As a prosecutor, the result is that you could prosecute the alleged thief for residential burglary. Now consider the perspective of the lawyer who represents the defendant. As a defense lawyer who also concludes that the State could prove each of the six elements, the legal result is that your client would likely be found guilty of the crime of residential burglary. Given your assessment of the Statute, as a practical matter you might conclude that you should use your best efforts to negotiate a plea bargain on behalf of your client.

B. Outlining Rules of Law with Factors

Like traditional rules that have required elements, when you evaluate a rule of law that has factors or discretionary criteria, it is also important to list separately each criterion or factor identified in the rule of law. Consider the following statutory language:

> In determining the amount to be ordered for support, the court shall consider the following circumstances of each party: (a) Earning capacity and needs. (b) Obligations and assets. (c) Age and health. (d) Standard of living. (e) Other factors the court deems just and equitable.

In the above example, notice the term "shall"—what does it mean? The statutory language signals that the judge is *required* to consider the enumerated "circumstances that follow." However, notice that the "circumstances" are broad, general factors rather than standards or required elements that someone must prove or satisfy. The statute gives the judge the discretion to weigh each of the factors listed in (a) through (d). Here, the judge has the discretion to decide that certain factors are more important than other factors, and therefore weigh them more heavily when deciding an appropriate monetary amount for support payments. In addition, the statute specifically authorizes the judge to consider any "other factors the court deems just and equitable" when determining the amount of the award for monetary support.

Because factors are only guidelines and not required elements, outline the factors in any manner that seems logical and reasonable to you, being careful not to omit any enumerated factor. In the above illustration, you might decide to change the order in which the factors are listed in the statute in order to make it easier for you to evaluate the law. One way you might outline the rule of law is:

> In determining the amount to be ordered for support, the court must consider each party's:
> 1. earning capacity
> 2. assets
> 3. needs
> 4. financial obligations
> 5. standard of living
> 6. age
> 7. health
> 8. other factors the court deems just and equitable

Consider why the drafter here reorganized the factors from the statute. In contrast to the order in which the factors were originally listed in the statute, what logical order does the above outline now follow?

Another logical way to outline the above rule of law would be to make the different conceptual categories explicit:

In determining the amount to be ordered for support, the court must consider each party's:

    A. Financial resources, including:
        1. earning capacity
        2. assets
    B. Liabilities, including:
        1. present and future needs
        2. financial obligations
        3. standard of living
    C. Physical Conditions, including:
        1. age
        2. health
    D. Other factors the court deems just and equitable

The above outline merely clarifies the writer's conceptualization of the different types of factors courts evaluate when considering an award of financial support. There is no single "right" way to outline a discretionary rule of law. However, be careful to include every listed factor in your outline, including the generic "other factors" criterion that many discretionary rules of law include.

III. EXERCISES IN OUTLINING
RULES OF LAW

The following exercises include both the more traditional type of rule structure with a set of elements and a discretionary rule structure. Carefully review each rule below, identify the type of rule structure the rule of law illustrates, and then outline each rule.

When outlining a rule structure with a set of elements, remember that it is important to identify each separate element of the rule, even when the statute itself does not clearly reflect the separate elements. When outlining discretionary rules, there are often a number of ways in which they can be outlined. You may or may not decide to change the order in which factors are enumerated. You may or may not decide to add subsections that conceptualize different criteria for you, or to reorganize any subsections that already appear in the rule of law.

Exercise 6-1

Or. Rev. Stat. § 163.212(1)—Unlawful use of an electrical stun gun, tear gas or mace in the second degree.

A person commits the crime of unlawful use of an electrical stun gun, tear gas or mace in the second degree if the person recklessly discharges an electrical stun gun, tear gas weapon, mace, tear gas, pepper mace or any similar deleterious agent against another person.

Exercise 6-2

42 U.S.C. § 2000e-2—Unlawful Employment Practices.

It shall be an unlawful employment practice for an employer—

(1) to fail or refuse to hire or to discharge any individual, or otherwise to discriminate against any individual with respect to his compensation, terms, conditions, or privileges of employment, because of such individual's race, color, religion, sex, or national origin; or

(2) to limit, segregate, or classify his employees or applicants for employment in any way which would deprive or tend to deprive any individual of employment opportunities or otherwise adversely affect his status as an employee, because of such individual's race, color, religion, sex, or national origin.

Exercise 6-3

N.Y. Ment. Hyg. § 9.61(e)(2)—Criteria for involuntary outpatient treatment

A court may order the involuntary administration of psychotropic drugs as part of an involuntary outpatient treatment program if the court finds the hospital has shown by clear and convincing evidence that the patient lacks the capacity to make a treatment decision as a result of mental illness and the proposed treatment is narrowly tailored to give substantive effect to the patient's liberty interest in refusing medication, taking into consideration all relevant circumstances, including the patient's best interest, the benefits to be gained from the treatment, the adverse side effects associated with the treatment and any less intrusive alternative treatments. Such order shall specify the type and amount of such psychotropic drugs and the duration of such involuntary administration.

Exercise 6-4

....

N.J. Stat. Ann. § 2C:12-1.2(a) — Endangering an injured victim

A person is guilty of endangering an injured victim if he causes bodily injury to any person or solicits, aids, encourages, or attempts or agrees to aid another, who causes bodily injury to any person, and leaves the scene of the injury knowing or reasonably believing that the injured person is physically helpless, mentally incapacitated or otherwise unable to care for himself.

IV. IDENTIFYING ISSUES FROM RULES OF LAW

After you have evaluated and outlined a rule of law, the next step in evaluating a client's problem is to identify the potential issues the rule of law raises for your client. Next to each separate element of the rule of law, make a note of the specific client facts that seem to relate to that element. From this initial evaluation, identify those elements that, on their face, are potential issues that might merit further research and analysis. These potential issues will guide your research and, ultimately, your written analysis of the law.

Be very careful before setting aside the elements you do not believe merit further analysis under the facts as you know them; you do not want to ignore an element only to find out later that the element was important. Therefore, keep an open mind and consider every client fact that might possibly present a potential issue under any possible interpretation of the language of each element. If you are uncertain whether an element merits further analysis, identify that element as a potential issue. It is better to be over-inclusive rather than under-inclusive in your research and analysis.

◎ ILLUSTRATION: Residential Burglary Problem

Assume that you represent the State of Illinois and have been asked to address whether the State can charge an individual with residential burglary. From the preliminary facts you received, you know that a man identified as Gerry Arnold has been apprehended for breaking into a garage owned by the Stripe family. One-third of the Stripe family's garage is used to store the family car, while the remaining two-thirds of the garage is used as a get-a-way by Michael Stripe, the couple's college-age son. A wall separates the two different areas of the garage. Michael Stripe's get-a-way has its own separate entry through a door. He spends two to three evenings a week and his free time on weekends in the garage, writing music. He also sometimes sleeps in the garage on a futon in a loft area. The garage is physically separated from the Stripes' home.

You also know that Arnold was apprehended with a bass guitar belonging to Michael Stripe and tools that would allow him to forcibly enter the garage. Michael Stripe claims that he left the guitar in his get-a-way earlier that day. Arnold has confessed that he entered the garage and took Michael Stripe's guitar. Arnold has also admitted that he does not know the Stripe family and did not have their permission to enter the garage. The Stripes would like the State to press charges.

Recall the residential burglary statute outlined earlier in this chapter. The outline reflects six elements the State has to prove in order to convict Arnold of residential burglary. Therefore, as the State's attorney, you would carefully consider each element and make a note of the facts that seemingly satisfy or fail to satisfy that element. Your notes would look like this:

A person commits residential burglary who:	
1. knowingly	Likely non-issue. No facts at this point to suggest unknowingly. Element likely satisfied.
2. and without authority	Non-issue. Arnold admits he did not have permission to enter the Stripe family garage. Element satisfied.
3. enters	Non-issue. Arnold was apprehended with a guitar Michael Stripe has identified as his guitar; Arnold had tools capable of forcing entry into the garage and admits he entered the garage. Element satisfied.
4. the dwelling place	Issue. Unclear whether the ⅔'s of the garage used as a get-a-way could be a "dwelling place" under the Statute.
5. of another	Non-issue. Garage clearly belongs to the Stripes.
6. with the intent to commit (a) felony, or (b) theft.	Non-issue under present facts. Arnold had tools to break and enter. He admits the guitar does not belong to him and that he took it from the garage.

Exercise 6-5

In Exercise 6-4 above, you outlined New Jersey Statute Section 2C:12-1.2(a), entitled "Endangering an Injured Victim," which provides that "[a] person is guilty of endangering an injured victim if he causes bodily injury to any person or solicits, aids, encourages, or attempts or agrees to aid another, who causes bodily injury to any person, and leaves the scene of the injury knowing or reasonably believing that the injured person is physically helpless, mentally incapacitated or otherwise unable to care for himself."

Referring to the Stripe illustration above as a guide, apply the following facts to the elements you outlined for this statute, noting which components are likely met, which are not met, and which warrant further legal research or further factual development.

Factual Situation: Seth Green was arrested and charged with violating New Jersey's Endangering an Injured Victim statute. Green hired you to prepare a defense, and as a starting point, you intend to analyze the facts you've learned thus far in conjunction with the statutory requirements. You have learned that Michael Reeves was injured in a 2-car motor vehicle crash when his car and Green's collided. It is unclear who caused the accident, but Green claims it was Reeves' fault. Green was driving with an expired license at the time, so he fled the scene without stopping to determine the severity of Reeves' condition, as he feared the legal repercussions of driving with an expired license. Reeves was knocked unconscious as a result of the impact and therefore unable to call for help. Another driver who witnessed the wreck stopped his vehicle and checked on Reeves. That driver dialed 9-1-1 to get help for Reeves, and Green was later apprehended by police.

CHAPTER IN REVIEW

Core Concepts:

THE BASICS:

1. "Original rule of law" is a term used in this textbook to refer to legal rules that arise from one of the three sources of law:
   a. Constitutions;
   b. Statutes;
   c. Common Law.
2. Original rules of law are intended to apply prospectively to a large group of people; therefore, they are usually written in broad, general terms.

THE STRUCTURE OF AN ORIGINAL RULE OF LAW

1. a. An element or set of elements (most common), or
   b. Factors or guidelines; *and*
2. A word or phrase that reflects whether it is mandatory, prohibitory, or discretionary; *and*
3. A result that occurs after evaluating the elements or factors.
4. Sometimes, a rule of law also contains an exception or group of exceptions.

OUTLINING AN ORIGINAL RULE OF LAW

1. Rules of Law with Elements (Most Common)
   a. *Definition*: Each element is a standard or requirement that, if proven, compels a particular result.
   b. To evaluate a rule of law with elements, identify and make a list of each separate element:
      i. Look for separate words or phrases that relate to a single idea. *E.g.*, "Dwelling place of another" would constitute two elements, rather than one, because it relates to two separate ideas; it is possible for someone to enter a dwelling place (satisfying that requirement), but the dwelling place might not be that "of another" (not satisfying this requirement).
      ii. Each word or phrase that embraces a single idea becomes a separate element of the rule of law.
2. Rules of Law with Factors or Guidelines
   a. *Definition*: A rule of law that identifies factors, or guidelines, to guide judges in their decision-making process.
   b. List separately each factor identified in the original rule of law.
   • Outline in any manner that seems logical and reasonable, organizing the factors by conceptual classifications that will make it easy for you to evaluate.

IDENTIFYING ISSUES FROM RULES OF LAW

1. Next to each separate element, list all of the client facts that seem to relate to that idea.
2. For each element, carefully evaluate whether the client facts present an *arguable* case that the element has or has not been satisfied.
3. If it is arguable whether the client facts satisfy or fail to satisfy a specific element, that element becomes a potential issue to research and evaluate.
   • In contrast, when it is very clear that the client facts satisfy or fail to satisfy a specific element, without the need to evaluate the law, that element becomes a "non-issue."

EVALUATING A CASE

I. HOW COURTS INTERPRET ORIGINAL RULES OF LAW

A. Evolution of Rule Enactment and Refinement

Because original rules of law are broad and general, questions and disputes inevitably arise when attorneys attempt to evaluate how the law affects a client's unique factual situation. Attorneys bring these disputes to courts, asking courts to resolve what the law itself means (law-centered issues) and how the broad rule of law applies to a specific factual situation (fact-centered issues).[1] When a court interprets or applies an original rule of law, it does not create a new rule of law. Instead, you might visualize the court's legal interpretation of an original rule of law as a sub-rule of the original rule. For example, when a court is asked to consider whether a person's verbal statement constitutes an "offer" that would create a legally binding contract, the court's interpretation of the term "offer" does not create a new law. Rather, the interpretation merely illuminates the meaning of an "offer." To help distinguish this type of legal rule from original sources of law, this textbook will refer to judicial interpretations of original sources of law as *interpretive* rules of law.

As an example of this continuous evolution of rule enactment and refinement, consider the federal wiretap statute. Congress enacted the wiretap statute, in part, to curb perceived abuses of governmental wiretapping. One procedural limitation was designed to protect wiretap evidence from tampering during the time frame before trial. That section of the statute requires the government "immediately" to obtain the safeguard of a judicial seal after retrieving wiretap evidence. Should the government fail to obtain a judicial seal immediately, the statute provides the government with only one alternative: it must provide a "satisfactory explanation" for its failure to do so.[2] This original rule of law leaves many questions unresolved. What exactly is a

---

1. Review Chapter 3 for a more extended discussion of law-centered and fact-centered issues.
2. 18 U.S.C. § 2518(8)(a).

"satisfactory explanation"? Does a satisfactory explanation require that the government prove there was no possibility of tampering during the delay, or must the defendant prove tampering was possible? Is a mere mistake a satisfactory explanation, or must the government prove that it had a legitimate law enforcement reason for the delay?

These unresolved questions require courts to define in more concrete terms what a "satisfactory explanation" means, separate and apart from the client's factual situation—a law-centered issue. Even with a more concrete definition, courts also have to determine whether specific types of explanations satisfy the new legal definition—fact-centered issues.

1. Interpretive Rules of Law: Law-Centered Definitions & Interpretations

When a court resolves what an original rule of law actually means, its interpretation of the law effectively changes how the original rule will be applied. Where once the law was silent, a court has now supplied a definition that will, in itself, become a test, or new standard, for litigants to satisfy. Using the federal wiretapping statute as an example, a court was asked to define the term "satisfactory explanation." In resolving the question, the *Gigante* court held that a satisfactory explanation requires proof that the government acted with "reasonable diligence" to obtain the required judicial seal.[3] This new definition is an interpretive rule of law. The court interpreted the original rule—the statutory term "satisfactory explanation"—and gave it further definition. And, by interpreting the statutory language to require proof that the government acted with "reasonable diligence," the court set a new factual standard for the government to satisfy. Thus, the interpretive rule effectively changed how the original rule would be applied. Where once the rule of law was silent, the *Gigante* court clarified that, at least within the Second Circuit, the statutorily mandated "satisfactory explanation" requires that the government prove that it acted with "reasonable diligence."

2. Interpretive Rules of Law: Fact-Centered Holdings

Even judicial interpretations of original rules of law leave many questions unanswered as attorneys evaluate how a newly defined rule affects their clients' unique factual situations. For example, even the "reasonable diligence" standard is vague. What set of facts might satisfy this standard? The *Gigante* court resolved only the specific factual question before the court—whether an innocent mistake might constitute a satisfactory explanation. The *Gigante* court held that a mistake is not a satisfactory explanation because it does not satisfy the "reasonable diligence" standard.

---

3. *United States v. Gigante*, 538 F.2d 502 (2d Cir. 1976).

This fact-centered holding is also an interpretive rule of law. By holding that governmental mistake does not satisfy the new definition, or standard, the court provided additional meaning to the original rule of law. We now know that, within the Second Circuit, innocent mistakes do not satisfy the "reasonable diligence" standard set by the court, and therefore do not constitute satisfactory explanations under the federal wiretap statute.

Although the *Gigante* court's fact-centered holding helped clarify the meaning of "reasonable diligence," new questions inevitably arise when courts face new fact patterns. For example, what if the government's delay was caused by something other than an innocent mistake? What if the delay was caused by the government's need to transcribe the tapes from Spanish to English, and the government faced a limited budget, equipment failure, and limited personnel? In *Vazquez*, a later court in the Second Circuit applied the "reasonable diligence" standard to this new set of facts. The *Vazquez* court held that the government satisfied the reasonable diligence standard because the government worked around the clock to minimize the sealing delay.[4] When the *Vazquez* court applied the original rule of law, as previously interpreted by the *Gigante* court, to a new set of facts, a rule of law also emerged from the *Vazquez* case. The rule of law emerging from the *Vazquez* case might be expressed as:

> The government acts with reasonable diligence when the delay is caused by a legitimate governmental purpose and the government makes reasonable efforts to minimize the delay.

To summarize, when a court interprets and defines an original rule of law, it creates an interpretive rule of law. Thus, the *Gigante* court interpreted the term "satisfactory explanation" to require that the government act with "reasonable diligence." When a court applies a rule of law to a specific factual situation, the fact-centered holding also creates an interpretive rule of law. The interpretive rule of law that emerges from the *Gigante* case's fact-centered holding is that an innocent mistake does not rise to the level of reasonable diligence. The interpretive rule of law that emerges from the *Vazquez* case is that the government acts with reasonable diligence when the delay is caused by a legitimate governmental purpose and the government makes reasonable efforts to minimize the delay.

The creation and refinement of a rule of a law can be illustrated as follows:

---

4. *United States v. Vazquez*, 605 F.2d 1269 (2d Cir. 1979).

ORIGINAL RULE OF LAW

E.g., Government must provide a "satisfactory explanation" for sealing delays."

INTERPRETED BY COURTS

**INTERPRETIVE RULE OF LAW:
LAW-CENTERED ISSUE**

E.g., Gigante: A satisfactory explanation requires "reasonable diligence."

INTERPRETIVE RULE OF LAW: FACT-CENTERED ISSUE	**INTERPRETIVE RULE OF LAW: FACT-CENTERED ISSUE**
E.g., Gigante: A mere mistake does not constitute reasonable diligence and is therefore not a satisfactory explanation.	*E.g., Vazquez:* The government acts with reasonable diligence when the delay is caused by a legitimate governmental purpose and the government makes reasonable efforts to minimize the delay.

II. EVALUATING CASES IN YOUR ROLE AS A LAWYER

In Chapter 3, you learned about the different components of a court opinion and how to brief cases for law school classes. As you read and study cases for a doctrinal class, your purpose is to learn about different legal doctrines, such as contracts and torts. However, in your role as a lawyer, you must not only be able to read and understand cases in the abstract, but also understand how the cases affect a client. Therefore, as a lawyer representing a client, your evaluation of cases will be affected by your client's unique factual situation. From a group of cases that address an issue you are researching, you will focus only on those cases that contain helpful interpretations of the original rule of law and/or facts that are analogous to your client's factual situation. Essentially, you will read cases to identify how courts define and interpret original rules of law that affect your clients. For fact-centered issues, you will also read cases to evaluate how courts have applied the rule of law to fact patterns analogous to your clients' factual situations so that you can predict how a court might resolve your clients' legal dilemmas. The remainder of this chapter describes how you will read and evaluate cases in your role as a lawyer, using the hypothetical residential burglary problem for purposes of illustration.

◎ ILLUSTRATION: Residential Burglary Problem, *People v. Thomas*

Recall the residential burglary illustration from Chapter 6. You were asked to assume the role of a young prosecutor for the State of Illinois who was evaluating whether the State could charge Gerry Arnold with residential burglary. Mr. Arnold had broken into a garage that was sometimes used as a retreat by the owners' son. After outlining the residential burglary statute, it became clear that the "dwelling" element posed an issue for further research. Specifically, the issue became whether a garage can be a "dwelling" under the Statute. Assume that you have researched Illinois law and found the *Thomas* case, a case interpreting the residential burglary statute. In *Thomas*, the Illinois Supreme Court held that the garage in that case was not a dwelling under the Statute. *People v. Thomas*, 561 N.E.2d 57 (Ill. 1990).

As you read the text of the *Thomas* case below, look for definitions or interpretations of the term "dwelling" and consider carefully how the facts in that case support the court's legal interpretations and its holding. The comments on the right hand column reflect how a lawyer might read the case, and the questions and steps the lawyer would choose to pursue having read the case.

People v. Thomas
137 Ill.2d 500, 148 Ill. Dec. 751,
561 N.E.2d 57 (1990)

Justice Ryan delivered the opinion of the court:

Defendant, Walter Thomas, was indicted by a Du Page County grand jury on four counts of murder (Ill. Rev. Stat. 1985, ch. 38, par. 9-1) [note], two counts of burglary (Ill. Rev. Stat. 1985, ch. 38, par. 19-1(a)), two counts of arson (Ill. Rev. Stat. 1985, ch. 38, par. 2 I(a)) and one count of aggravated arson (Ill. Rev. Stat. 1985, ch. 38, par. 20-1.1). A jury found defendant guilty of each offense. After separate hearings concerning the question of whether to impose the death penalty, the same jury found that Thomas was eligible for the death penalty and found that there were not sufficient mitigating factors to preclude impos-

> **Lawyer's Thoughts While Reading the Case:**

> Procedural history—will skim through and see if any of the history is relevant to my issue.

> Skimming through rest of procedural history—again, nothing relevant to my issue—can ignore.

ing the death sentence (Ill. Rev. Stat. 1985, ch. 38, par. 9-1). The trial court then sentenced Thomas to death.

The trial court also sentenced defendant to prison terms of seven years for burglary and 50 years for aggravated arson. The arson charge merged with the aggravated arson count. Defendant's death sentence was stayed (107 Ill.2d R. 609(a)) pending direct appeal to this court (107 Ill.2d R. 603). We affirm the convictions and the sentences.

> Court affirmed the lower court.

Facts

The facts are essentially as follows. On the morning of November 26, 1986, Detective James Davis of the Aurora police department investigated the scene of an apparent murder and arson at 302 Windstream in Aurora. There he found the body of Sophie Darlene Dudek on the floor of her garage. He observed fire damage in the rear of the garage and in the car that was parked there. He also found a broken perfume bottle. The perfume was used as an accelerant in the fire.

> These facts are not relevant to "dwelling" issue. Can skim and ignore.

Detective Davis then spoke with Allen Albus, who stated that earlier that morning he saw a black man, wearing a gray hooded sweat shirt, walking in front of Dudek's garage. Albus stated that several minutes later he saw smoke coming from the garage. Donnie Moore, who was defendant's employer, later informed Detective Davis that defendant was the leader of a cleaning crew that was working at Dudek's building on the day of the murder, and that defendant was wearing a gray hooded sweat shirt on that day.

Detective Davis, along with several other officers, later contacted Thomas, brought him to the Aurora police station and questioned him extensively. Defendant was again questioned on a different day. During the second day of interrogation, Thomas orally confessed and then signed a written statement in which he admitted committing the crimes with which he was charged.

> Skim and ignore—facts re: body and confession are not relevant to the dwelling issue.

Thomas stated in his confession that he had entered Dudek's garage, where she stored a large quantity of perfume that she was in the business of selling. Defendant stated that he opened a bottle of perfume, which he planned to remove from the garage, and that it fell on the floor, at which time Dudek entered the garage. Thomas stated that he tried to leave the garage but Dudek grabbed the back of his sweat shirt and began to scream. Defendant then, according to his written statement, removed a butterfly knife from his pocket and stabbed Dudek repeatedly. One of the stab wounds severed her spinal cord, killing her instantly. Thomas stated that he then poured perfume throughout the garage, in the car and on decedent's body, set it on fire with the hope of concealing the murder, and then left, later disposing of the knife. Based on this confession, and on other physical evidence, the indictments were forthcoming.

At trial, the State called Albus and Moore. It also called several law enforcement officials who testified generally as to the condition of the crime scene and decedent's body, and the circumstances surrounding defendant's confession. Following the presentation of the State's and the defendant's evidence, the jury returned guilty verdicts for all the crimes charged.

Burglary Conviction

Defendant's third point of error involves his burglary conviction. He contends that the facts, as presented by the State, establish that he committed, if anything, residential burglary rather than burglary. As such, he argues, he was improperly charged and convicted. We reject this argument.

The decedent's body was found in her garage. This garage is part of a multi-unit structure. All of the living units and garage units are attached and are under the same roof. Decedent stored perfume products in her garage, which provided defendant with the incentive to enter it.

Given these facts, the prosecution chose to charge defendant with burglary, rather than residential burglary. The crime of residential burglary was severed from the burglary statute in 1982 to create a four-year mandatory sentence for those convicted of entering the dwelling place of another without authority to do so. We held, in *People v. Bales*, (1985), 108 Ill. 2d 182, 91 Ill. Dec. 171, 483 N.E.2d 517, that the residential burglary statute is constitutional because it is distinct from the crime of burglary and, therefore, it does not confer unbridled discretion

Skim and ignore.

Good—here's the gist of the issue—was it burglary or residential burglary? Court holds it was not residential burglary.

These facts may be important—take note:
1. Garage is attached to multi-unit structure;
2. Perfume is stored in the garage;
3. Perfume gave defendant the incentive to enter the garage.

History of burglary statute—I can just skim through this to make sure the court doesn't say anything about dwellings.

This is my issue—focus on what court says...

Great—a definition of dwelling! Wait a minute—this definition is now part of the statute itself.

Note: check out that statutory section.

Bingo! Key language. I wonder what the court means by: "at least in this instance." Does that mean that in other instances a garage *might* be a residence? Also, the court says "whether attached... or not"—does that imply that a *detached* garage could possibly be a residence? Check and see whether there is other language in the case that answers these questions. Also check to see whether other cases clarify this language.

Check out the *Dawson* case because there a garage was a dwelling.

Check out the *Bales* case and see how it changed the law.

Is *Dawson* still good law after *Bales*? Check this out.

Shepardize *Thomas*—check to see whether any of these questions have been answered post-*Thomas*.

upon the State to choose which crime to charge. Defendant argues in the present case that, because he entered decedent's attached garage, he committed residential burglary. Therefore, defendant argues, to allow the State to charge him with burglary illustrates an instance in which the State has acted arbitrarily. We disagree.

We hold here that an attached garage is not necessarily a "dwelling" within the meaning of the residential burglary statute. In *Bales*, we stated that a dwelling is a structure that is "used by another as a residence or living quarters in which the owners or occupants actually reside." (108 Ill. 2d at 191, 91 Ill. Dec. 171, 483 N.E.2d 517.) This definition was later essentially codified by the legislature in the statute defining "dwelling." (Ill. Rev. Stat. 1987, ch. 38, par. 2-6(b).)

A garage, at least in this instance, whether attached to the various living units or not, cannot be deemed a residence or living quarters. As such, the prosecution, armed with the residential burglary statute (Ill. Rev. Stat. 1985, ch. 38, par. 19-3) and *Bales,* appropriately determined that defendant Thomas should be charged with burglary. Ill. Rev. Stat. 1985, ch. 38 par. 19-1.

We understand that the conclusion in this case is contrary to that in *People v. Dawson*, (1983), 116 Ill. App. 3d 672, 72 Ill. Dec 260, 452 N.E.2d 385, which involved essentially the same facts, and held that one who enters another person's attached garage commits residential burglary. *Dawson*, however, was decided before this court decided *Bales* and before the legislature adopted the new definition of "dwelling." Our decision today is not, therefore, necessarily inconsistent with the reasoning in *Dawson*. We leave to another day the question of whether the entry of an unoccupied portion of the second floor (*People v. Suane* (1987), 164 Ill. App. 3d 997, 115 Ill. Dec 933, 518 N.E.2d 458) or the porch (*People v. Wile* (1988), 169 Ill. App. 3d 140, 120 Ill. Dec. 433, 523 N.E.2d 1344) of a house constitutes the unlawful entry of a residence.

A. Identify Useful Interpretations of the Original Rule of Law

As in the *Thomas* case, courts often provide useful commentary about what an original rule of law means. This commentary might range from a discussion of the law's impact on public policy, to a survey of earlier court decisions that have interpreted the original rule of law, to a valuable definition buried within a single sentence in the opinion. The court's definition of the original rule of law often imposes a new standard that a party must satisfy. For example, the *Gigante* court interpreted the "satisfactory explanation" element of the federal wiretapping statute to require that the government must act with "reasonable diligence." As a practical matter, the "reasonable diligence" definition imposed a new standard with which the government must comply. Although not the original rule of law, each of these judicial pronouncements can loosely be described as rules of law that have been interpreted by the courts.

When you research and read cases, keep in mind that courts often address and evaluate many different issues within the body of a single opinion. Only those aspects of a case that relate to the precise issue you are researching for a client will be helpful to you as you evaluate your client's problem. In the *Thomas* illustration, note how the lawyer skimmed through the judge's commentary on legal elements that did not concern the issue the lawyer was researching for the client. In contrast, the lawyer focused very intently on the parts of the court's opinion that analyzed the issue relevant to whether a structure is a dwelling. Note how the lawyer paused and considered various questions the court's language inspired.

Again using the *Thomas* decision for purposes of illustration, consider the court's commentary regarding the residential burglary statute:

> We held in *People v. Bales* that the residential burglary statute is constitutional because it is distinct from the crime of burglary and, therefore, it does not confer unbridled discretion upon the State to choose which crime to charge.

The above statement is clearly a judicial comment about the residential burglary statute. You might even find the statement interesting because you learned something new about the residential burglary statute. However, that statement is totally irrelevant to the issue being researched—whether a garage can be a dwelling under the Statute. Therefore, you would not jot down this statement in your notes about the case because it would only distract you from your goal of finding language that clarifies the meaning of the statutory term "dwelling."

Although the above commentary is not helpful, the *Thomas* court did make two relevant statements about the "dwelling" element. Your notes on how the *Thomas* court interpreted the dwelling element might look like this:

1. "[A]n attached garage is not necessarily a dwelling."

   Question: What does the word "necessarily" mean? Could it mean that a garage *may* be a dwelling under the residential burglary statute with the right set of facts? Or maybe it means that only *attached* garages might be a dwelling with the right set of facts? Check this out.

2. "A dwelling is a structure used... as a residence or living quarters."

   Note to me: Court seems to be emphasizing the use of a structure as an important factor. This definition was incorporated into the Statute. Check the Statute to verify.

As the above notes illustrate, a court's interpretations and definitions of an original rule of law often prompt additional questions and the need for additional inquiry. For example, the meaning of the word "necessarily" can be properly understood only by scouring the rest of the court's opinion for facts and language that might provide added insight.

B. Identify How the Court Applied the Rule of Law to Facts

1. Identify the Fact-Centered Holding

To identify the court's holding, look for a statement that answers the legal question presented to the court. In *Thomas*, the question was whether the garage in that case was a dwelling. The court's statement that "a garage is not necessarily a dwelling" under the Statute does not answer that question. The court merely concluded that a garage may or may not be a dwelling. A few sentences later, the court answers the question before it: "A garage, at least in this instance, whether attached to the various living units or not, cannot be deemed a residence or living quarters." Your notes might look like this:

Holding: The garage, although attached to the living unit, was not considered a dwelling because it was not a residence or living quarters.

> **Note to me:** Will want to verify all of the facts that support this holding—e.g., how the owner used the garage—why it wasn't a residence or living quarters.

> **Another note to me:** Check out the significance of the phrase "although attached to the living unit"—is there any language to support the inference that physical attachment was at least a relevant factor to the court?

2. Identify Relevant Case Facts and Factors

a. Identify the Legally Significant Facts

Before arriving at any firm conclusion, make an initial list of every fact you think may have been relevant to the court. As you take notes, you will not simply make a list of each fact in isolation. Rather, you will be attempting to determine why certain facts were important to the court. When speculating as to why certain facts were important, the starting point for your analysis is the court's holding and rationale. Courts usually provide legal interpretations of the law (*explanatory reasoning*) and/ or a summary of the important facts that support their holdings (*application reasoning*, in which the law is applied to the case facts).[5] If the court proffered a legal interpretation(s) of the law to support its holding, write down each reason on a notepad or on your computer. For example, in its rationale, the *Thomas* court defined a dwelling as a "residence or living quarters"; this would be one such starting point. If the court didn't interpret or define the original rule of law in any helpful manner, then list the components of the original rule of law you are evaluating as your starting point.

Keeping the original rule of law and the court's legal statements in mind, write down each fact that seems to illustrate or relate to each statement. Sometimes courts expressly identify the facts they find to be important when they justify their holdings. For example, suppose the *Thomas* court had stated: "The garage was not a dwelling in this case because the owner only used the garage to store perfume, a commercial product. Notably, she did not use the garage for any living-type activities." When a court recites the facts it found relevant, these facts are clearly significant and should be identified in your notes. However, even when a court has articulated specific factual reasons to support its holding, consider whether any other facts in the case may have been *implicitly* important to the court. Just because a court may not have explicitly repeated a case fact in its rationale doesn't necessarily render that fact irrelevant. Your decisions about these facts will often be judgment calls over which reasonable lawyers may differ.

b. Identify the Underlying Factors that Support the Court's Holding

After you have written down each fact that may have been important to the court, the next step is to group together facts that seem to be similar and that reflect a common idea, or theme. After evaluating each factual grouping, you may decide a specific grouping of facts has several themes and is, accordingly, somewhat unwieldy and over-broad. If that is the case, subdivide the facts into smaller groupings until each grouping of facts reflects a manageable, common idea, or theme. These common themes can also be called "factors," because they reflect the underlying ideas the court

---

5. Review Chapter 3 for a more extended discussion of explanatory and application reasoning.

considered when justifying its holding.[6] At this early stage of the analysis, however, don't be overly concerned with the precise wording of the factors you are evaluating—you will likely modify your wording anyway as you read additional cases, deepen your understanding of the law, and begin the writing process itself.

It might be helpful at this point to define further what we mean by a "factor." Whether consciously or subconsciously, we weigh factors in every decision we make. For example, when deciding whether to purchase a car, we might weigh such factors as the cost of the car or the performance and appearance of the car, along with the car's age and reliability. Whether we overtly express them or not, factors guide our decisions. Similarly, when a court determines how an element of a rule of law should be applied to a specific factual situation before it, the court weighs different factors as well. In some cases, courts explicitly state the factors that guide them in their decision-making process. More often, however, the guiding factors are implicit, and lawyers must deduce the guiding factors by carefully evaluating the facts, holding, and rationale of a case.

Using the *Thomas* case for purposes of illustration, the court in *Thomas* did not clearly identify the specific facts or factors that supported its holding. However, when justifying its holding (the rationale), the *Thomas* court made three relevant statements about the original rule of law: (1) that "an attached garage is not necessarily a dwelling"; (2) that "a dwelling is a structure used . . . as a residence or living quarters"; and (3) that "a garage, at least in this instance, whether attached to the various living units or not, cannot be deemed a residence or living quarters." Separately considering each statement and the facts that seem to relate to that statement, your notes might look like this:

> **1. "Dwelling"**   *—court interprets this element as:* "An attached garage is not necessarily a dwelling."
>
> *Relevant Facts*
> *or Factors?*   Can't tell from this statement—too vague.

---

6. Note, however, that the use of the word "factor" here differs from the word's use in Chapter 6. Chapter 6 discussed factor tests, in which a legislature or court *specifically* provides a list of factors that judges are to consider when deciding a particular issue. The use of "factor" in this instance involves a common-sense grouping of facts (by you as the legal reader) that seem to belong together within a common idea.

2. **"Dwelling"**	—*court also defines this element as:* "A dwelling is a structure used... as a residence or living quarters."
Relevant Facts?	There are no facts here to indicate residential use. However, using the garage to store perfume is a *commercial* use and relates to this statement. The garage's use for *commercial* purposes is also consistent with the court's holding that this garage is not a "residence or living quarters."
Relevant Factor?	The important idea here seems to be the *use of the structure* as a residence or living quarters;
	There is no dictum that suggests any specific facts that might indicate what would constitute a "residential" use.
3. **Holding:**	"A garage, at least in this instance, *whether attached to the various living units or not,* cannot be deemed a residence or living quarters."
Relevant Facts?	Seemingly non-critical facts—a garage was attached to multi-unit structure and shared the same roof with living units.
Factor?	By this phrase, the court seems to be referring to the idea of the structure's attachment/detachment, or "proximity" to the house.
My thoughts:	By stating "whether attached... or not," the court implies that attachment vs. detachment to the residence isn't very important—particularly when coupled with the court's emphasis on the *type of use* as the dispositive factor. However, I'm not sure whether I should totally discount this fact and factor. What if the court merely meant that an attached garage is not automatically part of the dwelling?

3. A Word about Elements, Standards, and Facts

You may be wondering at this point why it's important to identify the underlying factors that may have implicitly guided a court in its decision. Sometimes it's not necessary at all. In some cases, the underlying elements of the rule of law a court is interpreting might be sufficiently clear and concrete for you simply to rely on the elements themselves to guide your analysis. Often, however, elements and legal standards are too broad and general to serve as effective analytical tools. At the opposite extreme, case facts, standing alone, are too specific and narrow to serve as effective analytical tools. Therefore, it can be helpful to break down a broad element or standard into more concrete and useful conceptual ideas—the factors that guided a court's decision.

a. Elements and Standards

As Chapter 6 discussed, statutes and common law rules typically impose elements that a party must satisfy in order to prevail. These elements, in effect, impose a legal standard that must be met. These criteria are the starting point for any legal analysis. However, when you consider the reasons why a court held as it did and, later, begin to make factual comparisons between a precedent case and your client's situation, these criteria, standing alone, are usually too broad and general to be useful. For example, consider the statutory requirement that the government provide a "satisfactory explanation" when it delays sealing wiretap evidence. This statutory element is too broad and unwieldy to be very useful when evaluating precisely why the *Gigante* court held that the government in that case failed to satisfy the "satisfactory explanation" standard under the specific facts of that case.

Even the standards that courts sometimes create when they interpret a statute or common law rule are often too broad and general to be useful analytical tools. For example, the *Gigante* court interpreted the statutory element "satisfactory explanation" to require that the government act with "reasonable diligence." Although this new legal definition, or standard, is helpful, it is too broad and vague to be of optimal usefulness when evaluating precisely why the *Gigante* court held that the government in that case failed to act with reasonable diligence.

The above discussion reflects the reality that many legal elements and standards are simply too broad and general to serve as the sole evaluative tool in legal analysis. However, it is also important to recognize that some elements and standards are concrete and narrow enough to serve as evaluative tools without the necessity of identifying underlying factors. For example, after reading the *Thomas* case, you might appropriately conclude that the statutory "living quarters" standard serves as a useful evaluative tool, in and of itself, without the need to identify any underlying factors. Nevertheless, clarifying in your own mind that the court seemed to be emphasizing the garage's "type of use" might be helpful to you as you evaluate the case and later consider how the case affects your client's situation. Moreover, although the "type of use" factor may seem obvious from reading the *Thomas* case in isolation, this factor might also be helpful later as you review other cases that evaluate the dwelling issue and attempt to reconcile the cases.

b. Case Facts

Relying solely on case facts to serve as the primary analytical tool creates the opposite problem. Unless your analysis is very simplistic and involves minimal case facts, case facts are usually too narrow and specific to be the most effective analytical tools. When determining which facts were relevant to the court, it would be virtually impossible to identify the legally significant facts in a vacuum, without reference to the court's holding and rationale, including the underlying factors the court seemed to weigh.

Just as importantly, it would be unwieldy and confusing to use case facts as your only analytical tool when you evaluate how the case affects your client's factual situation. Using the residential burglary problem for purposes of illustration, suppose you were to conclude only that the *Thomas* case illustrates that a garage used to store perfume is not a dwelling. Your narrow fact-specific evaluation of *Thomas* would not be very helpful to you in evaluating other structures in which the owners did not store perfume. By identifying "type of use" as an important factor in evaluating whether a structure is a dwelling, the *Thomas* case would now help you evaluate a client's situation that is similar, but not identical, to the facts of the *Thomas* case.

For example, assume that, as a young prosecutor for the State of Illinois, you are also evaluating whether you can prosecute someone under the residential burglary statute for breaking into a screened-in porch that is attached to a home. Relying solely on factual comparisons, without factors to guide you, you would likely find it difficult to compare a screened-in porch to a garage used to store perfumes. A screened-in porch simply does not appear to be "like" a garage, and you might be inclined to dismiss the case out-of-hand as being irrelevant. However, by using the "type of use" factor as an analytical tool, you would be more likely to recognize that the *Thomas* case could indeed serve as a useful basis for comparison—the "type of use" in *Thomas* (use of a garage to store perfume for commercial purposes) can be compared to the specific facts in the new situation (use of the screened-in porch for sitting, eating, and grilling food). And the "type of use" factor could help explain why the garage in *Thomas* was not a "dwelling" under the Statute, while the porch in another case, *People v. McIntyre*,[7] was a dwelling.

C. Formulate a Rule Statement

When courts interpret the law, they resolve what an original rule of law actually means (law-centered issue), and/or resolve how the original rule of law affects the factual situation before the court (fact-centered issue). In both cases, your challenge as a lawyer is to convert a court's holding(s) into a rule statement that accurately reflects how *and* why the court answered the legal question in the manner that it did. The goal is to draft a rule statement for each case that so clearly and accurately reflects how and why the court answered the legal question before it, that another lawyer would be able to grasp the import of the case just from reading your rule statement. These rule statements will be important to you as you seek to understand the legal requirements provided within court opinions, and as discussed later in this coursebook, they will be a critically important tool in educating and persuading the reader(s) of the legal documents you prepare, such as memoranda and briefs.

---

7. 578 N.E.2d 317 (Ill. App. Ct. 1991). This case will be examined in-depth in subsequent chapters of the book.

Sometimes courts expressly state how and why they answered the legal question in language that is clear, accurate, and artful. Under those circumstances, your task is easy—simply quote or paraphrase that language when formulating your rule statement. For example, suppose the *Gigante* court stated: "A mere mistake does not constitute reasonable diligence and is therefore not a satisfactory explanation under the federal wiretap statute." Because this is a fairly clear statement of why the court answered the legal question in the manner that it did, that statement might become your own rule statement for the *Gigante* case.

However, courts are usually not so artful or clear. Very few courts express their holdings as beautifully crafted statements that perfectly and clearly reflect why they answered the legal question in the manner that they did. For example, the *Thomas* court held only that "*a garage, at least in this instance, whether attached to the various living units or not, cannot be deemed a residence or living quarters.*" In one sense, this statement can be said to express the court's holding. However, this holding doesn't really capture why *Thomas* is important and unique. *Why* wasn't the garage "in this instance" a dwelling under the Statute?

In such situations, you must attempt to draft a rule statement that accurately reflects the take-away from the case opinion. Although there are many varieties of rule statements that can emerge from a judicial opinion, all rule statements contain two specific components: (1) a result and (2) a standard (often illustrated by the relevant factors). The result will focus on the specific legal issue you are interpreting. For the *Thomas* opinion, we focused specifically on whether a garage is considered a "dwelling" under the residential burglary statute. The court held that the garage, in that instance, was not a dwelling and then provided rationale to support that holding. Thus, when drafting a rule statement from the case on this issue, you may begin with something like "*A garage is not a dwelling under the Illinois residential burglary statute when…*"

Next, provide the standard for what it takes to satisfy that result. The standard is gleaned directly from the court's rationale—thus, take note of how the court *explained* the basis for its holding and any factors it seemed to be emphasizing. We learned in *Thomas* that the garage in that case, although attached to the living unit, was not a residence or living quarters, but was instead used to store perfume for the victim's business. On this basis, the court held that it was not a dwelling. In its reasoning, the court provided us with some express reasoning language to use—it told us that a resident's use of the space as a residence or living quarters is key. That key language from the opinion should be included within the standard of our rule statement. In addition, the specific factors/key facts involved in the case—the victim's use of the garage as a place to store perfume—relate directly to the basis for the holding. The victim did not use the garage as a place of residence, but instead used it in a storage capacity. With that knowledge, we must attempt to formulate a rule statement that captures both the reasoning language the court expressly gave ("residence or living quarters") and the implied take-away from the opinion (a garage is not a dwelling when it is used to store items such as perfume).

It is typical for a rule statement to *begin* with the result and *then* supply the standard for what it takes to satisfy the result. The reason for this particular order is reader-centered—in providing the result first, the reader's curiosity about the point of the sentence is satisfied at the outset. However, at times, it makes sense to reverse the order, particularly when the legal standard, and the factor(s) that often illustrate the standard, provide the reader with a clearer understanding of how the new sentence links back to the ideas in the previous paragraph and points forward to the discussion to follow. Again, the reason is reader-centered—in such cases, by providing the legal standard first, the reader's curiosity about the point of the sentence is satisfied at the outset. Further, you may find that your legal analysis reads less rigidly with variety in the sequencing of your rule statements.

In drafting rule statements, the challenge, in your role as an advisor to a client, is to formulate a rule statement that most accurately expresses the take-away from the case. At the same time, the ambiguities inherent in most courts' fact-centered holdings will also create opportunities for you in your role as an advocate. The ambiguous nature of courts' holdings will provide you with a fair degree of latitude to express holdings broadly or narrowly, depending upon which rule statements most effectively support your clients' interests. In other words, the unique rule of law a court's fact-centered holding expresses is not rigid but fluid. For example, in the *Thomas* case, a rule statement that embodies the court's holding might possibly be expressed in any of the following ways. As you are reading these rule statements, attempt to isolate both the result and the standard of each:

1. An attached garage is not a dwelling under the residential burglary statute when it is used to store perfume for business purposes.

2. An attached garage is not a dwelling under the residential burglary statute when it is used solely to store commercial products.

3. A garage is not a dwelling under the residential burglary statute when it is not used as a residence or living quarters, but is instead used solely to store commercial products.

4. A structure is not a dwelling under the residential burglary statute when it is not used as a residence or living quarters, but is instead used solely to store commercial products.

5. A structure is not a dwelling under the residential burglary statute when it is not used as a residence or living quarters, but is instead used primarily to store commercial products.

6. A structure is not a dwelling under the residential burglary statute when it is used to store commercial products.

Although each of the above statements attempts to reflect the case result and standard applied, your task as an advisor to the client is to formulate a rule statement that is both accurate and reasonable. Let's consider the accuracy and reasonableness of each possible rule statement.

1. *An attached garage is not a dwelling under the residential burglary statute when it is used to store perfume for business purposes.*

This rule statement is narrowly linked to the case facts. Under this statement, the *Thomas* rule is restricted not only to an "attached garage" but one used to "store perfume for business purposes." Under this statement of the *Thomas* rule, the court's holding would not necessarily be relevant to any structure other than an attached garage or to any use other than the storage of perfume. Under this very narrow rule statement, the *Thomas* court's holding would not apply, for example, to an attached garage used to store whippets rather than perfume. A later court would almost certainly not interpret *Thomas* this narrowly because the rule statement doesn't reflect the concerns and rationale underlying the court's holding.

2. *An attached garage is not a dwelling under the residential burglary statute when it is used solely to store commercial products.*

This second rule statement is somewhat broader, expanding the definition of impermissible use from perfume storage to one used "solely to store commercial products." Under this rule statement, any attached garage used for the sole purpose of storing commercial products would not be a dwelling. This rule statement would be a reasonable expression of the rule of law established in *Thomas*. Under this rule statement, an attached garage used only to store whippets would be interpreted in the same way as the garage in the *Thomas* case—the garage would not be a dwelling under the Statute.

3. *A garage is not a dwelling under the residential burglary statute when it is not used as a residence or living quarters, but is instead used solely to store commercial products.*

This third rule statement is even more expansive, expanding the *Thomas* rule to all garages, both attached and detached. If you were to apply this rule statement, any garage used only to store whippets would not be a dwelling under the Statute, regardless of whether the garage is attached or detached. This rule statement appears to be a reasonable expression of the rule of law established in *Thomas*. In addition, this rule statement contains explicit reasoning language from the case that further clarifies the requirements of a dwelling—that it be used as a residence or living quarters. Taking this key language straight from the opinion lends to its credibility and helps shield it from attack from an opponent. Under this rule statement, in a later case, a detached garage used to store commercial products would be interpreted in the same way as the garage in the *Thomas* case—the garage would not be a dwelling under the Statute.

4. *A structure is not a dwelling under the residential burglary statute when it is not used as a residence or living quarters, but is instead used solely to store commercial products.*

This fourth rule statement is more expansive yet, expanding the *Thomas* rule to all structures, not just garages. If you were to apply this rule statement, any structure used only to store commercial products would not be a dwelling under the Statute. Thus, a warehouse used to store whippets would not be a dwelling. Even a porch attached to a home would not be a dwelling if the porch was used only to store whippets. Again, this rule statement appears to be a reasonable expression of the rule of law established in *Thomas*. In fact, advocates might reasonably differ as to whether this rule statement more accurately reflects the *Thomas* case than the previous two rule statements.

5. *A structure is not a dwelling under the residential burglary statute when it is not used as a residence or living quarters, but is instead used primarily to store commercial products.*

This fifth rule statement is even more expansive, expanding the definition of impermissible use from a structure used solely to store commercial products to a structure used *primarily* to store commercial products. Under this interpretation of the *Thomas* rule, a porch attached to a home would not be a dwelling if the porch was used primarily to store whippets, even though the porch might have other uses as well (so long as those uses were not residential in nature). Again, this rule statement appears to be a reasonable expression of the rule of law established in *Thomas*.

6. *A structure is not a dwelling under the residential burglary statute when it is used to store commercial products.*

This sixth rule statement is more expansive yet, expanding the definition of impermissible use from a structure used primarily to store commercial products to a structure that stores *any* commercial products. Under this interpretation of *Thomas*, the *Thomas* court's holding would extend even to an attached porch used by a family for eating and sitting (residential purposes), so long as the owners stored a single box of commercial products in the corner of the sun porch. After considering the *Thomas* court's underlying concerns and the facts it emphasized in the opinion, a later court would probably reject this rule statement as being too broad—it doesn't seem to capture a reasonable interpretation of what the *Thomas* court likely meant. In addition, an opponent may attack this rule statement, arguing that it is not a clear reflection of the *Thomas* holding.

At this point, you should have a sense of the fluidity of rule statements and of the latitude you will have as an advocate to interpret case law. This fluidity can be visualized in the following diagram:

Narrowest Rule Statement

Thomas holding controls only that narrow category of future cases in which attached garages are used to store perfume

Broadest Rule Statement

Thomas holding controls a broad range of future cases in which the structures are used in *any way, however infrequently,* to store commercial products

Although holdings are "fluid," there is also a range of "reasonableness" within any two extreme interpretations of a court's holding. The above two extreme rule statements illustrate the limits of that latitude. A later court will not interpret an earlier court's holding in a manner that would create an absurd or unfair result. Therefore, in your role as an advisor to the client, your goal is to find a spot within the range of "reasonable" interpretations that accurately expresses the court's holding, even if that expression doesn't necessarily favor your client's own situation.

Later, as an advocate, should you actually be in the position of having to argue why a case favors your client's position, you might choose to adopt a more favorable interpretation of the holding than you would in your role as an advisor. Even then, however, you would still strive to fall within the "range of reasonableness" to avoid losing credibility before the court.

CHAPTER IN REVIEW

Definitions:

RULE OF LAW:

A generic term that can refer to:

1. Legal rules set forth in the original sources of law, e.g., constitutions, statutes, and the common law ("original" rules of law); and
2. Judicial interpretations and definitions of the original rules of law (interpretive rules of law).

Visually, rules of law can be depicted as follows:

RULES OF LAW
(Broad term that includes):

↓

"Original" Rules of Law (Chapter 6)

↙ ↓ ↘

Constitutions Statutes Common Law

↘ ↓ ↙

Interpretive Rules of Law (Chapter 7)

↓

Statements courts make when they define
and interpret original rules of law

ELEMENT:

Elements are separate requirements of a rule of law (legal standards) that a party *must* prove to compel a particular result.

FACTORS:

1. Factors are the underlying ideas that courts explicitly or implicitly weigh when evaluating whether a particular set of facts satisfy an element of a rule of law;

2. Some statutes also explicitly identify factors, or guidelines, to guide judges in their decision-making process.

RULE STATEMENT:

A statement you formulate that clearly and accurately reflects the court's holding and the "take-away" from the case.

STANDARDS:

When a court interprets an original rule of law, sometimes it defines the rule of law in a manner that effectively establishes a new requirement the parties must satisfy. The new requirement can be called a standard (*e.g.*, the *Gigante* court interpreted the term "satisfactory explanation" to require "reasonable diligence," which effectively became a new standard, or requirement, under the Statute).

....

Evaluating Cases

1. Review the opinion for useful interpretations of the original rule of law, noting:
   a. Whether the court *defined* the original rule of law, thereby creating a new legal standard or a helpful definition;

b. Whether the court voiced any *public policy* concerns; and

c. Whether the court furthered your understanding of the rule of law by *surveying earlier court decisions*.

☑ Make a list of each helpful interpretation of the original rule of law on your computer or legal notepad.

2. Evaluate how the court applied the rule of law to the case facts (if a fact-centered issue):

a. Identify the *holding*: How did the court answer the legal question before it?

b. List each reason the court used to justify its holding (the *rationale*), including any definitions or interpretations of the law.

c. Next, create a list of *case facts* that seem to illustrate or relate to the court's legal interpretations or to the components of the rule of law.

d. Then group case facts together that appear to be similar to each other, or that illustrate a similar point.

e. Identify the *common theme* each group of facts seems to illustrate

   i. If a specific grouping of facts seems to have several themes, subdivide the facts into smaller groupings until each grouping of facts reflects a common theme.

   ii. For each grouping of facts, label the theme, thereby identifying the underlying *factor* the court seemed to be weighing.

3. Formulate a *rule statement*:

a. Identify a result that reflects *how* the court answered the legal question before it; and

b. Summarize *why* the court answered the question as it did by showing the standard (often illustrated by factors) the court applied that showcases what it takes to meet the result.

   • For example, one rule statement for the *Thomas* case would be: "An attached structure is not a dwelling under the residential burglary statute when it is used only for commercial, rather than residential, activities."

EVALUATING HOW AN EARLIER CASE AFFECTS YOUR CLIENT

After you have thoroughly studied a precedent case, you are ready to assess how the case might be helpful to you in evaluating your client's situation. From your evaluation of relevant cases, you will have already identified helpful aspects of each case. A case might be helpful to you because it clearly interpreted or defined the original rule of law, or explored the policy implications of a rule of law. That same case might also have analogous facts that will help you predict what the law would have to say about your client's situation. Some cases might contain useful interpretations of the law but have no analogous facts. Other cases might have facts that closely resemble your client's situation but no helpful rationale. This chapter discusses how to evaluate a single case's effect on a client. Later, in Chapter 12, you will learn how to synthesize a group of relevant cases, and, in Chapter 18, how to select and prioritize case law for use in an office memorandum.

I. EVALUATING CASES WITH ANALOGOUS FACTS

A. Comparing Case Facts to the Client's Facts

When an earlier case's facts appear analogous to your client's situation, your goal is to evaluate how the factual analogies might dictate the outcome in your client's situation. Using your notes from the precedent case to guide you, separately consider each factor that guided the earlier court. For each factor, list the case facts that fall within the umbrella of that factor and then create a parallel list of any client facts that relate to that factor. Don't be concerned if only one of several factors in an earlier case applies to your client's situation. Unlike elements of a rule of law, factors are only guidelines to be weighed and evaluated. All of the factors do not have to be present in order to evaluate whether an element has been satisfied. However, the absence of a factor may affect how you evaluate the strength of your client's case when compared to the precedent case.

As you took notes from the earlier case, you may have determined that the court articulated a concrete, narrow standard or definition that guided its decision. Recall that concrete, narrow standards serve the same purpose as factors—they provide the court, and you, with concrete concepts that serve as evaluative tools. If you have decided that the legal standard or definition itself is so clear and specific that factors are not necessary analytical tools for your analysis, use the standard or definition instead. Simply list the case facts that fall within the umbrella of that standard or definition and then create a parallel list of client facts.

After you have created parallel lists of facts, evaluate how your client's facts compare to the precedent case facts. If you determine that your client's legally significant facts are similar enough to the case facts to merit the same result, then you would conclude that your client's situation would likely be resolved the same way as the precedent case. On the other hand, if you determine that your client's facts are distinguishable from the case facts in a legally significant way, then you would conclude that your client's situation would likely be resolved differently than the precedent case.

◉ ILLUSTRATION: Residential Burglary Problem
People v. Thomas and the Stripe Garage

Recall the residential burglary problem and the *Thomas* case discussed in Chapter 7. In *Thomas*, the court held that a garage used to store perfume for commercial use was not a dwelling under the residential burglary statute. After evaluating how the court interpreted the term "dwelling," the lawyer concluded that the garage's "type of use" was the critical factor that guided the court's holding. The court emphasized a structure's "use" by defining a dwelling as a "living quarters" in which the owner "actually resides." (This definition was codified and is now a part of the statutory language.) The *Thomas* court reasoned that a garage used to store perfume did not satisfy this definition. Equipped with that information, as a prosecutor for the State of Illinois, you would be ready to assess how the *Thomas* case would help you decide whether to charge Mr. Arnold with residential burglary for breaking into the Stripe family's garage.

At this point, as the prosecutor, assume that you have the following information about your case: Gerry Arnold has been apprehended for breaking into a garage owned by the Stripe family. The garage is physically separated from the Stripes' home. One-third of the Stripe family's garage is used to store the family car while the remaining two-thirds of the garage is used as a get-a-way by Michael Stripe, the couple's college-age son. A wall separates the two different areas of the garage. Michael Stripe's get-a-way has its own separate entry through a door.

The son, Michael Stripe, spends two to three evenings a week and his free time on weekends in the garage, writing and listening to music on his stereo system. Michael is the lead singer in a band, R.E.N., that plays once a month in clubs around town. The band practices in the garage most Sunday mornings and stores some equipment in the garage. Michael has an expensive sound system in his get-a-way section of the garage. He also keeps a portable five-inch T.V. in the garage and a mini-refrigerator that stores soda and beer. The garage has electricity and a space heater, but no running water or heat. During the summer and fall when his parents are in town, Michael sleeps in the garage on a futon in a loft area. When his parents travel to Florida during the winter and spring, Michael sleeps in the house in the bedroom in which he was raised.

You also know that Arnold was apprehended with a bass guitar belonging to Michael Stripe and tools that would allow him to forcibly enter the garage. Michael Stripe claims that he left the guitar in his get-a-way earlier that day. Arnold has also confessed that he entered the garage and took Michael Stripe's guitar, and that he does not know the Stripe family and did not have their permission to enter the garage. The Stripes would like the State of Illinois to press charges.

Your notes evaluating how *Thomas* might affect your ability to prosecute Mr. Arnold for residential burglary would look like this:

Based on the "type of use" factor, your ability to prosecute Mr. Arnold under the residential burglary statute seems fairly promising. In other words, you have determined that the facts in your case are distinguishable from the *Thomas* case facts in a legally significant way. Michael Stripe used the garage for living-type purposes while the victim in *Thomas* used the garage only for commercial storage purposes. However, before arriving at a definitive conclusion, you would also address a potentially troubling distinction you noticed when comparing your case to *Thomas*. Recall that the *Thomas* court mentioned, on two occasions, that the garage in *Thomas* was attached to the multi-unit apartment building. You do not know for sure what the court was thinking when it noted the garage was attached. Perhaps it meant that a structure's physical attachment or detachment to a primary residence is irrelevant. However, suppose it merely meant that an attached garage is not automatically a dwelling because it is attached to a home. This ambiguity becomes problematic because, unlike the garage in *Thomas*, the garage you are evaluating is detached from the owner's home. Is it possible that an attached garage is more likely to be considered part of the dwelling than a detached garage? Thus, you should evaluate this factor as well:

Factor: Type of Use **Thomas** Case	Factor: Type of Use Client's Situation	Compare Type of Use Factor Per Court's Rationale
<u>Why this factor is important:</u> *Thomas* definition: dwelling must be used as a residence or living quarters		Unlike the act of storing perfume to sell for business purposes, Michael Stripe used the garage for living-type activities—these activities seem to be the type of activities with which the *Thomas* court was concerned.
<u>*Thomas* Facts:</u> ˙ Stored perfume to sell in business	<u>Client Facts:</u> ˙ Used as get-a-way to: (1) Play music (2) Listen to music (3) Sleep ½ the year (4) Relax, eat snacks, and watch T.V.	Is it a problem that Michael's band practices in the garage and the band makes money playing around town—a commercial activity? Probably not. This activity seems secondary to its use as a part-time living quarters. Check out whether there are other cases in which the occupant used a structure for both residential and commercial use.

Factor: Proximity to Home **Thomas** Case	Factor: Proximity to Home Client's Situation	Compare Proximity Factor Per Court's Rationale
<u>Why potentially important:</u> <u>2 statements</u> "An attached garage is not necessarily a dwelling." "A garage, at least in this instance, whether attached to the various living units or not, cannot be deemed a residence or living quarters."		Potentially troubling distinction. A garage physically removed from the principal dwelling could be considered less likely to be a part of the dwelling than an attached garage.
<u>*Thomas* Facts:</u> ˙ Attached to a multi-unit apartment dwelling.	<u>Client Facts:</u> ˙ 30 feet behind the Stripes' home	However, given the court's emphasis on the *use* of the garage, and the fact that the Stripes' garage was sometimes used as a living quarters, I don't think this distinction would change my initial conclusion that the Stripes' garage is a living quarters. In other words, the garage could be considered a living quarters in and of itself. I am not trying to make the argument that, merely because of its proximity/ attachment to the primary home, the garage is, by extension, also part of the home.

Exercise 8-1: Social Host Liability

To: Summer Law Clerk
From: Senior Attorney
Date: [Date exercise is assigned]
Re: Social Host Liability

Recently, a client named Ben Smith came to our firm to sue and hopefully recover money damages from John Havanother. Havanother had recently hosted a poker night, and Smith feels that Havanother was directly responsible for severe injuries Smith suffered in a fight.

Havanother hosted this strictly social Friday night poker party several months ago. Philip Douglas attended the party, as did Ben Smith. Havanother served three alcoholic drinks to Douglas, although Douglas definitely appeared past the point of intoxication. Smith did not drink.

Douglas and Smith began to drive home at the same time in separate cars. At the end of Havanother's driveway, Douglas' car hit Smith's car at a very slow speed, causing little damage. Despite the small amount of damage, Douglas started a fight on Havanother's front lawn. Witnesses will testify that Douglas began to "lose it," ranting and raving and beating Smith brutally. Smith will probably incur medical expenses for rehabilitative physical therapy for the rest of his life.

Douglas was found to have a blood alcohol level of .172 at the time of the fight. This level indicated acute alcohol intoxication of at least nine drinks.

A summary of a relevant case, *Linn v. Rand*, 356 A.2d 15 (N.J. 1976), follows. Evaluate the similarities and distinctions between the client's facts and the facts of *Linn*, and assess the strengths and weaknesses of your client's claim in light of *Linn*.

Linn v. Rand: The plaintiff sued the defendant for negligence in serving an excessive amount of alcoholic beverages to Rand, a minor, while she was a guest at the defendant's home. The plaintiff further claimed that the defendant negligently permitted Rand to drive her car from defendant's home just prior to Rand's running down and seriously injuring the plaintiff. The trial court granted summary judgment in favor of the defendant, concluding that liability in negligence for the sale or serving of alcoholic beverages to intoxicated persons is specifically limited to tavern keepers and to those in a strictly business setting. The appellate court reversed, rejecting the defendant's claim that social hosts are immune from liability in negligence for the serving of alcoholic beverages to intoxicated persons. The court concluded that the defendant's potential liability was a jury question. Specifically, the court stated that "a jury might well determine that a social host who serves excessive amounts of alcoholic beverages to a visibly intoxicated minor, knowing the minor was about to drive a car on the public highways, could reasonably foresee or anticipate an accident or injury as a reasonably foreseeable consequence of his negligence in serving the minor." The court further pointed out that "[t]his becomes devastatingly apparent in view of the ever-increasing incidence of serious automobile accidents resulting from drunken driving."

B. When Case Facts and Client Facts Do Not Seem Analogous

Sometimes you may not easily be able to identify how an earlier case's facts might be useful to you as a basis for comparison. For example, in Chapter 12 you will read the *People v. McIntyre* case, another case that interprets the residential burglary statute. In that case, the court evaluated whether a porch attached to a home was a dwelling within the meaning of the Statute. Superficially, the burglary of a porch does not seem to be analogous to the burglary of a garage located thirty feet behind a residence. Before discarding the case as an unhelpful case, first try broadening the level of generalization to see if you can find a common characteristic, or theme, between the two groups of facts that might prove to be legally significant.

From a narrow interpretation of the facts, the facts in *McIntyre* do not seem to share a common characteristic with the Stripe family's garage. A porch attached to a home is not "like" a garage located thirty feet behind a building. However, by broadening the level of generalization, we can find a common characteristic, or theme, that both facts share—they are both "structures" measured in part by their closeness to or distance from the main residence. This common characteristic becomes a helpful factor, or analytical tool, when evaluating how the *McIntyre* case affects the Stripe family's garage—a structure's proximity to the primary dwelling.

Of course, not all cases will be helpful to you as a basis for factual analogy. If you are forced to broaden the level of generalization to a point that the common characteristic doesn't make any sense, then the case would not be helpful as a basis of comparison or distinction.

Exercise 8-2: Finding an Analogy Between Dissimilar Fact Patterns

Assume you represent a client who was injured in an automobile accident. The other driver, an employee of a "deep-pocket" employer, was clearly at fault. During your investigation, you discover the following facts. The other driver was a traveling salesman, and his job required him to drive thousands of miles a year. When the employer hired the salesman, it did not check his driving record. In fact, the salesman had numerous speeding tickets. When researching whether your client can sue the employer for negligently hiring the employee, you discover the following rule of law: an employer is liable for negligently hiring an employee if the employer knew or should have known of the employee's dangerous proclivities.

Assume that you are unable to find any case that involves an accident caused by an employee's speeding. You cannot even find a single case that involves an accident caused by an employee's negligent acts. In fact, the only cases you can find are cases involving intentional torts or actual crimes committed by an employee. Consider how you might use the following such case as a basis of comparison to your client's situation:

In case X, an employee assaulted a customer on the work premises during working hours. The employee's job duties required him to circulate among the customers. When the employer hired the employee, it did not check his criminal record, which would have disclosed a prior assault conviction. In case X, the court held that the employer negligently hired the employee, reasoning that the employer knew or should have known of the employee's dangerous proclivities because of the employee's criminal record.

What common characteristic do these two factual scenarios share? How might you use this common characteristic to argue that the employer in your case negligently hired the traveling salesman?

II. EVALUATING POLICY STATEMENTS

Some cases openly discuss the policy implications of a particular rule of law. Such policy implications can help you evaluate how the rule of law would be applied to a client's factual situation. Even the implicit policy concerns underlying a court's analysis of a rule of law can be helpful as you evaluate how the rule might be applied to a client. If a particular outcome would further the policy underlying the rule, a court is more likely to rule in a manner consistent with that outcome. On the other hand, if a particular outcome would thwart the policy underlying the rule of law, a court is more likely to rule in a manner that would not promote that outcome.

◎ ILLUSTRATION: Residential Burglary Problem
People v. Silva and the Stripe Garage

In Illinois, the legislature amended the residential burglary statute to incorporate the *Thomas* court's definition of "dwelling" into the Statute. The Statute now defines a dwelling as a "living quarters in which at the time of the alleged offense the owners or occupants actually reside or in their absence intend within a reasonable period of time to reside."[1] Following *Thomas*, the *Silva* court was asked to interpret the codified definition of the term "dwelling." The court reviewed the legislative purpose underlying the statutory amendment and quoted the following statement of Senator Sangmeister during the Senate Proceedings:

---

1. 720 Ill. Comp. Stat. 5/2-6 (1987).

Yes, it was even brought to our attention by the Illinois Supreme Court in a number of cases that *** there should be a better definition to the dwelling house. We are having people prosecuted for residential burglary for breaking into *** unoccupied buildings such as garages. Therefore, very simply, we have redefined dwelling to mean a house, apartment, mobile home, trailer, or other living quarters in which at the time of the alleged offense the owners or occupants actually reside in or *** in their absence intend within a reasonable period of time to reside. So that still covers, in my opinion, the vacation home; you intend to reside in that and if you burglarize that, you would still be committing residential burglary, but it tightens up some of these cases where we got old abandoned buildings around our garages and stuff that *** would not be residential burglary.[2]

If you were evaluating whether to charge Gerry Arnold with residential burglary for breaking into the Stripes' garage, this policy statement would at least be relevant to your decision. Superficially, the statement seems problematic—Senator Sangmeister implied that people could not be prosecuted for breaking into garages. However, consider that the penalty for breaking into a residence is more severe than the penalty for breaking into a warehouse. What underlying policy concerns might be implied from reading the *Silva* court's examination of the legislative history? You might argue that Senator Sangmeister's own statement reflects the legislative concern with protecting human life. The senator was concerned that people were being prosecuted under the Statute for breaking into "unoccupied buildings"—buildings where no living-type activities take place. Because Michael Stripe uses the Stripes' garage as a retreat and frequent living quarters, its very use as a living quarters addresses the legislative concern for human life. Therefore, the garage is arguably more like a living quarters than an unoccupied garage.

---

2. *People v. Silva*, 628 N.E.2d 948, 951 (Ill. App. Ct. 1993).

CHAPTER IN REVIEW

Core Concepts:

EVALUATING CASES AND THEIR IMPACT ON THE CLIENT

A case might be relevant to your client's situation in one of the following ways:

a. The case may contain a helpful definition or interpretation of the rule of law;

b. The case may contain useful rationale, such as public policy considerations underlying the rule of law; and/or

c. The case may contain analogous facts.

WORKING WITH CASES WITH ANALOGOUS FACTS

1. Separately list each factor the precedent court seemed to consider.
   - Alternatively, if the court articulated a concrete, narrow standard that can serve as a useful evaluative tool in lieu of a factor, use that standard instead.

2. Under each factor (or standard), create parallel lists of the case facts and the client facts that fall within the umbrella of that idea.

3. For each parallel list of facts:
   a. Compare the client facts to the case facts and determine whether the client facts are similar to, or distinguishable from, the case facts.
   b. Considering the court's rationale, evaluate whether the factual dissimilarities weaken or strengthen your client's situation vis-à-vis the precedent case.

4. Review the separate lists of facts *in total* and, considering the court's rationale, determine:
   a. Whether the client's facts, as a whole, are similar enough to suggest that a court might resolve the client's situation in the same manner as the court in the precedent case, or, alternatively,
   b. Whether the client's facts, as a whole, are different enough from the case in legally significant ways to suggest that a court might resolve the client's situation in a different manner than the court in the precedent case.

WHEN THE CASE FACTS AND CLIENT FACTS DO NOT SEEM TO BE ANALOGOUS

1. Broaden the level of generalization between the two sets of facts until you find a common characteristic, or theme, that both sets of facts share.

- *E.g.*, A common characteristic the Stripes' garage and the *McIntyre* porch share is that both structures are measured, in part, by their closeness to, or distance from, a home.

2. If you are forced to broaden the level of generalization to a common characteristic that does not make sense, the case is not factually analogous enough to be useful.

THE OFFICE MEMORANDUM

An Overview

I. INTRODUCTION

Lawyers regularly convey legal analysis in a document that is called an office memorandum. Office memoranda are in-house documents that are typically drafted by more junior lawyers in response to legal questions senior lawyers in their law office have asked them to research and analyze. The context in which office memoranda are drafted will help you better understand the purpose and structure of an office memorandum.

In a typical situation, a client asks the senior lawyer for legal advice. Instead of researching and analyzing every legal question presented by every client, senior lawyers routinely delegate many research issues to more junior lawyers in their office. Although you will often be asked to research and write memos in your role as a junior lawyer in a law office, paradoxically you will become the expert on the particular areas of the law you research. Although the senior lawyer might be more experienced than you and have a better idea of the "bigger picture," the senior lawyer won't have an understanding of how the subtleties of complex laws affect a client's unique legal question. That's why the senior lawyer will have asked you to research the law in the first place.

Because legal analysis is often complex and detailed, you will typically relay your analysis in written form, in a document known as an office memorandum. Typically, you will sum up your analysis by either advising whether the client can lawfully engage in specific conduct, or predicting how a decision-maker is likely to rule on the client's existing legal problem.

Because your intended readers will be trained lawyers, they will expect the information within the memo to conform to the ways in which lawyers evaluate the law. Thus, they will expect to review first the relevant rule or rules of law, followed by an identification of the issue or issues presented by the rule of law, followed by an exploration of previous cases that have interpreted and applied the rule of law, followed by an examination of how the rule of law and previous cases impact the client's situation. You will want to conform to these expectations when writing legal memos. This section of the book provides you with basic guidelines that reflect commonly understood writing practices within the legal community.

II. INFORMATION CONVEYED IN AN OFFICE MEMO

A good office memo should evaluate every significant aspect of the relevant rules of law and issues, the previous cases that have interpreted the law, and the effect of the law and case precedent on the client's factual situation. The information in the office memo should be so thorough that the lawyer reviewing your memo will understand the nuances of how the law affects the client's situation without having to read the relevant cases discussed in the memo. The memo should be so thorough that a senior lawyer would be able to sit down with you and discuss your interpretation of a case cited in the memo without personally having to read the case. Finally, it should be so thorough that the senior lawyer would feel comfortable giving the client advice based on the legal analysis contained in your memo.

The most common mistake first-year law students make when drafting office memos is "bottom-lining" their analysis—conveying only a summary of their conclusions. Students often say that they do so out of the belief that, because a senior lawyer is an expert in the law, they would insult the senior lawyer's intelligence by disclosing too much information. They fear that a senior lawyer might be insulted by the presumption that he or she did not already know the details of the law.

This fear is misplaced for a number of reasons. First, even an expert in a particular area of the law cannot possibly maintain a thorough knowledge of every nuance in the law. A tax lawyer may be an expert on tax law. However, numerous volumes of books contain the tax code, and literally hundreds of thousands of cases interpret the code. Only a handful of these will be helpful in resolving a client's specific factual problem.

Second, even when the senior lawyer understands what the law requires or permits in the abstract, that lawyer cannot be expected to know, from thousands of cases, the details of the specific applicable cases that might be helpful in resolving the client's problem. Therefore, even though the senior lawyer may understand the general requirements of a particular law, that lawyer will expect *you* to become the expert on how the law would affect a client's very specific problem.

Third, even though a senior lawyer might understand the general elements of a particular rule of law you are researching, the office memo should be a self-contained document. It should contain the relevant content of every rule of law and court opinion that helped you arrive at your legal conclusion. The reviewing lawyer will expect to see the logical links of your analysis within the body of the office memo itself. You do not want to force the reviewing lawyer to have to go to the library and read the original rule of law and cases that interpret it.

Finally, like any reader, the senior lawyer who is reading your memo is not a passive reader but an active participant in the unfolding analysis. Readers have an on-going dialogue in their head as they try to make sense of what they are reading. If too little information is conveyed, the lawyer's internal dialogue might be saying: "wait a minute; why did the court hold that…?" or "I think I've missed a step here—what does this mean?" or "I'm not sure why this point is legally significant." On the other hand, if irrelevant information is conveyed, the lawyer's internal dialogue might be saying: "what does this have to do with…? I'm lost."

This internal dialogue is, of course, distracting to the reader and counter-productive to your goal of conveying a clear, complete legal analysis. You can quiet the reader's distracting inner dialogue only by conveying enough relevant detail in your analysis so that the lawyer's questions are resolved when they arise. Therefore, your goal as the writer is to spell out each of the relevant details about the law, and each and every step of your analysis so that the reviewing lawyer's internal dialogue says: "yes, that makes sense" and "right, I'm with you."[1]

III. THE PREDICTIVE FUNCTION OF THE OFFICE MEMO

Office memos explore the relevant rules of law and then predict how the law would apply to a client's factual situation. The senior lawyer who reviews an office memorandum will make recommendations to the client about future conduct based on the analysis contained in your memo. Therefore, you want to evaluate very carefully every aspect of the legal problem, including the legal arguments an opponent might make. Recall that the office memo is reviewed only by members of your own law office. You need not be concerned that your exploration of weaknesses in the client's position might be exposed to opposing counsel. Instead, the reviewing partner and client need to know the potential risks involved if the client takes or fails to take certain actions. Failure to evaluate the risks could ultimately result in losing the client or facing a malpractice claim filed by the client. Therefore, office memos describe all of the legal arguments that support the client's conduct, as well as all of the legal arguments that do not favor the client.

IV. THE STRUCTURAL FORMAT OF THE OFFICE MEMO

Office memos generally follow a standard format that most lawyers find to be the clearest means of communicating legal analysis. The general format of the typical office memorandum is premised on two notions. First, because senior lawyers are

---

1. *See also* Linda H. Edwards, *Legal Writing: Process, Analysis, and Organization* 159 (2d ed. 1999).

usually very busy, the overall format of a standard office memo allows the reviewing lawyers to obtain a quick and insightful overview of the legal problem first (the Question Presented and Short Answer) followed by a more thorough analysis of the details of the problem (the Fact and Discussion sections).

Second, the overall format of an office memo reflects the fact that readers automatically search for context when reading new material. Because legal analysis is often extremely complex, the need for context is particularly important in documents that evaluate the law. Therefore, an office memo provides the reviewing lawyers with general context, or roadmaps, before analyzing the specific details of the legal problem. The roadmaps serve as a foundation, or starting point, for the reader to grasp the more specific details that follow. This format of providing context before details begins with the very first component of the typical memorandum—the Question Presented, and continues through the heart of the memorandum itself—the Discussion section.

Some students chaff at the thought of being compelled to follow a rigid organizational structure when they draft their memos. However, it is important to follow a structure that meets the expectations of the reviewing lawyer. Lawyers are skeptical readers, trained to assess the validity of legal analysis. Because the organizational structure of your memo is the most visible part of your analysis, an unstructured memo invites a reviewing lawyer to doubt whether the analysis itself is reliable and credible. Moreover, a lawyer who is met with structural surprises is less likely to be receptive to the information you are trying to convey.

Although office memos generally reflect a common pattern of analysis, some law offices have their own internal formats the lawyers in that office are expected to follow. For example, they may refer to certain sections of the office memo by specific titles that differ somewhat from the titles used in this book. When you begin practicing law, you will of course follow the preferred format that exists within your law office. Any such variations in format will be primarily cosmetic and easy to pick up as you begin practicing law.

A typical office memo follows the basic structure illustrated below:

MEMORANDUM

To: Senior Attorney
From: Junior Attorney
Date: [Date memo is submitted]
Re: XYZ Client Matter

QUESTION PRESENTED

This is the section that identifies the legal question or questions the memo will evaluate. (Chapter 15 discusses the Question Presented in greater detail.)

SHORT ANSWER

After identifying the legal question, this section provides a brief answer to the question. As the name implies, the Short Answer simply answers the Question Presented and provides a very brief summary of the reasons that support the answer. (Chapter 15 discusses the Short Answer in greater detail.)

STATEMENT OF FACTS

The Statement of Facts section of the memo simply tells the client's factual story. Included within the description of that story are all of the legally relevant facts and any background facts that help tie the story together. This section includes relevant facts that are favorable to the client as well as any relevant facts that are unfavorable to the client. (Chapter 15 discusses the Statement of Facts in greater detail.)

DISCUSSION

The Discussion section is the heart of the office memorandum, where the relevant law is evaluated and then applied to the facts of the client's situation. Because the Discussion section of a formal memo can be fairly lengthy and complex, this section of the memo is further comprised of the following components:
- An overview paragraph that lays the foundation for the discussion;
- A thesis paragraph that summarizes the issue under discussion;
- Paragraphs that explain and evaluate the law concerning the issue (*Rule Explanation*);
- Paragraphs that apply the law to the client's factual situation (*Rule Application*); and
- A conclusion for the client's situation.

(Chapters 11, 13, and 14 discuss the Discussion section of an office memo in greater detail.)

CONCLUSION

In this section, you will "close up" the memorandum by reiterating the conclusions you provided in both the overview and thesis paragraphs of the Discussion section. Note that if your memorandum contains only a single legal issue and is fairly short and simplistic, this separate section introduced with a heading may be unnecessary, as the conclusion you provided at the close of the Discussion section may be sufficient.

At this point, you may wish to take a look at Sample Memo A in Appendix A to see how the residential burglary problem and the Stripe family's garage was evaluated in a memo.

THE DISCUSSION SECTION

The Basic Template for Analysis

I. CHAPTER IN FOCUS

MEMORANDUM

To: [Senior Attorney]
From: [Junior Attorney]
Date: [Date of Submission of Memo]
Re: [XYZ Client Matter]

QUESTION PRESENTED

. . .

SHORT ANSWER

. . .

STATEMENT OF FACTS

. . .

DISCUSSION ⬅

. . .

CONCLUSION

. . .

II. THE DEDUCTIVE WRITING PATTERN

A. The Shift from Inductive to Deductive Analysis

After you have fully evaluated a rule of law and the cases that interpret the rule of law, you are ready to begin the drafting process. The drafting process can be challenging, and even frustrating at times, because the writing process tends to illuminate the complexity and ambiguities inherent in ideas that often seem so clear in the abstract. Moreover, the very nature of the pre-drafting analytical thought process presents an additional challenge during the shift from the pre-drafting to the drafting process. When you evaluate rules of law and cases, you separately examine each court's holding, reasoning, and numerous case facts to identify any underlying factors that guided the court, and to formulate a rule statement that captures the essence of the case. This analytical process of examining specific facts and reasoning to identify broad rules of law is *inductive*. The inductive process involves the examination of specific details to arrive at general principles.

Although the inductive reasoning process makes sense in the pre-drafting stage, a written analysis patterned on the same inductive process would be extremely confusing for a reader to follow. Imagine forcing a reader to meander through the same lengthy, winding path you traveled when evaluating the law. Imagine the reader's mounting frustration as the reader reviews case after case, all the while wondering where the path is leading and why the details of various cases will ultimately become important. To avoid that result, when drafting a legal discussion, you must totally reverse your pre-drafting analytical process to a *deductive* analytical pattern. The deductive writing pattern is premised on the notion that readers can absorb information more easily if they understand its significance as soon as they see it. The best way to assure immediate understanding is to present the context of an idea before describing its details.[1] The context provides a basis, or "foundation," for understanding the details that will follow. Therefore, a deductive analytical pattern is one that progresses from a broad conclusion to narrow, specific illustrations of why the conclusion is sound.

To appreciate the importance of the deductive writing pattern, compare the following set of instructions.

> (1) After you have turned onto Highway 170 South, take Forest Parkway East.
>
> Before that you will have to take the appropriate exit from Highway 70 going east.
>
> Look for Big Bend Boulevard. You will not turn at that street but will continue going straight until you see the law school.
>
> Begin the journey, however, by taking exit 235C at Cypress Road. Take Cypress road to Highway 170 South.
>
> Forest Parkway East becomes Millbrook. At that point, you will have followed Forest Parkway to its conclusion, which is the law school.

---

1. Stephen V. Armstrong & Timothy P. Terrell, *Thinking Like a Writer: A Lawyer's Guide to Effective Writing and Editing*, 3-3 through 3-5 (Clark, Boardman, Callaghan 1992).

As a reader who has been given no context, or foundation, for understanding the above directions, what did you experience while reading these directions? Did you try to guess where the directions were taking you? Were you at all frustrated (or might you be if this were something important for you to understand)? Now review the second example, and note how this time, you have been given context, or a roadmap, before reading the details.

(1) To get from the airport to the law school, follow the signs to exit the terminal and then take exit 235C at Cypress Road.

Take Cypress road to Highway 70 East.

After three miles, exit to Highway 170 South.

From Highway 170 South, take the "Forest Parkway East" exit.

Take Forest Parkway East for about two miles until it becomes Millbrook Avenue.

Go straight on Millbrook through one stoplight (Big Bend is the cross street).

After going past that intersection, the law school will be on your right. Turn right into the law school parking lot.

Even though the second set of instructions conveyed the same substantive information, this set was easier to follow. Notice how, in the second example, the information was presented in an order that met your expectations of how directions should be given (from the beginning of the journey to the end). Also, in the second set of instructions, you were given the appropriate context to understand why you were reading the paragraph. The writer let you know immediately that you would be reading instructions from an airport to a law school.

B. The Deductive Pattern in Legal Analysis

In the legal setting, a deductive analytical pattern is equally as important. In the Discussion section of an office memo, a written legal analysis also begins at the logical starting point—the rule of law upon which your entire analysis will rest. Legal writers also let the reader know up-front the general roadmap for the Discussion and the writer's conclusion. Unlike a mystery novel, legal readers want to know your conclusion up-front—again, it provides a context for understanding the detailed legal analysis that will follow. The remainder of the Discussion illustrates and proves why the conclusion is sound.

The broad framework of a written legal analysis might be visualized as follows:

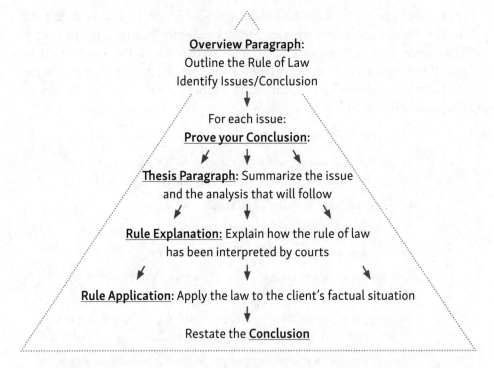

Overview Paragraph:
Outline the Rule of Law
Identify Issues/Conclusion

For each issue:
Prove your Conclusion:

Thesis Paragraph: Summarize the issue
and the analysis that will follow

Rule Explanation: Explain how the rule of law
has been interpreted by courts

Rule Application: Apply the law to the client's factual situation

Restate the **Conclusion**

In the above diagram, note how the deductive analytical pattern resembles a pattern with which you may be familiar from other courses in law school—IRAC, an acronym for: Issue → Rule → Apply Rule → Conclusion. In a very general sense, the deductive pattern of analysis follows a pattern similar to IRAC. However, the organizational structure of a legal discussion is somewhat more complicated, and fluid, than a literal adherence to IRAC might otherwise suggest.

III. ORIGINAL RULE OF LAW AS THE TEMPLATE

Drafting a Discussion that reflects legal analysis is not unlike formulating a mathematical equation. Like a mathematical equation, each piece of your analysis should logically build from an earlier section of the analysis and logically lead to the section that will follow. Because the structure of your analysis is, in a sense, formulaic, you must have a basic grasp of the "formula" your memo will follow before you begin writing. Because the formula of each memo is based on a rule of law, the original rule of law you are evaluating serves as the template for the Discussion.

If you determine that the original rule of law has several elements, but only one element actually presents a legitimate issue that merits discussion, your memo would discuss in depth only one issue. Therefore, you would follow the template for a single-issue memo outlined below.

If, however, you determine that two or more elements of a rule of law merit discussion, the structure of your memo would of necessity have to accommodate each issue. Adding another issue to the equation is not complicated because the basic template for each separate issue does not vary. Instead, the template for a single issue discussion is duplicated (for a two-issue memo), tripled (for a three-issue memo), and so on. The following very broad outlines illustrate the macro template of a single-issue discussion and a multiple issue discussion.

A. Outline of the Single-Issue Memo

DISCUSSION

1. Lay the Foundation (*Overview Paragraph*):

If the original rule of law has more than one element or factor, it is generally good practice to begin your analysis with an overview of the original rule of law. This paragraph lays the foundation for the analysis by stating the ultimate (overall) conclusion, outlining the elements (or factors) of the original rule of law, identifying those elements that are not issues, and identifying the element that will be discussed—the "legal issue." Chapter 14 discusses the components of the overview paragraph in greater detail.

2. Summarize the Issue (*Thesis Paragraph*):

Unlike the more general framework provided in the overview paragraph, the thesis paragraph provides a focused roadmap of the specific legal issue that will be discussed in the memo. This paragraph summarizes the analysis that will follow by stating what the rule of law means and by describing any relevant factors that guide courts in evaluating the issue. Chapter 14 discusses the components of the thesis paragraph in greater detail.

Prove Why Your Conclusion Is Valid:

3. Explain the Law (*Rule Explanation*):

Because this section of the memo evaluates in detail the element of the rule of law that presents an issue, this section may span pages of your memo. Your evaluation of the law may include an analysis of how earlier cases have interpreted and applied the rule of law and, in the case of a statutory rule of law, may also include statutory interpretation and an examination of legislative history. Chapters 11 and 13 discuss in detail this section of the memo and the different formatting options that relate to this specific section of the memo.

4. Apply the Law to the Client's Factual Situation (*Rule Application*):

This section evaluates how the law affects the client's situation. Like the rule explanation section of the memo, this section may also span a number of pages. Chapters 11 and 13 discuss in detail this section of the memo and the different formatting options that relate to this specific section of the memo.

(a) *Favorable Rule Application*:

If there is any way in which the law has a favorable impact on a client's situation, lawyers typically evaluate how the law supports the client's position before addressing unfavorable rule application.

(b) *Unfavorable Rule Application*:

After evaluating the ways in which the law favors the client with respect to a specific idea, the Discussion then evaluates any counter-arguments that relate to that same idea. This section of the memo is very important. In your role as an advisor to the client, you have a responsibility to advise the client about unfavorable arguments as well as arguments that favor the client.

5. Conclusion

Most memos end with a brief conclusion that again answers the issue. Depending upon the complexity and length of the memo, the conclusion might appear within the body of the Discussion section itself, or may appear under a separate heading—the "Conclusion."

B. Template of the Multi-Issue Memo

If you determine that two or more elements of a rule of law present issues that merit discussion, you will need to adjust the template of your Discussion to accommodate both issues. With a two or more issue Discussion, the pattern of analysis for each individual issue does not change from that of the single issue memo. You will simply duplicate the template for a one-issue memo and add headings to serve as visual signposts for the reader.

Headings that serve as visual signposts are often called "point-headings." In order for point-headings to be useful to a reader, they should be very clear and relatively short. Simply by glancing at the point-heading, your reader should be able to grasp the direction in which the memo is headed. Some lawyers prefer simply to identify the issue with a short word or phrase. For example, assume in the residential burglary hypothetical problem that the prosecutor has identified two issues that merit analysis: whether the Stripe garage is a dwelling, and whether Mr. Arnold had the requisite intent to commit a theft. The two point-headings might be identified as:

> I. The Stripes' garage as a dwelling.
> II. Intent to commit a theft.

Other lawyers prefer to frame their point-headings as conclusions, signaling to the reader the writer's bottom-line. Stated as conclusions, the two point-headings would be described as follows:

> I. The Stripes' garage is a dwelling under the Statute.
> II. Mr. Arnold had the requisite intent to commit a theft.

When drafting point-headings for multi-issue memos, follow the preference of your professor or the senior lawyer who asked you to draft the memo.

The basic template of the multi-issue memo is as follows:

DISCUSSION

Lay the Foundation (*Overview paragraph*):

Identify the separate elements of the rule of law and the two or more elements that are issues to be evaluated in the memo.

  I. Issue One Heading (e.g., "The Stripes' garage is a dwelling.")

    1. Summarize Issue 1 (*Thesis paragraph*): Provide a roadmap for Issue

        1. Prove Why Your Conclusion Is Valid:

    2. Explain the Law (*Rule Explanation*): Explain how previous cases interpret the law.

    3. Apply the Law to the Client's Factual Situation (*Rule Application*):

      a. *Favorable Rule Application*: If there are favorable arguments that can be made, examine how the rule of law for this issue favorably affects the client's factual situation.

      b. *Unfavorable Rule Application*: Identify and evaluate any unfavorable arguments from the rule of law for Issue 1 (if applicable).

    4. Conclusion: Restate the answer to Issue 1.

 II. Issue Two Heading (e.g., "Mr. Arnold had the intent to commit a theft.")

    1. Summarize Issue 2 (*Thesis paragraph*): Provide a roadmap for Issue

2. Prove Why Your Conclusion is Valid:

2. Explain the Law (*Rule Explanation*): Explain how previous cases interpret the law.

3. Apply the Law to the Client's Factual Situation (*Rule Application*):

   a. *Favorable Rule Application*: If there are favorable arguments that can be made, examine how the rule of law for this issue favorably affects the client's factual situation.

   b. *Unfavorable Rule Application*: Identify and evaluate any unfavorable arguments from the rule of law for Issue 2 (if applicable).

4. Conclusion: Restate the answer to Issue 2.

CONCLUSION

Depending on the length of the memo and the preferences of your professor or assigning attorney, you may provide a short conclusion that summarizes each of the issues that have been separately evaluated in the memo.

C. Template of the Multi-Claim Memo

Sometimes when researching a problem on behalf of a client, you might not only have to address more than one legal issue, but more than one legal claim. For example, assume you represent a client who was terminated from her employment. After researching a number of potential claims she might have against her employer, suppose you conclude that she might have a viable claim for breach of her employment contract, and might also have a viable claim for sexual discrimination under Title VII of the Civil Rights Act of 1964. For this research project, you are, in essence, evaluating two separate legal claims that relate to the same client and the same factual situation. Therefore, although you will be addressing two separate legal claims, it makes sense to discuss the two claims in one document.

Like adding a second issue to an office memorandum, adding another claim to the equation is not complicated. The format for discussion of each individual claim and each individual issue conforms to the templates illustrated above. You need only add appropriate point-headings to guide the reader through the analysis. The outline of a multi-claim memo resembles two separate memos combined in a single document.

The following macro-outline presumes that the first claim (breach of contract) involves two issues, while the second claim (sexual discrimination) involves only a single issue.

DISCUSSION

Introductory Paragraph: Because the memo will address two separate claims, many attorneys insert a brief introductory paragraph prior to the first point-heading. The paragraph provides a roadmap for the entire Discussion by separately identifying each of the claims that will be discussed in the memo.

   I. <u>Claim One Heading</u> (e.g., "I. <u>Breach of Contract</u>")

     A. <u>Issue One Heading</u> (e.g., "A. <u>Terms of the Offer</u>")

         . . . .

     B. <u>Issue Two Heading</u> (e.g., "B. <u>Breach of Contract</u>")

         . . . .

  II. <u>Claim Two Heading</u> (e.g., "II. <u>Sexual Discrimination under Title VII</u>")

         . . . .

CONCLUSION

Multi-claim memos often conclude with a separate section that summarizes the conclusions of each claim discussed in the memo.

THE DISCUSSION SECTION

Drafting the Analysis (Single Case)

I. CHAPTER IN FOCUS

<u>MEMORANDUM</u>

To: [Senior Attorney]
From: [Junior Attorney]
Date: [Date of Submission of Memo]
Re: [XYZ Client Matter]

<u>QUESTION PRESENTED</u>

. . .

<u>SHORT ANSWER</u>

. . .

<u>STATEMENT OF FACTS</u>

. . .

<u>DISCUSSION</u> ←

Overview Paragraph
Thesis Paragraph
Rule Explanation ←
Rule Application ←

<u>CONCLUSION</u>

. . .

II. SINGLE CASE / SINGLE ISSUE MEMO

After evaluating how the law impacts your client's situation, you are ready to convey your legal analysis in writing. If you take a moment to consider the logic underlying the organizational format of the Discussion section of your memo, you might save yourself some time later when you attempt to translate your analysis into writing. Recall that readers need to understand the "context" of a legal analysis before they can absorb the myriad details. Because your entire analysis will be based on your interpretation of the original rule of law, the law itself is the logical starting point for your Discussion. Likewise, readers need to understand how earlier courts have interpreted the law before bringing their attention to your client's factual situation. Therefore, as a courtesy to the reader's need for context, you will explain the law in detail ("rule explanation") before evaluating how the rule of law affects the client's unique factual situation ("rule application").

A. Drafting the Rule Explanation

When describing a case that has interpreted the original rule of law, it is usually safe to assume that the senior attorney who asked you to draft the memo has not reviewed the case or evaluated the original rule of law. Even if the senior attorney has previously read the case, he or she presumably has not thoroughly evaluated the case; otherwise, you would not have been asked to draft a memo that evaluates the issue. Given these assumptions, your goal is to convey every important aspect of the case without distracting the reviewing attorney with irrelevant information.

1. A Typical Format for Discussing a Factually Relevant Case

a. The Thesis Sentence

The clearest introduction to a case discussion is to begin with a thesis sentence that describes a rule of law that expresses the court's holding—in other words, the rule statement you formulated when evaluating the case. The rule statement should identify: (a) *how* the court answered the legal question before it; and (b) *why* it responded in the manner that it did. When summarizing why the court responded in the manner that it did, incorporate the important factors (or narrow legal standard) that guided the court in its decision. By drafting the rule statement as the thesis sentence, the first sentence of the paragraph provides the foundation for the case discussion that follows. Thus, an ideal thesis sentence alerts the reviewing attorney to the crux of why the case is important and why the attorney will be reading that case discussion.

Again using the residential burglary problem for purposes of illustration, consider the *McIntyre* case and its interpretation of the "dwelling" element of the residential burglary statute. That case, and the lawyer's "thinking notes" from that case, are reproduced in Chapter 12, and the memo in its entirety is reproduced in Appendix A.

When evaluating the *McIntyre* case, the lawyer formulated the following rule statement that expresses the *McIntyre* court's holding: "*An enclosed, attached porch is considered a 'dwelling' when it is frequently used for residential activities as part of the living quarters of a home.*" This rule statement both identifies how the court answered the legal question (the porch is a "dwelling") and the relevant factors that guided its decision ("attached porch" "frequently" "used for residential activities" is part of the home's living quarters). This rule statement can easily become the thesis sentence that introduces the discussion of that case:

An enclosed, attached porch is considered a "dwelling" when it is frequently used for residential activities as part of the living quarters of a home. *People v. McIntyre*, 578 N.E.2d 314 (Ill. App. Ct. 1991). 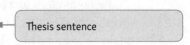 Thesis sentence

b. The Relevant Case Facts

Although there are several ways you can format your discussion of a case, one of the easiest ways to structure your case discussion is to follow the thesis sentence with a description of the case facts you determined were relevant to the court. If the case facts have a chronological order, describe the facts chronologically to make it easier for the reader to absorb the factual story underlying the case. The case facts provide the reader with a foundation, or context, from which the reviewing attorney can understand the significance of the court's holding and rationale. Thus, the two types of facts you should include in this section are background facts to provide context to the reader, and legally significant facts, which are facts the court actually relied on in making its determination.

It is important to keep in mind that in this section of the memo you are not describing any of the facts of your *client's* factual situation. It would be too difficult for a reader to absorb the factual story of a precedent case while simultaneously attempting to decipher analogies to the client. In the rule explanation section of your memo, you are only describing the facts of the relevant case. Again using the *McIntyre* case for purposes of illustration, the thesis sentence is followed by a description of the relevant case facts:

In *McIntyre*, the owners used an attached, screened porch for "sitting, eating, and cooking." *Id.* at 315. They ate most of their meals on the porch in the summer and cooked meals there four or five times a week in the winter. The owners furnished the porch with wrought-iron furniture and a barbecue grill that reflected its use. The porch was enclosed, locked, and attached to the home, although three locks separated the porch from the home. *Id.*

Description of the relevant case facts.

c. The Court's Holding & Rationale

Just as the thesis sentence gives the reader context for the entire case discussion, the factual story of the case provides context for the reader to appreciate why the court held the way that it did. To avoid distracting the reader with unnecessary "throat-clearing," the clearest way to state the holding is to simply identify how the court answered the legal question. For example, in the residential burglary illustration, you might state: "*The court held that, under these facts, the porch was a living quarters, and therefore, a dwelling under the Statute.*"

The holding, in turn, provides context for the reviewing attorney to understand *why* the court held as it did (the rationale). When describing the court's rationale, you might be tempted to restate all of the case facts you described earlier in the case discussion. However, this would not only be unnecessarily repetitive for your reader, but would also add an extra layer of confusion. Instead, what the reader really wants to know is this—from all of the information you've already given me, what were the *most important reasons* why the court answered the legal question the way that it did?

One way to distill rationale down to its essence is to use the factors (or legal standard) described in the thesis sentence as guideposts that lead the reader through your explanation of the court's rationale. However, to avoid merely repeating the thesis sentence, your explanation of the court's rationale should expand on each factor a bit by educating the reader as to why the court found each factor to be important. The following example, excerpted from Sample Memo A in Appendix A, illustrates how the holding and rationale in the *McIntyre* case were described:

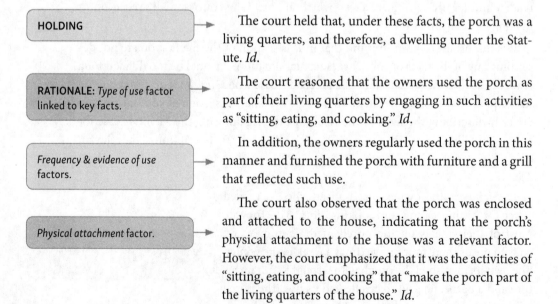

HOLDING

The court held that, under these facts, the porch was a living quarters, and therefore, a dwelling under the Statute. *Id.*

RATIONALE: *Type of use* factor linked to key facts.

The court reasoned that the owners used the porch as part of their living quarters by engaging in such activities as "sitting, eating, and cooking." *Id.*

Frequency & evidence of use factors.

In addition, the owners regularly used the porch in this manner and furnished the porch with furniture and a grill that reflected such use.

Physical attachment factor.

The court also observed that the porch was enclosed and attached to the house, indicating that the porch's physical attachment to the house was a relevant factor. However, the court emphasized that it was the activities of "sitting, eating, and cooking" that "make the porch part of the living quarters of the house." *Id.*

d. The Importance of Proper Sequencing

When drafting the rule explanation section, it is important to be thoughtful of the order of information you present. Consider, for a moment, that you are reading a letter from someone. Do you expect certain information to appear in specific places? Would it be odd for the author to sign the letter at the top and address the recipient at the bottom? Yes, because we expect to read the letter with the greeting at the beginning and the salutation at the end.

When readers read your rule explanation section, they expect to be educated about the case without having to read the full case opinion. If they are trained legal readers, they expect that information will be presented in a specific order, which is the order noted above: (1) thesis sentence, (2) facts, (3) holding, and (4) rationale. However, even if the readers aren't legally trained, the order of information matters because of how some information provides context, and how other information builds on each other. Read the following rule explanation example and determine if, as someone who has never read the case opinion, it is challenging to follow in this order:

> In *People v. Kulwin*, 593 N.E.2d 717 (Ill. App. Ct. 1992), the court noted that the defendant, due to his financial condition, was particularly susceptible to influence from others, and he had expressed an unwillingness to engage in the criminal activity. He only acquiesced to the State's repeated inducement to consummate the drug deal because of the pressure on him and the stress he was under due to his financial debts. The court noted that he was "coaxed" by the government agents who persuaded him to commit the illegal acts with full knowledge of his financial challenges.
>
> The appellate court held he was not predisposed to commit the drug offense. The defendant became friendly with the owner of a restaurant, but unbeknownst to the defendant, the owner was a former drug trafficker turned informant. The defendant confided in the owner about his problems, including his debts. After the defendant asked the owner if he could borrow money to pay the debts and to avoid the foreclosure of his home, the owner said he was "not in the business of lending money," but that the defendant could make money fast by selling cocaine. The owner put the defendant in touch with an undercover officer posing as a drug dealer, and the defendant took part in a drug sale transaction. He was later arrested and convicted of a controlled substance charge, but he appealed that ruling to the state appellate court.

Reading the rule explanation in that order, were you able to follow the story and understand the court's reason for its holding, or did the order of information leave you with questions along the way? Presenting you with reasoning language before

providing the context of the story with case facts, likely left you confused and searching for clarity from the beginning. This is why providing the information in an order
that will make a seamless read for the reader is so important. Now read a new version
of this rule explanation, but with the components presented in the appropriate order:

> A defendant is not predisposed to engage in an illegal drug sale when there
> is evidence that government agents preyed upon his vulnerabilities in pressur-
> ing him to engage in the sale. *People v. Kulwin*, 593 N.E.2d 717 (Ill. App. Ct. 1992).
> In *Kulwin*, the defendant became friendly with the owner of a restaurant, but
> unbeknownst to the defendant, the owner was a former drug trafficker turned
> informant. The defendant confided in the owner about his problems, including
> his debts. After the defendant asked the owner if he could borrow money to pay
> the debts and to avoid the foreclosure of his home, the owner said he was "not
> in the business of lending money," but that the defendant could make money
> fast by selling cocaine. The owner put the defendant in touch with an undercov-
> er office posing as a drug dealer, and the defendant took part in a drug sale
> transaction. He was later arrested and convicted of a controlled substance
> charge, but he appealed that ruling to the state appellate court.
>
> The appellate court held that the State failed to prove that the defendant
> was predisposed to commit the crime, as is required to rebut a defense of en-
> trapment. The court noted that the defendant, due to his financial condition,
> was particularly susceptible to influence from others, and he had expressed an
> unwillingness to engage in the criminal activity. He only acquiesced to the
> State's repeated inducement to consummate the drug deal because of the pres-
> sure on him and the stress he was under due to his financial debts. The court
> noted that he was "coaxed" by the government agents who persuaded him to
> commit the illegal acts with full knowledge of his financial challenges. Because
> of this, the State failed to prove beyond a reasonable doubt that the defendant
> was predisposed to commit the crime.

Did you find this second version much easier to follow from the beginning? Starting with a thesis sentence that describes the rule of law, or "take-away," from the case
and then providing a factual story before discussing the court's holding and rationale provides a logical, easy to follow framework for the reader to absorb the case
information.

2. An Alternative Format for Discussing a Factually Relevant Case

The above format for discussing a case can be a relatively easy and straightforward
way of capturing each component of the court's opinion. At the same time, if the case

discussion itself is not very complex, the format described above can be unnecessarily wordy and repetitive. Think about the case facts and the rationale of the case you will be describing in your memo. If the case facts are fairly simplistic and the court's rationale is relatively succinct, you might find it more effective to draft an abbreviated case discussion that avoids unnecessary repetition or wordiness. Under this format, your case discussion would be organized as follows:

1.   Thesis Sentence: Rule Statement
2.   Court's Rationale, including:
   a.   The key reasons the court held as it did (organized by factors or legal standards), linked to:
   b.   The important case facts that illustrate each key reason the court held as it did.

In this alternative format, notice two distinctions from the first format described above. First, the factual story of the case is woven into the description of the court's rationale. In other words, rather than having separate "case facts" and "rationale" components of your case discussion, they are condensed into a single discussion.

Second, in this alternative format, the rule statement itself serves as the statement of the court's holding. Even though the rule statement expresses the court's holding under the first format as well, under the first format it's usually helpful to remind the reader of the court's holding again after you've finished telling the reader about the relevant case facts. With a more simplistic case discussion, however, this added step isn't usually necessary because you will have moved directly from your rule statement (which describes the holding) to a discussion of the court's rationale and key facts.

Cautionary Advice: When the factual story and/or the court's rationale is fairly complex and lengthy, it's more challenging to use this alternative format effectively. This format requires that you accomplish two goals at once—(1) to tell the reader "what happened" in the case (the case facts); and (2) to explain the legal significance of each fact (the rationale). If the factual story is complex, it can be difficult to combine these two components (case facts and rationale) while still presenting to the reader a clear and cogent story of "what happened" in the case. After drafting a case discussion under this alternative format, ask yourself whether a reader who hasn't read the case would be able to follow the factual story. If not, you might want to revise the discussion to see whether the other format might be more workable for you.

The following example illustrates how the *McIntyre* case might be described under this alternative format:

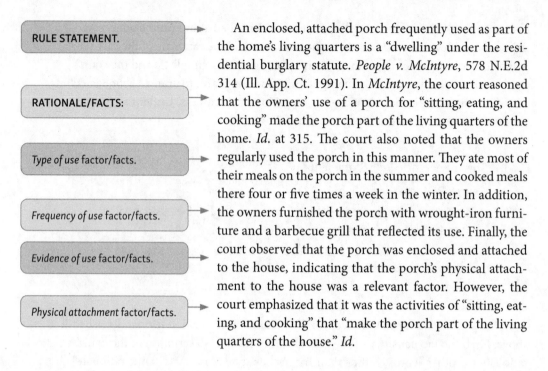

An enclosed, attached porch frequently used as part of the home's living quarters is a "dwelling" under the residential burglary statute. *People v. McIntyre*, 578 N.E.2d 314 (Ill. App. Ct. 1991). In *McIntyre*, the court reasoned that the owners' use of a porch for "sitting, eating, and cooking" made the porch part of the living quarters of the home. *Id.* at 315. The court also noted that the owners regularly used the porch in this manner. They ate most of their meals on the porch in the summer and cooked meals there four or five times a week in the winter. In addition, the owners furnished the porch with wrought-iron furniture and a barbecue grill that reflected its use. Finally, the court observed that the porch was enclosed and attached to the house, indicating that the porch's physical attachment to the house was a relevant factor. However, the court emphasized that it was the activities of "sitting, eating, and cooking" that "make the porch part of the living quarters of the house." *Id.*

B. Rule Application

After satisfying the reader's curiosity about how a court has interpreted the law, the lawyer reviewing your memo is now in a position to consider how the case affects your client. In the rule explanation section of the memo, you identified the important factors and/or legal standard that guided the court in its decision. In the rule application section of the memo, you will evaluate how each factor or legal standard impacts the client.

Each factor (or standard) will be used as an analytical tool to evaluate the client situation. For purposes of simplicity, the term "factor" will be used during the remainder of this discussion to refer to the term "standard" as well. Whether your analysis involves factors or standards, these evaluative tools will become the organizational lynchpins of your analysis.

1. Outlining the Framework for Analysis

a. Consider the Relative Weight of Each Factor

Before drafting your analysis of how the law affects a client situation, you can save yourself time by first outlining the basic framework of your analysis. As a starting point, each factor you previously identified as important will become the topic of a separate paragraph or group of paragraphs. Therefore, you can begin your outline by jotting down each factor you've identified as important, for example: (1) Type of Use…. (2) Frequency of Use…. (3) Evidence of Use…. (4) Proximity to Residence….).

If there is a logical order in which you think the ideas should be discussed, then organize your outline according to that logical order. If you can't think of any logical order for discussion, begin with the most important factor, followed by the second most important idea, and so on. If each factor seems equally important, begin with the idea that seems most favorable to the client. The final organizational idea to keep in mind is that, if two or more factors are interrelated, it's helpful to discuss these factors one after the other, rather than inserting an unrelated factor in the middle of the analysis.

As an example, in the residential burglary problem, the factors of "type of use," "frequency of use," and "evidence of use" are interrelated because they bring out interrelated facts from the client's situation. On the other hand, the "physical attachment" factor is more unrelated because it brings out an entirely different nuance from the client's factual situation. Therefore, you wouldn't want to insert the "physical attachment" factor into the midst of your discussion about the interrelated factors.

b. Opposing Arguments

i. Unfavorable Arguments that Are Related to Favorable Arguments

As you contemplate the different arguments you will make, one or more of the factors, or ideas, you are evaluating will likely be susceptible to an *unfavorable* as well as a favorable argument. If a factor is susceptible to credible arguments that both favor and damage the client's position, discuss the favorable argument first. This makes sense given your role as an advocate for your client; if there's a valid favorable argument that can be made, your client (and the senior lawyer reviewing your memo) will usually want to know about that argument first.

At the same time, the senior lawyer reviewing your memo will also want to know about any "problems" with your argument. The best time to address the problems with a particular argument is when the reader is already thinking about the topic. Therefore, in order to satisfy the reader's curiosity, insert any opposing arguments relating to a favorable argument *directly following* the favorable argument you have just made. In other words, the senior lawyer will want to review both the favorable and unfavorable implications of an idea before moving on to a different topic. For example, in the residential burglary problem, if there had been a credible opposing argument relating to the "type of use" factor, the young prosecutor would have inserted that argument immediately following the favorable discussion of the "type of use" factor.

ii. Unfavorable "Stand-Alone" Arguments

Some unfavorable arguments aren't directly related to any of the favorable arguments that are made in a legal discussion, but instead bring out an entirely separate idea. With this type of "stand-alone" argument, it's usually more effective to save the opposing argument until the end of your legal discussion. Again, in your role as an advocate for your client, the senior lawyer reading your memo will usually be interested in hearing the favorable arguments that can be made before thinking about the "stand-alone" unfavorable arguments. For example, in the residential burglary problem, the "proximity" factor is an unfavorable idea that stands alone from the rest of the arguments; it is unrelated to any of the favorable arguments that are made in the memo. Therefore, the young prosecutor waited until the end of the legal discussion before discussing the proximity factor.

As with any rule, there are always exceptions. If your client's legal situation is so bleak that the unfavorable arguments very clearly outweigh any possible favorable arguments that can be made, then you might want to address the unfavorable arguments first. That way, you directly address the likelihood that the client will not prevail first, and then end the discussion with any favorable, albeit unlikely, arguments that could be made.

Using the residential burglary problem and the *McIntyre* case for purposes of illustration, a template for the rule application section would look like this:

1. Type of Use (the most important factor)

2. Evidence of Use (sub-factor of the first factor and therefore logically related to the first factor)

3. Frequency of Use (sub-factor of the first factor and therefore logically related to the first factor)

4. Proximity of the structure to the residence (arguably the least important factor and also a factor that will be used solely as an opposing argument)

2. Filling in the Framework for Analysis

Some lawyers find it time efficient to fill in their outline with further details before they begin to draft their legal analysis. Doing so can save time later because you will have already reasoned through the specific details of each argument before you begin drafting. And, to some lawyers, reasoning through the permutations of each argument in an outline format can be less confusing than trying to do so while they are simultaneously struggling with writing decisions. If you have a tendency to encounter writer's block, filling in a more complete outline before you begin writing can help prevent that problem.

On the other hand, some lawyers prefer to begin the drafting process as soon as they complete a "big picture" outline of the arguments they will address in the memo. For these writers, the writing process itself helps trigger the creative process, and they aren't overly concerned with a messy first draft and the cutting and pasting process.

If you're not sure which process works best for you, you may wish to experiment by trying a more detailed outline first. Should you elect to begin with a more thorough outline, you would fill in the framework for your analysis by listing the relevant client facts and case facts that fall within the "umbrella" of each argument you will be making. Again using the residential burglary problem and the *McIntyre* case for purposes of illustration, a more detailed outline of the rule application section would look like this:

1. **Type of Use Factor**

   Thesis = Like the owners in *McIntyre*, Michael Stripe ("M.S.") uses the garage as a living quarters.

   Proof of thesis =
   - M.S. uses the garage to play and listen to music, and for snacking, sleeping, and watching T.V.—like the *McIntyre* acts of "sitting, eating, and cooking"
   - Sleeping seems even more residential than the activities in *McIntyre*

2. **Evidence of Use**

   Thesis = Furnishings reflect its use as a living quarters.

   Proof of thesis =
   - Futon, T.V., mini-refrigerator, and sound system—these furnishings are like the *McIntyre* grill, wrought-iron chairs, and table

3. **Frequency of Use**

   Thesis = Like the porch in *McIntyre*, the frequency of use reflects its use as a "living quarters."

   Proof of thesis =
   - M.S. spends 2–3 evenings a week and weekends—like *McIntyre*, in which the porch was used 4 to 5 times a week
   - M.S. sleeps there during the summer and fall—this is a greater frequency than the 4–5 times a week in *McIntyre*

4. **Proximity to Residence** (factor that will be raised by opponent)

   Basis for opponent's argument = the garage's detachment from the Stripes' home prevents it from being a living quarters.

   Proof of opponent's thesis =
   - *McIntyre* porch was attached; the court emphasized the porch's attachment to the residence in its rationale.

   My conclusion re: opponent's argument = lacks merit

My proof:

- It was more important to the *McIntyre* court that the owners used the porch as a living quarters than it was that the porch was attached—quote from court opinion to illustrate.
- The porch was separated from the home by 3 locks—it was not an open part of the primary residence; therefore, the porch is not really that different from M.S.'s separate living quarters.

3. Drafting the Rule Application—Favorable Arguments

a. Introduce Each New Idea with a "Legally Significant" Thesis Sentence

As the above outline reflects, each factor you evaluate will become an analytical tool that leads a separate argument, whether favorable and/or unfavorable. The thesis sentence for each new paragraph should satisfy the reader's curiosity by stating your ultimate conclusion about how the client's facts relate to the factor in a legally significant way. Therefore, your thesis sentence should identify the (1) factor (idea) the paragraph will be discussing, and (2) your legally significant conclusion about that factor.

It can be challenging to draft a thesis sentence that states a factual conclusion that is legally significant. Novice legal writers commonly fail to explain why the thesis sentence is legally significant. Instead, they tend to draft thesis sentences that identify why the client's facts are "like" or "unlike" a precedent case's facts with respect to a specific factor. Unfortunately, that type of thesis sentence makes it very difficult for the reader to grasp immediately the legal significance of the paragraph.

As importantly, a poorly written thesis sentence that doesn't illustrate a *legally significant conclusion* makes it difficult, as a writer, to draft a persuasive paragraph that illustrates why the client facts are legally significant. Instead, if your thesis sentence merely states that your client's facts are "like" or "unlike" a precedent case, it's easy to fall into the trap of merely proving why the client's facts are like, or unlike, the precedent case's facts.

A Tip: Before drafting a thesis sentence, ask yourself the following question: How does this factor, and the client facts that relate to this factor, help prove whether the client does (or does not) satisfy the question that I'm discussing? For example, in the residential burglary problem, the prosecutor is evaluating whether the Stripes' garage is a "living quarters," and therefore a "dwelling," under the Statute. Therefore, when thinking about how to draft a thesis sentence for the "type of use" factor, the goal is to draft a sentence that links the "type of use" factor to the legal issue conclusion (whether the garage is a "living quarters," and therefore a "dwelling," under the Statute). How does the garage's "use" help prove (or disprove) that the garage is a "living quarters" under the Statute?

Compare the following examples:

> **Not:**   Michael Stripe's use of the garage is like the use in *McIntyre*.
>
> **Instead:** Like the owners in *McIntyre*, Michael Stripe uses the garage for activities commonly associated with a "living quarters."

In the above example, the first thesis sentence would set you up for failure. If you attempted to prove why the premise in the thesis sentence was valid, the resulting paragraph would only prove that the client's facts are "like" the precedent case's facts. This is not an effective argument strategy because it fails to explore why the client's facts are *legally significant*. In contrast, the second thesis sentence would make it easier for you to construct an argument that has legal significance.

A Final Cautionary Note: As you begin to draft thesis sentences that have "legal significance," it can be tempting to slide into an analysis of whether the client facts "satisfy" a factor. Remember, factors are only guidelines, not a legal standard or element that must be proven. Therefore, if you set up factors as the ultimate legal conclusion you are trying to prove, you will have forced an analysis that is misleading. Compare the following two illustrations:

> **Not:**   Michael Stripe's use of the garage satisfies the "type of use" factor.
>
> **Instead:** Like the owners in *McIntyre*, Michael Stripe uses the garage for activities commonly associated with a living quarters.

The first illustration incorrectly implies that Michael Stripe's conduct should be satisfying a particular factor. The second illustration correctly states the writer's premise about the "type of use" factor and its relationship to the broader legal question—whether Michael Stripe used the garage for activities commonly associated with a living quarters.

b. Prove Why the Premise in the Thesis Sentence Is Valid

After stating the premise of your paragraph within the thesis sentence itself, the remainder of the paragraph should prove why the premise is valid. It might help to think of the rest of the paragraph as your "evidence." Which client facts serve as evidence that your premise is valid? What analogies to the precedent case can serve as useful evidence that your premise is valid? As a novice writer, it is very easy to fall into the habit of making comparison after comparison without letting the reader know why the comparisons are legally significant. Therefore, make sure that you spell out the legal significance of the client facts and comparisons you are making. Consider the following example:

> **Example 1:**
>
> Michael Stripe's use of the garage is like the owners' use of the porch in *McIntyre*. In the present case, Michael Stripe played and listened to music and watched television. He also relaxed in his garage get-a-way retreat. In *McIntyre*, the owners engaged in eating, sitting, and cooking activities. Michael Stripe also sleeps in his garage retreat. The owners in *McIntyre* did not sleep on their porch.

While the facts and comparisons in the above example are accurate, the legal significance of each fact is only implied, forcing the reader to stop and consider why the comparisons are important. From the thesis sentence through the remainder of the paragraph, the analysis is structured as "this is what happened in the precedent case" and "the case facts are like the client facts." Thus, the analogies themselves become the focal point of the paragraph, and the reader is left wondering why the factual similarities are important from a legal perspective.

In Example 2 below, the paragraph focuses instead on how the client facts illustrate the *legally significant premise* described in the thesis sentence. The statements that clarify the legal significance of facts and comparisons are underlined so that you can easily identify the few changes that enhance the clarity of the analysis. Note how each added explanation simply spells out for the reader why specific facts and analogies are important to the issue being evaluated. By clearly spelling out the legal import of each fact and analogy, the reader isn't forced to stop and mull over why you're highlighting certain facts and analogies.

> **Example 2:**
>
> Like the owners in *McIntyre*, Michael Stripe uses the garage for <u>activities commonly associated with a living quarters</u>. Similar to the activities of "sitting, eating, and cooking" in *McIntyre*, Michael Stripe's use of the garage for relaxing, playing and listening to music, watching television, and eating snacks <u>are uses commonly associated with a living quarters</u>. In addition, <u>Michael Stripe's use of the garage as a sleeping quarters</u> during the summer and fall makes his use of the garage even more of a typical living quarters than the porch in *McIntyre*. Unlike the *McIntyre* activities of barbecuing, eating, and sitting, <u>which can occur outside of a dwelling, sleeping is an activity uniquely associated with a living quarters</u>.

4. Drafting the Rule Application—Unfavorable Arguments

a. Introduce the Argument with a Thesis Sentence

In many ways, drafting unfavorable arguments is like drafting favorable arguments. Just like rule application paragraphs that discuss favorable arguments, a paragraph (or group of paragraphs) that evaluates an unfavorable argument begins with a thesis sentence that states a legally significant factual premise. However, because the thesis sentence is introducing an *unfavorable* argument, the legally significant factual premise often begins with a statement such as: "the [opponent] may argue that…." Thus, in the residential burglary problem, the lawyer began an unfavorable argument with the following statement:

> The Defendant may argue that, despite Michael Stripe's frequent use of the garage for activities associated with a living quarters, the garage's physical detachment from the Stripes' home prevents it from being a "living quarters" in which the owners "reside."

b. Explain the Basis for the Unfavorable Premise

Just as with favorable arguments, next describe the "evidence" the opposing counsel would likely use to prove why the opposing premise is valid. Figuratively placing yourself in the shoes of the opposing counsel, describe any language in the precedent case that might be problematic for the client, and/or client facts that could prove to be problematic. For example, in the residential burglary problem, the lawyer elaborated on why the opponent might argue that the Stripes' detached garage is not a living quarters:

> Under this theory, the Defendant would argue that the garage, standing alone, is not a living quarters in which anyone resides. The garage has no running water, bathroom facilities, or heat. Thus, the garage's status as a dwelling is dependent upon whether it can reasonably be viewed as an extension of the Stripe family's living quarters within the home itself. The Defendant would argue that the fact that the *McIntyre* porch was physically attached to the family's home was essential to the court's holding. Only because it was physically attached to the home could the porch reasonably be viewed as an extension of the family's living quarters. In contrast, the Stripes' garage stands thirty feet away from their residence.

c. State Your Premise, or Conclusion, About the Unfavorable Argument

After fully elaborating on the opposing counsel's unfavorable argument, next state your own conclusion about the merit of that argument. If you believe the unfavorable argument has little merit, you might state: "While having some merit, this argument should fail." If you believe that the unfavorable argument has substantial merit, you might state something like: "This argument has considerable merit. However, the court may well find [summarize your favorable position]." If you can think of *no credible argument* in response to the unfavorable argument, you might state: "This argument has merit and, unfortunately, the court is likely to find…"

d. Prove Why Your Favorable Premise Is Valid

Unless you can think of no credible favorable rebuttal to the opposing argument, next prove why the unfavorable argument is faulty, or weak, or should not prevail. If the unfavorable argument itself merely explores an unfavorable nuance from a favorable argument that you have *already discussed*, this last section of the argument will likely be relatively brief—you will have already explored the details of your rebuttal within the favorable argument you have already discussed. In that case, you need only summarize the important reasons why the favorable analysis is more persuasive than, or at least as credible as, the unfavorable argument.

However, if the unfavorable argument is a discussion of an entirely new factor that has *not* previously been discussed, this section of the analysis will, of necessity, require more explanation. Thus, in the residential burglary problem, the prosecutor's rebuttal to the proximity factor is detailed and thorough. The following paragraph is excerpted from the residential burglary memorandum in Appendix A:

> While having some merit, this argument should fail. Although the *McIntyre* court did note that the porch was physically "attached and enclosed," it concluded that it was the owners' "activities" and *use* of the porch that made the porch "part of the living quarters of the house." 578 N.E.2d at 314. Thus, the court implied that the activities for which the porch was used were more important than the porch's attachment to the home. Moreover, the fact that the porch was separated from the utility room of the owners' home by a door with "three locks" lends less significance to the attached/detached distinction. The presence of three locks implies that the porch area was not an open part of the main residence, but was instead physically separate from the main residence. Like the physically separate porch in *McIntyre*, the Stripes' garage is used as an extension of the Stripe family's living quarters.

5. Concluding on the Legal Issue

Finally, end the rule application section by concluding on the client's legal issue. The following sentence, excerpted from the residential burglary memorandum in Appendix A, demonstrates the legal issue conclusion:

> In conclusion, the Stripes' garage is a living quarters in which Michael Stripe resides and is thus a "dwelling" for purposes of prosecuting Arnold under the Statute.

III. SINGLE CASE / MULTI-ISSUE MEMO

At times, you might have a single case that evaluates more than one issue. Thankfully, the rule explanation and rule application sections of a multi-issue memo don't really differ from the analysis of a single-issue memo. For a multi-issue memo, you would simply repeat the same outlining and drafting steps you performed for the first issue—except this time you would repeat the process twice. For example, assume that the hypothetical residential burglary fact pattern revealed a second issue: whether Mr. Arnold had the requisite "intent to commit theft." Your template for the analysis of this second issue would be identical to your template for the analysis of the first issue. For the second issue, you would again discuss the case that interpreted the "intent to commit theft" element of the statute (rule explanation), followed by a discussion of how the factors for this issue affect the client situation (rule application).

Using the same precedent case to explore each issue in a multi-issue memo presents only one additional drafting challenge. It's generally not a good idea to discuss the precedent case only once and hope that the reader will remember the discussion by the time she finally reads the discussion of the second issue. That's asking too much of the reader. As well, there will be some case facts and rationale that relate only to the first issue, and other case facts and rationale that relate only to the second issue. Therefore, it makes sense to discuss the case twice. However, it does takes some thought and finesse to separately identify and isolate those aspects of the case you will highlight in the first discussion, and those aspects of the case you will save for the second discussion.

For example, assume that the *McIntyre* court evaluated both the "dwelling" and "intent to commit theft" elements of the Statute. In your discussion of the *McIntyre* case for the "dwelling" issue, you would describe only those case facts, holding, and rationale that pertained to whether the porch was a dwelling. In your second discussion of the *McIntyre* case for the "intent to commit theft" issue, you would bring out for the first time those facts, holding, and rationale that pertained to whether the thief in *McIntyre* intended to commit theft.

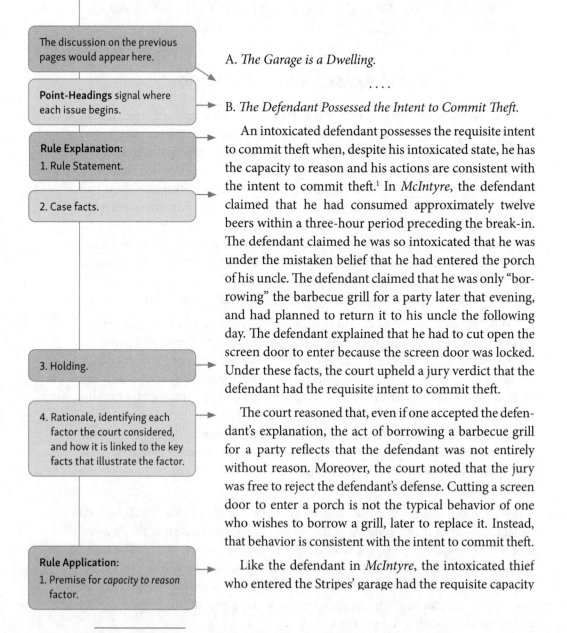

◎ ILLUSTRATION: Residential Burglary Problem

The following example illustrates the rule explanation and rule application sections of a memo discussing the "intent to commit theft" element of the residential burglary statute, the *McIntrye* case, and the Stripes' garage.

The discussion on the previous pages would appear here.	A. *The Garage is a Dwelling.* . . . . B. *The Defendant Possessed the Intent to Commit Theft.*
Point-Headings signal where each issue begins.	
Rule Explanation: 1. Rule Statement.	An intoxicated defendant possesses the requisite intent to commit theft when, despite his intoxicated state, he has the capacity to reason and his actions are consistent with the intent to commit theft.[1] In *McIntyre*, the defendant
2. Case facts.	claimed that he had consumed approximately twelve beers within a three-hour period preceding the break-in. The defendant claimed he was so intoxicated that he was under the mistaken belief that he had entered the porch of his uncle. The defendant claimed that he was only "borrowing" the barbecue grill for a party later that evening, and had planned to return it to his uncle the following day. The defendant explained that he had to cut open the screen door to enter because the screen door was locked.
3. Holding.	Under these facts, the court upheld a jury verdict that the defendant had the requisite intent to commit theft.
4. Rationale, identifying each factor the court considered, and how it is linked to the key facts that illustrate the factor.	The court reasoned that, even if one accepted the defendant's explanation, the act of borrowing a barbecue grill for a party reflects that the defendant was not entirely without reason. Moreover, the court noted that the jury was free to reject the defendant's defense. Cutting a screen door to enter a porch is not the typical behavior of one who wishes to borrow a grill, later to replace it. Instead, that behavior is consistent with the intent to commit theft.
Rule Application: 1. Premise for *capacity to reason* factor.	Like the defendant in *McIntyre*, the intoxicated thief who entered the Stripes' garage had the requisite capacity

---

1. This discussion of the *McIntyre* case is hypothetical for purposes of illustration only.

to reason. Mr. Arnold claimed that he consumed eight martinis the night of the break-in and was so intoxicated that he has only a hazy recollection of the events that transpired that night. However, Mr. Arnold also claims that his purpose in entering the Stripes' garage was to borrow a guitar for a "gig" later that night. Mr. Arnold claims that he is an acquaintance of Michael Stripe and knew the Stripes stored musical instruments in the garage because he had heard the band playing there before. Like the defendant's explanation in *McIntyre*, "borrowing" a guitar to play in a gig reflects that Mr. Arnold had the power to reason. In fact, Mr. Arnold was arguably less intoxicated than the defendant in *McIntyre*, who ostensibly ended up on the wrong porch. Here, Mr. Arnold actually planned to take the guitar from the Stripes' garage and was able to carry out that plan. These actions reflect that Mr. Arnold had not lost the capacity to reason.

Moreover, like the defendant in *McIntyre*, Mr. Arnold's actions are consistent with the intent to commit theft. Because the door to the garage was locked, Mr. Arnold used a glass cutter to cut the window pane next to the door. After he cut the window pane, he apparently reached in and unlocked the door from the inside. When Mr. Arnold was apprehended, he had cuts on his arm from reaching through the window. As the court noted in *McIntyre*, one does not typically forcibly break into a locked structure to borrow an implement from an acquaintance. Instead, such an act is more consistent with the intent to commit theft. Had Mr. Arnold indeed wanted to borrow Michael Stripe's guitar, he would have knocked on the door and, hearing no answer, left and come back later. The fact that Mr. Arnold was found with a glass cutter in his satchel strengthens the argument that his purpose was to commit theft. It is difficult to conceive of any lawful purpose Mr. Arnold might have had for carrying such a tool. Thus, the facts show that Mr. Arnold possessed the intent to commit theft when he entered the Stripes' garage.

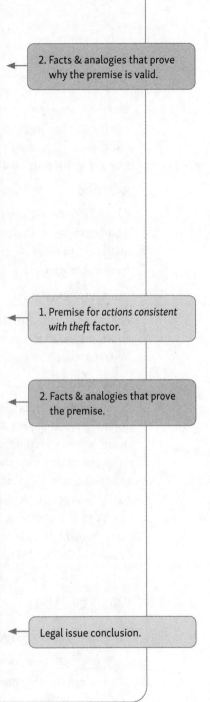

2. Facts & analogies that prove why the premise is valid.

1. Premise for *actions consistent with theft* factor.

2. Facts & analogies that prove the premise.

Legal issue conclusion.

CHAPTER IN REVIEW

Definitions:

ELEMENT:

Elements are separate requirements, or standards, of a rule of law that a party *must* prove to compel a particular result. If an element is very narrow and concrete, it might be used as an analytical tool in rule explanation and rule application paragraphs in lieu of factors.

FACTORS:

Factors are the underlying concepts that courts weigh when evaluating whether a particular set of facts prove an element of a rule of law. Factors are a common analytical tool in rule explanation and rule application paragraphs to lead the reader through the legal analysis.

RULE STATEMENT:

A statement you formulate that clearly and accurately reflects how *and* why the court answered the legal question in the manner that it did. Rule statements appear in thesis sentences that introduce important cases.

STANDARDS:

(1) Elements of an original rule of law impose standards a party must prove to compel a particular result. (2) In addition, when a court interprets an original rule of law, sometimes it defines the rule of law in a manner that effectively establishes a new requirement the parties must satisfy. The new requirement can also be called a standard (*e.g.*, the *Gigante* court interpreted the term "satisfactory explanation" to require "reasonable diligence," which effectively became a new standard, or requirement, under the statute). If a standard is very narrow and concrete, it might be used as an analytical tool in rule explanation and rule application paragraphs in lieu of factors.

Editing Checklist:

RULE EXPLANATION PARAGRAPHS

As you draft rule explanation paragraphs, consider whether the case discussion:

1. Begins with a thesis sentence that contains your rule statement. The thesis sentence should both:
   a. Identify the important standard (often illustrated by key factors) that guided the court in its decision; and
   b. Identify the court's answer to the legal question before the court.

- Alternatively, if the case discussion is a continuation of the same point raised in the preceding paragraph, the discussion may instead begin with a transition sentence.

2. Identifies the legally significant facts in the opinion.
3. States the court's holding (how it responded to the legal question before it).
4. Describes the court's rationale, or justification, for holding as it did. The rationale for a fact-centered holding should incorporate:
   a. Explanatory reasoning, if provided, which provides legal interpretations of the law and the key factors that guided the court in its decision; and
   b. Application reasoning, which links the key factors to a *brief* summary of the key facts that illustrate why each factor was important to the court.
      - If you selected the "alternative format" for discussing a case described in Section II, A.2. *supra*, your discussion of the court's rationale will include more detailed factual information within this section of the case discussion.

RULE APPLICATION PARAGRAPHS

1. *Outline* the framework for your analysis
   a. Review the legal standard (as illustrated by important factors) you will use as the basis for your analysis and consider:
      i. Whether there is a factor that should logically be discussed first;
      ii. If there is no logical starting point, begin with the factor that is most important;
      iii. If all factors are equally important, begin with the factor that has the most favorable application to the client.
   b. Opposing Arguments:
      i. If the opposing argument brings out an unfavorable idea that relates to a factor that also brings out a favorable analysis, insert the opposing argument *directly following* a favorable analysis of the same idea, or factor.
      ii. If the opposing argument relates to a factor that is entirely unfavorable, save the opposing argument until the end of your discussion. For example, in the residential burglary problem, the "proximity" factor is entirely unfavorable—there are no favorable arguments the prosecutor made with respect to that factor. Therefore, the prosecutor waited until the end of the favorable discussion to insert that opposing argument.
   c. You may find it helpful to fill in the framework for analysis even further before you begin drafting:

  i. List the client facts and case facts that fall within the umbrella of each factor (or legal standard); and

  ii. For each factor (or standard), summarize the favorable and unfavorable arguments you will evaluate with respect to that factor.

2. As you *draft* rule application paragraphs, consider:

  a. Whether the paragraph begins with a thesis sentence that identifies:

    i. The factor (or legal standard) the paragraph will discuss; and

    ii. Your factual conclusion about how the client facts illustrate that factor (or legal standard) in a legally significant way. *e.g.*, *<Factor>*: "Like the owners in *McIntyre*, *<Conclusion>*: Michael Stripe uses the garage for activities commonly associated with a living quarters."

      • To determine legal significance, ask yourself how your factual conclusion helps answer the broad legal question.

  b. Whether the remainder of each paragraph of rule application:

    i. *Elaborates fully* on the client's facts, explaining why the facts prove why the premise, or conclusion, set out in the first sentence of the paragraph is sound.

    ii. Makes direct, concrete *analogies* to the precedent case's facts.

    iii. Explains why the client facts and analogies are *legally significant*—*e.g.*, how they support the conclusion in the first sentence.

    Note: Restrict the ideas in the paragraph only to those factual details that prove why the conclusion in the first sentence is valid.

  d. Whether the credible *opposing arguments* are fully explained and evaluated.

    i. Begin with a thesis sentence that identifies (i) the factor (or legal standard) the paragraph will discuss; and (ii) the opposing counsel's likely conclusion.

    ii. Describe the opposing argument in as much detail as necessary to flesh out the opposing counsel's arguments.

    iii. State your *own* conclusion as to the relative merit of this argument; and

    iv. Unless you can think of no credible favorable rebuttal to the unfavorable argument, next provide your own evidence that illustrates why your own favorable premise is at least a viable rebuttal to the unfavorable argument.

  e. Whether, at the end of your rule application analysis, you clearly communicate your *legal issue and ultimate conclusions?*

    i. Your legal issue conclusion at the end of your discussion should be consistent with the legal issue conclusion stated in the thesis paragraph.

    ii. Your ultimate conclusion at the end of your discussion should be consistent with the ultimate conclusion stated in the overview paragraph.

   iii. Depending on the simplicity or complexity of the issues, you may or may not include a separate heading labeled "CONCLUSION."

EVALUATING MULTIPLE CASES

I. CASE SYNTHESIS

When researching a legal issue, typically you'll find more than one relevant precedent case. When evaluating multiple cases that address your legal issue, you have an additional challenge—to "synthesize" the diverse case facts and results. For example, assume you find three cases that address an issue you are researching. It is highly unlikely that any of these three cases will be identical to the client's factual situation or even to one another. In some cases, the plaintiff won; in other cases, the defendant won. In each of the cases, what happened between the plaintiff and the defendant will be different. Your ultimate goal is to take these diverse case results and case facts and advise your client how these cases, as a group, affect the client.

When evaluating an individual case, you engage in a process of *inductive* reasoning. The process of inductive reasoning requires that you examine specific facts to form broad conclusions. In other words, from a myriad of facts and details in an individual case, you formulate a broad rule of law that expresses the court's holding. When you evaluate two or more individual cases, you will engage in a similar inductive reasoning process. From a number of cases that interpret and apply a rule of law, you will also formulate a broad rule statement that synthesizes the cases as a group. The inductive reasoning process can be visualized like this:

Case 1	Case 2	Case 3
1) Useful interpretation of rule of law	1) No useful interpretation of rule of law	1) Useful definition of rule of law
2) Holding	2) Holding	2) Holding
3) Factors A & B seemed to guide court's holding	3) Factors B & C seemed to guide court's holding	3) Narrow standard that guided court's holding
4) Relevant facts that illustrate factors A & B	4) Relevant facts that illustrate factors B & C	4) Relevant facts that support court's application of the narrow standard
5) Rule statement reflecting the holding	5) Rule statement reflecting the holding	5) Rule statement reflecting the holding

Verify accuracy of factors

Synthesize legal standard in Case 3 with factors in Cases 1 & 2

Formulate synthesized rule statement that illustrates the cases as a group

◎ ILLUSTRATION: Residential Burglary Problem
Thomas, *McIntyre*, and *Silva* Cases

1. People v. McIntyre *Case*

After having read the *Thomas* case, assume that you next evaluated the *People v. McIntyre* case. As you read the lawyer's notes to the right of the court opinion, notice how the lawyer reads *McIntyre* from two perspectives: the *McIntyre* case as an opinion that stands on its own, and the *McIntyre* case as it relates to *Thomas*—the case the lawyer has already evaluated.

a. Court Opinion

People v. McIntyre

218 Ill. Dec. 187, 578 N.E.2d 314 (App. Ct. 1991)

JUSTICE KNECHT delivered the opinion of the court:

Defendant Bruce McIntyre was convicted of residential burglary (ILL. REV. STAT. 1989, ch. 38, par. 19-3) after a bench trial in the circuit court of Macon County. He was sentenced to a six-year term of imprisonment and now appeals, alleging he was not proved guilty of residential burglary beyond a reasonable doubt. We disagree and affirm.

Betty Houser of 3930 Bayview Drive, Decatur, was on vacation. While away, she asked her daughter, Jana Chisenall, and Jana's husband, Gary, to check on her house. On the evening of May 8, 1990, the Chisenalls checked the house and noticed nothing unusual. After leaving the house, they decided to drive around the block and go by the house again. On doing so they observed a white Dodge station wagon parked adjacent to the Houser property.

As they approached, they observed two men running from the backyard of the Houser property toward the white car. Gary observed two men get into the wagon but, as he and Jana pulled up in their car and looked inside, they saw only one person, whom they identified as defendant.

Jana asked the defendant if he needed help, but he only stared at them and sped off. They recorded the license-plate number. They then discovered a large gas grill in the middle of the Hauser backyard about 10 feet away from where they had seen the men running. The gas grill was always kept on the screened-in porch attached to the Houser residence. They called the police, who discovered the screen near the porch door had been torn, and the porch door had been unlocked and was open.

At trial, defendant testified he made two trips to the Houser residence on the evening of May 8, because he was in the company of Michael Houser, who was checking his parents' residence while they vacationed. Michael Houser

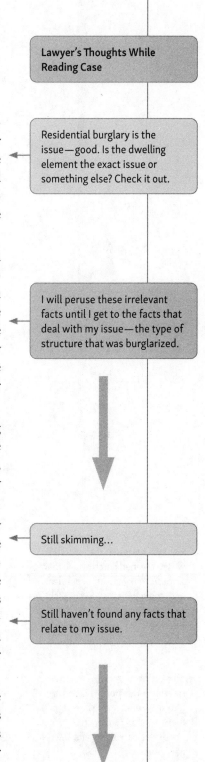

Lawyer's Thoughts While Reading Case

Residential burglary is the issue—good. Is the dwelling element the exact issue or something else? Check it out.

I will peruse these irrelevant facts until I get to the facts that deal with my issue—the type of structure that was burglarized.

Still skimming...

Still haven't found any facts that relate to my issue.

was also charged with residential burglary as a result of the incident. Defendant knew Michael socially, and had a vehicle for sale which Michael came to his residence to see. Because Michael had no vehicle, as a favor defendant drove him to his parents' home to check on the house. After arriving there, Michael remembered he had forgotten the house keys and defendant then drove Michael back to Michael's apartment to get them. They returned to the Houser residence, and Michael approached the house while defendant waited in his vehicle.

Shortly thereafter, the Chisenalls' van pulled up and Michael returned from the house and entered defendant's vehicle. Michael told defendant the woman in the van was his sister and to just drive away. Defendant did so without responding to the woman.

Defendant denied knowing Michael Houser intended to steal anything and denied seeing a gas grill. He also testified a prior serious injury and spinal operation pre-vented him from running or carrying heavy objects. Defendant's two prior felony convictions were admitted into evidence for impeachment purposes. The trial judge rejected defendant's version of the incident, and stated he did not believe his testimony. The finding of guilty was based primarily on the Chisenalls' testimony regarding two men running in the Houser backyard, their proximity to the gas grill that had been removed from the porch, and the identification of defendant as the driver of the vehicle that sped away.

Finally—my issue: The structure was a screened porch attached to a house. And yes—this case deals with the right issue—whether it was a dwelling.

Defendant raises two issues on appeal. First, he contends the State failed to prove a residential burglary because any entry that did occur was only to a screened porch attached to a house. Defendant argues the supreme court's decision in *People v. Thomas*, (1990), 137 Ill. 2d 500, 148 Ill. Dec. 751, 561 N.E.2d 57, *cert. denied* (1991), ___ U.S. ___ , 111 S.Ct. 1092, 112 L.Ed.2d 1196, and the definition of dwelling in section 2-6(b) of the Criminal Code of 1961 (Code) (Ill. Rev. Stat. 1989, ch. 38, par. 2-6(b)) require us to conclude a screened porch attached to a house is not part of a dwelling. We disagree.

Holding = this porch was part of the dwelling. Now I need to focus—I wonder why this porch was a dwelling and the garage wasn't?

Thomas held, for our purposes here, that an attached garage is not necessarily a dwelling within the meaning of the residential burglary statute. Our supreme court also stated it would wait until some future date to decide whether the unlawful entry of the porch of a house may constitute the unlawful entry of a residence. We need not decide whether every porch is part of a dwelling. We are satisfied this porch was a part of the Housers' living quarters.

The enclosed porch in this case is a wood frame structure with a wooden floor and dimensions of 8 by 10 or 12 feet. The porch includes both solid walls to a height of three feet and screen from that height to a roof. The floor, walls, and roof are all attached to the house. The porch has a metal door with glass inset and a lock to provide access to the backyard. A wooden door with glass inset and three locks connects the porch to the utility room of the house.

The Housers furnished the porch with a metal table, chairs, a wrought iron love seat, a small table and a large gas grill. The furniture was always kept on the porch regardless of the season.

The Housers used the porch in the summer for most of their meals, and in the winter cooked on the porch four or five times per week.

The Code defines "dwelling" for purposes of the residential burglary as "a house, apartment, mobile home, trailer, or other living quarters in which at the time of the alleged offense the owners or occupants actually reside or in their absence intend within a reasonable period of time to reside." (ILL. REV. STAT. 1989, ch. 38, par. 2-6(b).) In our view, the porch here is a part of the house.

It is attached, enclosed, and used for sitting, eating, and cooking. These activities make the porch part of the living quarters of the house. This conclusion is not inconsistent with *Thomas*.

Affirmed.

Side annotations:

Was my conclusion that the *Thomas* court was more interested in "use" than in its "attachment" to the house correct? I wonder if the type of structure is important—will a porch be treated the same way as a garage?

Court is describing the porch's physical dimensions—possibly important.

Court notes there was a lock between the house and the porch—possibly important.

Court is describing how the porch is furnished.

Now court is describing how the owners used the porch and how often—this is like the "type of use" factor in *Thomas*.

If "type of use" is relevant to this court, maybe that's why the court described the furnishings—they are evidence of the way in which the owners used the porch.

Court's definition of dwelling—quote is pulled right out of the Statute. Court restates holding—porch is part of the house.

Court reasons: it is "attached"—is attachment important? Rethink in light of *Thomas*. Court also emphasizes the activities of sitting, eating, and cooking—court states that it is "these activities" that make the porch part of the living quarters. This would clearly fit with *Thomas*.

b. Notes from *McIntyre* Case

After carefully reviewing the *McIntyre* case and writing down some "thinking notes," your notes would reflect the following important information:

---

1. Court's holding was fact-specific—*e.g.*, held only that this porch was a dwelling under the Statute.

2. Court emphasized the following facts and factors:

   a. *Factor #1*: <u>Type of activities on porch</u>

      Facts that support: Sitting, eating, drinking, and cooking meals

      Language that supports: "The porch here is a part of the house. It is…used for sitting, eating, and cooking."

   b. *Factor #1(a)*: <u>Amount of time spent on porch</u>

      Facts that support: 4-5 times a week

   c. *Factor #1(b)*: <u>Evidence of living-type activities</u>

      Facts that support: Gas grill, metal table, chairs, wrought iron love seat, and small table

   d. *Factor #2*: <u>Physical proximity & characteristics of structure</u>

      Facts that support: Porch with solid wall and screen; attached to home by wooden door with 3 locks

      Language that supports: "The porch here is a part of the house. It is attached, enclosed…"

3. My evaluation of factors:

   The <u>type of activities</u> that occurred on the porch, as reflected by the <u>frequency</u> of these activities (amount of time spent on porch) and <u>evidence of these activities</u> (furnishings) seemed to be critical. The porch's <u>attachment</u> to the house & maybe its <u>physical characteristics</u> as part of the house were also important to the court.

   Language that supports my conclusion: When supporting its holding, the court observed: "The porch is *attached, enclosed*…" and the court also stated that "these activities make the porch part of the living quarters of the house."

4. Rule statement:

   An attached porch frequently used for residential activities is part of the living quarters of a home and is therefore a dwelling under the residential burglary statute.

---

2. People v. Silva *Case*

After reading *Thomas* and *McIntyre*, assume that you next discovered the *People v. Silva* case. Having read that case, you determined that the facts in *Silva* were not particularly helpful as a basis of analogy to the Stripes' garage. However, the court did engage in an interesting policy discussion of legislative intent and also interpreted the *Thomas* case. Only the relevant portions of the *Silva* case have been reproduced below. As you read the *Silva* case, note how it enhances our understanding of *Thomas* and *McIntyre*, even though the case is not helpful as a basis of factual analogy:

a. Court Opinion

. . . .

During legislative debates, Senator Sangmeister explained the intent of the amendment as follows:

> "Yes, it was even brought to our attention by the Illinois Supreme Court in a number of cases that * * * there should be a better definition to the dwelling house. We are having people prosecuted for residential burglary for breaking into * * * unoccupied buildings such as garages. Therefore, very simply, we have redefined dwelling to mean a house, apartment, mobile home, trailer or other living quarters in which at the time of the alleged offense the owners or occupants actually reside in or * * * in their absence intend within a reasonable period of time to reside. So that still covers, in my opinion, the vacation home; you intend to reside in that and if you burglarize that, you would still be committing residential burglary, but it tightens up some of these cases where we got old abandoned buildings around our garages and stuff that * * * would not be residential burglary....". 84th Ill. Gen. Assem. Senate Proceedings, June 18, 1986, at 66-67 (statements of Senator Sangmeister).

> | Lawyer's Thoughts While Reading Case |

> | Legislative intent discussed—maybe this will help clarify my questions. This is not good—implies here that garages are not dwellings. But wait a minute—the key distinction seems to be between abandoned, vacant buildings vs. occupied homes—the Stripes' garage isn't abandoned so maybe we are fine. |

Burglary is a Class 2 felony with a statutory penalty range of not less than three years' nor more than seven years' imprisonment. (Ill. Rev. Stat. 1991, ch. 38, pars. 19-1(b), 1005-8-1(a)(5); now codified as 720 ILCS 5/19-1(b); 730 ILCS 5/5-8-1(a)(5) (West 1992).) Residential burglary

> | Court notes the difference in penalties between burglary and residential burglary. |

> Residential burglary carries the more severe penalty.

is a Class 1 felony with a statutory penalty rage of not less than four years' nor more than 15 years' imprisonment. (Ill. Rev. Stat. 1991, ch. 38, pars. 19-3(b), 1005-8-1(a)(4); now codified as 720 ILCS 5/19-3(b); 730 ILCS 5/5-8-1(a) (4) (West 1992).) "The overall legislative scheme evidences an intent to make clear that an offender may not be charged with residential burglary—a crime with a more severe penalty—when he unlawfully entered a structure that was not a 'dwelling place of another.'" *Edgeston*, 243 Ill. App. 3d at 10, 183 Ill. Dec. 196, 611 N.E.2d 49.

> Here is why the penalty is more severe: 1) protecting the sanctity of the home and 2) the greater potential for serious harm in homes than in businesses.

The residential burglary statute is designed to protect the "privacy and sanctity of the home," with a view toward the "greater danger and potential for serious harm from burglary of a home as opposed to burglar of a business." *Edgeston*, 243 Ill. App. 3d at 10, 183 Ill. Dec. 196, 611 N.E.2d 49.

> Great—court is evaluating how the structure's *use* implicates the public policy concerns underlying Statute—not "attachment."

The [structure] implicated the concerns for privacy, sanctity of the home, and the potential for serious harm which are addressed by the residential burglary statute....

> Even better—the court interprets *Thomas* just like I did!

Thomas did not hold that a garage *per se* is not a dwelling within the meaning of the residential burglary statute; rather, *Thomas* held that the particular garage involved in that case was not a dwelling.

The judgment of the circuit court is affirmed.

Affirmed.

b. Notes from *People v. Silva* Case

After carefully reviewing the *Silva* case and writing down some "thinking notes," your notes would reflect the following important information:

> 1. <u>Legislative intent</u>: to prosecute people for residential burglary when they break into occupied residences and places used as living quarters, but not to prosecute for residential burglary when the structure is an abandoned or vacant building.
>
> 2. <u>Public policy reflected in legislative intent</u>:
>   a. To protect the privacy and sanctity of the home.
>   b. To deter burglary of homes because of the greater danger posed to human life in homes.

3. My evaluation of policy statements & court's interpretation of *Thomas*:

This case supports my interpretation of *Thomas*—a garage can, under appropriate circumstances, be a dwelling.

Court clarifies the policy underlying the Statute—the concern for increased danger to homes as opposed to businesses (or, more clearly, vacant buildings and garages). This policy is consistent with the emphasis in both *Thomas* and in *McIntyre* re: the manner in which the owners use of the structure is critical in determining whether it is a living quarters.

I can argue that Michael Stripe's frequent use of the garage as a living quarters is consistent with the policy concerns underlying the Statute—a place used as a private retreat & living quarters poses an increased danger to human life. Also—to protect the sanctity of the home.

3. The Process of Case Synthesis

As you read the *Thomas, McIntyre* and *Silva* cases, notice how you did not read the cases in isolation. Although you will separately evaluate and make tentative conclusions about each case you read, other cases you have reviewed do affect your evaluation of each individual case. As you read each case, you cannot help but engage in an informal synthesis as your mind continually seeks to make sense of the wealth of information it is evaluating. Therefore, at this stage of your analysis, you will likely have arrived at some informal, tentative conclusions about the cases you have reviewed.

Before solidifying your conclusions and drafting a written analysis of your findings, first verify whether your initial assumptions about the cases are valid in light of all of the cases you may have reviewed. Recall that the human brain is self-confirming—it makes initial assumptions and then tries to prove that its initial presumption is right. Therefore, it's important at this stage to counter that natural tendency by actively questioning your initial assumptions.

a. Synthesize the Courts' Language

Sometimes courts simply quote the original rule of law and do not attempt to define the rule further. However, as you learned in Chapter 7, courts often interpret an original rule of law by explaining what they think the rule of law means. When reviewing several cases that contain definitions and explanations of an original rule of law, it may seem at first that each case has defined the original rule of law in a different way. Before concluding that the definitions are different and not reconcilable, consider whether the courts are merely using slightly different language to make the same point. Alternatively, consider whether, because of the unique set of facts before the courts, the courts are evaluating the original rule of law from different perspectives that are entirely reconcilable. If so, synthesize the various statements into one or more definitions or explanations that embody the ideas expressed in each of the cases. If one of the cases clearly and cogently interprets the rule of law in a manner that is consistent with each case, make note of that language, as you may decide to quote that language when you draft your memo.

Using the residential burglary problem as an example, the *Thomas* court defined dwelling as a "living quarters" in which the owners or occupants "actually reside." The legislature codified this definition, and it is now part of the original rule of law—the Statute. The *McIntyre* court chose not to define the term "dwelling" any further, and instead simply quoted the statutory definition of a living quarters. Therefore, these two cases do not provide any interesting new interpretations of the original rule of law. However, the *Silva* court considered the purpose underlying the Statute and reasoned that the Statute was designed to protect the "privacy and sanctity of the home" because of the "greater danger and potential for serious harm from burglary of a home as opposed to burglary of a business."

This new interpretation of the Statute is relevant because it would affect your analysis of whether the Stripes' garage is a living quarters under the Statute. This interpretation would also help you evaluate the *Thomas* and *McIntyre* cases. In other words, the legislative concerns expressed in *Silva* would affect your analysis of the relative importance of such potential factors as the "type of structure" and its "attachment to or detachment from the primary residence." If the legislative concern is to protect privacy and to reduce the potential for serious harm to human life, then the manner in which a structure is used, including the *type of use* and *frequency of use* of that structure, would seem to be far more important than the structure's attachment to a primary residence. Therefore, even when a structure such as the Stripe family's garage is not a complete residence in and of itself, its use as a part-time living quarters may be dispositive.

b. Synthesize Factors

As you consider the cases as a group, this is also an ideal time to consider whether the factors you tentatively identified from each case are reconcilable with the other cases you have evaluated. In other words, when you consider the factors from Case A, do these factors also explain the results in Cases B and C, or do you need to re-evaluate or refine your thoughts about a particular factor? As you evaluate the various court opinions, you can also get a better sense of which factors appear to be more or less important than other factors. You might find that one factor seems to be a common thread throughout each of the cases, while some of the other factors appear in a few, but not many, of the other cases. The presence of one factor in a particular case might explain why that court interpreted the law in favor of the plaintiff, while the absence of that factor in a second case might help explain why the second court interpreted the law in favor of the defendant.

For example, in the residential burglary problem, the different case results would support your initial tentative conclusion that the "type of use" factor is more important than the structure's physical attachment to the primary residence. In *Thomas*, the structure was not a living quarters when the owner used the garage only to store commercial products. In *McIntyre*, the structure was a living quarters when the owners frequently used the structure for such living-type activities as "sitting, eating, and cooking." In both cases, the structures were attached to the primary residence. Thus, to explain the diverse results, the manner in which the structures were used seems to be the most important factor. The structure's attachment to the primary residence did not compel a positive outcome in the *Thomas* case. However, because the *McIntyre* court also emphasized the porch's physical attachment to the residence, this factor cannot be totally discounted, even though it may not be as important a factor as the type of use.

Finally, consider whether the factors you identified are reconcilable with any legal definitions or standards one or more courts may have emphasized. For example, in the residential burglary problem, the *Thomas* court defined the term "dwelling" to be a "living quarters" in which the owners or occupants "actually reside." Assume that, while reading *McIntyre*, you identified the "type of use" of a structure as a potentially important factor. As part of your synthesis of the cases, you would evaluate whether the "type of use" factor in *McIntyre* is consistent with the *Thomas* court's legal definition. Obviously, when determining whether a structure is a "living quarters," one must look at the manner in which the structure is used; thus, the factor is consistent with the legal definition, or standard. The sub-factors identified from the *McIntyre* case are also consistent with this legal definition—the "frequency of use" and "evidence of use."

c. Synthesize Your Individual Rule Statements

When evaluating each case, you formulated a rule statement that embodied each court's holding. From these individual rule statements, it is also useful to broaden the individual rule statements into a general, "synthesized" rule statement(s) that accurately reflects the group of cases as a whole. If the cases do not appear to be reconcilable after your initial comparison, you would need to evaluate the cases further to determine whether they are in fact reconcilable. You will learn more about reconciling cases later in this chapter. However, assuming that the cases are reconcilable, use the common threads that run throughout the cases and synthesize them into broad rule statements that accurately depict the cases as a group.

In the residential burglary problem, your notes might look like this:

Rule statements I formulated from each case:

Thomas: An attached garage used primarily to store commercial products is not a dwelling under the residential burglary statute.

McIntyre: An enclosed, attached porch is considered a dwelling when it is frequently used for residential activities as part of the living quarters of a home.

Important Threads: "Type of Use" and "Attachment/Proximity" to Residence. These two factors are very different and bring up two very different nuances from the cases. Therefore, I'm going to draft two separate synthesized rule statements rather than one.

Rule Statements that Capture the Essence of Both Cases:

A structure is a living quarters when the owners frequently use the structure for activities that commonly occur in a dwelling. (This explains the result in both *McIntyre* and *Thomas*.)

Although a structure's attachment to the main residence is also relevant, physical attachment to the primary residence is not necessary. (This also explains the results in both *McIntyre* and *Thomas*.)

Exercise 12-1: Case Synthesis Exercise

Assume you are a lawyer who represents a private boarding school. Mr. Tetley, the principal of the school, has met with you and explained that one of the students is threatening to file a lawsuit against the school. Mr. Tetley explained that Holly Murphy, the student, had skipped three days of classes. Holly was captain of the school's tennis team and apparently skipped school to play tennis so that she would be in top form for an upcoming tennis tournament. As punishment, the principal gave Holly two thrashes with a paddle. The school's normal punishment for students who skip school is four thrashes with a paddle. Because of Holly's apparent remorse, the principal elected to give her only two thrashes.

After receiving her thrashes, Ms. Murphy began to limp out of the principal's office. Because she was unsteady, she fell against a file cabinet and wrenched the socket of her shoulder blade. She has had surgery to correct the shoulder problem, but the doctor believes she may never be able to play tennis again. Holly has threatened to file a lawsuit against the school for assault. You have researched the law to determine whether the school can be held liable for the thrashing. You have found the following two cases. Consider how you might reconcile the two cases and then draft one or more general rule statement(s) that accurately reflects the two cases as a group.

> **CASE 1:** In *State v. Pendergrass*, the state Supreme Court held that a teacher was not liable for assault and battery when the teacher whipped a six-year-old girl with a switch, causing marks on her body that disappeared within a few days. The Court reasoned that preserving discipline is a valid educational goal. The Court further stated that as long as the pain is only temporary, it does not matter how "severe the pain inflicted," even if the pain seems disproportionate to the child's offense. The Court concluded that, as long as the teacher acts without malice, the teacher is authorized to administer corporal punishment to her students.

> **CASE 2:** In *Drum v. Miller*, a teacher threw a pencil at a student to attract the student's attention. The pencil struck the student in the eye, causing partial blindness in that eye. The state Supreme Court held that the teacher would be liable if a jury found that a reasonable person would have foreseen that throwing a pencil at a student would result in permanent injury. The Court noted that a reasonable person need not foresee the precise permanent injury that actually occurred. A teacher is liable if it was reasonably foreseeable that the punishment would result in *any* permanent injury.

II. CASE RECONCILIATION

On occasion, you may read cases within the same jurisdiction that seemingly conflict with each other. This can happen, although it is not very common, because our system of jurisprudence is based on the principle that courts within the same jurisdiction follow the rules of law adopted by higher level courts within their jurisdiction. Nonetheless, this can happen when courts at the same level interpret the law differently, and a higher-level court hasn't definitively resolved the issue. For example, the court of appeals from the southern district of your state might interpret the law one way, while the court of appeals from the northern district of your state might interpret the law differently. In these relatively uncommon situations, you should follow the guidance of the courts within the district that governs your own situation.

However, before concluding that the two cases are irreconcilable, review again the language in each case and consider whether the courts have simply used different language to describe the same rule of law. Also consider whether there might be a relationship between the seemingly different standards that reconciles them. For example, one standard might express the general rule in the jurisdiction, while another standard might express an exception to the general rule. Also consider whether the differing standards are intended to apply to different factual situations. If after carefully re-evaluating the cases you still cannot reconcile them, you might wish to review secondary sources to determine whether a legal scholar has addressed the issue. Legal periodicals and the American Law Reports often discuss issues that are the subject of splits of authority. Such articles typically catalog the various court decisions that discuss the legal point and discuss the competing policy interests that affect the different courts' analyses. By surveying the law and synthesizing the different cases, secondary authorities can save you a significant amount of time.

Exercise 12-2: Social Host Liability

This exercise builds on Exercise 8-1 in Chapter 8. First review the fact pattern in that exercise. Then analyze and synthesize the following case notes, formulating general rule statements that accurately depict the group of cases, and the relevant factors that guide the courts' decisions.

Case Notes

Rappaport v. Nichols (1959): A tavern owner served alcoholic beverages to a minor, who became intoxicated. The minor later drove and caused a car crash, killing the other driver. The plaintiff sued the tavern owner under a negligence theory. The court decided that if a jury found that the tavern owner knew the patron was a minor, or if the tavern owner was on notice that the patron was intoxicated, then in either case the tavern owner could be responsible under a negligence theory.

Soronen v. Olde Milford Inn, Inc. (1966): A tavern owner served five drinks of alcohol to an adult patron who rose from his barstool, took several steps and fell, striking his head on a steel column. He later died. A doctor arrived quickly on the scene and later testified that there was "a very, very profuse, profound odor of alcohol" from the body and opined that he must have been in a state of acute alcoholism for at least two hours. The court decided that if a jury could find that the decedent was visibly intoxicated at the time he was served additional drinks of alcohol, then the tavern owner was liable to the decedent's estate, despite the fact that the decedent played a large role in his own death. The court reasoned that the liquor licensee's duty not to serve intoxicated persons is for the protection of the individual patron as well as the public.

Linn v. Rand (1976): A friend served a minor alcoholic beverages in the friend's home. The minor subsequently drove a car and hurt a pedestrian, who sued the driver's friend. The court decided that the jury should decide whether the host knew the minor would be driving, and thus, whether the host should be responsible in a negligence suit. The court declined to give social hosts any broad kind of immunity, and the court cited the public policy of curtailing "the ever-increasing incidence of serious automobile accidents resulting from drunken driving."

Kelly v. Gwinnell (1984): A friend (host) served liquor to an adult guest, knowing the guest would have to drive home. The host continued to serve drinks even after the guest was visibly intoxicated. The guest drove negligently and injured a third party. The court held that the host was liable to the third party under these facts, reasoning that the injury was reasonably foreseeable.

Griesenbeck v. Walker (1985): A father served two drinks to his adult daughter, who left in her car around midnight to drive three miles home. By 1:20 a.m., a blazing fire in her home killed the daughter, her husband, and one of her two children. The fire was caused by the daughter's cigarette left smoldering in a sofa. The expert toxicology report indicated the daughter's acute alcohol intoxication (at least nine drinks). The surviving child of the adult daughter sued her grandfather for negligence, on the theory that he served his daughter when she was visibly intoxicated and permitted her to go home impaired by alcohol, where she was so intoxicated that she caused the fire and was unable to save herself or help evacuate her other family members. The court held that the father was not liable because the fire was not a foreseeable or probable harm.

CHAPTER IN REVIEW

Core Concepts:

CASE SYNTHESIS:

1. *Defined*: the process of reconciling diverse case facts and results into workable rule statements and common factors that explain the diverse results.

2. The *Process*:
   a. Review your notes from each case you have evaluated.
      - Before solidifying your conclusions about each case, verify whether your initial assumptions about the case are valid in light of all of the cases you have reviewed.
   b. Reconcile the courts' different interpretations of the original rule of law.
      - Courts may use different language to make the same point or evaluate the original rule of law from different perspectives that are entirely reconcilable.
   c. Reconcile the factors you identified from each case.
      i. Consider whether the factors you have tentatively identified from each case are still viable when you study the cases as a group.

- • If so, consider whether you might want to rephrase one or more of the factors for clarity.
  - ii. Before discounting a factor, consider:
    - • Different cases might well be reconcilable because one of the factors is simply not that important; that factor's relative lack of importance might account for a pro-plaintiff result in one case and a pro-defendant result in another case.
    - • Different cases might well be reconcilable because one of the factors is important in one of the cases but is simply not present in another case.
  - d. Synthesize the rule statements you formulated from each case.
    - • From the individual rule statements you identified for each case, formulate one or more general rule statements that accurately reflects the group of cases as a whole.
    - • To formulate a general rule statement, find the common threads that run throughout the cases and synthesize them into broad legal principles that accurately depict the cases as a group.

CASE RECONCILIATION

1. Before concluding that cases are truly irreconcilable, determine whether:
   a. The courts have used different language to make the same point;
   b. There is a relationship between the two different interpretations that reconciles them—*e.g.*, a rule and an exception;
   c. The differing interpretations are intended to apply to different fact situations.

2. Dealing with irreconcilable cases within the same jurisdiction.
   a. Adopt the ruling of the highest level court, if there is one.
   b. If both rulings are from the same level court, adopt the ruling of the highest court within your district.
   c. If the rulings are from the same level court within the same district, consider:
      i. Date of the opinion; and
      ii. Public policy considerations expressed in the cases.

THE DISCUSSION SECTION

Drafting the Analysis (Multiple Cases)

I. CHAPTER IN FOCUS

MEMORANDUM

To: [Senior Attorney]
From: [Junior Attorney]
Date: [Date of Submission of Memo]
Re: [XYZ Client Matter]

QUESTION PRESENTED

. . .

SHORT ANSWER

. . .

STATEMENT OF FACTS

. . .

DISCUSSION ←

Overview Paragraph
Thesis Paragraph
Rule Explanation ←
Rule Application ←

CONCLUSION

. . .

II. MULTIPLE CASE MEMO

A. Similarity to Single Case Memo

In most respects, the same general writing principles described in Chapter 11 also apply to memos that explore more than one case. In other words, the macro-organization of the Discussion still follows the same general deductive writing pattern: you will explain how the rule of law has been interpreted (rule explanation) before evaluating how the rule of law applies to the client's factual situation (rule application). In addition, the micro-organization of each paragraph also follows the same deductive writing pattern: (1) each paragraph begins with a thesis sentence that expresses the thesis, or premise, of the paragraph; and (2) the remainder of the paragraph illustrates why your premise is valid. Finally, the substantive content of each paragraph also follows the same principles described in Chapter 11. A discussion of an important analogous case still describes for the reader each of the important aspects of the case (*e.g.*, the rule of law the case illustrates, the relevant case facts, the holding, and the rationale). Your analysis of how the law affects the client's situation also stays the same, with each paragraph evaluating how a legal standard or important factor affects the client's unique factual situation.

B. Deductive Analytical Pattern Becomes Fluid

When discussing only a single case that interprets a rule of law, the pattern of interplay between the "rule explanation" and "rule application" sections of your memo is fairly straightforward; you first explain how the rule of law has been interpreted (rule explanation) before evaluating how the law affects the client's unique factual situation (rule application). However, assume you want to discuss in detail four different cases that address a single issue. You can imagine how confusing it might be for a reader to read detailed discussions of four different cases before reading how each of the cases affects the client. Alternatively, assume you followed a discussion of each separate case with a discussion of how each case affected the client. If you were using two or more cases to illustrate the same point, this format might prove to be unnecessarily repetitive as you evaluated how the same client facts related to each of the cases.

Instead of arbitrarily deciding to format your Discussion according to either one of these alternatives, think of the interplay between the rule explanation and rule application sections as fluid. Sometimes it will make sense to insert a "rule application" paragraph or paragraphs immediately following a case discussion; at other times it will make sense to wait to insert a "rule application" paragraph(s) until after you have discussed a group of cases. Before discussing the options in greater detail, it may be helpful to visualize the first two options, very simplistically, as follows:

Option 1:
- Discuss Case 1
- Discuss Case 2
- Apply Factors from Cases 1 & 2 to Client Facts

Option 2:
- Discuss Case 1
- Apply Factors from Case 1 to Client Facts
- Discuss Case 2
- Apply Factors from Case 2 to Client Facts

1. Option 1: Discuss Cases as a Group Before Moving to Rule Application

Some factually analogous cases illustrate the same factors or legal principle and will generate factual comparisons to or distinctions from the same client facts. For example, assume that two cases were guided by the same legal principle or factors, but the different fact patterns yielded two different results—in one case the plaintiff won, and in the other case the defendant won. You might decide to explore each of these cases in detail because they might help you predict the result in your client's situation—are the client facts more like Case 1 or more like Case 2? The *McIntyre* and *Thomas* cases in the residential burglary memo are discussed in detail for that very reason (Sample Memo A in Appendix A).

When you elect to discuss two or more cases in detail that illustrate the *same* factors or legal principle and will generate factual comparisons to or distinctions from the *same* client facts, your formatting choice is guided by consideration for the reader. For example, consider the residential burglary memo. If you discussed the *McIntyre* case (RE), then evaluated how each of the factors from the *McIntyre* case affected the client situation (RA), then discussed the *Thomas* case (RE), and then evaluated how each of the factors from the *Thomas* case affected the client situation (RA), imagine how repetitive this would be from the reader's perspective. Because each case interprets the same factors and generates factual analogies to the same client facts, it wouldn't make sense to force the reader to follow this repetitive formatting choice.

Instead, it would make sense to discuss each case first (rule explanation) before evaluating how the cases collectively affect the client (rule application). This does not mean that each of the cases would be discussed in a single paragraph, or that the case discussions themselves would be intermingled. Instead, under this option, you would thoroughly evaluate each case before evaluating how the cases collectively affect the client.

In brief, formatting Option 1 makes sense when each case:

(1) Illustrates the *SAME* key factors or ideas; AND

(2) Generates factual comparisons to or distinctions from the *SAME* client facts.

Under this format, the outline of your discussion would look like this:

> **Rule Explanation:**
>
>   ¶ Case #1—discuss facts/holding/rationale—illustrating, *e.g.*, factors A & B
>
>   ¶ Case #2—discuss facts/holding/rationale—illustrating factors A & B
>
> **Rule Application:**
>
>   ¶ Apply Factor A to client facts (comparing to both Cases 1 & 2)
>
>   ¶ Apply Factor B to client facts (comparing to both Cases 1 & 2)

Test for Viability of Option 1: After completing your first draft, critically review your analysis from the perspective of a reader who is not familiar with the cases. Is the discussion clear and distinct, or is it confusing? If the discussion seems confusing, consider:

(1) Instead of the same factors, do the cases illustrate *different* factors? (Although the cases do not have to share every factor in common, the cases should illustrate several common factors.)

(2) Even if the cases illustrate common factors, do the factors engender analogies to and distinctions from *different* client facts rather than the same client facts? You might wish to review your pre-drafting notes. Are you comparing the same, or different, client facts to each of the cases?

If you responded affirmatively to either of the above questions, either Option 2 or 3 would be a more effective formatting choice.

2. Option 2: Insert Rule Application Following Each Case

When cases illustrate *different* factors or standards, each case should be discussed and then followed by a separate rule application section before discussing the other cases. Because the cases illustrate different ideas, the clearest way to convey your analysis is to follow each case discussion by evaluating how the unique factors or ideas brought out by the case affect the client's factual situation. Again, this option makes sense from the reader's perspective. If you are using two cases to illustrate two very different ideas, it would be confusing if the reader was forced to read all about Case 1, then read a discussion of how Case 2 illustrates an entirely different point, then read about how the ideas from Case 1 affect the client, and then jump back to reading about how the ideas from Case 2 affect the client. Under these circumstances, it makes more sense to separately evaluate how each case affects the client's situation.

This option should also be used when two cases illustrate the same idea or factors but will generate comparisons to *different* client facts. For example, review the sample kidnapping memo illustrated as Sample Memo B in Appendix A. In that memo, even though the *Enoch* case discusses the same factors as the *Lamkey* and *Franzen* cases, it is separately discussed and applied to the client facts because it generates analogies to a different group of client facts than the other two cases. In contrast, *Lamkey* and *Franzen* are grouped together (Option 1) because they not only illustrate the same factors, but generate factual comparisons to and distinctions from the *same* client facts. In brief:

Follow a case discussion with rule application paragraphs devoted only to factual comparisons to that case when the precedent cases:

(1)   Illustrate DIFFERENT factors or standards; OR

(2)   Illustrate the same factors or ideas but generate factual comparisons to or distinctions from DIFFERENT client facts.

Under this format, the outline of your discussion section would look like this:

Rule Explanation:

¶ Case #1—discuss facts/holding/rationale—illustrating factors A & B

Rule Application:

¶ Apply Factor A to client facts (comparing to Case 1)

¶ Apply Factor B to client facts (comparing to Case 1)

Rule Explanation:

¶ Case #2—discuss facts/holding/rationale—illustrating factor C

Rule Application:

¶ Apply Factor C to client facts (comparing to Case 2)

Test for Viability of Option 2: After you complete your first draft, review your discussion and evaluate how easily a reader would be able to follow the analysis. If you think the rule application paragraphs are unnecessarily repetitive or, alternatively, too broad and vague, consider why they might be ineffective. Format Option 2 can be repetitive or vague for any of the following reasons:

(1)   Do the cases explore the same idea or factors? AND

(2)   Do the cases engender factual comparisons to and distinctions from the same client facts?

If the answer to both questions is "yes," then Option 1 is a clearer formatting option.

3. Hybrid of Options 1 & 2

At times, you may have three or more cases that you elect to discuss in detail in a legal discussion. Two of the cases may discuss the *same* factors and generate factual comparisons to and distinctions from the *same* client facts (Option 1). However, a third case may discuss a *different* factor or, alternatively, discuss the same factor but generate factual comparisons to and distinctions from *different* client facts. Under these circumstances, simply use Option 1 to discuss the first two cases and use Option 2 to discuss and evaluate the third case that will generate different comparisons to the client facts.

Under this format, the outline of your discussion section would look like this:

Option 1:

Rule Explanation:
- ¶ Case #1—discuss facts/holding/rationale—illustrating factors A & B
- ¶ Case #2—discuss facts/holding/rationale—illustrating factor B

Rule Application:
- ¶ Apply Factor A to client facts (comparing to Case 1)
- ¶ Apply Factor B to client facts (comparing to Cases 1 & 2)

Option 2:

Rule Explanation:
- ¶ Case #3—discuss facts/holding/rationale—illustrating factor C

Rule Application:
- ¶ Apply Factor C to client facts (comparing to Case 3)

---

4. Option 3: Organizing the Entire Discussion by Factors

Recall that, with Options 1 and 2, individual factors serve as the analytical lynchpins in the rule application paragraphs—each rule application paragraph discusses a single factor (or sometimes two short interrelated factors). With Options 1 and 2, the discussion is factor-led *only* in the rule application paragraphs. In the rule explanation paragraphs, your discussion of each of the cases includes the rule statement, case facts, holding, and all of the factors the court weighed when justifying its holding.

However, there is another way in which you can format a legal analysis. Under this approach, the *entire discussion* (both rule explanation and rule application paragraphs) is organized around the factors—not just the rule application paragraphs. Under this approach, a case that evaluated three factors when reaching a decision might be separately discussed three times—once for each factor. This approach can be very effective, although it is significantly more difficult for a novice legal writer to draft effectively. This format option might be visualized, very simplistically, as follows:

Format Option 3:

Factor A:

    Rule Explanation per Factor A
      (How Cases 1 & 2 interpret Factor A)

    Rule Application per Factor A

Factor B:

    Rule Explanation per Factor B
      (How Cases 1, 2, & 3 interpret Factor B)

    Rule Application per Factor B

And so on . . .

One reason this formatting option can be challenging to draft is that it is difficult to divide a discussion of the same case into several distinct "mini-discussions" concerning the same issue. For each separate mini-discussion of a case, you should divulge only the specific information about the case that relates to the *specific factor* under discussion, while also including enough information to give the reader sufficient context to understand the case. This can be very challenging to do well. For example, suppose a court considered and weighed three factors when it evaluated the law. Under Option 3, specific, discrete aspects of that case would be discussed three different times—once for each relevant factor. Although that might sound easy enough, recall that your reader has likely not read the cases that are the subject of discussion in your memo. Therefore, you must also include enough background information about the case the first time you discuss it for the reader to be able to absorb the overall context of the case. At the same time, you don't want to confuse the reader by incorporating information that really relates to another factor.

Another reason this formatting option can be difficult to draft effectively is that some factors are so interrelated that it is very difficult to discuss what happened in a case without describing each of the interrelated factors that guided the court's decision. In addition, interrelated factors may also generate a discussion of the same client facts. Under those circumstances, a Discussion formatted under Option 3 would likely be repetitive.

In brief, you can, but need not, use Option 3 when:

(1)   Within each separate discussion about a given case, you can provide enough background information about the case to give the reader

necessary background context while still restricting the discussion to a single factor; AND

(2) The factors are independent enough to make it possible to discuss how the court evaluated one factor in isolation, without reference to the remaining factors; AND

(3) The factors will generate factual analogies to or distinctions from DIFFERENT client facts.

Although challenging to strike the right balance, this approach is often used very effectively by experienced writers. Sample Memo C in Appendix A illustrates how the residential burglary problem could be formatted using Option 3.

Factor A:

Rule Explanation:

¶ Examine Factor A, as illustrated by Case #1—(discuss only those facts/holding/rationale that relate to Factor A)

¶ Examine Factor A, as illustrated by Case #2 and perhaps Case #3 (again discussing only those components of each case that illustrate Factor A)

Rule Application:

¶ Apply Factor A to client facts (comparing to Cases 1, 2, & 3)

Factor B:

Rule Explanation:

¶ Examine Factor B, as illustrated by Case #1—(discuss only those facts/holding/rationale that relate to Factor B)

¶ Examine Factor B, as illustrated by Case #2 (again discussing only those components of each case that illustrate Factor B)

Rule Application:

¶ Apply Factor B to client facts (comparing to Cases 1 & 2)

Factor C:

Rule Explanation:

¶ Examine Factor C, as illustrated by Case #1—(discuss only those facts/holding/rationale that relate to Factor C)

¶ Examine Factor C, as illustrated by Case #2 and perhaps Cases #3 & #4 (discussing only those components of each case that illustrate Factor C)

Rule Application:

¶ Apply Factor C to client facts (comparing to Cases 1, 2, 3, & 4)

Test for Viability of Option 3: After completing the first draft of your memo, critically review the Discussion from a reader's perspective. Is the analysis clear, or is it repetitive or confusing? If the Discussion is repetitive or confusing, you may want to switch to one of the other Options.

Exercise 13-1: Formatting Option Exercise

This example evaluates an issue that often arises when an employee injures someone. The injured party, seeking the deeper pocket of the employer, seeks to hold the employer liable under a theory of "respondeat superior." Under that theory, an employer may be liable for an employee's behavior if the particular activity was "within the scope" of the employee's employment. Assume that an insurance salesman injured someone while playing for the company softball team. Assume that in a roadmap paragraph, the drafting attorney indicated that the following factors were important in determining whether an employee's conduct occurred while the employee was acting within the scope of his or her employment: (1) whether the employer specifically authorized the conduct; (2) whether the employer repeatedly approved of the conduct; (3) whether other similarly situated employees engaged in similar conduct; and (4) whether the employee previously had engaged in similar conduct.

Review the following Discussion based on these four factors and evaluate whether Option 3 has been drafted effectively. Specifically, consider:

(1) Is each factor truly different from the other factors, or just another way to state the same point?

(2) Does each factor generate a discussion of the same, or different, client facts from those used to evaluate the other factors? *Query:* If a factor generates a discussion of the same client facts as those used to evaluate another factor, which formatting option would be a more effective selection?

(3) Has the writer provided enough information in each case law paragraph for you to assess how the factor relates to the case as a whole?

DISCUSSION

[Rule Explanation: "Specific Authorization" Factor]

Where an employer specifically authorizes the conduct in which the employee is engaged, the employee is acting within the scope of his or her employment. In *Riviello v. Waldron*, the owner of a restaurant specifically authorized his chef to visit with the patrons in the dining room of the restaurant and to perform knife tricks while doing so. 391 N.E.2d 1278, 1280 (N.Y. 1979). On one occasion, the chef mishandled the knife while tossing it in the air, and a restaurant patron was injured when the knife struck her in the eye. *Id.* Under these facts, the Court held that the chef was acting within the scope of his employment while tossing the knife. *Id.* The Court reasoned that the owner of the restaurant had specifically authorized and approved of the conduct that resulted in the patron's injury. The Court noted that the employer hired the chef based on the chef's ability to perform the knife tricks and frequently asked the chef to go "perform" in the dining room among the patrons. *Id.*

[Rule Application: "Specific Authorization" Factor]

Similarly, the employer specifically authorized Mr. Henderson to participate in the conduct that resulted in the client's injury. The insurance company both sponsored the softball team and allowed its employees in the Albany office to leave early on Thursdays to participate in the team's games. Under *Riviello*, Mr. Henderson was acting within the scope of his employment when he injured the client.

[Rule Explanation: "Repeated Approval" Factor]

Additionally, where an employer repeatedly approves of the conduct in which the employee is engaged, the employee is acting within the scope of employment. In *Riviello*, when concluding that the chef was acting within the scope of his employment while tossing the knife, in addition to considering whether the owner of the restaurant specifically authorized the chef's knife tossing, the Court pointed out that the owner had also repeatedly approved of the conduct that resulted in the patron's injury by frequently visiting the kitchen and asking the chef to go "perform" in the dining room among the patrons. *Id.*

[Rule Application: "Repeated Approval" Factor]

Similarly, the employer repeatedly approved of Mr. Henderson's participation in the conduct that resulted in the client's injury. The insurance company both sponsored the softball team and allowed its employees in the Albany office to leave early on Thursdays to participate in the team's games. Under *Riviello*, Mr. Henderson was acting within the scope of his employment when he injured the client.

[Rule Explanation: "Previous Conduct" Factor]

Additionally, where the employee previously had engaged in the same or similar conduct as that which resulted in injury, the employee is acting within the scope of employment. In *Lundberg v. State*, the Court held that an employee broker was acting within the scope of his employment when he negligently struck another member of an aerobics class in the eye. 255 N.E.2d 177, 179 (N.Y. 1969). The Court reasoned that "the broker here involved was a routine and regular participant in the class." *Id.* at 182.

[Rule Application: "Previous Conduct" Factor]

Similarly, Mr. Henderson was a "routine and regular participant" in the softball games. Under *Lundberg*, this "routine and regular" participation brings the games within the scope of his employment.

[Rule Explanation: "Acts of Other Employees" Factor]

Finally, where other similarly situated employees within the company engaged in substantially similar conduct as that which resulted in injury, the employee is acting within the scope of his employment. In *Lundberg*, the owner of a brokerage house encouraged all of his employees to participate in a noon-time aerobics class to reduce stress. The class occurred in the gymnasium on the premises of the brokerage house. 255 N.E.2d at 179. The Court held that a broker was acting within the scope of his employment when he negligently struck another member of the class in the eye. The Court reasoned that "all eight of the brokers in the brokerage house participated in the noontime aerobics class at the prompting of their employer." *Id*. at 181.

[Rule Application: "Acts of Other Employees" Factor]

Similarly, all six of the insurance salesmen in the company's Albany office played for the company-sponsored softball team. In fact, the salesmen here perceived the contact with the clients at the games as a necessity for advancement within the company, whereas there was no mention in *Lundberg* that the brokers felt similarly. Accordingly, this case is an even stronger case for liability than *Lundberg*.

CHAPTER IN REVIEW

···

Editing Checklist:

FORMAT OF THE DISCUSSION

When discussing two or more cases in depth, the interplay between the rule explanation and rule application sections of your memo becomes fluid.

OPTION 1: When cases address the *same* ideas and generate comparisons to the *same* client facts, select Option 1.

Illustration:

- Discuss Case 1

  (Rule Statement/Facts/Holding/Rationale illustrating, *e.g.*, factors A & B)

- Discuss Case 2

  (Rule Statement/Facts/Holding/Rationale illustrating, *e.g.*, factor B)

- Apply Factor A to Client's Facts

  (comparing to case 1)

- Apply Factor B to Client's Facts

  (comparing to both cases 1 & 2)

OPTION 2: When cases address *different* ideas and/or generate comparisons to *different* client facts, select Option 2.

Illustration:

- Discuss Case 1

  (Rule Statement/Facts/Holding/Rationale illustrating, *e.g.*, factors A & B)

- Apply Factor A to Client's Facts

  (comparing to Case 1)

- Apply Factor B to Client's Facts

  (comparing to Case 1)

- Discuss Case 2

  (Rule Statement/Facts/Holding/Rationale illustrating, *e.g.*, factor C)

- Apply Factor C to Client's Facts

  (comparing to Case 2)

OPTION 3: If the factors are fairly independent and will generate comparisons to different client facts, you may choose to organize your entire Discussion by factors.

Illustration:

Factor A:

- Discuss Case 1 as it relates to Factor A
- Discuss Case 2 as it relates to Factor A
- Apply Factor A to Client's Facts

  (comparing to Cases 1 & 2)

Factor B:

- Discuss Case 1 as it relates to Factor B
- Discuss Case 3 as it relates to Factor B
- Apply Factor B to Client's Facts

  (comparing to Cases 1 & 3)

THE DISCUSSION SECTION

Drafting Roadmap Paragraphs

I. CHAPTER IN FOCUS

II. DRAFTING THE OVERVIEW PARAGRAPH

A. The Overview Paragraph

The deductive writing pattern satisfies the reader's curiosity by stating your ultimate conclusion right away and by providing a roadmap of the analysis that will follow. Imagine yourself as a reader and, for a moment, assume the role of a senior lawyer who has asked a more junior lawyer to evaluate a legal problem. Using the hypothetical residential burglary problem as an example, assume that you have not read any of the cases that discuss the circumstances under which a structure would be a dwelling under that Statute. Instead, assume that you asked another lawyer in your office to determine whether you can prosecute someone for residential burglary of a detached garage.

What information would you like to read first? Would you want to know the answer to your question? Or would you rather pick up the memo and begin reading about the specific facts and holding of the *Thomas* case? Would you prefer to begin reading about the law by learning that a garage used to store perfume products is not a "living quarters" under the Statute? Or would you rather begin at the beginning, by learning the key elements of the Statute you would have to prove in order to prosecute the thief under the residential burglary statute?

Hopefully you can appreciate the reader's dilemma. As a reader who isn't familiar with the specific details of the law, you would likely be confused if you were to begin reading about the specific facts and holding of the *Thomas* case. Without a foundation, or context, for the analysis, you would not understand why the specific details of the *Thomas* case might be important. As well, you might be frustrated if the junior lawyer forced you to read about the details of the *Thomas* case before you learned the answer to your question, or had a mental roadmap that prepared you for the detailed analysis that will follow.

Because your legal analysis will be based on a rule of law, it is logical to begin your legal analysis by describing the rule of law upon which you are building your legal analysis. And, because the reader will appreciate knowing each separate component of the rule of law upon which you are building your analysis, satisfy the reader's curiosity up-front by including within your overview paragraph the separate elements or factors of the law that you are evaluating. This gives the reader a context to appreciate the structure of your argument. However, some components of the legal rule may not actually merit any legal discussion given the unique factual situation you are evaluating. In that case, identify for the reader those elements that you won't be discussing, and then focus in on those elements that you will actually be evaluating in the memo. Finally, satisfy the reader's curiosity by responding to the ultimate question paramount in the reader's mind—your answer to the ultimate question.

B. When an Overview Paragraph Is Unnecessary

When the original rule of law you are evaluating has more than one element or factor, it is usually helpful to describe the rule's components in a separate overview paragraph. The overview paragraph sets the stage for the detailed discussion of the issues that will follow by alerting the reader to which elements are not at issue, and those elements that will be the subject of discussion. With that said, some original rules of law contain only a single element. As such, the reader wouldn't need to peruse an outline of the rule of law because it only has one element. Under these circumstances, an overview paragraph is usually unnecessary, and you can describe the rule of law in a thesis paragraph instead. The thesis paragraph then becomes the single roadmap paragraph for your memo.

C. Structural Format of an Overview Paragraph

The structural format of the overview paragraph is guided by the same deductive writing pattern that guides the overall organization of a legal discussion itself. Again with the reader's expectations in mind, the elements of the rule of law provide the foundation, or context, for a discussion of the elements that do and do not present issues for the client. Therefore, describe the elements of the rule of law before identifying those elements that are non-issues and those elements that present issues that merit discussion. Depending on the preference of your professor or the assigning attorney, state the ultimate conclusion in either the first or final sentence of the overview paragraph. Some lawyers prefer to begin the overview paragraph with the ultimate conclusion in order to satisfy the reader's curiosity immediately. Other lawyers prefer to wait until the end of the paragraph because the rule of law provides context for the reader to understand the basis for the ultimate conclusion.

The Overview Paragraph Checklist:

1. State your *ultimate conclusion* (or, alternatively, wait until the end of the paragraph).
2. Describe the *elements* or components of the original rule of law.
3. Identify the elements that do not present issues under the client's unique factual situation (i.e., *non-issues*).
4. Identify the *elements that are at issue* and merit further discussion.

◎ ILLUSTRATION: Residential Burglary Problem,
An Overview Paragraph

In the following illustration, there is actually not just one, but two statutory sections that are relevant to the ultimate issue the junior prosecutor is researching—whether the State can prosecute Arnold under the residential burglary statute. Therefore, both statutory sections are described in the overview paragraph. The first statutory section describes the broad elements of residential burglary. The second statutory section has a narrower focus than the first section—it focuses in on the dwelling element itself. When two or more sections of a statute affect a problem you are evaluating, discuss the broad statutory section first, because it provides the foundation, or context, for understanding the narrower, more specific, statutory section. In the residential burglary example, the broad elements of the residential burglary statute provide the foundation, or context, for the more specific statutory section that defines the "dwelling" element. Therefore, the broader, more basic section is described first.

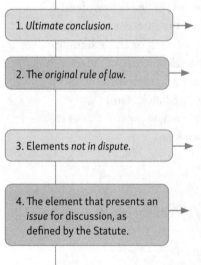

1. *Ultimate conclusion.*

2. The *original rule of law.*

3. Elements *not in dispute.*

4. The element that presents an *issue* for discussion, as defined by the Statute.

The State likely can prosecute Arnold for residential burglary under Illinois' Residential Burglary Statute (the "Statute"). To prosecute Arnold successfully under the Statute, the State must prove that Arnold "knowingly and without authority enter[ed] the *dwelling place* of another." 720 Ill. Comp. Stat. 5/19-3 (2004) (emphasis added). There is no real dispute that Arnold "knowingly" "entered" the Stripes' garage or that his entry was "without authority." Whether the garage is a "dwelling place" is more problematic. The Statute defines a dwelling as "a house, apartment, mobile home, trailer or *other living quarters* in which … the owners or occupants *actually reside*…." 720 Ill. Comp. Stat. 5/2-6(b) (2004) (emphasis added). This memorandum addresses whether the Stripes' garage is a "living quarters" in which Michael Stripe "actually resides," and therefore a dwelling.

As an additional note, if your legal problem centers on an original rule of law containing numbered elements, it is important in the overview paragraph to identify the elements by number when disposing of any non-issue(s) and highlighting the element(s) at issue. This will help your reader to effectively track which components are easily met, and which components warrant further analysis. Also, if the original rule of law identifies, but doesn't expressly enumerate the separate elements, you can add numbers to your description to help clarify the relevant elements of the original rule of law. For example, the residential burglary statute's language doesn't separately enumerate elements, but it is easy to add numbers to clarify the rule of law for the reader. Review the following illustration of the residential burglary example with numbered elements

The State can likely prosecute Arnold for residential burglary under Illinois' Residential Burglary Statute (the "Statute"). To prosecute Arnold successfully under the Statute, the State must prove that Arnold: (1) knowingly, (2) without authority, (3) entered (4) the *dwelling place* of another. 720 Ill. Comp. Stat. 5/19-3 (2004). There is no dispute that elements (1), (2), and (3) are satisfied, as Arnold "knowingly" "entered" the Stripes' garage, and his entry was "without authority." The question for analysis is whether element (4), requiring that Arnold entered a "dwelling place," is met. The Statute defines a dwelling as "a house, apartment, mobile home, trailer or *other living quarters* in which… the owners or occupants *actually reside.…*" 720 Ill. Comp. Stat. 5/2-6(b) (2004) (emphasis added). This memorandum addresses whether the Stripes' garage is a "living quarters" in which Michael Stripe "actually resides," and therefore a dwelling.

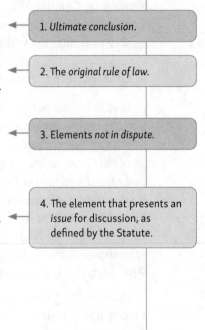

1. *Ultimate conclusion.*

2. The *original rule of law.*

3. Elements *not in dispute.*

4. The element that presents an *issue* for discussion, as defined by the Statute.

III. DRAFTING THE THESIS PARAGRAPH

Even though the thesis paragraph physically appears in the memo before the rest of your legal discussion, you may wish to delay writing the thesis paragraph until after you have drafted the rest of your legal discussion. Some lawyers find this approach to be time-efficient, because drafting a thesis paragraph requires a sophisticated understanding of the law and how the law affects the client's situation. Ideally, you would have acquired the requisite level of understanding during the pre-drafting process as you evaluated the rule of law and relevant cases. However, the writing process itself often reveals that some ideas that seemed so clear in the abstract are in fact only partially-formed. Therefore, even when you believe you have a solid grasp of the cases from your pre-drafting analysis, the writing process often reveals unanticipated gaps in thinking. Because this is a fairly common experience, many lawyers deliberately choose to wait until *after* they have drafted the remainder of the Discussion section before drafting a thesis paragraph.

In a single-issue memo, such as the residential burglary problem, the thesis paragraph simply follows the overview paragraph without a separate point-heading. In a multi-issue memo, it is helpful to introduce each issue with a separate point-heading. To aid clarity for the reader, each *legal issue conclusion* might also be stated within the point-heading, as in the attractive nuisance Sample Memo D in Appendix A (*e.g.*, "A. Trespassing Children Were Foreseeable"). While the point-heading "Foreseeability of Trespassing Children" also serves as a guidepost to introduce the issue, stating the legal issue conclusion within the point-heading is even clearer here.

A. Content of the Thesis Paragraph

Like overview paragraphs, thesis paragraphs also serve as roadmaps. However, while overview paragraphs merely provide a broad roadmap of the basic law upon which the entire memo is based, thesis paragraphs are more focused and specific. They only summarize the specific *element* of the original rule of law that will be discussed in the memo (or the section of the memo that discusses that specific element). In the residential burglary memo, for example, the overview paragraph describes the basic elements of the residential burglary statute (a thief must knowingly and without authority enter the dwelling place of another). In contrast, the thesis paragraph focuses on the specific issue being evaluated—whether the Stripes' garage is a "living quarters" in which Michael Stripe "actually resides," and is thus a "dwelling."

Because the thesis paragraph serves as a roadmap for the legal discussion of a specific issue, it summarizes the most important points that will be explored in the discussion that follows. If your memo does not include an overview paragraph that has already identified the issue to be discussed, begin the thesis paragraph by identifying the issue you will discuss. The thesis paragraph then states the conclusion as to how the issue affects your client's situation, followed by a brief summary of the reasons why your conclusion is sound.

In proving why the conclusion is sound, summarize the rules of law expressed in the case law, including any standards or factors that courts consider when interpreting and applying the original rule of law. These rules of law, standards, and factors serve as guideposts that will help lead the reviewing senior attorney through the discussion that follows. Finally, to the extent the complexity of the memo requires, conclude the thesis paragraph by briefly summarizing how the rules of law, factors, and/or guidelines apply to the client's facts, thereby justifying the conclusion.

B. When a Thesis Paragraph Is Necessary

Because thesis paragraphs summarize the law pertaining to a specific issue, as a general rule, each issue discussed in a memo usually merits a separate thesis paragraph. Thus, a one-issue memo would contain a single thesis paragraph, a two-issue memo would contain two thesis paragraphs, and so on. (*See, e.g.,* the templates of one-issue, multi-issue, and multi-claim memos illustrated in Chapter 10, and Sample Memo D in Appendix A).

However, like overview paragraphs, in some circumstances you may not find it necessary to draft a thesis paragraph for an issue. If you are evaluating a relatively minor issue that can be thoroughly addressed in a few paragraphs, a thesis paragraph may be unnecessary. In that case, you might instead simply introduce the rule of law in a thesis sentence introducing your first case discussion. A good rule of thumb is that when your legal discussion is of any length or complexity, it is good practice to introduce that discussion with a thesis paragraph. In contrast, a succinct and simplistic legal discussion usually doesn't require a separate thesis paragraph.

C. Organizational Format of a Thesis Paragraph

The same deductive writing pattern that dictates that context should be introduced before details also applies to the internal structure of the thesis paragraph. Therefore, if your memo doesn't have an overview paragraph that identifies the issue to be discussed, begin the thesis paragraph by identifying the issue under discussion. The issue provides a necessary framework for the discussion to follow. In turn, the applicable legal rule, standards, and/or factors provide the context, or foundation, for a summary of how they affect the client's facts. As with the overview paragraph, some lawyers prefer to begin the thesis paragraph with their conclusion, while other lawyers prefer to end the thesis paragraph with the conclusion.

> **The Thesis Paragraph Checklist:**
> 1. Describe the *original rule of law* and *issue* (if not already explained in the overview paragraph).
> 2. State your *legal issue conclusion* as to how the law affects the client's factual situation for the issue under discussion (or, alternatively, wait until the end of the paragraph).
> 3. Identify any *factors or standards* that guide courts as they apply the rule of law.
> 4. Synthesize your individual rule statements from each case into a *general rule statement(s)* that accurately reflects the cases as a group.
> 5. *Briefly apply* the factors or standards to the client's factual situation, showing how they support the legal issue conclusion.

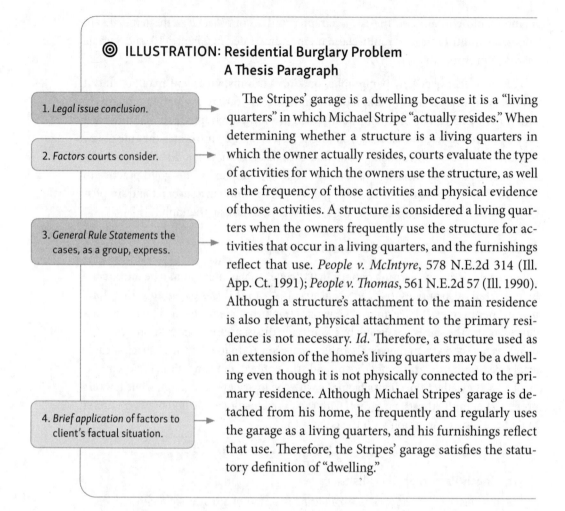

◎ ILLUSTRATION: Residential Burglary Problem
A Thesis Paragraph

1. Legal issue conclusion.

2. Factors courts consider.

3. General Rule Statements the cases, as a group, express.

4. Brief application of factors to client's factual situation.

The Stripes' garage is a dwelling because it is a "living quarters" in which Michael Stripe "actually resides." When determining whether a structure is a living quarters in which the owner actually resides, courts evaluate the type of activities for which the owners use the structure, as well as the frequency of those activities and physical evidence of those activities. A structure is considered a living quarters when the owners frequently use the structure for activities that occur in a living quarters, and the furnishings reflect that use. *People v. McIntyre*, 578 N.E.2d 314 (Ill. App. Ct. 1991); *People v. Thomas*, 561 N.E.2d 57 (Ill. 1990). Although a structure's attachment to the main residence is also relevant, physical attachment to the primary residence is not necessary. *Id.* Therefore, a structure used as an extension of the home's living quarters may be a dwelling even though it is not physically connected to the primary residence. Although Michael Stripes' garage is detached from his home, he frequently and regularly uses the garage as a living quarters, and his furnishings reflect that use. Therefore, the Stripes' garage satisfies the statutory definition of "dwelling."

Exercise 14-1: The Social Host Problem

This exercise builds on Exercises 8-1 and 12-2. First review the fact pattern in the social host exercise (Exercise 8-1). Then review the cases that were summarized in Exercise 12-2 and your notes from that exercise. Draft a thesis paragraph that: (1) identifies the issue; (2) incorporates any relevant standards or factors that guided the courts; (3) contains a rule statement(s) that accurately expresses the group of cases; (4) states a conclusion; and (5) briefly summarizes how the standards or factors support the conclusion.

CHAPTER IN REVIEW
···

Editing Checklist

OVERVIEW PARAGRAPH → In your overview paragraph, did you:

1. State your *ultimate conclusion*?
2. Describe the separate *elements* of the original rule of law?
   - If the courts interpreted or defined the original rule of law in an important way, include such definitional statements.
3. Identify any elements that do not present issues under the client's unique factual situation (i.e., *non-issues*)?
4. Identify the elements that merit further discussion (i.e., *issues*)?

THESIS PARAGRAPH → In your thesis paragraph, did you:

1. Describe the *original rule of law* and identify the element of the rule of law that presents an *issue* (if your memo did not merit a separate overview paragraph)?
2. *State your legal issue conclusion as to* how the law affects the client's factual situation for the issue under discussion?
   - You can either begin or end the thesis paragraph with your conclusion, depending upon your or your professor's preference.
3. Identify any *factors* that guide courts as they evaluate and apply the element of the rule of law to factual situations?
   - Synthesize the factors or standards from the diverse cases into factors or standards that accurately reflect the cases as a group.
   - If courts use different language to refer to the same factor, select the language that most clearly depicts the idea.
4. Synthesize your individual rule statements from each case into a general rule statement(s) that accurately reflects the cases as a group?
5. *Briefly apply* the factors to the client's factual situation, to show how they support the legal issue conclusion?

DRAFTING AN OFFICE MEMO

Completing the Draft

I. CHAPTER IN FOCUS

> **MEMORANDUM**
>
> To: Senior Attorney
> From: Junior Attorney
> Date: Date of Submission of Memo
> Re: XYZ Client Matter
>
> **QUESTION PRESENTED**
>
> . . .
>
> **SHORT ANSWER**
>
> . . .
>
> **STATEMENT OF FACTS**
>
> . . .
>
> **DISCUSSION**
>
> Overview Paragraph
> Thesis Paragraph
> Rule Explanation
> Rule Application
>
> **CONCLUSION**

II. DRAFTING THE HEADING

Now that you have completed a draft of the Discussion section of your memo, you are in a position to add the remaining sections. Drafting the heading is fairly straight-forward. The centered "<u>MEMORANDUM</u>" title informs the reader that the document is an office memorandum. In the remaining portions of the heading, include the name of the person to whom you are writing the memo (the "To" designation), your own name (the "From" designation), and the date you submitted the memo (the "Date" designation). The date is important because it represents that your analysis is accurate as of the date you submitted the memo. Should you or another attorney later decide to revisit the issue evaluated in the memo, the date serves as a reminder that the analysis is complete only as of the date designated on the memo and that the research will need to be updated. The "Re:" designation refers to the client matter that is the subject of the memo. Because many clients have numerous matters that are pending within a law office, include enough information about the client matter and file so that other attorneys in your office will be able to identify easily the client matter that is the subject of the memo.

III. DRAFTING THE QUESTION PRESENTED

A. Purpose

Following the heading, the next section identifies for the reviewing attorney the issue or issues that will be discussed in the memo. The issue statement is commonly called the "Question Presented," although some law offices label the issue statement as the "Issue" or the "Issue Presented." You should follow the format preferred by your professor or the law office in which you work. The purpose of the Question Presented is to frame the legal question(s) that will be evaluated in the memo. The Question Presented should provide the reviewing attorney with an accurate, focused overview of the issue or issues the memo will discuss, including the component of the rule of law that is at issue and the critical client facts that present an issue under that rule of law.

As you might imagine, it can be quite challenging to draft a clear, succinct Question Presented that accomplishes such goals. Therefore, although the Question Presented is the first section of the memo itself, many lawyers wait until after they have drafted the Discussion section of the memo before drafting the Question Presented. Even more so than the thesis paragraph, drafting an effective Question Presented requires a sophisticated understanding of the law and how the law affects the client's situation. Unless you have first struggled with and deepened your understanding of the nuances of the law while drafting the Discussion section of your memo, you might find yourself spending an inordinate amount of time trying to capture the issue in a well-crafted Question Presented only to end up frustrated and discouraged. If you find that to be the case, try drafting and polishing the Discussion first and then come back to the Question Presented and Short Answer section of your memo.

B. The Question Presented in a One-Issue Memo

1. Content

Unless you have been informed otherwise, you should presume that the senior attorney who will read your memo does not understand the intricacies of the specific client facts that pose a legal problem. If the senior attorney understood the intricacies of the client problem at that depth, you probably would not have been asked to research the law and draft a memo on the matter. Therefore, your Question Presented should (1) inform the reviewing attorney of the element of the rule of law that presents an issue for the client, and (2) summarize those important client facts that create the issue. Because your goal is to capture the essence of the issue that will be addressed, it is important to summarize both the important client facts that *support* your legal issue conclusion, as well as any important client facts that are particularly problematic.

2. Format

Recall that readers need to know the context of what they are reading before they can understand details. The same principle is true when reading Questions Presented. Therefore, the most effective format is one that first identifies the element of the rule of law that presents the issue before summarizing the important client facts. The rule of law presents the context for the issue itself. The format follows this form:

"Can... [identify the *element* of the rule of law that presents an issue] when... [summarize the *important client facts* that present the issue]?

A typical Question Presented would look like this:

> **QUESTION PRESENTED**
>
> *<Rule>* Is a detached garage a "dwelling" that is a "living quarters" in which the owners "actually reside" under Illinois' Residential Burglary Statute,
>
> *<Facts>* when it has been converted into a retreat for the owners' college-age son, who uses it on a weekly basis as a getaway and sleeps there half the year, although the retreat does not have plumbing facilities?

The above illustration begins with the word "is," followed by the question. Other common verbs that follow this format are: "Was...?" or "Can...?" or "May...?"

Instead of forming a question within the Question Presented, some lawyers prefer to begin the Question Presented with the word "whether" rather than with a verb that signals a question. This format follows the same sequence as the above illustration—the rule of law followed by a summary of the important facts. However, this form of a Question Presented ends with a period rather than a question mark. Thus, the Question Presented illustrated above could also be framed like this:

> ### QUESTION PRESENTED
>
> Whether a detached garage is a "dwelling" that is a "living quarters" in which someone "actually resides" under Illinois' Residential Burglary Statute, when it has been converted into a retreat for the owners' college-age son, who uses it on a weekly basis as a getaway and sleeps there half the year, although the retreat does not have plumbing facilities.

A final option includes what is known as the under-does-when format.[1] This format provides the Question Presented with three specific pieces: (1) the area of law for the "under," (2) the specific legal issue for the "does" (or, alternatively, "is," or "can,"), and (3) the client problem's most legally significant facts pertaining to the legal issue for the "when." Therefore, the Question Presented illustrated above could also be framed like this:

> ### QUESTION PRESENTED
>
> Under Illinois' Residential Burglary Statute, is a detached garage a "dwelling" that is a "living quarters" in which the owners "actually reside," when it has been converted into a retreat for the owners' college-age son, who uses it on a weekly basis as a getaway and sleeps there half the year, although the retreat does not have plumbing facilities?

3. Avoiding Common Traps

It is easy when drafting a Question Presented to fall into the trap of including your conclusion within the statement of the issue itself. For example, the issue illustrated above could be erroneously drafted as follows:

---

1. This format was introduced in Laurel Currie Oats, et al., *The Legal Writing Handbook* § 5.9.2 (1993).

QUESTION PRESENTED

Incorrect:

Whether a detached garage is a dwelling *when it is a living quarters* in which the owners' son resides on a weekly basis.

Note how the above example contains the legal conclusion within the issue statement itself—it presumes that the detached garage is a "living quarters." There can only be one answer to a question that presumes that a structure is a living quarters. Instead, carefully review your draft to ensure that you have not crafted a question that inadvertently contains the legal issue conclusion itself.

Similarly, be careful not to include any rule language within the factual section of your Question Presented. Doing so creates a similar problem as providing a legal conclusion—it makes the Question itself circular and leaves no room for analysis. As an example, recall the rule for what constitutes a "living quarters" under the Residential Burglary Statute. We noted in Chapter 14 that "a structure is considered a living quarters when the owners frequently use the structure for activities that occur in a living quarters, and the furnishings reflect that use." Now, read the following Question Presented that improperly implements that rule language within the factual section of the question:

QUESTION PRESENTED

Incorrect:

Under Illinois' Residential Burglary Statute, is a detached garage a "dwelling" that is a "living quarters" in which the owners "actually reside," when the owners frequently use the structure for activities that occur within a living quarters, and the garage's furnishings reflect that use?

You can see the clear problem with this draft. In answering the question by applying the rule's language within the fact section of the Question Presented, there is nothing there to analyze—the answer must be "yes" regardless of the actual facts of the case. Instead of including rule language within the factual section of the Question Presented, focus on the client's legally significant facts within your question. Review the following draft to see *case facts*, rather than rule language, properly utilized:

> **QUESTION PRESENTED**
>
> *Correct:*
>
> Under Illinois' Residential Burglary Statute, is a detached garage a "dwelling" that is a "living quarters" in which the owners "actually reside," when it has been converted into a retreat for the owners' college-age son, who uses it on a weekly basis as a getaway and sleeps there half the year, although the retreat does not have plumbing facilities?

4. Personalizing the Question Presented

There are several schools of thought as to whether it is preferable to personalize the Question Presented, or instead to refer to the client by a more abstract characterization. Lawyers who prefer to personalize the issue statement reason that the memo involves a specific client; thus, the Question Presented itself should also refer to the client by name. In the residential burglary example, the issue statement would refer to the "Stripes' garage" rather than to the more generic label of "a detached garage." Other lawyers prefer instead to characterize the client by a generic label, reasoning that other lawyers who review the memo will more easily be able to grasp the import of characterizations. For example, a reviewing attorney who is not intimately familiar with the facts of a specific client problem may find it easier to grasp the significance of labels such as "landowner" or "child trespasser" rather than by the specific names of the parties involved. As with other formatting issues that involve individual preferences, follow the formatting preference of your professor or of the senior attorney who has asked you to draft the memo.

C. The Question Presented in a Multi-Issue Memo

In a multi-issue memo, it can be challenging to draft a single Question Presented that identifies the original rule of law, the separate issues, and the critical facts that relate to each separate issue. Often in a multi-issue memo, lawyers add an "umbrella" question that (1) contains the ultimate question the memo will address and (2) the elements of the rule of law that present issues for discussion. Underneath the umbrella question, each issue becomes a separate Question Presented. Each separate issue is drafted just like a Question Presented in a one-issue memo. The following example is excerpted from Sample Memo D in Appendix A:

QUESTION PRESENTED

Do the clients have a valid claim against landowners under Florida's attractive nuisance doctrine, which requires proof that: (a) the landowners could reasonably foresee the presence of trespassing children on their property, (b) the property contained a hidden danger, and (c) the landowners failed to exercise reasonable care to protect the child from injury?

> The *"Umbrella" question* that identifies:
> 1. The ultimate question; and the
> 2. Elements of the rule of law.

    A. *Is the presence of trespassing children reasonably foreseeable when* the property is located next to an elementary school; a pond on the property contains inner-tubes, ducks, and fish; and the landowners have previously discovered school children trespassing?

> **1st issue:**
> 1. *The element of the rule of law &*
> 2. *Key facts under that element.*

    B. *Is a dock a hidden danger to a six-year-old child when* it is covered by moss and algae, provides the only means of access to the pond, and is so deteriorated that it collapsed under the weight of the child?

> **2nd issue:**
> 1. *The element of the rule of law &*
> 2. *Key facts.*

    C. *Do landowners fail to exercise reasonable care to protect children from foreseeable injury when* they do not lock the gate to the property, repair the dock, or post warning signs of the deteriorating condition of the dock, although they erected a chain link fence around the property and posted a "Do Not Climb Fence" sign on the fence?

> **3rd issue:**
> 1. *The element of the rule of law &*
> 2. *Key facts.*

IV. DRAFTING THE SHORT ANSWER

A. The Short Answer in a One-Issue Memo

After identifying for the reader the issue or issues the memo will address, the memo next provides an answer to the Question Presented. The Short Answer both (1) answers the question, and (2) provides a brief, succinct summary of the key reasons that justify the answer.

Many lawyers prefer that the Short Answer begin with a simple responsive statement, such as "yes" or "no." However, unless you are comfortable that your analysis supports a "yes" or "no" conclusion, it is perfectly acceptable to allow your conclusion to reflect any uncertainty you may have. Therefore, your Short Answer can begin with a "probably," "probably not," or "most likely not," as well. Another way of framing the conclusion is to begin the Short Answer with a declarative sentence that expresses your opinion as to the strength or validity of the client's claim or defense. Thus, instead of framing the conclusion with a "probably," you might state: "The client has a *strong* claim (or defense)..." A more tentative favorable conclusion might be framed as: "The client has a *viable* claim (or defense)..." Avoid, however, responding to the Question Presented with a term such as "possibly" or "it is possible." Anything in life is "possible"; your conclusion should provide the reviewing attorney with more direction than an "anything in life is possible" response.

After stating your conclusion, next provide a brief summary of the most important reasons that support your conclusion. If you have identified a legal standard or factors that guide courts as they interpret the rule of law, incorporate the relevant standard or factors into the basis for your conclusion within the Short Answer. However, unless you provide rules of law (as demonstrated in the second example below), do not cite to cases or statutes in this section of the memo. This section of the memo should be very brief, and the first example shows an option that allows the reviewing attorney to absorb the essence of your conclusion without being weighed down by an extensive evaluation of the law or client facts.

The following illustration reflects a Short Answer that begins with a simple direct response to the question. It also stays consistent with the drafting choice reflected in the Question Presented to refer to the owners and their garage generically rather than by their names.

SHORT ANSWER

Most likely, yes. A detached garage used as a retreat and seasonal sleeping place is a "living quarters" under the Statute. The owner frequently and regularly uses the garage for activities typically associated with a living quarters. The garage is furnished to reflect that use.

The following Short Answer illustrates another way to draft the Short Answer. It provides a more detailed analysis to back up the "yes" or "no" answer. This example incorporates three basic components to both provide an answer and to support it: (1) the bottom line answer to the question asked, which may be "probably yes" or "most likely no," or something similar; (2) the rule of law pertaining to the legal issue identified in the Question Presented; and (3) a brief application that applies the client's most legally significant facts (relating to the legal issue) to the rule statement just provided. When using this more detailed format, it is advisable that the writer cite authorities within the second component, since those rule statements come directly from legal authorities. This example also presumes that the Question Presented referred to the client by name, instead of by a generic classification.

SHORT ANSWER

Most likely, yes. A structure is considered a "dwelling" when the owners frequently use the structure for activities that occur in a living quarters, and the furnishings reflect that use. *People v. McIntyre*, 578 N.E.2d 314 (Ill. App. Ct. 1991); *People v. Thomas*, 561 N.E.2d 57 (Ill. 1990). The Stripes' detached garage, used as a retreat and seasonal sleeping place, is probably a "living quarters" under the Statute. The Stripes' son frequently and regularly uses the garage, for activities typically associated with a living quarters, such as watching television, writing and listening to music, and practicing with his band. The garage is also furnished to reflect that use, with a futon, space heater, television, and mini-refrigerator. Thus, it likely qualifies as a dwelling under the Statute.

B. The Short Answer in a Multi-Issue Memo

In a multi-issue memo, the Short Answer should track the Question Presented section. In other words, if there is an umbrella question and three separate questions that are each sub-parts of the umbrella question, then the Short Answer should include an umbrella answer and three separate answers that are sub-parts of the umbrella answer. The actual content of each Short Answer is no different than a Short Answer in a single-issue memo. The following example is excerpted from Sample Memo D in Appendix A:

SHORT ANSWER

Yes, the clients have a strong claim against the landowners for injuries sustained by their child under the doctrine of attractive nuisance.

> *The answer to the ultimate question.*

    A. *First, their child's presence on the property was reasonably foreseeable because the landowners' property is both visible and accessible from an area that young children frequent, it contains objects or conditions that attract children, and*

> **1st issue:**
> 1. *Answers the issue;* and
> 2. Identifies the general factors that support the answer.

the landowners had previously discovered school children trespassing on their property.

B. *Second, the deteriorating dock was a hidden danger* because a six-year-old child is too young to appreciate its dangerous condition.

C. *Finally, the landowners failed to exercise reasonable care to protect trespassing children from the danger of the dock* because the burden of taking reasonable precautionary measures was slight when compared to the risk of harm to foreseeable child trespassers.

2nd issue:
1. *Answers the issue*; and
2. Identifies the general factors that support the answer.

3rd issue:
1. *Answers the issue*; and
2. Identifies the general factors that support the answer.

EXERCISES 15-1 THROUGH 15-4

Review the Statement of Facts and thesis paragraph for the kidnapping memo illustrated in Appendix A as Sample Memorandum B. Compare the following examples and consider their respective appeal to a busy partner. For each exercise, respond to the following questions:

1. Does the Question Presented:
   a. Identify the element of the rule of law that is at issue?
   b. Clearly and succinctly summarize the key client facts? If not, how might the facts be more effectively presented?
   c. Follow a format that provides the reader with context before details? If not, how might the Question Presented be restructured?

2. Does the Short Answer:
   a. Answer the question?
   b. Identify the element of the rule of law that frames the answer?
   c. Inform the reader of the reasons that support the answer?

Exercise 15-1

QUESTION PRESENTED

Does a defendant have a viable defense under Illinois' Aggravated Kidnapping Statute when he confined a friend to a chair in his living room?

SHORT ANSWER

He may have a viable defense under the Aggravated Kidnapping Statute.

Exercise 15-2

QUESTION PRESENTED

If a defendant ties a friend to his chair in the living room of his home, and the living room is on the first floor of his home, which is primarily surrounded by a large picture window with a small amount of brick surrounding the entrance, and the home is twenty feet from a moderately-traveled road, and the front door is two steps up from the sidewalk, making it visible to passersby, but he does not answer the telephone or doorbell, does he have a viable defense under Illinois' Aggravated Kidnapping Statute that he did not "secretly" confine his friend under the Statute?

SHORT ANSWER

Yes. He has a viable defense that he did not "secretly" confine his friend.

Exercise 15-3

QUESTION PRESENTED

Under Illinois' Aggravated Kidnapping Statute, does a defendant have a viable defense that he did not "secretly" confine another under the Statute, when he confined a victim in the victim's home in front of a large picture window visible to neighbors and passersby, and made no effort to conceal the victim, although he failed to answer the telephone or doorbell?

SHORT ANSWER

Yes, a defendant has a viable defense that he did not secretly confine another under the Statute. The defendant selected a visible location near a public area from which witnesses were likely to view the confinement, and he made no effort to conceal the victim in a less visible location. In view of the location's visibility to potential witnesses, the fact that the defendant failed to answer the telephone or doorbell should not make the confinement "secret."

Exercise 15-4

QUESTION PRESENTED

Does a defendant have a viable defense under Illinois' Aggravated Kidnapping Statute that he did not "secretly" confine another under the Statute, when he confined a victim in front of a large picture window visible to neighbors and passersby?

SHORT ANSWER

Yes, a defendant has a viable defense that he did not secretly confine another under the Statute. The defendant selected a visible location near a public area from which witnesses were likely to view the confinement.

V. DRAFTING THE STATEMENT OF FACTS

A. Purpose

The Statement of Facts simply tells the factual story of the client's situation. The Statement of Facts serves several purposes. First, the factual story serves as context for the legal analysis in the Discussion section of the memo. Just as with every other section of the memo, your reader will appreciate understanding the underlying context of the client's situation before focusing on the aspects of the client situation that create an issue under the relevant rule of law.

Second, a thorough factual statement gives the reviewing attorney the opportunity to correct any misunderstandings. It is not uncommon for a senior attorney to relate the facts to a junior attorney during an office conference that is subject to telephone calls and other interruptions. As a practical matter, a senior attorney may inadvertently neglect to inform you of a fact that may prove to be legally significant. On other occasions, you and the senior attorney may both be present during a client meeting; however, you may each leave the meeting with two different impressions of certain facts. Therefore, the factual statement provides an opportunity to correct any misunderstandings.

Third, because your analysis and legal conclusions will be based on the existence of certain facts, the Statement of Facts protects you. Should additional facts later be revealed, it will be clear from the memo itself that your conclusion in that memo is premised on a specific set of facts and might be different in light of any additional facts.

Finally, an office memo is a self-contained document. Should other lawyers in the office review your memo at a later date, or should you decide to refer to the memo as you research a related matter, it is important that all of the relevant information be contained within a single document.

B. Content

The Statement of Facts section of an office memo contains two different types of facts: (1) those facts that are legally significant; and (2) those helpful background facts that provide context for the factual story. Legally significant facts are those facts that are significant to your analysis of how the law affects the client's situation. You will not know which facts are legally significant until after you have researched the law, carefully evaluated the cases, and analogized and compared their facts to the client's situation. In fact, as you research the law, you may change your mind a number of times as to which facts are significant and how they are significant. Because the senior attorney and client will rely on your analysis of the law in making future decisions, it is important that you fully apprise them of all of the legally significant facts, unfavorable as well as favorable. Therefore, it is important to include the legally significant facts that do not favor your conclusion as well as those facts that support your ultimate conclusion.

Every legally significant fact that appears in your Statement of Facts should also appear somewhere in your Discussion section. Therefore, your Statement of Facts can serve as a useful editing tool when you revise and finalize your memo. After completing the Statement of Facts, check to make sure that every legally significant fact is incorporated in the Discussion section as well.

Although this may seem repetitive to you as the writer, the reader won't see it that way. Because the Statement of Facts serves a different purpose than the Discussion section of the memo, you will be presenting the facts differently in this section than in the Discussion section. In the Statement of Facts, the reader learns all about the factual story, including what the client did or didn't do and what happened to the client. In this section of the memo, you should refrain from making any legal conclusions about the facts. Legal conclusions would both distract the reader from understanding "what happened" and also inappropriately insert your own conclusions into what should be an impartial statement of "what happened." In contrast, in the Discussion section you will have incorporated the facts into your legal discussion solely for their legal significance. In that section of the memo, you will be incorporating key facts as "evidence" to illustrate different arguments you are making.

C. Format

Like the roadmap paragraphs in the Discussion section of the memo, begin the Statement of Facts with a sentence or two that can provide context for the factual story that follows. Depending on the complexity of the case, these contextual facts may absorb a paragraph or may only require a single sentence. You may also wish to include in the opening paragraph a brief description of the procedural posture of the case. However, although some lawyers prefer to include a brief statement of the procedural posture in the first paragraph, other lawyers prefer to wait until the end of the Statement of Facts. You should follow the format preferred by your professor or assigning attorney. The following introductory paragraph is excerpted from Sample Memo A in Appendix A:

> On August 10, 20XX, Defendant, Gerry Arnold, broke into Carl and Rita Stripes'
> two-car detached garage and removed some of their personal property. The
> State has charged Mr. Arnold under the Residential Burglary Statute. Mr. Ar-
> nold's attorney has moved to dismiss the charge, contending that the Stripes'
> garage is not a "dwelling" within which the Stripes "reside," as required by the
> Statute.

The remaining paragraphs of the Statement of Facts can be organized chronologically, or by issue, or by a combination of both approaches.

1. Chronological Order

Because readers are accustomed to absorbing facts chronologically, detailing the
factual events in chronological sequence can be a clear and effective means of telling
the story. In fact, if the factual situation you are describing lends itself to a chronology of events, a reader would have difficulty understanding the factual story if you
didn't tell it in sequence. Consider the following example:

> **Example 1:**
>
> On August 10, 20XX, when a police officer stopped Mr. Arnold, he noticed the
> stolen equipment in the back seat of the car and arrested Mr. Arnold. The police
> officer observed Mr. Arnold driving erratically. Gerry Arnold had broken into the
> Stripes' garage by breaking a window. After breaking a window in the garage,
> Mr. Arnold then unlocked the door and made three trips to his car, carrying with
> him Michael Stripe's guitar, a sound system, and a T.V.

In the above illustration, if you weren't already very familiar with the story, you
would find it difficult to absorb what happened without going back and rereading
certain sentences. Without the context that a chronological sequence would provide,
it's difficult to follow the story. For example, the first sentence in Example 1 describes
a police officer stopping Mr. Arnold and arresting him because of stolen equipment in
the back seat of the car. Without knowing that Mr. Arnold had earlier broken into the
Stripes' garage and taken away certain equipment, that part of the factual story lacks
context. In addition, the story describes the police officer's search of the car before
disclosing why the police officer stopped the car in the first place. Assuming such facts
were relevant to the issue to be evaluated in the memo, the following example describes
the factual story in chronological sequence, making it easier for the reader to follow.

Example 2:

On August 10, 20XX, Gerry Arnold broke into the Stripes' garage by breaking a window. Mr. Arnold then unlocked the door and made three trips to his car, carrying with him Michael Stripe's guitar, a sound system, and a T.V. While fleeing from the scene, a police officer observed Mr. Arnold driving erratically. When the police officer stopped Mr. Arnold, he noticed the stolen equipment in the back seat of the car and arrested Mr. Arnold.

2. Grouping Facts Per Issue or Factor

Sometimes facts do not have a chronological order. Instead, they simply describe an object or person or general events. For example, in the residential burglary problem, the facts relating to whether the Stripe family's garage is a dwelling do not have a chronological order. When facts don't lend themselves to a chronological sequence of events, group the facts according to the common issue to which they relate. Thus, if courts are guided by A, B, and C factors when interpreting a rule of law, you might tell the factual story by separately grouping the client facts that relate to each factor. For example, consider the following paragraph excerpted from the Statement of Facts for the residential burglary memo (Sample Memo A in Appendix A):

The Stripes' garage is equipped to accommodate Michael Stripe's interests. In addition to a futon, the garage contains an expensive sound system, a portable five-inch television, and a mini-refrigerator. The garage has electricity and a space heater, but no running water or heat.

In the above example, this factual paragraph groups together all of the facts that describe the manner in which the Stripes' garage was furnished, a factor relevant to courts in determining whether a garage is a "living quarters" under the residential burglary statute. As the sample memo reflects, each of the remaining paragraphs in the Statement of Facts is also grouped by issue. The paragraphs separately describe the physical characteristics of the garage, Michael Stripe's use of the garage, and the frequency of Michael's use of the garage.

3. Combining the Two Formatting Strategies

Often, a client's story involves some facts that have a chronological order and other facts that do not. Under such circumstances, a combination of both formatting strategies can be effective. When combining the two strategies, try and structure the story so that paragraphs relating to specific issues do not interrupt the chronology of events. Therefore, when possible to do so, place the paragraphs that are grouped according to an issue or factor so that they either *precede* or *follow* the paragraphs describing the chronological flow of events. For example, in the Statement of Facts for the residential burglary memo, the paragraphs describing the Stripes' garage and its uses and structure (issue grouping paragraphs) follow a paragraph describing the events that happened on August 20 (chronology of events paragraph).

D. Deducing Inferences from Facts

Clients do not usually provide their lawyers with all of the facts that may be relevant to their legal problem. Even though clients try to provide their lawyers with all of the relevant information concerning their legal problem, clients are typically not trained to deduce important inferences from facts. The skill of deducing inferences from facts is an important one that you will learn and practice in law school. Essentially, the art of deduction involves examining the facts that you know are true. From those facts you know to be true, deduce the existence of other facts that must also be true. For example, if a client were to walk in the door with snow sprinkled over her winter coat, you would deduce that it is snowing outside. Such inferences will be valuable to you as you evaluate client problems.

The following example illustrates this process of deductive reasoning. In this example, assume that the lawyer who drafted the following Statement of Facts represents a defendant who has been charged with a crime. The Government's case against the defendant rests solely on transcripts of wiretap tapes the Government intercepted from the defendant's home telephone. The Government lost the tapes for a period of two months. Because the Government lost the tapes and cannot assure the court that the tapes were not altered during that time period, the lawyer will evaluate in a memo whether a judge would "suppress" the tapes, thereby depriving the Government of the ability to introduce the tapes into evidence during trial.

Assume that prior to drafting the Statement of Facts, the drafting attorney had the following information concerning the Government's loss of the wiretap tapes: (1) Agent Friday placed the tapes in a cardboard box on Sept. 7 and states she placed a label on the box indicating it was to go to the courthouse for the court to "seal" the tapes; (2) Agent Friday states that she sealed the box of tapes; (3) her office of 5,000 people moved offices on Sept. 8th; (4) a janitor saw the box of tapes in an office supply room at the new location but did not realize what it was—the box of tapes was not labeled and "was open. You could look right in and see what was inside."; (5) until Agent Friday discovered the tapes two months later in the storage room, the Government was not aware the tapes were missing; (6) the Government cannot explain why the box of tapes was open when it was found; and (7) this case was Agent Friday's only responsibility during the relevant time period.

Keeping that background in mind, review the following Statement of Facts. The facts that have been inferred from known facts are <u>underlined</u> to help you identify them. As you consider the facts that have been inferred, identify the known fact that is the source of the inference.

> The client, Mr. Joseph Hart, has been indicted with . . . [a statutory violation]. Wiretap tapes the Government obtained from a wiretap on Mr. Hart's home are the sole basis of the Government indictment. On September 6 and 7, the Government obtained the tapes they are using as the sole basis for Mr. Hart's indictment.
>
> On September 7, 2020, Agent T. Friday removed the tapes from the surveillance van parked near Mr. Hart's home and took them to the investigating bureau's office. <u>Although Agent Friday had to have been aware</u> that the Bureau was moving offices the next day, she dropped the tapes in a plain cardboard box <u>that was identical to the thousands of cardboard boxes used for the move.</u> Although Agent Friday testified that she placed a label on the box indicating that the box was to be transported to the courthouse, the building janitor testified that no label appeared on the box of tapes. Although Agent Friday testified that she sealed the box of tapes, the building janitor testified that the box of tapes "was open. You could look right in and see what was inside." (R. at 14.) The Government has not explained these factual discrepancies.
>
> <u>After the Bureau moved offices, Agent Friday never telephoned or appeared at the courthouse to ensure the tapes arrived for sealing. Agent Friday never asked the court clerk to confirm whether a judge had sealed the tapes.</u> And, despite the fact that Agent Friday had no responsibilities other than this case during the entire period of August to November, 2020, <u>Agent Friday apparently did not make a single attempt to locate her only evidence in this case.</u>
>
> On or about November 8, 2020, Agent Friday finally found the missing tapes while looking for party decorations. (R. at 12.) The Government speculates that the tapes sat exposed in an open box in the unlocked office supply room for over two months. (R. at 12.) The exposed tapes sat in the busy supply room amidst note pads, pencils, office supplies, and party decorations, <u>open to the 5,000 occupants of the building who frequent the room for coffee and office supplies.</u>

Note the factual discrepancies between Agent Friday's testimony and the janitor's testimony. In the Statement of Facts, these factual discrepancies are merely noted, without arguing why the discrepancies are legally significant. The Statement of Facts thereby sets the stage for the lawyer to later argue in the Discussion section why such discrepancies are legally significant. Thus, the lawyer would later explore the legal consequences of the inferences raised from such discrepancies—either an unknown individual later removed the tapes from a box that Agent Friday sealed, or Agent Friday did not originally place the tapes in sealed envelopes or seal the box itself. Either inference would have legal ramifications.

Exercise 15-5: Factual Inferences

Assume that your client was sued for stealing trade secrets from her former employer and selling them to a competitor with whom she is now employed. During the lawsuit, the plaintiff (former employer) asked the court to dismiss the lawsuit after it discovered that your client was not, in fact, the culpable party. Your client seeks monetary sanctions against her former employer for filing a lawsuit that was not "well-grounded in fact" after a "reasonable investigation." The applicable court rules require lawyers to conduct a "reasonable investigation" before filing a lawsuit to ensure that the factual basis for the lawsuit is "well-grounded in fact." Your job is to evaluate whether you should file a request for sanctions on the ground that the former employer did not reasonably investigate its claim before filing suit.

During the discovery process, the plaintiff described all of the information it had available that indicated your client was culpable, and all of the steps it took to investigate the matter before filing the lawsuit: (1) your client had access to and used the trade secret information while employed by the plaintiff; (2) your client became employed by the competitor immediately after leaving the plaintiff's employ; (3) approximately six months after your client began working for the competitor, the competitor began marketing technology based on trade secret information; (4) the employer's employment records reflected that your client was the only employee who left its employment to become employed by the competitor; and (5) the plaintiff asked each of its ten present employees who have access to the trade secrets to take a lie detector test; all passed the test.

At least superficially, the plaintiff appears to have taken reasonable steps to investigate the claim. Nevertheless, your job is to infer from the known facts the existence of other facts that might reveal that the investigation was, in fact, superficial in scope and not reasonable. For this exercise, you can assume that the plaintiff failed to take any potential investigative step not described above.

As you evaluate the facts, consider the following:

(1) **Factual possibilities the plaintiff failed to consider:** List other groups of culprits, or alternative explanations, the plaintiff failed to consider while pursuing its investigation.

(2) **Steps the plaintiff failed to take:** List any other steps the plaintiff could have taken when investigating this matter to strengthen the factual basis for its complaint.

(3) **Faulty inferences from the facts it had available:** Consider whether the plaintiff's incorrect conclusion that your client was the culpable party was based on any faulty inferences from the facts it had available. List any faulty inferences the plaintiff made.

CHAPTER IN REVIEW

Editing Checklist:

QUESTION PRESENTED

1. If you are drafting a multi-issue memo, did you begin with an "umbrella" question that identifies: (a) the ultimate question the memo will address; and (b) the elements of the original rule of law that present issues? (*See* Sample Memo D in Appendix A)
   - *Note*: If the issues and important facts are not very complex in a multi-issue memo, you may not need to draft an umbrella question.

2. In each Question Presented, did you: (a) begin the question with a summary of the element of the rule of law that presents an issue (the legal issue); and (b) conclude with a summary of the important client facts that create the issue?
   - Did you avoid the trap of including your conclusion within the statement of the issue itself?
   - Did you avoid the trap of including rule language instead of facts within the factual portion of the question?
   - Did you include both a summary of the facts that support your conclusion as well as any important facts that may be problematic?

SHORT ANSWER

1. If you drafted an "umbrella" question for a multi-issue memo, did you draft an "umbrella" conclusion to the overall question presented? (*See* Sample Memo D in Appendix A)

2. In each Short Answer, did you (a) begin with a conclusion that answers the question presented; (b) followed by a summary of the most important reasons that support your conclusion?
   - If your Discussion section identifies a legal standard or factors that guide courts as they interpret the rule of law, did you use the legal standard or factors to illustrate why your answer is sound?

STATEMENT OF FACTS

1. Did you include in your Statement of Facts all of the legally significant facts that also appear in the Discussion section of your memo?
    -   Check both sections of your memo to ensure that no legally significant fact is omitted from either your Statement of Facts or your Discussion section.
2. Did you incorporate in your Statement of Facts all of the helpful background facts that provide context for your reader to understand the legally significant facts?
3. If the facts have a chronological order, did you provide your reader with context by following a chronological sequence in describing the events? (*See* Sample Memo B in Appendix A)
4. If the facts do not have a chronological order, did you group the client facts according to the issue or factor to which they relate? (*See* Sample Memo A in Appendix A)
5. If some facts have a chronological order while others do not, did you use a combination of formatting strategies, such that the facts grouped per issue or factor do not interfere with the facts that follow a chronological sequence?

REVISING AND FINALIZING THE MEMO
Content and Organizational Structure

I. THE IMPORTANCE OF THE REVISION PROCESS

Prior to law school, you may not have had much practice in reviewing, editing, and finalizing your written work. However, in the practice of law, it is common for lawyers to go through many drafts of their written work before submitting it to their colleagues or to their clients or judges. Clear and persuasive legal writing requires two, three, and even four or more rewrites. The process of revising and finalizing written work is extraordinarily important. Although a first draft is a necessary first step in the drafting process, it would be a mistake to view the first draft as a work product that would be satisfactory in a legal setting.

The following excerpts from a letter forwarded by a corporate employer to a law school dean provide a graphic illustration of the value of the revision process. The corporate employer forwarded this letter to the law school dean following that employer's experience interviewing law students for employment.

Excerpts from a corporate employer's letter:

> Dear _____:
>
> The Office of Legal Counsel of… has concluded a successful recruiting season. We are writing to express our gratitude for your assistance.
>
> We have hired four second-year students for our Summer Intern Program. The successful candidates are…
>
> Our pleasure with these fine recruits is tempered, however, by concern and disappointment in the quality of the writing samples submitted by applicants for summer positions. We have enclosed a representative sample from one of

your students. *The sample's flaws include sloppy editing, poor organization, significant grammatical and syntactical errors, as well as poor logic, reasoning, and analysis.* (Emphasis added.)

Our concern is multifaceted. First, the writing sample a student submits should be representative of the student's writing ability. If the enclosed writing sample is truly typical, these students lack a vital skill required for success. If not typical, the students displayed poor judgment in submitting such samples to prospective employers. Second, submission of writing samples like the enclosed example reflects a basic misunderstanding about the significance of writing samples. If students believe that recruiters do not scrutinize the samples carefully, they are sorely mistaken. In our office, each writing sample is read and evaluated by a minimum of three attorneys. Many students who were well regarded after the office interviews were deleted from our 'potential hire' list or moved several places down the list because of the poor quality of the writing sample....

A law school should counsel its students on the importance of quality communication (both oral and written) and on the importance of the writing samples that students provide on their career opportunities. We wanted to alert you to the problems we perceived this year and over the last few years. If you share our concern, will you please inform your students of the importance attached to their writing ability and choice of writing samples.

[Signature]

As the above letter illustrates, whether submitting your written work to a professor, a potential employer, or a senior attorney in a law office, submitting a first draft as a final draft can lead to unfortunate consequences. Because the revision process is so important, this textbook devotes two chapters to discussing the reflection and revision strategies that will help you become an effective editor of your own work.

After composing the first draft of your memo, it's important to keep an open mind about the draft itself. When reviewing our own work, it is very easy to become invested in what we have written, particularly when we have spent a significant amount of time thinking through the analysis, organizing the analysis, and finding the right words to express our thinking. After all of that time and effort, our tendency is to defend the written work product. However, it is so very important to review initial drafts from the perspective of a detached observer—a challenging prospect. The passage of time makes it easier to see the draft from the fresh perspective of the intended reader. Therefore, whenever possible, allow time within your drafting schedule to put the draft away for a few days.

II. REVIEWING THE SUBSTANTIVE CONTENT

As you review your draft, first consider the substantive content of your analysis. Openly question whether you have provided enough information to the reader about the rule of law and the relevant cases that interpret the rule of law. If the reader had not studied the original rule of law or any of the cases that have interpreted the law, would the reader understand every relevant aspect about the law? Next consider whether you have adequately informed the reader about the law's effect on the client's factual situation. Have you evaluated the impact of each standard or factor on the client's situation? Consider whether you have thoroughly elaborated on the significance of each legally significant fact from the client's situation, including the unfavorable as well as the favorable arguments that can be made. Review again your Statement of Facts to ensure that each legally significant fact described in your factual statement is evaluated within the Discussion section as well. As you carefully review your draft, consider whether any of the substantive content is unnecessary or repetitive and should be deleted. You may realize at this point that some of the information originally included in your analysis was not ultimately legally significant.

III. EVALUATING THE ORGANIZATIONAL STRUCTURE

A. Macro-Organization of the Discussion

Drafting a legal discussion is a fluid, on-going process. Often, lawyers end up trying different formatting options in later drafts, sometimes ultimately deciding to stay with their initial decisions, and sometimes deciding to adopt a different organizational format. Therefore, consider whether your organizational format allows for a clear evaluation of the law and its effect on the client. If you conclude that at least part of the Discussion seems confusing or repetitive, review again the three basic formatting options discussed in Chapter 13 that reflect the interplay between the rule explanation and rule application sections of a memo.

There are several ways you can test whether your overall structure seems to work. In a well-organized memo, each thesis and transition sentence should reveal a cohesive, logical, step-by-step argument. To determine whether your structure works, copy and paste each thesis and transition sentence in the Discussion section of your memo onto a blank document. Does each thesis and transition sentence flow together to create a cohesive argument? Or are there gaps in your analysis or unnecessary repetition? If you see problems in the flow of your argument, move the thesis/transition sentences around by cutting and pasting them into a different order, or, in the case of repetitive paragraphs, you can merge two sentences into a single sentence. This strategy can be an effective way of verifying whether your argument flows well because it avoids the distraction of all of the "content" within each separate paragraph.

Another way to review the macro-organization of your argument is to print out a draft of your Discussion. In the margin next to each paragraph, jot down a few words that capture the principal purpose or idea expressed in that paragraph. If you can identify more than one idea that a particular paragraph illustrates, then jot down the essence of each separate idea that appears in the paragraph. After you've reviewed the entire legal discussion, go back and review your margin notes. For paragraphs that contain more than one primary idea, separate the paragraph into two or more paragraphs until each paragraph illustrates one primary idea. You might also find that a thread of an idea appears in two or more different paragraphs throughout your analysis. In that case, you may wish to take that thread of a recurring idea and create a separate paragraph addressing that idea.

B. The Micro-Format of Each Paragraph

Under the deductive writing pattern, roadmap paragraphs provide the context for the details that will follow in the Discussion section of the memo. Even on the smaller scale of an *individual paragraph*, the paragraph itself should follow a deductive analytical format, transitioning the reader from old information to new information. On the smaller scale of a paragraph, thesis and transition sentences provide the context that transitions a reader from old information to the new information that will follow within a particular paragraph.

The thesis or transition sentence in a paragraph identifies the broad thesis or premise the paragraph will explore and illustrate. The remaining information in the paragraph illustrates and proves with supporting details why the broad thesis or premise is sound. Therefore, each paragraph also follows a deductive format, with the thesis sentence reflecting the paragraph's broad premise and providing the context for the details that will illustrate the premise.

1. Thesis and Transition Sentences

At this stage of the reflection process, consider whether each thesis and transition sentence clearly serves the purpose for which it is intended. Thesis and transition sentences serve as visual "sign posts" that guide a reader through a discussion. Thesis and transition sentences assume a critical role in legal analysis because of the very complexity of legal analysis. The more complex the substantive content, the more difficult it is for a reader to follow the train of analysis. To serve as effective sign posts, thesis and transition sentences should both:

1. **Relate back** to information the reviewing attorney has already read; and
2. **Signal forward** to the essence of the new information that will follow.

By both relating back to old information and signaling forward to new information, thesis and transition sentences serve as valuable links that allow a reader to follow the logical flow of the analysis.

a. Thesis Sentences

Whenever you introduce a new idea in a legal discussion, a thesis sentence should alert the reader to the introduction of the new idea. Because a thesis sentence introduces a new idea, and because readers understand information best if they understand the relationship of the new idea to old information, an effective thesis sentence should both state the paragraph's thesis, or premise, (the "new information") and its relationship to the entire document (the "old information"). An effective way to accomplish this goal is to use the roadmap paragraphs (overview and thesis paragraphs) as the *source* for thesis sentences. Recall that roadmap paragraphs summarize for the reader the elements of the rules of law and any legal standards or factors that guide courts when they interpret the law. Restating the relevant parts of that same information in a thesis sentence effectively: (1) reminds the reviewing attorney of the "old information" from the roadmap paragraphs; and (2) alerts the attorney that the "new information" to be discussed in the upcoming paragraph will elaborate on a particular aspect of the old information.

i. Thesis Sentences Introducing a Case Discussion

When discussing a relevant case, the thesis sentence identifies both how the court answered the legal question before it, and the relevant standard and/or factors that help show why the court answered the legal question in the manner that it did. When possible, use the same language used in the roadmap paragraphs to describe the relevant factors the court weighed. By using the same language, the paragraph's connection to the earlier analysis is instantly clear to the reader. Unlike a typical undergraduate essay, varying the language to avoid presumed boredom will not excite the reader! Instead, using different language to describe the same idea can confuse the reviewing attorney. In your roadmap paragraphs, you assigned specific legal meaning to certain language. Varying the language could imply that the new language has a different *legal meaning* than the old language.

Using the residential burglary memo as the basis of illustration, the following thesis sentence is excerpted from Sample Memo A in Appendix A. In the thesis paragraph of that memo, the following factors were identified as important guiding factors that illustrated the legal standard ("living quarters"): (1) type of use, including the frequency and evidence of use; and (2) the structure's proximity to the home. The rule of law that captures the essence of the *McIntyre* case reflects how the court applied both factors in that case to frame a standard that answers the legal question. The thesis sentence is illustrated as follows:

> An enclosed, attached porch frequently used as part of the home's living quarters is a dwelling under the residential burglary statute. *People v. McIntyre*, 578 N.E.2d 314 (Ill. App. Ct. 1991).

ii. Thesis Sentences Introducing Rule Application

When applying law to a client's factual problem, the thesis sentence should state the factual conclusion, or premise, the paragraph will reach as it applies the law to the client's facts. In that manner, the thesis sentence both relates back to old information (the law as previously evaluated) and alerts the reviewing attorney to the essence of the new information that will follow (how the law affects the client). Thesis sentences incorporate both: (1) the standard and/or factor(s) the paragraph will be discussing, and (2) your factual conclusion about how the client's facts illustrate that standard or factor in a legally significant way. Again using the residential burglary memo as the basis of illustration, the following thesis sentence is excerpted from Sample Memo A in Appendix A.

> Like the owner's use of the porch in *McIntyre*, Michael Stripe used the Stripes' garage for activities commonly associated with a living quarters.

The above thesis sentence identifies the factor that will be discussed in the paragraph (the "type of use" factor), and states a legally significant premise (that the client used the garage for purposes commonly associated with the statutorily-required "living quarters"). As you evaluate each thesis sentence introducing a rule application paragraph, consider whether the thesis sentence relates to the *client* or to the *case law*. In the above illustration, note that the premise of the thesis sentence relates to the *client*, not to case law. The paragraph's premise is that Michael Stripe used the garage for activities associated with a living quarters. It does not restate the thesis from the *McIntyre* case (*e.g.*, "The *McIntyre* court observed that the use of a structure is important in determining whether it is a living quarters."). By framing the thesis around the client, the sentence accurately signals that this will be a paragraph of rule application rather than rule explanation.

As you evaluate each thesis sentence, also consider whether the premise from each sentence identifies why the client facts are *legally significant*. Novice legal writers commonly fail to explain why the facts and factor that are described in the thesis sentence are legally significant. Instead, they tend to adopt a premise that identifies why the client's facts are "like" or "unlike" a precedent case's facts with respect to a specific factor. (For example, a draft thesis sentence might state: "Michael Stripe's use of the garage is similar to the use of the porch in *McIntyre*.") This type of thesis sentence sets the writer up for failure. As the writer attempts to prove the premise in the thesis sentence, the resulting paragraph would only prove that the client's facts are like the precedent case's facts. This is not an effective argument strategy because it fails to explore why the client's facts are legally significant, which is the whole point of the analysis.

As you consider whether each thesis sentence identifies a legally significant premise, ask yourself whether the premise helps prove why the client's facts do or do not satisfy the legal standard that is the subject of the analysis. For example, in the residential burglary problem, the drafting attorney is evaluating whether the Stripes' garage is a "living quarters" under the Statute. When formulating the thesis sentence illustrated above, the sentence identifies how the client's facts that illustrate the "type of use" factor help prove why the garage is a "living quarters" under the Statute—the legal issue that is the subject of discussion.

b. Transition Sentences

Transition sentences serve the same function as thesis sentences, insofar as they help orient a reader to the relationship between old information and new information. In contrast to thesis sentences, however, transition sentences signal the continuation of a discussion of the same general idea. Transition sentences show readers the connection between information in a previous paragraph and in a new paragraph that explores the same general idea.

The following sentences are also excerpted from the residential burglary memo illustrated as Sample Memo A in Appendix A. One argument the writer explores is a potential opposing argument that a garage can never be a dwelling under the residential burglary statute. In the previous paragraph, the writer explored the State's rebuttal to this argument by examining the language and reasoning in the *McIntyre* case. The first sentence in the illustration below is the final sentence in that previous paragraph. The final sentence of that paragraph reflects the writer's conclusion that, even though the Stripes' garage is detached, it is still an extension of the family's living quarters. The transition sentence that leads the next paragraph signals to the reader that the *Thomas* case bolsters the conclusion reached in the previous paragraph.

> .... Like the physically separate porch in *McIntyre*, the Stripes' garage is used as an extension of the Stripe family's living quarters.
>
> *People v. Thomas* lends further support to this conclusion....

2. Remainder of Each Paragraph: Illustrating the Thesis

a. Rule Explanation Paragraphs

As Chapter 11 discusses, there are several ways in which you can organize the discussion of a factually comparable case that will be discussed in depth (*e.g.*, that you will discuss for its factual significance, holding, and rationale). The thesis sentence should serve as the context for the specific details that will follow. As you re-examine each paragraph of rule explanation, verify that you have adequately laid a foundation for each sentence of the paragraph. Consider whether you have omitted to tell the reader any background information that would help the reader understand the significance of your analysis. When describing the factual story of a case that lends itself to a chronological description of the events, consider whether there are any confusing lapses in the chronology.

Exercise 16-1: The Micro-Organization of a Paragraph

The following illustration reflects the importance of providing context within each paragraph. This case discussion contains the four components of a rule explanation paragraph that evaluates a case of primary importance: (1) a rule statement; (2) holding; (3) relevant case facts; and (4) rationale. While reading this example discussion of the *McIntyre* case, identify each sentence that does not have the necessary foundation for a reader to understand easily its significance. Note how the order in which the four different components are presented interferes with clarity.

> In *People v. McIntyre*, 578 N.E.2d 314 (Ill. App. Ct. 1991), the owners furnished the porch with wrought-iron furniture and a barbecue grill that reflected its use. They ate most of their meals on the porch in the summer and cooked meals there four or five times a week in the winter. The porch was enclosed, locked, and attached to the home. They used an attached, screened porch for "sitting, eating, and cooking." *Id.* at 315.
>
> The court observed that the porch was enclosed and attached to the house, indicating that the porch's physical attachment to the house was a relevant factor. The court reasoned that the owners used the porch as part of their living quarters by engaging in such activities as "sitting, eating, and cooking." *Id.* The court held that, under these facts, the porch was a "living quarters" under the Statute. *Id.* In addition, the owners regularly used the porch in this manner and furnished the porch with furniture and a grill that reflected such use. However, the court emphasized that it was the activities of "sitting, eating, and cooking" that "make the porch part of the living quarters of the house." *Id.* An enclosed, attached porch frequently used as part of the home's living quarters is a dwelling under the residential burglary statute.

At this point, you are already familiar with the *McIntyre* case and have even read the case. Nevertheless, you probably had some difficulty following the train of analysis in the above illustration. Imagine the difficulty a reader would have who had never read the *McIntyre* case.

Exercise 16-2: Editing a Rule Explanation Paragraph

Assume that you are reviewing and editing the first draft of an office memorandum that will ultimately become Sample Memo D in Appendix A. Review the Editing

Checklist at the end of this chapter and list the problems you see in the first draft of this rule explanation paragraph.

> **1st Draft:** In *Ansin*, the defendant's pond contained a floating dock. 98 So. 2d 87. A dock was a dangerous condition in *Ansin*. The court noted that a nine-year-old boy could not be expected to recognize its danger. *Id*. at 88. The court upheld a jury's finding that the dock was a dangerous condition.

Identify each change in the revised paragraph below. For each change, describe the purpose the change serves and why the revised or added language is more effective than the language in the first draft.

> **Revised Paragraph:** When a dangerous condition is hidden to a child because of the child's age and immaturity, it constitutes a hidden danger, or trap. *Ansin*, 98 So. 2d 87. In *Ansin*, the defendant's pond contained a floating wooden dock that extended into the water about twelve feet, well over a child's head. A make-shift raft that was "prone to tip" floated in the water at the end of the dock. A nine-year-old child jumped from the dock onto the tipsy raft and then drowned in the pond after playing on the raft. *Id*. at 88. The court held that the pond, floating dock, and tipsy raft combined to constitute a hidden trap. The court observed that the tipsy raft floated in water of a depth well over the child's head. The court reasoned that a nine-year-old boy could not be expected to recognize its danger. *Id*.

b. Rule Application Paragraphs

The detailed information in each paragraph of rule application should illustrate and prove why the premise, or conclusion, that is identified in the first sentence of the paragraph is a sound conclusion. Therefore, carefully review each paragraph of analysis to ensure that the detailed information in each paragraph only illustrates and supports the major idea reflected in the first sentence of that paragraph. If you see that part of the information in a paragraph relates to a different point, now is the time to use the cut and paste function of your word processor. If you become confused while evaluating each paragraph, print out your analysis and take notes in the margin, jotting down the specific points each sentence in the paragraph makes. Making margin notes can sometimes help an editor begin to see the "forest through the trees."

If you are discussing a factor that contains several different sub-factors, you may or may not decide to include a discussion of the different sub-factors in the same paragraph. If each sub-factor is complex enough to merit its own paragraph of analysis, then review your draft to ensure that you have restricted each such paragraph only to that specific sub-factor. Sometimes, however, different sub-factors are minor enough that they can be adequately discussed within a single paragraph. If you have selected this alternative, review your draft to ensure that you have fully evaluated and concluded your discussion about one sub-factor before moving on to the next sub-factor. It is difficult for a reader to absorb the logical flow of an analysis when the discussion itself jumps back and forth between different sub-factors. When discussing a factor that brings out several different sub-factors, check to see whether you can clarify your analysis by introducing each sub-factor with a new premise—even within a single paragraph. Again, the premise for each sub-factor provides the necessary broad context for the reader to understand the factual details that will follow.

For example, in the residential burglary problem, the "type of use" factor has several interrelated sub-factors: frequency of use and evidence of use. The discussion of each sub-factor is complex enough that they should be discussed in separate paragraphs. Assume, however, that while drafting a memo based on this problem, your first draft evaluated both sub-factors within the same paragraph. As you review each example, consider the comments in the margin that identify the organizational format of each paragraph.

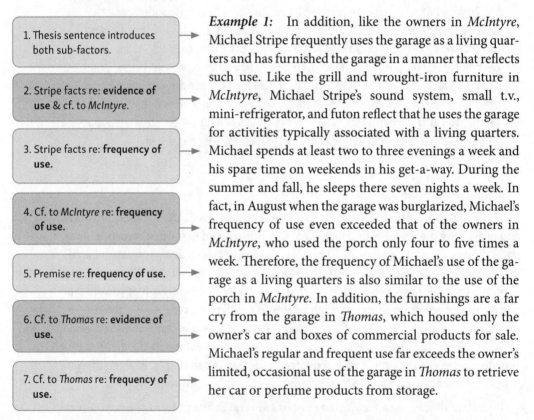

1. Thesis sentence introduces both sub-factors.

2. Stripe facts re: **evidence of use** & cf. to *McIntyre*.

3. Stripe facts re: **frequency of use**.

4. Cf. to *McIntyre* re: **frequency of use**.

5. Premise re: **frequency of use**.

6. Cf. to *Thomas* re: **evidence of use**.

7. Cf. to *Thomas* re: **frequency of use**.

Example 1:   In addition, like the owners in *McIntyre*, Michael Stripe frequently uses the garage as a living quarters and has furnished the garage in a manner that reflects such use. Like the grill and wrought-iron furniture in *McIntyre*, Michael Stripe's sound system, small t.v., mini-refrigerator, and futon reflect that he uses the garage for activities typically associated with a living quarters. Michael spends at least two to three evenings a week and his spare time on weekends in his get-a-way. During the summer and fall, he sleeps there seven nights a week. In fact, in August when the garage was burglarized, Michael's frequency of use even exceeded that of the owners in *McIntyre*, who used the porch only four to five times a week. Therefore, the frequency of Michael's use of the garage as a living quarters is also similar to the use of the porch in *McIntyre*. In addition, the furnishings are a far cry from the garage in *Thomas*, which housed only the owner's car and boxes of commercial products for sale. Michael's regular and frequent use far exceeds the owner's limited, occasional use of the garage in *Thomas* to retrieve her car or perfume products from storage.

In Example 1 above, note how several organizational problems impeded the clarity of the analysis. First, the writer jumped back and forth between an analysis of each sub-factor. Second, the writer jumped from facts describing the "evidence of use" sub-factor to facts describing the "frequency of use" sub-factor, without first inserting a premise that would introduce the new sub-factor. Instead, the writer waited until *after* describing the new facts before stating a premise about those facts. This organizational format can be confusing because it describes facts that do not have a context, thereby forcing the reader to wonder why such facts are important.

Compare the previous example to the following revised version:

Example 2: In addition, like the owners in *McIntyre*, Michael Stripe frequently uses the garage as a living quarters and has furnished the garage in a manner that reflects such use. Like the grill and wrought-iron furniture in *McIntyre*, Michael Stripe's sound system, small t.v., mini-refrigerator, and futon reflect that he uses the garage for activities typically associated with a living quarters. These furnishings are a far cry from the garage in *Thomas*, which housed only the owner's car and boxes of commercial products for sale. In addition, the frequency of Michael's use of the garage as a living quarters even exceeded that of the owners in *McIntyre*. In *McIntyre*, the owners used the porch only four to five times a week, while Michael sleeps in his getaway seven nights a week during the summer and fall. Moreover, he spends at least two to three evenings a week and his spare time on weekends in his getaway. Michael's regular and frequent use far exceeds the owner's limited, occasional use of the garage in *Thomas* to retrieve her car or perfume products from storage.

> 1. Thesis sentence introduces both sub-factors.

> 2. Stripe facts re: **evidence of use** & cf. to both *McIntyre* and *Thomas*.

> 3. Premise re: **frequency of use**.

> 4. Cf. to both *McIntyre* and *Thomas* re: **frequency of use**.

In Example 2 above, the writer clarified the analysis by introducing each sub-factor with a premise and then fully evaluating that sub-factor before moving on to a new idea. Thus, the facts relating to the "evidence of use" factor were fully discussed and analogized to the precedent cases before the writer introduced the premise and facts relating to the "frequency of use" factor.

Exercise 16-3: Editing a Rule Application Paragraph

Assume that you are reviewing and editing the first draft of an office memorandum that will ultimately become Sample Memo D in Appendix A. Review the Editing Checklist at the end of this chapter and list the problems you see in the first draft of this rule application paragraph that addresses the "hidden danger" factor.

1st Draft: The Hurts' dock is like the raft and dock in *Ansin*. The *Ansin* raft and dock were floating, and the court held that it was a hidden danger. Here, the Hurts' dock was solid, but it was deteriorating and is therefore like the floating dock in *Ansin*. The child in *Ansin* did not know the dock was unsafe. Mikey also did not know the dock was unsafe.

Identify each change in the revised paragraph below. For each change, describe the purpose the change serves and why the revised or added language is more effective than the language in the first draft.

Revised Paragraph: Like the dock and raft in *Ansin*, the Hurts' dock was a hidden danger, or trap. In fact, the deceptive safety of the Hurts' dock made it inherently more hidden, and therefore more dangerous, to a child trespasser than the raft in *Ansin*. A wooden, anchored dock has a seemingly solid foundation. Children simply do not expect that the "ground" might collapse out from under them. It is precisely because of its illusion of safety that Mikey stayed on the dock. Mikey knew that he did not swim well and deliberately stayed out of the water on a seemingly solid foundation. To a child who does not swim well, the dock promised a safety that it did not deliver. In contrast, a child is more likely to foresee the danger that one might fall from a raft that floats on the water, particularly the "visibly tipsy raft" in *Ansin*. Unlike Mikey, the child in *Ansin* deliberately risked the danger of the water by jumping from a floating dock onto a floating raft. In short, the Hurts' dock was even more dangerous than the floating raft in *Ansin* because its danger was more hidden.

CHAPTER IN REVIEW

Editing Checklist:

As you review the Discussion section of your memo, consider the following:

A. **OVERVIEW PARAGRAPH** → In your overview paragraph, did you:

1. State your *ultimate conclusion* to the broad question?
2. Describe the separate *elements* of the original rule of law?
3. Identify any elements that do not present legal issues under the client's unique factual situation (i.e., *non-issues*)?

    4. Identify the elements that merit further discussion (i.e., *issues*)? (Chapter 14—*Drafting Overview Paragraphs*)

B. **THESIS PARAGRAPH** → In your thesis paragraph, did you:

    1. Describe the *original rule of law* and identify the element that presents an *issue* (if your memo did not merit a separate overview paragraph)?

    2. *State your legal issue conclusion* as to how the law affects the client's factual situation for the issue under discussion?

    3. Identify any *factors or useful definitions* that guide courts as they evaluate and apply the element of the rule of law to factual situations?

    4. Synthesize the separate rule statements you formulated for each individual case into a *general rule statement(s)* that accurately reflects the cases as a group?

    5. *Briefly apply* the standard/factors to the client's factual situation, showing how they support the legal issue conclusion? (Chapter 14—*Drafting Thesis Paragraphs*)

C. **RULE EXPLANATION** → For each case that you emphasize as a primary case, did you:

    1. Begin with a *thesis sentence* that describes the rule of law that expresses the court's holding (i.e., your "rule statement")? Does your rule statement:

      a. Identify the legal standard (often illustrated by key factors) that guided the court in its decision, and

      b. Identify how the court answered the legal question before it?

    2. Include all of the *facts* of the case that are relevant to the court's holding?

    3. State the court's *holding* (its answer to the specific legal question before it)?

    4. Describe the court's *rationale* that justifies its holding? When describing the rationale, did you:

      a. Incorporate the key factors the court weighed in justifying its holding?

      b. Link the key factors to a brief summary of the key facts that illustrate why each factor was important to the court? (Chapter 11—*Drafting the Analysis*)

D. **RULE APPLICATION** → When applying the case(s) to the client's facts, did you:

    1. Use the *factors* as organizational tools to lead each paragraph (with one factor, or several minor interrelated factors, per paragraph)?

- Alternatively, if a court relied on a concrete, narrow definition (legal standard) in lieu of a factor, that definition would serve as an organizational tool.

2. Format your analysis to begin with the factor or legal standard that should logically be discussed first, or, if there is no logical starting place, the factor or standard that is most important?

3. For each paragraph of rule application, did you:

   a. Begin the paragraph with a *thesis sentence* that (i) identifies the factor the paragraph will be discussing; and (ii) your factual premise, or conclusion, about how the client's facts illustrate the factor in a legally significant way?

   b. *Elaborate fully* on the client's facts, explaining why the facts prove why the premise, or conclusion, set out in the first sentence of the paragraph is sound?

   c. Make direct, concrete *comparisons* to the precedent case's facts?

   d. Explain why the client facts and *comparisons* are *legally significant*—i.e., how they support the conclusion in the first sentence?

   e. Restrict the ideas in the paragraph only to those factual details that prove why the conclusion in the first sentence is sound?

4. Clearly state and evaluate the reasonable *opposing arguments* that can be made?

   - Each opposing argument should directly follow a favorable analysis of the same idea, or factor.

5. At the end of your rule application analysis, clearly communicate your *legal issue and ultimate conclusions*?

   a. Your legal issue conclusion at the end of your Discussion should be consistent with the legal issue conclusion stated in the thesis paragraph.

   b. Your ultimate conclusion at the end of your Discussion should be consistent with the ultimate conclusion stated in the overview paragraph.

   c. Depending on the simplicity or complexity of the issues, you may or may not include a separate heading labeled "CONCLUSION." (Chapter 11—*Drafting the Analysis*)

REVISING & FINALIZING THE MEMO
Sentence Structure & Word Choice

I. SENTENCE STRUCTURE

At this stage in the drafting process, when you are fairly confident that the content and format of your analysis will not change, you are now in a position to consider how you might modify the structure of each sentence and clarify your word choices so that they more clearly express your ideas. Effective legal writing is not legalese or long, contorted sentences that would take a devoted and willing senior attorney hours to decipher. Most senior attorneys, clients, and judges do not have the time or inclination to puzzle over convoluted sentences to discern their meaning. Instead, your goal is to take complex legal issues and communicate them in a manner that appears to be simple and straightforward.

A. Use "Micro" Roadmaps Within Sentences to Transition Reader

As is true on the larger scale, readers understand information more easily if each sentence shows its link to old information before it conveys new information. In order to achieve this, each sentence begins with old information and ends with new information. You might picture each sentence in a paragraph as follows: (Old → New) → (Old → New) → (Old → New). Note: A reader's knowledge base is "old" information.

1. Writing Tips
a. Repeat Part of the Prior Sentence's Content

At or near the beginning of a sentence, repeat part of the preceding sentence's content, using the same words or easily recognizable synonyms. Consider how the following example excerpted from Sample Memo A in Appendix A transitions the reader from "old" to "new" information. To help you identify the transitions, the *old information is italicized* and the <u>repetition of that information is underlined</u>.

> Moreover, the fact that the porch in *McIntyre* was separated from the utility room of the owners' home by a *door with "three locks"* lends less significance to the attached/detached distinction. <u>The presence of three locks</u> implies that the porch area was not an open part of the main residence, but was instead physically kept separate from the main residence.

b. Use Transitional Words and Phrases

At or near the beginning of a sentence, use a word or phrase of transition that shows the sentence's logical connection to the previous paragraph or sentence—does it qualify it? add to it? rephrase its point? Transitional expressions are a wonderful means of showing the logical relationship between "old" and "new" information. They can enhance the clarity of any idea, including ideas expressed in a thesis or transition sentence. However, use care when selecting a transitional expression. Use of an inappropriate transition can mislead and confuse the reader, making it more difficult for the reader to follow the train of analysis.

2. Examples of Transitional Expressions[1]

(1)   To add a new point:

and	further
also	furthermore
in addition	moreover
in fact	next
finally	second, third, etc.

(2)   To indicate a difference:

alternatively	in contrast
but	on the other hand
contrary to	rather than
conversely	to the contrary
however	

---

1. Transitional expressions adapted in part from Laurel C. Oates, et al., *The Legal Writing Handbook* (Aspen L. & Bus. 1993); Helen S. Shapo, et al., *Writing and Analysis in the Law* 147–48 (3d ed. Found. Press 1995).

(3)   To indicate a similarity:

also	likewise
as	similarly
like	

(4)   To illustrate or explain an idea:

after all	in other words
as an example	simply put
for example	specifically
for instance	to illustrate
in fact	under such circumstances
in particular	

(5)   To conclude:

accordingly	in summary
as a result	therefore
consequently	thus
in conclusion	

In the following example excerpted from Sample Memo A in Appendix A, transitional words and phrases are used throughout the paragraph, beginning with the thesis sentence and continuing throughout the discussion. To help you identify the transitions, the transitional words are <u>underlined</u>.

<u>Finally</u>, like the use of the porch in *McIntyre*, the frequency of Michael's use of the garage <u>also</u> reflects the garage's use as a living quarters. Michael spends at least two to three evenings a week and his spare time on weekends in his getaway. <u>Moreover</u>, during the summer and fall, he sleeps there seven nights a week. Michael's regular and frequent use far exceeds the owner's limited, occasional use of the garage in *Thomas* to retrieve her car or perfume products from storage. <u>In fact</u>, in August when the garage was burglarized, Michael's frequency of use exceeded even that of the owners in *McIntyre*, who used the porch only four to five times a week.

Exercise 17-1: Using Internal Roadmaps

Assume that you represent a client who was injured in a softball game by a player on the opposing team. The members of the opposing team are all employed by Ajax Cleaning & Plumbing ("Ajax"). You are evaluating whether you can sue the employer, Ajax, under a theory of "respondeat superior." Under that theory, an employer may be liable for an employee's behavior if the particular activity was "within the scope" of the employee's employment. Assume that you have drafted the following rule explanation paragraph:

> Where an employer specifically authorizes the conduct in which the employee is engaged, the employee is acting within the scope of his employment. In *Riviello v. Waldron*, the owner of a restaurant specifically authorized his chef to visit with the patrons in the dining room of the restaurant and to perform knife tricks while doing so. 391 N.E.2d 1278, 1280 (N.Y. 1979). On one occasion, the chef mishandled a knife while tossing it in the air, and a restaurant patron was injured when the knife struck her in the eye. *Id.* Under these facts, the Court held that the chef was acting within the scope of his employment while tossing the knife. *Id.* The Court reasoned that the owner of the restaurant had specifically authorized and approved of the conduct that resulted in the patron's injury. The Court noted that the employer hired the chef based on the chef's ability to perform the knife tricks and frequently asked the chef to go "perform" in the dining room among the patrons. *Id.*"

In the following rule application paragraph, add transitions that clearly link old information to new information. Consider: (1) repeating key language within the beginning of a new sentence to link the new information in that sentence to old information; and (2) adding transitional words and phrases to link new information to old information.

> Ajax specifically authorized Mike Jones to play softball as part of his job duties. Ajax hired Mr. Jones as a salesperson. Ajax selected Mr. Jones over other qualified applicants, in part, because of his reputation as a softball player. Ajax prides itself on winning the Division I title every year. Its star catcher resigned last year. Ajax actively sought to hire someone who would be a strong replacement. Ajax provides its team members with shirts that bear the Ajax logo. It allows its employees to leave work early when necessary in order to compete in softball games that require the team to travel.

B. Use the Active Voice

When reading, a reader's eyes automatically search for "who did what to whom." Sentences written in the active voice easily and clearly satisfy the reader's natural curiosity because they describe an actor (the subject) → acting upon → the object. In other words, the sentence structure is as follows: subject → acts upon → an object.

In contrast, the passive voice forces the reader to work harder to discover "who did what to whom." In a passive voice sentence, the writer states: this object → was acted upon → by this actor. This structural format satisfies the writer's curiosity in reverse order, forcing the reader to "think backwards." The reader has to wait until the end of the sentence to find the actor, or subject, and then has to review the sentence again to determine the action in which the actor engaged. This problem becomes even more pronounced when the writer hides the actor entirely. This writing style problem, called the "truncated" passive voice, requires the reader to pause and consider the identity of the missing subject. In addition to forcing the reader to think harder, passive voice sentences usually require more words to make the same point. Therefore, as a general rule, write in the active voice.

1. Example of Passive Voice that Hides the Actor

Compare the clarity of the following two sentences:

Original:	Two to three evenings a week and free time on weekends are spent in the getaway writing, listening to music, and watching television.	Who is writing, listening, & watching t.v.?
Revised:	Michael spends two to three evenings a week and his free time on weekends in the getaway writing, listening to music, and watching television.	

2. Example of How Passive Voice Requires More Words

Compare the clarity and wordiness of the following very simple sentence:

Original:	A futon in a loft area of the garage is used by Michael to sleep. [15 words]	Object → Verb → Subject
Revised:	Michael sleeps in the garage on a futon in a loft area. [12 words]	Subject → Verb → Object

3. Two Exceptions: When Passive Voice Is Preferable to Active Voice

Very rarely is writing in the passive voice preferable to writing in the active voice, but there are two situations in which a legal author would intentionally choose the passive voice. First, the author may not know the identity of the actor. In that situation, writing in the passive voice is the author's only option. Second, the author may have a strategic reason for de-emphasizing the actor's role in the action. For example, imagine you are the attorney for a defendant in a civil battery matter, and you are drafting a brief to the court, asking for a dismissal of the case. You dispute that your client touched the plaintiff in a harmful or offensive way, but the plaintiff testified in a deposition that your client, Mark, hit her with his fist during an argument. Consider these two options for how you may word this fact within your factual section:

> **Active:**   The plaintiff testified that Mark hit her with his fist during the argument.
>
> **Passive:**   The plaintiff claimed in deposition testimony that she was struck in the face during an argument.

It is clear in this circumstance that writing in the passive voice is the strategically better choice. Positioning the action as the subject and removing the actor's identity better serves the client in this situation.

◎ EDITING TIP

Ask: Who is the actor in this sentence? In other words, "who/what did this?" Once you identify "who/what did this," check to see whether the actor is also the subject of the sentence. If the actor is also the subject of the sentence, the sentence is "active," with the actor appearing before the verb. In contrast, if the actor is not the subject of the sentence, the sentence is passive, with the verb "acting upon" the actor. Only utilize the passive option if the actor's identity is truly unknown, or if de-emphasizing the actor's identity is strategically sound.

C. Keep Sentences Relatively Short

Because readers automatically search for "who did what to whom" when reading a sentence, they generally expect to find a single actor, verb, and object within a single sentence. When several ideas are combined within a single sentence, the reader's eye will often skim over the second and third ideas and miss their significance entirely. Therefore, in legal writing, where every expressed idea is important to the writer's understanding of the legal analysis, generally restrict each sentence to one main idea. However, incorporating several *interrelated* ideas within a single sentence can be effective. As a general rule of thumb, most sentences should have approximately twenty-five (25) words. Sentences that run significantly longer than that risk confusing the reader. Sentences that run significantly less than twenty-five words may appear less fluid and choppy. Use the following techniques to help transform run-on sentences into sentences of a more manageable length.

1. Make Dependent Clauses "Independent"

Dependent clauses are clauses that do not stand on their own because they are introduced with words that depend on another clause to complete their thought (*e.g.*, although, even though). Run-on sentences often contain one or more dependent clauses that either begin the sentence, or interrupt the sentence in the middle somewhere. One way of simplifying the sentence is to remove the dependent clause from the run-on sentence and create two sentences from the original sentence.

To clarify the link between the two newly created sentences, use a transitional word to introduce the second sentence. The transitional word should incorporate the *same transitional idea* as the word that introduced the original dependent clause. In the following example, the transitional word "however" in the second illustration reflects the same transitional idea as the word "although" in the original sentence.

Original:	Although a structure's proximity to the main residence is a relevant factor, a structure that is not physically connected to the primary residence may still constitute a living quarters because the owner's use of the structure is a more important factor. **[41 words]**
Revised:	A structure's proximity to the main residence is a relevant factor. **[11 words]** However, a structure that is not physically connected to the primary residence may still constitute a living quarters because the owner's use of the structure is a more important factor. **[30 words]**

◎ EDITING TIP

When reviewing an overly lengthy sentence, check for dependent clauses that you might remove and incorporate into a separate sentence. To find dependent clauses, look for the following words that often introduce dependent clauses:

Although	Despite	Rather than	Unless
Because	Even if	Since	While
Before	Even though	Though	

2. Eliminate Superfluous Statements

Superfluous statements purport to alert the reader of why a sentence is important without really adding any new meaning to the sentence itself. They are often called "throat-clearing" statements. They can introduce a sentence (*"You should note that…"*), or can appear in the middle of a sentence following a dependent clause ("Although the court held x, y, z, *it is important to point out that…"*). Because such superfluous statements unnecessarily clutter the purpose of the sentence, check your writing for such phrases and then remove them as you edit your work.

Original:	It is important to note that the proximity of the structure to the main residence is also relevant.
Revised:	The proximity of the structure to the main residence is also relevant.

The following example illustrates a slightly less obvious form of the superfluous statement.

Original:	In *People v. McIntyre*, the court addressed the dwelling issue, holding that an attached porch was a living quarters under the Statute.
Revised:	In *People v. McIntyre*, the court held that an attached porch was a living quarters under the Statute.

In the above example, the fact that the *McIntyre* court addressed the dwelling issue is already obvious because the entire memo discusses that issue. Thus, the underlined phrase in the original example is superfluous.

◎ **EDITING TIP**

The following phrases are typical examples of "throat-clearing":

It is interesting to note that…	I should emphasize that…
Another important point that…	Please note that…
Here it should be pointed out that…	It is significant that…

D. Keep the Actor, Verb, and Object Together

Recall that readers automatically seek to find the subject, verb, and object in each sentence (*e.g.*, who did what to whom?). Dependent clauses can confuse a reader when they separate the subject from the verb or the verb from the object. By separating key components of the sentence, they interrupt the reader's natural focus on "who did what to whom." To eliminate the problem of dependent clauses that break up the actor, verb, object sequence, either move the dependent clause to the beginning or end of the sentence, or break the sentence into two sentences.

1. Example of Moving the Dependent Clause

Original: Moreover, the <u>court</u>, by limiting the holding to the specific facts before it, <u>left open</u> the possibility that a garage could, given the appropriate use, constitute a living quarters under the Statute.

Revised: Moreover, by limiting the holding to the specific facts before it, the <u>court left open</u> the possibility that a garage could, given the appropriate use, constitute a living quarters under the Statute.

2. Example of Breaking the Sentence into Two Sentences

Original: Moreover, the <u>court</u>, by limiting the holding to the specific facts before it, <u>left open</u> the possibility that a garage could, given the appropriate use, constitute a living quarters under the Statute.

Revised: Moreover, the <u>court limited</u> the holding to the specific facts before it. Thus, <u>the court left</u> open the possibility that a garage could, given the appropriate use, constitute a living quarters under the Statute.

E. Use Parallel Structure

When you express two or more ideas of a similar nature, express them in parallel form. For example, if the first verb in a sequence ends with the letters "ing," the remaining verbs in the sentence that continue the sequential description should also end with the letters "ing."

> **Original:**   He learned <u>to swim</u>, <u>to play</u> tennis, and horseback <u>riding</u>.
>
> **Revised:**   He learned <u>to swim</u>, <u>to play</u> tennis, and <u>to ride</u> horses.

> **Original:**   At camp, they enjoyed such activities as <u>swimming</u> and horseback <u>riding</u> and <u>played</u> tennis.
>
> **Revised:**   At camp, they enjoyed such activities as <u>swimming</u>, horseback <u>riding</u>, and <u>playing</u> tennis.

II. CLARITY OF WORD CHOICE

A. Substitute Simple Words for Longer Words

Many law students have the mistaken impression that, as an attorney, they should use sophisticated, formalistic language. To the contrary, effective attorneys take complex ideas and communicate them in simple, concrete, clear language. In the following illustration, notice how much easier it is to grasp the purpose of the sentence in the revised example:

> **Original:**   Defendant may <u>set forth the proposition that</u>, despite the <u>usage</u> of the garage by Michael as a getaway, the <u>edifice's</u> physical detachment from the Stripes' <u>principal place of habitation</u> prevents it from being a living quarters.
>
> **Revised:**   Defendant may <u>argue</u> that, despite Michael's <u>use</u> of the garage as a getaway, the <u>garage's</u> physical detachment from the Stripes' <u>home</u> prevents it from being a living quarters.

B. Use Active Verbs, Not Nominalizations

As readers subconsciously search for "who did what to whom," they automatically think in terms of short, concrete active verbs. By writing in the active voice and using short active verbs that reflect exactly "who did what to whom," you will easily satisfy the reader's natural curiosity. To emphasize people and what they do, place the action in the sentence in the verb itself. As you review your writing for clarity, check to see whether you have inadvertently converted verbs into nouns. A verb that has been converted into a noun is called a "nominalization." Nominalizations obscure the action in a sentence—the action verb becomes a noun, while the remaining verb within the sentence often becomes a detached abstraction.

Example of How Nominalizations Obscure Clarity

Original: Michael <u>engages in sleeping activities</u> on a futon in a loft area of the garage.

Revised: Michael <u>sleeps</u> on a futon in a loft area of the garage.

In the above example, the action verb "sleeps" becomes the noun "sleeping" in the original sentence. To replace the verb "sleeps," the writer necessarily has to use another verb. The replacement verb, "engages," is a detached abstraction that does not convey the action in the sentence.

◎ EDITING TIP

When reviewing your writing, ask yourself what the actor in the sentence is really doing.[2] In the above example, is Michael Stripe "sleeping," or is he "engaging"? As you consider whether you have inadvertently converted a verb into a noun, watch for words with the following endings:

tion	(e.g., *violation* vs *violate*)
sion	(e.g., *decision* vs *decide*)
ence	(e.g., *deterrence* vs *deter*)
ance	(e.g., *assistance* vs *assist*)
edge	(e.g., *knowledge* vs *know*)
ment	(e.g., *statement* vs *state*)

---

2. Laurel C. Oates, Anne Enquist & Kelly Kunsch, *The Legal Writing Handbook: Analysis, Research, and Writing* 644 (2d ed., Aspen L. & Bus. 1998).

C. Use Concrete, Specific Words Rather Than Vague, Abstract Language

Perhaps more so than in any other form of written communication, legal analysis must be communicated in specific language that clearly conveys the attorney's thinking. First, legal analysis often requires the reader to follow and absorb complex ideas that may have taken the drafting attorney literally days or weeks to evaluate and analyze. Using concrete, specific words that have a definite meaning helps the reader readily absorb the complex analysis. Second, many words have specific legal significance. Thus, your choice of words can have tremendous ramifications. Loose, vague language could potentially propel your client into a lawsuit or cost the client significant sums of money.

First drafts often contain vague language, in part because ideas are often not fully crystallized until the drafting process itself reveals gaps in the writer's understanding. In short, vague language often reflects thinking that has not been fully developed. Therefore, as you review your early drafts, it is very important to ask yourself probing questions: "What exactly do I mean by this statement?" "What exactly is the purpose of this paragraph?" You may even find it helpful to verbalize your questions. The goal is to find areas in your analysis that are not fully developed and clarify the written expression of your thinking.

In the following example, the vague language in the original illustration obscures the clarity of the writer's analysis. The revisions simply clarify the writer's thinking. Upon reviewing the first draft, the writer would have prompted the revision by asking: "What exact point do I want to make about the *Thomas* case? What exact point about the *Thomas* court's discussion of the garage am I trying to make here?"

> **Original:**   In *Thomas*, the court <u>discussed the garage</u>.
>
> **Revised:**   In *Thomas*, the court <u>minimized the importance of the garage's physical attachment to the main residence</u>.

D. Use the Proper Tense

It is important to use the proper tense when evaluating the law so that the reader can properly assess the sequence of events and the present status of factual events and the law. The present tense refers to facts or rules of law that exist as of the moment you are drafting a memo. The past tense refers to facts and events that are in the past—they happened before you began drafting the memo.

1. Client's Factual Situation

When discussing a client's factual situation, use the past tense to refer to events that have already occurred, and use the present tense to refer to conditions that presently exist. Thus, in the following example, because the event that occurred on August 20 is in the past, the drafting attorney uses the past tense to refer to that event. In contrast, because the Stripes' garage still exists today, the description of the garage is in the present tense.

> On August 10, 20XX, Defendant, Gerry Arnold, <u>forcibly entered</u> Carl and Rita Stripes' two-car detached garage and <u>removed</u> personal property belonging to them. The garage <u>is</u> located approximately thirty feet behind the Stripes' home.

2. Discussion of Precedent Case

The actual events that occurred and were reported in a case all occurred in the past. Therefore, use the past tense to describe the factual events of a case. Because the court's holding and reasoning also occurred in the past, refer to the court's holding and rationale in the past tense, but use present tense when providing rule language within the rationale section. As demonstrated in an example below, this may mean you will need to switch back and forth between past and present tense when providing the court's rationale. Further, because your rule statement (thesis) illustrates a rule of law that is valid at the present time, use the present tense when crafting rule statements.

- Thesis sentence describing *Rule Statement*: Present Tense
- *Case Facts*: Past Tense
- *Holding*: Past Tense
- *Rationale*: Past Tense for the court's actions and decisions, and its discussion of case facts; Present tense for rule language

a. Description of Actual Case "Events"—Past Tense

> In *McIntyre*, the owners <u>used</u> the porch for such activities as "sitting, eating, and cooking."… The court <u>held</u> that the attached porch was part of the living quarters of the home. The court <u>reasoned</u> that the owners used the porch as part of their living quarters by engaging in such activities as "sitting, eating, and cooking…."

b. Description of Rule Statement—Present Tense

> An enclosed, attached porch frequently used as part of a home's living quarters <u>is</u> a dwelling under the residential burglary statute.

c. Description of Rationale—A Combination of Past and Present Tense

Explanatory reasoning: The court <u>reasoned</u> that "an attached garage <u>is</u> not necessarily a 'dwelling' within the meaning of the residential burglary statute."

Application Reasoning: The court <u>held</u> that the attached garage, "at least in this instance," <u>was</u> not a dwelling because it <u>was</u> not used as a "living quarters."

E. Strike the Appropriate Tone of Formality

Because legal analysis concerns matters that are important and serious to the client, your writing should avoid the informality of colloquialisms, or jargon. Moreover, unless the client is a minor, avoid referring to an individual client by first name, instead respectfully referring to the client by last name. Finally, avoid use of the first person when drafting a legal document. As with colloquialisms and first names, writing in the first person implies a level of informality that is not appropriate in most legal writing.

1. Eliminate Colloquialisms and Jargon

Original: During the summer and fall when his <u>folks</u> are in town, Mike <u>crashes</u> on a futon in the loft.

Revised: During the summer and fall when his <u>parents</u> are in town, Michael Stripe <u>sleeps</u> on a futon in the loft area of the garage.

2. Refer to Adults by Last Names

Original: <u>Carl</u> and <u>Rita's</u> garage is located thirty feet behind their home.

Revised: The Stripes' garage is located thirty feet behind their home.

Or revised: Mr. and Mrs. Stripes' garage...

3. Refer to Children by First Names

Original: Mr. Stripes, the client's 6-year-old child, was home when the burglary occurred.

Revised: Randy, the client's 6-year-old child, was home when the burglary occurred.

4. Avoid Using the First Person

Original: In <u>my opinion, we</u> can successfully prosecute Mr. Arnold under the Residential Burglary Statute.

Revised: <u>The State</u> can successfully prosecute Mr. Arnold under the Residential Burglary Statute.

In the above example, the first person reference is also an example of "throat-clearing." Unless otherwise indicated, readers presume that the opinions expressed in a memo are the writer's opinion.

F. Avoid Sexist Language

Sexist language has the potential to offend a reviewing attorney, client, or adjudicator. Of course, if you are referring to a specific person who happens to be male, then you would refer to that person by the pronoun "he." For example, if you are referring to a specific defendant in a case who happens to be a male, use a pronoun that reflects his male gender. If, however, you are referring to people in general rather than to a specific person, avoid using language that presumes the hypothetical person is a male. Because the English language has not evolved to the point where commonly used gender-neutral phrases have replaced sexist phrases, avoiding sexist language skillfully and artfully takes some practice. The following examples illustrate different ways you can avoid using sexist language.

1. Avoid the Generic Use of the Pronoun "He"

The most common way in which sexist language appears in the English language is through variations of the pronoun "he." Instead, try any of the following alternatives: (1) use the plural form rather than the singular form; (2) substitute other pronouns for the pronoun "he"; (3) omit pronouns altogether by rewriting the sentence to make the pronoun unnecessary; (4) substitute articles for the pronoun "he"; (5) repeat the original noun rather than refer to the pronoun "he"; or (6) if all else fails, refer generically to each gender—"he or she."[3]

a. Use the Plural Form

When converting a sentence from the singular to the plural form, check to make sure that you have also made the subject of the sentence plural. The subject, pronoun, and verb must all reflect the same form.

> **Original:** Skilled writers know that a reader understands information best when <u>he is</u> presented with context before details.
>
> **Revised:** Skilled writers know that <u>readers</u> understand information best when <u>they are</u> presented with context before details.
>
> **Not:** Skilled writers know that a <u>reader</u> understands information best when <u>they are</u> presented with context before details.

b. Substitute Another Pronoun

> **Original:** <u>He</u> should carefully evaluate every aspect of the legal problem in an office memorandum.
>
> **Revised:** <u>One</u> should carefully evaluate every aspect of the legal problem in an office memorandum.

c. Omit Pronouns Altogether

If the pronoun itself is not important, you can avoid sexist language by omitting the pronoun altogether.

> **Original:** A skilled writer knows that a reader understands information best <u>when he is presented</u> with context before details.
>
> **Revised:** A skilled writer knows that a reader understands information best <u>when presented</u> with context before details.

---

3. Ideas adapted from Linda H. Edwards, *Legal Writing: Process, Analysis and Organization* 223–24 (Aspen L. & Bus. 1996); Helene S. Shapo, *Writing and Analysis in the Law* 173 (3d ed., Foundation Press 1993) (adapting recommendations from the "Guidelines for the Nonsexist Use of Language" written for the American Philosophical Association by Virginia L. Warren, published in 59 Proceedings and Addresses of American Philosophical Association, No. 3 (Feb. 1988)).

d. Substitute Articles or Nouns for the Pronoun

> **Original:** In an office memo, the writer should make sure that <u>he</u> carefully evaluates every aspect of the legal problem.
>
> **Revised:** <u>An office memo</u> should carefully evaluate every aspect of the legal problem.

e. Repeat the Original Name

> **Original:** When preparing to draft an office memorandum, an attorney has two primary decisions to make. First, <u>he</u> must consider the actual substantive content of the memo.
>
> **Revised:** When preparing to draft an office memorandum, an attorney has two primary decisions to make. First, <u>the attorney</u> must consider the actual substantive content of the memo.

f. Refer Generically to Each Gender

> **Original:** The Question Presented and Short Answer provide the reviewing attorney with a quick overview of the legal problem. The Discussion section provides the reviewing attorney with a more thorough analysis of the law when <u>he</u> has more time to consider a detailed analysis of the problem.
>
> **Revised:** The Question Presented and Short Answer provide the reviewing attorney with a quick overview of the legal problem. The Discussion section provides the reviewing attorney with a more thorough analysis of the law when <u>he or she</u> has more time to consider a detailed analysis of the problem.

2. Avoid Generic Use of Gender-Specific Nouns

Another common example of how the English language embraces sexist phrases is through the use of gender-specific nouns (*e.g.*, "chairman"). To avoid this, whenever possible, replace the gender-specific noun ("man") with a gender-neutral term ("person"). The following are some common examples of gender-specific nouns and their gender-neutral counterparts.

Examples:

Brother/sister	→	Sibling
Chairman	→	Chair or Chairperson
Fireman	→	Firefighter
Husband/wife	→	Spouse
Maid	→	Housekeeper
Mailman	→	Mail Carrier
Man, woman	→	Person
Newsman	→	News reporter
Policeman	→	Police Officer
Stewardess	→	Flight attendant

III. EFFECTIVE USE OF QUOTATIONS

Because it is critical to convey the law accurately, the use of quotations is important in legal writing. Nevertheless, novice legal writers often rely too heavily on case quotations. A blind reliance on quotations can create several problems. First, many statutes and court decisions are not models of clarity. Although judges may admonish lawyers to write clearly, many judges do not follow their own advice. Thus, quoting a poorly written sentence from a case would not serve your goal of clear communication. Second, by relying heavily on quotations, you may be tempted to neglect your own careful pre-drafting synthesis of the relevant cases. Third, in your written legal analysis, you will refer to rules of law and factors by specific language; that specific language will assume legal significance to the reader. If a court has not used that identical language when referring to a rule of law or factor, the reader may not see the link between the legally significant information that appears elsewhere in your analysis and the quoted language. Finally, every writer has a unique style. It can be disconcerting to a reader to jump frequently from your style to the various writing styles of different judges or legislation. Therefore, your goal is to find the proper balance between a blind reliance on quotations and a failure to use quotations at all.

When quoting, it is critically important that you provide the quoted words accurately. When a legal reader sees quotation marks around words from a legal authority, the reader rightly presumes that the language within that quote is exactly as it appears within the source. If the author alters the quote in any way, such alterations must be clearly displayed. For example, an author may choose to remove words from a quote. To showcase this change, the author would replace the omitted words with an ellipsis (…). If the author chooses instead to alter a word within a quote, the author would demonstrate this change by placing brackets around the altered word. Review the following examples of properly altered quotes.

Original:

"A person commits residential burglary when he or she knowingly and without authority enters or knowingly and without authority remains within the dwelling place of another, or any part thereof, with the intent to commit therein a felony or theft." 510 Ill. Comp. Stat. §5/16 (2004).

Altered with Language Omitted:

"A person commits residential burglary when he or she knowingly and without authority enters... the dwelling place of another, or any part thereof, with the intent to commit therein a felony or theft." 510 Ill. Comp. Stat. §5/16 (2004).

Original:

"A person commits residential burglary when he or she knowingly and without authority enters or knowingly and without authority remains within the dwelling place of another, or any part thereof, with the intent to commit therein a felony or theft." 510 Ill. Comp. Stat. §5/16 (2004).

Altered with Language Changed:

"A [defendant] commits residential burglary when [the defendant] knowingly and without authority enters or knowingly and without authority remains within the dwelling place of another, or any part thereof, with the intent to commit therein a felony or theft." 510 Ill. Comp. Stat. §5/16 (2004).

In addition, it can be challenging to determine when quotation marks are necessary to give proper attribution to the author of a source. A common rule of thumb in legal writing is to quote language when 7 or more words are taken directly from a source. However, you may choose to use quotation marks on critically important language, even if the number of words taken are fewer than 7, because you wish to clearly demonstrate that these precise words were taken word-for-word from the source.

A. Quotations from Cases

Effective lawyers use case quotations sparingly and with purpose, quoting only vitally important components of a relevant case whose meaning might otherwise be lost if paraphrased. Because the court's rationale is critically important to an understanding of why the court held as it did, it is often effective to quote critical parts of a court's reasoning. However, restrict your quotes to language that is clearly written and otherwise important. If the language is less than a model of clarity, either paraphrase the court's rationale or quote only a critical word or phrase—it is not necessary to quote an entire sentence. You should quote an entire paragraph only in very limited circumstances when the court has so clearly and beautifully articulated a critical point that any attempt to paraphrase would not capture the meaning of the quoted language. Whether quoting language or paraphrasing ideas, you must *always* cite to the source of your quotation.

1. Example of Effective Case Quotations

In the following example, the writer quotes only selected critically important phrases from the court's holding and reasoning, and then comments on the significance of the quoted language.

> The court held that the attached garage, "at least in this instance," was not a living quarters. *Id.* The court reasoned that "an attached garage is *not necessarily* a 'dwelling' within the meaning of the residential burglary statute." *Id.* (emphasis added). By that statement, the court implied that the owner's use of the structure is more important than its proximity to the main residence.

2. Example of Ineffective Case Quotations

In the following example, note how the writer has quoted the court's observations about the facts of the case, as well as the entire holding and stated rationale. This approach of "throwing in the kitchen sink" is not effective. Rarely does the manner in which the court states the facts merit a direct quote (unless the court has quoted a witness whose testimony the writer would like to emphasize). Moreover, by quoting the court's holding and reasoning in its entirety, the significance of the truly critical language is all but lost (i.e., "these activities make the porch part of the living quarters of the house").

> In *McIntyre*, the court was "satisfied this porch was a part of the Houser's living quarters." 578 N.E.2d at 315. In *McIntyre*, the owners used an attached porch "in the summer for most of their meals, and in the winter cooked on the porch four or five times per week." *Id.* "The Housers furnished the porch with a metal table, chairs, a wrought iron love seat, a small table, and a large gas grill." *Id.* The court held that, "in our view, the porch here is a part of the house. It is attached, enclosed, and used for sitting, eating, and cooking. These activities make the porch part of the living quarters of the house. This conclusion is not inconsistent with *Thomas*." *Id.*

B. Quotations from Statutes

When discussing statutory issues, you should quote the critical language from the statute, because it is the source of law under evaluation. It is important for the reader to see the statute's precise language, because the language chosen, and how courts have interpreted that specific language, is often central to a case's outcome. However, if a statute is poorly written and difficult to follow, you should instead paraphrase the non-critical language of the statute, and quote only key statutory words or phrases. Alternatively, you might quote most of the statutory language but insert transitional words between the elements to make the language more readable. When there are a number of different statutory elements, you can also use numbers as transitions, numbering each separate element for clarity.

1. Example of Selective Quotation of Statutory Language

Under the Dog Bite Statute, the plaintiff must prove that: (1) he was "peaceably conducting himself" (2) in a "place where he may lawfully be" (3) when, "without provocation," a dog owned by the defendant (4) "attacked or injured" him. 510 Ill. Comp. Stat. §5/16 (2004).

2. Example of Full Quotation of Statutory Language

The State must prove that the defendant "knowingly and without authority enter[ed] the *dwelling place* of another." 720 Ill. Comp. Stat. §5/19-3 (2004) (emphasis added). The Statute defines a dwelling as "a house, apartment, mobile home, trailer, or *other living quarters* in which… the owners or occupants *actually reside*…." 720 Ill. Comp. Stat. §5/2-6(b) (2004) (emphasis added).

CHAPTER IN REVIEW

Editing Checklist:

As you review your memo, consider the following:

SENTENCE STRUCTURE → For each sentence in the paragraph, did you:
1. Clarify each sentence's relationship to prior information by:
   a. Repeating part of a prior sentence's content, or
   b. Using transitional words and phrases?

2. Use the active voice? (*e.g.*, actor (subject) → acts upon → the object)
   E.g., from: "The ball was thrown by Jane." *to*: "Jane threw the ball."

3. Keep each sentence relatively short (about 25–30 words)?
   - To shorten sentences, consider the following tips:
     - Create two sentences from one sentence
     - Eliminate superfluous words or phrases

4. Keep the actor, verb, and object together?
   E.g., from: "The *court*, by limiting the holding to the specific facts before it, *held*..." *to*: "By limiting the holding to the specific facts before it, the *court held*..."

5. Use parallel structure?
   E.g., from: "He learned to swim and horseback riding." *to*: "He learned to swim and to ride horses."

CLARITY OF WORD CHOICE → For each sentence did you:

1. Substitute simple words for longer words?
   E.g., from: "Defendant may set forth the proposition..." *to*: "Defendant may argue..."

2. Use active verbs, not nominalizations (verbs made into nouns)?
   E.g., from: "Michael engages in sleeping activities..." *to*: "Michael sleeps..."

3. Use concrete rather than vague and abstract language?
   E.g., from: "In *Thomas*, the court discussed the garage." (What did the court discuss?) *to*: "In *Thomas*, the court minimized the importance of the garage's physical attachment to the main residence."

4. Use the proper tense?

5. Strike the appropriate tone of formality?
   a. Eliminate colloquialisms and jargon
   b. Refer to adults by last names
   c. Refer to children by first names
   d. Avoid using the first person

6. Avoid sexist language?

SELECTING CASES FOR
THE MEMO

I. ASSESSING THE VALUE OF EACH CASE

After you have researched a legal issue and found a number of potentially relevant cases, not every case will find its way into your memo. Instead, you will need to choose which cases to incorporate into your memo, and, from those cases, identify the reason you're including each case. At this point, you may be most familiar with cases that are factually comparable enough to your client's factual situation to merit a full case discussion—the facts, holding, and rationale. However, not all cases are factually comparable enough to merit a thorough evaluation of their facts, holding, and rationale. A case that is not very helpful factually may instead interpret the law in a manner that helps you understand what the law means. For example, the court may define the rule of law, or may express a standard or factors that should be used when evaluating the rule of law. A case may also include a useful discussion of the purpose underlying the rule of law, or the public policy considerations the law was designed to address.

Therefore, as you consider each case you think may be helpful to you in drafting your analysis of the law, think about the different ways in which the case could be helpful:

> Does the case contain:
> 1. Any helpful definitions or explanations about what the law means?
> 2. A helpful discussion about the underlying purpose of the rule of law or public policy considerations?
> 3. Relevant case facts that can serve as the basis of analogy to or distinction from the client's facts?

After you have carefully considered the different ways in which each case is useful to you, you are now ready to decide how you might incorporate each case in your memo. Some cases may be relevant in all three of the basic ways in which a case might be useful. These cases will obviously assume a significant role in your written analysis of the law. However, other cases may be useful for only a discrete point, meriting only a brief mention.

A. Cases with Useful Definitions or Interpretations of the Law

A case may be important to you solely because it contains a sentence or two that beautifully defines the original rule of law. The court's interpretation of the law may include a standard by which the rule of law must be measured or the factors that courts must consider when evaluating the rule of law. Sometimes a court's interpretation or definition of the law may be so important in the jurisdiction that it becomes what is known as a "landmark" decision—a case to which later courts routinely refer when evaluating the law. Unless such a case is also valuable to you for other reasons (i.e., an analogous fact pattern or policy discussion), you would likely refer only briefly to the case itself, simply quoting or paraphrasing the definition, standard, or factors.

To illustrate, the following cases, excerpted from Sample Memo D in Appendix A, are only referred to briefly in the memo to support a specific point about how the law should be interpreted. The courts' interpretations are paraphrased rather than quoted because the language in each case was not particularly clear.

> When evaluating whether a condition is a hidden danger, or trap, courts consider the inherent dangerousness of the condition and the age of the injured child. A condition constitutes a hidden danger, or trap, if its dangerous condition would be hidden to a child because of the child's age and immaturity. *Ansin v. Thurston*, 98 So. 2d 87, 88 (Fla. Dist. Ct. App. 1957). In addition, the dangerous condition that injures the child must have a connection with the object that initially attracts the child onto the property, such that the two conditions jointly contribute to the child's injury. *Starling v. Saha*, 451 So. 2d 516, 518–19 (Fla. Dist. Ct. App. 1984).

B. Cases that Describe the Underlying Purpose or Policy of the Law

Some cases may be useful because they describe the underlying purpose of the law or the law's effect on public policy. In the case of a statute, the court may comment on the legislative history and even incorporate relevant parts of the legislative history, such as congressional testimony or reports.

As an example, consider the residential burglary problem and the *Silva* case. In that case, the court remarked on the Statute's purpose and cited to legislative history within that discussion. Recall that the legislative history directly relates to an argument the lawyer needed to evaluate—whether the legislature intended to exclude garages as potential dwellings under the Statute. Therefore, as the following example reflects, the lawyer decided to address the *Silva* case only for that specific purpose. Because the case facts were not analogous, the case facts and holding were omitted from the case discussion.

> Defendant might also argue that the legislative history suggests that the legislators did not intend for the Statute to cover structures such as garages. As the court noted in *People v. Silva*, 629 N.E.2d 948 (Ill. App. Ct. 1993), the legislature amended the Statute in 1986 to clarify and to narrow the meaning of the term "dwelling." The court quoted the following statement of Senator Sangmeister made during legislative hearings: "It was even brought to our attention by the Illinois Supreme Court in a number of cases that... there should be a better definition to the dwelling house. We are having people prosecuted for residential burglary for breaking into... unoccupied buildings *such as garages*." *Id.* at 951 (emphasis added).
>
> This argument lacks merit. The *Silva* court noted that "[t]he residential burglary statute is designed to protect the 'privacy and sanctity of the home,' with a view toward the 'greater danger and potential for serious harm from burglary of a home as opposed to burglary of a business.'" 629 N.E.2d at 951 (*quoting People v. Edgesto*, 611 N.E.2d 49 (Ill. App. Ct. 1993)). Senator Sangmeister's concern that people are being prosecuted for breaking into "unoccupied buildings" is consistent with the general legislative purpose to deter residential burglary because of its potential for serious harm. An occupied garage used as a living quarters invokes the same legislative concerns for the sanctity of the home and the increased risk of harm that results from an invasion of that home. Moreover, the Illinois Supreme Court decided the *Thomas* case only a few years after the amendment. In *Thomas*, the court implied that a garage used as a living quarters would be a dwelling under the Statute.

C. Cases with Relevant Facts

Some cases may be useful because the court has evaluated how the law affects a factual situation that is relevant to the client situation you are evaluating. If you have more than one factually relevant case to consider, you may not discuss each of these cases in depth. Instead, you may decide to discuss a few of the cases in depth and refer only briefly to other cases. When deciding which cases to emphasize and which cases to omit or to incorporate only tangentially, consider the following:

1. Consider the Standard or Factors that Each Case Emphasized

First, consider the various standards and underlying factors that guided the courts' decisions. After you have identified the cases that can potentially illustrate each standard or factor that you will discuss, you're now ready to assess which cases are important enough to include in your office memo. Some choices are clear; if you have only one case that illustrates a particular standard or underlying factor that is relevant to your analysis, you would definitely include that case in your memo because the case is your only means of illustrating that idea.

Other choices are not as clear. If two or more cases seem to emphasize the same points (*i.e.,* the same standard or factors), consider the results in the cases. If two cases were guided by the same standard or factors but the different fact patterns yielded two different results, you may want to discuss both cases in detail. The cases can then illustrate how far the rule of law or standard extends in each direction. In the Residential Burglary Memorandum, the *Thomas* and *McIntyre* cases reflect this choice—they each discussed the same overall factors, but the different fact patterns yielded two different results. Because the Stripes' garage fell somewhere in between the two extremes, both cases were good choices to incorporate into the memo.

Suppose, however, that two or more cases each evaluate the same standard and factors, and the court in each case arrived at the same result. In that situation, you should consider whether the cases bring out different nuances of the law that could be relevant to your analysis. If so, you may decide to explore both cases in in depth. However, if each case seems to make similar points, you may instead decide to discuss one case in depth and refer to the other case only tangentially.

The following example, excerpted from Sample Memo D in Appendix A, illustrates how you might explore one case in depth while referring to another case only tangentially. In that sample memo, the lawyer decided to discuss both the *Ansin* and *Allen* cases. However, when evaluating the relative importance of each case, the lawyer decided that, while both cases were factually relevant, the *Ansin* case provided a stronger basis for factual comparisons. In addition, the lawyer concluded that the *Allen* case did not bring out any nuance of the law not already expressed in the *Ansin* case. Therefore, the lawyer elected to discuss fully the facts, holding, and rationale of the *Ansin* case and to use the *Allen* case only as supplemental support. The following example is excerpted from the "rule explanation" section of the first issue:

It is foreseeable that children will trespass on property when the property is attractive and alluring to children and the landowner has actual knowledge that children have previously trespassed on the property. *Ansin v. Thurston*, 98 So. 2d 87, 88 (Fla. Dist. Ct. App. 1957). In *Ansin*, the defendant's property contained an artificial pond with white sand banks, a floating dock, and a raft. *Id.* at 88. A child drowned in the pond after playing on the raft. The court upheld a jury's finding that the presence of child trespassers was reasonably foreseeable, holding that it was "certain that children would be attracted to such a place...." *Id.* The court reasoned that the pond was both visible and accessible to children, as it was close to well-traveled streets and homes. Moreover, the property was seven blocks from an elementary school. Finally, the owner knew that children had used the pond for swimming. *Id. See also Allen v. William P. McDonald Corp.*, 42 So. 2d 706, 707 (Fla. 1949) (holding that white sand banks adjacent to a pond were sufficiently alluring and attractive to children to entice them to trespass).

2. Consider Which Cases Serve a More Useful Predictive Function

a. General Rule of Thumb

When more than one case illustrates a particular point you are emphasizing, it's also important to consider which cases serve a more useful predictive purpose in evaluating your client's factual situation. Generally, a case grows increasingly more useful as a predictive tool the more closely it matches your client's factual situation. Thus, if two cases serve the same purpose (i.e., they illustrate the same factors or standard with the same result), the case that more closely matches your client's situation would be more useful as a predictive tool. In making that decision, you may find it helpful to create a graph of the cases. The following graph uses the residential burglary example to illustrate how you might create a graph to assess the relative importance of different cases in terms of their predictive function:

Not a Dwelling				Dwelling
⇐				⇒
Case 1:	**Case 2:**	Stripe garage	**Case 3:**	**Case 4:**
Empty warehouse in industrial district	Garage used to store perfume and attached to a dwelling	Detached garage used as a getaway	Attached porch used for sitting, eating, & cooking	Vacation home used occasionally on weekends as a getaway
Not a dwelling	*Not a dwelling*	*?*	*Dwelling*	*Dwelling*

In the above example, the Stripes' garage falls somewhere between Case 2 and Case 3. Because Case 2 and Case 3 yield different results, each case may be useful in evaluating whether the Stripes' garage is a dwelling. Your discussion would evaluate whether the Stripes' garage is more like the facts in Case 2 or, rather, more like the facts in Case 3. In contrast, the facts in Case 1 and Case 4 do not serve as useful a predictive function because Cases 2 and 3 have facts that are more closely analogous to the client's with respect to the particular factor being explored—the "type of use" factor. Therefore, you would either omit Cases 1 and 4 from the discussion entirely, or refer to them only tangentially to illustrate a specific point.

A Word of Caution: If you elect to chart cases on a graph, it's important to include on the graph only those cases that illustrate the *same* point (i.e., interpret and apply the *same* factor or legal standard). In other words, if you are evaluating how three entirely separate points apply to the client's situation, you might sketch three separate graphs—one for each point. If you combine all of the cases onto a single graph, you might mistakenly decide to omit a case that is not as factually similar to the client's situation as other cases, even though it is the only case that illustrates a unique point.

b. When a Case with Less Desirable Facts Produces a Favorable Result

Sometimes you will be fortunate enough to discover a case that reaches a favorable result (the result desired by your client), with analogous case facts that are actually *less desirable* than your client's situation. These cases are important for the following reason—if a case with less desirable facts produces the "right" result, then a court is even more likely to reach the same conclusion when evaluating your client's more desirable facts. This type of case is helpful because of the favorable distinctions you can make between the case and your client's factual situation. In other words, you would argue that the favorable factual distinctions actually *compel* the same favorable result. For that reason, in the illustration below, Case 2 would serve a more useful predictive function than Case 3 when evaluating the Stripes' garage. Although Case 3 might, for other reasons, merit being included in your memo, just because the prosecutor in Case 3 prevailed doesn't necessarily mean that *you* would prevail—the facts in Case 3 are simply better than in your own situation.

Not a Dwelling				Dwelling
⇐				⇒
Case 1:	Case 2:	Stripe garage	Case 3:	Case 4:
Empty warehouse in industrial district	Detached garage sometimes used as an artist studio by the owner	Detached garage used as a getaway	Attached porch regularly used for sitting, eating, & cooking	Vacation home used occasionally on weekends as a getaway
Not a dwelling	*Dwelling*	*?*	*Dwelling*	*Dwelling*

Exercise 18-1

Assume you represent a client who is being prosecuted for kidnapping. One of the elements of the state kidnapping statute is that the confinement must be "secret." You know the following facts: Your client, Mr. Tate, confined Mr. Campbell to a chair in Mr. Campbell's living room. Mr. Campbell's home is a large, renovated, two-story brownstone. The living room is on the first floor of the home. The walls of the first floor are dominated by a large glass picture window (an uninterrupted pane of glass). A small amount of brick surrounds the entrance and provides support at the exterior wall of the home. The picture window is not tinted or coated in any way to affect its transparency. The confinement took place in the evening; your client left a light on in the living room that evening. Your client did not close the drapes to obscure the view into the living room. The lot on which the home is situated is level, and the front door to the home is only two steps up from the sidewalk that leads to the home. The front door is solid wood with no window. The home sits back only twenty feet from the street. The street in front of Mr. Campbell's home is classified by the police as "moderately traveled," and is open to both commercial and residential traffic. A neighbor claims that she can see into the home at night when the lights are on, although she did not look into the home that particular evening.

In researching whether the confinement was "secret" under the kidnapping statute, assume you discovered the following four cases:

Case A—In this case the court held that the confinement was secret when the defendant confined the victim in a basement apartment. The confinement took place at night; the drapes were closed, and a friend trying to find the victim peered in through the window of the apartment and could not see anything.

Case B—The court held that the confinement was not secret when an enraged defendant, holding a gun, dragged the victim from the victim's private office into the lobby of an office building. A security guard was present in the lobby, and the enraged defendant caught the security guard's attention when he shouted that he would kill the victim unless the victim complied with his demands.

Case C—In this case, the court held that the confinement was secret. The defendant hid in the victim's garage one evening. The garage was attached to the victim's home, and the garage door was closed. When the victim left her home to enter her car, the defendant forced the victim to climb into the trunk of the car. The defendant drove the car to a deserted landfill, where he finally removed the victim from the trunk of the car. No one saw the victim at any time during this abduction.

Case D—The court held that the confinement was not secret when the defendant confined the victim in a small vestibule of an apartment building. The vestibule was a few steps up from a busy street, and the confinement took place during morning rush hour. A driver on the street saw the defendant holding the victim against her will and honked his horn.

After evaluating the above cases:

1. List the cases that would serve the most useful predictive function for your client.
2. List those cases that would serve the least useful predictive function for your client.
3. Explain your choices.

3. Consider the Rationale in Each Case

The extent and depth of the court's rationale is another factor to consider when deciding which cases to discuss in a memo. A case with relevant facts becomes more valuable when the court justifies its holding with a thorough discussion of both explanatory reasoning (in which the court explains the legal requirements of the original rule of law) and application reasoning (in which the court provides an in-depth discussion of why it applied the law to the case facts in the manner that it did). All other things being equal, a case with a thorough discussion of its holding is more useful than a case in which the rationale is fairly superficial. If a case with weak rationale has a specific point you would like to bring out, you might make that point by referring to the case in passing without necessarily discussing the case in detail.

D. Consider the Level of Court

When selecting cases for a memo, also consider the level of court that rendered each decision. A case decided by the highest level court in a jurisdiction has greater weight in the jurisdiction than a case decided by a lower level court. However, it would be a mistake to disregard lower-level cases solely because you may have also found a case decided by a higher court. The case decided by the lower court may be more valuable to you if, for example, the facts of that case are more analogous to your client.

E. Consider the Date of Decision

Finally, also consider the dates of the cases you are evaluating. All other things being equal, a recent case is more valuable than an older case, particularly when there is a wide difference in time. For example, a case decided in 2020 would potentially carry greater weight than a case decided in 1950, even though the 1950 case might still be "good law." This is particularly true in areas of the law where the law has undergone some transformation due to changing policy considerations. *Caveat:* An older case might still be an effective choice if it contains relevant facts or useful rationale.

Exercise 18-2

You represent Chester Tate and are defending him with respect to attempted murder charges filed by the State of Illinois. Another associate in the law firm has previously worked on Chester Tate's defense to kidnapping charges the State filed in connection with the same incident. To acquaint yourself with the factual and legal background underlying your representation:

A. Review the Sample Office Memo that analyzes a potential defense to kidnapping charges (Sample Memo B in Appendix A); and

B. Review the cases provided by your professor (as referenced in the Teacher's Manual). Carefully evaluate the cases and consider their relative importance and usefulness in analyzing the viability of Mr. Tate's intoxication defense to attempted murder.

After carefully evaluating and taking notes from each case:

1. Select the cases that you would emphasize as cases of "primary" emphasis in a memo that assesses the viability of an intoxication defense. Primary emphasis cases are those analogous cases that are of such primary relevance that they would merit a complete case discussion in an office memo, including a discussion of case facts, holding, and rationale. For each such case of primary emphasis, note:

   a. The case facts that you would use as a basis of comparison to or distinction from the client's facts; and

   b. The important rationale from the court's decision.

2. Select those cases that you would use as "tangential" cases in assessing the viability of an intoxication defense. Tangential cases are those cases that have some relevance to the client's problem but, because they are not as important as primary emphasis cases, do not merit an extended discussion in an office memo. Sample Memo D in Appendix A reflects the use of tangential cases (*see, e.g.,* the use of the *Allen, Bathey,* and *Newby* cases referenced in that memo). For each such tangential case, note:

   a. The specific purpose for which you would use such case in an office memorandum (*e.g.,* does it contain a good statement of a rule of law? A valuable interpretation of public policy? Would a few case facts be helpful in a parenthetical to support a factual analogy made by a primary case?); and

   b. State the specific language or case facts that you would select from the case to serve such purpose.

3. Identify those cases that you would not mention in an office memo at all (*e.g.*, because they have no relevance to the client's problem or because other cases reflect the same points more clearly).

CHAPTER IN REVIEW

Core Concepts:

POSSIBLE USES FOR A PRECEDENT CASE

1. Does the case contain a helpful *definition or explanation* about what the law means?
   - If that is all the case provides, consider using the case as a *tangential* case to define or explain the law. (*See* Sample Memo D, Appendix A—*Starling v. Saha, Johnson v. Bathey*, and *Newby v. West Palm Beach Water Co.*, in Section B(2))

2. Does the case contain a helpful discussion about the underlying *purpose* of the rule of law, or *public policy* considerations?
   - If that is all the case provides, consider using the case as a *tangential* case to illustrate the purpose of the law or policy considerations. (*See* Sample Memo A, Appendix A—*People v. Silva*)

3. Does the case contain *relevant case facts* that can serve as the basis of analogy to or distinction from the client's facts? If so:
   a. Is it the only case that illustrates a particular standard or factor? If so, describe the case in detail, including the rule of law, facts, holding, and rationale.
   b. If more than one case illustrates the *same* standard or factor:
      i. Do they yield two *different* results?
         - If so, consider discussing both cases in detail so that you can later compare and contrast the client's facts to both cases.
      ii. Do they yield the *same* result? If so:
         - Do they bring out different nuances of the law?
            - If yes, consider discussing both cases in detail.
            - If no, consider discussing one case in detail and bringing in the other case to make a tangential point (see (iii) below to determine which case to discuss in detail).
      iii. If two or more cases yield the same result, illustrate the same standard or factor, *and* do not bring out different nuances in the law, consider:

- Which case most <u>closely matches</u> the client's factual situation, thereby providing the strongest basis for factual comparisons? As a general rule of thumb, emphasize that case in your legal discussion.

- Do any of the cases produce a <u>favorable holding with less desirable facts</u> than your client's factual situation? If so, emphasize that case in your legal discussion.

- Which case(s) has the most extensive <u>rationale</u>? *All other things being equal*, emphasize the case with the most extensive and thorough rationale.

- Consider the <u>level of court</u> and <u>date of the decisions</u>. *All other things being equal*, emphasize the most recent cases from the highest level court.

DRAFTING SHORT MEMOS
The Thin-Sliced Analysis

As a practicing lawyer, the decision to draft a short memo rather than a longer, more formal memo will be dictated by practical concerns. In recent years, due to rising legal costs and the economy, short memos have become the norm, while longer, more formal memoranda tend to be used more infrequently. It typically takes more time, and costs clients more money in legal fees, for lawyers to draft, revise, and polish formal office memoranda than it does for them to draft short memos. Moreover, short memos are often more appropriate vehicles to discuss narrow, clearly defined legal issues that can be adequately discussed in a few pages. However, when the stakes are significant, a longer memorandum might be more appropriate, particularly when the legal issues are complex; complex legal issues often require a more thorough explanation in order to convey a legal analysis that is both clear and accurate. The individual idiosyncrasies of your client might also assume a role in your decision. A client who is deliberate and cautious and who wants to see the legal details laid out in a precise, step-by-step fashion might prefer a more formal legal memorandum. In contrast, a "big picture" client who is interested in knowing only the broad parameters of the legal issues might prefer a short memo.

As a young lawyer, you will also need to pay attention to the wishes of the senior lawyers who ask you to research and draft memos for them. In addition to the factors mentioned above, the culture of your law firm or legal environment will also assume an important role in dictating your choice. Whether you are receiving instructions from a client or from a senior lawyer in your law office, the need for clarity is essential. Does the senior lawyer want a thorough, complete rendition of the legal issues? Or does the senior lawyer want a shorter summary of the law, perhaps with additional details to be fleshed out in a meeting? It is also important to clarify the time frame under which the senior lawyer or the client expects to receive your response. Does the senior lawyer want a response in two hours, the end of the day, or next week? All of these factors should be considered, and ambiguities clarified, before you begin researching and drafting your legal analysis.

I. PRE-DRAFTING PROCESS

Drafting a short memo does not mean that it is acceptable for the memo to be poorly evaluated, poorly written, or poorly edited. In fact, although it might seem counter-intuitive, drafting a succinct, short memo requires greater expertise than drafting a longer, more formal legal memorandum. This is because short memos must not only be succinct, but also thorough, covering all of the important bases. The succinct but thorough analysis requires you to "thin-slice" your analysis by assessing what information is most important and what information can be omitted.[1] This is a real challenge that requires considerable thought and care. If you leave out important information the senior lawyer or client should know in order to understand the essence of your legal analysis, at best, you will have left your reader confused and frustrated; at worst, your omission of important information might have misled the client or senior lawyer to assume the legal case is more favorable (or less favorable) than it actually is.

Because it is so challenging to thin-slice a legal analysis, the pre-drafting process is critically important. The following chart identifies a pre-drafting process that will not only make the drafting of the short memo easier, but will also help you thin-slice your analysis to achieve the right balance between disclosing too much, or too little, information.

> **Step 1:** Identify the *rule of law*, and the elements of the rule you will be evaluating. (Ch. 6)
> - The elements of the rule of law will serve as a foundation for your discussion.
>
> **Step 2:** From your research, select the most important cases to discuss in your short memo. From that group of cases, select those cases that you will simply *mention* for a specific purpose (*e.g.*, policy point), and those cases in which you will *summarize the case facts* (your *primary emphasis* cases). (Ch.18)
>
> **Step 3:** Take a careful look at each of the important cases you have decided to include in your short memo as a "primary emphasis" case. Jot down the *holding* of each case, the critically important *case facts*, and the essential aspects of the court's *rationale* that fairly explain the holding.
>
> **Step 4:** Formulate a *rule statement* for each case that you will include as a "primary emphasis" case in your memo. (Ch. 7)

---

1. "Thin-slice" is a term coined by Malcolm Gladwell to describe how experts solve problems. Malcolm Gladwell, *Blink* (Little, Brown & Co. 2005).

◎ ILLUSTRATION: Residential Burglary Problem

Recall the residential burglary problem, which is illustrated in Appendix A of this textbook. In that problem, the lawyer evaluated whether an alleged thief could properly be charged under the state of Illinois' residential burglary statute. Under the Statute, the issue was whether a detached garage, sometimes used as a retreat for the homeowners' college-age son, was a "dwelling place" under the Statute. (You may wish to review again the Office Memorandum illustrated as Sample Memo A in Appendix A, which describes the facts and case law in greater detail.) Assume for present purposes that a senior prosecutor in your office has asked you to re-search Illinois' residential burglary statute and to draft a short memo conveying your legal analysis.

Step 1: Identify the Rule of Law & Its Elements

In your research, assume that you identified Illinois' residential burglary statute as the original rule of law upon which you will build your legal analysis. As you review the Statute, notice that there are two separate aspects of the Statute that apply to your research question: (1) Section 5/19-3, which defines residential burglary as the un-lawful entry into the "*dwelling place*" of another; and (2) Section 5/2-6(b), a defini-tional section that defines the term "dwelling place." Under this latter statutory sec-tion, the term "dwelling place" is defined as "*a house, apartment, mobile home, trailer, or other living quarters in which the owners or occupants actually reside....*"

When evaluating each of the definitional terms of a "dwelling place" under the Statute, consider which terms are probably irrelevant and which terms appear to be most relevant to the Stripes' garage. The Stripes' garage would likely not qualify as a "house," "apartment," "mobile home," or "trailer." However, it is possible that the ga-rage, as used by Michael Stripe, might be construed to be a "living quarters" in which Michael Stripe "actually resides." Assume that, as you researched the cases that inter-pret the Statute, you discovered that your initial assessment was correct—with struc-tures such as the Stripes' garage, the phrase "*living quarters in which the owners or occupants actually reside*" is indeed the phrase courts evaluate in these situations. Therefore, this latter element would be the foundation upon which you would build your analysis in the short memo.

Step 2: Select the Cases to Include in Your Short Memo

After researching the law and discovering numerous cases that interpret the resi-dential burglary statute, assume you discovered three cases that seem to be the most relevant and noteworthy: *People v. McIntyre, People v. Thomas,* and *People v. Silva.*

Each of these three cases brings out a different, and important, nuance that illustrates how Illinois courts interpret the term "living quarters" under the Statute.

Assume that you have decided to use both the *McIntyre* and *Thomas* cases as "primary emphasis" cases because the two cases produce two contrasting results and contain facts that you can analogize to your own situation. Although the *McIntyre* case involves an attached porch rather than a detached garage, the court's rationale is detailed and pertinent to your own situation, and the case has been cited numerous times by other Illinois courts. In addition, if you plotted out the cases and your own fact pattern on a graph (from the point of "clearly a dwelling" to "clearly not a dwelling"), your fact pattern seems to fall somewhere in between the *McIntyre* and *Thomas* cases. Therefore, by comparing the facts of your own situation to the facts of both cases, you can predict the likely result of your own situation—is the Stripes' garage more like the porch in *McIntyre* or more like the garage in *Thomas*?

Thomas	**Your Situation**	*McIntyre*	*Silva*
Not a Dwelling			**Dwelling**

In contrast, you have decided not to summarize the facts and holding of the *Silva* case because it isn't as factually relevant as the *Thomas* and *McIntyre* cases. In the *Silva* case, the court held that an unoccupied apartment that was undergoing a remodel was still a "dwelling" under the Statute. As you can see from the graph, the *McIntyre* facts are more closely comparable to your situation than the *Silva* case's facts, making the *McIntyre* case a better fit to discuss as a "primary emphasis" case. Nonetheless, you have decided to briefly mention the *Silva* case in your short memo because it does bring out a nuance that neither *Thomas* or *McIntyre* mention—the legislative purpose. You conclude that you could use the legislative purpose described in the *Silva* case to rebut an argument the defendant will surely bring out in his defense—that because the Stripes' garage stands thirty (30) feet away from the primary residence, it can't be considered part of the Stripes' dwelling. Therefore, it makes sense to include the *Silva* case in your memo for the limited purpose of rebutting an opposing argument.

Step 3: Jot Down the Holding, Rationale, & Key Facts of Each Case

In a short memo, your discussion of each case will be more abbreviated than in a longer, more formal memorandum. It can be particularly challenging to distinguish between information you really must disclose in order for the client and/or senior lawyer to understand why each case is important, and information that, while relevant, is not essential. For purposes of illustration, consider the *McIntyre* case. Your pre-drafting notes might look something like the following example. Pay particular attention to the "notes to self" discussion. The lawyer here decides which facts and rationale to emphasize, which facts to mention only briefly, and which facts to omit.

McIntyre **Holding** = Attached porch is a "living quarters" under the Statute

Rationale = Activities of "*sitting, eating, & cooking* make the porch part of the living quarters of the house"

NOTES to self: The "activities of sitting, eating, & cooking" seem to be out-come-determinative. Without these facts, the result would have gone the other way. So this is what I'll emphasize in my discussion of the court's rationale.

The court also mentions three other points: (1) the *frequency* with which the owners used the porch; (2) the porch was *attached* to the home; and (3) the porch's *furnishings* served as evidence that the owners actually used the porch.

As to point (1), this seems to have been somewhat important to the court. If the owners had only used the porch a few times a year, the result may have been different. Therefore, I'll briefly mention this point in my case discussion—that the owners frequently used the porch.

As to point (2), although the porch was attached, it was separated from the home by a lock. Also, the court didn't emphasize this factor in its opinion, making the "attachment" factor somewhat less important. However, because the Stripes' garage is 30 feet away from the residence, this is a distinction I shouldn't ignore—defense counsel may well raise this issue as a defense. Therefore, I'll mention that the porch was attached (to alert the senior lawyer), but because it didn't seem very important to the court, I won't go into detail about that part of the court's rationale.

As to point (3), the porch's furnishings seemed more superfluous to the court—more of a "make-weight" argument. Plus, the Stripes' garage was also furnished like a "living quarters," so I don't anticipate the defendant making any argument here. Because I don't see this as posing any real disputable issue, I will omit this aspect of the opinion.

Step 4: Formulate Rule Statements for Each "Primary Emphasis" Case

Formulating rule statements is no less challenging in a short memo than it is with a longer, more formal memorandum. You may want to review again the discussion of rule statements that appears in Chapter 7. Your rule statement should capture the essence of the court's holding; in other words, *how* and *why* the court answered the legal question the way that it did. It should contain a result, which centers on the legal issue involved, and a standard that illustrates what it takes to satisfy that result, which centers on a "take-away" from the court's reasoning regarding the legal issue. Using the residential burglary problem for purposes of illustration, the rule statement for the *McIntyre* case should incorporate both the "how" (court's holding) and the "why" (key reasons). In *McIntyre*, (1) the court's *holding* is: "the porch is a dwelling under the residential burglary statute because it is part of the living quarters"; and (2) the key *reasons* the court held as it did are the three factors you identified as being most important to the *McIntyre* court: "type of use," "frequency of use," and "attachment to home." Piecing these two components together, the essence of the *McIntyre* case's holding could be captured in the following rule statement:

> **Rule Statement Capturing Essence of *McIntyre* case:**
>
> An enclosed, attached porch is a dwelling under the residential burglary statute when it is frequently used as part of a home's living quarters.

Before reading further, consider how the above rule statement contains both the result and legal standard. The first part of the rule statement contains the result, while the second part of the statement describes the legal standard that satisfies the result, as illustrated by the *McIntyre* court's reliance on three factors.

As another example, a rule statement that captures the essence of the *Thomas* case would include its holding ("the garage is not a dwelling"), and the key reasons the court held as it did ("garage not used as a living quarters"). As you piece these two components together, your rule statement that would introduce a discussion of the *Thomas* case could be expressed as:

> **Rule Statement Capturing Essence of *Thomas* case:**
>
> An attached garage used only for storage purposes is not a dwelling under the residential burglary statute.

II. DRAFTING PROCESS

Step 1: Introductory "Roadmap" Paragraph(s)

Like more formal office memos, your short memo should follow a *deductive* writing pattern by providing "context" before "details." The introductory paragraph(s) provides the reader with context by outlining a roadmap of the memo that will follow. Depending upon the circumstances under which you have been asked to provide a short memo, you may or may not include within the introductory paragraph(s) an abbreviated summary of the important facts. For example, if a senior lawyer has asked you to research a discrete, narrow legal issue and is already intimately familiar with the facts, you would probably not begin your short memo with a summary of the facts. The facts would be unnecessary and detract from the principal purpose of your memo. On the other hand, if you are preparing a short memo for a client, and you want to ensure that you correctly understand some of the important factual details upon which your analysis is based, then it might be valuable to begin with an abbreviated description of the important facts.

If you include a factual summary within your short memo, your introductory paragraph(s) should identify: (1) the legal question you have been asked to evaluate; (2) the rule of law upon which you are basing your analysis; (3) the critically important client facts that you have relied upon in evaluating the law; and (4) your conclusion. Depending upon how many facts you need to recite in the memo, your introductory roadmap might range from a single roadmap paragraph to two or even three paragraphs or more.

If the circumstances suggest that a factual summary would be unnecessary, the introductory roadmap paragraph should identify: (1) the legal question you have been asked to evaluate; (2) the rule of law upon which you are basing your analysis; and (3) your conclusion. (Depending upon the circumstances and what seems to flow most naturally, you might satisfy the reader's curiosity by inserting the conclusion anywhere within the introductory, roadmap paragraph(s).)

Steps 2–4: The Discussion: Rule Explanation, Rule Application, & Conclusion

The remainder of your Discussion should follow the same deductive writing pattern as a longer memorandum. As with more formal memoranda, you need to tell your reader how the cases explain and interpret the rule of law (*Rule Explanation*). However, your discussion of the cases in a short memo will be more abbreviated and succinct than in a longer memorandum. After you have educated the reader about how the cases interpret the rule of law, next tell the reader how the law applies to the factual situation you are evaluating (*Rule Application*). Again, however, in a short memo you will not delve into as many details and nuances as you would in a longer office memorandum. Instead, you will need to identify and incorporate into your short memo only the most critically important aspects of the factual situation you are evaluating. Finally, unless the short memo is extremely short and this next step would seem repetitive and unnecessary, you should remind the reader of your conclusion.

The following chart summarizes each of the drafting steps involved in drafting a short memo:

Step 1: Draft an introductory, roadmap paragraph(s), that identifies:
  i. The *legal question* you've been asked to evaluate;
  ii. The *rule of law* you will be evaluating;
  iii. *Sometimes*, an abbreviated summary of the important *facts* of your case; and

iv. Your ultimate *conclusion*.

Step 2: Rule Explanation:
- For factually relevant cases, this includes: (1) a *rule statement* capturing the *holding* of the case, and (2) the most essential aspect of the court's *rationale/facts* that fairly explain the holding.
- For other cases, include the important *nuance or policy* point each case illustrates.

Step 3: Rule Application: Discuss how the cases impact your client's factual situation.

Step 4: If helpful to the reader, repeat your Conclusion.

◎ ILLUSTRATION: Residential Burglary Problem

1. Roadmap Paragraph

In the residential burglary problem, assume that the senior prosecutor who assigned you this research project was already fully aware of the facts and of the residential burglary statute and its separate elements. Suppose your assignment was to address only the narrow issue of whether a detached garage sometimes used as a retreat for the homeowners' college-age son could be considered a "dwelling" under the Statute. Because this is your intended reader's starting point, you wouldn't want to distract the senior prosecutor by discussing the factual details of the problem you are evaluating. Instead, your roadmap paragraph would begin with the narrow legal question you've been asked to research:

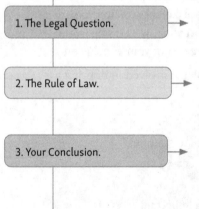

1. The Legal Question.

2. The Rule of Law.

3. Your Conclusion.

This memo addresses whether the Stripes' garage constitutes a "dwelling" under Illinois' Residential Burglary Statute for purposes of prosecuting Gerry Arnold under that Statute. The Statute defines a dwelling place as "a house, apartment, mobile home, trailer, or *other living quarters* in which... the owners or occupants *actually reside....*" 720 Ill. Comp. Stat. 5/2-6(b) (2004) (emphasis added). Although the law is not entirely clear, the Stripes' garage is likely a "living quarters" in which Michael Stripe "actually resides." Therefore, there is a strong argument that the Stripes' garage is a dwelling under Illinois' Residential Burglary Statute.

2. Rule Explanation: Discuss the Important Cases

Now that you have given the senior prosecutor a foundation, or context, for your short memo, the next step is to thin-slice the most important aspects of the law that the senior prosecutor would need to know in order to understand your conclusion, beginning with the relevant cases. For purposes of comparison, the first example illustrated below reflects the original discussion of the *McIntyre* case described in the longer, more formal memorandum.

As you read the original version illustrated below, consider what modifications you might make to this case discussion if you were to condense it into a short memo. Which case facts could be condensed or even omitted? Are there aspects of the court's rationale that you would condense or even omit? You might find it helpful to strike out the lines of discussion you think would be unnecessary in a short memo so that you can compare your ideas to the second example illustrated below that reflects a condensed discussion of the *McIntyre* case.

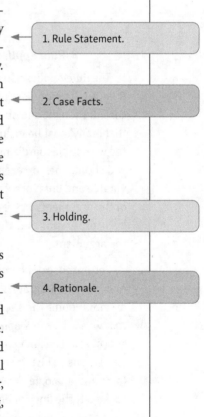

An enclosed, attached porch is considered a dwelling under the residential burglary statute when it is frequently used as part of the home's living quarters. *People v. McIntyre*, 578 N.E.2d 314 (Ill. App. Ct. 1991). In *People v. McIntyre*, the owners used an attached, screened porch for "sitting, eating, and cooking." *Id.* at 315. They ate most of their meals on the porch in the summer and cooked meals there four or five times a week in the winter. The owners furnished the porch with wrought-iron furniture and a barbecue grill that reflected its use. The porch was enclosed, locked, and attached to the home. The court held that, under these facts, the porch was a "living quarters," and thus a dwelling, under the Statute. *Id.*

1. Rule Statement.

2. Case Facts.

3. Holding.

The court reasoned that the owners used the porch as part of their living quarters by engaging in such activities as "sitting, eating, and cooking." *Id.* In addition, the owners regularly used the porch in this manner and furnished the porch with furniture and a grill that reflected such use. The court also observed that the porch was enclosed and attached to the house, indicating that the porch's physical attachment to the house was a relevant factor. However, the court emphasized that it was the activities of "sitting, eating, and cooking" that "make the porch part of the living quarters of the house." *Id.*

4. Rationale.

As you read the following abbreviated version of the case discussion that might appear in a Short Memo, identify the modifications that are made. Which facts are omitted, and which facts are condensed? Why? Which parts of the original rationale are omitted, and which parts of the rationale are condensed? Which parts of the rationale are still emphasized? Why? You might want to take another look at the Notes from the *McIntyre* case described in the *Illustration of the Pre-Drafting Steps: Step 3*. The Notes identify the lawyer's thought processes and decisions to include, minimize, or exclude certain facts and rationale.

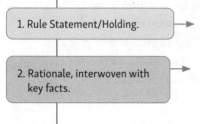

1. Rule Statement/Holding.

2. Rationale, interwoven with key facts.

An enclosed, attached porch frequently used as part of a home's living quarters is a dwelling under the residential burglary statute. *People v. McIntyre*, 578 N.E.2d 314 (Ill. App. Ct. 1991). In *McIntyre*, the court emphasized that the owners used the attached, screened porch for "sitting, eating, and cooking" at least four or five times a week. *Id.* at 315. The court held that these activities made the attached porch "part of the living quarters of the house." *Id.*

3. Rule Application: Apply the Law to Your Factual Situation

The Rule Application part of your short memo should be a succinct version of the Rule Application section of a longer, more formal office memorandum. It takes careful thought and skill, however, to distinguish between the factual arguments that really must be included in the memo and those arguments that could be omitted without jeopardizing the accuracy and integrity of the memo. In a short memo, you should include each important factual argument that can be made—both favorable and unfavorable arguments. At the same time, instead of fleshing out each of the arguments in great detail, you will instead thin-slice each of the arguments by incorporating only the most basic points necessary for the reader to understand the argument.

For purposes of comparison, the first example below reflects the original Rule Application paragraphs as set forth in the longer, more formal residential burglary memorandum. The second illustration reflects a revised Rule Application section that would be more appropriate for a short memo. As you read the original discussion below, consider what modifications you might make to these Rule Application paragraphs. Which facts and analogies could be condensed or even omitted? Which facts and analogies would you still emphasize? Why? You might find it helpful to strike out the lines of discussion you think would be unnecessary in a short memo so that you can compare your ideas to the second example illustrated below.

Like the owners of the porch in *McIntyre*, Michael Stripe used the Stripes' garage for activities commonly associated with a living quarters. Similar to the activities of "sitting, eating, and cooking" in *McIntyre*, Michael Stripe's use of the garage for playing and listening to music, watching television, and eating snacks are uses commonly associated with a living quarters. In addition, Michael Stripe's use of the garage as a sleeping quarters during the summer and fall makes his use of the garage even more of a typical living quarters than the porch in *McIntyre*. Unlike the *McIntyre* activities of barbecuing, eating, and sitting, which can occur outside of a dwelling, sleeping is an activity uniquely associated with a living quarters. Moreover, Michael Stripe's use of the garage is clearly distinguishable from that in *Thomas*, where the owner used the garage only for storage purposes.

In addition, like the owners in *McIntyre*, Michael Stripe furnished the garage in a manner that reflects its use as a living quarters. Like the grill and wrought-iron furniture in *McIntyre*, Michael Stripe's sound system, small TV, mini-refrigerator, and futon reflect that he uses the garage for activities typically associated with a living quarters. Again, the furnishings are a far cry from the garage in *Thomas*, which housed only the owner's car and boxes of commercial products for sale.

Finally, like the owners' use of the porch in *McIntyre*, the frequency of Michael's use of the garage also reflects the garage's use as a living quarters. Michael spends at least two to three evenings a week and his spare time on weekends in his getaway. During the summer and fall, he sleeps there seven nights a week. Michael's regular and frequent use far exceeds the owner's limited, occasional use of the garage in *Thomas* to retrieve her car or perfume products from storage. In fact, in August when the garage was burglarized, Michael's frequency of use even exceeded that of the owners in *McIntyre*, who used the porch only four to five times a week.

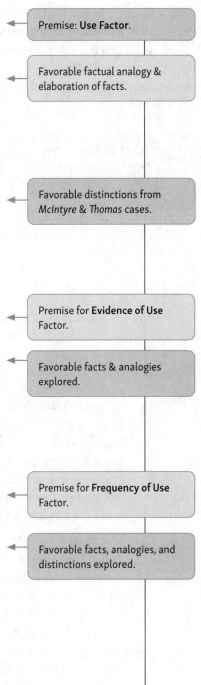

Premise: **Use Factor**.

Favorable factual analogy & elaboration of facts.

Favorable distinctions from *McIntyre* & *Thomas* cases.

Premise for **Evidence of Use** Factor.

Favorable facts & analogies explored.

Premise for **Frequency of Use** Factor.

Favorable facts, analogies, and distinctions explored.

As you read the abbreviated version of the case discussion below, identify the modifications that were made. Which facts and analogies are omitted? Which facts and analogies are condensed? Why? Which facts and analogies are still emphasized? Why?

> **1. Conclusion.**
>
> **2. Favorable Argument** re: *Type of Use* and *Frequency* factors, with favorable analogies and distinctions to both cases.

Like the owners of the porch in *McIntyre*, Michael Stripe uses the Stripes' garage more like a living quarters than a typical garage. Similar to the activities of "sitting, eating, and cooking," Michael Stripe uses the garage as an extension of the living quarters of the Stripes' home. The garage is Michael Stripe's getaway retreat in which he writes and plays music, watches television, and eats light meals. During the summer and fall, he even sleeps in the garage every night on a futon that has been set up in the loft area of the garage. Like the owners in *McIntyre*, Michael Stripe regularly and frequently uses the garage as part of the living quarters of the house. Michael Stripe's use of the garage as a retreat and part-time sleeping quarters is a far cry from the garage in *Thomas*, in which the owner used the garage only for storage purposes.

In the above example, notice that each of the critically important arguments are still included in the discussion; however, each argument is distilled down to its essence, with little elaboration. Thus, the arguments relating to the most important factors (the "use" of the garage and the "frequency of the use") are still incorporated within the Rule Application section of this short memo. However, the "evidence of use" factor and analysis is omitted because it is more peripheral and not essential to the analysis. The "attachment" factor will be addressed below when the opposing arguments are explored.

Important Note: In a short memo, your Rule Application section may be longer than a single paragraph. In this particular fact pattern, the favorable arguments could legitimately be made within a single paragraph. However, that will not always be the case; in some instances, your Rule Application paragraphs might run even a few pages. The point is not how many paragraphs you "should" include in a short memo, but, rather, how many paragraphs it legitimately takes to summarize the important information the senior lawyer and/or client will need to know in order to understand your analysis and conclusion.

4. Rule Application: Discuss Important Opposing Arguments

As in a longer, more formal office memorandum, it's essential that your short memo alert the reader to important opposing arguments that might be made. In the residential burglary problem, the fact that the Stripes' garage is thirty (30) feet away from the primary residence is a potential problem, particularly because the porch in *McIntyre* (a "favorable result" case) was attached to the homeowners' residence. Therefore, as in a longer memorandum, you would include this argument, and your rebuttal, in a short memo. However, your discussion of the argument and rebuttal will be thin-sliced so that you incorporate only the "bones" of the argument.

For purposes of comparison, the first example illustrated below is excerpted from the original Rule Application paragraphs set forth in the longer, more formal memorandum. The second example illustrates a revised discussion of opposing arguments that would be more appropriate for a short memo.

The original version describes two opposing arguments: (1) the garage's physical detachment from the Stripes' home; and (2) a legislative history argument relating to structures such as garages. As you read the original discussion below, consider what modifications you might make to the discussion of the opposing arguments. Are both arguments necessary to include? Can they be condensed in some way? How might the discussion be pared down to its essence? Can some of the details from the precedent cases be pared down, while still retaining the essence of the opposing argument and rebuttal? You might find it helpful to strike out the language you think would be unnecessary in a short memo so that you can compare your ideas to the second example illustrated below.

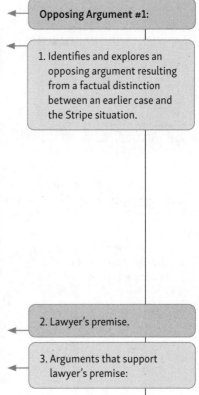

Opposing Argument #1:

1. Identifies and explores an opposing argument resulting from a factual distinction between an earlier case and the Stripe situation.

Defendant may argue that, despite Michael Stripe's frequent use of the garage for activities associated with a living quarters, the garage's physical detachment from the Stripes' home prevents it from being a "living quarters" in which the owners "reside." Under this theory, the Defendant would argue that the garage, standing alone, is not a living quarters in which anyone resides. The garage has no running water, bathroom facilities, or heat. Thus, the garage's status as a dwelling is dependent upon whether it can reasonably be viewed as an extension of the Stripe family's living quarters within the home itself. The defendant would argue that the fact that the *McIntyre* porch was physically attached to the family's home was essential to the court's holding. Only because the porch was physically attached to the home could it reasonably be viewed as an extension of the family's living quarters. In contrast, the Stripes' garage stands thirty feet away from their residence.

While having some merit, this argument should fail. Although the *McIntyre* court did note that the porch was physically "attached and enclosed," it concluded that it

2. Lawyer's premise.

3. Arguments that support lawyer's premise:

as fleshed out using rationale from the *McIntyre* case.

as fleshed out using rationale from the *Thomas* case.

4. Conclusion repeated for lengthy analysis.

Opposing Argument #2:

1. Identifies & discusses a 2nd opposing argument.

was the owners' "activities" and use of the porch that made the porch "part of the living quarters of the house." 578 N.E.2d at 314. Thus, the court implied that the activities for which the porch was used were more important than the porch's attachment to the home. Moreover, the fact that the porch was separated from the utility room of the owners' home by a door with "three locks" lends less significance to the attached/detached distinction. The presence of three locks implies that the porch area was not an open part of the main residence, but was instead physically separate from the main residence. Like the physically separate porch in *McIntyre*, the Stripes' garage is used as an extension of the Stripe family's living quarters.

People v. Thomas lends further support to this conclusion. In *Thomas*, the court minimized the importance of the garage's physical attachment to the main residence while emphasizing the garage's use. The court reasoned that "[a] garage, at least in this instance, *whether attached to the various living units or not*, cannot be deemed a residence or living quarters." 561 N.E.2d at 58 (emphasis added). By that statement, the court implied that the garage's physical attachment to the owner's home was not important. That statement, together with the court's earlier definition of a dwelling as a structure used as a "living quarters," implies that a detached garage used as a living quarters would be a dwelling under the Statute. Therefore, the fact that the Stripes' garage is physically detached from their residence does not deprive it of its status as a "living quarters" in which the owners "actually reside."

Defendant might also argue that the legislative history suggests that the legislators did not intend for the Statute to cover structures such as garages. As the court noted in *People v. Silva*, 628 N.E.2d 948 (Ill. App. Ct. 1993), the legislature amended the Statute in 1986 to clarify and narrow the meaning of the term "dwelling." The court quoted the following statement of Senator Sangmeister made during legislative hearings: "It was even brought to our attention by the Illinois Supreme Court in a number of cases that... there should be a better definition to the dwelling house. We are having people prosecuted for residential burglary for breaking into... unoccupied buildings *such as garages*." *Id.* at 951 (emphasis added).

This argument lacks merit. The *Silva* court noted that "[t]he residential burglary statute is designed to protect the 'privacy and sanctity of the home,' with a view toward the 'greater danger and potential for serious harm from burglary of a home as opposed to burglary of a business.'" 628 N.E.2d at 951 (*quoting People v. Edgesto*, 611 N.E.2d 49 (Ill. App. Ct. 1993)). Senator Sangmeister's concern that people are being prosecuted for breaking into "unoccupied buildings" is consistent with the general legislative purpose to deter residential burglary because of its potential for serious harm. An occupied garage used as a living quarters invokes the same legislative concerns for the sanctity of the home and the increased risk of harm that results from an invasion of that home. Moreover, the Illinois Supreme Court decided the *Thomas* case only a few years after the amendment. In *Thomas*, the court suggested that a garage used as a living quarters would be a dwelling under the Statute.

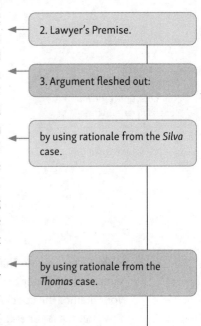

2. Lawyer's Premise.

3. Argument fleshed out:

by using rationale from the *Silva* case.

by using rationale from the *Thomas* case.

As you read the abbreviated version of the opposing arguments below, identify the modifications that have been made. There were originally two arguments, and now there is only one argument. Were either of the original arguments omitted entirely, or were they merely condensed into a single argument? How are the arguments condensed—by eliminating details from the precedent cases that lend support to the rebuttal arguments, or by some other means? Do you agree with the lawyer's choices? What risks might there be in abbreviating the arguments?

Defendant might argue, however, that despite Michael Stripes' frequent use of the garage for activities associated with a living quarters, the garage's physical distance from the Stripes' home distinguishes it from the porch in *McIntyre*, which was attached to the home. Unlike the attached porch in *McIntyre*, the Stripes' garage stands thirty (30) feet away from their home, and has no running water, bathroom facilities, or heat. Thus, the garage's status as a dwelling is dependent upon whether it can reasonably be viewed as an extension of the Stripe family's living quarters within the primary residence itself.

While having some merit, the Defendant's argument should fail. Both the *McIntyre* and *Thomas* courts emphasized the actual activities that occurred within the structures themselves, not the structures' proximity to the homes. Moreover, the legislative purpose underlying the

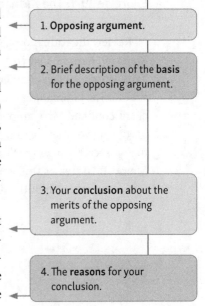

1. **Opposing argument**.

2. Brief description of the **basis** for the opposing argument.

3. Your **conclusion** about the merits of the opposing argument.

4. The **reasons** for your conclusion.

5. *Silva* case mentioned for the sole purpose of providing added support for your opposing argument.

Statute suggests that the legislators were concerned about the increased potential for danger when thieves break into homes. For example, in *People v. Silva*, the court noted that the reason the legislature enacted the residential burglary Statute, with more severe penalties than for other burglaries, is because of the "greater danger and potential for serious harm from burglary of a home as opposed to burglary of a business." 628 N.E.2d 948, 951 (Ill. App. Ct. 1993). The burglary of an occupied garage used as a living quarters carries the same potential for increased risk of harm as a burglary of a home.

5. Repeat Your Conclusion

In a short memo that extends beyond a few paragraphs, it is helpful to remind your reader of your conclusion. The conclusion also serves as a natural ending for your memo. The conclusion can be brief—unless the short memo is longer than a few pages, it is generally unnecessary to repeat the important reasons that support your conclusion. Thus, in the residential burglary problem, you could simply conclude the memo as follows:

> In conclusion, a strong case can be made that the Stripes' garage is a "living quarters," in which Michael Stripe resides, and thus a dwelling, for purposes of prosecuting Arnold under the Residential Burglary Statute.

Exercise 19-1: The Kidnapping Problem

Review the Kidnapping Memorandum that is illustrated in Appendix A as Sample Memo B. Assume that your law firm represents the defendant in that legal action, Mr. Tate, who has been charged with aggravated kidnapping under Illinois' kidnapping statute. The kidnapping statute requires that the State of Illinois prove that, when your client confined Mr. Campbell against his will, the confinement was "secret." A senior partner in your law firm has asked you to research whether the confinement was actually "secret" under the Statute. The office memorandum that is illustrated as Sample Memo B addresses this issue within the format of a formal, longer memorandum. Condense and redraft the discussion in Sample Memo B into a Short Memo.

PROFESSIONAL E-MAIL COMMUNICATIONS

I. PROFESSIONALISM CONCERNS

A. Striking the Appropriate Tone

Due to the speed and convenience of the Internet, e-mail communications have become a common means by which lawyers communicate with their clients, colleagues, and opposing counsel. Although you have likely been texting and e-mailing friends for many years, these informal, casual messages are very different from the professional e-mails you will be sending as a lawyer. In e-mails to friends and family, you might use colloquialisms (slang) to capture the more playful quality of a "live" exchange, and acronyms to convey commonly used expressions, such as LOL ("laughing out loud"), TTYL ("talk to you later"), BTW ("by the way"), or FYI ("for your information"). In informal e-mail exchanges, emoticons and the use of ALL CAPS are commonly used to convey "tone." For example, you might use the symbol :) to convey humor or happiness, the symbol :(to convey a frown or sadness, or CAPS, such as "CALL ME NOW," to convey a sense of urgency or importance.

In professional e-mail communications to clients, colleagues, and opposing counsel, these informal means of communicating both "content" and "tone" are inappropriate. In a professional communication, irrespective of whether the message is sent by e-mail, by letter, or by office memorandum, the message should strike a tone that is respectful of the professional relationship you have with the recipient. By whatever form of communication, your colleagues and clients will have an expectation that you behave with professionalism and impeccable judgment. A hastily written e-mail that treats the recipient with the same casual breeziness as your personal e-mail messages could cost you the recipient's respect and trust.

At the same time, communicating as a professional doesn't necessarily mean that you strike an overly formal and legalistic tone, either. Overly formal writing can be off-putting and can jeopardize the relationship you are attempting to cultivate with a client, colleague, or other professional. Within this fine balance between appearing unprofessional and overly casual on the one hand, and overly formal and rigid on the other, you might also take your cue from the personality and expectations of the recipient of your e-mail communication. Some people are, by nature, more formal and proper, particularly in a business setting. Others are more informal and relaxed, and appreciate a certain degree of levity. Even in the latter case, however, remember that clients expect you to behave like a professional (and they are generally paying you a significant hourly rate for the privilege of communicating with you). Therefore, even when a client has employed humor in an e-mail to you, or has used acronyms or emoticons, be very, very careful about responding in kind. Your client might have expectations of professionalism that hold you to a higher standard than the client's own e-mail communications. Moreover, even if the recipient of your e-mail might appreciate your humor, consider other recipients to whom the e-mail might be forwarded; they may not appreciate the same level of humor or levity, particularly if they do not already have a good working relationship with you.

B. Emotionally Sensitive Conversations

1. When E-Mail Is Not the Appropriate Medium

No difficult or emotionally sensitive conversation, particularly one laden with negative emotions, should be undertaken by e-mail. Sending difficult messages by e-mail runs the risk of fracturing the professional relationship you enjoy with the recipient. First, the recipient may well interpret the e-mail as a sign of disrespect or cowardice. A communication that has particular emotional importance to the recipient merits a personal meeting or telephone call.

As importantly, a written message carries the risk that your meaning will be misconstrued; this is particularly true when there is reason for the recipient to be sensitive to or upset with the message you are attempting to convey. Unlike with a verbal conversation, the recipient of your e-mail message can't "read" your non-verbal behavior and doesn't necessarily know whether your intention is to chastise and judge, or whether you are simply making a matter-of-fact point. When you are delivering bad news or attempting to resolve a difficult conversation with the recipient, the recipient is particularly apt to inaccurately assign negative motives to language that you intended to be neutral. This is one of the reasons emoticons are popular in electronic communications—you can soften a message, for example, by adding a smiley face :). Unfortunately, emoticons are not professional enough to be used in electronic communications with clients and other professionals.

Before sending an email that involves a difficult or emotionally sensitive matter, consider whether the discussion might be more appropriately, and respectfully, handled in an actual conversation rather than in an e-mail message. Should you decide to raise the matter in an e-mail message, take particular care in selecting your language. Remember that the recipient can't read your non-verbal behavior or the tone of your voice. Strive for language that is non-judgmental and that is not likely to cause defensiveness. If you can't think of a way to frame the language in a manner that is unlikely to cause defensiveness or emotional pain, then a written message is not the appropriate medium to convey the message.

2. Problems Associated with "Flaming"

One reason e-mail communications are so popular is the ease and speed with which we can communicate with others. However, the ease and speed of e-communications is also one of its dangers. After reading an e-mail that "triggers" an angry or unhappy reaction, it is all too easy to respond in kind and to click the "send" button while still angry or disturbed. Unfortunately, because there is no opportunity in an e-mail communication for the give-and-take of a verbal exchange, and the recipient has no opportunity to read cues from your non-verbal behavior, angry words expressed in an e-mail are apt to be magnified and to linger in the recipient's mind long after the message has been sent. Therefore, an angry e-mail is likely to trigger an angry rebuttal and to exacerbate the original problem without actually resolving it.

Moreover, because e-mails are in written form, they stand as permanent reminders of an outburst that, in a calmer moment, you might later regret. It can be momentarily satisfying to send an angry missive; far more lasting, however, is the resulting damage to the relationship, to your ability to continue to work effectively with the recipient, and even to your reputation. The most influential professionals are those people who have the ability to manage their emotions and to "respond" to unpleasant situations rather than "reacting" to them. A reactionary, angry missive is apt to damage your credibility and reputation, not only in the eyes of the recipient but also, potentially, to third parties whom you might not even know. This is because e-mails are so easy to forward to others; an e-mail fired off in a fit of anger might well be the only impression a third-party recipient of your e-mail ever has of you. An angry or curt missive can damage your reputation with the sweep of the "send" button, but can take literally years to repair.

A practical rule of thumb is never to send an e-mail message while angry or even mildly irritated. Instead, wait to send the message until after you have calmed down and have gained a clearer perspective about your ultimate goals and priorities. A good test is this: the stronger your desire to click the "send" button, the greater the likelihood that you are angry and that your message would benefit from further revisions after you have calmed down. If necessary, sleep on it (for several days, if necessary), until you confidently believe that you have achieved some perspective. Upon calmer reflection, you might even conclude that it is wiser not to respond at all.

◎ A CAUTIONARY TALE

The following infamous e-mail exchange occurred between a new law school graduate and a potential employer, a lawyer who practices law in Boston, Massachusetts. The lawyer had offered the law school graduate a job; however, during the second job interview, the lawyer apparently lowered the starting salary from the salary figure he had given in the first interview. The two stories conflict as to whether the law school graduate actually accepted the job offer. According to the potential employer, the graduate accepted the job offer; according to the graduate, she only *tentatively* agreed to the job offer. Because these were verbal communications not commemorated in writing, we can only speculate as to what was said and agreed to in the job interviews. However, the following e-mail exchange lives on in perpetuity. Following the second interview, the law school graduate sent the following e-mail to her prospective employer. In the e-mail, she stated:

> At this time, I am writing to inform you that I will not be accepting your offer. After careful consideration, I have come to the conclusion that the pay you are offering would neither fulfill me nor support the lifestyle I am living in light of the work I would be doing for you. I have decided instead to work for myself, and reap 100% of the benefits that I sew [sic]. Thank you for the interviews.[1]

Before reading on, consider how you might feel upon reading this e-mail, particularly if you had already ordered stationary and business cards for the new law school graduate, and had reformatted a computer and set up an e-mail system for her. Would you expect that, given the subject matter of the e-mail, this might be a more appropriate topic for an actual conversation rather than an e-mail communication? Would you feel disrespected? What language in the e-mail might offend you? Why? What implied judgment and criticism might you glean from this message? What judgments have you formed about the sender of this e-mail message?

The employer responded:

> Given that you had two interviews, were offered and accepted the job (indeed, you had a definite start date), I am surprised that you chose an e-mail and a 9:30 PM voicemail message to convey this information to me. It smacks of immaturity and is quite unprofessional. Indeed, I did rely upon your acceptance by ordering stationary and business cards with your name, reformatting a computer and setting up both internal and external e-mails for you here at the office. While I do not quarrel with your reasoning, I am extremely dis-

---

1. Anne P. Mitchell, *When Emails Haunt You—The Saga of William Korman and Dianna Abdala*, Internet Patrol (Feb. 23, 2006), https://www.theinternetpatrol.com/when-emails-haunt-you-the-saga-of-william-korman-and-diana-abdala/.

appointed in the way this played out. I sincerely wish you the best of luck in your future endeavors.[2]

Before reading on, consider how you might feel upon reading this e-mail. Would you feel disrespected? What language in the e-mail might offend you? Why? What implied judgment and criticism might you glean from this message? What language is likely to inflame the recipient's anger? How might you have responded instead? What might be a more professional response?

Less than four hours later, the law school graduate sent this brief retort:

A real lawyer would have put the contract into writing and not exercised any such reliance until he did so. Again, thank you.[3]

How might you feel upon reading this e-mail message? Why? Is any productive purpose accomplished by this message? Does the "thank you" at the end of the message soften the message? Why or why not? What purpose do you think the law school graduate might have had in sending this e-mail? Is she attempting to defend herself? What might have been a more professional response?

Seventeen (17) minutes later, the lawyer responded:

Thank you for the refresher course on contracts. This is not a bar exam question. You need to realize that this is a very small legal community, especially the criminal defense bar. Do you really want to start pissing off more experienced lawyers at this early stage of your career?[4]

Is there any language in this e-mail that could be misconstrued, or interpreted to be a threat? Is any productive purpose accomplished by this message? What purpose do you think the lawyer might have had in sending this e-mail? What would have been a more professional response? Was a response necessary? Desirable?

Eleven (11) minutes later, the law school graduate sent her final three-word missive:

bla bla bla[5]

Perhaps it was momentarily satisfying to draft these e-mails and angrily hit the "send" button. However, the potential damage to reputation lingered long after the actual e-mail exchanges themselves. Perhaps not surprisingly, the lawyer forwarded the e-mail exchange to a friend, who forwarded it to other friends. The exchange quickly "began whipping through cyberspace, landing in e-mail in-boxes around the

---

2. *Id.*
3. *Id.*
4. *Id.*
5. *Id.*

city and country, and, eventually, across the Atlantic. In short order, it has become yet another cautionary tale that you should definitely not put in an e-mail anything you wouldn't want the rest of the world to read."[6]

In the Boston Globe article reporting on the e-mail exchange, then Boston Bar Association president-elect Jack Cinquegrana was quoted as follows: "You should never write an e-mail that you are not willing to see preserved forever in history.... The dangers created by this new world we live in, where everything is recorded for history, are not only that you could be second-guessed at every stage in the context of a civil dispute or government investigation, but that your reputation can be affected by words you don't think you're preserving for posterity—but really are."[7]

C. Balancing Speed with Professionalism Concerns

One of the benefits of e-mail communications is the speed and ease with which you can communicate with others. In informal exchanges with friends and family, misspelled words, abbreviations, acronyms, and even a lack of a greeting ("Dear X") or signature ("Best regards, Y") are commonly accepted practices; they are simply a by-product of the speed and ease of this form of communication. In contrast, the recipients of your professional e-mail communications have different expectations of you—they expect a level of professionalism and polish that is more akin to a professionally drafted letter or office memo than to the informal e-mail exchanges you share with friends.

A hastily drafted e-mail message that contains typographical errors or that is not carefully thought out conveys a general impression of unprofessionalism and carelessness. Once that seed is planted in the mind of a client or colleague, it is difficult to displace. As an example, assume that you went to a doctor complaining of abdominal pain, and that the doctor requested that you undergo x-rays and an MRI. Following these procedures, assume that you received the following e-mail message from the physician:

X-rays show abdominal obsturction. Call offce and make appt for sergury ASAP. Questions? Call 555-1279.

Would you entrust your health to a physician who sent you such a message? You might be forgiven for leaping to the conclusion that the physician was (a) unprofessional; (b) careless; and (c) incompetent. To many people, even the lack of a greeting or signature would be construed to be curt (at best), or disrespectful (at worst). It is doubtful that you would want to place your life and physical health into this physician's care. Would you even be inclined to give this physician a second chance?

---

6. Sacha Pfeiffer, *2 E-mailers Get Testy, and Hundreds Read Every Word*, Boston Globe, Bus. (Feb. 16, 2006).
7. *Id.*

Your clients and colleagues expect a similar level of professionalism from you. At the same time, they are also likely to expect that you respond to an e-mail communication promptly. This can place you in a quandary—should you respond quickly, or should you take more time to respond thoughtfully and carefully? The answer is: both. If you can respond promptly with a simple reply that doesn't require significant thought or research, then do so. However, even with quick responses that do not require significant thought or analysis, it's important to proofread your e-mail messages for clarity, typographical errors, and incomplete sentences before sending them out.

In contrast, if an e-mail asks you for legal advice and your response merits some research or careful thought, then it would be a mistake to send a quick, off-the-cuff response that is either incomplete or inaccurate. The ease of sending an e-mail can seduce you into sending your legal analysis prematurely, before you've had the opportunity to think about it and mull over the implications of your advice. Instead, you can send the client or colleague a prompt response indicating that you have received the e-mail and that you will provide an in-depth response later, after you have had the opportunity to research the issues and/or evaluate the problem. This satisfies the recipient's expectations that you will promptly respond to the e-mail inquiry. At the same time, by specifying a realistic time frame within which you will send a follow-up response, you can avoid misunderstandings as to the timing of your follow-up response.

D. Other Professionalism Issues: Courtesy & Respect

You might think that the most important aspect of your professional e-mail communications is the legal "content" they convey. Although it is important that the substantive content of your e-mails be both accurate and thorough, there is more to being a professional than conveying good legal advice. There are other courtesies of being a "professional" that are less easy to define, but that will also be important to your success as a lawyer. The recipients of your e-mail communications will expect that you comply with their own unwritten expectations concerning professional courtesy and respect. If you violate these expectations, you can unwittingly harm the professional relationship you share with them.

What makes this such a challenge is that each of us has different ideas about what it means to be courteous and respectful. Some people are more casual than others, and some people are more tolerant of other people's failure to comply with social "niceties." Because of the differing ideas your clients and colleagues might have as to what constitutes respectful behavior, it is better to err on the side of caution. What follows are a few of the more common conventions that are, to many people, considered to be important signs of courtesy, respect, and professionalism.

1. Greetings & Endings

Although your personal e-mail communications might omit a formal greeting or signature, you should not ignore these professional courtesies in your e-mail communications. As an example, assume you have scheduled a meeting with a colleague, and that, the day before the meeting, you received the following e-mail from your colleague:

> From: Joseph Langston
> Subject: Meeting Tomorrow
> To: [You]
> Date: [Present Date]
>
> This confirms our meeting tomorrow at 9:30 AM.

What is your initial impression of the e-mail? Does it seem professional and to-the-point? Or does it instead seem rather curt and abrupt? Does it convey a sense that your colleague looks forward to your meeting? That your colleague "likes" you? Or would this not matter to you? For some people, this e-mail might be well-received; it serves the purpose (relaying important information) and doesn't waste either the sender's or the recipient's time with irrelevant details. However, for other people, this e-mail would not be as well-received. To some people, the message might seem curt and off-putting because it ignores the social convention of beginning a message with a greeting and ending it with a signature. Because you usually won't know for sure how the recipient might respond, it is better practice to take the extra few seconds and add a greeting and a signature to your e-mails.

A professional greeting can begin with a "Dear Ron," or "Hi Ron," (depending upon your familiarity to and relationship to "Ron"). You should close your e-mails with a professional signature. The following are common professional terms to close an e-mail: "Sincerely"; "Best regards"; "Regards"; and "Very truly yours." After "signing" your name, a professional signature should also include: your professional title; your law office's name and address; your telephone number; and your e-mail address.

The following example conveys the same message as the e-mail communication illustrated above. However, in this message, the sender has added a greeting ("Dear Ron"), an ending ("Best regards, Joe"), a professional signature, and a sentence to soften the message ("I look forward to seeing you then"). The added information is italicized for purposes of comparison. For some recipients, the different tone that this e-mail message conveys could affect their regard for the sender and their opinion of the sender's professionalism. Therefore, although it might have taken only a few more seconds to draft the message, the following e-mail conveys a more professional and respectful "tone."

From: Joseph Langston
Subject: Meeting Tomorrow
To: [You]
Date: [Present Date]

Dear Ron,

This confirms our meeting tomorrow at 9:30 AM. *I look forward to seeing you then.*

Best regards,

Joe

Joseph Langston
Langston & Jones, LLP
1005 Broadway
Los Angeles, CA 92925
(309) 555-1234
josephlangston@langston_jones.com

2. The Dilemma of First Names vs Surnames

Like with greetings and signatures, failing to address people by their surnames can be viewed by some people as either presumptuous or disrespectful. The following rule of thumb avoids such issues. When addressing clients or other professionals for the first time, always refer to them by their surnames using the appropriate title (e.g., "Mr. Jones" rather than "Jim"). Women present a bit more of a dilemma, as many women prefer to be referred to as "Ms.," while some married women prefer to be referred to as "Mrs." As a general rule, it is better practice to refer to women as "Ms. [Jones]" rather than "Mrs. [Jones]," unless she has made it clear that she prefers the title "Mrs." If the recipient has a professional title, use the professional title rather than the more generic gender title (for example, "Dr. Jones," or "Judge Jones" rather than "Mr.," "Ms.," or "Ma'am"). Some prefer that you not utilize pronouns at all, and if this is what the recipient has communicated to you, you should respect that request and refer to that person by the requested name. For example, a client may prefer "they" as a neutral pronoun. Although using "they" as a singular pronoun is typically viewed as a grammatical mistake, it would be appropriate to use it as a singular pronoun when the client requests that designation.

After you have addressed the recipient by the appropriate surname (if applicable), wait and see how your salutation is received. In a personal conversation, the recipient can make his preference very clear: "Please, call me Ron." In an e-mail communication, the invitation towards greater informality is usually more indirect. When the recipient of your e-mail responds to your more formal salutation, check the recipient's signature. Does the recipient end with: "Sincerely, Mr. Jones," or does the recipient end with: "Sincerely, Jim." In the latter case, the recipient has given you an implicit invitation to refer to him by his first name. With that said, there are some e-mail correspondents whose titles merit greater deference than others. Even if a judge were to refer to herself as "Lucy" in responding to your e-mail, it is usually wiser to respond with the deferential title "Judge Jones" rather than "Lucy."

3. Acknowledgments

As a lawyer, the sheer volume of the e-mails you receive might seem daunting at times, particularly when you are attempting to balance many competing demands on your time. It can be tempting to respond only to those e-mails that absolutely require a response, and to ignore such courtesies as thanking a client or colleague for sending you a helpful document or for extending you a favor. Resist this temptation. While there are always e-mails you can ignore, any time a client, colleague, or other lawyer extends a favor to you or spends the time to help you in any way, it is not simply a courtesy, but also professionally smart, to respond with an acknowledgement and a "thank you."

Within the larger scheme of your day, it may not seem that important to spend the time to send such e-mails. Nonetheless, such gestures take very little time and can pay dividends for you as a professional. For example, assume a colleague has agreed to review a draft of a legal argument you are preparing to submit to the court, and sends you an e-mail with her comments and suggestions. Do you send her a "thank you" for her time and thoughtful comments, or do you decide that it's not that important in the larger scheme of things because she surely knows that you appreciate her time? When a young lawyer in the office asks for help in the future, do you think that colleague would rather extend herself to support the efforts of someone who always seems to appreciate her past efforts, or someone who doesn't seem to appreciate them? An acknowledgement doesn't require a significant investment of time, and can simply be a quick: "Thank you for getting back to me so quickly. I appreciate your feedback and look forward to reviewing your comments." This is a simple gesture that can pay dividends in your professional career.

E. Special Issues of Confidentiality

As a lawyer, communications relating to information about your clients are confidential. In fact, you have an ethical duty to maintain the confidences of your clients.[8] However, e-mail communications present special concerns with confidentiality issues, in part because they can so easily be forwarded to anyone, anywhere. Moreover, the

---

8 Model R. Prof. Conduct 1.6 (ABA 2002). Comments 16 and 17, which clarify the meaning of Rule 1.6, require lawyers to act "competently" to preserve confidentiality by taking "reasonable precautions to prevent the information from coming into the hands of unintended recipients." *Id.*

speed of e-mail communications increases the likelihood of mistakes in delivery. For example, it would be the rare professional who has not received an e-mail communication by mistake because the sender accidentally clicked the "reply all" rather than the "reply" button, or clicked the "reply" rather than the "forward" button. These mistakes can not only be embarrassing, but they can also have serious ethical consequences.

E-mail communications can also be subject to compelled disclosure in lawsuits. Therefore, think carefully about the potential implications of any e-mail message before sending it. A hastily written e-mail can come back to haunt you. Consider, for example, the Enron employees who failed to consider the legal implications of their e-mails when they noted: "[t]his week is not good. I have too large a pile of documents to shred."[9] Employers also have a lawful interest in monitoring the e-mail communications of their employees. Therefore, you should refrain from sending sensitive or confidential information to your clients' workplace e-mail addresses.

Finally, there are special confidentiality issues that can arise from the "metadata" that is discoverable from documents that are sent by e-mail. Unless you take affirmative steps to remove the metadata from electronic documents, the recipient can scour the document's history and identify any changes, deletions, and additions that were made to the document, as well as the people who at any time have accessed the document. A document's history could well disclose confidential client information and undermine your client's interests.

For example, assume you represent a client who has sued his spouse for divorce. Following a meeting with your client, assume that you drafted a settlement agreement proposing a division of the parties' marital assets. After sending the agreement to your client, suppose that he suggested various modifications that would provide him with a greater percentage of the marital property; perhaps he even inserted electronic comments noting those property interests he would readily concede and those interests that he very much wanted to retain. Assume that you revised the agreement in accordance with your client's instructions and e-mailed it to the opposing counsel without taking affirmative steps to remove the metadata. Under this scenario, the opposing counsel could potentially mine the document's history and discover the electronic revisions and messages you shared with your client. This confidential information could provide the other party with leverage and with the upper-hand in negotiating the terms of the agreement. In some states, it is ethically improper to mine documents for metadata, while in other states this practice is permitted. The safest solution is either to purchase software that removes metadata from documents, convert the document to a PDF, or send sensitive documents by hard copy rather than electronically.

Due to the special confidentiality issues that arise with e-mail communications, most lawyers also prominently display cautionary language within any confidential e-mail communication that the e-mail itself contains "confidential communications,"

---

9. Sacha Pfeiffer, *2 E-mailers Get Testy, and Hundreds Read Every Word,* Boston Globe Bus. (Feb. 16, 2006).

or "confidential attorney-client communications." Even with that cautionary language, however, the problem isn't entirely eliminated; a confidential e-mail message can still be forwarded to third parties, whether inadvertently or otherwise. Therefore, use discretion when determining the information that you disclose in an e-mail communication. Generally, do not include in an e-mail communication any information that is confidential or that you would not be willing to have made public. As an example, if you represented a client in a divorce proceeding, it would be unwise to refer to the client's extra-marital affair in an e-mail communication to the client.

In sum, e-mail communications can be a useful, quick, and expedient way to communicate with clients and other professionals. Nonetheless, the very ease and speed of the electronic medium presents special challenges and opportunities for professional mishaps. Most of these mishaps can be avoided if you take the time to slow down and proofread your messages for clarity, accuracy, and "tone." However, you must also be particularly sensitive to the inherent risks to confidentiality that electronic messages pose, and take reasonable precautions to minimize that risk.

II. DRAFTING EMAILS CONTAINING LEGAL ANALYSIS

As discussed earlier, communicating through e-mail has become more and more commonplace, and this holds true for communications containing substantive legal analysis. A client may prefer to send a question via e-mail, hoping for a thorough, yet quick, written response. Similarly, a firm partner may prefer a shorter, more concise emailed response to a legal inquiry instead of a lengthier, more detailed memorandum. The partner may be preparing to meet with the client later that day, and the need for a quick response could be paramount. However, the partner still requires an understanding of the basis for the answer, and thus it is important to learn how to convey substantive legal analysis in a concise, professional way.

Providing legal analysis through e-mail is not unlike drafting legal analysis in memo form. Just like with a memorandum, your reader expects to first understand the issue addressed and receive an answer to that issue. The reader then expects you to "show your work" and prove that the answer is valid. You can do this just as you would with any other legal analysis—you explain the law and then apply it to the client facts (if applicable).

Thus, the basic template for an emailed legal analysis would look like this:

1. Statement of the issue and your conclusion about that issue
2. Explanation of the law, from the most general to the most specific
3. Application of the law (if applicable)
4. Restatement of your conclusion

Below is an example of an email prompt from a firm partner. The partner is preparing for a client meeting, and he needs the associate attorney to promptly research an issue and educate him on the legal requirements surrounding that issue.

From: Jack Randall
Subject: Retaining a Tenant's Security Deposit
To: Anna Michaels
Date: [Present Date]

Hi Anna,

I need your help with a research issue. Could you please let me know if a landlord in Michigan is legally entitled to retain a security deposit when the tenants move out and leave the rental property dirty?

I'll be in and out of court today and need your analysis ASAP. Please email me your response before close of business today.

As always, thanks for your help,

Jack Randall
Randall & Jones, LLP
1515 W. 9th St.
Grand Rapids, MI 49501
(616) 555-1234
jrandall@randall_jones.com

Notice that in this prompt, there are no client facts provided. Because of that, there are no facts to apply to the law. Review the following sample answer to this question, which begins with the issue addressed, and then provides an answer to that issue and an explanation of the law supporting the answer, with a focus on black letter law.

From: Anna Michaels
Subject: Re: Retaining a Tenant's Security Deposit
To: Jack Randall
Date: [Present Date]

Dear Jack,

As you requested, I researched Michigan's Landlord-Tenant Relationship Act (LTRA) to determine whether a landlord may retain a tenant's security deposit when property is left in an unclean state. My research uncovered that landlords may not retain a deposit for this reason because the applicable statute requires "damage" to property, and "dirtiness" does not constitute damage.

Regarding security deposits under the LTRA, the statute provides that a security deposit may be utilized to "reimburse the landlord for actual damages to the rental unit... that are the direct result of conduct not reasonably expected in the normal course of habitation of a dwelling." Mich. Comp. Laws Ann. §554.607 (West 2001). The statute does not define the term "damages," but Michigan courts have held that "where a term is not defined by the statute, it is to be given its plain and ordinary meaning...." *Smolen v. Dahlmann Apartments, Ltd.*, 338 N.W.2d 892, 894 (Mich. Ct. App. 1983). As Webster's Dictionary defines the ordinary meaning of "damage" as "that of injury to something," the *Smolen* court concluded that a "rental unit requiring cleaning has not been damaged." *Id.* In addition, because the Legislature "specified that [a] security deposit could only be used to pay for 'actual' damages to the premises," the court found the term "actual" alerts landlords that they "could no longer stretch the meaning of the term 'damages' to include such fabricated 'damages' as grimy appliances and dirty floors." *Id.* at 895. Furthermore, the LTRA requires the landlord to provide "an itemized list of damages," which includes an estimated repair cost of each property item damaged. Thus, the statute "contemplates that damage is the sort of condition remedied by repair." *Id.* As a result, the court deemed the "Legislature must have intended that premises requiring cleaning" do not suffer damages, and a landlord may not retain the security deposit due to the "dirty" nature of the rental property. *Id.* This seminal case still stands as undisputed law today.

Please let me know if I can help you any further.

Thanks,

Anna Michaels
Randall & Jones, LLP
1515 W. 9th St.
Grand Rapids, MI 49501
(616) 555-1235
amichaels@randall_jones.com

In the previous example, the firm partner did not provide any client facts that called for an application of the law to facts. The next sample includes those facts, and in the sample answer, the facts are applied to the law in the application section of the response.

From: Jack Randall
Subject: Retaining a Tenant's Security Deposit
To: Anna Michaels
Date: [Present Date]

Hi Anna,

I need your help with a research issue. Our client, Madison Evans, owns several rental properties in the area. She is rather new to the leasing industry and often seeks our counsel on some of the issues involving her leases. One such issue arose today, and she needs our assistance.

The lease period expired on one of her rental properties, and the tenants, the Jacksons, recently moved out. When the Jacksons moved into the house, they put down a $1500 deposit on the property per the lease's requirements. The lease they signed provides that if they leave the house "damaged," Ms. Evans (the landlord) may retain any portion(s) of the deposit needed to cover expenses related to the damage.

After the Jacksons moved out, Ms. Evans discovered that several of the appliances were dirty, the toilets in the house were not well cleaned, and some of the cabinets were pretty filthy. Ms. Evans hired a cleaning service to take care of these issues and to clean the home in full. She paid $250 for this service. Ms. Evans would like to deduct this $250 from the deposit to cover the cleaning expense. I'm not sure if she can do this, and I need you to look into it for me.

I will be in and out of court today and need your analysis ASAP. Please email me your response before close of business today so that I can counsel our client in a timely manner.

As always, thanks for your help,

Jack Randall
Randall & Jones, LLP
1515 W. 9th St.
Grand Rapids, MI 49501
(616) 555-1234
jrandall@randall_jones.com

Below is the associate's response to this question, with the client (and her specific facts) named:

From: Anna Michaels
Subject: Re: Retaining a Tenant's Security Deposit
To: Jack Randall
Date: [Present Date]

Dear Jack,

As you requested, I researched Michigan's Landlord-Tenant Relationship Act (LTRA) to determine whether Madison Evans has valid grounds to deduct $250 from the Jacksons' security deposit to cover cleaning expenses. I believe she may not do so, and I will explain why below.

Regarding security deposits under the LTRA, the statute provides that a security deposit may be utilized to "reimburse the landlord for actual damages to the rental unit… that are the direct result of conduct not reasonably expected in the normal course of habitation of a dwelling." Mich. Comp. Laws Ann. § 554.607 (West 2001). The statute does not define the term "damages," but Michigan courts have held that "where a term is not defined by the statute, it is to be given its plain and ordinary meaning…." *Smolen v. Dahlmann Apartments, Ltd.*, 338 N.W.2d 892, 894 (Mich. Ct. App. 1983). As Webster's Dictionary defines the ordinary meaning of "damage" as "that of injury to something," the *Smolen* court concluded that a "rental unit requiring cleaning has not been damaged." *Id.* In addition, because the Legislature "specified that [a] security deposit could only be used to pay for 'actual' damages to the premises," the court found the term "actual" alerts landlords that they "could no longer stretch the meaning of the term 'damages' to include such fabricated 'damages' as grimy appliances and dirty floors." *Id.* at 895. Furthermore, the LTRA requires the landlord to provide "an itemized list of damages," which includes an estimated repair cost of each property item damaged. Thus, the statute "contemplates that damage is the sort of condition remedied by repair." *Id.* As a result, the court deemed the "Legislature must have intended that premises requiring cleaning" do not suffer damages, and a landlord may not retain the security deposit due to the "dirty" nature of the rental property. *Id.*

As a result, it appears that Ms. Evans does not have valid grounds to withhold $250 from the Jacksons' security deposit for reimbursement of cleaning services. Retaining the deposit requires a showing of "damage," *id.* at 894, and Ms. Evans simply found the appliances, toilets, and cabinets were dirty. Since this does not constitute "damage" under Michigan law, as it is not remedied with a "repair," *id.*, she may not retain any portion of the Jacksons' security deposit for that purpose.

Although Ms. Evans does not have valid grounds to retain the $250 for cleaning services, she may have valid grounds to retain a portion of the security deposit if she can show actual property damage requiring repair that was caused by the Jacksons' unreasonable conduct. I advise that she inspect the property to check for any such areas.

Please let me know if I can help you any further.

Thanks,

Anna Michaels
Randall & Jones, LLP
1515 W. 9th St.
Grand Rapids, MI 49501
(616) 555-1235
amichaels@randall_jones.com

In this example, the author of the email has bad news to deliver to the firm partner—unfortunately, the client does not have grounds to retain a portion of the security deposit for the dirty rental unit. However, notice that the author suggests an alternative idea for the client and also offers to further assist in the matter. Including such niceties can soften the blow when the research results are not favorable, and they leave a positive impression for the reader, who will likely appreciate the author's commitment to fully assisting with the matter.

Exercise 20-1: Drafting an Email Response

Review the prompt below and draft an email response, following the template given earlier in this chapter. As you prepare to draft the email, note whether the question contains client facts that should be included within an application section of your answer.

Prior to drafting the answer, review the following case opinion, which will serve as your legal authority, and highlight the relevant black letter law to include within your answer: *McInnis v. OAG Motorcycle Ventures, Inc.*, 35 N.E.3d 1076 (Ill. App. Ct. 2015).

From: Rachel Wayne
Subject: Consideration Needed for Non-Compete
To: [You]
Date: [Present Date]

Hi [your name],

I need your help with a research issue. Our client is an Illinois-based company that wishes to sue to enforce a non-compete agreement that it entered into with a former employee. This employee claims the non-compete lacks valid consideration, and I need to know Illinois' requirements for sufficient consideration for a non-compete agreement.

I'll be in and out of court today and need your analysis ASAP. Please email me your response before close of business today.

As always, thanks for your help,

Rachel Wayne
Wayne & Associates, P.C.
2929 N. Main Street
Buffalo Grove, IL 60069
(847) 555-1234
RachelWayne@waynelaw.com

DRAFTING CLIENT LETTERS

I. TYPES OF CLIENT LETTERS

Letter writing is the bread-and-butter of a lawyer's practice. Lawyers routinely communicate with their clients by letter, whether the letter is sent to the client through the U.S. mail or by an e-mail communication. Client letters can be grouped into three basic types. The first type of letter does not involve legal analysis; instead, these letters convey "non-legal" information, such as confirming a meeting, summarizing a telephone conversation, notifying a client of the status of the client's legal matter, or forwarding a document to the client. Given the ease and speed of the Internet, this type of letter is often sent as an e-mail communication.

In addition to such commonplace letters, lawyers also convey *legal analysis* in letter form. The first type of letter conveying legal analysis is a formal document called an "opinion letter." Opinion letters state the law firm's conclusion that the client's actions comply or do not comply with the law. These letters are highly specialized, formal documents. They express the legal opinion of the law firm as to the *legal validity* of a client's proposed action. The potential legal ramifications from these letters can be enormous. If the client relies on a lawyer's opinion letter and is later sued or criminally sanctioned because of those actions, the law firm itself could be vulnerable to liability in a malpractice action. Because of these legal ramifications, many law firms will not issue an opinion letter until at least two law partners have reviewed the letter and "signed off" on it, representing that the firm has complied with certain due diligence procedures.

The "advisory letter" is by far the more common type of client letter that conveys legal analysis. This type of letter is similar to an office memo insofar as the letter presents a well-balanced analysis of the law, although the legal discussion itself is more succinct than in an office memo. In addition, the client advisory letter often includes a discussion of the client's options, both legal and non-legal, and a brief summary of the advantages and disadvantages of each of the client's available options.

Because you can expect to draft advisory letters on a routine basis as a lawyer, the remainder of this chapter discusses the nuts and bolts of drafting advisory letters.

II. CLIENT ADVISORY LETTERS

An advisory letter typically has five basic sections. Like any letter, an advisory letter begins with an introductory paragraph that introduces the purpose of the letter. Next, the advisory letter contains a summary of the relevant client facts that relate to the issue under discussion. Following the factual summary, the letter evaluates the law. This section is akin to an abbreviated version of the rule explanation and rule application sections of an office memo. Next, the letter summarizes each of the client's available options. Finally, the letter concludes by suggesting a "next step."

A.   Introductory Paragraph

B.   Factual Summary of Relevant Facts

C.   Legal Discussion
   1. Roadmap Paragraph(s) Containing Conclusion & Legal Rules
   2. *Sometimes*, Additional In-Depth Rule Explanation Paragraph(s)
   3. Rule Application Paragraph(s)

D.   Discussion of Available Options

E.   Closing Paragraph

A. Introductory Paragraph

An introductory paragraph accomplishes the following three purposes:
   (1)   It states the issues or questions the letter will address;
   (2)   It briefly answers the questions; and
   (3)   It sets the proper tone of the letter.

1. Setting the Tone

Because the introductory paragraph is the very first paragraph the client reviews, it is important to set an appropriate tone. Before you begin to draft a letter, stop and consider your client. Although every client advisory letter should be professional in tone, your client's preferences may dictate a slightly more formal or informal tone. An extremely formal letter written to a client who prefers informality may not establish the kind of rapport you ultimately want to develop with the client. In contrast, a letter that is too informal in tone may convey a lack of professionalism and consideration for what is, to the client, a very serious matter. Also consider your client's educational level and relative sophistication. Does your client have a high school education or an advanced degree? Is your client a blue-collar worker or an executive of a major corporation? Your goal is to convey information in language the client will readily understand and in a manner that will inspire trust and confidence.

In setting the appropriate tone, consider not only the client's background and personal preferences, but also the particular circumstances that have brought the client to your office and the information you will convey in the letter. For example, when writing to a client who has retained you to represent the client following the loss of a child, your language should convey your sensitivity to the client's loss. To illustrate, consider the following example:

> **Example 1:**
>
> Dear Mr. and Mrs. McLean,
>
> It was great meeting with you. After our meeting, I checked out the law regarding "attractive nuisance," and I have some good news. We have a very good shot at collecting money against the Hurts' insurance company in the death of your son! The upshot of my research is that the Hurts probably violated the law by leaving the gate to their pool open in which your son was drowned.

In the above example, the phrases "great meeting with you" and "good news" reflect the lawyer's insensitivity to the tragedy the clients have endured. The informality of the words "checked out," "good shot," and "upshot of my research" belie the seriousness of the matter and could be viewed as insulting by the clients. Finally, the lawyer's insensitivity to the clients' tragedy is further reflected by the exclamation mark following the reference to the death of the clients' son. Grieving clients would be left with the impression that the lawyer cavalierly expects them to rejoice that they have a "good shot at collecting money" from the insurance company.

Now consider the different tone reflected in Example 2 that has been excerpted from Sample Letter B in Appendix B:

> **Example 2:**
>
> Dear Mr. and Mrs. McLean,
>
> It was a pleasure to meet you last week, although I am sorry that it was under such sad circumstances. Following our meeting, I researched the law in Florida and confirmed that property owners who own pools are generally responsible for any injuries to young children who gain access to the pool through unlocked gates. From my research, I believe we have a very strong legal claim against the Hurts should you wish to pursue legal action against them.

In Example 2, what language conveys the lawyer's respect and regard for the tragedy the clients have just experienced? Why do you suppose the lawyer deleted the reference to the clients' son? Notice, too, the shift from informality to language that is more professional. The informal phrase "checked out" has been replaced with the word "researched," and the phrase "very good shot" has been replaced with the phrase "very strong legal claim."

2. Stating the Issue and Answering the Question

The client to whom you are writing the letter has likely been eager to learn the results of your research. Therefore, it makes sense to open the letter by (a) reminding the client of the legal question you have been asked to address; and (b) answering the legal question you've been asked to research. In Example 2 above, the introductory paragraph serves each of these purposes. It both identifies the legal question the lawyer has been asked to research (whether property owners are legally responsible for injuries to children who gain access to the pool through an unlocked gate) and answers the question (the clients have a "very strong legal claim").

A Caveat: It is easy to tell clients good news, but not as easy to give your clients answers they don't want to hear. When the answer is unfavorable, many lawyers still convey the unfavorable news within the introductory paragraph, reasoning that the client deserves to know the "bottom-line" immediately. They reason that the client has requested an answer, has paid for an answer, and is anxious to know the bottom-line without sifting through a lengthy analysis of the legal problem. However, some lawyers prefer to wait until later in the letter to deliver unfavorable news. They reason that the client will view the answer more favorably after they have walked the client through the legal analysis.

You should follow your own inclination in any given situation, based on your knowledge of the client and your own beliefs. In either event, when you must provide the client with an unfavorable answer, it's important to strike an appropriate tone that will serve to strengthen your future relationship with the client. For example, in the illustration below, the word "unfortunately" conveys a sense of regret and alliance with the client's interests. The following introductory paragraph is excerpted from Sample Letter A in Appendix B.

Dear Mr. and Mrs. Johnson:

> 1. Identifies the issue & purpose of letter.

It was a pleasure meeting you last week. As you requested, I have analyzed the viability of a legal claim against your landlord to recover for the injuries you suffered when you fell on an icy sidewalk at your apartment complex. This letter summarizes the facts as I understand them and my analysis of Missouri law concerning a landlord's legal duty to keep common walkways free from

snow and ice. My research suggests that we could make a
viable legal claim that your landlord was negligent under
Missouri law. Unfortunately, however, the law is less than
clear, and we would face some legal hurdles in recovering
damages against your landlord.

> 2. States the conclusion.

B. Factual Statement

Because your clients are presumably aware of the facts that involve their legal problems, it may seem counter-intuitive to include a factual statement in client letters.
However, the factual statement is important because your advice will be based on
facts you believe to exist. If you misunderstand the facts in any way, or if the client
neglected to tell you about an important factual detail, this could affect your legal
conclusion and advice. Clients often fail to inform their lawyers of relevant facts, not
because they wish to deceive their lawyers, but because they are not aware that the
facts are legally important. Incorporating the relevant facts in the advisory letter provides the client with an opportunity to review the facts as you understand them and
to let you know if the facts are incomplete or inaccurate in any way.

In drafting the factual statement, include all facts you believe are legally relevant to
the issue you are evaluating, as well as any helpful background facts that provide
fluidity to the factual story. Your goal is to achieve a tone that portrays the facts objectively and respectfully, yet reflects empathy for the client. The following factual
paragraphs are excerpted from Sample Letter B in Appendix B.

Before I discuss the law and your legal alternatives, I'd
like to review my understanding of the facts so that I can
confirm that I have an accurate understanding of what
happened. As you may know, the factual background of
any legal case is critically important, as lawsuits are often
won or lost based on factual nuances. I am uncomfortably
aware of how painful it must be to think back to the tragic incident; however, it's important that my understanding
is correct. Please let me know if my understanding of the
facts is incorrect in any way.

> What 2 purposes does this
> paragraph achieve?

As I understand the facts, on Sunday, May 28, 20XX,
your six-year-old son, Mikey, and two of his friends entered the Hurts' property through an unlocked gate. The
Hurts' property has a man-made pond and dock that has
attracted small children to their property for a number of
years. Ten years ago, after an elementary school was built
on property adjacent to their property, the Hurts erected
a fence around their property. It is your understanding
that the fence installer tried to persuade the Hurts to build

> There is a fair amount of factual
> detail conveyed in these three
> paragraphs. Can you identify
> why each of these facts might
> be legally significant?

a privacy fence around their property rather than a four-foot high chain-link fence, because the installer believed that the chain-link fence would not deter school children from entering the Hurts' property. Nonetheless, the Hurts declined to purchase the more expensive privacy fence and elected instead to erect the inexpensive chain-link fence with a "No Trespassing" sign posted on the fence.

> Notice the degree of detail concerning the past history of child trespassers. How is this relevant?

Unfortunately, the chain-link fence did not keep young children from entering the Hurts' property. In the past, the Hurts did not object to children feeding the ducks through their chain-link fence. However, when two of Mikey's friends climbed the fence to feed the ducks that were swimming in the pond, the Hurts told the children that they "should get back to school." After that incident, some of the older students began to dare each other to climb the fence without getting caught. Apparently to prevent the students from climbing the fence, the Hurts removed the "No Trespassing" sign and replaced it with a "Do Not Climb Fence" sign.

> Notice how the lawyer refrains from calling the clients' son a "trespasser." What purpose does this serve?

On May 26th, the Hurts left town for the holiday weekend, leaving the gate unlocked while they were away. On Sunday, May 28th, Mikey and two friends decided to visit the pond and entered the Hurts' property through the unlocked gate. Mikey's friends ran across the dock and dove into the water to swim, but Mikey stayed on the dock to feed the ducks. Unfortunately, the dock was decaying and rotting, but the decay was partially hidden by moss and algae growing on the dock. While Mikey was standing on the dock, it collapsed from under him, and Mikey was not able to swim to safety. You have learned that the Hurts planned to replace the dock, but had postponed the repairs until the winter months.

> Notice the language used to describe the fatal accident. Why didn't the lawyer (more accurately) state that Mikey drowned?

C. Discussion of the Law

When drafting your legal analysis, you will need to decide how significantly you should "thin-slice" your analysis. Should you provide your client with the depth of analysis that would be akin to the legal analysis conveyed in a short memo? Or should you instead provide merely a brief summary of the law? Your response will vary depending upon the personality and needs of your client and the complexity of the law you are addressing.

As you consider how in-depth or abbreviated your legal discussion should be, first consider your client. Some clients have a strong desire to know every detail of the legal analysis and are willing to pay for the time it will take to convey detailed information to them in writing. For such clients, you might present a more thorough, formal analysis of the law. Other clients may prefer to know only the "big picture" and aren't interested in sifting through a complex legal analysis replete with legal citations.

Consider as well the client's presumed knowledge base. Your client might be the in-house legal counsel of a major corporation. If your client happens to be a lawyer, you can presume that the client has a basic understanding of the law and understands legal citations. When writing to a non-lawyer, however, you may need to explain certain basic legal concepts within the body of the letter. Non-lawyers may not understand legal citations and may not wish to be burdened with an endless stream of supporting citations.

Finally, consider the clarity of the law itself. If the law is fairly complex, or the success of your client's claim is relatively uncertain under the law, you will need to provide the client with enough legal background so that the client can grasp why the law is unclear. For example, in Sample Letter A in Appendix B, the client's road to success in a lawsuit is complicated, and it would likely take a significant investment of time and money for the client to vindicate his legal rights under the law. In order to convey that information, the legal discussion itself is, of necessity, more extended.

In contrast, if the law is clear-cut and the client's legal options are fairly straightforward, a legal discussion can be abbreviated. Again, practicalities dictate the length and depth of your legal analysis. If you can educate the client about the law and the client's legal rights fairly succinctly, then you should do so. Sample Letter B in Appendix B illustrates a more abbreviated discussion of the law.

Whether your discussion is a lengthy analysis of the law or a more abbreviated version of that analysis, your legal discussion will follow the same deductive writing pattern as a legal discussion in an office memo. The legal discussion should begin by discussing the relevant law, followed by a discussion of how the law affects the client.

1. Roadmap Paragraph(s)

Depending upon the length and complexity of the legal discussion in your client letter, the roadmap paragraph in a client letter can provide a framework for the more extended legal analysis that will follow. In a lengthier client letter, this framework for the discussion is similar to the roadmap paragraph(s) you might draft in an office memo. (Sample Letter A in Appendix B illustrates this format.) Alternatively, in a client letter with a very brief legal discussion, the roadmap paragraph might constitute most or all of your entire legal discussion of the case law. (Sample Letter B in Appendix B illustrates this format.)

a. Roadmap Paragraph(s) in an Extended Legal Discussion

Sample Letter A in Appendix B illustrates a legal discussion that requires a more in-depth analysis of the complexities in the law. In that letter, the lawyer sets up the legal discussion with a three-paragraph roadmap of the legal analysis that will follow. The first paragraph is akin to an overview paragraph in an office memo, providing the client with general background information about the law of negligence, as well as the conclusion. The next paragraph is akin to a thesis paragraph in an office memo, providing a more detailed explanation of the law of negligence and explaining why the law does not favor the client. The third roadmap paragraph summarizes the basis for potential success against the back-drop of unfavorable law.

Overview paragraph:
1. States conclusion; and
2. Identifies legal theory

Based on these facts, I researched Missouri law and found that, although the law is not entirely clear, we have a viable legal claim against your landlord for negligence. Under the legal theory of "negligence," we would argue that your landlord had a *legal duty* to keep the common premises safe from foreseeable injuries, and that he violated that duty when he failed to keep the walkways free from snow and ice.

Thesis paragraphs:
Summarizes rule of law, including:
1. General rule statements; and
2. Summary of how courts have interpreted the law; and

When determining whether your landlord violated his legal responsibility to you under the law of "negligence," the court would examine previous court decisions to determine how other courts have interpreted the law of negligence. In similar cases, courts have held that landlords are legally responsible for injuries suffered by their tenants only if the landlord had a "legal duty" to the tenants. Courts have found that landlords have a duty to keep an apartment building's "common" areas safe from permanent hazards. Although the walkway is part of the "common" area, unfortunately, Missouri courts have distinguished cases where the danger in the common areas is caused by a *temporary* weather hazard, such as snow. When the danger is caused by snow, courts have not imposed a duty upon landlords to shovel the snow from common walkways. Courts have justified this rule by noting that the duty to remove snow would "subject the landlord to an unreasonable burden of vigilance and care."

3. Summary of recent developments in the law that provide the basis for a potential legal claim

However, a trend in landlord/tenant court decisions does offer some hope. The last reported Missouri opinion that decided the issue of snow removal is forty years old. Even in that forty-year-old decision, the court noted that the more "modern" rule adopted in other states imposed a duty on landlords to shovel snow from their common walkways. We could argue that more recent Missouri Supreme Court opinions reflect this state's willingness to follow a national trend to protect tenants' rights to a greater degree than they have been protected in the past.

b. Roadmap Paragraph(s) in an Abbreviated Legal Discussion

Sometimes you can abbreviate the legal discussion in a client letter while still conveying the important information your clients will need to understand before evaluating their available options. Under those circumstances, the roadmap paragraph(s) can constitute most or all of your entire legal discussion of the case law. Sample Letter B in Appendix B illustrates this format. In that problem involving attractive nuisance, the law is clear-cut. There are three elements the clients must prove in order to prevail, and each of the elements is fairly easy to satisfy. Because of the ease and relative brevity with which the law can be described, most of the legal discussion of the law itself was condensed into a single roadmap paragraph, as follows:

Based on these facts, I have researched Florida law. Should you wish to pursue a legal action, I think we have a strong claim against the Hurts under a legal theory called "attractive nuisance." Under this legal theory, landowners are legally responsible for injuries sustained by children when: (1) they have a dangerous condition on their property; (2) they have reason to foresee that children would be attracted to the dangerous condition; and (3) they failed to exercise reasonable precautions to protect trespassing children from the dangerous condition.

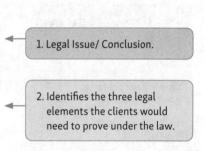

1. Legal Issue/ Conclusion.

2. Identifies the three legal elements the clients would need to prove under the law.

2. Discuss the Relevant Law: Rule Explanation

In a client letter with an abbreviated legal discussion, you might omit this section of the legal analysis entirely. However, in a client letter that merits a more extended legal discussion, you will need to summarize for the client the most important aspects of the case law. Even then, however, consider your client when evaluating the relative formality and tone of the extended legal analysis. Consider carefully the client's education, vocabulary, and familiarity with the law. For example, does the client know what "negligence" is? An artful analysis of the law is useless if the client doesn't understand the basic rule of law on which your analysis is based, or legal vernacular.

At the same time, it's important that you provide the client with enough information about the law for the client to understand how the law supports your conclusion. You might summarize the cases into broad legal principles, focusing only on black letter law rules rather than on full case discussions with case facts and holdings. Or, you might need to inform the client of the relevant facts, holdings, and rationale of the most important case or cases. If there is case law that supports a *contrary* conclusion, you should discuss those cases as well, and illustrate why they are not dispositive. When a client decides to take action based on your recommendations, it is critical that the client know the legal risks involved in taking that action. Moreover, should the client decide to take a risky course of action, and ultimately find herself in legal trouble, your written communication to the client informing the client of such risk will be important.

Sample Letter A in Appendix B is an example of a client letter that provides the client with a fairly extensive analysis of the law. In the following paragraph excerpted from that letter, the lawyer evaluates the law by discussing two cases. The lawyer decides here to omit citations to the cases because the clients are not lawyers and are not accustomed to reading legal analysis. The lawyer also avoids using terms of art, such as "holding" or "held," instead using language that is more commonly understood by lay people ("found").

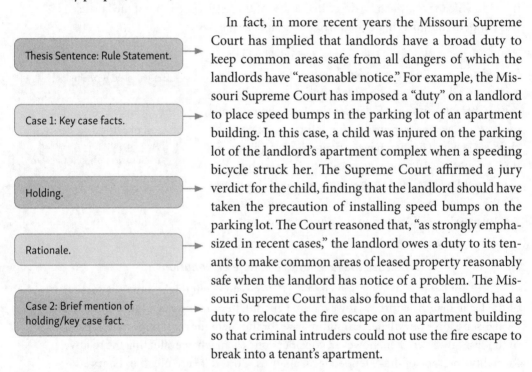

Thesis Sentence: Rule Statement.

Case 1: Key case facts.

Holding.

Rationale.

Case 2: Brief mention of holding/key case fact.

In fact, in more recent years the Missouri Supreme Court has implied that landlords have a broad duty to keep common areas safe from all dangers of which the landlords have "reasonable notice." For example, the Missouri Supreme Court has imposed a "duty" on a landlord to place speed bumps in the parking lot of an apartment building. In this case, a child was injured on the parking lot of the landlord's apartment complex when a speeding bicycle struck her. The Supreme Court affirmed a jury verdict for the child, finding that the landlord should have taken the precaution of installing speed bumps on the parking lot. The Court reasoned that, "as strongly emphasized in recent cases," the landlord owes a duty to its tenants to make common areas of leased property reasonably safe when the landlord has notice of a problem. The Missouri Supreme Court has also found that a landlord had a duty to relocate the fire escape on an apartment building so that criminal intruders could not use the fire escape to break into a tenant's apartment.

3. Apply the Relevant Law to the Client's Facts: Rule Application

Just as in an office memo, after the client has had an opportunity to absorb the broad parameters of the law, the client is in a position to consider how the law affects the client's own situation. Again, the depth or brevity of your analysis will depend upon how much information the client needs to know in order to understand how the law impacts the client's own situation.

a. Rule Application: Evaluating Favorable & Unfavorable Law

If the law is not entirely clear, and there are some valid arguments that might realistically be made on both sides of an issue, you should address both the favorable and the unfavorable arguments in a client letter. The client deserves to know the problems with the case and the potential risks involved in pursuing a legal course of action. At the same time, if there are valid arguments you can make that support the client's desired position, explore those arguments before evaluating any opposing arguments. The practical reason for this is that clients want to know that you are their advocate—that you are on the "client's side." Although you have a responsibility to alert clients to potential problems in their cases, by first stating the favorable arguments that you might make, you reinforce your role as their advocate and soften the "bad news." Sample Letter A in Appendix B illustrates this technique by exploring the favorable argument first:

Under the broad language and shifts in policy reflected in the more recent Missouri Supreme Court opinions, we can argue that the landlord owed you a duty to keep the sidewalk free from ice because the landlord had "reasonable notice" of the danger. The landlord had actual notice that snowy and icy conditions existed, as public and private schools in the City of St. Louis were closed for two days prior to your injury. Given the known snow and ice conditions, the landlord arguably had "reasonable notice" that a tenant might slip and fall on the icy sidewalk. Under this argument, by failing to keep the sidewalk safe, the landlord violated his duty to you under the law. If a court were to adopt this interpretation of the law, the law would permit you to recover damages for injuries you suffered as a result of the landlord's breach of duty.

Rule Application: Favorable Argument

1. Premise.

2. Facts that illustrate the favorable argument that could be made.

In the paragraph that follows, the lawyer next evaluates the weaknesses in the client's position.

Unfortunately, these more recent Missouri Supreme Court cases did not have the opportunity to address whether the older "temporary hazard" cases involving snowy conditions are still valid law in this state. Despite a policy trend that favors tenants, and broad policy language that favors us, the latest Missouri Supreme Court decisions do not explicitly reject any of the older cases that absolve landlords from liability involving temporary conditions such as snow. Because the older cases are the

Rule Application: Unfavorable Argument

1. Identifies the weakness in the client's position.

2. Explains more fully the basis of the problem, including:

only higher-level court cases that address a landlord's responsibility to protect tenants from temporary hazardous conditions, a trial court would probably follow these older cases. (A trial court judge has to follow the law announced by higher level courts.) More realistically, our best chance to prevail in such a lawsuit would be before a higher court, most likely the Missouri Supreme Court.

| the nuances of our legal system. |

b. Rule Application: Brief "Rule Explanation" Woven In

In a client letter that contains a more abbreviated discussion of the law, at times it makes sense to weave a brief explanation of the law into one or more of the "rule application" paragraphs. This format makes sense when you are addressing two or more legal elements, but the succinct nature of the legal discussion doesn't merit full-blown rule explanation paragraphs.

For example, in the attractive nuisance problem depicted in Sample Client Letter B in Appendix B, the three elements of attractive nuisance can be succinctly and clearly summarized for the client. The three elements are: (1) foreseeability of child trespassers; (2) dangerous, hidden condition; and (3) reasonable precautions to minimize the potential for harm. Nonetheless, the "reasonable precaution" element merits a brief mention of how courts balance competing interests. Although this idea doesn't require a separate "rule explanation" paragraph, a condensed summary of this point is woven into the "rule application" section of the client letter.

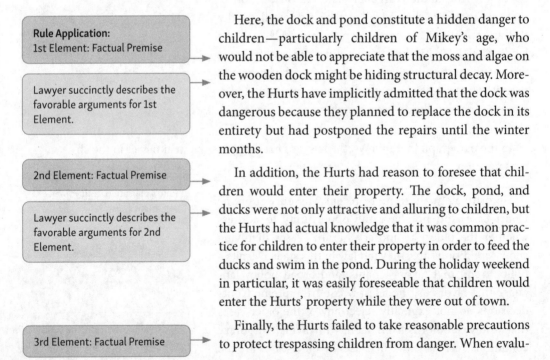

Rule Application:
1st Element: Factual Premise

Lawyer succinctly describes the favorable arguments for 1st Element.

2nd Element: Factual Premise

Lawyer succinctly describes the favorable arguments for 2nd Element.

3rd Element: Factual Premise

Here, the dock and pond constitute a hidden danger to children—particularly children of Mikey's age, who would not be able to appreciate that the moss and algae on the wooden dock might be hiding structural decay. Moreover, the Hurts have implicitly admitted that the dock was dangerous because they planned to replace the dock in its entirety but had postponed the repairs until the winter months.

In addition, the Hurts had reason to foresee that children would enter their property. The dock, pond, and ducks were not only attractive and alluring to children, but the Hurts had actual knowledge that it was common practice for children to enter their property in order to feed the ducks and swim in the pond. During the holiday weekend in particular, it was easily foreseeable that children would enter the Hurts' property while they were out of town.

Finally, the Hurts failed to take reasonable precautions to protect trespassing children from danger. When evalu-

ating whether a landowner has taken "reasonable precautions," courts balance the degree of danger posed by the
hidden dangerous condition against the preventive measures the landowner took to prevent injury. As the likelihood of harm increases, the landowner's burden to protect
children from that harm also increases. Here, it was easily
foreseeable that children would trespass on the Hurts'
dock while the Hurts were out of town and that the dangerous condition of the dock could seriously injure a child
who entered their property. Moreover, the Hurts could
have easily prevented this tragedy by taking such minimal
protective measures as locking the gate or posting a sign
warning of the dock's dangerous condition. Therefore, we
have a strong legal claim that they failed to take reasonable
precautions to protect children from harm.

> Lawyer provides legal frame-
> work for the analysis (RE).

> Lawyer succinctly describes the
> favorable arguments for 3rd
> Element (RA).

4. Discussion of the Available Options

Clients usually have more than one option available to them and will need to decide which of the available alternatives would best satisfy their underlying interests.
Just because a client *could* file a lawsuit doesn't necessarily mean that filing a lawsuit
would be in the client's best overall interests. The decision to file a lawsuit will have a
significant impact on your client's life. Lawsuits are time-consuming, stressful, and
often expensive. They often affect your clients' emotional and psychological well-being, and they might even impact your clients' ability to focus on other business or
family pursuits. Even when a client has been sued and is the defendant in a lawsuit,
the client still has options. Should the client vigorously defend the lawsuit and seek
vindication following a trial, or would it be more effective to try to settle the case as
quickly as possible? Or should the client see whether the other party is willing, instead, to engage in an alternative dispute resolution process such as mediation?

With that said, some clients realistically have more options than others. In the
slip-and-fall case described in Sample Letter A in Appendix B, the tenuous nature of
the client's legal claims provides him with fewer options than he might otherwise
have. Thus, in that letter, the lawyer essentially provided the client with two options:
(1) file a lawsuit and push for a quick settlement of the legal claims; or (2) try to negotiate an out-of-court settlement of the client's legal claims. In contrast, the law is
more favorable in the attractive nuisance case described in Sample Letter B in Appendix B, and the amount of damages at stake is far greater. Therefore, these clients have
a wider range of options available to them.

The client letter is an ideal vehicle to broach the various options available to the
client. Unlike a client meeting, where the client must absorb myriad bits of information at a fairly fast conversational clip, a letter provides the client with the luxury of

time. The client can mull over the options you have outlined, carefully consider the potential advantages and disadvantages of each option, and take some notes of the questions that inevitably arise. It is for this reason that lawyers often send their clients an advisory letter summarizing the law and outlining their options before setting up a follow-up client counseling meeting.

The following discussion excerpted from Sample Letter B in Appendix B illustrates the typical range of available options in a litigation setting:

Option 1: Lawsuit

Given the strength of your legal claim, there are a number of options available to you. First, we could file a lawsuit against the Hurts; in my opinion, such a lawsuit would be successful. Although no legal remedy could ever begin to compensate you for the loss you have suffered, this option would likely allow you to recover substantial monetary damages from the Hurts. However, a lawsuit is also time-consuming and would be emotionally painful, as well, given the tremendous loss that you have suffered. On the other hand, a lawsuit has the potential for you to exact justice against the Hurts and, perhaps, to use the legal system to help protect other children from such tragedies in the future.

Potential costs and benefits of this option.

Option 2: Out-of-Court Negotiations

A second alternative would be to enter into out-of-court settlement negotiations with the Hurts' lawyer. Under this option, I would meet with the Hurts' lawyer and attempt to settle your legal claims out-of-court. An advantage of this option is that you would not be constrained by the legal remedies the law can offer, but could agree to non-legal remedies as well. For example, in addition to a monetary settlement, you could insist that the Hurts replace their fence with a more expensive fence that might help prevent other injuries in the future. You could also insist that the Hurts replace their dock immediately or agree to fill in their pond with dirt to remove the attractive nuisance entirely. Of course, the Hurts would have to agree to this option and to any such terms in order for this alternative to be successful. Nonetheless, if the Hurts were unwilling to enter into an out-of-court settlement agreement, your other legal options would still be preserved.

Potential costs and benefits of this option.

Option 3: ADR

A third alternative would be to explore alternative dispute resolution ("ADR") processes such as mediation or arbitration. On the spectrum of available options, the option of pursuing ADR falls somewhere between an out-of-court negotiation and a lawsuit itself. Both of these processes would require the agreement of both parties. However, if both parties agree to enter into an ADR process, these processes are generally quicker and less expensive than a formal lawsuit. At the same time, they might bring greater pressure to bear on the Hurts than an informal out-of-court negotiation.

> Overview of what this means, and

> Potential benefits.

In a mediation proceeding, both parties would select a neutral person to mediate the dispute and to help the parties reach an out-of-court agreement. This can sometimes be a successful way of settling a legal dispute should out-of-court negotiations between the two lawyers prove to be unsuccessful. However, this option would likely take more time than an informal negotiation and would also be more expensive, as both parties are responsible to pay for the mediator's time and expenses.

> **ADR Altern. 1:** Mediation

> Summary of what this means, and

> Potential costs and benefits of this option.

In terms of legal formality, a legal arbitration proceeding is a step up from mediation, but less formal than a lawsuit. Like with mediation, the parties would select a neutral third-party to oversee the process. However, unlike a mediator, who works with both parties to achieve a settlement agreement, an arbitrator assumes the role of a "judge" in the case. In that role, the arbitrator listens to testimony, considers the "evidence," and issues a legal ruling in favor of one party or the other. In that sense, arbitration is like an abbreviated lawsuit; however, an arbitration proceeding would be scheduled much sooner than a trial, and would likely be less expensive as well.

> **ADR Altern. 2:** Arbitration

> Summary of what this means,

> and possible benefit.

Finally, after thinking all of this over, you might decide that you are not interested in pursuing any legal option at all. You mentioned during our meeting that you weren't entirely sure whether you were willing to put yourselves in the position of having to re-live the trauma of this tragic event. I understand completely if you should decide that this option best serves the needs of your family.

> **Option 4:** Do Nothing

> Possible benefit of this option.

5. Conclusion and Recommendation

Clients routinely report that one of the major sources of dissatisfaction with their lawyers is their lawyers' failure to communicate and to keep them informed. You can minimize the potential for misunderstandings by concluding your letter with a clear and concrete proposed course of action. Without an explicit course of action, misunderstandings can all too easily arise. For example, you might legitimately believe that, by sending the client a letter, the client will initiate the next round of communications. The client, however, might legitimately believe that, as the lawyer, you will assume the lead role and initiate the next round of communications. The resulting lapse in communication could foster the impression that you don't believe the client's problem is important enough to merit your continuing attention.

To avoid any potential for misunderstanding, end any client letter with a proposed course of action that: (1) clearly informs the client of the steps the *client* should take (*e.g.,* give you a call to set up a meeting; write a letter; wait for you to contact the client); and (2) clearly informs the client of the steps *you* intend to take (wait to hear from the client; contact the client again; engage in additional research).

In addition, if there is a relevant statute of limitations, you should also include the relevant limitations period within the body of your letter. This alerts clients to the parameters within which they must make up their minds should they elect to pursue their legal rights via a lawsuit. Further, memorializing the statute of limitations can protect you later should a client initially decide not to file a legal action but later change her mind.

Sample Letter B illustrates a typical concluding paragraph:

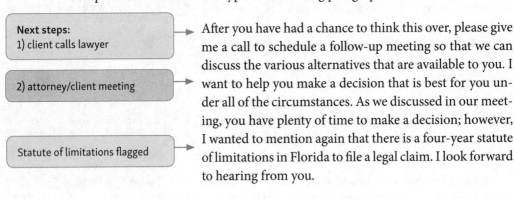

Next steps:
1) client calls lawyer

2) attorney/client meeting

Statute of limitations flagged

After you have had a chance to think this over, please give me a call to schedule a follow-up meeting so that we can discuss the various alternatives that are available to you. I want to help you make a decision that is best for you under all of the circumstances. As we discussed in our meeting, you have plenty of time to make a decision; however, I wanted to mention again that there is a four-year statute of limitations in Florida to file a legal claim. I look forward to hearing from you.

THE LAWYER AS ADVISOR/COLLABORATOR

Counseling the Client

I. UNDERSTANDING YOUR ROLE

Because clients hire you for your legal expertise, it might seem logical to envision your role as one in which you tell your clients what to do. However, this is only partially true. It is true in this sense—if you determine that the law doesn't allow a client to embark on a proposed course of action, you have a duty to be honest with the client and to tell the client he can't do it. This duty of candor is not always easy. Nonetheless, ethical rules require that you be honest with your clients, even if your response isn't something they necessarily want to hear.[1]

Often, however, the law will allow a client to move forward on a proposed course of action. The question then becomes whether the client *should* pursue the course of action, or which of a number of available legal options the client *should* take. Under these circumstances, it is the client, not you, who should make the ultimate decision about what to do. In fact, the Model Rules of Professional Conduct require that lawyers abide by the client's decisions concerning the objectives of the legal representation, so long as the objectives are otherwise lawful and ethical.[2]

The reason for this deference is because it is the client who will have to live with the outcome of the choices that are made, not you. In addition, it is the client who is in the best position to know how the various options might impact the client's life—economically, psychologically, emotionally, and pragmatically. Although a client might have a legal right to file a lawsuit, perhaps the costs outweigh the ben-

---

1. Rule 2.1 of the Model Rules of Professional Conduct requires lawyers to "render candid advice" when counseling clients, even when the legal advice "involves unpleasant facts and alternatives that a client may be disinclined to confront." Model R. Prof. Conduct 2.1, cmt. 1 (ABA 2002). And Rule 1.2(d) prohibits lawyers from counseling or assisting clients "in conduct the lawyer knows is criminal or fraudulent." Model R. Prof. Conduct 1.2(d) (ABA 2002).

2. Rule 1.2 of the Model Rules of Professional Conduct states that "a lawyer shall abide by a client's decisions concerning the objectives of representation and... shall consult with the client as to the means by which they are to be pursued." Model R. Prof. Conduct 1.2(a) (ABA 2002).

efits of vindicating the client's rights in court. Perhaps a lawsuit might prove to be too time-consuming and distracting to a client who is trying to organize a new business venture, or to care for a terminally ill parent or spouse. Or perhaps the expense of the lawsuit would curtail the client's ability to afford other items that are more important to the client, such as sending a child to college or buying a vacation home. These are all "impact" issues that you simply can't presume to evaluate on behalf of a client.

This does not mean, however, that you will assume a passive role in the client counseling meeting. You have an important role—that of a wise collaborator and advisor. Your clients lack your legal background and legal expertise; as a lawyer, you are in the best position not only to assess the relative strengths and weaknesses of your clients' legal positions, but also to identify the various legal options that are available to them. Moreover, although clients have a unique perspective about how the various options might impact their lives, they often lack the perspective to appreciate many of the costs and benefits associated with such options. For example, a client might theoretically understand that a lawsuit is "time-consuming," but might not understand that a lawsuit can take years to wind its way through the court system. Nor would the client understand that the lawsuit can consume countless hours of the client's time responding to discovery requests, preparing for and participating in depositions, and collaborating about the myriad strategic decisions that are part-and-parcel of a lawsuit. Without a clear understanding of what is actually involved in a lawsuit, your client would be ill-prepared to assess whether the potential benefits of filing a lawsuit would outweigh the costs.

In addition, clients are often so embroiled in the day-to-day details of the legal problem that they fail to see the bigger picture—metaphorically they become so lost in the trees that they can't see the forest. Although a client's personal dealings with an adverse party can sometimes help the client predict how the adverse party might react to a specific legal strategy, the client's "emotional brain" can also skew her perspective. Anger or frustration with another party can impair the client's ability to accurately foresee how the other party might react; further, some clients minimize potential problems as a way of controlling their own anxiety about the future. Therefore, as an objective collaborator and advisor, you will bring your own unique perspective to the collaboration because you will have a better sense of how people *typically* respond to certain tactics. As well, you can identify those instances in which a client seems to be blinded by emotion or impaired perspective so that you can be particularly careful to ensure that the client considers and weighs all of the costs and benefits. (Chapters 4 & 5 discuss some of the psychological impediments that impair perspective and judgment.) These are important aspects of your role—to provide clients with enough information to enable them to make sound decisions, and to offer the wise perspective of an objective, thoughtful advisor and collaborator.

◎ ILLUSTRATION OF THE RESPECTIVE ROLES: Business Setting

Most business deals involve a myriad of business decisions that the client is in the best position to evaluate (for example, whether a market exists for a corporate expansion). At the same time, there are also legal considerations the client has to consider and various legal alternatives the client could choose to pursue. For example, assume that you have been hired to negotiate a business deal on behalf of a client. Your client has designed a logo for a sports team, and the sports team is interested in using the logo on some of its merchandise. Even with this relatively straightforward business transaction, your client has several available options—your client might sell the logo outright to the sports team, or, alternatively, your client might enter into a licensing agreement with the sports team whereby the client would receive a percentage of the profits earned from merchandise containing the logo.

There are advantages and disadvantages to each of these options, many of which the client will likely not have considered. With an outright sale, the client could receive the money quickly in a lump sum payment. If the merchandise doesn't sell very well, then a lump sum payment might prove to be the most financially lucrative option for the client. However, if the merchandise sells well, a licensing agreement might prove to more financially lucrative. As the client's lawyer, you will have the privilege and responsibility of helping the client flesh out the costs and benefits of each option. This is how you "add value" to the business client.

On the other hand, the client is in a better position than you to weigh the relative *importance* of these costs and benefits. For a client who is risk adverse, a lump sum payment might be more satisfying than a licensing agreement, even though a licensing agreement might ultimately prove to be more lucrative financially. Alternatively, perhaps the client enjoys taking risks and/or would enjoy having a long-term relationship with the sports team itself. In that event, the client might prefer to enter into a licensing agreement with the team, even though there is a risk that this option might not be as financially rewarding. Or perhaps the client is looking to purchase his first home within the next few months. How might that "non-legal" factor potentially affect the client's choice? As you can begin to appreciate, the collaborative relationship you share with the client requires the active participation of both you and the client in order to ensure that the client makes a choice that will best serve the client's interests.

◎ ILLUSTRATION OF THE RESPECTIVE ROLES: Litigation Setting

In a litigation setting, you might be surprised at the breadth of the client's choices that will require your advice and counsel. Even if your research suggests that your client would likely prevail if the client were to file a lawsuit, the client still has choices. At the two extremes, the client could decide to file a lawsuit or decide to do nothing at all, having decided that the risks outweigh the benefits.

Somewhere in between the two extremes, there are other options for the client to consider. The client might decide to pursue an out-of-court settlement of the client's claims. If the client were to pursue this option, you would sit down with the lawyer representing the other party and try to negotiate a settlement agreement that serves the interests of both parties. You can enter into settlement negotiations with the other party's lawyer at any time—as an alternative to a lawsuit, before filing a lawsuit, or during a lawsuit.

Mediation is an option that is somewhat more formal and expensive than an out-of-court negotiation, but typically less expensive, and less formal, than filing a lawsuit or entering into arbitration. Like negotiations, mediations are designed to find solutions that are workable for both parties. However, in a mediation proceeding, both parties agree to hire a neutral third party who has special training as a mediator. The mediator sits down with both parties and their lawyers to help them settle the dispute. This can sometimes be helpful when the parties can't seem to settle the dispute on their own, but don't want to pursue the more expensive, and lengthier, option of filing a lawsuit.

Another alternative is the option of entering into arbitration. Assuming both parties are agreeable to entering into arbitration, they select a neutral third party to oversee the proceedings. However, in contrast to the settlement orientation of mediations and out-of-court settlement negotiations, arbitrations are more akin to a trial. In an arbitration proceeding, the arbitrator assumes the role of a "judge," hearing testimony, weighing evidence, and rendering a "legal" opinion as to which party wins and which party loses. Although arbitration resembles a lawsuit in some important ways, this option is typically less expensive than a lawsuit. Moreover, although this option takes longer than an out-of-court negotiation or a mediation, it also takes less time than a more traditional lawsuit to resolve.

As a lawyer advising and collaborating with a client about each of these options, you have an important role. Consider, for example, a hypothetical client who believes she was unlawfully terminated from employment. Although your client would likely understand in a broad sense what it means to file a lawsuit, she would not understand some of the specific advantages and disadvantages of this option. In your role as her legal advisor, you would advise the client that if she were to file a lawsuit, she would be restricted to the legal remedies that are provided under the relevant federal and state statutes. You would also advise the client about the likely damages she could expect to receive. However, it would be within your client's province to weigh the import of this information and to determine whether the legal remedies you describe would best satisfy her objectives.

II. THE CLIENT COUNSELING MEETING

A. Preparation for the Meeting

In your role as an advisor and collaborator, you can't begin to counsel clients about their options until you first research the law and determine their legal rights and obligations. Then, assuming the law permits a client to move forward, you need to spend some time thinking about your client's options. Because each option has its own set of advantages and disadvantages that require a careful evaluation of both short-term and long-term consequences, it is good practice to map out the advantages and disadvantages of each option prior to the client meeting. It can be helpful to bring this chart with you to the client meeting; the chart can serve as a useful template that you can flesh out during the meeting itself.

Prior to client counseling meetings, lawyers often send letters to their clients memorializing the results of their research and the legal options that are available to their clients. Client letters afford clients an opportunity to review their options carefully and thoughtfully prior to the client meeting. A client letter also affords clients the luxury of time to mull over any concerns the letter raises and to think of questions they want to ask during the meeting. Sample Letter B in Appendix B illustrates a typical letter that would be sent to a client preparatory to the client counseling meeting.

B. The Overview Phase

When the client arrives for a follow-up client counseling meeting, you will have already met with the client at least once and perhaps exchanged e-mail messages and phone calls. Nonetheless, the client will not have had an opportunity to talk with you in this type of setting before—a setting in which you will discuss and weigh the potential costs and benefits of the client's legal options. Therefore, after you have engaged in small talk and put your client at ease, it's important to confirm the client's goals and to provide a framework for the meeting. In this phase of the meeting, you should accomplish three goals: (1) confirm your client's goals and concerns; (2) provide the client with an overview of what to expect in the meeting; and (3) provide an appropriate summary of the client's legal rights and obligations.[3]

---

3. Many of the ideas in this chapter have been developed from materials in the following textbooks: David A. Binder et al., *Lawyers as Counselors: A Client-Centered Approach* (2d ed., West 2004); Robert F.

1. Confirm the Client's Goals & Concerns

In one sense, it might seem redundant to review again the client's goals and concerns, because you would have already discussed the client's goals and concerns during the initial client interview. However, this step is actually important for a couple of reasons. First, clients' priorities and concerns often shift during the time lag between the initial interview and the follow-up client counseling meeting. Perhaps the legal problem they came to see you about has taken a turn for the worse in the intervening weeks, or perhaps it has improved. Or perhaps something has changed in the client's life that has nothing to do with the legal problem itself but that affects the client's priorities and concerns. Second, given the sheer volume of factual information the client gave you in the initial meeting, you may have overlooked or minimized a priority or concern that is important to the client.

Therefore, before embarking on a legal discussion of the various options, it's important that you confirm and possibly update your understanding of what it is the client actually wants. Consider the example of a client who has been terminated from employment. If what the client really wants is a financial severance package from the employer that would provide her with a source of income while she searches for other employment, a lawsuit won't satisfy that objective. The client needs a source of income now, not in a year or more from now.

2. Give the Client an Overview of the Meeting

As with the initial client interview, many clients don't know what to expect in the follow-up client counseling meeting. Therefore, before moving into an in-depth discussion of the law and the various options that are available to the client, this is the perfect opportunity for you to educate the client about what to expect. You might tell the client that you will outline some options for the client to consider, and that you and the client will then discuss and evaluate the potential advantages and disadvantages of each option. You might also reinforce your respective roles at this stage in the meeting—although you will help identify the potential costs and benefits of each option, it is the client's ultimate decision as to which option best serves the client's overall interests.

3. Summarize the Important Aspects of the Law

Before a client can evaluate whether she wants to take the risk of either filing a lawsuit or moving forward with various legal options, she first needs to understand the nature of the risk she would ultimately be assuming. By providing your client with an overview of the law and your assessment of the strengths and weaknesses of the

---

Cochran, Jr., John M.A. DiPippa & Martha M. Peters, *The Counselor-at-Law: A Collaborative Approach to Client Interviewing & Counseling* (2d ed., LexisNexis 2006); Robert M. Bastress & Joseph Harbaugh, *Interviewing, Counseling and Negotiation: Skills for Effective Representation* (LexisNexis 1990).

client's case, you can help the client appreciate the nature of the risk she faces. This can be challenging to do well. As a starting point, you must find a way to convey your legal analysis in plain language that your client can understand. For example, a client is unlikely to understand the meaning of "respondeat superior." However, most clients would understand an explanation that "the employer can be held legally responsible for the actions of Mr. Johnson, your supervisor."

You also need to determine how much information to convey. On the one hand, you don't want to provide the client with so much detail that she becomes lost in "information overload." On the other hand, you need to provide the client with enough detail about the law for her to understand the nature of the risk she might be undertaking. There are a few strategies you can use to help ensure that you achieve the appropriate balance. First, make a chart that lists each of the legal elements you must prove (or defend). As an example, consider again the hypothetical client who believes she was the victim of sexual discrimination when she was terminated from employment. Assume your research revealed that you must prove the following elements: (1) that your client is a member of a protected class (in this case the protected class is her gender); (2) that she was subject to an adverse employment decision; (3) that the adverse employment decision was motivated by her gender; and (4) that she was otherwise qualified for the position.

Now consider your client and the information she needs to understand in order to assess the risk she might be assuming. Of these four statutory elements, the first two elements are "slam dunk" winning points. No one can realistically dispute that she is a member of a protected class or that being terminated from employment is an "adverse employment decision." Therefore, you might not want to waste the client's time (and attention span) by describing these two elements. In contrast, it would be important for your client to understand that she must prove that the adverse employment decision was motivated by her gender, and that she was otherwise qualified and competent to perform her job duties. Therefore, these latter two elements should be conveyed to the client when summarizing the law.

Next, to the extent you can link each legal element to concrete, specific facts, you can help the client make sense of why each legal element is important. In describing the requirement that your client's termination from employment has to have been motivated by gender, you would discuss the most important facts of your client's case that relate to this element. You might explain, for example, that the employer would defend itself by claiming that she was fired for "insubordination," and then summarize the potential strengths and weaknesses of that defense. Perhaps this comes down to a "he said/she said" scenario that would require a jury to believe one person's story over another. Or perhaps there are incidents that could be possibly be construed as insubordination that the client would need to rebut. Or perhaps there are facts that would suggest the employer's proffered explanation of insubordination is merely "pretext" to camouflage the real discriminatory reason for the client's discharge. Each of these ideas should be fully explored so that the client has an opportunity to assess the relative merits and weaknesses of her own case.

Finally, when deciding how much or how little of the law to discuss with the client, another important factor to consider is the relative strength of the client's legal case. If the law clearly favors your client, then an abbreviated discussion of the law might be sufficient to apprise the client of the strengths of her legal case. Your discussion would instead focus more on whether it makes economic, psychological, and pragmatic sense for the client to proceed. In contrast, if the client's legal case has some holes and is likely to be met with strong opposition by the other party, then the client would need a more detailed explanation of the law in order to understand the nature of the risk she is contemplating taking, and to decide whether it is a risk worth taking.

C. Evaluate the Options Phase

1. Provide a Roadmap of the Options

Before moving into an in-depth discussion of the potential costs and benefits of each available option, first set the stage by outlining for the client each of the available options the client can pursue. This phase of the meeting should be relatively brief. Here, you are merely providing a roadmap of the range of available options so that the client can choose which option she wants to discuss first. With that said, unless the client happens to have a legal background, you will need to briefly explain what you mean by some of the options. For example, most lay people have a sense of what it means to "file a lawsuit," and you shouldn't need to explain what this option means at this stage in the meeting. However, many lay people would not understand the meaning of the terms "out-of-court negotiation" or an "alternative dispute resolution" proceeding. To satisfy the client's curiosity, you should *briefly* explain what each term of art means, while saving a more in-depth discussion for later. For example, an out-of-court negotiation might be briefly explained as follows: "An out-of-court negotiation would mean that the other lawyer and I would meet privately and try to negotiate a settlement agreement. Of course, you and I would discuss in advance what terms you would like for me to negotiate."

2. Discuss the Advantages & Disadvantages of Each Option

After you provide the client with a list of available options, the client should select the option she wishes to discuss first. By asking the client which option she wants to discuss first, you can glean some important information about the client's preferences. Most clients choose to discuss first the option that has the greatest initial appeal to them, and will say something like: "You know, I like the idea of trying to negotiate an agreement out of court, so I'd like to talk about that first." The client's initial preference can give you important information about your client's values or concerns.

After the client selects an option to discuss, the next step is to collaborate with the client as both you and the client weigh the possible costs and benefits of that option. This part of the meeting should ideally resemble a conversation, with input from both you and the client. If you dominate the conversation, you run the risk of allowing your own values and preferences to dictate the client's ultimate choice. Recall that, because the client will have to live with the consequences of the decision, it should be the client's ultimate decision, not yours. On the other hand, if you force the client to dominate the conversation, then you won't add much value to the decision-making process as the wise advisor and collaborator. Instead, you might envision the ideal discussion as a running commentary between you and the client, with each of you assuming an active role in the discussion.

With that said, there are times when it's more appropriate for the client to assume a more dominant role in the discussion, and times when it's more appropriate for you to assume a more dominant role. When you are discussing consequences that implicate the client's psychological or emotional well-being, or that impact the client's professional or personal life, the client is clearly in the best position to appreciate the relative importance of those consequences. Therefore, your role for such discussions is to help the client flesh out her concerns and, where appropriate, to add your perspective so that the client can better appreciate the consequences of each choice.

However, some options present costs and benefits that a typical client isn't likely to appreciate simply because the client doesn't have a legal background. These consequences provide an opportunity for you to assume a more dominant role in the discussion. For example, most clients have little understanding of what it means to enter into mediation, much less to appreciate the relative advantages and disadvantages of mediation. Therefore, you might assume a more leading role when discussing this option by first explaining what mediation actually entails, and then giving the client your sense of the advantages and disadvantages of mediation. After the client has a basic framework to understand what mediation is, as well as the typical advantages and disadvantages of this approach, the client is then in a better position to weigh in with her own sense of how she prioritizes the costs and benefits given her personality and pragmatic concerns.

After you have fully fleshed out the advantages and disadvantages of the first option the client elected to discuss, you should engage in the same process for each of the remaining options. An effective strategy is to ask the client what option she would like to address next, discuss the costs and benefits of that option, and then move on to the third option, repeating the process again. You might be able to appreciate at this point that you and the client will be evaluating a myriad of different issues and concerns. Given the breadth and depth of the discussion, it is easy for the client to get lost within the discussion. Therefore, it can be helpful to keep a written chart in which you summarize the pros and cons of each option. As you try to help the client reach a decision at the end of the meeting, you can refer to the chart as a means of summarizing the most important points you discussed.

D. The Decision Phase

After you and the client have thoroughly evaluated each option, the client may or may not be mentally ready to make a decision. You can help the client make the decision by summarizing the options and those advantages and disadvantages that seemed to be most important to the client. For example, if the client has already made it clear that the "lawsuit" and "arbitration" options should be off the table, it's not necessary to recap the advantages and disadvantages of those options again. However, the client could benefit from being reminded of the key advantages and disadvantages of the several options she is actively considering.

After you have summarized the salient advantages and disadvantages of the options the client seems to be favoring, some clients will be ready and eager to select a course of action and move forward immediately. Other clients might need to mull it over even further and discuss it with family members before deciding on a course of action. Either alternative is fine; clients should have the opportunity to take whatever time might be necessary to make a decision they can live with over the long-term. A hastily made decision that proves to be ultimately unsatisfying does not serve either the client or you.

Whether the client reaches a decision during your meeting or needs more time to think it over, before the client leaves your office you should clearly specify the "next steps" you and the client will be taking. If the client has asked you to try to resolve the matter through out-of-court negotiations, make sure that you agree on the details. What time frame have you agreed upon to explore this option? What result does the client want you to achieve? Does the client want her job back? If you aren't successful in negotiating for her to get her job back, what is the client's fallback position? Does the client want a financial settlement? If so, how much money would it take for the client to walk away happy? Is there a bottom line at which the client would prefer to halt negotiations and pursue another option instead? These are all details that should be clearly understood by the time the meeting is concluded.

PERSUASIVE WRITING STYLE STRATEGIES

In persuasive arguments, effective advocates seek a balance between strident advocacy and a predictive analysis of the law. Strident advocacy is not a particularly effective technique for several reasons. First, language that too obviously reflects your underlying strategy loses its persuasive appeal because the reader recognizes the strategy and subconsciously resists it. The goal is to paint a very *subtle* persuasive picture without the adjudicator or opposing counsel being consciously aware of the underlying strategy. Second, if your language is too strident, you risk losing credibility. In law, as elsewhere, lawyers who appear emotionally overwrought and prone to overstatement do not seem as credible as lawyers who simply appear to be stating a professional, objective analysis of the law. Third, strident language may offend an adjudicator. At the very least, it does not convey the degree of respect most adjudicators expect from lawyers who appear before them.

At the opposite end of the spectrum, it is equally unpersuasive to adopt an objective tone typical of a legal analysis found in an office memo or client advisory letter. In your role as an advocate, you have a responsibility to champion the client's legal position, not to present an objective, neutral recitation of the law. Therefore, the goal is to achieve a balance between the two extremes—persuasively arguing why the law compels a favorable outcome for the client while also appearing objective and reasonable. The following writing strategies illustrate effective persuasive techniques that will also help you achieve the proper persuasive tone.

I. PERSUADE THROUGH WORD CHOICE

Many words have both explicit and implicit meanings. In persuasive writing, advocates select words not only on the basis of their explicit meaning, but on their implicit meaning as well.

A. Verbs and Adverbs

Verbs and adverbs are powerful tools used by advocates to present the law and factual events in a light most favorable to their clients. In fact, psychological studies reveal that verbs can actually change one's perception about "what is happening." In one study, students were shown a film clip of an automobile collision and were then asked to estimate the speed of the cars at the time of the collision. However, different verbs were used to set up this question for different groups of students. Students were either asked how fast the cars were going when the cars (1) "smashed" into each other; (2) "collided" into each other; (3) "bumped" each other; (4) "hit" each other; or (5) "made contact" with each other. The verbs that were used to set up the question changed the students' perceptions of the rate of speed. The students' responses ranged from an average speed of 40.8 MPH in response to the verb "smashed," to 31.8 MPH in response to the verb (nominalization) "made contact."[1]

In the following sentence, compare the use of the adverb and verb "finally stumbled" to the verb "found." In which example does Agent Friday appear more careless?

> (1)   Agent Friday *found* the missing tapes while looking for party decorations.
>
> vs.
>
> (2)   Agent Friday *finally stumbled* upon the missing tapes while looking for party decorations.

In which of the following statements do the police appear reasonable? Unreasonable?

> (1)   The police *warned* the defendant.
>
> vs.
>
> (2)   The police *threatened* the defendant.

Consider the following word pairings and their connotations. In each pairing, which example would be a more effective advocacy statement if you represented the defendant? Why?

> (1)(a) The plaintiff *stated* that…
>
> vs.
>
> (b) The plaintiff *conceded* that…

---

1. Elizabeth F. Loftus & J.C. Palmer, *Reconstruction of Automobile Destruction: An Example of the Interaction Between Language & Memory*, 13 J. of Verbal Learning & Verbal Behavior 585 (1974).

(2)(a) The witness *remembers* seeing the defendant outside the liquor store.

vs.

(b) The witness *claims* the defendant was outside the liquor store.

(3)(a) The plaintiff *failed to act* with reasonable diligence.

vs.

(b) The plaintiff *did not act* with reasonable diligence.

B. Nouns and Adjectives

Strategic use of nouns and adjectives can also be an effective persuasive technique. In the following example, the noun/adjective "home telephone" implies an invasiveness that the noun "telephone" alone does not capture.

(a) The Government wiretapped Defendant's *home telephone*.

vs.

(b) The Government wiretapped Defendant's *telephone*.

C. Use Verbs and Nouns with Subtlety

Your goal as an advocate is to use verbs and nouns with such subtlety that the opposing counsel or adjudicator is unaware of your strategy. If your underlying strategy is obvious, at best the strategy will provide the reader with amusement; at worst, the reader will resist your strategy and lose confidence in your credibility. Consider how the subtlety of "home telephone" in the above example loses its persuasive appeal in the following example:

The Government wiretapped one of Defendant's most personal possessions, a possession he uses to discuss his private yearnings and dreams—his home telephone.

Exercise 23-1

Using stronger verbs and/or nouns, rewrite the following sentences to be more persuasive for the advocate.

    a. *Advocate for the employee in a Title VII sexual discrimination case*: "The supervisor told the employee she was fired but did not provide a reason for the termination."

    b. *Advocate for the employee in a Title VII sexual discrimination case*: "The employee's performance review was positive, but she was terminated."

    c. *Advocate for the employer in a Title VII sexual discrimination case*: "The supervisor discovered that the employee was tardy on more than one occasion."

II. PERSUADE THROUGH ACTIVE/PASSIVE VOICE AND ACTION VERBS

Another effective strategy is to use the *active voice and action verbs* to bind an actor visually with an action. For example, a prosecutor might write: "Tim Jones snatched the purse from the arm of a seventy-year-old woman." (Sentence structure: Actor (Subject) → action verb → object.) In contrast, you can use the *passive voice and non-action verbs* when you would prefer to distance your client from your client's "negative" behavior. For example, a defense attorney representing Tim Jones might write: "The purse was taken from the complainant's possession." (Sentence structure: Object → non-action verb → no actor identified.)

Exercise 23-2

Using active/passive voice, and action/non-action verbs, rewrite the following sentences as an advocate representing the *opposing* party, as noted after each sentence.

    a. *Advocate for the defendant writes*: "The document was not produced to Plaintiff in April, as the result of an oversight by a legal assistant. As soon as we discovered the error in June, Defendant promptly produced the document."

Redraft as an advocate for the plaintiff.

    b. *Advocate for the defendant writes*: "The death of the victim resulted from a stab wound allegedly caused by Defendant."

Redraft as an advocate for the prosecution.

III. PERSUADE BY USING CONCLUSIVE, RATHER THAN "OPINION," STATEMENTS

Another important writing style strategy is to use forceful, definitive statements rather than statements that appear to be only opinions over which reasonable people might differ. Effective advocates commonly use definitive statements as topic or thesis sentences to state favorable conclusions. However, definitive statements appear throughout persuasive writing. When reviewing your writing, evaluate how you can eliminate unnecessary introductory clauses and tentative language to transform "opinion" language into more forceful, and persuasive, definitive language.

In each of the following examples, select the statement from each pairing that appears more like an affirmative "truth" and, therefore, more persuasive. Are there any circumstances under which you would use the statement that appears more like an opinion?

---

(1)(a) *It is the Defendant's contention that* Plaintiff's complaint is meritless.

vs.

(b) Plaintiff's complaint is meritless.

---

(2)(a) *It has been argued that* the officers violated Defendant's Constitutional right to privacy.

vs.

(b) The officers violated Defendant's Constitutional right to privacy.

---

(3)(a) *One court has held that* when the government fails to obtain an immediate judicial seal, its alternative "satisfactory explanation" must provide the same level of protection as a judicial seal. *United States v. Johnson*, [citation].

vs.

(b) When the government fails to obtain an immediate judicial seal, its alternative "satisfactory explanation" must provide the same level of protection as a judicial seal. *United States v. Johnson*, [citation].

Exercise 23-3

Rewrite the following sentences to make them appear as affirmative, definitive "truths" rather than opinions.

a. "Two courts have interpreted the legislative history to mean that the statute does not cover activities such as political protests. [citations]"

b. "This Court can find that the employer's conduct rises to the level of racial harassment under Title VII."

IV. PERSUADE BY USING AFFIRMATIVE, RATHER THAN DEFENSIVE, STATEMENTS

The tone of persuasive writing is one that *affirms* the client's position rather than one that denies an opponent's position. By simply denying the opponent's position, you run the risk of appearing defensive and unsure of your client's legal position. In addition, any time you directly rebut the opponent's position and argue why that position is unsound, the adjudicator continues to view the law and facts from within the context of your *opponent's* framework, and to question whether that position is correct or incorrect. Instead, you will be more influential if you can convince the adjudicator to view the law and facts from within the context of your own favorable argument.

Caveat: At times it's necessary to directly rebut an opponent's argument (for example, when responding to arguments the opposing counsel has raised in a court brief). However, even then it is more persuasive to argue first why your client's position is sound, framing the issues in a manner that favors your client. Having first persuaded the adjudicator of the brilliance of your client's position, your direct rebuttal will be even more compelling. An opponent's argument loses much of its persuasive appeal if you have already convinced the adjudicator to view the problem from your client's perspective.

In the following example, an advocate for the defendant, Mr. Hart, seeks to suppress wiretap evidence the Government obtained from Mr. Hart's telephone. The wiretap statute requires that, in order for the evidence to be admissible in court, the Government must either obtain an "immediate" judicial seal safeguarding the evidence, or provide a "satisfactory explanation" for its failure to do so. The Government did not immediately secure the integrity of the wiretap evidence by obtaining a judge's seal. Hart's attorney seeks to convince the court that the Government also failed to provide the required alternative—a "satisfactory explanation." Compare the persuasive appeal of the following two examples of Mr. Hart's argument.

(1) The Government incorrectly contends that the wiretap tapes are admissible as evidence during trial. The federal wiretap statute requires that the Government either obtain the protection of an "immediate" judicial seal to safeguard the integrity of wiretap evidence, or provide a "satisfactory explanation" for its delay. The Government argues that, even though it did not obtain an immediate judicial seal, it had a "satisfactory explanation" because it did not know the tapes were not sealed. The Government points out that, as soon as it discovered its mistake, it obtained a judicial seal. However, the Government's argument should be rejected. Although the Government was unaware the tapes were not immediately sealed, it stored the tapes in an open box and misplaced them for over two months. Thus, its explanation was not "satisfactory."

> **Defending against opponent:** opponent "incorrectly contends"

> and stating the basis of the opposing argument.

> Finally, the **advocate's premise**: opponent's argument should be rejected, and why.

(2) The wiretap tapes the Government obtained from tapping Mr. Hart's home telephone are not admissible at trial. The evidence is inadmissible because the Government failed to comply with the requirements of the federal wiretap statute. The wiretap statute requires the Government to safeguard the integrity of wiretap tapes by obtaining an "immediate" judicial seal, or by providing a "satisfactory explanation" for its failure to do so. By waiting for over two months, the Government failed "immediately" to obtain the protection of a judicial seal. The Government also failed to provide a "satisfactory explanation" for its failure to do so. Instead, the Government lost this sensitive evidence as it allegedly sat exposed in an open box in a busy, unlocked storage room for over two months. By failing either to store the tapes in a manner that affords the same level of protection as an immediate judicial seal, or to act with reasonable diligence, the Government failed to offer a "satisfactory explanation" for its lengthy delay.

> **Advocate's thesis:** tapes are not admissible.

> **Proof of thesis:**

> Mr. Hart's favorable standard and why the Government has failed to satisfy the favorable standard.

Exercise 23-4

Assume you represent a plaintiff who has sued her former employer for damages, alleging that the former employer violated Title VII. Rewrite the following statement on behalf of the plaintiff to shift from an objective observation about the law to a persuasive declaration that affirms your client's position.

a. "In a Title VII suit, the plaintiff must prove that the employer unlawfully discriminated against an 'individual with respect to his terms, conditions or privileges of employment because of such individual's ... race.'"

Assume you represent the State in a criminal action against a man accused of murdering his spouse. You seek to admit into evidence the defendant's communications with his psychotherapist, in which he indicated his intent to murder his wife. The defendant's lawyer has filed a motion to suppress the evidence, arguing that the communications are protected by the patient/psychotherapist privilege. As the State's attorney, rewrite the following sentences into declarations that affirm the State's position.

b. "Communications between Defendant and his psychotherapist are not privileged communications and should not be withheld from the jury."

c. "The *Dixon* court 'assumed, without deciding, that such a privilege does exist.' However, that case was a civil case, not a criminal case. The court also noted that the plaintiff had advanced no policy interests in that case that might justify disclosure. Therefore, the *Dixon* case is not controlling, and this Court should not base its decision on *Dixon*."

V. PERSUADE BY USING JUXTAPOSITION AND PARALLELISM

A. To Attack Opponent's Credibility or Legal Theory

Juxtaposing conflicting statements can be extremely effective. Advocates use this technique to discredit their opponent's factual story or legal theory without sounding strident or obviously biased. For example, if you were to argue passionately that the opponent's story is absurd, or that the opponent is lying, you might appear so biased that you would risk losing credibility. On the other hand, if you can juxtapose conflicting statements so that the reader can draw the obvious conclusions from the discrepancy, you will have made the same point with much greater power—now the reader herself has drawn the obvious inference that the opponent is lying.

Compare the persuasive appeal of the following examples:

(1) Agent Friday testified that she placed a label on the box of tapes, indicating the box was to be transported to the courthouse. However, Agent Friday must be lying to this Court, because there was no label on the box two months later!

vs.

(2) Although Agent Friday testified that she placed a label on the box, indicating that it was to be transported to the courthouse, the building janitor testified that no label appeared on the box of tapes. The Government has not explained this factual discrepancy.

B. To Emphasize Similarities to Precedent Cases

You can also use juxtaposition and parallelism as a technique to emphasize the similarities between a client's facts and the facts of a precedent case. This strategy has a subtle psychological impact—the reader easily senses the parallels between your case and a precedent case when you use identical language to link key aspects of a case to key aspects of your client's situation.

Compare the persuasive appeal of the following examples:

> (1) In allowing the plaintiff to recover damages for his injury, the *Porter* court reasoned: "Under the pleadings, the defendants did not say the plaintiff was a bad check writer; they only caused him to appear to be one… to injure him in his reputation." *Id*. at 272.
>
> Similarly, in the present case, the Company attempted to imply that Martin received a $250,000 kickback in an effort to harm him.

In the above illustration, does the Martin situation seem to parallel the *Porter* case? Yes, perhaps in some ways. However, one cannot help but notice the distinctions as well. The *Porter* case deals with a bad check writer while Martin allegedly received a $250,000 kickback. Now consider the subtle writing style strategies that make the two cases appear more similar.

> (2) In allowing the plaintiff to recover damages for his injury, the *Porter* court reasoned: "Under the pleadings, the defendants did not **say** the plaintiff was a bad check writer; they only caused him to **appear** to be one… to injure him in his reputation." *Id*. at 272 (emphasis added).
>
> Similarly, in the present case, the Company did not **say** that Martin was fired because he received a $250,000 kickback. However, the Company certainly caused him to **appear** that way in an effort to injure Martin's reputation.

In the second example, the words "say" and "appear" are not emphasized by the court in the original opinion. However, the advocate enhanced the similarity between the case and the client's facts by adding the emphasis in the case discussion, and then paralleling the *same words* and *emphasis* when analogizing the case to the client's factual situation. Although this technique can be very powerful, use it selectively. If you use it with every case discussion, your strategy becomes transparent and loses its persuasive appeal.

VI. PERSUADE BY DE-EMPHASIZING NEGATIVE INFORMATION

Sometimes, a broad argument or precedent case that generally favors a client also contains within it information that is not as favorable to the client. Under those circumstances, you can use several persuasive writing techniques to de-emphasize the negative information.

Caveat: Be careful not to confuse this technique with the strategy of saving direct rebuttal to the end of your argument. Instead, this technique refers to instances in which you wish to de-emphasize certain language within the body of an *otherwise favorable argument*.

A. Make Negative Information Implicit

Sometimes it's possible to make "negative" information implicit rather than explicit. For example, assume you want to persuade a court to adopt a position taken by the Equal Employment Opportunity Commission ("EEOC"). However, the court is not required to adopt the EEOC's position because the EEOC regulations are merely persuasive, not mandatory authority. Consider the difference in persuasive appeal when the "negative" information is made implicit rather than explicit.

> (1)   While the EEOC Guidelines are interpretive regulations only and are not binding on courts, the United States Supreme Court has given courts the authority to look to the Guidelines as persuasive guidance when interpreting Title VII.
>
> vs.
>
> (2)   The United States Supreme Court has instructed lower courts to look to the EEOC Guidelines as persuasive guidance when interpreting Title VII.

B. "Bury" Negative Information

Sometimes "negative" information cannot be made implicit. Rather, you may either be ethically obligated to disclose the information, or you may elect to disclose it to avoid losing credibility. Under these circumstances, you can minimize the information's impact by "burying" unfavorable information in the middle of a sentence and/or paragraph.

For example, assume you represent Adams, a client who seeks to recover punitive damages for the defendant's gross negligence. You know that punitive damages are very rarely rewarded in such cases, yet you believe that you would lose credibility if you were to ignore that point.[2] Compare the following two examples and consider the

---

2. *See, e.g.*, Charles R. Calleros, *Legal Method and Writing* 311 (2d ed., Aspen L. & Bus. 1994).

difference in persuasive appeal when the negative information is buried in a dependent clause in the middle of the paragraph.

> (1) *It is true that punitive damages for negligence are not often awarded.* However, Adams is entitled to punitive damages in this exceptional case because the Defendant was grossly negligent in failing to repair the hole in the sidewalk even after three small children injured themselves by falling into the hole.
>
> vs.
>
> (2) Adams is entitled to punitive damages for the Defendant's gross negligence in this exceptional case, *even though such damages are not typically awarded in negligence actions*, because the Defendant failed to repair the hole in the sidewalk even after three small children injured themselves by falling into the hole.

Exercise 23-5

Again, assume that you represent the State in a criminal action against a man accused of murdering his spouse. After researching whether communications between the defendant and his psychotherapist are privileged, assume that you discover the *Burtrum* case. In that case, the court held that, due to the compelling state interests in *child abuse* cases, there was no psychotherapist and patient privilege. This is the first and only case in this jurisdiction in which a court has considered whether a privilege exists in a criminal case. Rewrite the following sentence to de-emphasize the distinction between child abuse cases and homicide.

"Although it is true that *Burtrum* involved the abuse of a minor child, the court's holding that the psychotherapist patient privilege does not exist should apply to these criminal proceedings for murder as well."

Exercise 23-6

Judge Cardozo wrote the following statement of facts in the famous *Palsgraf* case. The New York Court of Appeals ultimately held that the defendant railroad company was not negligent because the acts of its employees were not the "proximate cause" of the plaintiff's injuries. Judge Cardozo wrote the statement of facts in *Palsgraf* from a defendant's perspective, creating a visual picture that weakens the connection between the defendant's employees' actions and the plaintiff's injuries.[3]

---

3. *See* Diana V. Pratt, *Legal Writing: A Systematic Approach* 290 (2d ed. West 1993) (describing the writing style techniques used by Justice Cardozo in crafting the factual statement).

For this writing exercise, separately: (1) note the different persuasive style strategies Cardozo used in drafting this factual statement; and (2) redraft the following paragraph of facts from a perspective that favors the plaintiff.

CARDOZO:

Plaintiff was standing on a platform of defendant's railroad after buying a ticket to go to Rockaway Beach. A train stopped at the station, bound for another place. Two men ran forward to catch it. One of the men reached the platform of the car without mishap, though the train was moving. The other man, carrying a package, jumped aboard the car, but seemed unsteady as if about to fall. A guard on the car, who had held the door open, reached forward to help him in, and another guard on the platform pushed him from behind. In this act, the package was dislodged, and fell upon the rails. It was a package of small size, about fifteen inches long, and covered with newspaper. In fact it contained fireworks, but there was nothing in its appearance to give notice of its contents. The fireworks when they fell exploded. The shock of the explosion threw down some scales at the other end of the platform many feet away. The scales struck the plaintiff, causing injuries for which she sues.

CHAPTER IN REVIEW

Core Concepts:

1. For maximum persuasive appeal, find a balance between a neutral analysis of the law and strident advocacy.

2. When editing your writing, think about the following persuasive writing style strategies:

   a. Persuade through *word choice*: verbs & nouns.
   - *Editing Tip*: To make your language more persuasive, use a thesaurus to identify other words that can be used to subtly change the tone of your statement.
   - *Cf.* "The police *warned*…." vs "The police *threatened*…."

   b. Persuade through deliberate use of *active voice/action verbs* and *passive voice*.
   - To link your client to favorable acts, *or* to emphasize an opponent's unfavorable acts, use the active voice & action verbs (*e.g.*, "The defendant stabbed the victim.").
   - To distance your client from unfavorable acts, or to de-emphasize an opponent's favorable acts, use the passive voice. (*e.g.*, "The victim was stabbed.").

- *Editing Tip*: Active voice follows this format: actor (the subject) → acts upon → an object. Passive voice follows this format: this object → was acted upon → by this actor (subject).

c. Persuade by using *definitive* rather than "*opinion*" statements, which sound tentative and leave room for doubt.
  - *Editing Tip*: Check your sentences for introductory clauses that make the remainder of the sentence conditional.
  - *Cf.* "*The defense contends that* the plaintiff's argument is without merit." vs "The plaintiff's argument is without merit."

d. Persuade by using *affirmative*, rather than defensive, statements.
  - An affirmative statement is one that affirms the client's position rather than defends against an opponent's position.
  - *Cf.* "*The Government incorrectly contends* that wiretap tapes are admissible as evidence during trial." vs "The wiretap tapes the Government obtained are not admissible at trial."
  - *Exception*: In direct rebuttal, an advocate directly attacks the opponent's position and states why that position is incorrect.

e. Persuade by using juxtaposition & parallelism.
  i. Use this technique to attack the opponent's credibility or legal theory, as follows:
    - Juxtapose conflicting statements so that the reader can draw the obvious conclusions from the discrepancy.
    - *E.g.*, "Although Agent Friday testified that she placed a label on the box, there was no label on the box when the box was finally discovered. The Government has not explained this factual discrepancy."
  ii. Use this technique to emphasize similarities to a precedent case, as follows:
    - When describing a precedent case and then comparing it to the client's situation, use identical language to refer to the same important idea.
    - *E.g.*, "In *Porter*, the court reasoned that the defendants did not *say* the plaintiff was a bad check writer; they only caused him to *appear* to be one.... Similarly, in the present case, the company did not *say* that Martin was fired because.... However, they certainly caused him to *appear* that way...."

f. De-emphasize negative information.
  i. Make negative information implicit.
  ii. "Bury" negative information within the middle of a sentence or paragraph.

FACT-CENTERED ARGUMENTS
Pre-Drafting Strategies

I. THE CASE SELECTION PROCESS

From the numerous cases you might review and analyze, your goal is to select the most favorable cases to incorporate into the persuasive argument, while also considering the ethical and pragmatic considerations that might cause you to include cases that are less than entirely favorable. When evaluating the cases to incorporate into your argument, consider the following:

1. Whether the case is *mandatory or persuasive* precedent.
2. The court's *holding under the specific facts* before the court.
3. The *rationale* within the case.
4. The *date* of the case.
5. The *level of court* that decided the case.
6. Whether there are *ethical* or *pragmatic* reasons to include an unfavorable case into the argument.

A. Mandatory or Persuasive Precedent

The most important preliminary consideration is whether the case is mandatory or persuasive precedent. If there is solid mandatory case precedent addressing a legal issue, judges are often reluctant to rely on cases outside the jurisdiction. This is particularly true with state law issues, as the source of law varies from state to state. Therefore, as you research case law, first focus on cases within your jurisdiction. If there is good law within your jurisdiction, you may not want to expand your research to cases outside the jurisdiction. Many clients would not appreciate receiving a significant legal bill for researching persuasive case law that might only marginally benefit their argument.

B. Holding and Analogous Facts

Next consider the relative value of each court's holding under the unique fact pattern before the court. The following considerations are rules of thumb to consider when selecting factually analogous cases for a persuasive argument. However, use your judgment when deciding whether to include a case in your argument. For example, although factually analogous cases with favorable holdings are usually persuasive, an unfavorable policy statement or unfavorable dictum in the case might make that case an unwise selection for a persuasive argument. As another example, while two cases might both have favorable holdings with analogous facts, one of the cases might not produce as many favorable analogies to your client's situation.

1. Favorable Result Cases

Assuming you are evaluating cases that are all mandatory precedent (or are all persuasive precedent), prefer cases with favorable holdings. Of the cases with favorable holdings, the most persuasive cases have analogous case facts that are *less desirable* than the client's facts. These cases provide powerful fodder for a persuasive argument because you can highlight the point that, even with less desirable facts, the court nevertheless held in a manner favorable to your client. Then, as you apply the favorable case to the client's facts, your argument is relatively easy—if less desirable facts yielded a favorable holding, you should be able to highlight the favorable factual distinctions to argue that a court should clearly rule in your favor with respect to your client's more desirable facts.

The next most persuasive type of case with a favorable holding is a case in which the analogous case facts are *comparable* to your client's facts. A "comparable" case is one in which the client's facts are just as likely to satisfy, or fail to satisfy, a legal standard as the facts in the precedent case. If you can convince an adjudicator that a previous case is factually similar to your client's situation in every legally significant way, then the judge should apply the rule of law to your client's situation with the same result.

Somewhat less persuasive is the case with a favorable holding that has *more desirable* analogous facts than your client's factual situation. When a precedent case has more desirable facts than in the client situation, an adjudicator might conclude that the factual distinctions are legally significant. If the factual distinctions are legally significant, then the adjudicator would apply the law to your client's facts and potentially arrive at a different result. Nevertheless, if the distinguishable facts are not legally significant enough to compel a different result, then the precedent case might still be persuasive.

2. Unfavorable Result Cases

Cases with unfavorable holdings are generally less desirable precedent for the obvious reason that their holdings are unfavorable to the client. However, it is rare to research an issue and find only cases that have favorable holdings. You may sometimes find yourself in the enviable position of having enough favorable result cases to make a persuasive, credible argument without even having to incorporate an unfavorable result case into the argument. More typically, however, you must incorporate cases that have unfavorable holdings. It can be difficult to distinguish such a case from your client's situation without appearing defensive. However, cases with unfavorable holdings can also be persuasive as precedent if they are clearly distinguishable, particularly if the precedent court's rationale would seemingly compel a different result under a fact pattern similar to your client's. Thus, even cases with unfavorable holdings can support the client's position and can thereby be used as favorable cases within an argument.

When deciding whether to use a case with an unfavorable holding, consider: (1) whether, and how, you can distinguish the case on its facts; (2) whether you can craft a favorable distinction based on the court's rationale, including dicta; and (3) whether ethical and/or pragmatic considerations compel you to include a case in your argument that is less than entirely favorable.

a. Consider the Case Facts

Often advocates transform seemingly unfavorable cases into favorable law by distinguishing such cases on their facts. In evaluating whether an unfavorable result case is distinguishable enough to be included in your argument, consider how narrowly you can realistically construe the court's holding. If you can plausibly argue that the court's holding is dependent upon certain facts that are distinguishable from your client's facts, then the case might have persuasive value.

b. Consider the Court's Rationale

When evaluating a case with an unfavorable holding, also carefully review the court's rationale. Sometimes courts discuss policy considerations underlying the decision. If these policy considerations might dictate a different result under the client's fact pattern, then the case might have persuasive appeal. Strong policy statements within a court opinion can enhance the persuasive appeal of the factual distinctions.

Favorable dicta can also enhance the persuasive appeal of an unfavorable result case. Sometimes courts imply that the result might be different under a different set of facts. If a client's factual situation is similar to the hypothetical facts implied within the dicta, the case might have persuasive appeal. As you consider whether to incorporate such a case into your argument, evaluate how closely the client's factual situation seems to fit within the court's dicta and whether the case, as a whole, fits within the favorable argument you are constructing.

c. Consider Ethical and Pragmatic Factors

As a case with an unfavorable holding grows less distinguishable from the client's factual situation, it becomes less favorable as precedent. Some cases with unfavorable holdings cannot easily be transformed into favorable law. However, when you are presenting arguments before a court, you have an ethical obligation to disclose mandatory cases (higher level courts within the same jurisdiction) that are "directly adverse" to a client's position.[1] In a fact-centered argument, a case would not be considered "directly adverse" unless there were no legally significant factual distinctions between the case and the client's situation.

Even when you are not ethically compelled to disclose an unfavorable case or argument, you may decide to disclose and rebut the unfavorable law anyway. Sometimes, disclosing unfavorable law will best promote your client's interests. For example, an unfavorable case may be so important in the jurisdiction in which you are practicing law that you might damage your credibility by failing to disclose the case. Therefore, even when you are not ethically required to disclose a case with an unfavorable holding, consider: (1) whether disclosure is necessary to maintain your credibility with the court or other adjudicator; and (2) whether your disclosure and skillful advocacy can minimize the damage from your opponent's potential disclosure of the unfavorable law.

As you assess these pragmatic considerations, consider the following factors:

- Relative importance of the case in the controlling jurisdiction;
- Likelihood the opposing counsel will disclose and rely on the case; and
- Relative degree of harm the unfavorable law presents.

If it is likely that opposing counsel will rely on the case, and you can easily minimize its potential damage by distinguishing the case, then you would probably want to disclose the case in your own argument. You would prefer that the adjudicator first consider the unfavorable law within the context of your own skillful presentation rather than within the confines of your opponent's argument. If, however, an unfavorable case is fairly damaging, and it is questionable whether your opponent will rely on the case, you may well decide to omit any references to the adverse law. Instead, you may instead elect to anticipate and subtly rebut the damaging case through anticipatory rebuttal. Chapter 30 discusses anticipatory rebuttal in greater detail.

---

1. Model R. Prof. Conduct 3.3(a)(2) (ABA 2002).

3. Case Holdings and Facts at a Glance

A. Prefer cases with *favorable holdings* in the following order:
1.   Case facts that are *less desirable* than the client's facts.
2.   Case facts of the *same relative value* as the client's facts.
3.   Case facts that are *more desirable* than the client's facts, thereby not necessarily requiring a judge to reach the same result when evaluating the client's facts.

B. Prefer cases with *unfavorable holdings* in the following order:
1.   Case facts that are *far less desirable* than the client's facts, making the case easily distinguishable.
2.   Case facts that are *somewhat less desirable* than the client's facts, making the case distinguishable.
3.   Case facts that are of the *same relative value* as the client's facts (potentially unfavorable law to rebut).

Caveat:

Before ignoring an unfavorable case, consider whether *ethical* or *pragmatic* considerations suggest that it should be included within the argument.

C. Rationale

The reasoning within each case is also a critically important consideration. Rationale might transform an otherwise borderline case into a highly favorable or unfavorable case. Consider the facts the court emphasized in justifying its holding. Although your client's situation may be similar to a precedent case, upon further examination you may find that the facts the court found most significant are distinguishable from your client's facts. Do the distinctions help you advance your argument or hinder your ability to do so?

It is also important to review the rationale in cases that are not factually analogous, as well. Even though you would not discuss such a case in detail, you might refer to the case tangentially to highlight a favorable legal definition or policy statement. Does the court interpret the meaning of the law in a manner that favors, or damages, your client's interests? Based on the court's policy statements, can you argue that the relief requested by your client will promote favorable public policy?

D. Date and Level of Court

The date of each precedent case and the level of court that decided each case are also relevant, although somewhat less important than the above factors. All other things being equal, a more recent case is more valuable than an older case, and a case decided by the highest level court in the jurisdiction is more valuable than a case decided by a lower level court. However, lower courts are compelled to follow decisions of higher level courts within the jurisdiction. Thus, in most jurisdictions, an intermediate appellate court is just as binding upon a trial court as the highest appellate court. The level of court may have more relevance when the meaning of the law is unclear or the cases arguably conflict.

◎ ILLUSTRATION: Spousal Wiretap Problem

Consider the spousal wiretap problem that is the basis of the sample briefs in Appendix C. The federal wiretap statute prohibits individuals from recording telephone calls without the "prior consent" of one of the parties to the conversation. In the hypothetical fact pattern that is the basis of the briefs in Appendix C, a husband and wife (Mr. and Mrs. Harrison) have a history of recording all telephone calls into and out of their home for a limited period each time they hire a new nanny for their young son. They have done so out of a concern that the new nanny might abuse her telephone privileges. Each time, they have obtained the nanny's permission to record all calls. The present dispute arose when the husband and wife were legally separated but still living in the same home. The wife hired a new caretaker for the couple's son and then recorded all telephone calls for a limited period of time. Upon listening to the recordings, she discovered that her husband appeared to be engaged in marital misconduct.

The husband claims that he did not consent to his telephone calls being recorded. His best argument is the actual conversation the couple had about the telephone monitoring at the time the couple was legally separated and the wife hired a new caretaker for their son. The wife's statement is ambiguous; she stated that she "wanted to make sure the housekeeper did not make improper use of the telephone." The husband will argue, of course, that this statement did not give him notice that she intended to record all telephone calls into and out of the couple's home. The husband will also argue that the court must consider all of the surrounding circumstances when determining whether he consented—here, the couple were legally separated and relations were "strained." Under these circumstances, it would strain credibility to assume that he consented to such monitoring.

The wife claims that the husband did, indeed, impliedly consent to the recordings. In considering the surrounding circumstances, however, her argument will focus on the couple's *past practices,* not the present marital discord. Her best argument is the couple's past practice of recording all telephone calls when they hired a new caretaker for their child. She will argue that the ambiguous statement she made to her husband must be taken within the context of the couple's past practices. Taken within that context, her message was clear—all telephone calls would be recorded for a short period of time. When her husband told her to "go ahead and take care of it," she could only presume that he was consenting to the recordings.

Now that you are aware of the facts for this wiretap problem involving Mr. and Mrs. Harrison, consider the following options for selecting cases that will form the basis of each side's persuasive argument.

1. Cases that Are Not Factually Analogous

After reading the case law within the relevant jurisdiction, each lawyer discovers that there are four cases within the jurisdiction that address the issue of implied consent. One of the cases (*Lanoue*) is not factually analogous, but it does contain policy language that is highly favorable to Mr. Harrison, the plaintiff, who claims that he did not consent to the telephone monitoring. In that opinion the court stated:

> "Consent might be implied in spite of deficient notice, but only in a *rare case* where the court can conclude with assurance 'from surrounding circumstances... that the [party] knowingly agreed to the surveillance.' (citation omitted).... The surrounding circumstances must *convincingly* show that the party knew about and consented to the interception...." (emphasis added).

Therefore, even though the facts are not analogous, the plaintiff would elect to incorporate some of the language from the *Lanoue* case into his argument. The defendant, Mrs. Harrison, would not include *Lanoue* in her argument at all because the policy language is not favorable to her position, and the facts are not analogous.

2. Cases that Are Factually Analogous

a. The *Williams* Case

The three remaining cases are, to varying degrees, factually analogous—the *Williams, Griggs-Ryan,* and *Campiti* cases. The *Williams* case is probably the most factually analogous to the clients' factual situation. In *Williams,* as in the clients' situation, there was an ambiguous verbal communication about telephone monitoring and controversy about the actual communication itself. In *Williams,* the court held that the plaintiff did not consent to the telephone monitoring. Therefore, the holding is favorable to Mr. Harrison's position, who also claims that he did not consent. Because the facts are analogous, and the holding and rationale are favorable, Mr. Harrison's attorney easily elects to include this case in his argument.

Because the holding in *Williams* is unfavorable to the defendant, Mrs. Harrison's, position, the decision to include the *Williams* case in the defendant's argument is not as straightforward. However, because this is one of only a few factually comparable cases within the jurisdiction, the lawyer recognizes that Mr. Harrison's attorney will almost certainly rely on this case. She realizes that Mr. Harrison's attorney will highlight those aspects of the case that favor the plaintiff's position and will de-emphasize aspects of the case that favor the defendant's position. Therefore, she would prefer that the judge not read only the plaintiff's rendition of the *Williams* case. After carefully evaluating the case, the defendant's lawyer recognizes that the facts in *Williams* are different enough in legally significant ways for her to credibly distinguish the case. Thus, Mrs. Harrison's lawyer can minimize the damage from the plaintiff's argument by including the *Williams* case within her own argument and highlighting those aspects of the case that are more favorable to her client's position. After considering all of these factors, Mrs. Harrison's lawyer also elects to include the *Williams* case in her argument.

b. The *Griggs-Ryan* Case

The *Griggs-Ryan* case favors the defendant, Mrs. Harrison. In *Griggs-Ryan*, the court held that a tenant impliedly consented to his landlady's recording of his telephone calls. The court reasoned that the landlady repeatedly informed the tenant that all calls would be recorded; the tenant's subsequent use of the telephone constituted implied consent. Although this is a favorable result case from Mrs. Harrison's perspective, the facts in *Griggs-Ryan* are decidedly more desirable than in the client's situation. In *Griggs-Ryan*, there were very clear verbal communications warning the tenant about the monitoring; Mrs. Harrison's verbal communication to her husband was not as clear. Nonetheless, this is the only favorable result case in the jurisdiction, and Mrs. Harrison's attorney really cannot ignore it. Moreover, there are some factual nuances in the case that Mrs. Harrison's attorney can use to her advantage, as well as some favorable policy statements. Therefore, Mrs. Harrison's lawyer decides to include the *Griggs-Ryan* case in her argument.

Mr. Harrison, the plaintiff in the spousal wiretap problem, also has a decision to make with the *Griggs-Ryan* case. Because the *Griggs-Ryan* court held that the plaintiff did indeed consent to wiretapping, this case initially appears unfavorable. However, the very case facts that cause Mrs. Harrison's lawyer some concern (repeated, clear verbal warnings) make the case easily distinguishable from Mr. Harrison's situation. Moreover, because this is the only case in the jurisdiction that held that the plaintiff impliedly consented to monitoring, Mr. Harrison's lawyer also recognizes that the defendant will rely heavily on this case. Like the decision Mrs. Harrison's lawyer made with the *Williams* case, he would rather minimize any potential damage from *Griggs-Ryan* by including this case within his own argument. That way, he can emphasize the factually distinguishable aspects of the *Griggs-Ryan* case within his argument.

c. The *Campiti* Case

Although the holding in the *Campiti* case favors his client, Mr. Harrison's lawyer is faced with a dilemma—the facts in *Campiti* are more desirable than his client's facts. In *Campiti*, although the court held that the plaintiff, a prisoner, did not consent to the wiretapping of his telephone call, the court also found that the prison never provided *any* written or verbal communications advising prisoners that their telephone calls would be monitored. Thus, the facts in *Campiti* are significantly more desirable from the plaintiff's perspective than the Harrisons' factual situation. If one were to place the cases on a spectrum, the graph would look something like this:

No Consent			Consent
↑	↑	↑	↑
Campiti	*Williams*	Client	*Griggs-Ryan*

The Harrisons' factual situation probably falls close to the middle of the graph, just to the right of the *Williams* case. As the graph illustrates, when Mr. Harrison's lawyer uses case law to argue that his client did not consent to the monitoring, the *Williams* facts are more analogous to the client's situation. Therefore, unless the *Campiti* case has facts or rationale that might add a favorable nuance to Mr. Harrison's argument—a nuance that is not already present in the *Williams* case—Mr. Harrison's lawyer would not emphasize the *Campiti* case in his argument; the *Campiti* decision simply is not as factually analogous as the *Williams* case. Without an additional nuance not present in the other cases, Mr. Harrison's lawyer would likely make only a tangential reference to the *Campiti* case in his argument, providing a citation to indicate that there is another case in the jurisdiction that held the plaintiff did not consent.

After carefully evaluating the facts in *Campiti*, however, Mr. Harrison's lawyer does discover a favorable factual nuance that could add persuasive appeal to his argument. In *Campiti*, the prison had a past practice of monitoring prisoner calls. Despite this past practice, the court held that the prisoner did not consent to the monitoring. Mr. Harrison's lawyer realizes that he can emphasize this aspect of the case, and then ultimately use this case to rebut Mrs. Harrison's argument that the couple's past practice helped provide Mr. Harrison with notice of the telephone monitoring. Therefore, Mr. Harrison's lawyer elects to incorporate the case into his argument.

Now consider the choice facing the defendant's lawyer. Because the defendant, Mrs. Harrison, will argue that her husband consented to the recording of his telephone calls, the result in *Campiti* is unfavorable. However, the facts in *Campiti* are easily distinguishable from the client's facts because, in *Campiti*, there was never, at any time, any verbal or written communications warning the prisoners that their calls would be monitored. Therefore, this case is not wholly undesirable from the defendant's perspective. Moreover, there are other facts in the opinion suggesting that the prison's past monitoring practices were not as common as the prison contended. Because the defendant can easily distinguish *Campiti*, and, in fact, use her interpretation of the case to subtly rebut the plaintiff's interpretation of the case, Mrs. Harrison's attorney also decides to include the case in her own argument.

II. FORMULATING FAVORABLE INTERPRETATIONS OF THE LAW

A. Identify Favorable "Back-Drop" Statements

As you read the case law, consider whether any of the cases contain broad, general statements interpreting the law that might serve as a favorable "back-drop" for your argument. As an example, courts often include policy statements that can provide a favorable back-drop for an argument, such as whether the statute or common law rule of law should be interpreted broadly or narrowly. Favorable "back-drop" statements are too broad and general to serve as the vehicles that guide an argument. However, they can provide a favorable framework from which the court might view your argument. As you evaluate the case law, highlight any such language that might favorably promote your argument.

◎ ILLUSTRATION: SPOUSAL WIRETAP PROBLEM

Using the spousal wiretap problem as an example, recall that the *Griggs-Ryan* court held that a tenant impliedly consented to his landlady's recording of his telephone calls. As often happens, the *Griggs-Ryan* court made several broad, general statements about the statute (explanatory reasoning) before applying it to the factual situation before the court. A number of the court's statements are, not surprisingly, more favorable to the defendant, as the court ultimately concluded that the plaintiff impliedly consented to the monitoring. Thus, while reading the case, Mrs. Harrison's lawyer highlights these broad "back-drop" statements for later use in the defendant's brief. In *Griggs-Ryan*, the court made the following broad "back-drop" statements. In order to illustrate how an advocate might later emphasize the most favorable language from each statement, the most compelling language is italicized:

> "We agree with the Second Circuit that 'Congress intended the consent requirement to be *construed broadly*.'"

> "In this spirit, we—and other courts—have held that *Title III affords a safe harbor* not only for persons who intercept calls with the explicit consent of a conversant but also from those who do so after receiving *implied consent*."

> "Implied consent is inferred 'from surrounding circumstances indicating that the [party] knowingly agreed to the surveillance.'"

As often happens, the case does not just contain favorable language for only one party. Recall that Mr. Harrison's lawyer is arguing that he did *not* consent to the telephone monitoring. While reading the same case, Mr. Harrison's lawyer finds another broad "back-drop" statement that is more favorable to the *plaintiff's* position:

> "Of course, implied consent is not constructive consent. Rather, implied consent is '*consent in fact*' which is inferred 'from surrounding circumstances indicating that the [party] *knowingly agreed* to the surveillance.'"

Mr. Harrison's lawyer makes a note of this language for later use in his brief. As Mr. Harrison's lawyer scans the relevant case law for favorable "back-drop" statements, he finds another favorable statement from a case in which the court found the plaintiff did *not* consent to monitoring—the *Williams* case. In *Williams*, the court observed that:

> "In light of the prophylactic purposes of Title III, implied consent should *not be casually inferred*."

Note that two different courts within the same circuit have made two seemingly conflicting statements: that implied consent should be "construed broadly" (*Griggs-Ryan*), and that implied consent should "not be casually inferred" (*Williams*). The courts' differing positions are not entirely irreconcilable, nor are they that unusual. Like advocates, the courts have simply framed their task of statutory interpretation in a manner that provides favorable support for their holdings. In the written brief itself, effective advocates take advantage of these statements to "set the stage" for their persuasive arguments.

B. Formulate Favorable Rule Statements

Just as statutes often have vague, broad language that is susceptible to differing interpretations, the fact-centered holdings of courts are also susceptible to differing interpretations. As you read cases, look for statements that reflect how the court applied the law to the unique factual situation before the court. Sometimes, courts spell out a specific standard that a party either satisfied or failed to satisfy. In other cases, however, the court's reasoning is less clear, and advocates have greater leeway to formulate a favorable legal standard the court implicitly applied. Thus, the unique rule of law a court's fact-centered holding expresses is often not rigid, but fluid.

Whether a court's reasoning is express or implied, your ability to formulate favorable rule statements is critically important. These rule statements will form the backbone of your argument: they will ultimately help you organize the template of your argument and serve as thesis sentences introducing each case. As you consider how you might formulate favorable rule statements for each case and for a group of cases, first evaluate your client's factual situation and what you will need to prove in order to prevail. The goal is to formulate the most favorable, as well as credible, interpretation of each precedent case.

Although case law is susceptible to differing interpretations, it is important to keep in mind the parameters of ethical legal interpretation. Ethical rules of conduct prohibit lawyers from advancing legal theories or arguments that do not have a "basis in law and fact" or that are "frivolous."[2] Although there is room for creative interpretation, you must not stray into frivolous territory. Not only would such an interpretation violate ethical rules of conduct, but it would damage your credibility as well. Thus, your goal is to formulate the most favorable rule statements possible from case precedent while also retaining your credibility and honoring your ethical obligations to the court.

1. Cases with Clearly Expressed Standards

When courts explain their holdings, they sometimes spell out a legal standard that must be satisfied. Under such circumstances, you will not have a great deal of latitude in formulating a favorable rule statement, although you might emphasize certain favorable language to provide a favorable context for the standard. For example, in the spousal wiretap problem, the *Williams* court held that the plaintiff did not impliedly consent to the monitoring of his telephone calls. The court reasoned:

> There is no basis for us to conclude that the district court clearly erred in finding that [plaintiff] was not told… (1) of the manner—i.e., the intercepting and recording of telephone conversations—in which this monitoring was conducted; and (2) that he himself would be subjected to such monitoring.… Without at least this minimal knowledge on the part of [plaintiff], we do not see how his consent in fact to the monitoring could be inferred from this record.

The above passage makes it very clear that the *Williams* court applied a two-part test to determine whether the plaintiff consented to monitoring—whether the plaintiff was told in advance of the *manner* of the monitoring, and whether the plaintiff knew that the *scope* of the monitoring extended to his own telephone calls. Thus, when interpreting this case, an advocate would not have any freedom to formulate a rule statement that differs significantly from the above language. However, even using this two-part test, there are still subtle ways in which the plaintiff and defendant can formulate rule statements from the *Williams* case that will portray their clients' positions in a more favorable light.

---

2. Model R. Prof. Conduct 3.1 (ABA 2002).

a. Plaintiff's Favorable Slant

Mr. Harrison, the plaintiff in the spousal wiretap problem, argues that he did not impliedly consent to his telephone calls being recorded. Therefore, the *Williams* case is a highly favorable case for the plaintiff; his lawyer can easily use this standard to argue that Mrs. Harrison never told her husband of either the manner or the scope of the monitoring when she shared her concern about the new housekeeper's misuse of the telephone. Even though the court's rule statement is already favorable, Mr. Harrison's lawyer can still tweak the language a bit to emphasize a standard that would be more difficult for the defendant to overcome. Mr. Harrison's lawyer formulates the following rule statement from the *Williams* case. The added favorable language is italicized; the additional language is, of course, consistent with other language in the opinion and with the court's holding.

> When the target of wiretapping has not been *expressly notified* of both the manner and the scope of the interception, and has no *actual knowledge* that he himself will be a target of monitoring, implied consent may not be inferred.

In the above example, by emphasizing that the notice must be "express" and that the plaintiff must have "actual knowledge" of the monitoring, Mr. Harrison's lawyer makes the standard more difficult for the defendant to overcome. The lawyer also decides to draw out the second prong of the standard (the scope of monitoring) and create the appearance of two separate standards (the "scope" of monitoring and knowledge that "he himself will be a target"). Thus, the standard appears to be a three-part test rather than a two-part test. Finally, the lawyer subtly paints a picture of wrong-doing by referring to a "target of wiretapping." The term "target of wiretapping" subtly suggests a more alarming act than "monitoring," a more innocuous term.

b. Defendant's Favorable Slant

Superficially, the court's two-part test does not appear to be very favorable from the defendant's perspective. However, as an important case, the defendant cannot ignore the decision; and, because the language is clear, the defendant cannot ignore the court's standard. Nonetheless, Mrs. Harrison's lawyer can still use this standard to craft a persuasive argument. She will argue that Mrs. Harrison's ambiguous verbal statement must not be viewed in a vacuum, but must instead be construed in light of the couple's past practices. The couple's past practices, together with the defendant's verbal statement to her husband, sufficiently notified the plaintiff of both the scope and the manner of the monitoring.

Like the plaintiff's lawyer, Mrs. Harrison's lawyer can also subtly tweak the court's language to suggest a standard that would be easier for the defendant to satisfy. While the plaintiff's lawyer emphasized language that required "actual knowledge," the defendant's lawyer emphasizes language from the opinion suggesting that the party need only have "minimal knowledge." In addition, rather than emphasizing that the defendant must ultimately satisfy a two-part test, the defendant de-emphasizes the two-part nature of the test in the rule statement, making the "manner of the monitoring" prong implicit rather than explicit (the term "recording" suggests the manner of the monitoring). Finally, because Mrs. Harrison's lawyer will later attempt to distinguish this unfavorable result case, the lawyer formulates a standard that suggests that *only under the limited circumstances* illustrated by that case would the defendant not prevail (i.e., ... "does not imply consent to monitoring *only when* ..."). Again, the added language is italicized.

> A party's use of the telephone does not imply consent to monitoring *only when* he does not have even *minimal knowledge* that the scope of the monitoring would include the *recording* of his own telephone calls.

2. Cases with Ambiguous Standards

Sometimes, courts do not spell out a specific standard that one party did or did not satisfy in the case. Instead, these courts simply list the reasons why one party prevailed, leaving the advocate with the task of formulating a standard the court *implicitly applied*. Under these circumstances, advocates have a fair degree of latitude in formulating a favorable rule statement. As you think about how best to formulate a rule statement, consider whether the client's interests would best be served by advocating a rule statement *narrowly linked* to certain case facts, or a broader rule statement that, while still consistent with the facts and rationale, has *broader application*.

a. The *Griggs-Ryan* Case

Again using the spousal wiretap problem for purposes of illustration, the court in *Griggs-Ryan* did not expressly identify a legal standard that it applied to justify its factual holding. The court reasoned:

Plaintiff had been unmistakably warned on a number of occasions that all incoming calls were being monitored. In light of so sweeping a warning, he continued to receive calls and talk unguardedly on [the landlady's] personal line without the slightest hint of coercion or exigent circumstance. Plaintiff was free to use some other instrument; or since outgoing calls were not recorded, to return calls on the [landlady's] telephone and thus avoid any unwanted eavesdropping. Given 'the circumstances prevailing,' [citation omitted], it seems altogether clear that plaintiff 'knowingly agreed to the surveillance.' [citation omitted] His consent, albeit not explicit, was manifest. No more was required.

i. The Plaintiff's Favorable Slant

As is often the case, although the court detailed the facts that it found important, the court never expressly identified a legal standard that it was applying; instead, the standard is implicit in the court's reasoning. Therefore, Mr. Harrison's lawyer has some flexibility to draft a rule statement that is favorable to his client's position. Because the result in this case is unfavorable to the plaintiff's position, Mr. Harrison's lawyer will formulate a rule statement that suggests that *only under the limited circumstances* illustrated by that case would the plaintiff lose (i.e., "consent is implied *only when…*"). In addition, because Mr. Harrison's lawyer is arguing that Mr. Harrison did not impliedly consent to the telephone monitoring, the lawyer wants to draft a rule statement suggesting a standard for notification that would be very difficult for Mrs. Harrison to overcome.

The court's statement that the tenant was "unmistakably warned" of the monitoring is wonderful terminology from the plaintiff's perspective. Thus, the lawyer decides to link his rule statement to this favorable language, thereby imposing a standard that the communication *must* take the form of an "unmistakable warning" in order to be effective. In the argument itself, the lawyer can argue that Mrs. Harrison's ambiguous statement to her husband did not rise to the level of an "unmistakable warning." The plaintiff's lawyer drafts this rule statement:

> Consent is implied *only when* the target of a wiretap is *"unmistakably warned"* that all calls on a line will be monitored, and the target voluntarily continues to use the telephone despite that *express warning*.

ii. The Defendant's Favorable Slant

Although this is a favorable result case from Mrs. Harrison's perspective, the facts in *Griggs-Ryan* are decidedly more desirable than in the client's situation. Therefore, Mrs. Harrison's lawyer wants to minimize the unfavorable distinctions from the case (*e.g.*, "unmistakable warning" and the repeated nature of the warnings). Instead, the lawyer will draft a rule statement that describes a standard that will be easier for her client to satisfy. The lawyer accomplishes this goal by ignoring the unfavorable distinguishable facts and emphasizing the facts that are more similar to her client's situation. Thus, Mrs. Harrison drafts the following rule statement:

> When a party has been told that all incoming telephone calls would be recorded for an indefinite period of time, that party's continuing use of the telephone constitutes implied consent to the monitoring.

b. The *Campiti* Case

The *Campiti* court was even more ambiguous than the court in *Griggs-Ryan* when reasoning why a prisoner did not consent to the electronic monitoring of his telephone calls. After recounting the facts of the case, the court simply noted:

> [The defendant's argument] boils down to the proposition that [the prisoner] should have known his call would probably be monitored and he, therefore, gave consent.... To accept [this] theory of implied consent here would completely distort the plain words of section 2511(2)(c), legalizing an intercept where "one of the parties... has given prior consent to such interception." The district court did not err in finding that there was no consent for the monitoring. We hold that there was no implied consent.

Unlike the *Williams* case, where the court clearly applied a two-part standard when evaluating whether a party consented to monitoring, the *Campiti* court has no clear rationale. The result in *Campiti* is easily reconcilable with the two-part test in *Williams*, as there were no communications at all in *Campiti* that would suggest the prisoner was informed of either the scope or manner of monitoring. However, as illustrated earlier, it would be unnecessary and unpersuasive to use *Campiti* solely to illustrate the *Williams* standard. Instead, recall that both lawyers have elected to use *Campiti* for a different purpose altogether—to illustrate how past monitoring practices affect the outcome.

i. Plaintiff's Favorable Rule Statement

Mr. Harrison, as the plaintiff, argues that he did not consent to the monitoring of his telephone calls. His lawyer will therefore focus on language in the *Campiti* case in which the court was not persuaded that a common practice of monitoring telephone calls constitutes adequate notice of monitoring. Because the court did not really explain its holding, the plaintiff has the latitude to formulate this favorable rule statement:

> Even when a common practice might give rise to an "expectation" that telephone calls might be intercepted, a party does not impliedly consent to such interceptions absent express notice of the scope and manner of the interceptions.

ii. Defendant's Favorable Rule Statement

Because Mrs. Harrison will argue that her husband consented to the recording of his telephone calls, the holding in *Campiti* is unfavorable. However, recall that the *Campiti* case is easily distinguishable—in *Campiti*, there were *no* verbal or written warnings about monitoring. Because the *Campiti* case is so easily distinguishable, it is actually a favorable case for Mrs. Harrison's position. Unlike the plaintiff's lawyer, whose rule statement focuses more broadly on the prison's past practices, Mrs. Harrison's lawyer emphasizes the facts in *Campiti* that are distinguishable from her client's situation—the lack of any verbal or written warnings. Thus, the defendant's lawyer formulates the following rule statement from *Campiti* that is linked very narrowly to certain distinguishable case facts:

> A prisoner does not impliedly consent to monitoring when the prison staff never, on any occasion, notified the prisoners that their calls would be monitored.

CHAPTER IN REVIEW

Definitions:

RULE OF LAW:

A generic term that can refer to:

1. The original sources of law, *e.g.*, constitutions, statutes, and common law; and
2. Judicial interpretations and definitions of the original sources of law.

"BACK-DROP" STATEMENTS:

General policy statements courts make when interpreting a rule of law. Some of these statements can serve as a favorable "back-drop" for your argument (such as whether a statute should be interpreted narrowly or broadly).

ELEMENT:

Elements are separate requirements of a rule of law that a party *must* prove to compel a particular result.

RULE STATEMENT:

A statement you formulate that clearly and accurately reflects how *and* why a court answered the legal question in the manner that it did. As an advocate, the rule statement should be the most favorable credible interpretation of a court's holding.

STANDARD:

When a court interprets a rule of law, sometimes it defines the rule of law in a manner that effectively establishes a new requirement the parties must satisfy. The new requirement can be called a standard (*e.g.*, the *Williams* court interpreted the "consent" statute to require that the defendant warn the plaintiff of both the manner and scope of the monitoring—this becomes a standard that the defendant must satisfy in order to show implied consent).

Selecting Cases for the Argument

Assess the relative persuasive appeal of each case, considering:

1. Whether the case is mandatory or persuasive precedent
   - Prefer mandatory precedent over persuasive precedent.
2. The court's holding under the specific facts before the court
   a. Generally, prefer cases with favorable holdings in this order:
      i. Case facts that are *less desirable* than the client facts;
      ii. Case facts that are *comparable* to the client facts;
      iii. Case facts that are *more desirable* than the client facts.
   b. Generally, prefer cases with unfavorable holdings in this order:
      i. Case facts that are *far less desirable* than the client facts (making the case easily distinguishable);
      ii. Case facts that are *somewhat less desirable* than the client facts (making the case distinguishable);
      iii. Case facts that are of the *same relative value* as the client facts (potentially unfavorable law to rebut).

Caveat: Before ignoring an unfavorable case, consider whether *ethical* or *pragmatic* considerations suggest that it should be included within the argument anyway.

3. The court's rationale, including:
   a. Whether the court interprets the meaning of the law in a manner that favors your client's interests;
   b. Whether the court emphasizes facts in its rationale that favor your client's interests; and
   c. Whether there are any favorable policy statements that you might use as favorable "back-drop" statements in the argument (irrespective of whether the case is factually analogous enough to merit an extended factual discussion).
4. The Date and Level of Court
   - All other things being equal, prefer a higher level court.
   - All other things being equal, prefer a more recent case.

Formulate Favorable Rule Statements

1. First, consider the ultimate conclusion you want the court to adopt in your client's situation.
2. Next, for each case, consider the court's holding and rationale and determine how much latitude you have in formulating a favorable rule statement.

- You will have the most latitude in formulating a favorable rule statement when a court does not expressly apply a standard when explaining why a party did or not did not prevail.

3. Next, consider whether your client's interests are best served by advocating a rule statement that is narrowly linked to specific facts before the court or, alternatively, by a rule statement that is more expansive.

4. Finally, draft a rule statement that favorably expresses how the court applied the law to the facts before the court.

- The rule statement, when applied to your client's factual situation, should either compel, or at least justify, a favorable result.

FACT-CENTERED ARGUMENTS

Drafting the Argument

I. CREATING A TEMPLATE OF THE ARGUMENT

A. Determining the Number of Issues

1. Evaluate the Original Rule of Law

The initial step in creating a template of your Argument is to verify the number of issues you will be addressing. As Chapter 6 explained in detail, first evaluate the original rule of law and identify each of its separate elements or guidelines. If there is more than one element, carefully consider which of the elements presents an issue under the client's factual situation. If more than one element needs to be addressed, create a separate heading for each issue; the headings will lead a discussion of each separate issue.

If, however, there is only one element of the rule of law that creates an issue to be argued, you may or may not have a single-issue argument, depending upon the synthesized rule statements you will draft as your next step in the outlining process. As subsections 2 and 3 of this section discuss in further detail, your synthesized rule statements might dictate that the Argument be divided into separate issues, even though the original rule of law itself suggests that there is only one issue.

◎ ILLUSTRATION: Spousal Wiretap Problem

Recall the spousal wiretap problem that is the basis of the plaintiff's and defendant's briefs illustrated in Appendix C. In that hypothetical problem, the plaintiff's lawyer argues that his client did *not* consent to having his telephone calls recorded by his estranged wife (the *legal issue conclusion*), and that the defendant therefore violated the federal wiretap statute (the *ultimate conclusion*). The original rule of law is the federal wiretap statute itself. That statute authorizes a person to intercept a wire communication when "one of the parties to the communication has given prior consent to such interception." 18 U.S.C. § 2511(2)(d). Before the plain-tiff's lawyer even filed a lawsuit, he carefully considered the statute and deter-mined that the statute contains a number of elements—(1) whether there was a "communication," (2) whether there was "prior consent," and (3) whether there was an "interception." However, given the factual controversy surrounding Mrs. Harri-son's recording of Mr. Harrison's telephone calls, only one of these elements pres-ents an issue—whether Mr. Harrison gave "prior consent" to the recording of his telephone calls. Thus, the original rule of law itself suggests that the Argument will be a single-issue argument leading to a legal issue conclusion.

2. Formulate a Synthesized Rule Statement(s)

Next evaluate how courts have interpreted the rule of law. As you evaluate each case that you intend to discuss in your Argument, you will have already formulated separate rule statements for each case. Recall that, when you generated a rule statement for each individual case, you identified how each court applied a rule of law to the unique facts before the court, thereby justifying the holding. From these separate rule statements, the next step is to formulate a synthesized rule statement (or statements) for the cases as a *group*. As you review the cases as a group, consider whether each of the cases illus-trates a single rule statement (even though the law might be phrased and applied a bit differently under each case's unique set of facts), or whether the cases illustrate two or more different legal rules. Cases can illustrate the same favorable rule even if the cases do not use identical language to describe the legal test they are applying; it is sufficient if you can reconcile the decision in each case with the same rule statement.

Again using the spousal wiretap statute for purposes of illustration, recall that the plaintiff's lawyer decided to emphasize three cases in his argument—the *Griggs-Ryan* case, the *Williams* case, and the *Campiti* case. He has formulated the following sepa-rate rule statements for each case:

(1)   *Williams* case:

> When the target of wiretapping has not been *expressly notified* of both the man-ner and the scope of the interception, and has no *actual knowledge* that he him-self will be a target of monitoring, implied consent may not be inferred.

(2)   *Griggs-Ryan* case:

> Consent is implied only when the target of a wiretap is expressly and "unmis-takably warned" that all calls on a line will be intercepted, and the target volun-tarily continues to use the telephone.

(3) *Campiti* case:

> Even when a common practice might give rise to an "expectation" that tele-
> phone calls might be intercepted, a party does not impliedly consent to such
> interceptions absent express notice of both the scope and the manner of the
> interceptions.

Recall that *Williams* was the only case in which the court explicitly applied a legal standard when evaluating the factual situation before the court (i.e., that the defendant must notify the plaintiff of both the manner and the scope of monitoring). However, after evaluating each case, the plaintiff's lawyer recognizes that the other two cases are each reconcilable with the *Williams* standard; in other words, the *Williams* standard would explain the results in both *Griggs-Ryan* and *Campiti*. Because the *Williams* court explicitly applied this standard, and the standard is reconcilable with all three cases, the lawyer *must* include this standard in his synthesized rule statement.

However, as with the individual rule statements for each case, Mr. Harrison's lawyer wants to draft a synthesized rule statement that is as favorable to his client's position as possible—language that would create a difficult test for Mrs. Harrison to satisfy. The lawyer therefore decides to incorporate into his synthesized rule statement the *Griggs-Ryan* court's language that the warning be "unmistakable," and the *Williams'* rationale that the warning was not "express." To create a subtle impression that the standard is difficult to satisfy, the lawyer also decides to use language that would draw out the two-part test and make it appear more like a three-part test. Mr. Harrison's lawyer drafts the following synthesized rule statement that accurately, and persuasively, illustrates the holdings in all three cases:

> Consent is implied only when a party has been expressly and unmistakably
> warned of both the manner and the scope of the interception, and knows that
> he himself will be the target of monitoring.

Although the above rule statement accurately reflects the holdings in all three cases, recall that the plaintiff's lawyer has decided to use the *Campiti* case for a different purpose altogether. The attorney wants to include *Campiti* in the argument as a subtle rebuttal to the defendant's argument that the clarity of Mrs. Harrison's warning to her husband must be construed in light of the couple's past practice of recording telephone calls. In *Campiti*, the court held that the prisoner did not consent to monitoring even though the prison had a past practice of monitoring telephone calls. Therefore, the plaintiff's lawyer decides to add a second rule statement that brings out this nuance, while also retaining its connection to the first rule statement:

> An expectation that one's calls *might* be monitored, without unmistakable notice as to the manner and scope of interception, does not rise to the level of consent.

3. Identify the Separate Components of Each Synthesized Rule Statement

After you have drafted a synthesized rule statement or statements, consider how many components (separate factors or standards) each statement expresses. Next consider the components' relationship to each other and evaluate whether the factors or standards can be argued separately, or whether they should be argued together. If a court will evaluate the different components of the rule statement(s) together, create a template for a single-issue argument. However, if a court will separately evaluate two or more different components of the rule statement(s), each component will become a separate issue in the Argument, usually with separate sub-headings. Thus, if your synthesized rule statement has two different components that should be discussed separately, it is possible for a one-element statute to give rise to a two-issue argument.

a. Rule Statement that Suggests Separate Issues

As an example of a rule statement that should be decided separately, consider the *criminal* wiretap problem that is illustrated in Appendix E. In that problem, the defendant contends that the Government did not provide the statutorily required "satisfactory explanation" for its delay in sealing sensitive wiretap evidence. Notice that the statutory language itself lends itself to a single-issue argument—whether an explanation is "satisfactory." However, after reading the cases, the defendant's lawyer discovered that the courts apply two different tests to determine whether an explanation is "satisfactory." The lawyer formulated the following rule statement that synthesizes all of the cases:

> A satisfactory explanation requires both that the government's prefiling procedures ensured the tapes' integrity, and that it acted with reasonable diligence to obtain the required approval.

This synthesized rule statement contains two different standards that will force an adjudicator to focus on two separate ideas: (1) whether the Government stored the tapes in a manner that safeguarded their integrity; and (2) whether the Government acted with reasonable diligence in minimizing the sealing delay. Accordingly, the defendant's lawyer would begin his Argument template by drafting the following separate headings. Each of these headings will ultimately lead a separate factual argument within the defendant's appellate court brief:

> A. *The Government Failed to Store the Tapes in a Manner that Protected Them from Any Possibility of Tampering.*
>
> B. *The Government Failed to Act with Reasonable Diligence.*

b. Rule Statement that Suggests a Single Issue

As an example of a synthesized rule statement that embodies only a single issue, consider again the *spousal* wiretap problem illustrated in Appendix C. The plaintiff has drafted the following synthesized rule statements:

> 1. Consent is implied only when a party has been expressly and unmistakably warned of both the manner and the scope of the interception, and knows that he himself will be the target of monitoring.
>
> 2. An expectation that one's calls *might* be monitored, without unmistakable notice of the manner and scope of interception, does not rise to the level of consent.

Consider the first rule statement. Although it contains a number of words, the rule statement can actually be broken down into the following two basic components: a party cannot consent unless he is expressly and unmistakably warned of both the (1) manner and the (2) scope of the monitoring. The remaining language in the first statement only explains or modifies this two-part test. For example, knowledge that "he himself will be the target of monitoring" merely explains more fully the "scope of monitoring" component. Mr. Harrison's lawyer added this extra explanatory phrase primarily for persuasive purposes, to give the appearance of a more stringent standard and to clarify the exacting requirements of the notice—that the party must know that he himself will be monitored. The rest of the language in the rule statement only modifies the two-part test—the warning itself must be "express" and "unmistakable."

As the lawyer examines the relationship between the two basic components of the rule statement (manner and scope of monitoring), he realizes that both components must be discussed together—the same conversation, and the same past practices, will help prove whether Mr. Harrison received express and unmistakable warning of the "scope" and "manner" of monitoring. Any effort to separate these ideas into different issues would result in an unnecessarily repetitive argument. Therefore, after considering the relationship between the two components, the lawyer decides to argue both components of the rule of law within the same issue.

Next consider the second rule statement. This rule statement adds an additional component to the "manner and scope of monitoring" test—whether past practices can create an expectation that one's call might be monitored. Although this rule statement brings out an additional nuance of the law, it too must be argued within the same discussion as the first rule statement. A judge would consider the couple's past practices and Mrs. Harrison's verbal communication to her husband to determine whether the defendant provided Mr. Harrison with notice as to the manner and scope of monitoring. Again, any effort to separate this argument from the first argument would result in unnecessary repetition of the same client facts. Therefore, this second rule statement does not create a second issue, but only adds a nuance to the first issue.

B. The Persuasive Paradigm

After you have selected the cases you will emphasize in your Argument and have determined the number of issues for your Argument, you are in a position to outline and draft the Argument. As you consider your Argument, stay focused on your overall goal. Your overall goal is to convince the adjudicator that the precedent cases, as applied to your client's factual situation, compel a ruling that favors your client. How might you structure the Argument to compel the adjudicator to arrive at a favorable conclusion?

The structure of a persuasive argument paradigm leads the adjudicator, step by logical step, to the desired legal issue conclusion (which leads inexorably to the desired ultimate conclusion). The persuasive argument paradigm is a carefully constructed formula, with each step of the Argument leading to the next inevitable step. In fact, the structure of a persuasive argument is similar to the structure of the Discussion section of an office memorandum; the difference is that a persuasive argument does not discuss the weaknesses in the client's position, only the strengths. However, like the predictive analysis in office memos, arguments follow a deductive writing pattern. A persuasive argument begins with the *legal issue conclusion* the advocate wants the adjudicator to reach. Next, the advocate states, and then explains and illustrates, the favorable *rule statements* that support the legal issue conclusion. Finally, the advocate *applies* the favorable rule statements to the client's factual situation, illustrating how the law, as applied to the client's facts, inevitably leads to the legal issue conclusion.

The following template illustrates the basic persuasive argument paradigm for a single issue argument.

1. State the *legal issue conclusion* you want the judge to adopt.
2. State the *favorable rule statement(s)* you have synthesized from the case law. (The favorable rule statement(s), when applied to the client facts, should inevitably lead to the legal issue conclusion you want the judge to adopt.)

3. *Prove and explain* the favorable rule statement(s) by examining case precedent.

4. *Favorably apply* the components of the rule statement(s) to the client's factual situation by proving how each factual premise leads to the desired legal issue conclusion.

5. Conclude by summarizing how the favorable rule statement(s), as applied to your client's facts, leads to the *legal issue conclusion, and therefore the ultimate conclusion.*

C. Filling in the Template of Your Argument

Before drafting an Argument, many writers find it helpful first to sketch the basic template, or framework, of the Argument. As they construct the framework, they begin to identify any gaps in their thinking and ideas that need further clarification. In addition, they find that sketching the framework of an Argument before beginning the drafting process saves them time in the end; the template helps them stay focused during the drafting process.

1. Clarify the Ultimate Conclusion & Legal Issue Conclusion

First clarify in your own mind the ultimate conclusion and legal issue conclusion(s) you want the adjudicator to reach, and write down the desired conclusions: this will help you stay focused on the overriding goal. For example, in the spousal wiretap problem illustrated in Appendix C, Mr. Harrison's lawyer's ultimate goal is to convince the judge that the defendant violated the federal wiretapping statute (ultimate conclusion) because his client did not consent to the recording of his personal telephone calls (legal issue conclusion).

2. Consider the Cases that Will Explain and Illustrate Each Favorable Rule Statement

Next, list each synthesized rule statement that you have formulated. If you have more than one synthesized rule statement, list the most persuasive rule statement first, then the next most persuasive statement, and so on. Then, in a column under each synthesized rule statement, separately list the cases you have selected to explain and illustrate that statement. List the most persuasive case first, the second most persuasive case second, and so on. You may wish to review again Chapter 24, Section I to refresh your memory about how to evaluate the persuasive appeal of precedent cases. For each case, note the important facts and rationale you will highlight to explain why that case is helpful in illustrating your rule statement. Finally, under each case description, briefly note the client facts you will compare to the case facts. These notes will become your "thinking notes" from which you will outline and draft your Argument.

Checklist:

1. List each synthesized rule statement, beginning with the most favorable rule statement.

2. In a column under each rule statement:
   - Beginning with the most favorable case, list each case that explains
     and illustrates the rule statement and:
     (a) Note the key facts and rationale you will highlight;
     (b) List the case facts you will compare to the client's facts.

◎ ILLUSTRATION: Spousal Wiretap Problem

In the spousal wiretap problem, Mr. Harrison's lawyer has decided to use the
Williams and *Griggs-Ryan* cases to illustrate the first synthesized rule statement he
formulated, and the *Campiti* case to illustrate the second rule statement. The lawyer concludes that the first synthesized rule statement he formulated should be
argued first because that rule statement will bring out more favorable client facts.
When the lawyer later applies the first synthesized rule statement to the client's
factual situation, the argument will focus on the defendant's ambiguous verbal
statement, which is the strongest aspect of Mr. Harrison's argument. The second
rule statement he formulated, while also persuasive, will bring out comparisons to
the couple's past practice of recording telephone calls, the weakest aspect of Mr.
Harrison's argument. Thus, the lawyer's "thinking notes" would look something like
this:

1. Consent is implied only when a party has been expressly and unmistakably warned of both the manner and the scope of the interception, and
   knows that he himself will be the target of monitoring.

   (a) *Williams* case:
       - *Holding:* Plaintiff did not consent to the monitoring.
       - *Rule*: Case applies a two-part test—whether the plaintiff was clear-
         ly notified of both the manner and scope of the monitoring.
       - *Favorable facts*:
         - Even though the plaintiff was told that employees' calls were
           being monitored, he did not consent to his *own* calls being mon-
           itored.
         - Court found it unlikely that the plaintiff would have consented
           to monitoring because he was feuding with the defendants.

- • *Application to Client*:
  - Will favorably compare the ambiguous verbal statements the defendants made in *Williams* to Mrs. Harrison's ambiguous statement.
  - Will highlight the "feuding" aspect of the case to illustrate why Mr. Harrison would not have consented to monitoring during a divorce.

  (b) *Griggs-Ryan* case:
  - • *Holding:* The plaintiff consented to the monitoring.
  - • *Favorable distinguishable facts:*
    - The landlady repeatedly and "unmistakably" warned the tenant that she would record all in-coming calls.
  - • *Application to Client*:
    - Will favorably distinguish Mrs. Harrison's ambiguous verbal statement from the "unmistakable warning" the defendant repeatedly gave to the tenant in *Griggs-Ryan*.

2. An expectation that one's calls *might* be monitored, without unmistakable notice of the manner and scope of interception, does not rise to the level of consent.

    (a) *Campiti* case:
    - • *Holding:* The plaintiff consented to the monitoring.
    - • *Favorable distinguishable facts*:
      - Even though the prison had a past practice of monitoring telephone calls, the past practices did not create a presumption that the prisoner consented to the monitoring.
    - • *Application to Client*:
      - Will favorably compare the couple's past practice of monitoring to the prison's past practice of monitoring prisoner's calls.

3. Consider the Interplay Between the "Rule Explanation" and "Rule Application" Paragraphs

Thus far, you have identified the number of issues you will be addressing in your Argument, formulated synthesized rule statements, and identified the cases that will explain and illustrate your rule statements. As the persuasive paradigm reflects, the rule statements and case discussions ("rule explanation" paragraphs) set the foundation, or context, for how the law and facts of the precedent cases favorably affect your client's situation ("rule application" paragraphs).

Superficially, it might appear to be a simple matter to create an Argument template from your "thinking notes." However, like the format of an office memo, the basic persuasive argument template becomes a bit more complex when the Argument explores more than one precedent case in detail. For example, assume you want to describe four different cases in detail. You can imagine the potential for confusion if an adjudicator was required to read all four case discussions before considering how the cases affect the factual situation before the court. Alternatively, imagine how repetitious an Argument might be should the lawyer draft a separate rule application section following each of the four cases.

To avoid such confusion or repetition, the interplay between the "rule explanation" and "rule application" sections of the Argument becomes fluid when two or more cases are discussed in depth. If two or more of your important cases illustrate the same rule statement and will generate factual comparisons to and distinctions from the *same* client facts, it makes sense to discuss each of the cases fully before evaluating how the case law affects the client's situation. In contrast, if two or more of your important cases will generate factual comparisons to and distinctions from *different* client facts, it makes sense to insert your analysis of how a case affects the client's situation immediately following each case discussion. If your memory needs refreshing, you may wish to review again Chapter 13, which discusses these options in greater detail. However, very simplistically, the options can be visualized as follows:

Option 1:	Option 2
• Discuss Case 1	• Discuss Case 1
• Discuss Case 2	• Apply Case 1 to Client Facts
• Apply Cases 1 & 2 to Client Facts	• Discuss Case 2
	• Apply Case 2 to Client Facts

As an example, consider again the spousal wiretap problem illustrated in Appendix C. Mr. Harrison's lawyer seeks to convince the court that his client did not consent to the recording of his personal telephone calls. The lawyer will rely on three cases to explain and illustrate his rule statements: *Williams*, *Griggs-Ryan*, and *Campiti*. As he sketched his "thinking notes," he noted the following specific comparisons he wanted to make from each case:

1. *Williams* case:
   → *Application to Client*:
      • Will favorably compare the ambiguous verbal statements the defendants made in *Williams* to Mrs. Harrison's ambiguous statement.
      • Will highlight the "feuding" aspect of the case to illustrate why Mr. Harrison would not have consented to monitoring during a divorce.
2. *Griggs-Ryan* case:
   → *Application to Client*:

- Will favorably distinguish Mrs. Harrison's ambiguous verbal statement from the "unmistakable warning" the defendant repeatedly gave to the tenant in *Griggs-Ryan*.

3. *Campiti* case:
   → *Application to Client*:
      - Will favorably compare the couple's past practice of monitoring to the prison's past practice of monitoring prisoner's calls.

As the lawyer reviews his notes, he realizes that he will use both *Williams* and *Griggs-Ryan* for the same purpose—to compare and contrast the verbal statements made in those cases to Mrs. Harrison's ambiguous verbal statement. Therefore, he realizes that it makes sense to choose Option 1 for these two cases, explaining each case in detail before moving into his analysis of how the law and facts in each case reflect favorably on Mrs. Harrison's ambiguous verbal statements. Note that the lawyer will also use the *Williams* case for a second purpose, to illustrate why the couple's strained relationship suggests that Mr. Harrison would never have consented to the recording of his telephone calls. However, the mere fact that the *Williams* case will be used to illustrate an additional point that is not raised in the *Griggs-Ryan* case does not change the formatting decision. The Argument would be unnecessarily repetitive if the lawyer were to separately discuss how Mrs. Harrison's ambiguous verbal statement is like the statement in *Williams* and then, later, discuss again how the very same statement is distinguishable from the statement in *Griggs-Ryan*.

As the lawyer reviews his notes from *Campiti*, however, he realizes that he not only will be using *Campiti* to make a different point, but that it generates a discussion of different client facts altogether. While *Williams* and *Griggs-Ryan* will generate an argument about Mrs. Harrison's verbal statement, *Campiti* will generate an argument about the couple's past practices. Because *Campiti* will generate an entirely different factual analysis, he decides to select Option 2 for this case, separating the *Campiti* case discussion and analysis from the other two cases.

4. Consider the Organization of the "Rule Application" Paragraphs

At this point, you should have a fairly good idea of the various points you will make in your Argument, but you may be uncertain about how to create an outline or argument of these persuasive points. The discrete components of your synthesized rule statements will serve as the organizational lynchpins of your Argument. Whether the component is a factor to be weighed or a standard to be satisfied, each separate component will become the topic of a separate paragraph or group of paragraphs. In addition, any other persuasive points you identified when evaluating the cases and client facts will become sub-topics. As you consider how to organize the major points you will be arguing, sometimes there is a logical order in which the ideas should be discussed. However, if there is no logical order that must be followed, begin with the most persuasive idea, and then the second most persuasive idea, and so on.

◎ **ILLUSTRATION: Spousal Wiretap Problem**

After making further organizational decisions, Mr. Harrison's lawyer begins to fill in the Argument template. The outline looks like this:

1. *Legal Issue Conclusion*:	Plaintiff did not consent to monitoring.	
2. *1st Synthesized Rule Statement:*	Consent is implied only when a party has been expressly and unmistakably warned of both the manner and scope of the interception, and knows that he himself will be the target of monitoring.	
3. *Explain & Illustrate the 1st Rule Statement:*	*Williams* case: • Highlight ambiguous verbal statement. • Highlight feud. *Griggs-Ryan* case: • Highlight "unmistakable" and repeated warnings.	
4. *Apply the Rule Statement to the Client:*	*1st Factual premise*: Mr. Harrison was not expressly and unmistakably warned of the manner and scope of monitoring—Mrs. Harrison's verbal statement was ambiguous. *2nd Factual premise*: Given the surrounding circumstances of the divorce, Mr. Harrison would not have consented.	
5. *2nd Favorable Rule Statement*	An expectation that one's calls *might* be monitored, without unmistakable notice of the manner and scope of interception, does not rise to the level of consent.	
6. *Explain & Illustrate the 2nd Rule Statement:*	*Campiti*: Illustrate how prison's past practices did not create implied consent.	
7. *Apply the Rule Statement to the Client:*	*Factual Premise*: The Harrisons' past practices do not create a presumption that Mr. Harrison consented to the recording of his calls.	
8. *Restate the Legal Issue Conclusion:*	Therefore, the plaintiff did not consent to the monitoring.	

At this point, you may wish to begin drafting the Argument or, alternatively, fill in further details in your outline before beginning the drafting process. The choice you make will depend upon your personal style. Some lawyers prefer to begin drafting the Argument at this point because the drafting process itself helps them flesh out further details of the Argument. Other lawyers find it easier and more time-efficient to fill in the details of their outline even further, adding additional bullet-points to clarify their Argument. There is no right or wrong way to proceed to the next stage. Through a process of experimentation, you should discover an outlining and drafting strategy that is most effective for you.

Exercise 25-1

Review the fact-centered Argument for Sample Brief B that is illustrated in Appendix D (Motion to Quash). Draft a template of the fact-centered Argument, separately noting: (1) the ultimate conclusion and legal issue conclusions; (2) the favorable rule statements formulated by the advocate; (3) the case used to explain and illustrate the favorable rule statements; and (4) the factual premises that lead to the legal issue conclusions, and therefore, the ultimate conclusion.

II. DRAFTING THE ARGUMENT

A. Roadmap Paragraphs

1. Introduction Section

In many arguments before courts, the Argument section begins with an "Introduction" that precedes the statement of facts. Each of the sample trial level briefs illustrated in Appendices C and D contain a separate Introduction. In an appellate court brief, the introductory section is called the "Summary of Argument." A Summary of Argument is illustrated in the sample appellate court brief contained in Appendix E. Chapter 33 provides a more detailed explanation of a formal Summary of Argument. However, the introductory section of an Argument is critically important because it provides an adjudicator with the first glimpse of the issues and your theory of the case. When drafting an Introduction, seize the adjudicator's attention immediately by clearly describing: (1) the result you want the adjudicator to reach; and (2) the most persuasive and cogent reasons that would compel any reasonable person to agree with your conclusion. Because drafting an argument summary requires an intimate familiarity with the nuances of your Argument, you may find it more time efficient to wait to draft this section until after you have already drafted and polished the remainder of your Argument.

The following Introduction is excerpted from the plaintiff's brief in the spousal wiretap problem that appears in Appendix C:

Ultimate conclusion.	Plaintiff, Mr. Harrison, is entitled to recover compensatory and punitive damages, attorney's fees, and other reasonable litigation costs for the Defendant's unlawful interception of his telephone calls in violation of Section 2520 of the federal wiretap statute. 18 U.S.C. § 2520. The Supreme Court has long recognized the right to privacy, and has included within this right a constitutional right to privacy in wire communications. *Berger v. New York*, 388 U.S. 41 (1967). Thus, the federal wiretap statute expressly and unambiguously prohibits the interception of wire communications except under narrowly proscribed circumstances, such as when "one of the parties to the communication has given prior consent to such interception." 18 U.S.C. § 2511(2)(d).
A favorable "back-drop" statement to frame the analysis.	
Important statutory language—the advocate makes the language appear more favorable by framing it as: "narrowly proscribed circumstances."	
Additional favorable "back-drop" statements.	When evaluating whether a party has given consent to the interception of wire communications, the First Circuit Court of Appeals has directed that, "in light of the prophylactic purposes of Title III, implied consent should not be casually inferred." *Williams v. Poulos*, 11 F.3d 271, 281 (1st Cir. 1993). Indeed, implied consent is not constructive consent, but is consent in *fact*. Consent is implied "only in a *rare case* where the court can conclude with assurance 'from surrounding circumstances... that the party *knowingly agreed* to the surveillance.'" *United States v. Lanoue*, 71 F.3d 966, 981 (1st Cir. 1995) (emphasis added). The
Brief application of the law to the client's facts, leading to:	present controversy is not even close to such a rare case. Here, the uncontroverted testimony reveals that Mr. Harrison was never expressly informed that *any* telephone calls would be monitored, much less that he himself would be a target of the interceptions. Without even the most
Legal issue conclusion.	minimal knowledge that his telephone calls would be intercepted, Mr. Harrison could not, and did not, knowingly agree to the surveillance. Therefore, the Defendant is liable
Ultimate conclusion.	as a matter of law for violating the federal wiretap statute.

2. Overview Paragraph

In an Argument with two or more issues, an overview paragraph provides the adjudicator with the overall framework of your Argument. It identifies your ultimate conclusion about how the original rule of law applies to the client's factual situation and the required elements that will be discussed in the Argument itself. Thus, the overview paragraph simply provides the basic roadmap of the Argument itself. Because the spousal wiretapping problem has only one issue, the parties' arguments do not contain an overview paragraph. However, the sample Motion to Dismiss brief in Appendix D illustrates the components of an overview paragraph. In that problem, the defendant's attorney argues that his client, who is merely an "agent" of an employer, cannot be held liable in his individual capacity in a Title VII action.

Defendant, Ronald Crane, respectfully requests that this Court issue an order dismissing Plaintiff's complaint pursuant to Fed. R. Civ. P. 12(b)(6) for failure to state a claim upon which relief can be granted. Defendant is entitled to an order dismissing Plaintiff's complaint because he cannot provide the relief Plaintiff seeks. Plaintiff seeks from Mr. Crane in his individual capacity compensatory and punitive damages under Title VII and the 1991 Amendments to Title VII. However, those statutes apply only to employers, not to individuals in their individual capacities. Because Plaintiff is suing Mr. Crane in his individual capacity and because Mr. Crane does not qualify as an employer under the statutes, he cannot provide the relief Plaintiff seeks.

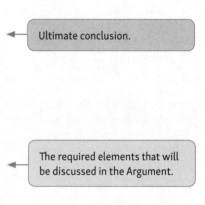

Ultimate conclusion.

The required elements that will be discussed in the Argument.

3. Thesis Paragraph

In a fact-centered argument of any complexity, each issue should be introduced with a thesis paragraph that contains the essential components of your argument *for that issue*. The essential components of your Argument should already be contained in your outline of that argument. Therefore, you need only convert your outline into narrative form, identifying: (1) any favorable "back-drop" statements that can provide a favorable framework from which the court might view your argument; (2) the favorable synthesized rule statements you have formulated; (3) a summary of why the client's facts, as illustrated by the rule statements, lead to your favorable legal issue conclusion; and (4) the ultimate conclusion the adjudicator must reach after accepting your legal issue conclusion. In the sample spousal wiretapping problem illustrated in Appendix C, Mr. Harrison's attorney drafts the following thesis paragraph. Because of the numerous favorable "back-drop" statements in the case law, this thesis paragraph is longer than many thesis paragraphs.

When evaluating whether a party has given consent to the interception of wire communications, the First Circuit Court of Appeals has directed that, "in light of the prophylactic purposes of Title III, implied consent should not be casually inferred." *Williams v. Poulos*, 11 F.3d 271, 281 (1st Cir. 1993). Indeed, implied consent is not constructive consent, in which one might be held to a standard that he "should have known" his telephone calls

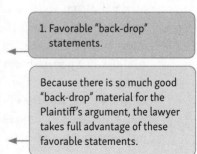

1. Favorable "back-drop" statements.

Because there is so much good "back-drop" material for the Plaintiff's argument, the lawyer takes full advantage of these favorable statements.

would be intercepted. *Campiti v. Walonis*, 611 F.2d 387, 393 (1st Cir. 1979). Instead, consent is implied "only in a *rare case* where the court can conclude with assurance 'from surrounding circumstances... that the party knowingly agreed to the surveillance.'" *United States v. Lanoue*, 71 F.3d at 981 (emphasis added). The First Circuit Court of Appeals has further directed that, when evaluating whether a party has given consent, "the surrounding circumstances must *convincingly* show that the party knew about and consented to the interception...." *Id.* (emphasis added).

2. Synthesized rule statements.

Thus, consent is implied only when a party has been expressly and unmistakably warned of both the manner and the scope of the interception, and knows that he himself will be the target of monitoring. *Williams*, 11 F.3d at 281; *Griggs-Ryan v. Smith*, 904 F.2d 112, 118 (1st Cir. 1990). An expectation that one's calls might be monitored, without unmistakable notice of the manner and scope of interception, does not rise to the level of consent. *Campiti*, 611 F.2d at 393.

3. Summary of factual premises that lead to the legal issue conclusion

Here, the uncontroverted evidence reveals that not only was Mr. Harrison never informed of the scope and manner of the interceptions, but he was never expressly informed that *any* telephone calls would be monitored. Absent such actual knowledge, Mr. Harrison did not knowingly agree to the interception of his telephone calls by his estranged

Legal issue conclusion.

wife.

4. Ultimate conclusion.

Because Mr. Harrison did not consent to the interceptions of his telephone calls, the Defendant is liable as a matter of law for violating the federal wiretap statute.

B. Rule Explanation Paragraphs

The body of your Argument should follow the template you created, explaining the case law (rule explanation) before applying the law to the client's facts (rule application). However, your description of a precedent case should differ, sometimes even markedly, from your description of that same case in an office memo. In a memo, your discussion of each case is candid and neutral because you are advising a senior attorney, and the client, of the strengths and weaknesses of the client's position. In contrast, in a persuasive argument, your ultimate goal is to persuade the adjudicator that your client's facts are at least as desirable, or better, than cases with favorable outcomes, and that the client's facts are easily distinguishable from the facts of cases with unfavorable outcomes. Drafting persuasive case discussions is an important step in this persuasion process. A persuasive case discussion both explains and illustrates the favorable rule statement described in the thesis sentence, and emphasizes the favorable aspects of the case while de-emphasizing any unfavorable information.

1. Begin with a Favorable Thesis Sentence

A persuasive case discussion begins with a thesis sentence that identifies the favorable rule statement the case illustrates—the favorable rule statements you formulated during the pre-drafting stage of your analysis (Chapter 24). The thesis sentence should highlight the favorable rule of law the case illustrates, and provide context for the favorable case facts, holding, and/or rationale you will highlight within your discussion of that case. Because you have already drafted a favorable rule statement for each case, simply insert these favorable rule statements as the first sentence of each case.

a. Plaintiff's Favorable Thesis Sentence

Using the spousal wiretapping problem to illustrate, Mr. Harrison's lawyer begins drafting the discussion of the *Griggs-Ryan* case with the following thesis sentence:

> Consent is implied only when the target of a wiretap is expressly and "unmistakably warned" that all calls on a line will be intercepted, and the target voluntarily continues to use the telephone despite the express warning.

b. Defendant's Favorable Thesis Sentence

Mrs. Harrison's lawyer has also elected to discuss the *Griggs-Ryan* case. Notice the different slant she has given to the *Griggs-Ryan* case in her thesis sentence introducing this case:

> When a party has been told that all incoming telephone calls would be recorded for an indefinite period of time, that party's continued use of the telephone constitutes implied consent to the monitoring.

2. Highlight Favorable Facts & De-Emphasize Unfavorable Facts

Following the thesis sentence, highlight favorable facts of the precedent case by elaborating on them. Do not summarize favorable facts by burying them within run-on sentences or dependent clauses. Instead, highlight favorable facts by describing them in great detail. In contrast, de-emphasize unfavorable facts by burying them within the middle of the paragraph or within a dependent clause within the middle of a sentence. Some unfavorable language can be omitted entirely if the omission does not make your characterization of the case misleading.

If the holding in the case is favorable, your goal is to emphasize every case fact that is *less desirable* or *comparable* to your client's factual situation and to de-emphasize the case facts that are *more desirable* than your client's facts. By doing so, the adjudicator will be left with the impression that if the outcome was favorable even under the less desirable facts of the precedent case, then the client should prevail here as well.

In contrast, if the holding in a case is unfavorable, your goal is to convince the adjudicator that your client's situation is distinguishable enough to merit a different outcome. Therefore, emphasize every case fact that is *distinguishable* from your client's factual situation, and de-emphasize every case fact that is *similar* to your client's factual situation.

In addition, when discussing a case in a persuasive argument, be sure to include only facts relevant to the specific issue at hand. For example, suppose the *Griggs-Ryan* decision discussed two issues—whether the landlady violated the federal wiretap statute when she intercepted her tenant's phone call, and whether the landlady violated the tenant's right to privacy when she set up hidden video cameras around the campground. When discussing the case facts for purposes of the federal wiretap claim, you would not include the case facts related to the hidden video cameras because they are not relevant to the wiretap claim. You would be selective and include just enough background facts to provide context to tell the story, and of course the legally significant facts related to the issue at hand (those relating to the wiretap).

a. Plaintiff's Description of the Facts in *Griggs-Ryan*

Although the *Griggs-Ryan* case is unfavorable from the plaintiff's perspective, it is easily distinguishable. Therefore, Mr. Harrison's strategy is to emphasize the facts in *Griggs-Ryan* that are distinguishable from his client's situation. Thus, he emphasizes the "repeated" nature of the warnings, and the court's characterization of the warnings as "unmistakable."

> The lawyer highlights favorable factual distinctions by quoting key language: "repeatedly informed," and by emphasizing the express nature of the warning: "*all*" telephone calls.

In *Griggs-Ryan*, the plaintiff was a tenant at a campground operated by the defendant, his landlady. Although the tenants did not have individual telephones, they were allowed to use the landlady's telephone. After receiving obscene telephone calls that she suspected were made by the tenant's friend, the landlady "repeatedly informed" the tenant that *all* telephone calls to her home were being recorded. *Id.* at 117. The tenant subsequently received a telephone call at the defendant's home. When the voice appeared to be that of the obscene caller, the landlady listened in on an extension telephone and then recorded the call. When she discovered that the parties were engaged in an illegal drug transaction, the landlady gave the tape to the police. *Id.* at 114.

b. Defendant's Description of the Facts in *Griggs-Ryan*

Although the holding in *Griggs-Ryan* is favorable to the defendant, the case facts are actually more desirable than the Harrison facts. Therefore, Mrs. Harrison's lawyer's strategy is to *de-emphasize* the case facts that are more desirable than the client's facts and to *emphasize* those case facts that are similar to or less desirable than the client's facts. Thus, the lawyer omits the fact that the warnings were both "unmistakable" and repeated. So long as the lawyer states that the landlady in *Griggs-Ryan* did indeed inform the tenants that she would record all incoming calls, the lawyer has not misled the court; the lawyer has merely de-emphasized the clarity of the notice.

Although the facts in *Griggs-Ryan* are generally more desirable than the client's facts, there is one interesting aspect to the case that is comparable to or less desirable than the client's facts. Because the purpose of the monitoring was to identify an obscene caller, a reasonable person might plausibly conclude that calls would be monitored only for the first few seconds of a telephone call—until such time as the landlady could assure herself that the call was not an obscene call. However, the landlady recorded the tenant's entire telephone call. Thus, the scope of the landlady's warning was arguably narrower than the actual monitoring itself. Therefore, the lawyer elects to highlight these favorable facts by describing them in great detail.

In *Griggs-Ryan*, the plaintiff was a tenant at a campground operated by the defendant, his landlady. The tenants did not have individual telephones and were therefore allowed to use the landlady's telephone. The defendant informed the tenants that, because she was being plagued by obscene telephone calls, she would record all incoming calls. *Id.* at 114. Although it would have been reasonable for a tenant to assume the landlady would stop taping once she realized that a specific call was not obscene, the landlady did not explicitly inform the tenants of this practice. *Id.* at 118. However, it was in fact the landlady's practice to stop taping calls once she realized a call was not obscene or threatening. The plaintiff subsequently received a telephone call at the landlady's home. After notifying the plaintiff that he had a telephone call, the defendant listened in on an extension telephone and then recorded the entire call. When she discovered that the parties were engaged in an illegal drug transaction, the landlady gave the tape to the police. *Id.* at 114.

> ← Unfavorable fact buried within ¶.

> ← The lawyer highlights facts that are less desirable than the client's facts by describing them in detail and by commenting on the implications of such facts.

3. Persuasively Frame the Holding

Rather than simply identifying how the court responded to the legal question, an advocate can often persuasively frame the holding by juxtaposing the holding with favorable facts. Thus, if the holding in the case is favorable, you might juxtapose the holding with facts that are similar to or less desirable than your client's position. In contrast, if the holding in a case is unfavorable, you might emphasize the favorable distinction by incorporating key distinguishable facts into the statement of the court's holding.

In addition, remember that when you provide the case's holding, your focus is on the specific issue at hand. For the spousal wiretap problem, the lawyer is considering whether Mrs. Harrison violated the federal wiretap statute for failing to gain Mr. Harrison's "consent" for the recordings as required by the statute. Assume, again, that the *Griggs-Ryan* case, which the lawyer is explaining, involves two claims—whether the landlady violated the federal wiretap statute by taping the tenant's phone call, and whether the landlady violated the tenant's right to privacy by installing hidden cameras around the campsite. When discussing the case's holding in his own argument, Mr. Harrison's lawyer will not provide the *Griggs-Ryan* case holdings for both of these issues—the lawyer will only note the holding relevant to his client's legal issue—the one related to "consent" under the federal wiretap statute.

a. Plaintiff's Statement of the *Griggs-Ryan* Holding

From the perspective of Mr. Harrison, the fact that the warnings in *Griggs-Ryan* were "unmistakable" and repeated is the most easily distinguishable fact from that case. Therefore, Mr. Harrison's lawyer highlights the favorable distinction by linking them to his statement of the *Griggs-Ryan* court's holding. The favorable juxtaposition of facts is italicized in the following illustration:

> *In light of such "unmistakable warnings" that were repeated on a "number of occasions,"* the court held that the tenant impliedly consented to the monitoring of his telephone calls. *Id.* at 118.

b. Defendant's Statement of the *Griggs-Ryan* Holding

Although the holding in *Griggs-Ryan* is favorable from the defendant's perspective, the facts in *Griggs-Ryan* are generally more desirable than the client facts—not an ideal situation from the advocate's perspective. However, recall that the scope of the warning in *Griggs-Ryan* was arguably narrower than the actual monitoring—the tenant could plausibly have believed that the landlady would record only the first few seconds of his telephone calls. Therefore, Mrs. Harrison's lawyer highlights this favorable fact by incorporating it in the statement of the court's holding:

> *Even though the stated purpose of the monitoring was limited to screening obscene callers,* the court held that the plaintiff impliedly consented to his telephone calls being monitored *in their entirety.*

4. Highlight Favorable Rationale

As with favorable facts, highlight any language within the case that supports your client's position. Be careful not to bury favorable rationale in a run-on sentence; instead, provide each and every detail of the favorable rationale. Selectively quoting favorable language is an effective way to emphasize favorable rationale. At the same time, you do not want your case discussion to be a string of quotes. Therefore, carefully select the most favorable, and important, language to quote. Because readers tend to recall the beginning and ending of paragraphs more than the middle, another way to emphasize favorable rationale is to place the most highly favorable language in the very last sentence of the case discussion.

Remember to include only the rationale in the precedent case that directly relates to the legal issue you are arguing on behalf of your client. Your reader does not need a summary of the rationale of the entire case, and of reasoning related to other issues and other legal claims. Indeed, that would be distracting and confusing for the reader. Be selective on the rationale you include, and ensure it relates directly to the issue you are analyzing.

a. Plaintiff's Portrayal of the *Griggs-Ryan* Rationale

Mr. Harrison's lawyer has already highlighted the important factual distinction in *Griggs-Ryan* by emphasizing the "unmistakable" and repeated warnings aspect of the case in the thesis sentence, in the description of the case facts, and in the court's holding itself. Likewise, the lawyer also mentions this important factual distinction within the description of the *Griggs-Ryan* court's rationale. However, because there is no other favorable language in the court's rationale to emphasize, the plaintiff's description of the rationale is therefore brief:

The court reasoned that the tenant "effectively acquiesced in the interception" when he opted to converse on the landlady's telephone after repeatedly and expressly being told of the monitoring. *Id.*

> The phrase "repeatedly and expressly" is highlighted by placing it at the end of the final sentence in the paragraph.

b. Defendant's Portrayal of the *Griggs-Ryan* Rationale

Within the description of the case facts and holding, the defendant's lawyer has already highlighted the possible discrepancy between the warning and the scope of the monitoring. At the same time, throughout the case discussion, the lawyer has de-emphasized the unfavorable factual distinction from *Griggs-Ryan*—the repeated and "unmistakable" warnings. This strategy continues as she describes the court's rationale:

> The lawyer highlights the possible discrepancy between the warning and the actual scope of monitoring by describing these facts in great detail.

The court reasoned that the plaintiff "effectively acquiesced in the interception" when he opted to converse on the defendant's telephone after being told that all calls would be recorded. *Id.* at 118. Even though the purpose of the monitoring was to screen for obscene callers, the court was not persuaded by the fact that a tenant might reasonably presume the scope of any monitoring would be limited to the initial greeting phase of a telephone call. Instead, the court emphasized that, when the landlady informed the plaintiff that she would record all in-coming calls, she did not expressly limit the scope of the monitoring to the greeting phrase of the telephone call. Absent an express verbal statement limiting the scope of the monitoring, the tenant could not later claim that the landlady's authority was limited to screening for obscene callers. By continuing to receive calls on the defendant's telephone line, the tenant "knowingly agreed to the surveillance." *Id.*

> The lawyer ends the discussion by quoting favorable language.

Importantly, the court concluded: "[The tenant's] consent, albeit not explicit, was manifest. No more was required." *Id.*

Exercise 25-2

Review the *Diana* case discussion contained within the first fact-centered argument for the criminal wiretap problem illustrated in Appendix E. The first fact-centered argument contends that the Government failed to store the tapes in a manner that protected the tapes from any possibility of tampering. As you review the *Diana* case discussion, identify how Hart's attorney emphasizes: (1) the favorable rule of law the case illustrates; (2) the favorable facts within the *Diana* case; and (3) favorable rationale.

C. Favorable Rule Application

This section of the Argument explores and proves why the client must prevail when the law is applied to the client's factual situation. The favorable rule statements you formulated from the cases guide this part of the Argument as you illustrate how the law, when applied to the client's facts, inexorably leads to the legal issue conclusion(s), and, therefore, the ultimate conclusion.

1. Begin with a Favorable Thesis Sentence

Thesis sentences are very important, because the remainder of the paragraph (or group of paragraphs) proves why the factual premise identified in the thesis sentence is sound. The thesis sentence should illustrate a factual premise that, if proven, inexorably leads to the legal issue conclusion. Note, however, that a factual premise may take more than one paragraph to prove. Use transition sentences to begin subsequent paragraphs that merely continue the same argument.

2. Prove Why the Factual Premise Is Sound

After identifying the factual premise in the thesis sentence, the body of the paragraph or group of paragraphs proves why the factual premise is sound. To prove a factual premise: (1) highlight and elaborate on each client fact that illustrates and proves the factual premise; (2) make concrete, favorable analogies and distinctions to the case law whenever their use can help you prove why your factual premise is valid; and (3) explain the factual and legal significance of the client facts and analogies.

a. Plaintiff's Favorable "Rule Application"

Mr. Harrison's lawyer argues that the client did not consent to the recording of his telephone calls—the legal issue conclusion. One important factual premise that inexorably leads to the legal issue conclusion is that Mr. Harrison's wife did not give him "express" and "unmistakable warning" of the manner and scope of the monitoring. The most favorable evidence that supports this factual premise is his wife's ambiguous verbal statement. Therefore, the lawyer begins his argument by focusing on the ambiguous verbal statement. Because this argument is very important, it consumes four paragraphs. The initial paragraph of his argument, excerpted from Appendix C, is as follows:

Like the plaintiff in *Williams* and unlike the plaintiff in *Griggs-Ryan*, Mr. Harrison was not expressly and "unmistakably warned" of either the manner *or* the scope of any interceptions. In fact, Mr. Harrison was not notified that any telephone calls would be recorded *at all*, much less his own. Thus, Mr. Harrison had even less notice than the plaintiff in *Williams*, who was at least notified of the partial scope of the interceptions—that "monitoring" was in place to deter telephone abuse by employees. Here, Defendant's description of her intentions was far more ambiguous than in *Williams*. Defendant testified that she told Mr. Harrison she "was hiring a housekeeper" and that, among a laundry list of other requirements for the new housekeeper, she "wanted to make sure that the housekeeper did

> Factual Premise from favorable rule statement.

> Elaboration of how the client facts prove the factual premise, bringing in favorable distinctions from *Williams*. Notice how the facts are described in detail.

not make improper use of the telephone." (K. Harrison Dep. 52:4-54:7.) Expressing a concern that the housekeeper might make "improper use of the telephone" simply does not constitute express, unmistakable notice that the Defendant would be recording all of the home's in-coming and out-going calls. This alleged "notice" was made even more ambiguous by the fact that the Defendant's expressed concern about the housekeeper's improper use of the telephone was buried within a long laundry list of other concerns. (K. Harrison Dep. 52:4-54-7.)

> Spells out the legal significance of a fact—that it does not satisfy the legal standard.

b. Defendant's Favorable "Rule Application"

Mrs. Harrison's lawyer argues that the plaintiff consented to having his telephone calls recorded—her legal issue conclusion. One important factual premise that inexorably leads to this legal issue conclusion is that Mrs. Harrison did, indeed, notify the plaintiff of both the manner and scope of monitoring. The most favorable evidence that supports this factual premise is the couple's past practices. Because Mrs. Harrison's verbal statement was ambiguous, the lawyer must convince the judge that the couple's past practices provide a context for the ambiguous verbal statement and give it meaning. Because the couple's past practices provide important context to interpret the ambiguous verbal statement, the lawyer begins her argument by describing the couple's past practices (the first two paragraphs of the argument). Only after laying this favorable backdrop does the lawyer argue that the verbal statement constituted notice of the manner and scope of monitoring and that Mr. Harrison actually gave verbal consent to the monitoring. Although her argument extends through eight paragraphs, only the initial paragraph of her argument is excerpted here. Notice that, unlike other paragraphs of her argument, there are no case analogies within this paragraph. Because neither *Williams* nor *Griggs-Ryan* involved past practices, there are no favorable analogies to be made.

> Factual Premise.

> The lawyer sets the stage for arguing why past practices are important—they are a "surrounding circumstance."

> Highlights favorable facts from the couple's past practices, emphasizing that the "scope" included the recording of Mr. Harrison's telephone calls.

As in *Griggs-Ryan*, the Plaintiff in the present case was notified of both the scope and the manner of monitoring. Mrs. Harrison's verbal communication to her husband concerning the monitoring of the telephone must not be viewed in a vacuum, but instead must be construed in light of the couple's past practices. As the *Griggs-Ryan* court instructed, all of the surrounding circumstances must be considered when determining whether consent has been implied.

From the time the couple hired their child's first nanny, the couple engaged in a practice of recording all telephone

calls—in-coming and out-going—for a period of approximately one month. In other words, the scope of the recording included not just the nanny's calls, but also Plaintiff's telephone calls and Mrs. Harrison's telephone calls.
(K. Harrison Dep. 106:12; M. Harrison Dep. 77:20.) Both
spouses agreed that recording all telephone calls for a period of time was necessary to help them assess whether a
new caretaker was someone they trusted and wanted to
retain as an employee. (K. Harrison Dep. 105:12-106:18;
M. Harrison Dep. 77:4-77:22.) Plaintiff has acknowledged   ◄— Highlights Mr. Harrison's
that he not only agreed to such monitoring, but thought   favorable admission by quoting
it was a "good idea." (M. Harrison Dep. 77:22.)   favorable testimony.

Exercise 25-3

Review the rule application paragraphs for the first fact-centered argument in the
criminal wiretap problem illustrated in Appendix E. The first fact-centered argument
contends that the Government failed to store the tapes in a manner that protected the
tapes from any possibility of tampering. For each of the four rule application paragraphs within that argument, separately identify: (1) the factual premise of each paragraph; (2) the client facts used to prove the factual premise; (3) the favorable analogies
to and distinctions from the precedent cases; and (4) the factual and legal significance
of client facts and analogies.

CHAPTER IN REVIEW

Definitions:

"BACK-DROP" STATEMENTS:

General policy statements courts make when interpreting a rule of law. Some of
these statements can serve as a favorable "back-drop" for your argument (such
as whether a statute should be interpreted narrowly or broadly).

ELEMENT:

Elements are separate requirements of a rule of law that a party *must* prove to
compel a particular result.

RULE STATEMENT:

A statement you formulate that clearly and accurately reflects how *and* why a court
answered the legal question in the manner that it did. As an advocate, the rule
statement should be the most favorable credible interpretation of a court's holding.

STANDARD:

When a court interprets a rule of law, sometimes it defines the rule of law in a manner that effectively establishes a new requirement the parties must satisfy. The new requirement can be called a standard (*e.g.*, the *Williams* court interpreted the "consent" statute to require that the defendant warn the plaintiff of both the manner and scope of the monitoring—this becomes a standard that the defendant must satisfy in order to prove implied consent).

SYNTHESIZED RULE STATEMENT:

A statement you formulate that clearly and accurately reflects how a *group* of cases apply the rule of law to different fact patterns.

CREATE A TEMPLATE OF THE ARGUMENT

1. For each issue, outline the template of your Argument.
   a. Clarify the legal issue conclusion you want the judge to reach.
   b. For each synthesized rule statement, create a list of the cases you will use to illustrate the rule statement. For each case, note:
      i. The important case facts and rationale that will illustrate the rule statement; and
      ii. The client facts you will compare to the case.
   c. After reviewing your list of cases that illustrate a synthesized rule statement, consider the interplay between the "rule explanation" and "rule application" paragraphs:
      i. If two or more cases will generate factual analogies to and distinctions from the *same* client facts, discuss each case before moving to the "rule application" paragraphs.
      ii. If two or more cases will generate factual analogies to and distinctions from *different* client facts, insert rule application paragraphs following each such case.
   d. Organize the cases and arguments by arguing the most favorable cases and arguments first.

Editing Checklist:

ROADMAP PARAGRAPHS

1. In your *Introduction* section, if any, consider whether it clearly describes:
   a. The result you want the judge to reach; and
   b. The most persuasive reasons that support your conclusion.
2. In your *Overview paragraph* (used in arguments with two or more issues), consider whether you have identified:

    a. Your ultimate conclusion about how the law applies to your client's factual situation;

    b. The different elements that will be discussed in the Argument; and

    c. Your legal issue conclusion for each separate legal issue argument.

3. In your *Thesis paragraph* for each issue, consider whether you have identified:

    a. Any favorable "back-drop" statements;

    b. Your favorable synthesized rule statements;

    c. A summary of why the rule statements, as applied to your client's facts, lead to your favorable legal issue conclusion; and

    d. The legal issue conclusion you want the judge to reach.

RULE EXPLANATION PARAGRAPHS

As you draft rule explanation paragraphs, consider whether each discussion of an important factually analogous case:

1. Begins with a *thesis sentence* that favorably expresses how the court applied the law to the facts before the court (your rule statement);

2. Highlights the *favorable facts* of the case while de-emphasizing any unfavorable facts;

3. Favorably frames the *holding* by juxtaposing desirable facts with the court's holding; and

4. Draws out in detail the favorable aspects of the court's *rationale*, while de-emphasizing unfavorable rationale.

RULE APPLICATION PARAGRAPHS

As you draft rule application paragraphs, consider whether each new argument:

1. Begins with a *thesis sentence* that persuasively identifies your factual premise;

    • The factual premise, if accepted, should lead to your legal issue conclusion.

2. *Elaborates fully* on the favorable client's facts, explaining why the facts prove why the factual premise is sound;

3. Brings in *favorable factual comparisons* to the cases; and

4. Explains the *legal significance* of the facts and comparisons.

LAW-CENTERED ARGUMENTS

Working with Mandatory Case Precedent

I. INTRODUCTION

As a lawyer, you will sometimes address legal issues in which the meaning of the law itself is unclear, separate and apart from how the law might affect a client's factual situation. This chapter discusses argument strategies when at least one higher level court in your jurisdiction has arguably addressed a disputed legal issue, but the court opinion is unclear. Of course, if mandatory precedent were crystal clear, you and your opposing counsel would not be disputing the law's meaning—a lower court would be compelled to follow such precedent. The fact that you and your opposing counsel are actually disputing the significance of legal precedent in your jurisdiction means that the precedent is less than clear. For example, it may be unclear whether a precedent case actually resolved the issue at all. Alternatively, perhaps there are several cases in a jurisdiction that seem to conflict.

When previous higher level courts in your jurisdiction have left the meaning of the law unclear, you must convince the court that it has the *legal authority* to adopt your legal interpretation. Recall that, under our legal system of stare decisis, courts must follow the previous legal interpretations of higher level courts within the relevant jurisdiction ("mandatory authority"). Therefore, you must not only convince the judge that the original rule of law itself supports your interpretation, but that mandatory precedent gives the judge the legal authority to adopt your interpretation. To distinguish this type of argument from other types of arguments, this book will refer to such arguments as "*case justification*" arguments. A case justification argument illustrates how prior *mandatory precedent* either compels, or at least justifies, a favorable decision.

A. Options When Evaluating Each Individual Case

When the meaning of a mandatory case precedent is ambiguous, the case can potentially be construed in one of three ways. First, after careful consideration of the prior case's language, you might argue that the court actually interpreted the rule of law in a manner favorable to your client. As an advocate, this is the most favorable option—if mandatory case precedent actually adopts your favorable rule, our system of stare decisis would *compel* the judge to adopt your legal interpretation.

Second, you might argue that the prior case failed to resolve the legal issue at all. If no prior higher level court in the jurisdiction has definitively resolved the legal question, the issue is actually one of first impression. Therefore, the judge would be justified in interpreting the rule of law in whatever manner the judge deems appropriate.

Finally, you might conclude that the court did, indeed, adopt your opponent's unfavorable interpretation of the rule of law. Of course, as a practical matter you typically would not be constructing such an argument unless there were other more favorable cases in the jurisdiction that at least arguably conflicted with the adverse case. Ordinarily, you would not be attempting to convince a judge to adopt a position that is flatly inconsistent with mandatory precedent. The rare exception might be when you are arguing for a change in the law and are prepared to take the issue up to the highest-level court. More typically, however, under this scenario you would argue that, because previous case law is inconsistent, the judge is justified in interpreting the legal rule in either manner.

The Options at a Glance

Option 1: Prior case adopts your favorable interpretation of the rule of law.

Option 2: Prior case does not resolve the issue.

Option 3: Prior case adopts your opponent's interpretation of the rule of law. (You would make this concession only if there were other cases in the jurisdiction that conflict with the adverse case, or, in rare cases, if you are advocating for a change in the law.)

---

1. Arguing that a Prior Mandatory Case Has Adopted Your Favorable Rule Interpretation

Before arguing that a higher level court in your jurisdiction has already resolved the issue in a manner favorable to your legal position, review the previous court decision with an excruciatingly precise attention to detail. Carefully review each and every word of the case, including the footnotes, noting the specific quoted language that supports your argument. Consider all of the reasons underlying the previous court's decision, both expressed and implied. To successfully persuade a judge that a previous higher level court has already resolved the issue, your argument concerning that individual case would look like this:

> **Thesis Sentence:** State your conclusion—that the case has adopted your favorable interpretation.
>
> **Prove why your conclusion is valid:**
>
> 1. Highlight and quote *specific language* in the opinion that supports your conclusion;
> 2. Emphasize how the court's overall *holding* supports your conclusion; and, if possible,
> 3. Describe how *logic or policy* considerations support your conclusion that the court adopted your favorable legal interpretation.

◎ ILLUSTRATION: Fifth Amendment Problem

As an example, consider the Fifth Amendment problem that is the basis of Sample Brief B in Appendix D. *Background*: In that hypothetical problem, the Government is prosecuting the defendant, Mr. Browne, for unlawful distribution of drugs. The Government has issued a subpoena to obtain Mr. Browne's personal diary. The Government contends that the diary contains entries that reflect Mr. Browne's illegal drug activities. Rather than turning over the diary to the Government, Browne's lawyer has filed a Motion to Quash the subpoena. Browne's lawyer argues that Mr. Browne's personal diary is protected by the Fifth Amendment of the United States Constitution. The Fifth Amendment protects people from self-incrimination. However, the language is vague and general, leaving courts to resolve specific issues as to the Amendment's meaning. The Amendment states that: "No person... shall be compelled in any criminal case to be a witness against himself...." U.S. Const. amend. V.

The Government's lawyer argues that the Fifth Amendment should be narrowly construed only to protect persons from incriminating themselves with their *oral* testimony. The Government argues that the Fifth Amendment does not also protect persons from incriminating themselves with their *written* documents. Browne's lawyer argues, however, that the Fifth Amendment should be broadly construed to protect persons from incriminating themselves with their written documents as well as their oral testimony. Browne has a favorable Supreme Court case that has adopted this position. As we will see later, however, this Supreme Court case is an old case, and its holding has been eroded over the years. Nevertheless, Browne must use the old case to persuade the judge that mandatory authority has adopted Browne's broad interpretation of the Fifth Amendment. Therefore, Browne's lawyer argues:

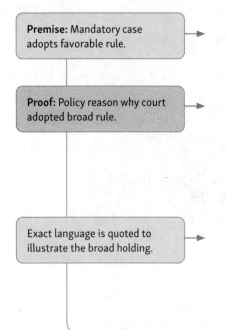

Premise: Mandatory case adopts favorable rule.

Proof: Policy reason why court adopted broad rule.

Exact language is quoted to illustrate the broad holding.

The Supreme Court has long held that the Fifth Amendment protects personal papers as well as oral testimony. *See United States v. Boyd,* 116 U.S. 616 (1886).

In *Boyd*, the Court equated seizing a person's personal documents as evidence against him with compelling that person to be a witness against himself: "And we have been unable to perceive that the seizure of a man's private books and papers to be used in evidence against him is substantially different from compelling him to be a witness against himself." *Id.* Additionally, the Court admonished that "any forcible and compulsory extortion of a man's own testimony or of his private papers... is within the condemnation of [the Fifth Amendment]," *id.* at 630, and "contrary to the principles of a free government." *Id.* at 635–36.

2. Arguing that a Prior Mandatory Case Failed to Resolve the Legal Issue at All

As with the first option, before arguing that a higher level court in your jurisdiction failed to resolve a legal issue, carefully review the previous court decision with a painstaking attention to detail. Carefully review each and every word of the case, including the footnotes, noting the specific quoted language that supports your argument that the court did not resolve the issue. To successfully persuade a judge that a previous higher level court failed to resolve the issue, your argument concerning that case would look like this:

Thesis Sentence: State your conclusion—that the case failed to resolve the legal issue.

Prove why your conclusion is sound:

1. Highlight and quote *specific language* in the opinion that supports your conclusion;

2. Emphasize how the court's *holding* was extremely narrow, resolving only the precise narrow issue in dispute in that case (i.e., an issue that differs from the issue you are disputing); and, if possible,

3. Emphasize how *logic or policy considerations* compel the conclusion that the court intended a very narrow holding; and, if possible,

4. Emphasize how *logic or policy* considerations compel the conclusion that the court could not possibly have intended to resolve the present disputed issue.

Again using the Fifth Amendment problem as an example, the defendant's lawyer also had to address several other Supreme Court cases that are more recent than the century-old *Boyd* case. More recent Supreme Court decisions have criticized *Boyd* and even questioned its present viability. Therefore, in order to convince the court that it is compelled to follow *Boyd*, Browne's lawyer must also persuade the court that the recent Supreme Court cases (*Fisher* and *Doe*) did not actually address the narrow legal issue before the court—whether a written personal document is protected by the Fifth Amendment. Because the recent Supreme Court cases held that *business records* are not protected by the Fifth Amendment, Browne's lawyer must distinguish business records from the personal documents that are at issue in Browne's situation. If the court accepts Browne's argument that *Fisher* and *Doe* did not resolve the narrow question of personal documents, the court would be compelled to follow the earlier *Boyd* case—the *Boyd* case would be the only mandatory precedent that actually resolved the precise issue before the court. In the following example excerpted from Sample Brief B in Appendix D, the defendant argues that two recent Supreme Court cases did not actually resolve the question before the court:

Although the Supreme Court recently concluded that *Boyd* does not protect *business* documents, it has preserved *Boyd's* protection of personal papers. *See Doe*, 465 U.S. at 610; *Fisher*, 425 U.S. at 403. In *Fisher*, the Court held that the Fifth Amendment does not protect the contents of tax records prepared by the defendant's accountant. *Id.* at 393. The Court based this holding on the fact that business documents do not implicate the privacy interests of personal papers: "special problems of privacy [that] might be presented by subpoena of a personal diary are not involved here." *Id.* at 407 n.7.

> **Premise:** Recent cases did not resolve issue.

> **Proof:** 1st case: Narrow holding—only tax records. Public policy illustrates narrow holding.

Additionally, the Court preserved *Boyd's* protection of personal papers by emphasizing that "[w]hether the Fifth Amendment would shield the taxpayer from producing his own tax records... is a question not involved here; for the papers demanded here are not his 'private papers.'" *Id.* at 414.

> Quotes exact language that illustrates narrow holding.

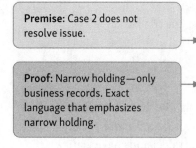

Premise: Case 2 does not resolve issue.

Proof: Narrow holding—only business records. Exact language that emphasizes narrow holding.

Similarly, *Doe* preserved *Boyd's* protection of personal papers. In *Doe*, the Court held that the Fifth Amendment did not protect the contents of business records in the possession of the owner of a sole proprietorship. 465 U.S. at 617. However, the *Doe* Court preserved *Boyd's* protection of personal papers by premising its holding on the corporate nature of the documents. The Court carefully noted that "each of the documents sought here pertained to [the defendant's] business." *Id*. at 610 n.7.

B. Constructing an Argument Strategy for a Group of Cases

If your research reveals only one mandatory authority case that has arguably addressed the disputed legal issue, the preceding discussion illustrates two straightforward options. You might argue that the case resolves the issue in a manner favorable to your client, or argue that the case fails to resolve the issue at all. However, when your research reveals two or more mandatory authority cases within your jurisdiction that have arguably addressed the legal issue you are disputing, your argument strategy is more challenging. Under such circumstances, you must not only decide how you want to interpret each individual case's holding, but must also look at the cases as a collective group.

When dealing with more than one mandatory authority case, you must be careful to ensure that your treatment of each individual case within the group is consistent with your overall goal. Your goal is to frame each court's holding in such a way that the group of cases, collectively, supports your legal argument. When viewed collectively, all of the individual cases' outcomes must either *compel* the judge to adopt your favorable interpretation of the rule of law or *allow* the judge to adopt that interpretation.

For example, if Browne's lawyer in the Fifth Amendment problem had relied only on the favorable *Boyd* case, the lawyer might well have won that narrow argument but lost the case. Without Browne's artful advocacy, the Government might have been able to convince the judge that the two recent Supreme Court decisions resolved the question of personal papers and implicitly overruled *Boyd*. Therefore, when evaluating more than one prior case, it's important not to lose sight of how the cases, as a group, lead to your desired conclusion.

In considering the cases as a collective group, there are four possible ways to structure your argument.

1. First, you might argue that each case within the collective group has adopted your favorable interpretation of the rule of law or, alternatively, that the highest court in the jurisdiction adopted your favorable interpretation. This is the most favorable construction, but is not always realistically possible to argue.

2. Second, you might argue that one or more cases within the collective group has adopted your favorable interpretation of the rule of law, while the remaining cases have not resolved the legal issue at all. This is the second most favorable construction.

3. Third, you might argue that none of the cases within the collective group has actually resolved the legal issue. This is the third most favorable construction.

4. Finally, you might argue that one or more cases within the collective group has adopted your favorable interpretation of the rule of law, while one or more of the remaining cases has adopted an unfavorable interpretation of the rule of law (i.e., a split of authority within the jurisdiction). This is the least favorable construction, although sometimes it is the only credible construction possible.

1. Each Case Within the Group (or the Highest Level Court) Has Adopted Your Favorable Interpretation

Assuming the cases in your jurisdiction can reasonably be construed as having adopted your favorable legal interpretation, this is a highly favorable argument construct—if each of the higher level courts within the jurisdiction has already adopted your favorable rule, the judge would be compelled to adopt that legal interpretation. Assuming there are two such cases that have adopted your favorable rule, the template of your case justification argument would look like this:

Conclusion & Consequences	Mandatory precedent has adopted your favorable interpretation of the rule of law. Therefore, the court is compelled to adopt your favorable interpretation.	
	Proof of Conclusion:	
Case 1:	Premise:	Adopts your favorable interpretation of the rule of law.
	Proof:	Highlight and quote *specific language*, the favorable *holding* and, if possible, the *logic or policy considerations* that support your conclusion.
Case 2:	Premise:	Adopts your favorable interpretation of the rule of law.
	Proof:	Highlight and quote *specific language*, the favorable *holding* and, if possible, the *logic or policy considerations* that support your conclusion.
Restate conclusion & consequences	Because Cases 1 & 2 have adopted your favorable interpretation of the law, the court is compelled to follow Cases 1 & 2.	

2. Some Cases Adopt Your Favorable Interpretation & Remaining Cases Fail to Resolve

Conclusion & Consequences		Mandatory precedent has adopted your favorable interpretation of the rule of law. Therefore, the court is compelled to adopt your favorable interpretation.
		Proof of Conclusion:
Case 1:	Premise:	Adopts your favorable interpretation of the rule of law.
	Proof:	Highlight and quote *specific language*, the favorable *holding* and, if possible, the *logic or policy considerations* that support your conclusion.
Case 2:	Premise:	Fails to resolve the issue at all.
	Proof:	Highlight and quote *specific language*, the *narrow holding* and, if possible, the *logic or policy considerations* that support your conclusion.
Restate conclusion & consequences		Because Case 1 has adopted your favorable interpretation of the law, and Case 2 has failed to resolve the issue, the court is compelled to follow Case 1.

The Fifth Amendment brief illustrates this type of argument construct. In the Motion to Quash, Browne's lawyer argued that *Boyd* adopted the favorable rule interpretation (the Fifth Amendment protects personal papers from compelled disclosure), and that remaining mandatory authority failed to address the issue at all (*Fischer* and *Doe* narrowly addressed the compelled disclosure of business records but did not address private papers).

3. No Case Within the Collective Group Has Resolved the Issue

After carefully reviewing each precedent case, you might conclude that none of the cases actually addresses or resolves the narrow question you are disputing. If no prior case in the jurisdiction has definitively resolved the legal question, the issue becomes one of "first impression." When a court addresses an issue of first impression, the court is justified in interpreting the rule of law in whatever manner the court deems appropriate. Assuming again there are two cases within the jurisdiction that are the subject of your inquiry, the template of your case justification argument would look like this:

Conclusion & Consequences	Mandatory precedent has not addressed or resolved the issue before the court. Therefore, the court is justified in adopting your favorable interpretation.

Proof of Conclusion:

Case 1:	Premise:	Failed to resolve the issue at all.
	Proof:	Highlight and quote *specific language*, the *narrow holding* and, if possible, the *logic or policy considerations* that support your conclusion.
Case 2:	Premise:	Failed to resolve the issue at all.
	Proof:	Highlight and quote *specific language*, the *narrow holding* and, if possible, the *logic or policy considerations* that support your conclusion.

Restate conclusion & consequences	Because Cases 1 & 2 failed to address or resolve the issue, the court is justified in adopting your favorable interpretation.

Using the Fifth Amendment problem as an example, if the *Boyd* case did not exist, Browne's attorney would argue that, because neither *Fischer* nor *Doe* definitively resolved the issue, the court would be justified in adopting the defendant's broad interpretation of the Fifth Amendment.

4. The Cases Conflict

The fourth argument construct is the least desirable option. It not only allows the court to adopt either your favorable interpretation of the rule of law or your opponent's unfavorable interpretation, but you must convince the judge to reject the unfavorable law. Under this argument construct, you would argue that one or more mandatory cases have adopted your favorable interpretation of the law and that one or more mandatory cases adopted your opponent's unfavorable interpretation of the law. You must also *motivate* the court to follow the favorable cases and reject the unfavorable cases. For purposes of clarity, we will refer to the latter type of arguments as "motivating" arguments. Motivating argument strategies are discussed below in Section II. Setting the details of motivating arguments aside for the moment, when structuring a case justification argument, argue the favorable case first. Thus, the general template of your case justification argument would look like this:

Conclusion & Consequences		Mandatory precedent has adopted your favorable interpretation. The favorable precedent should be followed because… Unfavorable mandatory precedent should be ignored because…
		Proof of Conclusion:
Case 1:	Premise:	Case has adopted your favorable interpretation of the rule of law.
	Proof:	Highlight and quote *specific language*, the favorable *holding* and, if possible, the *logic or policy considerations* that support your conclusion.
Case 2:	Premise:	Case incorrectly interpreted the rule of law and should be ignored.
	Proof:	Argue why the case *incorrectly interpreted* the rule of law, and/or how the court's unfavorable holding would have *adverse policy ramifications*.
Restate conclusion & consequences		Because Case 1 correctly interpreted the rule of law, and Case 2 incorrectly interpreted the law, the court should follow Case 1.

II. MOTIVATING ARGUMENTS

A. Motivate the Judge to Adopt Your Interpretation

1. Argue the Favorable Implications of Your Interpretation

Rarely is an advocate so convinced of the merits of the case justification argument that the advocate summarily ends the argument there. If mandatory precedent was so clearly one-sided, two lawyers would not be disputing the meaning of that precedent. Therefore, it is good practice to also convince the judge why the favorable cases are reasonable and just. In other words, your goal is to motivate the judge to approve of your favorable interpretation of the law. Like most people, judges strive to "do the right thing." If you and an opposing counsel each argue that the same case should be interpreted in two conflicting ways, a judge is more likely to climb out on a limb and accept your argument if the judge believes that your interpretation of the mandatory case law would produce better law.

a. Argue Policy

Courts strive to interpret the law in a manner that will have a positive impact on society. Conversely, they are reluctant to interpret the law in a manner that would have a negative impact on society. Therefore, if possible, illustrate how your favorable interpretation of the law would positively affect society and how the opposing attorney's interpretation would have a negative impact on society. Review Chapter 27 for a detailed discussion of the various types of policy arguments that can help persuade judges to adopt a favorable interpretation of the law.

b. Statutory Arguments

If the source of the law is statutory, you might argue how the statutory language and the statutory scheme support your favorable interpretation. You would also argue how the statute's legislative history supports your favorable interpretation. Review Chapter 28 for a detailed discussion of the specific types of statutory arguments that can help persuade judges to adopt a favorable interpretation of a statute.

2. Incorporating Motivating Arguments into the Argument Structure

As you consider how to incorporate motivating arguments into your argument structure, there are two basic formatting options, and a hybrid of the two basic options, available to you. First, you can weave the motivating arguments into the case justification argument, arguing not only what the precedent court held, but why the court's holding is sound policy. Second, you can argue the justification and motivating arguments separately, first arguing one type of argument and then arguing the other type of argument. Finally, you can format your argument based on a hybrid of the two other alternatives, weaving some motivating arguments into your case justification arguments, but also including a separate section that explores the motivating arguments in greater detail.

a. Weave the Motivating Arguments into the Case Justification Argument

Often, the two arguments relate to each other—the precedent court ostensibly adopted your favorable interpretation of the rule of law because of sound policy reasons. Under these circumstances, it is very effective to weave the motivating arguments into the justification arguments—any argument appears more reasonable when supported by policy and logic. You may find it helpful to outline the case justification argument first, and then weave into the outline specific motivating arguments that support a particular point. Then, if there are some motivating arguments that do not dovetail into the justification argument, they can be incorporated into the beginning and/or end of the argument (the hybrid option).

Again using the Fifth Amendment problem for purposes of illustration, Sample Brief B illustrates the hybrid option. Recall that Browne's lawyer seeks to quash the subpoena of the client's personal diary, arguing that the diary is protected from compelled disclosure by the Fifth Amendment. In the first and second paragraphs illustrated below, Browne's lawyer introduces the argument with the strong public policy interests that underlie the Fifth Amendment (motivating arguments). In the third and fourth paragraphs, Browne's lawyer argues how mandatory precedent has adopted a favorable, expansive interpretation of the Fifth Amendment (case justification arguments). Throughout the case justification arguments, Browne's lawyer also weaves in policy arguments.

Browne begins the argument by emphasizing the broad policy that underlies the Fifth Amendment.

The privilege against compulsory self-incrimination derives from the Fifth Amendment's "'respect [for] a private inner sanctum of individual feeling and thought'... that necessarily includes an individual's papers." *Bellis*, 417 U.S. at 91. In particular, it recognizes that "compelling self-accusation... would be both cruel and unjust." *Boyd*, 116 U.S. at 629. While the privilege may at times protect the guilty, the Supreme Court has admonished that "the evils of compelling self-disclosure transcends any difficulties... in the detection and prosecution of crime." *United States v. White*, 322 U.S. 694, 698 (1944). These evils include subjecting people to "iniquitous methods of prosecution," *id.*, betraying "the inviolability of the human personality," risking encroachment on the basic liberties of all citizens, and undermining the adversarial system. *Murphy*, 378 U.S. at 55. Accordingly, the Fifth Amendment proscribes invasion into "the privacies of life." *Boyd*, 116 U.S. at 630.

These policy concerns set up the favorable conclusion that the protections of the Fifth Amendment must be broadly construed to protect personal papers.

Personal papers are part of "the privacies of life." Failure to protect personal papers would thwart their development, thus inhibiting creativity and suppressing expression. Moreover, failure to protect personal documents would adversely affect the innocent as well as the guilty. *Boyd*, 116 U.S. at 629. Finally, failing to protect personal documents would create an artificial distinction between an individual's oral testimony and writings, even if the two are substantively identical. The Fifth Amendment does not contemplate such an anomalous result.

Policy reasons why personal papers should be protected under the Fifth Amendment.

The previous policy reasons set up Browne's favorable interpretation of *Boyd*. Even in this case justification paragraph, policy is woven into the argument to show why the court's holding is good policy.

Accordingly, the Supreme Court has long held that the Fifth Amendment protects personal papers as well as oral testimony. *See Boyd*, 116 U.S. at 633. In *Boyd*, the Court equated seizing a person's documents as evidence against him with compelling that person to be a witness against himself: "And we have been unable to perceive that the seizure of a man's private books and papers to be used in evidence against him is substantially different from compelling him to be a witness against himself." *Id.* Additionally, the Court admonished that "any forcible and compulsory extortion of a man's own testimony or of his private papers ... is within the condemnation of [the Fifth Amendment]," *id.* at 630, and "contrary to the principals of a free government." *Id.* at 635–36.

Since *Boyd*, the Supreme Court has reiterated *Boyd's* protection of personal papers. For example, in *Bellis*, the Supreme Court acknowledged that "[i]t has long been established ... that the Fifth Amendment ... protects an individual from compelled production of his personal papers." 417 U.S. at 87. And, in *White*, the Supreme Court observed that it is the Fifth Amendment's "historic function [to protect an individual] from compulsory incrimination through his own testimony or personal records." 322 U.S. at 701. In each of these cases, the Supreme Court could not have been clearer; the Fifth Amendment protects individuals from the compelled production of their personal papers.

> Browne bolsters the case justification argument with two additional Supreme Court cases that adopted the favorable interpretation of the 5th Amendment.

b. Argue Case Justification and Motivating Arguments Separately

Sometimes motivating arguments do not neatly dovetail into a case justification argument. For example, if you argue that earlier mandatory cases have not addressed or resolved an issue, then presumably the courts did not consider the policy or other arguments that relate to the issue. It is still possible under this scenario to weave in motivating arguments. However, you might decide that motivating arguments would interfere with your ability to present your case justification argument clearly and effectively.

Should you choose to argue your case justification and motivating arguments separately, you can argue either type of argument first. Each choice has advantages and can be used effectively depending upon the legal issue in question. From a logical perspective, the case justification argument is the threshold issue. If a judge doesn't have the authority to adopt a particular interpretation of a rule of law, it doesn't matter how compelling the motivating arguments might be. The judge is bound by stare decisis to follow mandatory precedent. Therefore, if the justification argument is hotly disputed and will require a detailed, sophisticated argument, a judge would probably want to consider that argument first. Under this scenario, after advancing your case justification argument, you would then motivate the judge by elaborating on all of the sound reasons why your favorable interpretation is the better rule.

However, if your strongest arguments are motivating arguments, and your case justification argument is somewhat weak, it can be persuasive to argue the motivating arguments first. The convincing policy and other considerations in the motivating argument might enhance the likelihood that a judge would also accept your case justification argument. Nevertheless, if the case justification argument is so important that it really must be argued first, this option is not viable. Instead, you can choose an alternative format that accommodates the competing concerns—the hybrid option.

c. The Hybrid Option

For the reasons stated above, you may sometimes conclude that the case justification argument should be argued first, even though it is the weaker of the two types of arguments. Under such circumstances, you can strengthen the case justification argument by expanding the roadmap paragraphs that introduce the body of the argument itself to include the crux of your motivating arguments. In other words, you can set the stage for your case justification argument by enlarging and enhancing your introductory roadmap paragraphs so that they persuasively summarize your most compelling motivating arguments. Then, when the judge begins reading the first argument—the case justification argument—the thrust of the motivating arguments will have already been laid out as a backdrop in the introductory paragraphs.

B. Motivate the Judge to Reject the Opponent's Case Law

You face an additional challenge when the mandatory cases in your jurisdiction arguably conflict, with one or more cases adopting your favorable interpretation and one or more cases adopting your opponent's unfavorable interpretation. Under such circumstances, you must not only convince the judge why sound policy and other reasons support your favorable cases, but why the unfavorable cases should be rejected. Chapter 30 discusses in detail how to address and rebut unfavorable law. When convincing a judge to reject unfavorable mandatory precedent, you can attack the unfavorable court's reasoning and/or argue that the unfavorable case is no longer "good law." Both of these strategies are discussed and illustrated in Chapter 30.

CHAPTER IN REVIEW

Definitions:

LAW-CENTERED ARGUMENT:

When the meaning of the law itself is unclear, advocates attempt to convince the judge to interpret the vague language in a manner favorable to their clients' interests.

CASE JUSTIFICATION ARGUMENT:

A form of a law-centered argument —when there is mandatory precedent that has at least arguably interpreted the law, an advocate must convince the judge that the mandatory precedent gives her the legal authority to adopt the advocate's favorable interpretation of the law.

MOTIVATING ARGUMENTS:

A form of a law-centered argument—these are arguments that persuade a judge that your favorable interpretation of the law is the most reasonable interpretation of the law. Advocates use policy arguments (Chapter 27) and, in the case of a statute, statutory construction arguments (Chapter 28) to motivate the judge to "do the right thing."

POSSIBLE INTERPRETATIONS OF A CASE:

As you read the mandatory precedent in your jurisdiction, consider whether each case:

1. Arguably *adopts* your favorable interpretation of the rule of law;
2. *Does not actually resolve* the issue at all; or
3. Adopts your *opponent's interpretation* of the rule of law.

POSSIBLE ARGUMENT CONSTRUCTS FOR A GROUP OF CASES

1. When your research reveals that two or more mandatory authority cases have arguably addressed the legal issue you are disputing, there are four possible ways to construct such an argument:
   a. Each case within the group of cases has adopted your favorable interpretation or, alternatively, that the highest level court in the jurisdiction adopted your favorable interpretation;
   b. Some cases have adopted your favorable interpretation and the remaining cases have failed to resolve the issue at all;
   c. No mandatory precedent has actually resolved the disputed issue; or
   d. The cases conflict, with at least one case adopting your favorable interpretation and at least one case adopting an unfavorable interpretation.
2. *Drafting Strategy*: Argue the most favorable case first, then the next most favorable, and so on. If there is a split of authority, save the unfavorable case for last, arguing why the court should ignore that case.

MOTIVATING ARGUMENTS

1. Effective advocates also use policy and statutory construction arguments to argue why their favorable interpretation of the law is sound.
2. There are three possible *drafting strategies*:
   a. Weave motivating arguments into the case justification argument;
   b. Argue motivating arguments separately;
      i. If the case justification argument is hotly contested, the judge will likely want to read that argument first, and the motivating arguments later.

      ii.   If the motivating arguments are much stronger than the case justification argument, consider arguing them first.

  c. Weave a summary of the motivating arguments into the roadmap paragraphs leading into the case justification argument, while addressing them in more detail later.

LAW-CENTERED ARGUMENTS

Working with Policy

I. FORMULATING FAVORABLE INTERPRETATIONS OF THE LAW

Whether the source of law is statutory or common law, rules of law often give rise to disputes about what the law means, separate and apart from how that law might be applied factually to a client's factual situation. Consider the federal wiretap statute that was introduced in Chapter 7. Congress enacted the wiretap statute, in part, to curb perceived abuses of governmental wiretapping. One procedural requirement was designed to protect wiretap evidence from tampering during the time frame before trial. That section of the statute requires that the government "immediately" obtain the safeguard of a judicial seal after retrieving wiretap evidence. Should the government fail to obtain a judicial seal immediately, the statute provides the government with only one alternative: it must provide a "satisfactory explanation" for its failure to do so.[1] This statutory rule of law left many questions unresolved. What exactly is a satisfactory explanation? Does a satisfactory explanation require that the *government* prove there was no possibility of tampering during the delay, or must the *defendant* instead prove that tampering actually occurred? Is a mere good faith mistake a satisfactory explanation, or must the government prove that it had a legitimate law enforcement reason for the delay?

The statute's vague language and the resulting questions that inevitably arise require courts to define in more concrete terms what a "satisfactory explanation" means—a law-centered issue. If a higher level court in a jurisdiction had already clearly resolved these questions, lawyers would not be disputing the law's meaning—a lower court judge would be compelled to follow such precedent. Thus, this chapter discusses how to construct a law-centered argument based on policy when no mandatory precedent exists.

---

1. 18 U.S.C. § 2518(8)(a).

The first step in formulating policy arguments is to clarify how you want the adjudicator to interpret the law. When no mandatory precedent exists, advocates have room to argue that the vague language of a rule of law should be interpreted in a manner that advances their clients' interests. When evaluating a vague legal standard, any interpretation you advocate must be a good faith and reasonable interpretation of the statute or common law rule. With that in mind, there is usually enough ambiguity for effective advocates to proffer different interpretations of the law.

As you consider how to formulate a favorable rule of law from ambiguous language, carefully consider your client's factual situation and what you will need to prove in order to prevail. Then consider how the rule of law's ambiguous language might help you formulate a winning interpretation. As you consider how you might construct a favorable interpretation of the law, research the case law in other jurisdictions to determine how courts have interpreted the statute or common law rule. Although these cases do not have the force of mandatory precedent, they serve two purposes. First, persuasive precedent can provide you with ideas that will help you formulate a favorable interpretation of the law. Second, the persuasive precedent will ultimately serve a purpose in the written argument you draft—you will refer to these cases to support your favorable interpretation of the law.

As you contemplate your client's factual situation and what you will need to prove in order to prevail, consider whether you want to interpret the rule of law in a manner that would make the legal standard very difficult to satisfy, or, alternatively, interpret it in a manner that would make the legal standard easy to satisfy. How you interpret the rule of law depends on who you represent and the factual situation before you. For example, if your client must satisfy a legal standard to avail itself of *privileges* under a statute, you would advocate an interpretation of the standard that your client could easily satisfy. If, on the other hand, your client must satisfy a standard before being *penalized* under a statute, you would advocate an interpretation of the statute that your client would not satisfy.

The same strategies apply when the opposing party must satisfy a standard. If your client's interests dictate that the opposing party not satisfy the standard, then you would consider how you might define the standard in a manner that would be difficult to satisfy. Alternatively, if your client's interests dictate that the opposing party satisfy the standard, then you would consider how you might define the standard in a manner that would be easy to satisfy. Again, any interpretation that you advocate must be a reasonable and fair interpretation of the law. Ethical rules prohibit lawyers from advocating any position that is "frivolous" or for which there is "no basis in law or fact."[2]

---

2. Model R. Prof. Conduct 3.1 (ABA 2002).

⊚ ILLUSTRATION: Criminal Wiretap Problem

Using the federal wiretap statute as an example, consider the two parties' differ-ing interpretations of the term "satisfactory explanation." In the fact pattern for the sample brief in Appendix E, the Government did not immediately obtain a judicial seal that would safeguard sensitive wiretap evidence. The Government's explana-tion for its delay is that the tapes were lost during an office move. The tapes were missing for two months and were finally discovered in an open box in an office supply room. Immediately upon discovering the tapes, the Government took them to a judge for sealing.

A. Government's Lawyer

Assume you represent the Government in this case, and that no higher-level court in your jurisdiction has yet interpreted the meaning of the statutory phrase "satisfactory explanation." Therefore, you are free to advocate a standard that is both a reasonable interpretation of the statute, as well as a favorable interpreta-tion. Under this set of facts, you have a bit of a problem because the Government made an easily avoidable mistake. Therefore, the Government would have great difficulty in satisfying a standard that would require the Government to fulfill strin-gent requirements. For instance, an easily avoidable mistake would likely not satis-fy a standard that would require the Government to act with "reasonable diligence."

As you research cases from other jurisdictions, you would not only read such cas-es to obtain a better understanding of how courts have interpreted the law, but also to discover whether any courts from other jurisdictions have adopted a lenient defi-nition of the "satisfactory explanation" requirement. If such cases exist, you would urge the court to adopt that lenient interpretation, and would later cite to such cases in your written argument as support for your position. If, on the other hand, courts have not yet interpreted the statutory language, you would consider and promote a standard that is both a reasonable interpretation of the law and favorable to your client. You might argue, for example, that the government supplies a "satisfactory explanation" any time it has a "good faith" explanation for the delay in sealing. Even an easily avoidable mistake could be deemed to be in "good faith." In fact, under that interpretation, almost all governmental explanations would be deemed satisfactory unless the defendant could produce evidence that the government acted in bad faith.

B. Defendant's Lawyer

Now assume that you represent the defendant, Mr. Hart, and want to argue that the Government's explanation for its mistake was not "satisfactory." As an advocate representing Mr. Hart, you would urge the court to adopt a very stringent standard that would be difficult for the Government to satisfy. You recognize that the Government has two problems. First, the Government was not very diligent—the mistake easily could have been avoided because the government agents knew in advance that the bureau was moving offices the next day. To avoid the mistake, the Government could easily have arranged for a courier to deliver the tapes to the courthouse rather than putting the tapes in a box that was identical to thousands of moving boxes. Second, the Government can't account for the tapes' whereabouts for two months. Although the box of tapes was ultimately discovered in an office supply room, the tapes could have been anywhere during the two-month delay. The Government's inability to explain what happened to the tapes during the two-month period means that it can't prove that it safeguarded the tapes from any possibility of tampering before it obtained the required judicial seal.

As Mr. Hart's lawyer, you would have researched case law in other jurisdictions and found cases in which courts have imposed very stringent standards on the government. Adopting the standards imposed by these courts, you would argue that a governmental explanation is not "satisfactory" unless the government can prove *both* that: (1) prior to judicial sealing, the government stored the tapes in a manner that safeguarded them from any *possibility* of tampering; and (2) the government acted with "reasonable diligence" to obtain the required judicial seal. This interpretation of the statute would make it almost impossible for the Government to prove that it complied with the statute.

II. CONSTRUCTING PROOF

Formulating a favorable interpretation of the rule of law is just the first step in the process. You must also convince an adjudicator that your favorable interpretation of the law is more reasonable than your opponent's interpretation. When urging an adjudicator to adopt a favorable interpretation of the law, advocates rely on two broad types of arguments: policy arguments and statutory construction arguments. This chapter discusses the policy arguments available to advocates. Chapter 28 discusses the special types of arguments that are also available to advocates when interpreting statutes.

A. Social Policy Arguments

Courts strive to interpret the law in a manner that will have a positive impact on society and, in the case of statutes, further the underlying purpose of the statute. Conversely, courts are reluctant to interpret the law in a manner that would have a negative impact on society. Policy arguments are very important, particularly when the court is faced with two reasonable interpretations of the law. Therefore, advocates persuade adjudicators to adopt their favorable interpretations of the law by illustrating how their legal interpretation would positively affect society and, if possible, why the opponent's interpretation would have negative policy implications. When arguing why the opponent's interpretation would have negative policy implications, advocates often use a "slippery slopes" argument that shows how the opponent's interpretation would lead to a "parade of horribles." To make such an argument, consider the logical consequences of your opponent's theory if taken to an absurd extreme. In fact, you have already had an opportunity to witness such an approach first-hand in your law school classes. Law professors often lead students down a slippery slope to an absurd extreme (the "parade of horribles") as a means of teaching students how to think critically.

Using the criminal wiretap problem as an example, the following paragraph is excerpted from the sample brief that appears in Appendix E. In the excerpted paragraph, the advocate argues both why his favorable interpretation of the statute has a positive effect on public policy, and why the opponent's interpretation would negatively impact society.

Only procedural safeguards can ensure that the integrity of sensitive wiretap evidence remains inviolate. Procedural safeguards are necessary because tape-recorded evidence is highly vulnerable to tampering and is cost-prohibitive to prove. In fact, with modern technology, it is often impossible to detect. *Johnson*, 696 F.2d at 124.

> Defendant argues that only his rule will have positive policy effects.

Tapes that are made for use in criminal investigations can be falsified, even by relatively unskilled persons, in ways that are superficially convincing.… Such alterations, moreover, are likely to go undetected because a highly skilled forensic examiner who is an expert in the fields of tape recording, signal analysis, and speech communication, using the best available analysis equipment, can take weeks and even months to establish with reasonable certainty the fact that a tape has been falsified. The advantage, in terms of effort, time, and cost is clearly with the forger.

> Defendant then illustrates the negative policy implications of the opponent's interpretation.

Id.

B. Equity Arguments

When determining a law's meaning, courts also want to arrive at a judgment that will be fair and equitable to the parties before the court. Therefore, consider how your favorable interpretation of the law would result in a fair and just outcome to the parties. For example, in the criminal wiretap problem, the Government lost its wiretap evidence for two months before it submitted the tapes to a judge for sealing. In that case, it was the Government's mistake in losing the wiretap evidence that created the problem before the court. Therefore, the defendant's lawyer uses that mistake to appeal to the court's sense of fairness, as follows:

> Finally, fairness mandates that the Government bear this burden. "Inasmuch as a need for a 'satisfactory explanation' only arises when those in charge of the wiretap operation fail to do their homework and to present the tapes for immediate sealing, any doubts about the integrity of the evidence should be laid at law enforcement's doorstep." *Mora*, 821 F.2d at 868.

Defendant appeals to judge's fairness.

C. Prudential Concerns

When evaluating the meaning of rules of law, courts are also concerned about the impact their judgments might have on the court system; this type of concern is called a "prudential concern." As an example, courts are reluctant to interpret a statute in a manner that might "open the floodgates" of litigation. Thus, by invoking a "slippery slopes" argument, you might argue that the unfortunate result of the opponent's interpretation would be to open the floodgates of litigation, creating an unmanageable case load within the court system. Courts are also understandably concerned with judgments that might impede the ability of courts to manage their caseloads efficiently. For example, a judge might be concerned about interpreting the law in a manner that would require courts to engage in costly and time-consuming fact-finding inquiries. Using the criminal wiretapping problem to illustrate this type of argument, an appeal to the court's prudential concerns is subtly buried within the following paragraph:

Defendant reminds the court that if it does not adopt the defendant's favorable rule, litigants will have to conduct "costly" and "time-consuming" fact-finding inquiries.

> ... Congress carefully incorporated external safeguards within the statute to avoid the costly, time-consuming, and inconclusive expert inquiries that inevitably result from fact-finding expeditions. By proving it held the tapes in a manner that ensures their integrity remained inviolate, the Government's satisfactory explanation not only affords the level of protection of an immediate seal, but avoids the problems Congress sought to avoid.

CHAPTER IN REVIEW

Definitions:

SOCIAL POLICY ARGUMENTS:

Arguments that appeal to the judge's desire to achieve a result that will have a positive impact on society.

EQUITY ARGUMENTS:

Arguments that appeal to the judge's desire to achieve a result that will be fair and equitable to the parties involved in the litigation.

PRUDENTIAL ARGUMENTS:

Arguments that appeal to the judge's desire to achieve a result that will avoid an adverse impact on the court system.

CONSTRUCTING LAW-CENTERED ARGUMENTS BASED ON POLICY:

As you read a statute or common law rule of law:

1. First consider how you might interpret the rule of law in a manner that is both credible and favorable to your client's interests.
   - *Caution*: Any favorable interpretation of the rule of law must also be a good faith and reasonable interpretation of the law.
   - If the rule of law is statutory, consider the types of arguments described in Chapter 28 and how they might support your interpretation of the statute.
2. Next, consider why your favorable interpretation of the law would have positive policy implications and why your opponent's interpretation would have negative policy implications.
   - Consider the following types of policy arguments:
     a. Social policy arguments;
     b. Equity arguments;
     c. Prudential arguments.

LAW-CENTERED ARGUMENTS
Working with Statutes

I. PRELIMINARY ASSESSMENT OF THE STATUTE

When a statute is the original source of law, you must convince the adjudicator that the statutory scheme itself supports the favorable legal interpretation you are advocating. Even if an adjudicator might agree that your legal interpretation best serves public policy, the adjudicator will not adopt your theory unless the source of law—the statute—permits that interpretation. Therefore, when interpreting statutory language, first carefully evaluate and outline the separate statutory elements, as discussed in Chapter 6. As you consider the statute's language, also verify your preliminary assessment by looking beyond the exact section of the statute you are evaluating. For example, many statutes have definitional sections that define key language used in the statute.

When considering the meaning of the statutory language, also review the statutory scheme as a whole. An adjudicator is not likely to interpret a section of the statute in a manner that would make the statute internally inconsistent or that would thwart the purpose of the statute as revealed by the statutory scheme. Reviewing the statutory scheme in its entirety may not only help you interpret the statutory language at issue, but may also help you determine whether any other statutory provisions may be relevant in evaluating the client's legal problem. Therefore, when considering the meaning of the statute's plain language, carefully evaluate: (1) the language of the statutory section that is at issue; (2) the definitions contained elsewhere in the statute, if applicable; and (3) the entire statutory scheme.

You are now in a position to consider the potential meaning of the statutory language and how you might use the statutory language to advance your client's interests. As the reading in Chapter 27 suggests, your goal is to formulate an interpretation of the statute from which your client will ultimately prevail. As you consider how to formulate a favorable rule of law from ambiguous language, first consider your client's factual situation and what you will need to prove in order to prevail.

Then consider how the statute's ambiguous language might help you formulate a winning interpretation.

II. CONSTRUCTING PROOF

After formulating a favorable interpretation of statutory language, you must convince an adjudicator to adopt your favorable interpretation of the statute. The fact that other courts in *other* jurisdictions agree with your interpretation, while perhaps persuasive, would not itself convince an adjudicator to adopt your interpretation. When a statute is the original source of law, you must convince the adjudicator that the statute itself supports the favorable legal interpretation you are advocating. When interpreting a statute's meaning, adjudicators consider some or all of the following:

1. The *plain language* of the statutory section at issue;

2. The *statutory scheme* as a whole, including:
   a. Any *definition sections* of the statute that define key language;
   b. The *title* or any *preamble* that might indicate the statute's purpose;
   c. The *remaining sections* of the statute to evaluate how the sections might interrelate;

3. The *legislative history*, if any, to determine the legislative purpose;

4. Any *canons of construction* that might help the court interpret the statutory language;

5. The *public policy* ramifications of its interpretation of the statute (discussed in Chapter 27); and

6. The interpretations adopted by *other courts and legal scholars*.

You can use each of these tools of statutory construction not only to advance arguments illustrating why your interpretation of the statute is sound, but also to argue why your opponent's interpretation of the statute is unsound. Therefore, as you consider each of these tools of statutory construction, evaluate them from two perspectives. First, consider how each tool of statutory construction might be used to advance an argument that favors your interpretation. Second, consider how the same tool of construction might be used to attack your opponent's argument.

Chapter 27 discusses how advocates use policy arguments to persuade an adjudicator to adopt their favorable interpretation of a rule of law. Policy arguments are persuasive tools whether the source of law is statutory or common law. The remainder of this chapter, however, describes the unique tools of persuasion that advocates employ when working with statutes.

A. Language of the Statute

The statute's language is the starting point. Does the language either compel or support your favorable interpretation of the statute? Sometimes, of course, the statutory language is so vague and unclear that it is not susceptible to any "plain language" argument. For example, the term "satisfactory explanation" in the federal wiretap statute is not defined within the statutory scheme itself, and the term is so broad and vague that it doesn't lend itself to an argument based on the language of the statute. Instead, the vague term "satisfactory explanation" would permit the judge to interpret that language in any reasonable manner. Because that language is so broad and vague, your legal argument wouldn't contain a "plain language" argument. Often, however, the language of the statute either clearly supports a particular interpretation, or at least lends itself to an argument based on the statutory language. In such cases, the language of the statute would be the cornerstone of your argument.

◎ ILLUSTRATION: Title VII Problem

As an example, consider the Title VII problem that is the basis of Sample Brief A in Appendix D. *The background*: Title VII prohibits employers from discriminating against employees on the basis of their sex, among other protected classifications. The statute prohibits any "employer" from discriminating against its employees, and defines the term "employer" to include "any agent" of the employer. The term "agent" lends itself to an argument based on the statute's language. Prior to 1991, when Title VII was amended, some lawyers argued that the term "agent" merely incorporated *respondeat superior* liability into the statute, with the employer thereby liable for the acts of its agents. Other lawyers argued that the term "agent" made supervisory employees liable as *individuals*. However, prior to 1991, the conflicting interpretations had little practical effect on the outcome because plaintiffs could recover only injunctive relief (reinstatement or hiring), or up to two years of back-pay.[1] These remedies are available only against an employer, not individual employees.

In 1991, Congress amended Title VII to allow plaintiffs to recover compensatory and punitive damages.[2] The expanded remedies intensified the debate. Following the amendment, some lawyers argued that, by expanding the available remedies, Congress also expanded the group of potential defendants to include individual employees who were supervisors. They argued that the term "agent," together with the expanded remedies available to plaintiff, made certain supervisory employees personally liable for both compensatory and punitive damages. Other lawyers argued that when Congress amended Title VII in 1991, it intended only to increase the

---

1. 42 U.S.C. § 2000e-5(g).
2. 42 U.S.C. § 1981a.

monetary award plaintiffs could recover. These lawyers argued that the amendments did not also expand the class of potential defendants from employers to supervisory employees. They argued that the term "agent" merely incorporated *respondeat superior* liability into the statute, with the employer thereby liable in compensatory and punitive damages for the acts of its agents.

1. Example of Argument Based on Statutory Language—Plaintiff

The plaintiff claims that a former supervisor sexually harassed her in violation of Title VII. She seeks to recover damages not only from her former employer, but also from her former supervisor. Therefore, her lawyer advocates for a broad definition of the term "agent" that would hold the former supervisor personally liable. In the following example, note how the language of the statute is the engine that drives the argument. The underlying purpose of the statute is woven into the argument to bolster the plaintiff's interpretation of the statutory language.

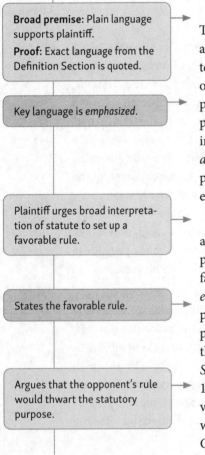

Broad premise: Plain language supports plaintiff.
Proof: Exact language from the Definition Section is quoted.

Key language is *emphasized*.

Plaintiff urges broad interpretation of statute to set up a favorable rule.

States the favorable rule.

Argues that the opponent's rule would thwart the statutory purpose.

The statute's plain language could not be any clearer. Title VII prohibits any "*employer*" from "discriminat[ing] against any individual with respect to his compensation, terms, conditions, or privileges of employment, because of such individual's…sex…." 42 U.S.C. § 2000e-2(a) (emphasis added). Title VII broadly defines the term "employer" to include "a person engaged in an industry affecting commerce who has fifteen or more employees… and *any agent* of such a person…." 42 U.S.C. § 2000e(b) (emphasis added). Thus, the statutory language, on its face, encompasses "any agent" of the employer.

In interpreting the scope of agency, Title VII must "be accorded a liberal interpretation in order to effectuate the purpose of Congress to eliminate the inconvenience, unfairness, and humiliation of ethnic discrimination." *Rodgers v. E.E.O.C.*, 454 F.2d 234, 238 (5th Cir. 1972). Thus, a person is properly an agent under Title VII when "he participates in the decision-making process that forms the basis of the discrimination." *Jones v. Metro. Denver Sewage Disposal Dist.*, 537 F. Supp. 966, 970 (D. Colo. 1982). Any other interpretation "would encourage supervisory personnel to believe that they may violate Title VII with impunity." *Hamilton v. Rodgers*, 791 F.2d 439 (5th Cir. 1986).

In the above illustration, the plaintiff's lawyer not only argues how the plain language of the statute supports the plaintiff's favorable interpretation, but how the opponent's interpretation would thwart the statutory purpose.

2. Example of Argument Based on Statutory Language—Defendant

The defendant supervisor, on the other hand, wants to avoid personal liability. He would argue that the term "agent" must be read narrowly to mean that only an employer is liable for the acts of its agents. The following argument is excerpted from the defendant's argument that appears in Sample Brief A in Appendix D:

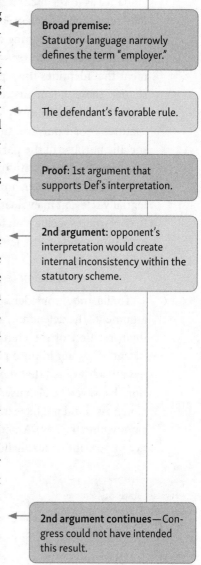

When prohibiting employers from discriminating against their employees, Title VII narrowly defines employer as "a person engaged in an industry affecting commerce who has fifteen or more employees... and any agent of such a person...." 42 U.S.C. §2000e(b). By defining employer as a "person... who has fifteen or more employees... and any agent of such a person," Congress codified its intention to exclude individuals in their individual capacities from liability for violations of Title VII. First, individuals in their individual capacities do not qualify as "person[s]... who ha[ve] fifteen or more employees." Individuals do not have employees, employers do.

Broad premise: Statutory language narrowly defines the term "employer."

The defendant's favorable rule.

Proof: 1st argument that supports Def's interpretation.

Second, interpreting the statutory language to include individuals in their individual capacities would produce an absurd result. The conjunctive term "and" links the term "any agent" to the phrase "person... who has fifteen or more employees." Thus, as an "agent" of an employer, an individual employee's liability would depend on whether the employer employed fifteen or more employees. Individuals who are "agents" of employers with fewer than fifteen employees would be exempt from liability—as an agent of an employer with fewer than fifteen employees, they would fall within the statutory exemption. In contrast, individuals who are "agents" of employers with fifteen or more employees would be liable in their individual capacities. Because their employer would not fall within the exemption, they would similarly not be exempt. Congress could not have intended this result. *Hudson v. Soft Sheen Prods.*, 873 F. Supp. 132, 135 n.2 (N.D. Ill. 1995).

2nd argument: opponent's interpretation would create internal inconsistency within the statutory scheme.

2nd argument continues—Congress could not have intended this result.

> Again, in the above example, the defendant not only argues why a favorable interpretation is sound, but attacks the opponent's theory as being inconsistent with the statutory scheme and as creating an absurd result that Congress could not possibly have intended.

B. The Statutory Scheme as a Whole

When evaluating statutory language, the entire statutory scheme often provides guidance as to the meaning of a particular section of a statute. The statutory scheme may reveal what the legislature intended when it enacted the statute, thereby shedding light on the meaning of the disputed language. When considering the statutory scheme, check first to see whether the statute begins with a preamble or policy statement that identifies the legislature's policy concerns and the reasons it enacted the statute. These statements can usually be found at the beginning of the overall statute. Next, peruse the statutory scheme as a whole to gain a clearer perspective of the legislature's broad purpose in enacting the statutory scheme. Then consider how the specific purpose of the particular section with which you are concerned might help effectuate the broad statutory purpose. Reviewing the statutory scheme in its entirety will also help you determine whether any additional statutory provisions may be potentially relevant in evaluating the client's legal problem. Finally, courts are reluctant to construe a specific statutory section in a manner that would create an inconsistent or absurd result when viewed in conjunction with other statutory sections.

1. Example of Argument Based on Statutory Scheme

To illustrate, consider again the Title VII problem and the defendant employee's argument. The defendant, a supervisory employee, urges the court to adopt a narrow interpretation of the statutory term "agent." The defendant argues that the term "agent" does not impose personal liability on individual employees. The defendant has already argued that the specific statutory language itself supports his interpretation. However, he also uses other sections within the statutory scheme to argue that Congress could not have intended this result. The defendant uses the damages provisions within the 1991 Amendments to bolster his argument that the term "agent" does not impose individual liability.

Premise: Statutory scheme supports Def's interpretation.
Proof: Def. points to the provisions in another section of the statute that limit liability for employers.

The elaborate liability scheme of the 1991 Amendments confirms that Congress intended to preserve Title VII's provision of exclusive employer liability. In expanding the scope of remedies available to victims of Title VII violations to include compensatory and punitive damages, Congress also carefully limited the damages to which an employer could be subjected depending upon the number of employees employed by the employer. For example, on the low end, Congress subjected an employer who employs between fourteen and 101 employees to no more than $50,000 in compensatory and punitive damages. 42 U.S.C. § 1981a(b)(3)(A). On the high end, Congress subjected an employer who employs more than 500 employees to no more than $300,000 in compensatory and punitive damages. *Id.* § 1981a(b)(3)(D). Congress' failure to include a damage cap for individuals reflects that it did not contemplate individual liability for compensatory and punitive damages under the Amendments. *See Hudson*, 873 F. Supp. at 135 ("[I]f Congress had envisioned individual liability under Title VII for compensatory and punitive damages, it would have included *individuals* in this litany of limitations…") (quoting *Miller*, 991 F.2d at 588 n.2).

> Def. argues that the absence of damage limits for individuals means that Congress did not intend to make individuals liable.

C. Legislative Purpose

The legislative purpose underlying a statute's enactment is also relevant when interpreting a statute. Adjudicators strive to interpret statutory language in a manner that will further the underlying statutory purpose. Conversely, they are reluctant to interpret statutory language in a manner that would thwart the statutory purpose. As the above examples illustrate, the statutory purpose can be gleaned from the statutory scheme as a whole. Indeed, the statutory purpose can be woven into a "plain language" or "statutory scheme" argument to enhance the persuasive appeal of such arguments.

You can also discover the probable purpose of a statute by examining the statute's legislative history, if any. Federal statutes, and some state statutes, contain legislative history that can be helpful in identifying the statute's underlying purpose. A statute's legislative history may contain committee reports and hearing transcripts that reflect the reasons the legislature enacted the statute. Note, however, that legislative history is generated by legislators and administrators who are usually invested in the outcome of a particular piece of legislation. Therefore, portions of the legislative history may contain statements that might not accurately reflect the consensus of the legislative body that enacted the statute. A legislative body votes on statutes as they are written, not on the committee reports and hearing transcripts. For these reasons, if an adjudicator determines that the plain language of a statute differs from the legislative intent as revealed in the statute's legislative history, the adjudicator will often (although not always) interpret the statute according to its plain language. Adjudicators reason that their responsibility is to interpret statutes as they were written and enacted, not as some members of the legislature may have wished the statute to have been written.

As you consider the purpose underlying the statute, and its legislative history, keep in mind that some portions of the legislative history might benefit your interpretation of the statute while other portions of the legislative history might benefit your opponent's interpretation. There are often a number of different purposes underlying a statute, as the legislature attempts to strike a reasonable balance between competing interests. Again using the Title VII problem for purposes of illustration, the defendant argues that, in 1991, Congress intended only to expand the scope of remedies available to plaintiffs and did not intend to expand the class of potential defendants.

1. Example of Argument Based on Legislative History

Premise: legislative history supports Def's interpretation.
Proof: Absence of history for individual liability is signif. Instead: replete with references to *employer* liability.

The legislative history to the 1991 Amendments also confirms that Congress intended only to expand the scope of remedies available, not to expand the class of defendants against whom victims of Title VII violations could proceed. None of the Committee Reports, including the House Reports on the 1991 Amendments and the Senate Reports on the precursor bill to the 1991 Amendments, even mention individual liability. *See Hudson*, 873 F. Supp. at 136 (detailing the failure of the legislative history to mention individual liability). Instead, the legislative history is replete with references to *employer* compensation and the possibility of *employer* deterrence. For example, Congress focused on the need for employers to compensate wronged employees. The House Reports reflect Congress' intent to prevent "employers who intentionally discriminate [from avoiding] any meaningful liability." H.R. Rep. No. 41, 102nd Cong., 1st Sess., pt. 2, at 4 (1991). The Senate Reports addressed the need to make "employers liable for all losses—economic or otherwise—[that] are incurred as a consequence of prohibited discrimination." *Id*. at 5.

Def. weaves in legislative purpose argument—that dual purposes of compensation and deterrence are adequately fulfilled by employer liability.

The legislative concern with deterrence also focused on employers, not on individual employees. The Senate Reports noted that employers must provide "punitive damages... in cases of intentional discrimination if the employer acted with 'malice'...." *Id*. The reports also observed that employer liability "will serve as a necessary deterrent to future acts of discrimination...." *Id*. Even the suggested mechanisms for deterrence are restricted to mechanisms an employer might implement, not an individual. Congress hoped to "encourage employers to design and implement complaint structures [that] encourage victims to come forward by overcoming fear of retaliation and fear of loss of privacy.... Data suggests that employers do indeed implement measures to interrupt and prevent employment discrimination when they perceive that there is increased liability." *Id.* at 18 (statement of Dr. Klein).

Moreover, the vocal dissenters to the Amendment failed to mention individual liability in their complaints. Had they considered individual liability even a remote possibility, they would have objected.

> Def. argues that Congressional silence supports the Def's interpretation.

[T]he dissenters supplied exhaustive, thoughtful, and even caustic responses to the Amendments. On such issues as the cost of business, number of litigants, and remuneration of lawyers, [Congress] apparently thought of every conceivable negative outcome and shouted it from the rooftops.... [H]ad they considered individual liability a conceivable outcome, they would also have considered it a negative one and denounced it in a similar fashion. Yet they never mentioned it.

> Def. quotes a compelling argument from a persuasive authority case to bolster the argument.

Hudson, 837 F. Supp. at 138.

D. Canons of Construction

Canons of construction are guidelines that suggest possible ways to interpret statutory language and can also be useful tools of statutory interpretation. However, canons of construction are often criticized because their use may not actually promote the legislative purpose. No court will apply a canon of construction if it defeats the purpose of the statute. Nevertheless, effective advocates often employ canons of construction to argue why statutory language should be interpreted in a manner that benefits the client's position. In fact, because they are only broad guidelines, two different canons of construction can sometimes suggest two totally different interpretations of the same statutory language. Because canons of construction do not necessarily provide accurate guidance of legislative intent, judges may use canons of construction more to justify their decisions rather than to assist them in interpreting statutory language.[3] The following are a few of the better-known and often used canons of construction.

---

3. Richard K. Neumann, Jr., *Legal Reasoning and Legal Writing: Structure, Strategy & Style* 161 (4th ed. Aspen L. & Bus. 2001) (citing Karl N. Llewellyn, *The Common Law Tradition* 521–35 (Little, Brown & Co. 1960)).

1. Criminal Statutes Narrowly Construed

One of the more widely known canons of construction suggests that criminal statutes be interpreted narrowly in favor of the criminal defendant. The broad policy underlying this canon is that, in our society, people should not be punished for conduct unless they have reasonable notice that the conduct is prohibited. Therefore, when the language of a criminal statute does not expressly and clearly prohibit or apply to a particular defendant's conduct, you might use this canon to argue that the statute should be interpreted narrowly in favor of the criminal defendant.

2. Remedial Statutes Broadly Construed

Another popular canon of construction advocates that remedial statutes should be broadly interpreted in favor of the plaintiff who seeks to recover remedies under the statute. The policy underlying this canon is that when the legislature seeks to compensate a class of individuals, the statute should be broadly construed to ensure that the intended victims will have redress under the statute. Examples of remedial statutes are workers' compensation laws, which provide money damages to employees who are injured while at work, and Title VII, which provides relief to persons who have been discriminated against in the terms of their employment due to race, sex, religion, color, or national origin.

3. Ejusdem Generis

Under the canon of *ejusdem generis*, when a statute mentions specific items to which it applies, followed by a general, sweeping phrase, the general phrase should be narrowly interpreted to include only those items that have the same characteristics as the specific items that were previously mentioned. Consider how this canon of construction might be applied to a residential burglary statute. An Illinois residential burglary statute prohibits the burglary of "dwellings," and defines a "dwelling" as: "a house, apartment, mobile home, trailer or *other living quarters* in which at the time of the alleged offense the owners or occupants actually reside...."[4] Using this canon of construction, the term "other living quarters" might be narrowly interpreted to include those living quarters that share the same physical characteristics as a house, apartment, mobile home, or trailer.

4. Expressio Unius est Exclusio Alterius

Under this canon of construction, when a statute expressly lists the conduct or items that it covers, any conduct or items not explicitly mentioned is construed to be excluded. The argument is that if the legislature did not include the conduct or item at issue, the omission was intentional, and that conduct or item should not be covered

---

4. 720 Ill. Comp. Stat. § 5/2-6(b) (2004) (emphasis added).

by the statute. Unlike with statutory language that includes a "catch all" at the end of a specific list of included conduct or items, such as the "*other living quarters*" example within Illinois' residential burglary statute, the argument is that a statutory list that does not include a catch-all should be deemed an exclusive list.

For example, in a criminal case involving the offense of driving under the influence (DUI), the Oklahoma Court of Criminal Appeals considered whether a defendant violated the DUI statute when he drove drunk on a road in a privately-owned trailer park.[5] The DUI statutory language did not extend beyond driving under the influence on "highways, turnpikes, or public parking lots."[6] With these specific locations noted and no "catch-all" included, a privately-owned trailer park was deemed excluded. The court noted that "[u]nder the facts presented here, we are unable to sustain the [defendant]'s conviction because the State did not prove he was driving on a highway, turnpike, or public parking lot." The court urged the legislature to amend the language to include the prohibition of drunk driving beyond those specified boundaries, and the legislature responded and did just that.[7]

CHAPTER IN REVIEW

Core Concepts

EVALUATING A STATUTE

As you evaluate a statute:

1. First carefully review the statutory language, and outline its separate elements.

2. Next, consider the possible interpretations of the disputed statutory language.

3. Next, review the statutory scheme as a whole to determine whether any other statutory provisions may be relevant in evaluating the issue.

4. Next, research the case law from other jurisdictions to determine how courts have interpreted the statutory language and the arguments they use to support their legal interpretations.

---

5. *Fenimore v. State*, 78 P.3d 549 (Okla. Crim. App. 2003), *overruled by State v. Silas*, 470 P.3d 339 (Okla. Crim. App. 2020).

6. *Id.* at 551.

7. *See Silas*, 470 P.3d at 341-42 (noting that the court urged the legislature to amend the DUI statute following *Fenimore*, and it "responded . . . by adding language expanding the scope of the statute and making it clear that private property was included within that scope").

5. Finally, consider how you might interpret the statute in a manner that is both favorable to your client's interests and a good faith, reasonable interpretation of the statute.

   a. If your client must satisfy a standard to avail itself of statutory *privileges*, if possible, advocate an interpretation your client can easily satisfy.

   b. If your client must satisfy a standard before being *penalized* under the statute, if possible, advocate an interpretation that would be difficult for your client to satisfy.

   c. The same considerations apply when advocating a standard that an opposing party must satisfy.

CONSTRUCTING PROOF

To convince an adjudicator to adopt your favorable interpretation, consider the following tools of statutory construction:

1. Can the *plain language* of the statute be construed to support your interpretation?

2. Are there *other sections of the statute* that might support your interpretation?

   • Is there a definition section of the statute that defines a key term?

   • Does the title or preamble to the statute indicate a statutory purpose that favors your interpretation of the statute?

   • Do any of the remaining sections of the statute bolster your interpretation of the statute and its purpose?

3. Is there any *legislative history* that supports your interpretation of the statute, including the plain language and/or the legislative purpose?

4. Are there any *canons of construction* that support your favorable interpretation of the statute? For example:

   • Criminal statutes should be narrowly construed in favor of the defendant.

   • Remedial statutes should be broadly construed.

   • *Ejusdem Generis*—general phrases should be narrowly interpreted to include only those items that have the same characteristics as specific items that were specifically mentioned.

   • *Expressio Unius est Exclusio Alterius*—when a statute expressly lists the conduct or items that it covers, any conduct or items not explicitly mentioned is thereby excluded.

5. Are there favorable *policy* ramifications from your interpretation of the statute, and/or unfavorable policy ramifications from your opponent's interpretation of the statute? (*See* Chapter 27)

- *Note*: Public policy considerations are usually linked to the statutory purpose—courts strive to interpret statutes in a manner that will further the underlying purpose of the statute and have a positive impact on society.

6. Are there court decisions from other jurisdictions that support your statutory interpretation?

DRAFTING LAW-CENTERED ARGUMENTS BASED ON STATUTES & POLICY

I. YOUR FAVORABLE INTERPRETATIONS OF THE LAW AS THE FOCAL POINT

Chapters 27 and 28 discuss the types of arguments available to you when you draft law-centered arguments based on policy and statutory analysis. How might you organize the various arguments into a persuasive, coherent written argument? A good focal point is the favorable interpretation of the law you want to persuade the adjudicator to adopt. Your overall goal is to convince the adjudicator to adopt your interpretation of the statute or common law rule. As you outline and then draft your argument, keep your focus on this goal. Every paragraph should help lead the reader to the conclusion that your interpretation of the statute or common law rule is superior to any other interpretation and should, therefore, be adopted. Thus, every paragraph should help prove how your interpretation favorably affects public policy and, in the case of a statute, why the statutory language supports your interpretation, why the statutory scheme supports your interpretation, and/or how your interpretation furthers the underlying purpose of the statute.

As you advance these arguments, you should weave in arguments that illustrate how your opponent's interpretation fails to accomplish these goals. Keeping your focus on the ultimate goal can also help you edit and polish your initial drafts. As you review your initial drafts, make margin notes describing the premise of each paragraph. If the paragraph does not serve any of these purposes, then it does not belong in a persuasive argument.

II. ASSESS THE PERSUASIVE APPEAL OF
YOUR SEPARATE ARGUMENTS

Consider the various arguments you have identified from reading both the statute or common law rule, and persuasive precedent. By the time you sit down to outline and draft your argument, you should have a list of each of the arguments that support your favorable interpretation of the law. Most of your ideas have likely been gleaned from reading persuasive case precedent. You may have discovered other ideas from reading law review articles or other secondary sources. You may also have identified other arguments from your own evaluation of the rule of law. Whatever the source, review your list of arguments and begin to rank them, from "most persuasive" to "least persuasive." You ultimately will draft a brief that begins with your strongest argument, followed by the next strongest argument, and so on.

As you review your list of potential arguments, omit entirely any arguments that are so weak that they might dilute the strength of other arguments or weaken your credibility. Include only those arguments that a reasonable person would find persuasive in evaluating the meaning of the statute or common law rule of law.

A. When a Statute Is the Source of Law

When a *statute* is the source of law, the statute's plain language is the first step of any court's inquiry into a statute's meaning. After all, the statutory language itself is the strongest proof of the statute's meaning. If the statutory language supports your conclusion, this is your strongest argument—begin your argument by arguing why the statutory language compels, or at least supports, your interpretation. Recall, however, that not every statute lends itself to such an argument. For example, the term "satisfactory explanation" in the federal wiretap statute is so broad and vague that it does not lend itself to an argument based on the language of the statute. Therefore, include this argument only if it makes sense to do so with the statutory language you are interpreting.

Also consider how the statutory scheme as a whole may support your argument; next to the statutory language of the disputed provision, this type of argument is often the next most persuasive argument. As you consider how the statutory language or statutory scheme supports your favorable interpretation, also consider how the legislative purpose of the statute supports your interpretation. After the statutory text itself, the next best evidence of a statute's meaning is the underlying purpose of the statute. The legislative purpose is often referenced in the statute's legislative history. A statute's legislative history can be an effective tool to bolster a plain language argument. However, it is difficult to persuade an adjudicator to ignore a statute's plain language when the statutory purpose, as reflected in its legislative history, seemingly conflicts with the text of the statute. Indeed, if the statutory language is clear enough, courts often refuse to examine the statute's legislative purpose to arrive at a contrary interpretation.

B. Weaving in Persuasive Precedent

1. Generally, Use Persuasive Precedent Merely to Support Your Arguments

As you evaluate the importance of various arguments, it can be a challenge to decide whether, and how, to include persuasive case precedent into the argument. Generally, the policy and statutory arguments described in Chapters 27 and 28 are the engine that runs a persuasive argument; persuasive authority cases are generally not used as separate arguments in and of themselves. For example, an advocate does not argue: "Title VII does not impose individual liability because the Fifth Circuit Court of Appeals said so." Such outright appeals to follow another court's decision are not persuasive because an adjudicator's responsibility is to interpret the *rule of law*, not to follow courts in other jurisdictions.

Instead, incorporate persuasive case precedent into your argument to add weight and credibility to the statutory and policy arguments that you are advocating in your brief. Therefore, as you evaluate the strength of each of your statutory and policy arguments, make a note of the cases from which you obtained these ideas, and those cases that agree with your ideas. Citations to such cases will add credibility to your statutory and policy arguments when you attempt to persuade the adjudicator to adopt your favorable interpretation of the law. (Moreover, it would be considered plagiarism to fail to cite to cases from which you obtained your ideas.) If the language from a case is clear and persuasive, you might quote such language to illustrate a particular point from a policy or statutory interpretation argument. If not, simply craft the argument in your own words and then cite the case to lend credibility to your argument.

For example, in the following illustration excerpted from the sample Title VII brief in Appendix D, the writer argues that imposing liability on individual employees for violating Title VII would create an absurd result. The lawyer found a case from another jurisdiction that agrees with this argument. After developing his argument, the lawyer simply cited to the case, as follows:

> ... Individuals who are "agents" of employers with fewer than fifteen employees would be exempt from liability—as an agent of an employer with fewer than fifteen employees, they would fall within the statutory exemption. In contrast, individuals who are "agents" of employers with fifteen or more employees would be liable in their individual capacities. Because their employer would not fall within the exemption, they would similarly not be exempt. Congress could not have intended this result. *Hudson v. Soft Sheen Prods.*, 873 F. Supp. 132, 135 n.2 (N.D. Ill. 1995).

Later in the argument, the lawyer found language in another case that was so persuasive he decided to quote the language:

> "It is unreasonable to think that Congress would protect small entities from the costs associated with litigating discrimination claims and limit the available compensatory and punitive damages based on the size of the... employer, but subject an individual supervisory employee to unlimited liability." *Haltek*, 864 F. Supp. at 805.

In the above illustrations, notice that the lawyer did not begin each argument by highlighting the court opinions themselves. For example, the lawyer didn't argue: "The Northern District of Illinois found that 'it is unreasonable to think that Congress would....'" Emphasizing a district court case from another jurisdiction doesn't serve a persuasive purpose; in fact, the emphasis on the court itself tends to make the argument appear to be an opinion over which reasonable courts could differ rather than a statement of "truth." Instead, the above arguments advance the policy arguments the lawyer gleaned from reading the *Hudson* and *Haltek* cases, citing to these two cases only as support for the policy arguments themselves.

2. When Persuasive Precedent Can Be Its Own Argument

Although persuasive precedent often does not serve as its own separate argument, there are exceptions. Cases from other jurisdictions become a separate argument when the cases have their own persuasive impact, separate and apart from the statutory interpretation or policy arguments you are advocating. Persuasive case precedent has its own persuasive impact when the majority of circuits that have evaluated the disputed issue have adopted your favorable interpretation. Cases from other jurisdictions also have their own persuasive impact when the cases help prove that your favorable interpretation represents a trend in the law. Under these circumstances, make the case law from other jurisdictions a separate argument. For example, you might argue:

> The majority of circuits that have considered this issue have correctly interpreted the statute in accordance with its plain language. *See, e.g.,* [string cite of cases supporting this proposition].

3. Sometimes, Emphasize the Identity of the Court Itself

When the identity of a court has particular persuasive appeal, it is persuasive to emphasize the court itself. For example, you might find a favorable idea or quote from a decision of the United States Supreme Court or of a higher-level court within your jurisdiction. These decisions would not, of course, have resolved the disputed legal issue—if they had, you would not be arguing what the statute or common law rule of law means. Although these decisions may not have resolved the disputed legal issue, they may, nevertheless, contain language that supports your underlying argument. The following example illustrates how to draw the judge's attention to the court itself:

> As the United States Supreme Court made abundantly clear, "the purpose of the legislation, which was passed in 1968, was effectively to prohibit… *all* interceptions of oral and wire communications *except those specifically provided for in the Act*." *United States v. Giordano*, 416 U.S. 505, 514 (1974) (emphasis added).

III. OUTLINING YOUR ARGUMENT

After you have prioritized your arguments according to their relative strengths, you are in a position to sketch a template of your argument. Recall the deductive writing pattern of an office memo. The deductive writing pattern begins with broad principles and then illustrates the broad principles with specific information. You will use the same deductive writing pattern when structuring an argument. However, the deductive pattern will be focused on achieving your ultimate goal—to persuade an adjudicator to give your client the relief the client desires. The most effective way to achieve that goal is by using an organizational structure that is so logical and reasonable that the reader cannot help but agree with your conclusion. As Judge Aldisert, Senior United States Circuit Judge for the Third Circuit Court of Appeals, notes:

> Your objective… should be to start with a proposition that the court—whatever its bent—must accept; then reason, logically, step by step, to your conclusion. If you do this well, you will arrive at your destination with the court right beside you. Your conclusion will make sense, not just because you say so, but because the court will have reasoned along with you.[1]

A. Create a Skeleton Outline of Your Argument

How might you achieve this goal of logically, step by step, leading an adjudicator to your conclusion? First, write down the ultimate conclusion you want the adjudicator to reach—your favorable interpretation of the statute. Next, review your list of arguments and fill in the essential, major points you will need to make in order to prove why your interpretation is sound ("*major premises*"). These major premises provide the skeleton outline of your argument. Using the Title VII argument excerpted from Appendix D for purposes of illustration, a skeleton outline of the defendant's argument would look like this:

---

1. Ruggero J. Aldisert, *Winning on Appeal: Better Briefs & Oral Argument* 146 (NITA 1992).

Ultimate conclusion to prove: Title VII, including the 1991 Amendments, imposes liability only on employers, not individual employees.

Major premises:

I. The plain language of Title VII imposes liability only on employers and not on individual employees.

II. The 1991 Amendments expanded only the scope of available remedies and did not expand the class of defendants to include individual employees.

III. Restricting liability to employers achieves Title VII's goals of compensation and deterrence.

B. Fill in the Broad Supporting Points that Prove Each of the Major Premises

After you have drafted the major premises you will use to prove your conclusion, next consider the arguments that support each of the major premises. You might visualize the process as an unfolding accordion, with the broad skeleton outline as a closed accordion. The accordion begins to unfold in this step, as you fill in the skeleton outline, as follows:

Ultimate conclusion to prove: Title VII, including the 1991 Amendments, imposes liability only on employers, not individual employees.

I. **1st Major Premise:** The plain language of Title VII imposes liability only on employers and not on individual employees.

Two Broad Supporting Points:

1. Title VII's definition of "employer" reflects its intention to impose liability only on employers.

2. Original remedies available to plaintiffs under Title VII confirm that liability is imposed only on employers.

II. **2nd Major Premise:** The 1991 Amendments expanded only the scope of available remedies and did not expand the class of defendants to include individual employees.

Three Broad Supporting Points:

1. The original definition of "employer" and "agent" was left undisturbed.

2. The new damages provisions reflect that Congress intended to make employers exclusively liable.

3. Legislative history under the 1991 Amendments reflects the intent to restrict liability to employers.

III. **3rd Major Premise:** Restricting liability to employers achieves Title VII's goals of compensation and deterrence.

Three Broad Supporting Points:
1. 1991 Amendments ensure that plaintiffs will be adequately compensated from the entity best able to provide compensation—the employer.
2. 1991 Amendments serve a deterrent purpose because employers now have an incentive to police their workplaces.
3. Individual employees are already adequately deterred.

C. Fill in the "Proof" for Each Broad Supporting Point

Before beginning the drafting process, many lawyers create an even more detailed outline, filling in the structure of the "proof" that will support each broad supporting point. They reason that the outlining process ultimately saves them time while drafting the Argument because they can begin the drafting process with a clear idea of each of the arguments they will need to make. Other lawyers prefer to begin drafting at this point, reasoning that they can think more clearly as they draft; after drafting the Argument, they cut and paste various sections of the Argument to ensure that the final draft is logical and persuasive. Choose the process that works most effectively for you. However, whether you fill in the details of your outline further or begin drafting at this point, the template of your final draft should resemble a fully opened accordion that clearly lays out each step of your analysis.

1. Template of the Argument

The template of a completed Argument should look like this:

I. Ultimate Conclusion
   A. First major premise that proves the conclusion
      1. First broad supporting point that proves the major premise
         a. 1st proof for first broad supporting point
         b. 2nd proof for first broad supporting point
         c. And so on
      2. Second broad supporting point that proves the major premise
         a. 1st proof for second broad supporting point
         b. 2nd proof for second broad supporting point
         c. And so on
      3. And so on
   B. Second major premise that proves the conclusion

1. First broad supporting point that proves the second major premise
   a. 1st proof for first broad supporting point
   b. 2nd proof for first broad supporting point
   c. And so on
2. Second broad supporting point that proves the second major premise
   a. 1st proof for second broad supporting point
   b. 2nd proof for second broad supporting point
   c. And so on
3. And so on

C. Third major premise that proves the conclusion

And so on…

2. Illustration of Detailed Outline for the Title VII Argument

Ultimate conclusion to prove: Title VII, including the 1991 Amendments, imposes liability only on employers, not individual employees.

A. **1st major premise:** The plain language of Title VII imposes liability only on employers and not on individual employees.
   1. Title VII's definition of "employer" reflects its intention to impose liability only on employers.
      a. Only employers can have 15 or more employees.
      b. Because the statute links the word "agent" to the term "employer," imposing individual liability would create an absurd result—individual liability would be dependent on whether the employer had more than 15 employees.
      c. Imposing liability on individuals would thwart Congress' purpose in shielding entities with limited resources.
   2. Original remedies available to plaintiffs under Title VII confirm that liability is imposed only on employers.
      a. Original remedies are restricted to remedies only an employer can provide.

B. **2nd major premise:** The 1991 Amendments expanded only the scope of remedies available to plaintiffs and did not expand the class of defendants to include individual employees.
   1. The original definition of "employer" and "agent" was left undisturbed.
      a. If Congress had wanted to change the definition, it would have done so.

> 2. The new damages provisions reflect that Congress intended to make employers exclusively liable.
>   a. Congress calibrated the damage caps based only on employer size, not individuals.
>   b. Imposing individual liability would create absurd results, either:
>   i   Unlimited individual liability, or
>   ii. Individual liability tied to the size of the employer.
> 3. Legislative history under the 1991 Amendments reflects the intent to restrict liability to employers.
>   a. Congress focused exclusively on employers, both in terms of:
>   i. Compensation, and
>   ii. Deterrence.
>   b. Legislative history is silent re: individuals.
> C. **3rd major premise:** Restricting liability to employers achieves Title VII's purposes of compensation and deterrence.
>   1. 1991 Amendments ensure that plaintiffs will be adequately compensated from the entity best able to provide compensation.
>   2. 1991 Amendments serve a deterrent purpose because employers now have incentive to police their workplaces.
>   3. Individual employees are already adequately deterred:
>   a. Professional and social sanctions
>   b. Civil and criminal liability

Exercise 29-1

Carefully review the sample brief in Appendix E that evaluates the federal wiretap statute. Then draft an outline of the law-centered argument following the first point-heading: I. AS PART OF ITS "SATISFACTORY EXPLANATION," THE GOVERNMENT MUST PROVE THAT ITS PRE-SEALING PROCEDURES PROTECTED THE WIRETAP TAPES FROM ANY POSSIBILITY OF TAMPERING.

In your outline, begin with the conclusion the advocate wants the judge to adopt. Following that conclusion, outline the template of that argument, including: (1) the major premise or premises that support the conclusion; (2) the broad supporting points that support each major premise; and (3) the more detailed proof that supports each broad supporting point.

IV. ROADMAP PARAGRAPHS

A. The Introduction Section—Briefs Before Courts

After you have drafted the argument, you are in a position to draft "roadmap" paragraphs that will ultimately make your argument easier for an adjudicator to follow and, therefore, more persuasive. In many arguments before courts, the argument begins with an "Introduction" that precedes the statement of facts. Each of the sample trial level briefs illustrated in Appendices C and D contain a separate Introduction. In an appellate court brief, the introductory section is called the "Summary of Argument." Chapter 33 provides a more detailed explanation of a formal Summary of Argument, and illustrates that section of a brief submitted to a court.

B. The Overview Paragraph

Whether or not your written argument is submitted to a court, your argument will begin with roadmap paragraphs that outline for the reader the basic points your argument will make. If your argument spans two or more issues, you may wish to draft an overview paragraph that provides a roadmap of the argument that will follow. The overview paragraph would simply identify the separate elements of the statute or common law rule of law that will be the subject of your argument. However, if you have already provided the adjudicator with a roadmap of the argument in a separate Introduction section, an overview paragraph may be unnecessary and repetitive.

C. The Thesis Paragraph

For each issue of any complexity, draft a thesis paragraph that provides a roadmap of the specific issue under discussion; a fairly simplistic issue may not require a separate thesis paragraph. Because you are drafting a document that is intended to persuade the reader, the thesis paragraph is a wonderful opportunity to summarize the most important reasons why your interpretation of the law is sound. In a thesis paragraph: (1) identify the important statutory language, if any; (2) summarize the major premises that support your legal issue conclusion; (3) depending upon the complexity of the issue, summarize the broad supporting points that prove each major premise; and (4) state the ultimate conclusion you want the adjudicator to adopt. Depending upon the complexity of the issue and your development of the argument, the conclusion can be stated at the beginning of the thesis paragraph or after you have laid the groundwork for why the conclusion is sound. As an example, the criminal wiretap brief that is illustrated in Appendix E begins the law-centered argument with the following thesis paragraphs:

Statutory rule of law.

> Title III states in no uncertain terms: "The presence of the seal as provided for by this subsection [an immediate seal], or a satisfactory explanation for the absence thereof, shall be a *prerequisite* for the use or disclosure" of the

tapes. 18 U.S.C. § 2518(8)(a) (emphasis added). In this issue of first impression, the plain language of Title III requires that the Government comply with one of two procedures as a "prerequisite" to introducing wiretap tapes into evidence during trial. Concerned with the abuse of electronic surveillance techniques, Congress enacted the first prerequisite, the immediate sealing requirement, as an external safeguard to ensure that the integrity of wiretap tapes would remain inviolate.

> Persuasive explanation of the statutory language that supports the advocate's major premise (broad supporting proof).

When the Government fails to protect the integrity of the tapes by immediately obtaining a judicial seal, the Government's alternative satisfactory explanation must ensure a similar level of protection. Whether the Government satisfies the legislative requirement of obtaining an immediate seal, or takes the scenic route to obtain the seal, the Government must prove that its *procedures* protected the integrity of the tapes. Without such a safeguard, the statutory protective device of immediate judicial supervision would be rendered meaningless. *United States v. Johnson*, 696 F.2d 115 (D.C. Cir. 1981). Accordingly, the District Court erred in failing to require the Government to prove that its pre-sealing procedures protected the tapes from any possibility of tampering. As a pure question of law, this issue is subject to de novo review.

> Major premise.

> Conclusion.

> Broad supporting proof as to why the major premise is sound.

CHAPTER IN REVIEW

Core Concepts

PRE-OUTLINING STRATEGY

1. Keeping in mind the favorable construction of the rule of law you want to convince the adjudicator to adopt, review your notes, considering the range of possible statutory construction and policy arguments available to you.

2. Consider the relative strength of the various arguments and rank them in order from the strongest to the weakest argument.
   - *Tip*: As you evaluate the relative strength of possible arguments, consider the following:
     i. If the *plain language* of the statute can be construed to support your favorable interpretation, begin with that argument.

ii. If there are *other sections of the statute* that support your favorable interpretation, such an argument would usually follow a plain language argument.

- *Exception*: When the other statutory sections do not clearly support your position, and you have other, stronger arguments listed below

iii. A statute's *legislative history* can also be persuasive, particularly if the history clearly supports a common sense reading of the statute.

iv. Public policy arguments can also be strong arguments.

v. Canons of construction, while valid tools to construe statutes, are not usually as compelling as the arguments listed above.

vi. Generally, do not list persuasive case precedent as separate arguments, but use them instead to lend support and add credibility to the statutory construction and policy arguments listed above.

- *Exception*: When a majority of circuits have adopted your favorable interpretation, draw attention to those line of cases.
- *Exception*: When your favorable interpretation represents a trend in the law, draw attention to the line of recent cases that have adopted your favorable interpretation.

OUTLINING AND DRAFTING YOUR ARGUMENT

1. Write down the ultimate conclusion you want the adjudicator to adopt—your favorable interpretation of the rule of law.

2. Next, fill in the essential, major points you will need to make in order to prove why your interpretation is sound ("major premises").
   - These major premises will serve as your skeleton outline—therefore, leave enough space between each point to flesh out the outline further.

3. Next, under each major premise, list each broad supporting point that illustrates why the major premise is sound.

4. Depending upon your individual writing style:
   a. Make notes of the more detailed proof that illustrates each broad supporting point; or
   b. Begin writing, allowing the more detailed proof to take form as you draft the argument.

5. After drafting the argument, then draft persuasive roadmap paragraphs.

ADDRESSING UNFAVORABLE LAW
AND ARGUMENTS

As you evaluate the cases you might incorporate into a persuasive argument, one of the first decisions you must make is whether to exclude any of the cases from your argument that have unfavorable language in them. If you have uncovered a case that is both binding precedent and also "directly adverse" to your client's legal position, you actually have an ethical duty to disclose the case.[1] In other words, if mandatory precedent interprets the rule of law in a manner that's unfavorable to your client's position, you have an ethical duty to disclose the binding precedent. With that said, if an adverse case is factually distinguishable from your client's situation in a legally significant way, then the case is not considered "directly adverse." Instead, it is merely unfavorable precedent that, while potentially damaging, is not considered to be "directly" adverse.

Even if you have no ethical obligation to disclose an adverse case, there may be pragmatic reasons for you to do so. An unfavorable case may be so important that you might damage your credibility by failing to disclose the case, or you may be able to minimize the damage from your opponent's potential disclosure of the unfavorable law by skillfully distinguishing the case. If you decide to disclose the case, you must also decide whether to emphasize the favorable components of the case, thereby distinguishing it from your client's situation, or to directly attack the case as unsound. Chapters 24 and 25 discuss how to factually distinguish cases with unfavorable holdings. This chapter discusses how to directly and indirectly rebut unfavorable law.

Rebuttal takes two basic forms: direct rebuttal and anticipatory rebuttal. You can directly rebut unfavorable law in two ways. First, you can directly attack an opponent's *interpretation* of the law as unsound. Under this approach, the attack is not on the adverse law itself, but on the opponent's interpretation of that law. Alternatively, you can directly attack an *adverse case* itself as unsound. Under this approach, you

---

1. Model R. Prof. Conduct 3.3(a)(2) (ABA 2002).

would directly attack the reasoning of the adverse case. Direct rebuttal is discussed and illustrated in Part I of this chapter.

Anticipatory rebuttal, on the other hand, is more subtle. As its name suggests, when engaging in anticipatory rebuttal, you will anticipate an opponent's argument and subtly weave into your own arguments indirect suggestions and innuendos that subtly rebut the opponent's argument. Part II of this chapter discusses and illustrates anticipatory rebuttal.

I. Direct Rebuttal

A. Direct Rebuttal of the Other Side's *Potential Arguments*

When responding to arguments the opposing counsel has already made, you will rebut those arguments because you won't want an adjudicator to consider only the other side's interpretation of the law. However, for ethical or pragmatic reasons, you may also decide to rebut unfavorable interpretations of the law even when your opposing counsel has not yet flagged the adverse law. To anticipate your opponent's arguments, figuratively place yourself in the opposing counsel's shoes. As you evaluate a statute or group of cases, consider not just your own favorable arguments, but the arguments the opposing counsel is likely to make from the same statute or group of cases. Assuming the role of the opposing counsel, consider every argument you might make to win the case. Still playing the role of opposing counsel, make note of the following arguments:

1. In the case of a statute, whether the *statutory language and/or its legislative history* supports the opponent's argument;

2. Whether there is *language in any case* that supports the opponent's argument (both favorable and unfavorable cases may have language that supports the opponent);

3. Whether there are *factual distinctions* to and *comparisons* from precedent cases that support the opponent;

4. Whether any *policy* considerations support your opponent's argument; and

5. Whether there are any *common sense* arguments you think would favor the opponent, even if not directly addressed in a case or statute.

With respect to each potential opposing argument, consider your response. For example, if there is statutory language that favors the opposing party, is there other statutory language that favors your client? If not, does your interpretation more closely further the legislative purpose? If there is language or facts from a precedent case that favors the opposing party, is there competing language or facts that minimizes or undercuts the adverse impact of such language? If policy considerations favor the opposing party, are there competing policy concerns that favor your client's argument?

B. Direct Rebuttal of an *Adverse Case* Itself

For ethical or pragmatic reasons, you may decide to directly rebut an adverse case or group of cases upon which the other side has already relied or certainly will rely. When directly rebutting the reasoning or validity of an adverse case itself, you can minimize the impact of the adverse case by saving the direct rebuttal until the end of your own argument. It is far more persuasive to argue first why your own position is "right" so that the adjudicator is already persuaded of the soundness of *your* position before considering the unfavorable law. An opposing argument loses much of its persuasive appeal when the adjudicator is already viewing the problem from your own favorable perspective before reading a discussion of the unfavorable case. Moreover, by arguing the favorable law first, you provide the adjudicator with a favorable conceptual framework, or lens, from which to consider the adverse law.

When convincing an adjudicator to reject an unfavorable case, you can either attack the unfavorable court's reasoning or argue that the unfavorable case is no longer "good law."

1. Attack the Unfavorable Court's Reasoning

The examples in Chapter 28 illustrate how you can attack the other side's *position*. When attacking a specific court's reasoning, however, your focus should be on the faulty reasoning within the unfavorable case itself. For example, you might argue how the reasoning of the unfavorable case would produce an inequitable and unfair result to the parties (the *equities* argument from Chapter 27). You might also argue how the unfavorable case would have negative public policy ramifications (the *public policy* argument from Chapter 27). You might also argue how the unfavorable case would negatively impact the functioning of the court system (the *prudential concerns* argument from Chapter 27). If the source of the law is statutory, you might also argue how the court ignored the plain language of a statute, failed to consider the statutory scheme as a whole, or ignored the statutory purpose (the *plain language*, *statutory scheme*, and *legislative purpose* arguments from Chapter 28).

The following example builds on the Title VII problem illustrated in Sample Brief A in Appendix D. Title VII prohibits employers from discriminating against employees on the basis of their sex, among other protected classifications. The statute defines the term "employer" to include "any agent" of the employer. The term "agent" is ambiguous. Prior to 1991, when Title VII was amended, some lawyers argued that the term "agent" merely incorporated *respondeat superior* liability into the statute, with the employer thereby liable for the acts of its agents. Other lawyers argued that the term "agent" made supervisory employees personally liable. However, prior to 1991, the conflicting interpretations had little practical effect on the outcome because plaintiffs could recover only injunctive relief (reinstatement or hiring) or up to two years of back-pay.[2] These remedies are available only against an employer, not individual employees. In 1991, Congress amended Title VII to allow plaintiffs to recover compensatory and punitive damages.[3] The expanded remedies only intensified the debate.

Sample Brief A in Appendix D illustrates the defendant's arguments. For purposes of this present discussion, however, assume that the defendant decides to attack an unfavorable case directly—the *Jendusa* case. Assume that the defendant is arguing the case before a federal district court in Illinois. The *Jendusa* case is also a federal district court case within Illinois. Because the *Jendusa* case is not a higher level court, it is not binding on another federal trial court judge. Nevertheless, it is certainly persuasive, and the defendant therefore elects to attack directly the *Jendusa* case.

Premise: Court incorrectly interpreted the law by ignoring legislative intent.

In *Jendusa*, the court ignored the overwhelming evidence that Congress did not intend to expand liability under Title VII to individual employees. 868 F. Supp. at 1016.

Proof: Court misinterpreted isolated reference in legislative history.

Instead, the *Jendusa* court took a single isolated reference in the Committee Reports and misinterpreted it. The *Jendusa* court reasoned that Congress must have envisioned individual liability because the Committee Reports cite *Zabkowicz* as one example of why the 1991 Amendments were necessary. In citing *Zabkowicz*, the Committee Reports note that the "corporate employer and its officers" had violated Title VII. *Id.* From that isolated reference to an employer's "officers," the *Jendusa* court leapt to the faulty conclusion that Congress must have intended to make individuals liable.

Openly identifies two flaws in the court's reasoning.

The *Jendusa* court's reasoning has two flaws. First, the court failed to recognize that in *Zabkowicz*, the supervisory employees were liable in their official capacity only, not in their personal capacity. The plaintiff in that case recovered only back-pay. Second, the Congressional lament in citing *Zabkowicz* was the *paucity* of the award (only two months back-pay), not the limited *scope* of the award. *Hudson*, 873 F. Supp at 136. In other words, Con-

---

2. 42 U.S.C. § 2000e-5(g).
3. 42 U.S.C. § 1981a.

gress was concerned that individuals were not able to recover fair compensation for their injuries, not that they
were restricted to seeking damages from employers.

2. Argue that the Unfavorable Case Is No Longer "Good Law"

Another way to attack an adverse case is to argue that the precedent is no longer
"good law." If the adverse case is older than the favorable case you want the adjudicator to follow, you might argue that the older case no longer reflects present policy,
and/or that it has been implicitly overruled by more recent case law. To illustrate this
type of argument, consider the Fifth Amendment problem discussed and illustrated
in Chapter 26 (Sample Brief B in Appendix D). In that hypothetical problem, the
Government is prosecuting the defendant, Mr. Browne, for unlawful distribution of
drugs. The Government has issued a subpoena to obtain Mr. Browne's personal diary. The Government contends that the diary contains entries that reflect Mr. Browne's
illegal drug activities. Rather than turning over the diary to the Government,
Browne's lawyer has filed a Motion to Quash the subpoena. Browne's lawyer argues
that Mr. Browne's personal diary is protected by the Fifth Amendment of the United
States Constitution. The Fifth Amendment protects people from self-incrimination.
However, the language is vague and general, leaving courts to resolve specific issues
as to the Amendment's meaning. The Amendment states that: "No person... shall
be compelled in any criminal case to be a witness against himself...." U.S. Const.
amend. V.

Browne's lawyer argues that the Fifth Amendment should be broadly construed to
protect persons from incriminating themselves with their written documents as well
as their oral testimony. Browne has a good Supreme Court case that has adopted this
position—the *Boyd* case. However, this Supreme Court case is an old case, and its
holding has been eroded over the years. As Chapter 26 discussed and illustrated,
Browne's lawyer attempted to convince the court that more recent Supreme Court
cases (*Fisher* and *Doe*) had not overruled *Boyd*. In attempting to convince the court of
that argument, Browne narrowly interpreted the holdings in *Fisher* and *Doe* so as to
preserve the holding in the earlier *Boyd* case.

For present purposes, however, consider the Government's argument. The Government's lawyer would argue that the Fifth Amendment should be narrowly construed to protect persons from incriminating themselves only with respect to their
oral testimony. The Government would argue that the Fifth Amendment does not
also protect persons from incriminating themselves with their *written* documents.
Thus, the Government would argue that the holdings in *Fisher* and *Doe* should be
broadly construed and that they implicitly overruled the early *Boyd* case. The Government would attempt to convince the court to ignore the early *Boyd* case as no
longer "good law":

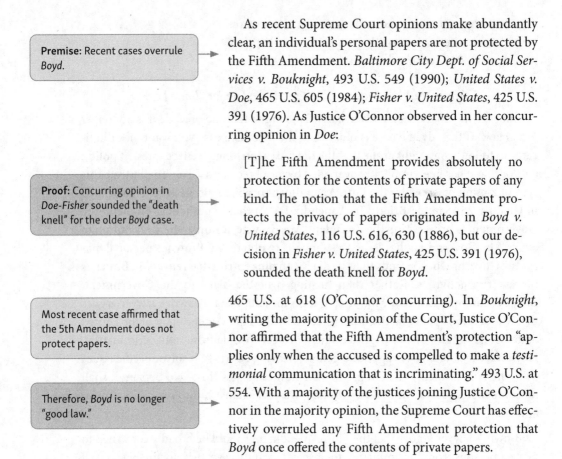

Premise: Recent cases overrule *Boyd.*

As recent Supreme Court opinions make abundantly clear, an individual's personal papers are not protected by the Fifth Amendment. *Baltimore City Dept. of Social Services v. Bouknight*, 493 U.S. 549 (1990); *United States v. Doe*, 465 U.S. 605 (1984); *Fisher v. United States*, 425 U.S. 391 (1976). As Justice O'Connor observed in her concurring opinion in *Doe*:

Proof: Concurring opinion in *Doe-Fisher* sounded the "death knell" for the older *Boyd* case.

> [T]he Fifth Amendment provides absolutely no protection for the contents of private papers of any kind. The notion that the Fifth Amendment protects the privacy of papers originated in *Boyd v. United States*, 116 U.S. 616, 630 (1886), but our decision in *Fisher v. United States*, 425 U.S. 391 (1976), sounded the death knell for *Boyd*.

Most recent case affirmed that the 5th Amendment does not protect papers.

465 U.S. at 618 (O'Connor concurring). In *Bouknight*, writing the majority opinion of the Court, Justice O'Connor affirmed that the Fifth Amendment's protection "applies only when the accused is compelled to make a *testimonial* communication that is incriminating." 493 U.S. at 554. With a majority of the justices joining Justice O'Connor in the majority opinion, the Supreme Court has effectively overruled any Fifth Amendment protection that *Boyd* once offered the contents of private papers.

Therefore, *Boyd* is no longer "good law."

C. Drafting Strategy

1. Affirm Client's Position First

There are several ways in which you might engage in direct rebuttal: in an opening brief before a judge, or, alternatively, in a responsive or reply brief. In briefs before courts, the moving party typically files the first brief, and the opposing party has an opportunity to file a responsive brief. Often, the moving party then has an opportunity to file a reply brief. However, whether filing an initial brief, responsive brief, or reply brief, the drafting strategy remains essentially the same—argue first why the law favors your client's position before attacking the position of the opposing party. You want the judge to view the law and facts from within the context of your own favorable interpretation of the law rather than from the opponent's position. If you were to attack the other party's position first and argue why that position is unsound, you would be inviting the judge to view the law and facts from within the context of the other party's framework rather than your own. Instead, by first convincing the judge of the persuasive appeal of your *client's* position, your direct rebuttal will be even more compelling. The other side's argument loses much of its persuasive appeal when you have already convinced the judge to view the problem from *your* perspective first. Thus, the favorable argument constructs discussed in Chapters 25, 26, and 29 remain intact whether or not you also elect to directly rebut the other side's interpretation of the law.

To review an illustration of this argument strategy, see Sample Brief A in Appendix D, in which the advocate argues that Title VII does not impose liability on individual employees. In that argument, the lawyer contends that the plain language of the statute itself restricts liability to employers—an argument affirming the client's position. Directly following that plain language argument, the advocate directly criticizes any opposing interpretation of the statutory language. Next, the lawyer argues that the statutory scheme as a whole supports the defendant's favorable interpretation—again, an argument that affirms the client's position (*see* first full paragraph under Section II.B). Only then, after arguing his own position first, does the advocate argue why the statutory scheme is inconsistent with the opponent's argument—a direct attack on the opponent's argument.

2. A Note About Reply Briefs

If you are in the position of filing a reply brief, you will have already educated the judge about the persuasive appeal of your argument in the first brief you filed with the court. Because the opposing counsel filed a brief in *response* to your opening brief, an important purpose of the reply brief is to attack the soundness of the arguments that were made in that responsive brief. However, even in a reply brief, it's important to argue the law from within your own favorable argument structure rather than from the other side's less favorable framework.

This can be challenging for several reasons. First, you understandably do not want to try the judge's patience by repeating your earlier argument in detail. Nonetheless, you do want to remind the judge of the force of your own arguments, particularly because the reply brief may well be the last brief the judge reads, and the arguments will linger in the judge's mind. Second, you must also resist the temptation to appear defensive as you rebut each of the other party's arguments point by point. To accomplish the dual goals of reminding the judge of the force of your own arguments while also attacking the soundness of the opposing counsel's arguments, first summarize for the judge the important points of your argument. Then, point by point, after first *summarizing* why your argument is sound, attack the soundness of the opposing party's position.

II. ANTICIPATORY REBUTTAL

After evaluating relevant ethical and pragmatic considerations, suppose you decide not to rebut directly an adverse case or an unfavorable interpretation of the law you anticipate the opponent might make. However, just because you decide not to openly rebut an argument does not mean that you should wholly ignore the adverse law or unfavorable legal interpretation. There is always the risk that opposing counsel may well artfully advance the argument you have chosen to ignore. If you have not anticipated your opposing counsel's argument and taken steps to minimize the damaging nature of that argument, the adjudicator will consider the argument for the first time while reading the other party's very persuasive argument. To avoid this result, effective advocates weave into their own arguments indirect suggestions and innuendos that anticipate and subtly rebut an opponent's argument. This strategy is called "anticipatory rebuttal."

Anticipatory rebuttal can protect you from either consequence of the calculated risk not to rebut an adverse case or argument directly. Should the opposing counsel fail to address the adverse argument, you will not have unnecessarily educated the other party about a plausible argument. On the other hand, should the opposing counsel ultimately advance the unfavorable argument, you will have defused the persuasive impact of that adverse argument by subtly anticipating and rebutting it within the body of your own argument. Moreover, you will usually have the opportunity to file a reply brief and directly rebut the opponent's argument later. If the relevant procedural rules don't permit you to file a reply brief later, you should take that procedural limitation into account when you calculate the risk of relying on anticipatory rebuttal rather than direct rebuttal.

You can use anticipatory rebuttal to anticipate and rebut a single unfavorable fact, an entire unfavorable case, or a single unfavorable part of a case that may otherwise be favorable. Therefore, you can weave anticipatory rebuttal into any part of an argument, from the introductory paragraph, through the factual statement, through the body of the argument itself. Depending on the adverse law you are rebutting, anticipatory rebuttal can be as subtle as a single adjective, or sweep through an entire argument. Because anticipatory rebuttal can be woven into any part of an argument, anticipatory rebuttal is an effective strategy even when you have decided to engage in direct rebuttal of an argument or adverse case. Thus, the seed for direct rebuttal may subtly be planted within the introductory paragraph, the factual statement, or during the discussion of a case. Such seeds, planted earlier in the argument, can predispose the adjudicator to view your direct rebuttal in a more favorable light.

How might you anticipate and plan an anticipatory rebuttal strategy? In Part I, we evaluated how you would openly rebut an opponent's unfavorable arguments. The pre-drafting strategy does not change for anticipatory rebuttal. Prior to drafting the argument, consider the opponent's arguments by figuratively placing yourself in your opponent's shoes. Assuming the role of your opponent, consider every argument the opponent might make to win the case and then consider your responses to such arguments.

After carefully considering your opponent's arguments and your rebuttal to each argument, you are ready to weave anticipatory rebuttal into the argument itself. Depending on the adverse law you are rebutting, anticipatory rebuttal can be as subtle as a single adjective, or sweep through an entire argument.

◎ ILLUSTRATION: Spousal Wiretap Problem

Recall the sample spousal wiretap problem illustrated in Appendix C. The plaintiff's attorney argues that his client, Mr. Harrison, did not consent to his former wife's recording of his telephone calls. Mr. Harrison's best argument is the ambiguous nature of his former wife's "notice" about recording telephone calls. In that conversation, the defendant told her estranged husband that she was concerned that the housekeeper "not make improper use of the telephone." The lawyer's pre-drafting notes might look something like this:

My Argument	Opponent's Response
1. The Defendant's "notice" was ambiguous and did not warn my client that *any* recording would occur, much less the manner and scope of monitoring.	1. But the conversation must be taken within the context of the couple's past practices of recording telephone calls—the *Griggs-Ryan* court states that the fact-finder must consider the "surrounding circumstances"—the couple's past practices are important surrounding circumstances.
2. I agree that the "surrounding circumstances" must be considered, but the important surrounding circumstances here are the couple's legal separation and pending divorce. • *Williams* case—concluded that it was unlikely the plaintiff would have consented to the recording of his telephone calls because he was in a "feud" with the defendants. • As in *Williams*, my client would not have consented to the recording of his telephone calls because he was in the midst of divorce proceedings.	2. There is a critical distinction between the feud in *Williams* and the couple's strained marital relationship. Mr. Harrison loves his child and has testified that his child's best interests are paramount—that's why he not only consented to the recording of his telephone calls in the past, but conceded that it was a "good idea" so that the couple could ensure they made good hiring decisions with their child's caretakers. Therefore, despite the pending divorce, there is no reason to believe that Mr. Harrison would not again take the necessary action to ensure his child was in good hands.

3. This is not the same type of situation as in the past. When the couple hired the last two nannies, the nannies were young and immature; the new housekeeper is thirty years old, and there was no reason to believe that she might misuse her telephone privileges.

3. But during the conversation in which Mrs. Harrison told my client that she was concerned about the new housekeeper's misuse of the telephone, my client told her to "go ahead and take care of it." This constitutes express consent.

4. Because the couple were legally separated and relations were "strained," my client was not attending to the details of the conversation. His remark to "go ahead and take care of it" simply meant that his wife should proceed with the details of hiring the new housekeeper.

After carefully evaluating each party's argument, the plaintiff's lawyer realizes that the entire thrust of Mrs. Harrison's argument will focus on the couple's past practice of monitoring telephone calls. He also recognizes that he has two valid responses to the other party's emphasis on the couple's past practice: (1) the parties' pending divorce changed the circumstances, making it unreasonable to presume that his client would have consented to the recording of his personal telephone calls; and (2) the difference in the ages of the caretakers created a different expectation as to the manner in which the new employees would be treated. Therefore, the lawyer decides to directly rebut Mrs. Harrison's emphasis on the couple's past practice of monitoring telephone calls. He also decides to sprinkle subtle anticipatory rebuttal throughout the entire factual statement and argument.

A. Direct Rebuttal

Having decided to directly rebut the defendant's argument that the couple's past practices provided the plaintiff with sufficient notice of monitoring, the lawyer decides to build his own case first and save the rebuttal argument for the end of the argument. Therefore, the lawyer waits to directly rebut the defendant's anticipated argument about the couple's past practices until *after* he has first argued why Mrs. Harrison's verbal statement was too ambiguous to constitute notice of monitoring. The following direct rebuttal is excerpted from the last paragraph of the plaintiff's argument illustrated in Appendix C:

As the court in *Campiti* made clear, the fact that the Harrisons monitored the telephone calls of former nannies several years earlier does not create a presumption that Mr. Harrison consented to the interception of his own telephone calls during an acrimonious divorce. On the two occasions in the distant past in which the couple briefly monitored the home's telephone calls, they did so out of a concern for the relative youthfulness and potential immaturity of their child's nannies, who were only eighteen and twenty years old, respectively. This concern should not have been present when the Defendant hired a new housekeeper in November 2020. The new housekeeper was not only thirty years old, but their child was also more mature and better able to demand that the housekeeper be available to cater to his needs when necessary. Tape recordings made years earlier simply do not create an expectation that the Defendant, estranged from her husband, would unilaterally decide to again begin recording telephone calls. Because no telephone calls have been intercepted for at least two years, the Harrisons could not be deemed to have engaged in a common practice of intercepting telephone calls. However, as the *Campiti* court made clear, even a "common practice" of intercepting telephone calls does not constitute implied consent, without an express, unmistakable warning that telephone calls would be intercepted.

> • Favorable Factual Premise.

> • Weaves the divorce (part of his rebuttal) into his premise.

> • Highlights a primary defense—the difference in age between the former nannies and the present housekeeper, thereby justifying a different practice.

> • Emphasizes lapse in time as evidence that there was no "practice" of monitoring or expectation of monitoring.

> • Uses favorable rule statement from *Campiti* as final attack on the defendant's argument.

Although the above paragraph directly attacks the other party's anticipated argument, it does so from an affirmative, rather than a defensive, posture. Notice that the paragraph does not begin like this:

> The Defendant will likely argue that the couple's past practices of monitoring the telephone calls of new caretakers provided Mr. Harrison with the requisite notice of monitoring. However, this argument should fail.

Such an introduction inevitably makes the lawyer's argument appear defensive. Instead, the lawyer's direct rebuttal affirms his own position rather than defends against the defendant's position:

> As the court in *Campiti* made clear, the fact that the Harrisons monitored the telephone calls of former nannies several years earlier does not create a presumption that Mr. Harrison consented to the interception of his own telephone calls during an acrimonious divorce.

In trial court briefs, lawyers either end the Argument with a one-sentence conclusion requesting that the court grant them the relief they seek, or end the Argument with a formal "conclusion" paragraph. Here, because the plaintiff's argument ends with an open rebuttal of the *weakest* aspect of the plaintiff's case, the lawyer elects to insert a formal conclusion into the argument so that he can end the Argument on a stronger note.

B. Anticipatory Rebuttal

Even though the lawyer has elected to directly rebut the defendant's anticipated emphasis on the couple's past practices, he also subtly inserts anticipatory rebuttal throughout the brief. Anticipatory rebuttal first shows up in the Statement of Facts. Recall that, during his evaluation of the case, the plaintiff's lawyer anticipated that the defendant would argue that the important "surrounding circumstances" the judge should consider are the couple's past practices of recording telephone calls. His rebuttal to this argument is that the important "surrounding circumstances" are the couple's pending divorce—this new circumstance changed the plaintiff's expectations about the privacy of his telephone calls and suggests that the plaintiff would never have consented to such an invasion of his privacy. The couple's pending divorce is also part of the plaintiff's theory of the case that Mrs. Harrison's ambiguous verbal statement is the *only* relevant evidence, and that the couple's past practices are not relevant. Because the pending divorce is therefore one of the plaintiff's strongest arguments, the lawyer begins the introductory section of the Statement of Facts with an emphasis on the divorce. Thus, the entire opening section of the plaintiff's Statement of Facts is, in essence, anticipatory rebuttal:

Plaintiff, Michael Harrison, and Defendant, Kathryn Harrison, were divorced on February 6, 2021. Four days after the couple became legally separated on November 1, 2020, Defendant began intercepting Mr. Harrison's out-going and in-coming telephone calls. (M. Harrison Dep. 35:5; K. Harrison Dep. 10:15.) Because the couple was in the midst of divorce proceedings, relations were very "strained." (K. Harrison Dep. 11:15.) In fact, the Harrisons' marriage had deteriorated to the point that, while still living in the same house, the couple slept in separate bedrooms and "strived to keep contact at a minimum." Additionally, sexual relations between the couple had ceased, and Defendant accused Mr.

Harrison of engaging in an extramarital affair. (M. Harrison Dep. 15:9-22.) Mr. Harrison has testified that he "had no idea she was recording my telephone calls, nor would I have ever agreed to such an invasion...."

The organizational format of the Statement of Facts is also, in a sense, anticipatory rebuttal. The lawyer cannot ignore the couple's past practices; he must acknowledge it. However, he waits to discuss the couple's past practices until after he has described the status of the couple's marital relationship and the ambiguous nature of Mrs. Harrison's verbal statement that she was concerned that the new housekeeper "not make improper use of the telephone." Then, when the lawyer finally discusses the couple's past practices, he subtly begins to rebut its significance. The italicized language reflects the subtle nature of anticipatory rebuttal.

The couple had *briefly* monitored the home's telephone calls on two previous occasions a *number of years earlier. Nine years ago*, in 2012, when the Defendant was in the process of hiring Dillon's first nanny, the Defendant was concerned that the nanny might spend "too much time on the telephone when she should be spending time with Dillon." (K. Harrison Dep. 105:12.) The *Defendant concedes* that one of the reasons the couple decided to monitor the telephone was because of the *nanny's relatively young age*—she was only *nineteen (19) years old at the time*. (K. Harrison Dep. 105:14.) Therefore, the couple agreed that, for an "indefinite period of time, all telephone calls into and from the house would be recorded." (K. Harrison Dep. 106:18; M. Harrison Dep. 77:4-77:22.) Seven years later, when the couple hired a new nanny, they were again concerned about her *relatively young age*—*age twenty-one*. Therefore, they agreed to again record all incoming and out-going telephone calls for a period of approximately one month until they were confident that they had made a sound decision in hiring the nanny. (K. Harrison Dep. 110:5-111:2; M. Harrison Dep. 78:11-79:15.) *At the time of each of these previous instances, there was no marital discord* in the couple's marriage, and both husband and wife decided to monitor the telephone calls *only after clearly discussing the issue and mutually agreeing to that course of action*. (K. Harrison Dep. 112:16-112:25; M. Harrison Dep. 82:11-82:24.)

Within the body of the argument itself, the lawyer's decision to emphasize the feud in the *Williams* case and to compare the couple's divorce proceedings to the *Williams* feud is also, in a sense, anticipatory rebuttal. The lawyer would have emphasized this favorable analogy in any event because the pending divorce suggests that Mr. Harrison would not have consented to the recording of his personal telephone calls. In that sense, the pending divorce is part and parcel of the lawyer's favorable argument. At the same time, the difference in marital status also subtly rebuts the defendant's argument that the couple's past practices led Mr. Harrison to conclude that his own telephone calls would be recorded.

Exercise 30-1

Consider again the fact pattern and legal arguments that support the criminal wiretap brief (Sample Brief in Appendix E). For purposes of this exercise, assume that you represent the defendant, Hart, whose telephone calls were intercepted, and that the matter is before a district court judge within the District of Columbia. Further assume that, prior to drafting a brief attempting to suppress the wiretap evidence, you find a precedent case in which the court held the Government's explanation for its sealing delay was "satisfactory." That case, *United States v. Elsinore*, was decided in 1970 by the United States Court of Appeals for the District of Columbia. In that case, the court accepted the Government's explanation as satisfactory, even though the Government's pre-sealing procedures were inadequate to protect the tapes from any possibility of tampering. However, the court stated: "Where, as here, the Government has proven through reliable expert testimony that the tapes were not in fact tampered with prior to sealing, the defendant was not prejudiced by the sealing delay. Therefore, the Government's explanation for the sealing delay is satisfactory and the tapes were properly admitted into evidence."

During your research, assume that you discover another case arising out of the District of Columbia. In *United States v. Wilmore*, the United States Court of Appeals for the District of Columbia held that the Government's explanation was not satisfactory. That case was decided in 1990. In *Wilmore*, the court held that the Government's pre-sealing procedures were inadequate to protect the tapes from any possibility of tampering. However, unlike the *Elsinore* court, the *Wilmore* court declined to allow the Government to produce expert testimony to prove that the tapes had not in fact been altered during the sealing delay. The court observed: "In recent years, technological advances have made forgery virtually impossible to detect. Alterations are likely to go undetected because a highly skilled forensic examiner who is an expert in the field of audio technology, using the most sophisticated equipment available today, can take months to establish with reasonable certainty that a tape has been falsified. This court declines to open the door to such lengthy and costly proceedings that might in themselves be inconclusive." In *Wilmore*, the court did not address the earlier *Elsinore* decision.

A. Under these circumstances, would you have an ethical obligation to discuss the unfavorable *Elsinore* decision? Why or why not?

B. Assume that you decide to address the *Elsinore* decision. Draft a paragraph that addresses both the *Wilmore* and *Elsinore* cases.

CHAPTER IN REVIEW

....

Core Concepts:

DIRECT REBUTTAL

1. Direct rebuttal takes two forms. You can:
   a. Directly rebut an *opponent's interpretation* of the law (whether or not opposing counsel has already filed a written argument); and/or
   b. Directly rebut the reasoning of an *adverse case* itself.
2. Direct rebuttal of an opponent's interpretation of the law
   - Place yourself in your opponent's shoes and consider:
     i. If a statutory dispute, whether the *statutory language* or any part of the *legislative history* supports the opponent's interpretation;
     ii. Whether the *language in any case* supports the opponent's interpretation;
     iii. Whether there are *facts in any of the cases* that might serve as the basis for favorable analogies for the opponent;
     iv. Whether there are any *policy* considerations that support the opponent's argument;
     v. Whether there are any *client facts* that favor the opponent's argument.
3. Direct rebuttal of an *adverse case* itself. Consider:
   a. Attacking the adverse court's *reasoning*.
     i. In the case of a statute, did the court ignore the statutory language, statutory scheme, or legislative purpose?
     ii. Would the case have negative policy implications?
   b. Arguing that the adverse case is no longer "*good law*"—i.e., it no longer reflects present policy, and/or it has been implicitly overruled by more recent case law.
4. *Drafting* Strategy: Insert direct rebuttal immediately following your own favorable argument relating to the same idea.

ANTICIPATORY REBUTTAL

1. *Defined*: Indirect suggestions and innuendos woven into an argument that anticipate and subtly rebut an opponent's argument.
   - Anticipatory rebuttal can be used both with and without direct rebuttal.
2. *Pre-Drafting* Strategy:
   - Place yourself in your opponent's shoes and consider:
     i. If a statutory dispute, whether the *statutory language* or any part of the *legislative history* supports the opponent's interpretation;

      ii.   Whether the *language in any case* supports the opponent's interpretation;

     iii.   Whether there are *facts in any of the cases* that might serve as the basis for favorable analogies for the opponent;

     iv.   Whether there are any *policy* considerations that support the opponent's argument;

     v.   Whether there are any *client facts* that favor the opponent's argument.

3. *Drafting* Strategy:

   a. Anticipatory rebuttal can be as subtle as a single adjective, or sweep through an entire argument.

   b. Thus, you can weave it into any part of the Argument, from the introductory paragraph, through the factual statement, through the body of the argument itself.

TRIAL & APPELLATE
COURT BRIEFS

I. OVERVIEW OF A BRIEF

Pre-Trial Briefs: A brief is a generic term that refers to any written argument submitted to a court. Some briefs are filed with a trial court judge prior to trial. This type of brief usually accompanies a "motion" requesting the court to grant the client relief in some manner. For example, upon receiving a Complaint, a defendant's lawyer might file a "Motion to Dismiss," requesting the court to dismiss the lawsuit against the client. Motions are typically very short and to the point. They ask the judge to grant the client specific relief and may also include the bottom-line reasons the client is entitled to the relief requested. Because lawyers don't want the judge to rule on the motion before having an opportunity to argue its merits, they often file written arguments with the motion that are generically referred to as briefs. In fact, they are often technically labeled as "Memorandum [or "Suggestions"] in Support of" or "Memorandum [or "Suggestions"] in Opposition to" the motion. Both parties have an opportunity to file a written argument, so long as they comply with the time and space constraints imposed by the court.

Trial Briefs: Other trial court briefs are filed during or following the trial. For example, sometimes lawyers try their cases before a trial court judge rather than a jury. Following the trial, the trial court judge sometimes asks the lawyers to submit written briefs that address specific issues raised during the trial. This type of brief is referred to as a "Post-Trial Brief."

Appellate Court Briefs: Other briefs are filed when a case is appealed from a trial court to an appellate court. In an appellate court brief, the losing party appeals the lower court judgment. That party is called the "appellant" or "petitioner"; the other party is referred to as the "appellee" or "respondent." In an appellate court brief, the appellant argues why the lower court erred with respect to very specific points that become the issues on appeal.

Chapter 23 discusses common persuasive writing style strategies that enhance the appeal of any persuasive argument. Chapters 24 through 30 discuss the different argument constructs and strategies involved in both law-centered and fact-centered arguments. The previous chapters pertain to persuasive arguments in general, whether or not the persuasive argument assumes the form of a brief filed before a court. When such arguments appear in a brief, however, they must also comply with specialized rules adopted by the court.

II. STRUCTURE OF A TRIAL COURT BRIEF

Prior to filing a brief before a trial court, check the local court rules to determine whether you must comply with any special rules of court. For example, local court rules often specify that briefs cannot exceed a certain number of pages and must comply with certain font and margin requirements. Other court rules might require briefs of a certain length to contain a Table of Contents and a Table of Authorities. These components of a brief are required in all appellate court briefs and in some trial court briefs, and are discussed below in Part 3. Most trial court briefs, however, contain the following sections: (1) an Introduction; (2) a Statement of Facts; (3) an Argument; and (4) a Conclusion.

A. Introduction

If the trial court brief is lengthy enough to merit a summary of the argument, the brief begins with an Introduction section. In the Introduction, you would state why your client is entitled to a favorable judgment and summarize the most compelling reasons that support your conclusion. The trial court briefs illustrated in Appendices C and D each contain a persuasive Introduction section that summarizes the argument.

B. Statement of Facts

The Statement of Facts provides you with an opportunity to convey a persuasive story of the underlying facts that relate to the argument. In the Statement of Facts, your goal is to subtly begin to persuade the judge while also appearing fair and ethical. Chapter 32 discusses the strategies involved in crafting persuasive factual statements, and Chapter 34 examines persuasive fact-writing techniques within briefs accompanying a specific type of motion known as a summary judgment motion.

C. Argument and Conclusion

The Argument is the heart of the brief, where you argue why the client should prevail. In a law-centered argument, you would argue why the law should be interpreted in a manner favorable to your client. In a fact-centered argument, you would argue why the law should be applied to the client's factual situation in a manner that compels a favorable judgment. These argument constructs are discussed at length in Chapters 24 through 30. Whatever argument construct you follow, in a multi-issue brief you would use point-headings to provide the court with persuasive roadmaps of the argument. Persuasive point-headings are discussed more fully in Chapter 33.

For a lengthy brief, the Argument may end with a short section entitled "Conclusion." For a shorter brief, the Argument may end with a simple prayer for relief: "Accordingly, Plaintiff respectfully requests that this Court grant Plaintiff's Motion to Dismiss and for such other and further relief as this Court deems proper."

III. STRUCTURE OF AN APPELLATE COURT BRIEF

Appellate courts have specialized rules with which lawyers must comply. Many appellate courts have specialized clerical rules that govern the typeface used in the brief, the margins, the size of the pages, and even the color of the pages. Other rules govern the mandatory components of the brief and the order in which they must be presented. Most courts also limit the number of pages within the brief. Before filing an appellate court brief, it's important to carefully review and then comply with the specialized rules that govern briefs filed before that court. Failure to comply with the court's rules could result in dismissal of an appeal.

Although different courts of appeal have specific rules with which lawyers must comply, most appellate courts require appellants to include the following components in their briefs:

A. Cover Page

The cover page identifies for the court important identifying information about the case. Such identifying information includes the court in which the brief is being filed, the parties' names, the party filing the brief, the docket number, and the names and addresses of the attorneys of record. If the pertinent court rules specify how you must prepare the cover page, you must comply with those rules exactly. However, the cover page for the brief illustrated in Appendix E is an example of a typical cover page.

B. Table of Contents

The Table of Contents describes each section of the brief and the page number on which each section begins. It is a map of the entire argument. Therefore, for purposes of clarity, separately identify each issue and sub-issue contained within the Argument. As you identify the issues, frame each issue as a declarative statement of the conclusion you want the court to adopt. Avoid identifying the issues generically (*e.g.*, Argument I), or stating the issues in question form. Take a look at the brief in Appendix E to view a typical Table of Contents and the manner in which the issues are identified. For obvious reasons, wait to draft the Table of Contents until after you have finalized the brief itself. Any last minute changes reflected in the brief must be duly noted in the Table of Contents as well.

C. Table of Authorities

As the name suggests, the Table of Authorities identifies the authorities cited within the brief. Usually, all of the cases are cited first, arranged alphabetically by the level of court. The list of cases is followed by a list of relevant statutes and constitutional authorities, followed by any secondary sources you may have cited in the brief. Next to each authority, you must include all of the page numbers within the brief on which the authority is cited. Thus, if you cite to an authority four separate times throughout the brief, you must include the page number of each reference. However, if you cite a particular case or other authority so frequently throughout the brief that page citations would be almost meaningless, you may use the term "passim" to replace page numbers. The Latin term "passim" denotes that the case is cited "everywhere" within the brief. Be careful not to use this term unless you can confidently state that the authority is truly used "everywhere" within the brief. The sample brief in Appendix E contains a typical Table of Authorities.

As with the Table of Contents, wait to draft the Table of Authorities until after you have finalized your brief. It is very important that the page numbers and other references be accurate and complete. Appellate court judges often refer to the table to locate the citation to a specific authority or to refer to the specific places in the brief where the authority is cited.[1] First impressions are important: incorrect page references or any other inaccuracy can result in a loss of credibility. You certainly don't want the judges to question your competence and credibility before they even begin to read your argument.

D. Statement of Jurisdiction

An appellate court must not only have subject matter jurisdiction to resolve the matter, but also have jurisdiction to hear an appeal at a particular point in time. In federal court, although there are specific, narrow exceptions, the appellant must appeal from a final appealable order. In state court, the appellant's ability to appeal an order is also restricted by state appellate court rules. Because the court cannot consider the substantive merits of your argument without jurisdiction, the Statement of Jurisdiction is often included as a separate component of the brief.

E. Statement of the Issues

The Statement of the Issues is also commonly called the Question(s) Presented. The Statement of the Issues is an extremely important part of the brief because it frames the issues the court has been asked to resolve. Careful consideration should be

---

1. Ruggero J. Aldisert, *Winning on Appeal: Better Briefs and Oral Argument* 100 (Rev. 1st ed. NITA 1996).

given to the issues you want the court to address and how you might frame the issues in a manner that is both favorable to your client and also fair and ethical. Chapter 35 discusses and illustrates this section of the brief.

F. Constitutional and Statutory Provisions

This section identifies the text of relevant constitutional or statutory provisions that are critical to the court's disposition of the issues on appeal. This section might also contain any court rules that are at issue on appeal. However, if a statutory or other provision is not critical to the issues under consideration, do not include the text of that provision in this section. Instead, simply refer to it in the Table of Authorities. Assuming the constitutional, statutory, or other provision is at issue on appeal, you may either quote the text of that provision or refer the court to the appendix in which the provision is reproduced. If the text is relatively short, quote the text of that provision within this section of the brief. If the provision is relatively lengthy, but only a specific part of that provision is at issue on appeal, quote only the part that is at issue. If the entire provision is at issue and it is lengthy and relatively complex, you might instead simply refer the court to the appendix in which the provision is reproduced.

G. Preliminary Statement

The Preliminary Statement briefly explains the procedural posture of the appeal by describing the order or judgment from which the party appealed and the relevant procedural events related to the appeal. The Preliminary Statement is sometimes called the "Proceedings Below" or "Nature of the Proceedings Below." To add to the confusion, some courts call the Preliminary Statement the "Statement of the Case," and label what is referred to in this book as the Statement of the Case, as the "Statement of Facts."[2] However, by whatever label, this section simply explains why the appeal is before the court. Again, refer to Appendix E to review a typical Preliminary Statement.

H. Statement of the Case

The Statement of the Case tells the relevant factual story underlying the controversy. This section of the brief is described more fully in Chapter 32.

I. Summary of the Argument

The Federal Rules of Appellate Procedure require each brief to contain a Summary of the Argument that precedes the formal argument itself.[3] This section of the brief is extremely important because it is the judges' first opportunity to review the most

---

2. Richard K. Neumann, Jr., *Legal Reasoning and Legal Writing: Structure, Strategy & Style* 382 (4th ed. Aspen L. & Bus. 2001).

3. Fed R. App. P. 28(a)(8).

important aspects of your argument. Chapter 33 discusses this section of the brief in greater detail.

J. The Argument

As its title suggests, the Argument section of the brief contains a complete articulation of the lawyer's arguments. Thus, in a law-centered argument, you would argue why the law should be interpreted in a manner favorable to your client. In a fact-centered argument, you would argue why the law should be applied to your client's factual situation in a manner that compels a favorable judgment. These argument constructs are discussed at length in Chapters 24 through 30. Whatever argument construct you follow, in a multi-issue brief you would use point-headings to provide the court with persuasive roadmaps of the argument. Persuasive point-headings are discussed more fully in Chapter 33.

K. Conclusion

In most cases, the conclusion should be a very brief, succinct statement of the exact relief you are requesting. For example, a brief commonly concludes with a simple statement such as:

> For the foregoing reasons, Appellant requests the Court to reverse the judgment of the District Court and to remand these proceedings with a direction to enter judgment in its favor.

Although the above illustration is the most common type of conclusion, some attorneys also include a brief recapitulation of the reasons why their client is entitled to the requested relief. Such brief summaries might be appropriate if the brief is unusually complex and lengthy. However, such recapitulations of the grounds for relief are not usually necessary. If they are included, they should not exceed a few sentences.

TRIAL & APPELLATE COURT BRIEFS

The Factual Statement

I. PRE-DRAFTING CONSIDERATIONS

A. Working with the Record

Before drafting a factual statement, you must work with the available record. The record is not just restricted to transcripts of testimony, but also includes affidavits, pleadings, prior court orders, and documents that were introduced into evidence. For example, if you were to draft a motion for summary judgment, you would work with pleadings, deposition testimony, documents, and responses to interrogatories. If you were to draft an appellate court or a post-trial brief, you would also work with the trial court record that contains the testimony of witnesses and the documents entered into evidence during the trial. Working with the record can be intimidating because it involves examining numerous pleadings, documents, and testimony that can span hundreds or even thousands of pages. Nevertheless, it is very important that you not only have a solid grasp of the factual record, but that you accurately incorporate the relevant facts into your brief.

As you review the record, you may find it helpful to keep a checklist of the facts you are seeking. First, as discussed more fully below, look for facts that will help you advance your theory of the case. Second, as you review the record, keep in mind that the factual statement must include every legally significant fact that will later appear in your argument. Legally significant facts include unfavorable as well as favorable facts. Third, look for any basic background facts that will help provide context for the factual story you will be telling. Finally, look for emotionally appealing facts that might appeal to the court's sense of fairness or equities.

> **Checklist:**
> 1. Facts that support your *theory of the case.*
> 2. Facts that are *legally significant,* including both favorable and unfavorable facts.
> 3. Facts that provide *context* for the story.
> 4. Facts that have *emotional appeal.*

Every statement of fact contained within a brief must appear somewhere within the record. In fact, you will be required to support every factual statement you make in the brief with a citation to the record. Therefore, as you review the record to identify the facts you will include within your brief, carefully note the pages from which you have extracted factual information. For a voluminous record, you might also wish to create a page-by-page summary of the record as you read the record for the first time. The summary will prove useful later as you refer back to the record to prepare your factual statement and argument.

B. Ethical Considerations

1. Legally Significant Facts

As you review the record, keep in mind that the factual statement must include every legally significant fact that will appear in your argument. Legally significant facts include unfavorable as well as favorable facts. Rules of professional conduct prohibit lawyers from "knowingly" making a "false statement of fact or law" to a court.[1] False statements not only include misrepresentations of the facts themselves, but also misrepresentations by *omission.* Therefore, should a lawyer fail to include relevant adverse facts within a factual statement, the lawyer not only risks losing the trust of the court, but also risks incurring ethical sanctions.

2. Factual Inferences

A false statement of fact also includes factual *inferences* that are stated as if they were facts themselves. Although you might properly include an inference of a witness that appears in the trial record, you must not state your own inferences as if they were facts.[2] To illustrate the distinction, consider an example from the criminal wiretap problem included in Appendix E. In that problem, Agent Friday testified that she sealed the box of tapes; nonetheless, the janitor testified that the box was open when he found the tapes. These statements are facts that would properly be included in the

---

1. *See, e.g.,* Model R. Prof. Conduct 3.3(a)(1) (ABA 2002).

2. *See, e.g., In re Greenberg,* 104 A.2d 46 (N.J. 1954) (holding that a lawyer improperly stated a factual inference as a fact).

factual statement of the defendant's brief. However, the following statement would be an impermissible inference from such testimony: "It is entirely possible that an unknown person opened the box of tapes at some point during the two-month time period in which they were missing." Although this is a permissible inference from the facts, it is not a fact itself. Therefore, although it would be permissible for the defendant's lawyer to argue this inference within the Argument section of the brief, it has no place within the factual statement. (Even in the Argument, however, it must be clear that the lawyer's conclusion is an inference from facts and not a fact itself.) Your review of the record will help you avoid stating inferences as fact. If a "fact" does not appear in the record itself, it is not a fact but instead an inference or an argument about the facts.

II. DRAFTING FACTUAL STATEMENTS

The factual statement in a trial court brief is commonly called a "Statement of Facts." In appellate court briefs, the factual statement is commonly called the "Statement of the Case." To confuse matters further, some appellate courts use the term "Statement of the Case" to refer to the "Preliminary Statement" of the procedural history of the case, reserving the term "Statement of Facts" for the statement of the factual story itself. To avoid confusion, this book uses the term "factual statement" to refer to the section of the brief that conveys the underlying factual story of the case.

As you draft the factual statement, keep in mind the dual purposes of the factual statement: (1) to inform the court of all legally significant facts; and (2) to persuade. You have a duty to the court to fairly and accurately inform the court of all facts that are legally significant, including unfavorable facts. At the same time, the factual statement is an ideal place to begin *subtly* painting a picture that portrays the client's position in an appealing, favorable light. Thus, you will want to emphasize facts that support your theory of the case and that have emotional appeal. This is a delicate balancing act. It will likely require many drafts to produce a factual statement that is both straightforward and fair, as well as subtly persuasive. However, the time you invest in drafting a persuasive factual statement is well worth the investment. As one federal appellate court judge observed: "[T]he statement of facts has tremendous significance to the outcome of the appeal. Cases turn far more frequently on their facts than they do the law."[3]

As you consider how to begin to persuade the court through your artful presentation of the factual story, consider the following guidelines. First, create an appealing story that emphasizes people rather than a detached commentary. Second, tell the story in a manner that emphasizes your theory of the case and highlights the favor-

---

3. Ruggero J. Aldisert, *Winning on Appeal: Better Briefs and Oral Argument* 155 (Rev. 1st ed. NITA 1996).

able facts. Third, de-emphasize and neutralize the unfavorable facts. Fourth, organize the factual story for clarity and persuasive appeal. Finally, edit your factual story to ensure that it is accurate, is supported by references to the record, and does not inadvertently include any argument or factual inferences.

A. Create an Appealing Story

People are captivated by other people's stories and how they experienced factual events. Stop and think for a moment about the real life stories that have affected you most strongly. It is probably safe to assume that most of us do not have a vivid recollection of detached commentaries about the economic forecast. However, we may recall a story about a family who was affected by the economy. We might not be personally moved by a news statistic that a mudslide killed hundreds of people in a country in another continent, but we would likely be moved by a story about specific people whose lives were tragically affected by that event.

A lawsuit is, on one level, a clash of competing stories. Like people everywhere, a judge will be drawn to the better story. A good story is one that focuses on people and portrays the story from the sympathetic perspective of the client. To read a story from the client's perspective, the reader must be able to sense what it must have been like to be there as the story unfolded. In other words, the reader must sense somehow what the people in the story must have heard, seen, tasted, smelled, felt, and believed. These facts have emotional appeal and draw the reader into the story.

As an example, consider the spousal wiretap problem illustrated in Appendix C. In that problem, the plaintiff contends that his former wife violated the federal wiretap statute when she recorded his telephone calls without his knowledge or consent. The plaintiff's theory of the case is two-fold: (1) his former wife's verbal statement was too ambiguous to constitute notice that she would be recording his telephone calls, and (2) he would never have consented to such recordings because the couple was going through divorce proceedings. The plaintiff's lawyer decides to set the stage for this theory of the case in the opening paragraph of the Statement of Facts. With that in mind, consider the persuasive appeal of Example 1 below:

> **Example 1:**
>
> On November 1, 2020, the Defendant hired a housekeeper whose responsibilities included taking care of the Plaintiff's and Defendant's son. On November 5, 2020, the Defendant began monitoring the Plaintiff's telephone calls as part of an effort to ensure that the new housekeeper did not abuse her telephone privileges. However, because the couple was legally separated, the Plaintiff was not aware that the Defendant was recording his calls.

Were you moved by the above story? Did the story leave you with a sense that the defendant engaged in any wrongdoing? After reading the story, you likely do not have a sense of who Mr. Harrison is or why he would not have consented to the recording of his telephone calls. Notice how even Mr. Harrison's name is lost within the generic reference to the "plaintiff." Now consider the alternative opening paragraph in Example 2 below:

Example 2:

The Plaintiff, Michael Harrison, and Defendant, Kathryn Harrison, were divorced on February 6, 2021. Four days after the couple became legally separated on November 1, 2020, the Defendant began intercepting Mr. Harrison's out-going and in-coming telephone calls. Because the couple were in the midst of divorce proceedings, relations were very "strained." In fact, the Harrisons' marriage had deteriorated to the point that, while still living in the same house, the couple slept in separate bedrooms and "strived to keep contact to a minimum." Mr. Harrison has testified that he "had no idea she was recording my telephone calls, nor would I have ever agreed to such an invasion…"

The second illustration personalizes Mr. Harrison and the couple's strained marital relationship. Rather than simply noting that the couple were legally separated, it invites the reader to imagine what the relationship was really like—"strained"; "sleeping in separate bedrooms"; and "striv[ing] to keep contact at a minimum." By quoting Mr. Harrison's reaction to the monitoring, the second illustration also allows the reader to glimpse how strongly he felt about the telephone recordings; he labels the monitoring as an "invasion." As a result, this story has a better chance of motivating a judge to find that Mr. Harrison did not consent to the recording of his telephone calls.

B. Emphasize Favorable Facts that Advance the Theory of the Case

1. Pre-Drafting Strategy

As you consider how to incorporate the factual record into a compelling factual statement, carefully consider your overall strategy and theory of the case. Chapters 24 through 30 discuss the argument strategies involved in crafting a winning argument for different types of law-centered and fact-centered arguments. These argument strategies reflect the various ways in which courts can be persuaded to adopt favorable positions. When the issue before a court involves a factual determination, you must consider how the various argument strategies interrelate with the factual record. The factual record must not only support your legal argument, but should dovetail into that argument: the facts and law, viewed together, should make the court *want* to grant your client the relief you seek. Therefore, a well-crafted factual statement should artfully advance the theory of the case.

As an example, consider the criminal wiretap problem that is the basis of the sample brief in Appendix E. In that brief, Hart's lawyer argues that wiretap tapes must be suppressed because the Government failed to provide a "satisfactory explanation" for its delay in obtaining the safeguard of a judicial seal. Hart's lawyer argues that the court must adopt a two-prong legal standard that would require the Government to prove: (1) that its pre-sealing procedures protected the tapes from any possibility of tampering; and (2) that it acted with reasonable diligence to minimize the sealing delay. When framing these favorable rules of law, Hart's lawyer considered the factual record before the court. The fact that the Government lost the tapes for two months motivated the attorney to argue that the court adopt the first prong of the legal standard—under that standard, the Government cannot prevail because its pre-sealing procedure did not protect the tapes from any possibility of tampering. In addition, the Government's carelessness in handling the tapes prompted Hart's advocacy of the second prong of the legal standard. A careless mistake that is not remedied for two months would likely not satisfy the "reasonable diligence" standard.

2. Drafting Strategy: Highlight Favorable Facts

When drafting a factual statement, the facts should artfully advance your theory of the case. This is a challenge, indeed, because the factual statement can't contain legal argument or inferences from the facts. Moreover, the factual statement must include all of the facts that are described in the argument itself, both favorable and unfavorable. Nevertheless, as you draft your factual statement, focus on your theory of the case and consider how the facts support that theme. Facts that support the theme can be highlighted by prominently displaying all of their descriptive details. Therefore, instead of summarily dispensing with a favorable fact, parade out all of the details. If there is a statement within the transcript that graphically illustrates a favorable fact, then quote that statement within the factual story. Also consider how you might use the persuasive writing style strategies discussed in Chapter 23 to highlight favorable facts.

Again using the criminal wiretap problem for purposes of illustration, Hart's lawyer advances two themes. The first theme concerns the precautionary measures the Government must take to protect wiretap evidence from tampering. To advance this theory, Hart's lawyer wants to highlight facts reflecting the potential for tampering during the two month period in which the Government cannot account for the tapes' whereabouts. How compellingly does the following factual statement advance this theme?

Example 1:

... Agent Friday also testified that she labeled and sealed the box of tapes. (R. at 10.) The tapes were located in a supply room on Nov. 8, 2020. When the box of tapes was found, there was no label on the box of tapes, and the box was not sealed. (R. at 14.)

In Example 1 above, the facts relating to this theme are present, but not highlighted. The above statement is a rather summary description of the relevant facts that advance Hart's theory of the case. Now consider the persuasive appeal of the following alternative factual statement in Example 2:

Example 2:

... Agent Friday also testified that she placed a label on the box, indicating that the box was to be transported to the courthouse. (R. at 10.) In contrast, the building janitor testified that no label appeared on the box of tapes. (R. at 14.) The Government cannot explain this factual discrepancy. (R. at 15.) Finally, although Agent Friday testified that she sealed the box of tapes (R. at 10), the building janitor testified that the box of tapes "was open. You could look right in and see what was inside." (R. at 14.)

   ... The Government speculates that the tapes sat exposed in an open box in the unlocked office supply room for over two months. (R. at 15.) The exposed tapes sat in the busy supply room amidst note pads, pencils, office supplies, and party decorations, open to the 5,000 occupants of the building who frequent the room for coffee and office supplies. (R. at 14.)

What makes this second factual statement more persuasive? Instead of summarizing the evidence, Hart's lawyer highlights the favorable facts by drawing out their details. For example, the fact that the box of tapes was found in an open office supply room would appeal to the judge's concern that the tapes' integrity may well have been compromised. Therefore, Hart's lawyer highlights the underlying facts that emphasize the vulnerable nature of the supply room by noting the number of people who have access to that room, and the various and sundry reasons why people would have occasion to visit the supply room. Hart's lawyer also highlights the discrepancy between Agent Friday's testimony and that of the building janitor. Hart emphasizes the janitor's favorable testimony by quoting the janitor: "You could look right in and see the tapes." By highlighting facts that support this theory of the case, Hart's lawyer appeals to the judge's concern that tainted evidence may well be used to convict the defendant.

Also note the persuasive writing style strategies used in the above statement. How does Hart's lawyer use the strategy of "juxtaposition" to illustrate inconsistencies in the Government's stories? What verbs and adjectives does Hart use to appeal to the judge's concern that the tapes' integrity may have been compromised?

Consider now the second legal theory Hart's lawyer advances in the argument itself—that a "satisfactory explanation" requires the Government to act with "reasonable diligence." To advance this theme, Hart's lawyer wants to highlight facts that reflect carelessness and ineptitude, parading in great detail all of the precautionary steps Agent Friday failed to take and her ineptitude in locating the missing tapes. How effectively does the following factual statement advance that theme?

> **Example 1:**
>
> On September 7, 2020, Agent Friday removed the tapes from the surveillance van and placed them in the bureau office, requesting that they be transported to the courthouse for sealing the next day. On September 8, 2020, the Bureau moved offices. On October 10, 2020, Agent Friday called the courthouse to inquire whether the tapes had been sealed. (R. at 12.) That telephone call alerted Agent Friday for the first time that the tapes were missing. Following the telephone call, Agent Friday testified that she undertook an intensive search of the office building and personally called the movers. (R. at 12.) On November 8, 2020, Agent Friday found the tapes in the office supply room. (R. at 13.)

The factual statement illustrated in Example 1 above certainly informs the court of the facts underlying the two-month sealing delay. However, it does not advance Hart's theme of portraying the Government's actions as careless. Of course, Hart's lawyer cannot state that the Government was careless in the factual statement. Carelessness is a conclusion Hart's lawyer wants the judge to draw from reading the facts, but, as a factual inference, it is not a fact itself. In the following illustration, note the persuasive strategies Hart's lawyer uses to highlight the favorable facts that advance the theme:

> **Example 2:**
>
> For more than a month after the Bureau moved offices, Agent Friday never telephoned or appeared at the courthouse to ensure the tapes arrived for sealing. (R. at 11.) Agent Friday never asked the court clerk to confirm whether a judge had sealed the tapes. (R. at 11.) And, despite the fact that Agent Friday had no responsibilities other than this case during this entire time period,

> Agent Friday did not make a single attempt to locate her only evidence in this case. (R. at 12.)
>
> It was not until October 10, 2020, that Agent Friday finally called the courthouse to inquire whether the tapes had been sealed. (R. at 12.) It was not until then that Agent Friday began searching for the missing tapes. Although Agent Friday testified that she undertook an intensive search of the office building and personally called the movers (R. at 12), nearly a month elapsed before Agent Friday was able to locate the tapes. It was not until November 8, 2020, that Agent Friday finally stumbled upon the missing tapes while looking for party decorations. (R. at 13.)…

In the second illustration, Hart's lawyer highlights the favorable facts by describing them in detail. Hart's lawyer also uses several persuasive writing style strategies discussed in Chapter 23. For example, Hart's lawyer uses the active voice to link Agent Friday with her careless actions. The lawyer also uses strong verbs, adverbs, and adjectives to create a sense of incompetence: "*never* telephoned or appeared," "*single* attempt," "*only* evidence," "*not until*… that Agent Friday *finally* called," "Agent Friday *finally stumbled*," and "*party decorations*."

C. De-Emphasize Unfavorable Facts

As discussed earlier, you also have an ethical duty to inform the court of unfavorable facts that are legally significant. This ethical duty has a pragmatic counterpart. A lawyer who fails to disclose unfavorable facts risks losing the trust and respect of the court. Moreover, you will likely be able to portray an adverse fact in a more favorable light than your opposing counsel. Therefore, the treatment of unfavorable facts presents an interesting challenge—how to incorporate unfavorable facts into a factual story without portraying the client in an adverse light.

There are several ways to de-emphasize unfavorable facts. First, you can neutralize the negative impact of the fact by juxtaposing that fact next to favorable information. The juxtaposition of a negative with a positive fact is often introduced with terms such as "although," "even though," and "despite." These terms signal that contrasting facts will be introduced. When juxtaposing unfavorable with favorable information in two or more sentences, the word "however" similarly signals that a contrasting fact will be introduced. Consider the following sentence excerpted from the criminal wiretap brief in Appendix E. This sentence concedes Agent Friday's testimony that she undertook an intensive search of the office while juxtaposing it with the favorable fact that the search, nevertheless, took one month to complete.

> Although Agent Friday testified that she undertook an intensive search of the office building and personally called the movers (R. at 12), nearly a month elapsed before Agent Friday was able to locate the tapes.

Another way to de-emphasize an unfavorable fact is to bury the fact within the middle of a paragraph or sentence. Readers tend to pay the least attention to the information in the middle of a paragraph. In addition, rather than parading out the details of unfavorable facts, treat the unfavorable facts in a more summary fashion. However, when doing so, be careful to ensure that you have not summarized the unfavorable information to such an extent that the court would not recognize the fact that you dealt with the unfavorable information. You do not want to leave the impression that you are hiding important information from the court. Finally, you can de-emphasize unfavorable facts by using such persuasive writing strategies as the passive voice and non-action verbs to distance your client from unfavorable conduct (or to distance the opponent from favorable conduct). (Persuasive writing style strategies are discussed in Chapter 23.)

D. Organize the Facts to Present a Compelling Story

1. Emphasize Favorable Facts

a. Front-Load Favorable Facts

A reader's attention span is at its greatest during the first few paragraphs.[4] Therefore, highlight the favorable facts that advance your theory of the case by emphasizing such facts within the first few paragraphs of the factual statement. Of course, if it doesn't make logical sense to do so, don't blindly place such facts at the beginning of your factual statement. However, your story will be more persuasive if you can emphasize favorable facts that advance your theme *before* you acknowledge unfavorable facts that detract from your theme.

For example, in the spousal wiretap problem, recall that the plaintiff's theory of the case is two-fold: (1) his former wife's verbal statement was too ambiguous to constitute notice that she would be recording his telephone calls, and (2) because they were going through divorce proceedings, he would never have consented to such recordings. Therefore, the plaintiff's lawyer describes the details of the divorce and the ambiguous verbal statement within the first few paragraphs of the Statement of Facts. Only after he has discussed the facts that reflect his theory of the case does the lawyer refer to the couple's past practice of monitoring telephone calls.

In contrast, the defendant's theory of the case revolves around the couple's past practices. She likely can prevail only if she can convince the judge to interpret Mrs. Harrison's ambiguous verbal statement within the context of the couple's past practices. Therefore, the defendant's lawyer describes the couple's past practices in detail within the first few paragraphs of the Statement of Facts. Only after she has discussed the facts that reflect her theory of the case does the lawyer refer to the ambiguous

---

4. Richard K. Neumann, Jr., *Legal Reasoning and Legal Writing: Structure, Strategy, and Style* 348 (4th ed. Aspen L. & Pub. 2001); Linda H. Edwards, *Legal Writing: Process, Analysis & Organization* 346 (2d ed. Aspen L. & Pub. 1999).

verbal statement. By organizing the facts in this manner, the lawyer has, in a very real sense, forced the judge to consider the ambiguous verbal statement within the context of the couple's past practices.

b. End with Favorable Facts

Although readers pay the most attention at the beginning, some experts contend that "they remember longest the material at the end."[5] Because that information is the last thing the reader reads, it tends to linger in the mind. Therefore, end the factual statement with a compelling fact or facts that will create a favorable impression in the reader's mind. For example, in the criminal wiretap brief, the factual statement ends with this lingering image that advances Hart's theme:

> The exposed tapes sat in the busy storage room amidst note pads, pencils, office supplies, and party decorations, open to the 5,000 occupants of the building who frequent the room for coffee and office supplies. (R. at 14.)

2. Providing Context Within the Story: Chronological Order

Readers need to understand the context of a story before they can absorb its details. Therefore, make sure you include contextual information at the beginning of the factual statement so that the court can appreciate the story that follows. In addition, if the story relates events that unfolded over a time sequence, readers can best follow such stories when they are presented in chronological order. Therefore, this method can be a clear and effective means of telling the story. Review again the Statement of the Case within the criminal wiretap brief in Appendix E. Notice how the facts are presented chronologically, with favorable facts emphasizing the theories of the case woven into the chronological presentation.

Important caveat: Although readers can best follow a story from the beginning to the end, do not follow this approach if a chronological recitation does not highlight your theory of the case. For example, in the spousal wiretap problem, the plaintiff's theory of the case focuses on the most *recent* episode of telephone monitoring and the couple's recent separation and pending divorce. Therefore, the plaintiff's lawyer elected to begin the factual statement by focusing on the more recent events, bringing in the couple's past practices only at the end.

3. Issue Grouping

Some facts do not lend themselves to an unfolding story. For example, the facts concerning the content of a personal diary do not lend themselves to a story of unfolding chronological events. Instead, they concern an object and whether that object merits the protection of the Fifth Amendment. Such facts should be grouped together ac-

---

5. Linda H. Edwards, *Legal Writing: Process, Analysis & Organization* 347 (2d ed. Aspen L. & Pub. 1999).

cording to the common issue to which they relate. The Statement of Facts in the Fifth Amendment brief illustrates this approach (Sample Brief B in Appendix D). Often, advocates combine both approaches by telling the story in chronological fashion while, within the chronology, grouping certain facts together that relate to common issues.

Exercise 32-1

Review the Statement of Facts contained in Sample Memo D in Appendix A (which involves Fred and Thelma Hurts' liability under the attractive nuisance doctrine after a child drowned in their pond). That sample memo illustrates how a lawyer would write the facts and law on behalf of the injured child. Assume that this case is currently before a court and that you are drafting a persuasive brief on behalf of the other party—Fred and Thelma Hurts. Take the facts you see in the sample memo's Statement of Facts, and rewrite them persuasively as a Statement of Facts for a brief you are writing on behalf of the Hurts. Remember that as counsel for the Hurts, you want to present the facts in a light favorable to them.

CHAPTER IN REVIEW

Core Concepts:

PRE-DRAFTING CONSIDERATIONS

1. Working with the record: As you review the record, look for:
   a. Facts that support your *theory of the case*;
   b. Facts that are *legally significant*, including both favorable and unfavorable facts;
   c. Facts that provide *context* for the factual story; and
   d. Facts that have *emotional appeal*.
2. Ethical considerations for documents that are filed with courts:
   a. Rules of professional conduct prohibit attorneys from misrepresenting facts and failing to disclose relevant adverse facts.
   b. Rules of professional conduct also prohibit attorneys from stating factual inferences as if they were facts.
      * However, you can properly include a witness's inference that appears in the trial record.
      * *Note*: You can argue your *own* inferences in the Argument section of a brief.

DRAFTING FACTUAL STATEMENTS

1. Create an appealing story.
   a. Emphasize facts that portray the story from the client's perspective.

    b. Detail facts that have emotional appeal, and that invite the reader to sense what it must have been like to be there as the story unfolded.

2. Emphasize favorable facts that advance your theory of the case.

    a. Emphasize favorable facts by prominently displaying all of their descriptive details.

    b. If a statement within a transcript graphically illustrates your theory of the case, quote that statement within the factual story.

3. De-emphasize unfavorable facts by:

    a. Burying them within the middle of a sentence or paragraph;

    b. Juxtaposing an unfavorable fact with a favorable fact;

    c. Rather than parading out the details of an unfavorable fact, dispensing with an unfavorable fact in a more summary fashion; and

    d. Using persuasive writing style strategies, such as the passive voice and non-action verbs (see Chapter 23).

4. Organize the facts to present a compelling story.

    a. Front-load the favorable facts that reflect your theory of the case within the first few paragraphs of your factual statement.

    b. If possible, end the factual statement with favorable facts.

    c. Chronological order: If a story relates events that unfold over time, provide context by presenting the story in chronological order.

       • *Caveat:* Do not follow this approach if a chronological recitation does not highlight your theory of the case.

    d. Issue grouping: If the facts do not lend themselves to a story about events unfolding over time, group facts according to issues.

TRIAL & APPELLATE COURT BRIEFS

Drafting Roadmaps of the Argument

Chapters 24 through 30 discuss in detail how to formulate, outline, and draft different types of arguments. When incorporating such arguments into a trial or appellate court brief, you will need to add a few additional components to the argument. First, you will use persuasive point-headings to lead the court through your argument. In addition, you will incorporate into your argument an Introduction (trial court briefs) or Summary of the Argument (appellate court briefs). Finally, if you are drafting an appellate court brief, you will also draft a Statement of the Issues, which is discussed in Chapter 35, and comply with the technical requirements described in Chapter 31.

I. PERSUASIVE POINT-HEADINGS

Point-headings serve two purposes in a brief: (1) they serve as visual signposts that lend clarity to the argument; and (2) they serve a persuasive purpose. To satisfy both goals, point-headings should state the conclusions you want the court to reach, and should state these conclusions as clearly and succinctly as possible. Thus, in a multi-issue brief, each issue you will address should be introduced by a major point-heading. If a single issue has separate components, each separate component should also be introduced with point-headings. If the discussion of a particular sub-issue within an issue requires the development of two or more arguments, you might also include point-headings to lead the court through those arguments, as well. Point-headings follow this format:

I. 1ST MAJOR POINT-HEADING
  A. *1st Sub-Heading*
  B. *2nd Sub-Heading*
      1. 1st Secondary Sub-Heading (if applicable)
      2. 2nd Secondary Sub-Heading (if applicable)
II. 2ND MAJOR POINT-HEADING

Do not include an "A" if there is no "B," or a "1" if there is no "2." Instead, simply include the argument within an umbrella point-heading that captures the argument.

If you sketched the outline of your argument before drafting the argument, your outline will also help you create the point-headings for your argument. When you outlined your argument, you noted the ultimate conclusion and legal issue conclusion(s) you wanted the court to adopt and the major premises that logically lead to each legal issue conclusion (and, therefore, the ultimate conclusion). To illustrate, consider the criminal wiretap problem that is depicted in Appendix E. As an attorney for the defendant, the ultimate conclusion you are advocating is that the wiretap evidence is inadmissible under the federal wiretap statute. That ultimate conclusion appears up-front in the first paragraph of the Summary of Argument. The template for the legal issue conclusions can be depicted as follows:

A. Law-based argument: The Government is required to prove that its pre-sealing procedures protected the wiretap tapes from any possibility of tampering.
  1. *Favorable Rule Statement*: Title III requires that the Government prove that its procedures protected the integrity of any wiretap tapes that it intends to introduce as evidence at trial.
  2. *Proof and Explanation of the Favorable Rule Statement*:
     Statute: 18 U.S.C. § 2518(8)(a) — provides the required statutory language.
     Case 1: *United States v. Johnson* — proves & explains favorable rule.
     Case 2: *United States v. Gigante* — proves & explains favorable rule.
     Case 3: *United States v. Giordano* — proves & explains favorable rule.
  3. *Restate Legal Issue Conclusion*: The Government cannot enter the wiretap tapes into evidence without proving that its procedures safeguarded the evidence from any possibility of tampering.
B. Fact-based argument: The Government's explanation was not satisfactory.
  - *1st Premise for This Issue*: The Government failed to store the wiretap tapes in a manner that would protect them from any possibility of tampering.

1. *Favorable Rule Statement*: A satisfactory explanation requires the Government to prove that its pre-sealing procedures protected the tapes from any possibility of tampering.

2. *Proof and Explanation of the Favorable Rule Statement*:

    Case 1: *United States v. Diana*—proves & explains favorable rule & favorable facts.

    Case 2: *United States v. Mora*—proves & explains favorable rule & favorable facts.

    Case 3: *United States v. Johnson*—use as tangential case to bolster argument.

3. *Favorable Application of the Law to the Client*:

    a.   The complete lack of security measures did not safeguard the tapes.

    b.   Due to lack of security measures, tapes may well have been compromised.

4. *Restate Legal Issue Conclusion*: Because the Government's pre-sealing procedures did not protect the tapes from any possibility of tampering, the explanation is not "satisfactory."

- *2nd Premise for this Issue*: The Government failed to act with reasonable diligence.

1. *Favorable Rule Statement*: A satisfactory explanation requires that the Government also act with reasonable diligence.

    Sub-rule: Reasonable diligence exists only when the delay is caused by a legitimate law enforcement purpose, and the Government acts with diligence to minimize the delay.

2. *Proof and Explanation of the Favorable Rule Statement*:

    Case 1: *United States v. Gigante*: proves & explains favorable rule and illustrates how a mistake is not a satisfactory explanation.

    Case 2: *United States v. Vazquez*—proves & explains favorable rule and facts.

3. *Favorable Application of the Law to the Client*:

    a.   A mistake is not a legitimate law enforcement purpose.

    b.   Agent Friday failed to act with diligence:

        i.   When she lost the tapes; and

        ii. When she failed to locate the missing tapes in a timely manner.

C. *Restate the Legal Issue Conclusion*: The Government did not provide a satisfactory explanation because it both failed to store the tapes in a manner that would protect them from any possibility of tampering and failed to act with reasonable diligence to minimize the delay.

To draft persuasive point-headings for this brief, the arguments and supporting premises from this outline are simply converted into point-headings. For example, the major arguments and supporting premises set forth in the above outline are as follows:

> I. *1st Argument*: As part of its "satisfactory explanation," the Government must prove that its pre-sealing procedures protected the wiretap tapes from any possibility of tampering.
>
> II. *2nd Argument*: The Government's explanation was not satisfactory.
>
>   A. *1st premise for this issue*: The Government failed to store the wiretap tapes in a manner that would protect them from any possibility of tampering.
>
>   B. *2nd premise for this issue*: The Government failed to act with reasonable diligence.
>
>   1.   1st Secondary Sub-Heading (if applicable)
>
>   2.   2nd Secondary Sub-Heading (if applicable)

After identifying the separate components of the argument that you will introduce with point-headings, next consider your language. Each point-heading should be a clear, affirmative statement that identifies the conclusion you want the court to reach. Do not dilute the persuasive appeal of the point-heading by making the statement a request, or by stating the rule as your "opinion" rather than as a statement of affirmative truth. Using the criminal wiretap brief problem for purposes of illustration, the conclusion from the fact-centered argument (issue #2) is simply rephrased to add clarity and persuasive appeal. Thus, the conclusion is more persuasively stated as:

> **Correct:**
>
> II. THE GOVERNMENT FAILED TO PROVIDE A "SATISFACTORY EXPLANATION" FOR ITS TWO-MONTH DELAY IN SEALING THE WIRETAP TAPES.

In the above example, the conclusion was clarified by adding the underlying context for the issue. The advocate also enhanced the persuasive appeal of the desired conclusion by using the active voice and a strong verb ("failed") to link the Government with unfavorable conduct ("its delay"). Consider how much less effective that point-heading would be if it was phrased as an opinion rather than a conclusion:

> **Incorrect:**
>
> II. THE DEFENDANT ARGUES THAT THE GOVERNMENT FAILED TO PROVIDE A "SATISFACTORY EXPLANATION" FOR ITS DELAY IN SEALING THE WIRETAP TAPES.

Finally, point-headings that are too wordy and that contain too much information are also less effective. Consider how much less effective the point-heading would be if it were diluted with too much information:

> **Incorrect:**
>
> II. THE GOVERNMENT FAILED TO PROVIDE A "SATISFACTORY EXPLANATION" FOR ITS DELAY IN OBTAINING A JUDICIAL SEAL OF THE WIRETAP TAPES WHEN IT LOST THE TAPES IN AN OFFICE MOVE AND DID NOT SUBMIT THEM FOR SEALING UNTIL TWO MONTHS LATER WHEN IT FOUND THEM IN A SUPPLY ROOM.

Now that we've prepared the correct point-heading for the legal issue conclusion of the fact-centered argument (issue #2 in the brief), we can add the sub-headings for the two premises identified in our outline:

> II. THE GOVERNMENT FAILED TO PROVIDE A "SATISFACTORY EXPLANATION" FOR ITS TWO-MONTH DELAY IN SEALING THE WIRETAP TAPES.
> A. *The Government Failed to Store the Wiretap Tapes in a Manner That Would Protect Them from Any Possibility of Tampering.*
> B. *The Government Failed to Act with Reasonable Diligence.*

Exercise 33-1

Draft persuasive point-headings for the trial or appellate court brief your professor has previously assigned.

II. SUMMARY OF ARGUMENT

A. Importance of the Summary of Argument

All appellate and many trial court briefs contain a separate section that summarizes the most compelling components of the argument. Because it is a self-contained section outside of the Argument itself, this section is different from the overview and thesis paragraphs that might appear within the body of the argument. In an appellate court brief, the Summary of the Argument follows the Statement of Facts (which is often called the Statement of the Case). Therefore, the Summary of the Argument is sandwiched between the factual statement and the fully articulated argument. You may wish to review the sample brief in Appendix E to familiarize yourself with this section of the brief. A trial court brief of any length usually incorporates a summary of a similar nature, although it is called an "Introduction." An Introduction precedes both the Statement of Facts and the Argument itself. The sample briefs in Appendices C and D contain separate Introduction sections that precede the Statement of Facts. Whether drafting an argument summary for an appellate or trial court brief, the essential goals and components are the same. For purposes of brevity, this chapter generically refers to both the "Introduction" and the "Summary of Argument" as the "Summary of the Argument."

The importance of the Summary of Argument cannot be overstated. It provides a critically important persuasive roadmap of the argument that will follow. You cannot even begin to persuade a court to agree with the myriad reasons and details that support an argument unless the court first understands the broad parameters of that argument. Providing context in persuasive writing is particularly important in brief writing because of the intended audience. The typical judge is very busy, handling hundreds of cases that may range from a sophisticated anti-trust problem to a simple negligence claim. As one judge writes:

> Judges "tend to be very busy. As a result, they have highly selective reading habits. They need and expect to know what a given case is about, and the opening of the summary of argument should tell them immediately.... The introduction of your summary... must let the reader know in a few sentences the scope, theme, content and outcome of the brief. It sets the stage for the discussion to follow. It dispatches your argument to the reader at once in succinct, concise and minimal terms. It describes the equitable heart of the [argument]. It sets forth the brief's strongest point—the argument... [in a manner] most calculated to persuade the court to your point of view.... If you are unable to write a cogent, succinct, encompassing introduction, you probably do not have a solid grasp of the subject matter."[1]

---

1. Ruggero J. Aldisert, *Winning on Appeal: Better Briefs and Oral Argument* 176 (Rev. 1st ed. NITA 1996).

The Summary of Argument, or Introduction, is also important because it is often the first part of the argument the judge reads. Consider this statement from Judge James L. Robertson of the Mississippi Supreme Court:

> I think the most important part of the brief is the Summary of the Argument. I invariably read it first. It is almost like the opening statement in a trial. From clear and plausible argument summary, I often get an inclination to affirm or reverse that rises almost to the dignity of a (psychologically) rebuttable presumption. I do not mean to denigrate the importance of a fully developed and technically sound argument. But I read the subsequent argument in a "show me" frame of mind, testing whether it confirms my impression from the summary of the argument.[2]

B. Drafting a Summary of Argument

The Summary of Argument should seize the court's attention by clearly describing: (1) the result you want the court to reach; and (2) the very best and most cogent reasons that would compel any reasonable person to agree with your conclusion. In doing so, the argument summary also provides the court with the legal framework of your argument.

Drafting an argument summary requires an intimate familiarity with the nuances of your argument. Therefore, wait to draft your Summary of Argument until after you have already drafted and polished the body of your argument and have incorporated point-headings into the argument. If your argument has point-headings, they embody the basic roadmap of your argument; therefore, the Summary of Argument should incorporate the substance of each of your point-headings, with enough "filler" for the court to understand why such conclusions are sound. Because your point-headings should reflect your theory of the case, your theme should also be evident from reading the Summary of Argument.

Using the criminal wiretap brief for purposes of illustration, recall that the brief contains both a law-centered and a fact-centered argument. In the law-centered issue, the lawyer argues that the statutorily-required "satisfactory explanation" for sealing delays requires that the Government prove that its pre-sealing procedures protected the tapes from any possibility of tampering. In the fact-centered issue, the lawyer argues (1) that the Government's pre-sealing procedures did not, in fact, protect the tapes from any possibility of tampering and (2) that the Government failed to act with reasonable diligence in sealing the tapes. The Introduction section therefore incorporates all three arguments, as follows:

---

2. Aldisert, *supra* note 1, at 175-76 (quoting Robertson, *From the Bench: Reality on Appeal*, 17 Litig. 3, 5 (Fall 1990)).

Ultimate Conclusion.

Statutory context for issue.

States how the ultimate conclusion logically follows from the statute.

Identifies the 1st favorable standard.

Summarizes the policy reasons why this standard is proper (the law-centered argument).

Summarizes why the Government failed to satisfy this standard (the fact-centered argument).

Identifies the 2nd favorable standard.

Summarizes why the Government failed to satisfy this standard:

The evidence obtained by the Government from a wiretap on Mr. Hart's home telephone is inadmissible at trial because the Government failed to comply with the requirements of the wiretap statute. The wiretap statute requires the Government to safeguard the tapes by immediately "sealing" them or by providing a "satisfactory explanation" for its failure to do so. 18 U.S.C. § 2518 (8)(a). In this case, the Government failed to comply with its statutory obligation. After intercepting private telephone conversations from Mr. Hart's home telephone, the Government failed to surrender the tapes immediately to a judge who could have protected their integrity with a judicial seal. The Government also failed to provide a "satisfactory explanation" for its failure to seek immediate judicial protection.

A "satisfactory explanation" requires the Government to satisfy two standards. First, a "satisfactory explanation" requires the Government to prove that its pre-sealing procedures protected the tapes from any possibility of tampering. Congress enacted the immediate sealing requirement as an external safeguard to ensure that the integrity of wiretap tapes would remain inviolate. Therefore, when the Government fails to protect the integrity of the tapes by immediately obtaining the protection of a judicial seal, its alternative explanation must ensure a similar level of protection. Here, the Government wholly failed to provide any level of protection for its sensitive evidence. Instead, the wiretap tapes sat exposed in an open box in a busy, unlocked supply room for over two months. The box sat exposed and available for any one of the 5,000 occupants of the building, or any visitor to the storage room, to tamper with the tapes.

Second, a "satisfactory explanation" requires that the Government act with reasonable diligence to minimize the sealing delay. Again, the Government's conduct falls far short of this standard. The sealing delay was caused by a mistake, a mistake that was not only foreseeable but easily preventable. Although the Government knew that its bureau offices would be moving the following day, Agent Friday failed to take any precautions to ensure that the tapes would be safely delivered to the courthouse for sealing. Instead, she dropped the tapes into a box identical to the thousands of moving boxes used to move office files and supplies. To compound that initial carelessness, Agent Friday delayed over a month before she placed a single telephone call to ensure that the tapes had arrived at the courthouse for sealing. Upon finding the tapes were missing, it took Agent Friday almost another full month to locate the tapes, despite the fact that she ultimately found them in an open box in a busy supply room. The Government's lengthy delay in obtaining the protection of a judicial seal violates the mandatory provisions of the federal Wiretap Act.

> (1) A foreseeable mistake.
> (2) Mistake compounded by carelessness after the move.
> (3) Mistake compounded by the length of time it took to locate the missing tapes.

> Restates the conclusion.

Exercise 33-2

Draft an Introduction or Summary of Argument for the trial or appellate court brief your professor has previously assigned.

SUMMARY JUDGMENT
BRIEFS

In Chapter 31, you were introduced to the "brief," which is a document containing a written argument that is submitted to a court. You also learned that a brief often accompanies a "motion" that asks the court to take a specific action, and you read about the basic types of briefs you will encounter in practice—pre-trial briefs, trial briefs, and appellate court briefs. This chapter focuses on a specific type of pre-trial brief that you will likely draft (and draft often) if you practice civil litigation—the summary judgment brief. A summary judgment brief accompanies a motion for summary judgment, and it asks the trial court to find in favor of the moving party on the merits of the claim, without the need for a trial. Thus, the summary judgment motion is a very powerful tool. If the motion is successful, the client prevails without having to face a judge or jury in trial.

Attorneys typically file summary judgment motions after the case's discovery phase has concluded, although such motions could be filed sooner. A party moving for summary judgment seeks to show the court that under the case's record evidence (typically elicited during discovery), there is no need for a trial, because the outcome-determinative facts (called "material facts") are not in dispute. The attorney will show that under the relevant law, these undisputed material facts entitle the moving party to a judgment as a matter of law.

Any party to the litigation can move for summary judgment. A plaintiff seeking summary judgment would request a finding in her favor on one or more of the claims she presented in the Complaint. A defendant may respond to such motion in opposition, attempting to demonstrate that the plaintiff's motion should not be granted, and the defendant may also file his own motion for summary judgment, asking the court to find that the plaintiff's claims do not warrant relief as a matter of law. Further, if the defendant presented a counter-claim, the defendant could move for summary judgment on the merits of that claim, and the plaintiff would have the same options to respond to the claim in opposition and/or file her own summary judgment motion, asking the court to find that the counter-claim should fail as a matter of law.

Because most of the body of a summary judgment brief follows general brief-writing considerations already introduced in earlier chapters, this chapter will focus only on the distinct characteristics of a summary judgment brief by: (1) introducing you to the summary judgment standard, and (2) focusing on the nuances of drafting the factual portion of a summary judgment brief (called the Statement of Material Facts).

This is the basic structure of the summary judgment brief, with the focus sections of this chapter emphasized in boxes:

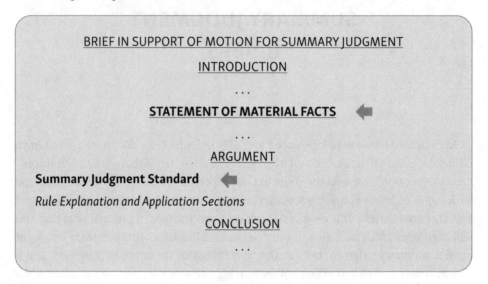

BRIEF IN SUPPORT OF MOTION FOR SUMMARY JUDGMENT

INTRODUCTION

. . .

STATEMENT OF MATERIAL FACTS

. . .

ARGUMENT

Summary Judgment Standard

Rule Explanation and Application Sections

CONCLUSION

. . .

I. THE SUMMARY JUDGMENT STANDARD

Before drafting a summary judgment brief, it is important to fully understand what the summary judgment standard requires. An attorney filing a summary judgment motion before a federal court would consult the Federal Rules of Civil Procedure to ascertain the relevant standard, and litigants filing such a motion in state court would consult that state's civil procedure rules. Often, state rules mirror the language of the federal rules, but it is important that you review the standard for your jurisdiction. Not only is the standard important for your understanding of the requirements, but you will provide the standard's language within the Argument section of your summary judgment brief.

Rule 56 of the Federal Rules of Civil Procedure provides:

A party may move for summary judgment, identifying each claim or defense—or the part of each claim or defense—on which summary judgment is sought. The court shall grant summary judgment if the movant shows that there is *no genuine dispute as to any material fact* and the movant is *entitled to judgment as a matter of law*.[1]

---

1. Fed. R. Civ. P. 56(a) (emphasis added).

State civil procedure rules often include a standard that is substantively similar to the federal rules. For example, Oklahoma's civil procedure rules provide that summary judgment should be granted "if the pleadings, the discovery and disclosure materials on file, and any affidavits show that there is no genuine issue as to any material fact and that the movant is entitled to judgment as a matter of law."[2]

Accordingly, it is your goal within the summary judgment brief to persuade the court both that the case's material facts are not in dispute and that the legal authorities require that judgment be entered in your client's favor. In the Argument section of the brief, you will provide your jurisdiction's standard for summary judgment, paying careful attention to your word choice. Recall that while writing a brief, your central goal is to persuade the court to find in your client's favor. This means that the full document will be drafted with a persuasive slant, including the recitation of the summary judgment standard. In Chapter 25 you learned the methods for drafting favorable, persuasive rule statements. In drafting any rule statement, one preliminary question you must ask is whether it will benefit your client to phrase the rule in a manner that would make the standard very difficult to satisfy or, alternatively, very easy to satisfy. Further, as you contemplate your word choice—do you want to make the desired result a mandatory choice under certain circumstances, or should you phrase the result as something that cannot be granted unless certain circumstances are present? The answer in this situation will depend on whether you are asking a court to grant your client summary judgment or, instead, asking the court to deny summary judgment to the opposing party. If you represent a party seeking summary judgment, you might phrase the relevant portion of Rule 56 as follows:

> Summary judgment *must* be granted when "the movant shows that there is no genuine dispute as to any material fact and the movant is entitled to judgment as a matter of law."

This rule statement is persuasive for the moving party because it showcases a steadfast requirement of the court—that summary judgment *must* be granted when specific circumstances are present. Consider now the following rule statement that is favorable for a party opposing a summary judgment motion:

> Summary judgment *may not* be granted *unless* "the movant shows that there is no genuine dispute as to any material fact and the movant is entitled to judgment as a matter of law."

---

2. Okla. Stat. tit. 12, § 2056(C) (2014).

This minor change to the standard's language is quite impactful—it showcases the difficulty in meeting the summary judgment standard, which is the impression the attorney hopes the court will have as it considers the merits of the opposing party's motion.

II. DRAFTING SUMMARY JUDGMENT FACTS

At the heart of the summary judgment brief is the Statement of Material Facts, which is the term used in summary judgment briefs for the Factual Statement that is included in trial and appellate court briefs. Because the summary judgment standard focuses squarely on the undisputed nature of a case's "material facts," a party moving for summary judgment must convincingly show the court that the case's most important facts are settled and not in dispute. These facts must also be presented in such a way that when they are later applied to the relevant law in the Argument portion of the brief, they demand a finding in the moving party's favor.

However, a party opposing a summary judgment motion may attempt to show the opposite—that the material facts *are* in dispute and that a trial is therefore required. While this chapter will focus on drafting facts that support a moving party's brief, information regarding the mechanics of drafting facts, and doing so persuasively, will apply equally to any party drafting a summary judgment brief, whether as the moving or non-moving party.

A. General Requirements for Composing the Material Facts

Courts are often quite particular about the required structure of the material facts section of a brief, and your jurisdiction's local rules will specify the requirements for this section of the brief. Local Rule 56.1 of the United States District Court for the Northern District of Illinois provides a typical example. This rule notes that a party moving for summary judgment shall provide "a statement of material facts as to which the moving party contends there is no genuine issue," and such statement "shall consist of short numbered paragraphs, including within each paragraph specific references to the affidavits, parts of the record, and other supporting materials relied upon to support the facts set forth...."[3] Thus, the material facts section is structured similarly to the allegations in a Complaint, with short, numbered paragraphs containing specific facts that an opponent can specifically reference when responding to the motion.

In addition, the facts in this section must be supported by evidence in the record, typically referred to as "record evidence." Rule 56 of the Federal Rules of Civil Procedure provides examples of materials that can support factual assertions, including "depositions, documents, electronically stored information, affidavits or declarations,

---

3. N.D. Ill. L.R. 56.1(a).

stipulations…, interrogatory answers, or other materials."[4] In addition to citing re-cord evidence, it is also permissible to note what is *absent* from the record, with a statement such as "Plaintiff never testified that ____," or "The contract does not con-tain a provision regarding ____."

When citing to the record evidence, you must provide the reader with a citation that allows the reader to easily locate the fact you provided. For example, if you found information for a statement of fact on line 5 of page 35 of a witness's deposi-tion transcript, provide that page and line number to the reader. There are various ways to cite to the evidence. Law firms often develop a unique method of record citing, and while the citations may vary slightly from one firm to the next, the gen-eral content is the same—the citation must identify the name of the document and direct the reader to the specific place to find the content. *The Bluebook* also provides guidance on citing to litigation documents, noting that the citation should include: "(1) the name of the document, abbreviated where appropriate," and "(2) the pin-point citation."[5] It also notes that the document's date should be included, "if re-quired."[6] Often, the date is included the first time the document is cited but will not be included thereafter, unless the date is necessary in later citations to pinpoint the specific document the author is citing (as with a witness, for example, who has tes-tified in more than one deposition). The Bluepages table BT1 supplies a list of abbre-viations, such as "Compl." for Complaint, "Dep." for deposition, and "Aff." for affida-vit,[7] and the Bluepages rules provide examples for supplying pinpoint pages.[8] For example, in citing a deposition transcript, *The Bluebook* provides the following ex-ample, with page 15, line 21 as the starting point and page 16, line 4 as the ending point: "Clark Dep. 15:21-16:4."[9] It also provides the following example for citing page 6 of an affidavit: "Hawkins Aff. 6."[10] The ALWD citation manual provides similar guidance for citing these documents.[11]

Using the Plaintiff's sample summary judgment brief in Appendix C, which focus-es on the spousal wiretap problem, note the following material facts excerpted from the brief that provide facts in short, numbered paragraphs and with citations to re-cord evidence per *Bluebook*:

---

4. Fed. R. Civ. P. 56(c)(A).

5. *The Bluebook: A Uniform System of Citation* B17.1, at 24-25 (Columbia L. Rev. Ass'n et al. eds., 21st ed. 2020).

6. *Id.*

7. *Id.* at 29 tbl. BT1.

8. *Id.* at B17.1, at 25.

9. *Id.*

10. *Id.*

11. Rule 25 of the ALWD Guide to Legal Citation (5th edition) provides the citation format for litiga-tion documents.

1. Plaintiff, Michael Harrison, and Defendant, Kathryn Harrison, were divorced on February 6, 2021. Four days after the couple became legally separated on November 1, 2020, Defendant began intercepting Mr. Harrison's out-going and in-coming telephone calls. (M. Harrison Dep. 35:5 (Mar. 13, 2021); K. Harrison Dep. 10:15 (Mar. 14, 2021).)

2. Because the couple was in the midst of divorce proceedings, relations were very "strained." Additionally, sexual relations between the couple had ceased, and Defendant accused Mr. Harrison of engaging in an extramarital affair. (K. Harrison Dep. 11:15.)

3. In fact, the Harrisons' marriage had deteriorated to the point that, while still living in the same house, the couple slept in separate bedrooms and "strived to keep contact at a minimum." (M. Harrison Dep. 15:9-22.)

With the facts presented in this manner and cited with specific pinpoints, the court can easily verify that the facts alleged in the brief are supported by the case's record evidence.

B. Persuasive Fact-Drafting Strategies

In Chapter 32, you learned about working with a record and how to draft factual statements that create an appealing story, that advance your theory of the case, and that highlight favorable facts and de-emphasize unfavorable ones. You also learned about effectively organizing your facts to tell the story in the way you want it told, how to create factual inferences, and the ethical importance of candor and truth in any statement you make to the court. Chapter 32 thus provides an important backdrop of considerations in telling the court your factual story, and these considerations directly apply to the material facts section of your summary judgment brief. Using the strategies from Chapter 32, along with additional considerations that are specific to summary judgment facts as supplied in this chapter, will prepare you for persuasive and thorough fact drafting in the summary judgment brief.

Recall from Chapter 32 that your factual statement must include every legally significant fact that will later appear in the Argument section of your brief. This means that before you begin drafting the material facts, you should thoroughly research the legal requirements of each cause of action or defense you will address in the brief and ensure you provide the facts needed for those requirements. For example, in the spousal wiretap problem discussed in the sample summary judgment briefs in Appendix C, the issue was whether the husband impliedly consented to the interception of his telephone calls. Binding case law provides that implied consent may be "inferred from surrounding circumstances indicating that the [party] knowingly agreed to the surveillance."[12] In the Plaintiff's Sample Brief in Appendix C, the plaintiff-husband moved for summary judgment, asking that the defendant-wife be found liable as a matter of law for violating the federal wiretap statute. The Statement of Material Facts included legally significant facts relating to the plaintiff's awareness and agreement to the surveillance: "Mr. Harrison has testified that he 'had no idea [the Plaintiff] was recording my telephone calls, nor would I have ever agreed to such an invasion . . . .' (M. Harrison Dep. 35:5.)." After providing this fact in the Material Facts section, the author is ready to assert that fact in the Argument section when applying the facts to the legal requirements.

Be careful, however, to avoid asserting legal conclusions or using rule language in your factual statement. Courts require that the Statement of Material Facts contain facts only, and many jurisdictions will specify this requirement within their court rules.[13] This section should contain only facts that come from testimony or other record evidence, and if a witness testifies in a deposition to a legal conclusion, you must avoid using that testimony and instead only reference the facts that the witness provided in the deposition testimony. The factual statement must also include basic background facts that provide context for the court and effectively tell your story. Although your facts are provided in numbered paragraph form, they should read like a story, with easy transitions from one fact to the next.

In addition, think about effective organization. If your brief covers one cause of action without multiple separate issues, it likely makes sense to provide the facts without the use of headings. However, if your brief will cover a spectrum of issues, all with facts that relate specifically to different issues, it may be confusing and overwhelming to provide all the facts in one fell swoop. Chapter 32 introduces issue grouping, which may help with organization in a complex brief. Grouping the facts by issue, and providing headings for each group, will aid the court in understanding the facts as they relate to each other.

For example, consider the attractive nuisance doctrine problem that forms the basis of Sample Memo D in Appendix A. Recall that the child in that case drowned after he fell in a pond on the defendants' property after the dock near the pond collapsed. The sample Memo analyzed three elements of the attractive nuisance doctrine—(1) whether the landowners could reasonably foresee the presence of trespassing children on their property, (2) whether the property contained a hidden danger, and (3) whether the landowners failed to exercise reasonable care to protect the child from injury. Suppose that the plaintiffs in that case filed suit and were prepared to move for summary judgment, requesting that the defendants be found liable for the child's death as a matter of law under the attractive nuisance doctrine.

---

12. *Griggs-Ryan v. Smith*, 904 F.2d 112, 116 (1st Cir. 1990).

13. *See, e.g.*, D. Neb. Civ. R. 56.1 ("The statement of facts must describe the parties and recite all facts supporting the court's venue and jurisdiction. The statement must not contain legal conclusions.").

In drafting the Statement of Material Facts for a summary judgment brief, the attorney would recognize that the facts relating to the separate elements of the doctrine are quite distinct. Accordingly, this would be a situation in which grouping them by issue would likely prove helpful to the factual organization. Below is an example of using headings to separate these groups. Note that the headings are factual and do not contain legal conclusions. The legal conclusion headings belong in the Argument section of the brief as point headings, as discussed in Chapter 33, and do not belong in the factual portion of your summary judgment brief.

NOTE: Assume this is an excerpt from the Statement of Material Facts section of the brief and that the author, in other areas of the factual statement, provided facts with context about the child's accident. As you review the factual headings, notice how the attorney avoids stating legal conclusions, which would be improper in this section of the brief. Compare "Location and Surroundings of the Property" (*factual heading*) to "Location and Surroundings of the Property Make Trespassing Foreseeable" (improper *legal heading*).

A. LOCATION AND SURROUNDINGS OF THE PROPERTY

1. Defendants' pond is man-made, and they have stocked it with fish and ducks. (F. Hurt Dep. 18:3-9.)
2. It is common for children to play near the pond, and Defendants' grandchildren fish in the pond, feed the ducks, and play on inner-tubes that Defendants leave in the pond. (F. Hurt Dep. 17:2-6.)
3. Reed Elementary School is located on property adjacent to Defendants' property, and children are known to travel near Defendants' property on a "continual basis" on their way to and from school. (T. Hurt Dep. 7:7-29.)

B. CHARACTERISTICS OF THE DOCK

4. Approximately twenty (20) years ago, Defendants installed a dock over the pond that extends about one foot above and fifteen feet over the pond. Because of the rocky shoreline, the dock is the only means of access to the pond. (F. Hurt Dep. 24:1-7; T. Hurt Dep. 6:14-22.)
5. Ms. Hurt admitted that on the date of the accident, the dock was in a state of disrepair, in that it was both "decaying and rotting." (T. Hurt Dep. 9:6-9.)
6. Ms. Hurt further admitted that the decay was partially hidden by a green shiny coating of moss and algae growing on the dock. (T. Hurt Dep. 11:11-19.)

C. DEFENDANTS' BEHAVIOR IN RELATION TO THE PROPERTY

7. Only an inexpensive chain-link fence surrounds Defendants' property. After the elementary school was built nearby, the fence installer

warned Defendants that the fence would not keep school children from entering the property, but Defendants were not persuaded to build a more secure privacy fence. (F. Hurt Dep. 30:2-10.)

8. As an alternative to erecting a more secure privacy fence, Defendants elected to post a "No Trespassing" sign on the chain-link fence. (F. Hurt Dep. 31:12-15.)

9. In addition, Ms. Hurt admitted that she commonly left the gate on the chain-link fence unlocked and that she had not locked it prior to the accident. (T. Hurt Dep. 24:16-25.)

Notice in the factual examples provided above that it is clear the author is the attorney representing the parents of the deceased child (the plaintiffs). This should be obvious given the narrative the facts are promoting. The facts create an inference that the defendants knew there were dangers on their property and that children would be exposed to those dangers. They further showcase, without directly stating, that the defendants chose to save money rather than erect a fence that could save the life of a child. If the facts in a summary judgment brief do not clearly favor the party for whom they are drafted, they are not drafted persuasively.

Also notice in the facts given above that although plaintiffs' counsel drafted the factual section, counsel chose to summarize and quote the *defendants'* testimony rather than rely simply on the plaintiffs' testimony. When choosing the evidence to include in your factual statement, there should be strategic thinking behind your decisions. If your factual statement contains testimony from only one witness, and that witness happens to be your client, it is challenging to label the facts as "undisputed." Rather, when possible, the facts should come from a spectrum of evidence and the testimony of multiple parties. In particular, if you have favorable testimony or evidence (such as an interrogatory answer or deposition testimony) that comes from your opponent, that is the best option for you. It becomes more challenging for the opposing party to dispute that there is "no genuine issue of material fact" if the evidence comes straight from the opponent. Thus, citing the opponent's deposition testimony, and quoting the opponent when appropriate, should be a strategic focal point when drafting your facts. However, that does not mean that you should not also cite evidence from your own client's testimony or documents—such evidence will also be needed to tell the whole story. But if the truly critical evidence comes from the opponent, that will strengthen your case considerably.

When it comes to quotations, again, strategy should be at the forefront. If you make the mistake of over-quoting within your factual statement, each quote will pack less of a punch, and, even worse, the reader may stop reading the facts closely, as readers do not enjoy reading a series of quotes. Instead, think about what testimony or other evidence is really critical, or which evidence is stated in such a way that it creates the inference you want. It is that sort of evidence, and evidence from your opponent that specifically advances your theory of the case, that you want to quote in your factual statement.

Exercise 34-1

In various chapters throughout this textbook, you have considered a hypothetical problem regarding a firefighter who was terminated from her job for "insubordination." The firefighter's name is Jessica Levy, and she believes her termination was due to sex discrimination. She has filed suit to recover damages under Title VII. Recall that the elements of her claim for sex discrimination claim include: (1) that she is a member of a protected class (in this case, the protected class is her gender); (2) that she was subject to an adverse employment decision; (3) that the adverse employment decision was motivated by her gender; and (4) that she was otherwise qualified for the position.

For purposes of this exercise, you represent Ms. Levy, and you are drafting a Motion for Summary Judgment with a brief in support of that motion. In particular, you are currently working on the Statement of Material Facts, and you are drafting facts that show Ms. Levy was **qualified** for her position as a firefighter. Using the fire chief's deposition excerpt below, draft the material facts relating *only* to this issue. Remember to draft them persuasively, but truthfully, to favor your client, and to use the format and citation parameters discussed earlier in this chapter. Remember also to provide only facts and no legal conclusions.

Excerpt from Deposition of Nathan Holloway

1   **Q: Mr. Holloway, did you hire Ms. Levy?**

2   A: Yes, I did. I hired her in 2019.

3   **Q: What made you select her as the candidate? Do you recall anything**
4   **about her application or interview with the fire department?**

5   A: Yes, I do. She interview well, and she had the necessary credentials. She
6   completed an associate's degree in fire science and had prior experience
7   with fire safety jobs. So we decided to hire her. We only had one position
8   open, and it came down to her and another applicant—I think his name
9   was Brian Reynolds. They were both good candidates, but she was more
10   experienced at that time, and we thought that her interview was better.
11   She seemed like the better candidate—that was, until she was here and
12   we got to know her. I later regretted that decision and wished I had hired
13   Brian.

14 Q: Was there anything about Ms. Levy's application that led you to believe
15 she was not qualified for the position?

16 A: No, there wasn't. I mean, we hired her. Like I said, she had the credentials
17 and the experience we were looking for. But when she arrived, she just had
18 this attitude. I would describe it as "insubordinate." It was like she always
19 wanted to push back against the orders I gave.

20 Q: Is that why you fired her?

21 A: Yes, it became too much. The insubordination was rubbing off on other
22 people. It was spoiling the well, or poisoning the well, or whatever that saying
23 is. It was affecting my crew and the respect that I expect around here. So it
24 was time for her to go.

25 Q: Ok, but tell us about her performance as a firefighter. Did she perform
26 the job she was hired to do?

27 A: Yes, she did the job. She showed up on time, and she responded to fire
28 calls promptly. She maintained and operated the fire equipment as directed.
29 I didn't see issues there. It was just her attitude—mostly her attitude
30 towards her superiors—that was a big problem.

APPELLATE COURT BRIEFS

Scope of Review & Statement of the Issues

I. THE STANDARD OF REVIEW ON APPEAL

Appellate courts review different types of questions under different standards of review. Standards of review range from the extremely deferential standard accorded to facts found by juries, to no deference at all accorded to questions of law adopted by lower courts. Therefore, it's important to know the appropriate standard of review that governs each issue on appeal. The lens through which the appellate court will be examining each issue will affect the way in which you frame your issues and argument; your arguments must show why, under the appropriate standard of review, your client should prevail.

A. Questions of Law

Questions of law are simply law-centered issues that concern the meaning of a rule of law itself, without regard to specific facts. An appellate court resolves questions of law under a "de novo" standard of review. Under the de novo standard of review, the appellate court does not have to defer to the lower court's interpretation of what a rule of law means; instead, the appellate court is free to substitute its own judgment for that of the trial court.

For example, the criminal wiretap problem illustrated in Appendix E contains the following question of law: What legal standard must the Government satisfy to provide a "satisfactory explanation" for a sealing delay under the federal wiretap statute? In that problem, the trial court determined that the Government provides a satisfactory explanation when it produces credible expert testimony that the wiretap tapes were not, in fact, altered during the sealing delay. On review, an appellate court is free to substitute its own judgment about the appropriate legal standard. Therefore, the appellate court would be free to conclude that a "satisfactory explanation" requires the Government to prove that its pre-sealing procedures protected the tapes from any *possibility* of tampering.

B. Questions of Fact

Facts are simply the historical and narrative accounts of "what happened" that were introduced into evidence during trial. A factual finding is simply the fact-finder's interpretation of that evidence. Pure factual findings are decided without reference to the law itself. For example, in the criminal wiretap problem, the fact-finder would answer such factual questions as whether the box was sealed or open, and whether the Government lost the wiretap tapes or, instead, whether the delay was deliberate.

1. Factual Questions Resolved by a Jury

Factual questions resolved by a jury provide appellate courts with a very limited scope of review. These questions fall at the opposite end of the spectrum from questions of law, in which the appellate court is free to substitute its own judgment for that of the lower court. An appellate court will not disturb a jury's factual findings unless there is no evidence at all from which the jury could arrive at that finding. Thus, an appellate court will generally not disturb a jury's factual findings unless those findings are not supported by any evidence. The deference accorded to jury verdicts stems in part from the parties' constitutional right to a trial by jury.

2. Factual Questions Resolved by a Trial Court

Factual questions resolved by a trial court are accorded slightly less deference than questions resolved by a jury. When reviewing a factual question resolved by a trial court judge, the appellate court reviews the judge's determinations under a "clearly erroneous" standard of review. In other words, the appellate court will not disturb that finding unless it concludes that the judge's decision was clearly erroneous. The "clearly erroneous" standard has been defined by the United States Supreme Court to mean that an appellate court "can upset a finding of fact, even when supported by some evidence, but only if the court has 'the definite and firm conviction that a mistake has been committed.'"[1]

C. Mixed Questions of Fact and Law: Ultimate Facts

Often, the fact-finder must determine whether the facts satisfy a certain standard under the law. Therefore, when arriving at an ultimate factual conclusion, the fact-finder must consider both the underlying historical facts that were introduced into evidence and the legal standard from which the facts should be evaluated. The resulting determination is called an ultimate factual conclusion.

Mixed questions of fact and law present interesting challenges for the appellate court. The appellate court may not disturb the basic *fact* component of the ultimate factual conclusion unless the fact-finder's determination was either not support by

---

1. Ruggero J. Aldisert, *Winning on Appeal: Better Briefs and Oral Argument* 63 (Rev. 1st ed. NITA 1996) (quoting *United States v. United States Gypsum Co.*, 333 U.S. 364, 395 (1948)).

any evidence (in the case of a jury determination), or "clearly erroneous" (in the case of a trial judge's determination). However, an appellate court may review the *law* component of the ultimate factual conclusion "de novo." In other words, the appellate court is free to substitute its own judgment when interpreting the meaning of a rule of law. Thus, the standard of review becomes complex, with part of the lower court's findings subject to a "clearly erroneous" standard and part of the lower court's findings subject to "de novo" review.

D. Questions Within the Trial Court's Discretion

The "abuse of discretion" standard is applied to matters that are within the trial court's discretion. For example, some statutes or court rules provide judges with the discretion to consider certain factors when resolving an issue. Under some statutes, judges have the discretion to award attorneys' fees. A trial court judge also has discretion over many matters of procedure. An appellate court might find an abuse of discretion when it finds the lower court's judgment to be "arbitrary, fanciful, or unreasonable" or when "no reasonable [person] would take the view adopted by the trial court."[2]

However, the "abuse of discretion" standard is somewhat difficult to define, in part because the scope of review depends on the breadth of the discretionary power conferred on the trial judge. If a trial judge has broad discretionary power to decide an issue, the corresponding scope of review should reflect that broad discretionary power. However, if the trial judge has more limited discretion, the scope of review should also reflect that more limited power.[3] Therefore, if you are appealing a trial court's use of discretion, you should research other cases involving the same or similar uses of discretion in order to gain a clearer idea of the deference the appellate court is likely to accord the trial judge.

II. STATEMENT OF THE ISSUES

All appellate court briefs contain a section that describes the issues the appellate court is being asked to resolve on appeal. In some courts, this section is called the "Statement of the Issues." In other courts, this section is called the "Questions Presented" or the "Issues Presented for Review." By whatever label, your statement of the issues should accomplish two purposes. First, it should clearly inform the court of the question or questions it has been asked to resolve. When clearly identifying each issue, the issues should correspond exactly to the arguments you will address in the body of your argument. If you will address one issue in your argument, draft only one issue. If you will address two issues in your argument, draft two issues.

---

2. *Id.* (quoting *Delno v. Market Street Ry.*, 124 F.2d 965, 967 (9th Cir. 1942)).
3. *Id.* at 68–72.

Second, each issue statement should very subtly persuade the court as to the merit of your position. Therefore, if possible, appeal to the court's sense of equities and fairness by framing each issue so that your position appears equitable and fair (and, by implication, the other party's position appears inequitable and unfair). For a fact-centered issue, incorporate the critical facts that are at the core of your theory of the case. The court should be able to know from reading each issue statement exactly what you intend to prove. As Judge Sol Wachter advised:

> The issues should be stated in such a way that the court will know immediately what you intend to prove. "The Defendant Was Denied Due Process" could lead anywhere; "The Defendant Was Denied Due Process When the Court Refused To Allow Him To Call Any Witnesses" lets everyone know where you are going.[4]

Successfully accomplishing these two goals will require significant thought and revision. Before drafting your issue, review the court rules to determine if they address whether issues must be stated in a question form, or whether they can be stated in a declarative sentence. If you have a choice, it is more persuasive to state the issue in a declarative sentence that describes your desired conclusion than to ask a question. Thus, in the above example, Judge Wachter identified the issue as a declarative statement: "The Defendant was denied due process when the court refused to allow him to call any witnesses." However, some courts require that issue statements be framed as questions. As a question, the same issue would be drafted as follows: "Did the court deny the Defendant due process when the court refused to allow him to call any witnesses?" When drafting an appellate brief for class, you should follow your professor's instructions. When drafting an appellate brief for a moot court competition, follow the rules of that competition.

A. Law-Centered Issues

When drafting an issue statement, it is challenging to achieve the fine balance between divulging too little information and too much. As an example, consider the criminal wiretap brief in Appendix E. In that argument, the defendant seeks to convince the court that the lower court erred when it interpreted the statutory requirement that the Government provide a "satisfactory explanation" for its sealing delays. Consider the following issue statement:

---

4. *Id.* at 121 (quoting New York's Chief Judge Sol Wachter).

> **Example 1:**
>
> Did the District Court err in defining the statutory term "satisfactory explanation"?

The first example is neither clear nor persuasive. It simply does not provide enough information for the appellate court to know what you intend to prove. Now consider whether the following example is any improvement.

> **Example 2:**
>
> Did the District Court err in finding that, as part of its "satisfactory explanation" for a two-month sealing delay, the Government need not prove that it sealed the tapes and placed them in a locked cabinet, and/or maintained a chain of custody, and/or placed them under guard, to prove that its pre-sealing procedures afforded the same level of protection as an immediate judicial seal would have provided, thereby protecting the wiretap evidence from any possibility of tampering during the sealing delay?

The second example does identify for the court the issue on appeal. However, it is weighed down by unnecessary details that obscure the heart of the issue. When the unnecessary factual details are eliminated, the issue looks like this:

> **Example 3:**
>
> Did the District Court err in finding that, as part of the Government's "satisfactory explanation" for its two-month delay in obtaining a judicial seal of wiretap evidence, the Government need not prove that its pre-sealing procedures protected the tapes from any possibility of tampering, which would afford the same level of protection as an immediate judicial seal would have provided?

In the third example, Hart's lawyer identifies the exact issue on appeal. In addition, the advocate appeals to the court's desire to promote the policy underlying the statute by noting that the level of protection Hart seeks is the same level of protection he would have received under the statute if the Government had obtained an immediate judicial seal. Hart's lawyer also appeals to the court's sense of fairness and equity by noting that the Government caused a two-month sealing delay, and that the standard Hart seeks will protect the evidence "from any possibility of tampering."

Assuming the relevant appellate court rules allow lawyers to frame issues in declarative sentences, the same issue could be stated more persuasively as follows:

> **Example 3 in a declarative sentence:**
>
> The District Court erred as a matter of law in finding that, as part of the Government's "satisfactory explanation" for its two-month delay in obtaining a judicial seal of wiretap evidence, the Government need not prove that its pre-sealing procedures protected the wiretap evidence from any possibility of tampering during the delay, which would afford the same level of protection as an immediate judicial seal would have provided.

B. Fact-Centered Issues

A well-drafted fact-centered issue should not only identify the exact issue before the court, but make the court *want* to decide the issue in your favor. To inspire the court to decide the issue in your favor, incorporate into the question the critical facts that are at the core of your theory of the case.

Again using the criminal wiretap brief in Appendix E as an example, Hart's lawyer argues that the Government failed to provide a "satisfactory explanation" for its sealing delay. Consider the appeal of the following example:

> Did the District Court err in finding that the Government provided a "satisfactory explanation" for its sealing delay when the Government lost the tapes for two months, only to find the tapes in an open box in an office supply room, and the Government can neither account for the tapes' whereabouts for the two month period in which they were missing or explain why the box of tapes had been opened?

In the above example, Hart's lawyer weaves into the question the critical facts that support the theory of the case. The lawyer highlights the possibility that the tapes could have been altered during the two-month sealing delay by noting that the tapes sat in an "open box in an office supply room." Hart's lawyer concludes the question with the highly favorable fact that the Government cannot account for the tapes' whereabouts or "explain why the box of tapes had been opened." The lawyer subtly portrays the Government as careless by emphasizing that the Government lost the tapes for two months and cannot account for the tapes' whereabouts.

Exercise 35-1

Draft a Statement of the Issues for a brief assigned by your professor.

Exercise 35-2

Review Sample Brief B in Appendix D. Assume the district court held that personal papers are not protected from compelled disclosure by the Fifth Amendment. Assume also that the defendant was ultimately convicted and now appeals the district court's order denying the motion to quash the subpoena. Draft a Statement of the Issue on behalf of the defendant.

ORAL ARGUMENTS

An oral argument serves several purposes. First and foremost, the oral argument provides judges with an opportunity to voice their concerns about the issues in a case by asking questions. In that sense, the oral argument is more like a Socratic dialogue than an oral presentation, and you should be prepared to respond to questions and to be interrupted. As you respond to the judges' questions, your goal is to persuade them to decide the case in your favor. Therefore, your responses to questions should demonstrate how your legal position satisfies the judges' concerns. An oral argument is also an opportunity for you to help the judges focus on the most important, fundamental aspects of your written argument while also reinforcing the theme, or theory of your case. Therefore, you should also arrive at the oral argument with a solid grasp of the few critical points you want to convey to the judges.

I. PREPARATION FOR THE ORAL ARGUMENT

A. Preparing an Outline of the Argument

By the time you begin preparing for an oral argument, you will have already drafted and filed your written brief and studied the brief of the opposing counsel. Therefore, you should already be very familiar with what it is you want the court to do and what you have to prove to win. You should also know how many points you must prove to win and whether they are mutually independent or dependent. Your written brief should also reflect the major premises that help prove your ultimate conclusions and the supporting proof for each issue. The supporting proof may consist of statutory analysis, legislative purpose and public policy arguments, and/or your interpretation of case precedent. In a fact-centered argument, your supporting proof would also include an argument about how the law favorably affects the client's facts.

You will not recite every detail of your written argument in your oral argument. You will be allotted only a limited amount of time to argue the merits of your case, and you can expect to be interrupted with numerous questions from the bench. Therefore, from the detailed arguments reflected in your written brief, your goal is to distill the very essence of your case and to communicate the most fundamentally important points you will need to make to win. As you consider which arguments are most important, take a step back from your brief for a moment and consider your theory of the case and why the judges should rule in your favor. Then consider which two or three points are the pivotal points you want to emphasize in the argument. Consider which points best promote and emphasize your theory of the case.

1. The Detailed Outline

From these fundamental points, create an outline of your argument. Avoid the temptation to draft a speech. An oral argument is a forum in which judges ask probing questions that reflect their concerns about the different legal positions being argued. An oral argument is more like a conversation than a rehearsed speech. Therefore, you will not have the opportunity to deliver a speech without interruption. Moreover, having a prepared speech would interfere with your ability to respond to the judges' questions and to move back and forth between your argument and your responses to questions. Instead, working from the conclusion you want the court to reach, create an outline of the most important points that support the conclusion. Begin with the strongest argument first, and then the second strongest argument, and so on.

Irrespective of the ultimate length of the outline you will actually bring with you to the podium at the oral argument, begin by drafting a relatively extensive "thinking" outline that will allow you to think through your arguments. For each issue, draft the most important points that support the conclusion. Under each point, bullet-point the most persuasive reasons why that point is sound. Next to each supporting reason, make note of the most important cases and references to the record that illustrate why that reason is sound. As you create a fairly extensive initial outline, consider how your main points and your supporting proof support your theory of the case. In the oral argument itself, you will want to weave your theme into the argument as well-placed "sound bytes." Thus, the major points and supporting proof should be designed to allow you to highlight your theme during the oral argument.

2. The Condensed Outline

After drafting a "thinking" outline, you will want to condense that outline into something more workable for the oral argument itself. Many advocates prefer to approach the podium with an outline of no more than a single-page that simply lays out the roadmap of their argument. A single-page outline avoids the problem of having to riffle back and forth between pages when responding to questions from the bench. With that said, if the thought of working from a single-page outline seems terrifying to you, then you might want to make your outline a bit more extensive. Whether a single-page or a couple of pages, the outline you bring with you to the podium should capture only the essential points you want to make in the argument. To make it easier for you to refer to your outline during the oral argument, use a large type-set that is easy for you to read at a glance. You may also wish to use wide margins on your outline so that you can include within the margins supporting data for each point. For example, you can include within the margins the names and citations of a few important authorities and critical pages from the record. Such an outline will provide you with a roadmap of the important points you want to make at oral argument.

3. Preparing for "Hot" and "Cold" Courts

As you consider the length and complexity of your outline, also think about the judges themselves and their level of preparation for the argument. Some courts are known as "hot" benches, meaning that the judges have meticulously reviewed the briefs in advance of the argument and interrupt frequently to engage counsel in extended dialogue. With a hot court, a longer outline might prove to be distracting. In addition, as you field numerous questions from the bench, a lengthy outline increases the likelihood that you might forget a critical point you wanted to make during the argument. During the heat of the moment, two or three critical points will stand out on a single-page outline but may become lost within a more extensive outline.

On the other hand, some courts are known as "cold" benches. In a cold court, the judges may not have carefully reviewed the briefs in advance and will usually not be prepared with a list of questions to ask the advocates. Therefore, the judges can be expected to listen fairly impassively with infrequent interruptions. With a cold court, you may wish to bring with you to the podium a more extended outline. Without the distraction of numerous questions, the extended outline may help you ensure that you make all of the points you want to make. With a cold court, you may not even use all of your allotted argument time.

In a moot court competition, you probably will not know in advance whether your judges will be "hot" or "cold." Therefore, you need to be prepared for either possibility. You may wish to prepare two outlines and bring both of them to the podium. The first outline would be an abbreviated one- or two-page outline that would be easier to use if you are engaged in a lively debate. The second outline would be a more extensive outline to which you could refer if the judges are more impassive.

B. Outlining Your Responses to Questions

Judges ask different kinds of questions during oral argument. Some questions are merely neutral requests for information. For example, a judge may ask you to supply the name of a case, or to identify where in the record certain testimony might be found. A judge might also ask you to identify the appropriate standard of review. It is important to know the standard of review for each issue before you arrive at the courthouse for oral argument. Unless the standard of review is at issue in the case, your thorough preparation should allow you to respond easily to such questions for information and clarification. Another type of question is the openly friendly question designed to help you promote your argument. These questions are sometimes called "softball" questions. For example, a judge might agree with your position and, through questioning, be trying to convince other judges on the panel of the merits of your position. Again, your thorough preparation of your own argument should allow you to respond easily to such questions. Other types of questions, however, are more challenging and require careful strategic thinking before the argument itself.

1. Positional Questions

One type of question for which you should prepare in advance are "positional" questions. Sometimes judges ask questions designed to force attorneys to "draw their line in the sand." Not unlike a law school professor in a Socratic classroom, judges sometimes test how far attorneys are willing to travel down the slippery slopes of their arguments. A judge might describe a worst case scenario that could follow from your proposed position and ask you whether you would advocate your position even under those extreme circumstances. A judge might attempt to probe how firmly you are committed to the position described in your brief, and to discover whether you are willing to concede part of that position.

To prepare for this type of questioning, carefully consider the ultimate conclusion you want the court to adopt. You identified and argued in your written brief the major points that lead to the desired conclusion. Now consider whether you can concede or modify any of these points without losing the ultimate argument. It may be that, although you would prefer that the court adopt a particular legal standard, your client might also be able to prevail under another standard that is not quite as favorable. However, there are always points you absolutely cannot concede and still prevail. On a sheet of paper, make a note of each of the points of your argument and how much you are willing to concede from your original positions. To help you identify the types of positional questions a judge might ask, review your opponent's brief. What are your opponent's positions? Are there any intermediate positions that lie somewhere between the two positions articulated by you and your opposing counsel? If your opponent has raised a "slippery slopes" argument that cautions the court about the "parade of horribles" that will result from adopting your position, be prepared to respond to questions that ask you to identify how far down the slippery slopes you are asking the court to slide.

As an example, consider the criminal wiretap brief that is illustrated in Appendix E. In that hypothetical problem, Mr. Hart's lawyer seeks to suppress wiretap evidence, arguing that because the Government failed to obtain an immediate judicial seal to protect such evidence, its pre-sealing procedures must provide the same level of protection as an immediate judicial seal. The trial court disagreed, holding that the Government could satisfy the statute if it produced credible expert testimony that the tapes were not altered during the sealing delay. Mr. Hart's lawyer asks the appellate court to reverse the trial court. In preparing for the oral argument, Mr. Hart's lawyer would be prepared to answer questions about his position. Therefore, the lawyer might draft the following question and answer in preparing for the argument:

> **Possible Question:** What if the Government's expert testimony is conclusive that the tapes were not tampered with during the delay? Wouldn't that testimony allay your concerns about tainted evidence being used to convict a person?
>
> **Response:** No, your Honor. As the District of Columbia Circuit Court of Appeals stated in *United States v. Johnson*, modern technology makes it difficult, if not *impossible*, to detect whether tampering has in fact occurred. Experts simply cannot provide the requisite level of proof that would ensure that tapes have not been tainted.

2. Questions that Probe the Weaknesses in Your Theory

The other type of question you should be fully prepared to address in oral argument includes oppositional questions that probe the weaknesses in your position. For example, judges might be concerned with potential adverse policy or equity ramifications should they adopt your position, or with whether mandatory case precedent allows them to adopt your position, or with whether a statutory scheme supports your position. Your responses to these core types of questions will be critical to your success at oral argument. Inexperienced advocates make the mistake of not preparing for these types of questions in advance. As a result, they waste the judges' time and patience with circuitous responses that do not really address the judges' concerns. Rather than taking thirty seconds to respond to the question, the advocate may have wasted several minutes of valuable argument time.

To anticipate these types of questions, carefully review your opponent's brief and any direct rebuttal in your own brief. You should be prepared to respond to each unfavorable argument raised in your opponent's brief. For each unfavorable argument you identify, draft an outline of your response. Don't make the mistake of outlining a detailed response that would take several minutes to express all of the myriad supporting details. Instead, front-load your answer. Begin with your answer to the question itself, such as "yes, your Honor," or "no, your Honor," or "I respectfully disagree, your Honor." Then follow the conclusion with the one or two best reasons that support your conclusion.

Again using the criminal wiretap problem for purposes of illustration, Mr. Hart's lawyer should be prepared for questions reflecting the judges' concern about allowing guilty people to avoid punishment:

Possible Question: Under your theory, guilty parties will avoid punishment simply because the Government's pre-sealing procedures were not fail-safe in every respect. In other words, I'm concerned that culpable parties would go free even though the Government could produce expert testimony that, almost to a 100% certainty, the tapes were not tampered with during the sealing delay. Isn't this too high a cost for us to pay?

Response: No, your Honor. It is true that a guilty person may avoid punishment under this standard. However, it is equally true that under the standard advocated by the Government, an innocent person might be imprisoned for a crime he didn't commit. As a society, that cost is too high, particularly when it is through the Government's own careless procedures that the tapes were not properly sealed. Compelling the Government to safeguard its own evidence would encourage the Government to act more carefully in the future.

After you have drafted your proposed responses to various questions, then condense the questions and answers into a brief outline with bullet-points that identify the crux of your responses. This step will encourage you not to read from your extensive outline as you respond to questions. Like the delivery of your argument itself, your responses to questions should be a conversation with judges rather than a dry recitation of your notes. Moreover, the very process of drafting responses and then condensing the responses into a brief outline will help cement your understanding of the issues. Ideally, you should be so well-prepared during the oral argument that you will not need to refer to your outline of questions and responses.

C. Preparing a Notebook for the Argument

You will not want to approach the podium armed only with a single-page outline, because you may need to refer to important cases or parts of the record when you respond to the judges' questions. On the other hand, you do not want to approach the podium armed with a pile of loose papers or index cards. They not only look unprofessional, but can also be distracting as you sift through pages or index cards trying to find an answer to a judge's question. For similar reasons, avoid bringing a yellow legal pad to the podium with you. Flipping through the pages can be visually distracting and can also create auditory interference from the microphone.

Instead, prepare a notebook to bring with you to the argument. Many lawyers prefer to use a three-ring binder with tabs that easily identify the components of the notebook. Other lawyers prefer to use a folder. Using a binder or folder, include the outline of your argument under one tab, together with an outline of your responses to the most important questions you anticipate the court will ask. Other tabs may be reserved for supporting data, such as a summary of the most important cases in the argument. For each case, include the case name, the court that decided the case, the year the case was decided, the holding, and any relevant facts and rationale. If a precedent case was decided by the court before whom you are arguing, also note the panel of judges that decided the earlier case; the judges may ask for that information. You might also want to include in another section of the notebook any critical testimony from the record, together with references to the pages in the record.

D. Rehearsing Your Argument

You should never arrive at the courthouse without having first gone through at least one dry-run of your argument. Many practicing lawyers ask other members of their law firm to help prepare them for an oral argument. In a moot court competition, if the rules of your moot court competition allow, ask other law students or professors to review the briefs in advance of your dry-run and to come prepared to ask you tough questions. Your colleagues may well have additional questions or introduce avenues of inquiry that had not occurred to you while preparing for the argument. Therefore, a practice session is a wonderful opportunity to spot any holes in your argument and to polish your responses and your delivery. To make the session successful, encourage your colleagues to give you constructive criticism. Although it can be difficult to receive criticism, it is far better that you hear it from friendly colleagues than allow your mistakes to potentially affect the outcome of the case.

E. Final Details

1. Updating the Law

Often, there is a significant time lapse between the date the brief is filed and the date of the oral argument. Therefore, before the oral argument, update your research to ensure that each of the cases on which you have relied is still "good law." Also check to see whether there is any recent case that may affect the argument itself. If so, you must let the court and opposing counsel know of the recent development in the law. If possible, notify the court and opposing counsel of the new law prior to the date of the argument so that the judges are not distracted with reading and absorbing new law during your argument.

2. Observing an Argument

If possible, prior to the date of your argument, visit the courtroom in which you will argue, preferably with the panel of judges before whom you will argue. Use this opportunity to acquaint yourself with the courtroom itself, noting where the lawyers are seated, the location of the podium and microphone, and how lawyers are notified that their time has expired. If the panel of judges is the same panel before whom you will argue, you will also get a sense of the type of questioning you can expect, and the kinds of arguments and behavior that appeal or do not appeal to the judges. If you cannot visit the courtroom in advance, arrive early for your argument and listen to other oral arguments.

In a moot court competition, you will likely not have the opportunity to listen to other students' arguments. However, you may find it helpful to pay an advance visit to the room in which you will be arguing. At the very least, you can familiarize yourself with the layout of the room. That advance familiarity will help alleviate any pre-argument anxiety. In addition, if your school has an intra-school moot court competition involving upper-level students, attend the final rounds of the competition. If your school is near a courthouse that has appellate court arguments, you might also consider visiting the courthouse to observe the arguments.

II. THE ORAL ARGUMENT

A. Setting of the Argument

Although a specific circuit may have twenty or more judges who sit on the appellate bench within that circuit, most appellate court arguments are heard by a panel of three judges from that circuit. Moot court competitions also commonly have panels of three judges. There are two counsel tables within the courtroom. Each counsel table is designated for lawyers who represent the appellant or the appellee. Thus, for example, as counsel for the appellant, you would sit at the table designated for the appellant. Lawyers address the judges from behind the podium. The judges sit facing the lawyers and the podium.

You will usually be sitting at the appropriate counsel table when the judges enter the room. A bailiff will announce the entry of the judges. Rise when the judges enter the room and remain standing until after all of the judges have been seated and the chief judge asks you to be seated. The chief judge will ask you if you are ready to proceed. When asked, stand up and announce that you are "ready, your Honor."

The court allots each party a designated amount of time within which to argue. Because the appellant is the moving party, the appellant's lawyer argues first. The appellant may, and should, reserve time for rebuttal. Any time reserved for rebuttal is subtracted from the time allotted to the opening argument. Thus, if the appellant has been allotted fifteen (15) minutes to argue, the appellant might reserve three (3) minutes for rebuttal, leaving twelve (12) minutes for the opening argument. After the appellant's counsel argues and sits down, the appellee's lawyer then stands up and approaches the podium to deliver the appellee's argument. The appellee cannot reserve time for rebuttal. In an appellate courtroom, the time is electronically monitored. In a federal courtroom, an amber button lights up to warn the advocate that two minutes remain in the argument. A red button lights up to signal that time has expired. In moot court competitions, a time-keeper typically uses flash cards to signal the interim warnings and the expiration of time.

In a moot court competition, two team members often represent each party, each of whom argues separate issues. In such a competition, the appellants argue in succession before the appellees argue. The appellant's team will have picked in advance the team member who will deliver the rebuttal. That team member delivers the rebuttal after both of the attorneys for the appellee have argued.

B. The Structure of the Argument

1. Introduction

After you have arrived at the podium, wait for the chief judge to let you know that the judges are ready for you to begin. Begin the argument by using the formal language used in all appellate arguments: "May it please the Court." Then state your name and the party you represent. If you are the appellant, tell the judges how much time you are reserving for rebuttal.

After stating your name, identify the issue on appeal in a manner that artfully captures your theme, or theory, of the case. Your statement of the issue should favorably frame your argument and make the court *want* to decide the appeal in your favor. Therefore, prior to the argument, carefully consider your theme and the issue or issues on appeal. What is at the heart of your appeal? Why should the court rule in your favor? What facts or policy favorably advance your theme? Because the way you frame the issue or issues is so important, spend some time drafting and then revising your preliminary statement to ensure that it has maximum persuasive appeal. After crafting a favorable statement, include the exact language of that statement in your outline.

As an example, consider again the criminal wiretap brief that is illustrated in Appendix E. In that hypothetical problem, Mr. Hart's theme, or theory of the case, is that the Government acted carelessly and that its haphazard pre-sealing procedures failed to protect the wiretap evidence from tampering. These themes are illustrated in the following introduction:

> May it please the Court. My name is Sandra Saunders, and I represent the appellant, Mr. James Hart. We ask the Court to reserve three minutes for rebuttal. After obtaining wiretap tapes on which the Government relied to convict Mr. Hart, the Government lost this sensitive wiretap evidence for a period of two months. The Government cannot account for the tapes' whereabouts for the two-month period in which they were missing, nor can the Government explain why the box of tapes, which had presumably been sealed, was found open in an office supply room, vulnerable to the 5,000 occupants of the building and their visitors. Under these facts, the Government's explanation for its sealing delay was not "satisfactory" under the federal wiretap statute.

2. Roadmap of the Argument

As former Wisconsin Chief Justice Judge Nathan S. Heffernan advises: "At the outset tell the judges what you are going to tell them, tell them, and if it appears necessary, tell them what you told them."[1] Just as with any written argument, it is important to provide the judges with a roadmap of your argument before presenting the argument itself. The roadmap should outline the two or three most important points you will make during the argument. The roadmap illustrated below would follow Ms. Saunders' introduction that is illustrated in the preceding example:

> The Government's explanation for its own delay in sealing the tapes is not satisfactory for two reasons. First, its pre-sealing procedures failed to safeguard the tapes from tampering because the Government cannot account for the tapes' whereabouts for the two-month period in which they were missing. Second, the Government's explanation is also not satisfactory because the Government failed to act with diligence in minimizing the sealing delay. The delay was caused by an easily preventable mistake and was exacerbated by the Government's carelessness and inattention to its own files.

3. Factual Statement

Advocates generally do not want to waste their limited argument time by providing the court with a detailed recitation of the factual statement that is already included with the written briefs. Usually, judges will have already read the briefs and will be familiar with the facts. If the judges have made it clear that they have read the briefs, or you know that the court generally reads the briefs in advance, you can assume that the judges are familiar with the facts. Do not spend precious argument time reciting a formal statement of the facts. Instead, weave into the argument itself the critical facts that support your theme and help develop your issues.

However, if you are not sure whether the judges have read the briefs, you should be prepared to provide a brief factual summary for the court. There are two schools of thought regarding how to handle this issue. Some advocates prefer simply to ask the court whether the judges would like to hear a brief summary of the facts. For example: "Would your Honors like for me to summarize the relevant facts?" Other advocates believe that it is better practice not to ask a direct question, reasoning that the judges might be offended by a question that suggests the judges are not familiar with the underlying facts. Instead, they prefer to give the court the opportunity to waive the reading of the facts without asking a direct question. Thus, they state: "I will briefly summarize the facts." After making that statement, they pause and give the judges the opportunity to waive the factual statement should they wish to do so.

---

1. Ruggero J. Aldisert, *Winning on Appeal: Better Briefs and Oral Arguments* 305 (Rev. 1st ed. NITA 1996).

Whichever method you choose, should you provide a factual summary, make sure that it is very brief and promotes your theory of the case. As the lawyer for the appellee, you will not need to restate the facts already provided by the appellant's counsel. However, the appellant's lawyer will have framed the facts in a manner that advances the appellant's theme. Therefore, as the lawyer for the appellee, you should be prepared to emphasize those few critically important facts that further your theory of the case.

4. Presentation of the Argument

Following a favorable statement of the issue or issues on appeal, a roadmap of your argument, and the few facts that illustrate your theory of the case, you are ready to present the argument itself. Your outline should identify the arguments you plan to make, beginning with your strongest argument. As you state your first argument, front-load the argument by beginning with the major premise that proves your point. If necessary, then continue by identifying a point or two that illustrates why your premise is sound. Avoid the details and nuances of the argument that are already described in great detail in your written brief. Through questioning, the judges will let you know which points they want to explore in greater detail.

5. Conclusion

When you are alerted that two minutes remain in your argument, if possible, try to begin leading to a concise, persuasive summary of why the court should rule in your favor. Ideally, you should save the last minute for a persuasive recap of your argument. If you finish your argument before time has expired, simply thank the court and sit down. If you have not finished your concluding statement when time has expired, stop and ask the court for permission to conclude your statement. If you are granted permission, your comments should not extend beyond 15 to 20 seconds, or you will risk incurring the wrath of the judges.[2]

With a "hot" bench, sometimes time expires while the advocate is in the middle of a response to a question from the bench. Should that happen to you, do not presume that you can continue your response and then state your conclusion following the expiration of your allotted time. Instead, when you are notified that time has expired, stop in the middle of your response and ask for the court's permission to briefly conclude. Very briefly complete your response to the question and state your conclusion. Again, your comments should not extend beyond a few seconds.

C. Responding to Questions

One of the most common complaints judges make against lawyers at oral argument is the failure to provide honest and direct responses to questions. When a lawyer

---

2. Aldisert, *supra* note 1, at 325.

attempts to evade a question or fails to acknowledge important aspects of the argument, the lawyer loses credibility with the court and risks the ire of the judges. With thorough preparation before the argument, you should be prepared to answer clearly and honestly any question asked of you during the argument. Of course, you cannot provide an effective response if you do not understand the question itself. It can be difficult to listen carefully when you are standing behind the podium attempting to respond to a seemingly endless stream of questions. It is all too easy to stop listening after the judge begins asking the question and begin preparing your response.

Instead, listen carefully to the entire question before considering your response. Before responding to any question, take a deep breath and pause to replay the question in your mind. What exactly has the judge asked of you? Also consider the type of question the judge has asked. Is the question merely seeking information, requiring only a brief response? Is the question one designed to hear your position on an issue? Does the question ask for a concession? Or is the question a "softball" designed to help you promote your argument and convince other judges on the bench? The judges will not begrudge your taking the time to reflect on the question before responding, particularly because your response is likely to be clearer and more concise following a thoughtful pause. If you are not sure that you understand what the judge has asked of you, ask for clarification. It is far better to ask the judge to repeat the question than to take the court's time responding to a question that was not asked.

When you have been asked a question, you must answer it at that time, not later. Don't make the mistake of telling the judges that you will respond to the question later in your presentation. You are there at the request of the court to respond to the judges' concerns. There is nothing more important than responding to a judge's question at the very moment the judge's curiosity has been piqued. Begin your response by stating your conclusion, and then provide the most important reason or reasons why your conclusion is sound. Wait for further questions from the bench before delving into the details of your reasoning. If further questions are not forthcoming, return to your argument.

Should you begin to be barraged with hostile questioning about one of your positions, consider the importance of the position. If the point is not necessary for you to prevail, and you suspect that the court will not become convinced of the merits of your position on that point, move on to other parts of your argument. You do not want to spend an inordinate amount of argument time rebutting a non-critical point of your argument. However, if the point is critical to the success of your argument, you must face the hostile barrage of questions and respond to the best of your ability. Again, with thorough preparation prior to the argument, such questions should not come as a surprise.

There may be times when a judge asks you a question to which you do not know the answer. Under such circumstances, do not try to bluff the court. When a court discovers through further questioning that an advocate has been bluffing, the advocate loses credibility. Moreover, the advocate's integrity has then been brought into question. Instead, simply acknowledge that you do not know the answer and will be pleased to supply the court with a supplemental response later.

D. Appearance and Delivery

1. Dress

When appearing before a court, dress conservatively and professionally. In a courtroom setting, conservative suits are appropriate attire that signal your respect for the court and the significance of the occasion.

2. Maintain Eye Contact

The oral argument should ideally be a conversation between you and the judges. As you would in ordinary conversation, maintain eye contact with the judges and communicate with them rather than attempting to read from your written notes. This is another reason why an extensive outline can hinder your effectiveness at oral argument. An extensive outline can encourage you to read from the outline rather than talk with the judges.

3. Body Language

As you stand behind the podium, try not to engage in mannerisms that will distract the judges from listening to what you have to say. Therefore, stay behind the podium and refrain from restlessly moving about or gesturing wildly with your hands. Of course, it is also important to appear natural. If you normally use your hands to gesture when you speak, then do so, but in moderation, so that your gestures do not detract from the force of what you are saying. At the opposite end of the spectrum, avoid the tendency to clutch the podium with clenched fists. During practice sessions before the argument, practice arguing behind a podium with your hands lightly resting on the podium.

4. Voice

Your goal during the oral argument is to speak clearly and firmly, exhibiting confidence in your position. Speak loudly and clearly enough for the judges to hear you without straining. As you practice for the oral argument, consider how you speak when you are nervous. Some people tend to speak too quickly, making it difficult for the listener to follow their statements. If this is your tendency, practice speaking very slowly—almost excruciatingly slowly—clearly enunciating every word. By slowing down your speech pattern during practice, your speech should achieve the proper balance with the added adrenalin the oral argument will provide. If, on the other hand, your tendency is to speak very softly and timidly when you are nervous, over-compensate for these tendencies during practice. During practice sessions, practice speaking loudly and with authority.

5. Demeanor

Your goal is to appear earnest and convinced of the soundness of your position, while also showing respect for the judges. Your demeanor should be one of "respectful equality. Don't be disturbed or pushed around simply because a judge disagrees with your position. Stand your ground firmly but with courtesy and dignity."[3] At the opposite end of the spectrum, resist the impulse to show any irritation, either verbally or with your body language. At times, judges ask questions that might seem irrelevant or off-track. Answer the question respectfully and then move back to your argument. Your demeanor should also show respect for the opposing party. Although you will attack the soundness of the opponent's legal positions, do not attack the opposing counsel or the opposing party personally. Finally, your manner of speech should reflect the seriousness of the occasion. Do not use slang or rhetoric.

6. References

Refer to the judges as a group as "Your Honors" or "the Court." Refer to a specific judge as "Your Honor" or "Justice [last name]." Refer to other lawyers as "counsel for the appellee" or "opposing counsel." Refer to the parties by their last name, such as "Mr." or "Ms." so-and-so, or "Dr." so-and-so.

CHAPTER IN REVIEW

Core Concepts:

PREPARATION FOR THE ARGUMENT

1. Prepare an outline of your argument.
   a. Considering your theory of the case, identify the two or three pivotal points you want to emphasize in the argument.
   b. From these pivotal points, create a fairly detailed "thinking" outline of your argument.
   c. Next, condense your "thinking" outline into a one- or two-page outline that lays out the roadmap of your argument.
2. Outline your responses to potential questions.

---

3. Aldisert, *supra* note 1, at 324.

    a. "Positional" questions—consider how far you can travel down a "slippery slope" before conceding your position. For each point, know in advance where you must draw the line.

    b. "Oppositional" questions—consider the weaknesses in your case and draft an outline of your response to each weak aspect of your position.

    c. Know the standard of review in advance of the argument.

3. Prepare a notebook or a folder to take to the podium with you.

   - Consider using tabs to divide the contents of your folder, including a tab for the outline of your argument, a tab for your responses to questions, and tabs for supporting data, including case summaries and references to the record.

4. Rehearse your argument with other law students and, if possible, law professors.

5. If possible, observe an argument in advance.

THE ARGUMENT

1. The structure of an oral argument

   a. First, introduce yourself: *e.g.*, "May it please the court. My name is xyz, and I represent abc."

   b. Next, state the issue on appeal—the issue should persuasively capture your theory of the case.

   c. Next, provide a roadmap of the two or three most important points you will make during the argument.

   d. Follow the rules of your school's competition in deciding whether to include a brief recitation of the factual record.

   e. Next, begin arguing the most important point you want to make in the argument.

       i. "Front-load" the argument by beginning with the major premise that proves your point.

       ii. Then identify a point or two that illustrates why your premise is sound.

   f. If possible, use the last minute or two to persuasively summarize your argument.

   - If time runs out when you are responding to a question, ask the court's permission to complete your response and conclude—your comments should not extend beyond a few seconds.

2. Responding to questions

   a. Listen carefully to the question and, if you need to, pause before responding.

     b. State your ultimate conclusion to the answer first, and then identify the one or two most important reasons that support your conclusion.

     c. Do not evade a question or tell the judge that you will respond to the question at a later time.

     d. Be respectful, even when the question seems irrelevant or inane.

3. Appearance and delivery

     a. Dress conservatively and professionally.

     b. Maintain eye contact with the judges—the oral argument should ideally be a conversation.

     c. Try not to engage in distracting mannerisms, such as gesturing wildly with your hands.

     d. Project your voice, and speak clearly and firmly at a measured pace.

     e. Your demeanor should be one of respectful equality.

DEMAND & SETTLEMENT LETTERS

Lawyers commonly transmit letters to opposing counsel seeking to assert clients' rights and settle legal disputes. In a demand letter, the advocate demands that another party comply with a legal requirement (*e.g.*, pay money due under a lease agreement), or that the other party cease from engaging in certain behavior (*e.g.*, landlord refusing to make repairs). Demand letters precede lawsuits, and are often settled without a resulting lawsuit. Settlement letters, on the other hand, have the goal of inducing an opposing party to settle a dispute by offering or accepting a sum of money that constitutes a compromise.

I. ACHIEVING THE PROPER TONE

Before drafting a demand or settlement letter, carefully consider the tone you want to achieve. Inexperienced lawyers make two common mistakes when writing letters to opposing counsel. Out of a desire to appear reasonable and fair, some lawyers make the mistake of unwittingly portraying their client in an unfavorable light. For example, they might state that they can "understand" how the opponent would feel justified in believing that the client acted in bad faith. Make no mistake: carelessly written words can come back to haunt an attorney. Moreover, it is not necessary to placate the opposing counsel in order to maintain a positive working relationship. At the other end of the spectrum, some advocates believe that a legal dispute is all-out war, and that "all is fair in love and war." The tone of such a letter is hostile and belligerent. Such letters also do not serve the client's interests because they are not likely to have the desired effect of encouraging a positive resolution of the dispute.

Effective advocates achieve a balance between the two extremes. Advocates are most effective when they affirmatively and clearly state their clients' position, yet do so in a manner that is respectful and professional. The goal of any demand or settlement letter is to persuade the opposing party to give your client a desirable result. The most effective way to achieve that goal is to convince the opposing counsel that your client's position is legally sound, and to do so in a manner that does not anger or belittle the opposing party. No one wants to compromise or concede when they are angry or feel belittled.

For purposes of illustration, consider the hypothetical problem that is the basis of the Client Letter A in Appendix B, and of Exercise 1 in this chapter. In that problem, Mr. Johnson was injured when he slipped and fell on an icy sidewalk outside his apartment complex. Mr. Johnson seeks damages from his landlord, claiming that the landlord should have shoveled the walkways to prevent such accidents. Johnson's lawyer faces the following problem: there are only a few cases that have evaluated whether a landlord has a duty to shovel common walkways, and they are very old. In those older cases, the courts did not impose such a duty on landlords. However, recent cases within the jurisdiction have eroded the broad protections landlords previously enjoyed, and have held landlords responsible for taking precautionary measures to prevent reasonably foreseeable injuries. Unfortunately, none of the recent cases has addressed whether landlords have a duty to keep walkways clear of snow and ice. Therefore, despite the shift in policy, the older cases are still "good law."

Johnson's lawyer recognizes that the only viable recourse within the judicial system is at the appellate court level. Trial court judges are compelled to follow the rulings of higher-level courts within the jurisdiction. Because the appellate process would be lengthy and expensive, Mr. Johnson has authorized his lawyer to explore settlement possibilities. Given this background, compare the persuasive appeal of the following three examples.

> **Example 1:**
> It's true that early Missouri courts have not imposed a duty upon landlords to shovel the snow from common walkways. However, these decisions are forty years old, and I respectfully request that you consider the policy implications from more recent decisions. Under these more recent decisions, I hope that you understand that we are justified in asking that your client be held responsible for my client's injuries.

In Example 1, Johnson's lawyer tries so hard to appear accommodating and fair that she ultimately appears defensive and unsure of her legal position. The language "it's true" appears defensive and weak. In conjunction with that defensive language, other language in the letter appears unduly deferential: "I hope you understand that we are justified"; "I respectfully request that you consider." This letter would not encourage anyone to settle the dispute. Now consider the tone of Example 2:

> **Example 2:**
>
> Your client is liable for Mr. Johnson's injuries. As you well know, recent Missouri Supreme Court decisions impose a broad duty on landlords to keep sidewalks free from snow and ice. Your client's blatant disregard for my client's safety has caused him injuries from which he will never fully recover. My client is justifiably angry and ready to take your client all the way to the Supreme Court if necessary.

In Example 2, Johnson's lawyer tries so hard to be a strong advocate that she ultimately appears strident and accusatory. The language "[a]s you well know" implicitly accuses the opposing counsel of acting in bad faith. The language "blatant disregard for my client's safety" is also insulting and would only incite the landlord to remain firmly entrenched in defending his legal position. The language suggesting that the client is ready to "take your client all the way to the Supreme Court if necessary" is so extreme as to appear hyperbolic. Most lawyers would not take such a "threat" seriously. This letter would likewise not encourage anyone to want to settle the dispute. Now consider the tone of Example 3:

> **Example 3:**
>
> Your client is liable in negligence for Mr. Johnson's injuries. Recent Missouri Supreme Court opinions impose a broad duty on landlords to keep sidewalks free from snow and ice. By failing to keep the sidewalk free from snow and ice, your client breached its duty of care owed to Mr. Johnson. This breach of duty was the proximate cause of his injuries.

In Example 3, the lawyer strikes the right balance between defensiveness and stridency. She appears professional and cordial while also clearly affirming the client's legal position.

II. FORMAT AND CONTENT

Letters to opposing counsel differ in length and complexity depending upon a number of factors, including the legal issue in dispute, the procedural posture of the litigation, the relative strength of the client's legal position, and the personalities and relationship of the lawyers themselves. In the early stages of litigation, while the facts are still unfolding, an advocate might elect to disclose very little information to opposing counsel. Disclosing information might force the client into factual or legal positions that may ultimately prove to be unfavorable as the factual investigation unfolds. On the other hand, a strong factual and legal position might make a lengthier, detailed argument very appealing.

The personalities and relationship of the lawyers also play a role. Some lawyers are more successful negotiating settlements verbally and prefer to express in person or over the telephone the reasons why the proposed settlement is fair. Other lawyers are more successful with the luxury of time and reflection that a letter provides—time to deliberate over the arguments and to select their language with care. Therefore, a determination as to how much, or how little, information to include in a demand or settlement letter is a decision you will make on a case-by-case basis as you practice law.

Although there are many variables that affect the length and complexity of a settlement letter, such letters also share certain common characteristics. Both demand and settlement letters incorporate the persuasive writing style techniques discussed in Chapter 23. Settlement letters also follow the persuasive argument paradigms discussed in Chapters 24-30. However, unless you are *responding* to an argument already raised by the opposing counsel, you generally would not directly rebut unfavorable law in an adversarial letter. Advocates generally emphasize only favorable law and do not attempt to address and distinguish unfavorable law.

The adversarial letter follows the same deductive pattern typical of office memoranda and other persuasive arguments. Such letters begin with an introductory paragraph that summarizes the purpose of the letter, followed by the favorable facts that support the advocate's position, followed by the favorable law (with an application of law to facts) that supports the advocate's position, and concluding with a statement of demands or an offer of settlement.

A. Introductory Paragraphs

In addition to setting the overall tone of the letter, the introductory paragraph serves the following purposes: (1) it identifies the lawyer's representative capacity, if the lawyer's representation has not already been established; (2) it briefly states the client's demands or offer of settlement, or response to such demands; and (3) it confirms in writing that the letter is the subject of confidential settlement negotiations and cannot be used as evidence during trial. Under the Federal Rules of Evidence and state evidentiary rules, settlement communications cannot be used as evidence during trial. Of course, you would not want a confidential letter you have written to be introduced into evidence by the opposing party. Therefore, lawyers protect their confidential communications with a written statement confirming the confidential nature of the letter. The following example of an introductory paragraph is excerpted from Sample Letter A in Appendix F. In that problem, the McLeans are seeking damages arising out of the drowning death of their child.

I represent Mr. and Mrs. McLean in the lawsuit they have recently filed against your clients in which they seek damages for the death of their young child. They are understandably anxious to seek full recovery under the law following the drowning death of their child in your client's man-made pond. However, to avoid protracted litigation, my clients are willing to allow me to explore settlement possibilities. My clients have authorized me to make the following offer: they will agree to dismiss this suit if your clients remit payment in the sum of $1,500,000. This offer will remain open until 5:00 p.m. on December 1, 20XX. This letter is intended as a confidential settlement communication pursuant to Rule 408 of the Federal Rules of Evidence and Rule 1-14.1 of the Florida Evidence Code. As such, it will not be admissible in the above proceeding, or any other proceeding, for any purpose.

B. Factual Support

The length of a factual statement may be very brief or rather lengthy, depending upon the complexity of the facts in dispute and the factual context of the letter. Consider, for example, a settlement letter designed to persuade an opposing party to settle a lawsuit following extensive pre-trial discovery. Because the facts have already been fully disclosed during the discovery process, you might incorporate a significant number of relevant, favorable facts designed to convince the opposing counsel that your client will ultimately prevail in the lawsuit. On the other hand, if you were to draft a settlement letter in the early stages of a lawsuit, you might incorporate fewer facts into the letter. In the early stages of a lawsuit, you would typically not be in possession of all relevant facts or have a final trial strategy. Therefore, to avoid making factual misstatements, or "tipping your hand" about a trial strategy that is still uncertain, you might incorporate only a few favorable facts.

Whether the factual statement is lengthy or brief, include only those favorable facts that support your client's legal position. The purpose of an adversarial letter is to *persuade*. Because unfavorable facts do not serve the purpose of persuasion, they are typically not disclosed in demand and settlement letters. Unfavorable facts might be disclosed only when the opposing counsel is clearly aware of, and emphasizing, the unfavorable facts, and the advocate can persuasively and easily argue why such facts are not legally significant. Consider the factual statement in Sample Letter A in Appendix F. In that problem, the lawyer emphasizes highly favorable facts that support her theory of the case—that the landowners simply did not take reasonable precautions to avoid a foreseeable injury. The following factual statement is excerpted from that letter:

As you are aware, on May 28, 20XX, my client's young son drowned in the Hurts' pond. Although your clients knew that young children enjoyed feeding the ducks on their pond, they left town for the holiday weekend, leaving the gate to the pond unlocked, and the dock in a state of disrepair. Their actions in leaving this attractive nuisance accessible to young children is even more troublesome in light of the fact that they knew the dock was dangerous and in need of repair. Yet they had delayed the long-needed repairs. Mikey McLean drowned in the Hurts' pond after the dock collapsed from under his slight weight.

In the above factual statement, the lawyer uses several persuasive writing style strategies to enhance the persuasive appeal of the factual story. First, she uses the strategy of "juxtaposition" discussed in Chapter 23 to juxtapose facts that make the Hurts appear to be very careless. Thus, she juxtaposes the Hurts' knowledge of trespassing children ("although your clients knew that young children…") with the fact that they nevertheless left town without taking precautions to protect trespassing children from their pond ("they left town for the holiday weekend, leaving the gate to the pond unlocked…"). The lawyer also juxtaposes the Hurts' knowledge of the decaying dock with the fact that they had delayed repairing the dock ("Yet they had delayed…"). The lawyer also uses the active voice to connect the Hurts with their careless actions: "they left town"; and "they knew the dock was dangerous"; and "they had delayed."

C. Legal Support—Explain the Law and Then Apply It to the Client Facts

The extent and nature of the legal support for your demand or settlement offer will vary depending upon how brief or detailed you decide to make the letter. In a simple demand letter, you would not include any legal support at all. For example, in a demand letter demanding that a tenant pay back-rent due and owing under a lease, the landlord's lawyer would support the demands by simply pointing out the applicable provisions of the lease. In such a letter, supporting case law would be unnecessary and distracting.

On the other hand, sometimes advocates seek to persuade opposing counsel by presenting a summary of all of the favorable law that supports their client. Again, when deciding how much information to disclose, it is critical to consider carefully each statement you make in the argument. Often during the litigation process, lawyers discover new factual information that affects their overall trial strategy. Thus, in presenting favorable law, it is important not to frame the resolution of the issue in a manner that could later foreclose other strategic decisions. In the following example, the advocate emphasizes the favorable law and facts in a summary fashion that is unlikely to foreclose later shifts in strategy. Again, the following example is excerpted from Sample Letter A in Appendix F:

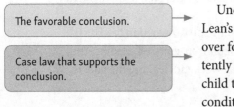

The favorable conclusion.

Case law that supports the conclusion.

Under Florida law, the Hurts are liable for Mikey McLean's death under the doctrine of attractive nuisance. For over forty years, a long line of Florida courts have consistently held landowners liable for the injuries sustained by child trespassers when the landowners leave a dangerous condition on their property and have reason to believe that children attracted to the dangerous condition will trespass onto the property. *See, e.g., Ansin v. Thurston*, 98 So. 2d 87 (Fla. Dist. Ct. App. 1957); *Samson v. O'Hara*, 239 So. 2d 151 (Fla. Dist. Ct. App. 1970).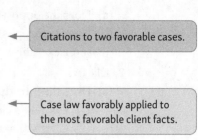

Citations to two favorable cases.

Here, the combination of the Hurts' dilapidated dock, the man-made pond, and the ducks that swam in the pond was dangerous, and yet inviting and attractive to small children. The Hurts both knew that the dock was dilapidated and dangerous, and knew that children from the neighboring elementary school trespassed onto their dock to feed the ducks. Yet they left this attractive nuisance open and accessible to children while they left town for the long holiday weekend.

Case law favorably applied to the most favorable client facts.

D. Conclusion

In the conclusion, clearly: (1) restate the demand or offer; (2) impose a specific time limit on the availability of the demand or offer; and (3) state the consequences should the opposing counsel fail to respond within the stated time. The following paragraph is excerpted from Sample Letter A in Appendix F:

The Hurts' liability under Florida law is clear. If this case is tried, the jury will not be focused on liability, but on the amount of damages to award the parents of their only child—a six-year-old son. After evaluating Florida law, I think you will agree that our $1,500,000 settlement offer is more than reasonable.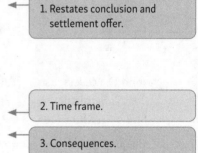

1. Restates conclusion and settlement offer.

Our offer remains open until 5:00 p.m. on December 1, 20XX. If I do not hear from you by then, I will be in touch with you to schedule depositions.

2. Time frame.

3. Consequences.

Exercise 37-1

Review Sample Client Letter A in Appendix B. Assume that you have forwarded that advisory letter to Mr. and Mrs. Johnson, your clients. After considering your recommendations, the Johnsons have decided to attempt to settle the dispute with their landlord, preferably without litigation. You have asked a more junior lawyer in the law office to draft a settlement letter to the landlord's lawyer. The junior lawyer has submitted a draft settlement letter for your review and comment.

When reviewing the draft settlement letter, consider the following:

    1. Practical Consequences:

    (a) Does the opposing counsel know what he is supposed to do?

    (b) Does the opposing counsel know the practical consequences of his response or failure to respond?

2. Clarity:

    (a) Does the introductory paragraph:

        (i) Contain a clear offer?

        (ii) Clarify that this letter is a confidential settlement communication?

    (b) Does the letter contain a clear factual statement?

    (c) Does the letter contain a clear thesis paragraph?

    (d) Does the letter contain legal and factual support for the client's argument?

3. Persuasive Appeal:

    (a) Does the letter use anticipatory rebuttal or direct rebuttal? Which would be a more persuasive strategy?

    (b) Does the letter affirm the client's position or defend against the opponent's argument?

    (c) Is the tone persuasive or neutral?

DRAFT SETTLEMENT LETTER FOR
REVIEW AND COMMENT

Charlotte Turley, Esq.
105 S. Central Ave.
St. Louis, MO 63105
April 15, 20XX

John D. Meyers, Esq.
201 N. Bemiston
St. Louis, MO 63105

Re: *Johnson v. Apartment Management Corp.*

Dear Mr. Meyers:

I met last night with my clients, tenants of Apartment Management Corp. Although my clients are anxious to press their claims, they would like to settle this dispute.

As you are aware, on December 18, 20XX, Mr. Johnson slipped and fell on an icy patch on the sidewalk at your client's apartment complex. On December 18, the sidewalk was icy and dangerous. Your client disclaims any responsibility to shovel the sidewalk or to salt the sidewalk.

Mr. Johnson's medical bills total $20,000.00 in actual out-of-pocket expenses. Moreover, Mr. Johnson is unable to continue his employment duties as a liquor driver. These duties require him to unload, lift, and carry heavy boxes. Doctors estimate he will not be able to return to work for three months. His lost wages total $6,000.00.

It is true that earlier Missouri court decisions have not imposed a duty upon land-lords to shovel the snow from common walkways. These courts have reasoned that landlords have no duty to keep an apartment building's "common premises" safe from temporary hazards such as snow. *See, e.g., Maschoff v. Koedding*, 439 S.W.2d 234 (Mo. Ct. App. 1969). Such earlier courts justify this rule by noting that the duty to remove snow "would subject the landlord to an unreasonable burden of vigilance and care...." *Id.* at 236. However, it is important to note that this decision is over forty years old.

More recently, in *Jackson v. Ray Kruse Const. Co.*, 708 S.W.2d 664 (Mo. banc 1986), the Missouri Supreme Court imposed a duty on a landlord to place speed bumps in the parking lot of an apartment building. In *Jackson*, the plaintiff child was injured on the parking lot of the landlord's apartment complex when a speeding bicycle struck her. *Id.* at 666. By so holding, the court extended the burden of a landlord's duty to keep common areas safe from foreseeable injuries beyond the scope of earlier court decisions. "As strongly emphasized in recent cases," the landlord owes a duty to its tenants to make common areas of leased premises reasonably safe. *Id.* The dissenting justice recognized this trend, noting that the court modified the law in order to com-pensate the injured plaintiff. The dissenting justice noted: "It must be obvious to those who care that the majority is bent on making the need for compensation the over-whelming function of the law of torts in Missouri." *Id.* at 671.

The landlord in *Jackson* had "reasonable notice" of the dangerous condition. Testi-mony established that safety bumps were standard safety devices used in parking lots to slow the speed of vehicles. *Id.* at 666. Thus, even though the landlord had no actu-al knowledge of the danger of speeding bicycles, the jury found that the landlord had "notice of a condition which required the installation of speed bumps." *Id.* at 667.

A more recent Supreme Court decision reflects this Missouri trend to protect ten-ants' rights, even at the expense of the supposedly "well recognized" legal principles set out in older cases. In *Aaron v. Havens*, 758 S.W.2d 446, 448 (Mo. banc 1988), the court held that a jury could find a landlord has the duty to relocate the position of a fire escape to make it impossible for criminal intruders to use the fire escape to break in to a tenant's apartment. Again, the dissenting justices reflect the changes in the law by expressing their concern at the Court's continued willingness to impose such du-ties on landlords. *Id.* at 450.

It is true that the recent Missouri Supreme Court cases did not have the opportu-nity to address whether the older "temporary hazard" cases are still valid in this state. Under the broad language and shifts in policy reflected in the most recent Supreme Court opinions, it is arguable that your client owed Mr. Johnson a duty to keep the sidewalk free from ice. Your client reasonably should have foreseen that a tenant would slip and fall on an icy sidewalk that is a common part of the premises. By failing to do so, your client breached its duty to Mr. Johnson under the law. In fact, the duty your client has assumed is less burdensome than the duties the Supreme Court imposed on the landlords in each of these recent cases. Also, the danger in our case is more obvious and known than the dangers presented in *Jackson* and *Aaron*. In point of fact, public and private schools in the City of St. Louis closed for two days. In contrast, in each of the recent cases, the landlords had no actual knowledge of the existing dangerous conditions.

After you have had an opportunity to digest and consider this letter, please give me a call and let me know whether you wish to settle this litigation. I will wait to hear from you.

Very truly yours,

Charlotte Turley

Exercise 37-2

Review the draft settlement letter in Exercise 37-1, and Sample Client Letter A in Appendix B. Redraft the letter in Exercise 37-1 to make it persuasive.

Appendix A

SAMPLE MEMOS

SAMPLE MEMO A:
ONE-ISSUE OFFICE MEMORANDUM

<u>MEMORANDUM</u>

To: Chief of Felony Prosecutions
From: Assistant Prosecutor
Re: Gerry Arnold case—Residential Burglary Prosecution
Date: August 15, 20XX

<u>QUESTION PRESENTED</u>

Is a detached garage a "living quarters" in which the owners "actually reside" under Illinois' Residential Burglary Statute, when it has been converted into a retreat for the owners' college-age son, who uses it on a weekly basis as a getaway and sleeps there half the year, although the retreat does not have plumbing facilities?

> **The Question Presented**
> 1. Relevant area of law.
> 2. Element of the law that presents the issue.
> 3. Critical facts that frame the issue.

<u>SHORT ANSWER</u>

Yes. A detached garage used as a retreat and seasonal sleeping place is a "living quarters" under the Statute. The owner frequently and regularly uses the garage for residential activities associated with a living quarters. The garage is furnished to reflect that use.

> **The Short Answer:**
> 1. Answers the question.
> 2. Briefly explains the answer.

<u>STATEMENT OF FACTS</u>

On August 10, 20XX, Defendant, Gerry Arnold, broke into Carl and Rita Stripes' two-car detached garage and removed some of their personal property. The State has charged Arnold under the Residential Burglary Statute. Arnold's attorney has moved to dismiss the charge, contending that the Stripes' garage is not a "dwelling" within which the Stripes "reside," as required by the Statute.

> This paragraph provides context by describing the foundational facts.

The garage is located approximately thirty feet behind the Stripe home. The Stripes have converted two-thirds of the garage into quarters for the couple's college-age son, Michael Stripe, to use as a getaway. They have walled-off that section of the garage from the section that stores the family car. The converted section of the garage has a window and a locked door.

Michael spends two to three evenings a week and his free time on weekends in the getaway, writing and listening to music and watching television. In addition, Michael is the lead singer of a band, R.E.N., that plays once a month in clubs around town. The band practices in the garage on Sunday mornings and stores some of their equipment there. During the summer and fall when his parents are in town, Michael sleeps in the garage on a futon in a loft area. When his parents travel to Florida during the winter and spring, Michael sleeps in the house.

The garage is equipped to accommodate Michael's interests. In addition to the futon, the garage contains an expensive sound system, a portable five-inch television, and a mini-refrigerator. The garage has electricity and a space heater, but no running water or heat.

DISCUSSION

The State can likely prosecute Arnold for residential burglary under Illinois' Residential Burglary Statute (the "Statute"). To prosecute Arnold successfully under the Statute, the State must prove that Arnold "knowingly and without authority enter[ed] the *dwelling place* of another." 720 Ill. Comp. Stat. § 5/19-3 (2004) (emphasis added). There is no real dispute that Arnold "knowingly" entered the Stripes' garage or that his entry was "without authority." Whether the garage is a "dwelling place" is more problematic. The Statute defines a dwelling as "a house, apartment, mobile home, trailer, or *other living quarters* in which… the owners or occupants *actually reside*…." 720 Ill. Comp. Stat. § 5/2-6(b) (2004) (emphasis added). This memorandum addresses whether the Stripes' garage is a "living quarters" in which Michael Stripe "actually resides," and therefore a dwelling.

The Stripes' garage is a dwelling because it is a "living quarters" in which Michael Stripe "actually resides."

The remaining paragraphs relate to the legally significant facts, grouped by issue (i.e., physical characteristics of the garage, type of use, frequency of use and evidence of use).

Note that details of the arrest are not included in the factual story because they are not relevant to the dwelling issue.

Overview paragraph:
1. Ultimate conclusion.
2. Elements of the rule of law.
3. Dispenses with non-issues.
4. Identifies the issue as defined by statute.

Thesis paragraph:
1. Legal issue conclusion.
2. Relevant factors.

When determining whether a structure is a living quarters, courts evaluate the type of activities for which the owners use the structure, as well as the frequency of those activities and physical evidence of those activities. A structure is considered a dwelling when the owners frequently use the structure for activities that occur in a living quarters, and the furnishings reflect that use. *People v. McIntyre*, 578 N.E.2d 314 (Ill. App. Ct. 1991); *People v. Thomas*, 561 N.E.2d 57 (Ill. 1990). Although a structure's attachment to the main residence is also relevant, physical attachment to the primary residence is not necessary. *McIntyre*, 578 N.E.2d at 315. Therefore, a structure used as an extension of the home's living quarters may be a dwelling even though it is not physically connected to the primary residence. Because Michael Stripe frequently and regularly uses the Stripes' garage as a living quarters, it satisfies the statutory definition of "dwelling."

> 3. Synthesized rule statements from cases.

> 4. Brief application of factors to client situation.

For example, an enclosed, attached porch frequently used as part of the home's living quarters is a dwelling under the residential burglary statute. *McIntyre*, 578 N.E.2d 314. In *People v. McIntyre*, the owners used an attached, screened porch for "sitting, eating, and cooking." *Id.* at 315. They ate most of their meals on the porch in the summer and cooked meals there four or five times a week in the winter. The owners furnished the porch with wrought-iron furniture and a barbecue grill that reflected its use. The porch was enclosed, locked, and attached to the home. The court held that, under these facts, the porch was a "living quarters" under the Statute. *Id.*

> **Rule Explanation — Case 1:**
> 1. Rule Statement from case 1.
> 2. Relevant case facts.

> 3. Holding.

The court reasoned that the owners used the porch as part of their living quarters by engaging in such activities as "sitting, eating, and cooking." *Id.* In addition, the owners regularly used the porch in this manner and furnished the porch with furniture and a grill that reflected such use. The court also observed that the porch was enclosed and attached to the house, indicating that the porch's physical attachment to the house was a relevant factor. However, the court emphasized that it was the activities of "sitting, eating, and cooking" that "make the porch part of the living quarters of the house." *Id.*

> 4. Rationale reflecting how the court evaluated each relevant factor.

Rule Explanation—Case 2:
1. Rule statement from case 2.

2. Relevant case facts.

3. Holding.

4. Rationale reflecting how the Court evaluated the relevant factor.

Rule Application Factor 1: Use

1. Conclusion.

2. Favorable analogy & elaboration of how client facts support the attorney's conclusion.

3. Favorable distinction from a favorable result case.

4. Favorable distinction from an unfavorable result case.

On the other hand, where a structure is attached, but used only for commercial, rather than residential activities, it is not a living quarters. *People v. Thomas*, 561 N.E.2d 57 (Ill. 1990). In *Thomas*, a garage was attached to a multi-unit apartment building. All of the garages and apartment units shared the same roof. The owner used the garage to park her car and to store large quantities of perfume for a commercial business. The Court held that the attached garage, "at least in this instance," was not a living quarters. *Id.* at 58.

The Court implicitly reasoned that a garage used only to store products for sale in a commercial business is not a living quarters, even when attached to the owner's apartment building. However, the Court left open the possibility that a garage could, given the appropriate use as a living quarters, constitute a dwelling under the Statute. The Court reasoned that "an attached garage is not *necessarily* a 'dwelling' within the meaning of the residential burglary statute." *Id.* (emphasis added). That language implies that a garage, appropriately used as a residence or living quarters, could be a dwelling under the Statute. *See also*, *People v. Silva*, 628 N.E.2d 948, 953 (Ill. App. Ct. 1993) (noting that *Thomas* left open the possibility for a garage to be a dwelling under the Statute).

Like the owner's use of the porch in *McIntyre*, Michael Stripe uses the Stripes' garage for activities commonly associated with a living quarters. Like the activities of "sitting, eating, and cooking" in *McIntyre*, Michael Stripe's use of the garage for playing and listening to music, watching television, and eating snacks are uses commonly associated with a living quarters. In addition, Michael Stripe's use of the garage as a sleeping quarters during the summer and fall makes his use of the garage even more of a typical living quarters than the porch in *McIntyre*. Unlike the *McIntyre* activities of barbecuing, eating, and sitting, which can occur outside of a dwelling, sleeping is an activity uniquely associated with a living quarters. Moreover, Michael Stripe's use of the garage is clearly distinguishable from that in *Thomas*, where the owner used the garage only for storage purposes.

In addition, like the owners in *McIntyre*, Michael Stripe furnished the garage in a manner that reflects its use as a living quarters. Like the grill and wrought-iron furniture in *McIntyre*, Michael Stripe's sound system, small t.v., mini-refrigerator, and futon reflect that he uses the garage for activities typically associated with a living quarters. Again, the furnishings are a far cry from the garage in *Thomas*, which housed only the owner's car and boxes of commercial products for sale.

> **Rule Application Factor 1(a): Evidence of Use**

> Facts & analogies explored for sub-factor.

Finally, like the owners' use of the porch in *McIntyre*, the frequency of Michael's use of the garage also reflects the garage's use as a living quarters. Michael spends at least two to three evenings a week and his spare time on weekends in his getaway. Moreover, during the summer and fall, he sleeps there seven nights a week. Michael's regular and frequent use far exceeds the owner's limited, occasional use of the garage in *Thomas* to retrieve her car or perfume products from storage. In fact, in August when the garage was burglarized, Michael's frequency of use even exceeded that of the owners in *McIntyre*, who used the porch only four to five times a week.

> **Rule Application Factor 1(b): Frequency of Use**

> Facts & analogies explored for "frequency" sub-factor.

Defendant may argue that, despite Michael Stripe's frequent use of the garage for activities associated with a living quarters, the garage's physical detachment from the Stripes' home prevents it from being a "living quarters" in which the owners "reside." Under this theory, Defendant would argue that the garage, standing alone, is not a living quarters in which anyone resides. The garage has no running water, bathroom facilities, or heat. Thus, the garage's status as a dwelling is dependent upon whether it can reasonably be viewed as an extension of the Stripe family's living quarters within the home itself. Defendant would argue that the fact that the *McIntyre* porch was physically attached to the family's home was essential to the court's holding. Only because it was physically attached to the home could the porch reasonably be viewed as an extension of the family's living quarters. In contrast, the Stripes' garage stands thirty feet away from their residence.

> **Opposing Argument #1:**
> 1. Identifies and explores an opposing argument resulting from a factual distinction between an earlier case and the Stripe situation.

While having some merit, this argument should fail. Although the *McIntyre* court did note that the porch was

> 2. Writer's conclusion re: validity of the opp. argument.

3. Arguments that support attorney's conclusion.

physically "attached and enclosed," it concluded that it was the owners' "activities" and *use* of the porch that made the porch "part of the living quarters of the house." 578 N.E.2d at 314. Thus, the court implied that the activities for which the porch was used were more important than the porch's attachment to the home. Moreover, the fact that the porch was separated from the utility room of the owners' home by a door with "three locks" lends less significance to the attached/detached distinction. The presence of three locks implies that the porch area was not an open part of the main residence, but was instead physically separate from the main residence. Like the physically separate porch in *McIntyre*, the Stripes' garage is used as an extension of the Stripe family's living quarters.

Note how the writer uses deductive reasoning to create an argument based on the fact that the porch was locked.

People v. Thomas lends further support to this conclusion. In *Thomas*, the Court minimized the importance of the garage's physical attachment to the main residence while emphasizing the garage's use. The Court reasoned that "[a] garage, at least in this instance, *whether attached to the various living units or not*, cannot be deemed a residence or living quarters." 561 N.E.2d at 58 (emphasis added). By that statement, the Court implied that the garage's physical attachment to the owner's home was not important. That statement, together with the Court's earlier definition of a dwelling as a structure used as a "living quarters," implies that a detached garage used as a living quarters would be a dwelling under the Statute. Therefore, the fact that the Stripes' garage is physically detached from their residence does not deprive it of its status as a "living quarters" in which the owners "actually reside."

Note how the writer uses exact language from the earlier cases to support the writer's conclusions.

4. Conclusion repeated for lengthy analysis.

Defendant might also argue that the legislative history suggests that the legislators did not intend for the Statute to cover structures such as garages. As the court noted in *People v. Silva*, 628 N.E.2d 948 (Ill. App. Ct. 1993), the legislature amended the Statute in 1986 to clarify and narrow the meaning of the term "dwelling." The court quoted the following statement of Senator Sangmeister made during legislative hearings: "It was even brought to our attention by the Illinois Supreme Court in a number of cases that... there should be a better definition to the dwelling house. We are having people prosecuted for res-

Opposing Argument #2:
1. Identifies & discusses a 2nd opposing argument.

idential burglary for breaking into . . . unoccupied buildings *such as garages.*" *Id.* at 951(emphasis added).

This argument lacks merit. The *Silva* court noted that "[t]he residential burglary statute is designed to protect the 'privacy and sanctity of the home,' with a view toward the 'greater danger and potential for serious harm from burglary of a home as opposed to burglary of a business.'" 628 N.E.2d at 951 (quoting *People v. Edgesto*, 611 N.E.2d 49 (Ill. App. Ct. 1993)). Senator Sangmeister's concern that people are being prosecuted for breaking into "unoccupied buildings" is consistent with the general legislative purpose to deter residential burglary because of its potential for serious harm. An occupied garage used as a living quarters invokes the same legislative concerns for the sanctity of the home and the increased risk of harm that results from an invasion of that home. Moreover, the Illinois Supreme Court decided the *Thomas* case only a few years after the amendment. In *Thomas*, the court suggested that a garage used as a living quarters would be a dwelling under the Statute.

CONCLUSION

The State can likely prosecute Arnold for residential burglary under the Statute, because the Stripes' garage should be deemed a "dwelling" under the Statute. Not only does Michael Stripe use the garage for residential activities, but he uses it frequently and regularly, and the furnishings reflect that use. The mere fact that the garage is not attached to the primary residence does not deprive it of its status as a living quarters. Therefore, as a living quarters, the Stripes' garage is a "dwelling" under the Statute.

2. Writer's conclusion re: validity of opposing arg.

3. Arguments that support the conclusion.

Again, the attorney uses deductive reasoning—noting the significance of the dates of the *Thomas* decision and the legislative amendment.

Ultimate and legal issue conclusions.

SAMPLE MEMO B
ONE-ISSUE OFFICE MEMORANDUM

*Question Presented and Short Answer Purposefully Omitted
from this Memo: Subject of Exercises, Chapter 15*

MEMORANDUM

To: Senior Attorney
From: Junior Attorney
Date: August 1, 20XX
Re: Chester Tate

STATEMENT OF FACTS

On July 19, 20XX, Mr. Chester Tate tied Mr. Aaron Campbell to a chair in Mr. Campbell's living room and shot him in the shoulder. The State has charged Mr. Tate with assault and aggravated kidnapping. This office has agreed to represent Mr. Tate.

Mr. Tate and Mr. Campbell have been friends for a number of years, and Mr. Tate has frequently been a visitor at Mr. Campbell's home. In early July, 20XX, Mr. Tate and Mr. Campbell argued about a loan Mr. Tate had made to Mr. Campbell that had not been repaid. After that argument, Mr. Campbell and Mr. Tate did not see or speak to each other until July 19. At 1:30 p.m. on July 19, Mr. Tate arrived unexpectedly at Mr. Campbell's home. When he arrived, the two friends talked for several minutes on the front porch. Afterwards, they decided that they would let bygones be bygones, and they walked into the house to have a beer.

After they entered the house, Mr. Campbell noticed the strong smell of alcohol on Mr. Tate's breath and suggested that it would not be a good idea to have a drink. Mr. Tate became upset, and the two friends began quarreling again. The argument escalated, and Mr. Tate put his arm around Mr. Campbell's neck in what Mr. Campbell described as a "headlock." Mr. Tate then put the nose of a gun he carried with him into Mr. Campbell's side and ordered Mr. Campbell to seat himself in a living room chair. Mr. Tate then tied Mr. Campbell's hands behind him and his feet to the chair. At some point during their argument, Mr. Tate shot Mr. Campbell in the shoulder while he was tied to the chair.

At approximately 4:00 p.m. that afternoon, Ms. Marva Stewart arrived at Mr. Campbell's home to meet with Mr. Campbell regarding some interior design work he had engaged her to perform. She rang the doorbell repeatedly. When there was no answer, she walked around to the back of the house, thinking that Mr. Campbell might be in his back yard gardening. When she did not find him there, she knocked on the back door repeatedly. When there was no answer, she returned to the front of the home, where she saw Mr. Campbell's car sitting by the curb. Thinking that he must be home, she tried calling him from her cell phone. When, after repeated rings, there was no answer, she assumed that he must be sleeping and left. She made no attempt to look into the windows of the home.

Because of his intoxicated state, Mr. Tate does not recall how long he stayed with Mr. Campbell in his living room. However, he does recall hearing the telephone ring and the doorbell chime. He did not answer the telephone or open the door. Mr. Tate also recalls the living room lamp switching on from an automatic timer. (The timer is set to go on at 8:00 p.m.) A friend of Mr. Campbell's discovered him at 9:00 that evening blindfolded, gagged, bleeding from a gunshot wound to the right shoulder, and bound to a chair in his living room.

Mr. Campbell's home is a large, renovated, two-story brownstone. The first floor is primarily a glass picture window (a large, uninterrupted pane of glass), with a small amount of brick surrounding the entrance and providing support at the exterior wall of the home. The picture window is not tinted or coated in any way to affect its transparency. The second floor is primarily brick with two windows facing the street. The lot on which the home is situated is level, and the front door to the home is only two steps up from the sidewalk that leads to the home. The front door is solid wood with no window. The home sits back only twenty feet from the street. The street in front of Mr. Campbell's home is classified by the police as "moderately traveled" and is open to both commercial and residential traffic.

Ms. Gretchen Kraus, Mr. Campbell's neighbor directly across the street, has stated to police that she saw Mr. Tate arrive at Mr. Campbell's home in the early afternoon of July 19. She observed Mr. Campbell greet Mr. Tate with a smile and a handshake. Although she did not actually see the two men enter the home, she did see them on the small, concrete, two-step "porch" together. She assumed that the two men were going to enter Mr. Campbell's home. Ms. Kraus is able to see into Mr. Campbell's living room from her porch; in particular, during daylight, she is able to see figures and movement, and at night, when the living room lights are on, she is able to make out the activities within the room more clearly. However, she did not attempt to see into Mr. Campbell's living room on the afternoon or evening of July 19.

DISCUSSION

For the State to prosecute Mr. Tate for aggravated kidnapping, it must prove that Mr. Tate "knowingly... and secretly confined another against his will... while armed with a dangerous weapon." 720 Ill. Comp. Stat. § 5/10-1 (2004). There is no real dispute that Mr. Tate "confined another against his will... while armed with a dangerous weapon" because Mr. Tate tied Mr. Campbell to a chair and shot him with a gun. While the "knowingly" requirement may be an issue due to Mr. Tate's apparent intoxication, this memorandum focuses only on whether Mr. Tate's actions satisfy the "secretly" requirement.

Illinois courts have defined "secretly" to mean "concealed; hidden; not made public;... kept from the knowledge or notice of persons liable to be affected by the act." *People v. Franzen*, 622 N.E. 2d 877, 887 (Ill. App. Ct. 1993). When considering whether a confinement is secret, courts evaluate the visibility of the location of the confinement, as evidenced by its proximity to a public area and by whether there were, or could have been, witnesses, and the defendant's attempts to conceal the victim from the knowledge of others. When a defendant confines the victim in a location clearly visible to witnesses, and makes no attempt to conceal the victim, the confinement is not secret. *People v. Lamkey*, 608 N.E. 2d 406, 409 (Ill. App. Ct. 1993); *Franzen*, 622 N.E. 2d at 887. Because Mr. Tate confined Mr. Campbell in front of a large window visible to potential witnesses, and did not attempt to conceal Mr. Campbell from the knowledge of others, the confinement was not secret.

Further, when the defendant confines the victim in a location close to a public area that is visible to potential witnesses, and makes no attempt to conceal the victim, the confinement is not secret. *Lamkey*, 608 N.E. 2d at 409. In *Lamkey*, the defendant confined the victim in the vestibule of an apartment building that had commercial space on the first floor. The vestibule was two steps up from one of Chicago's busiest streets and was separated from the sidewalk by a glass door. From within the vestibule, the victim was able to see cars and passersby. Moreover, a passing motorist witnessed and interrupted the assault. On these facts, the court held that the confinement was not "secret" and overturned the defendant's conviction. The court reasoned that the attempted assault occurred "within public view... in an area clearly visible to anyone walking or driving down the street." *Id*. Moreover, the court found it "significant" that the defendant made no attempt to conceal the victim by moving her to a more concealed location within the building. *Id*.

On the other hand, when the defendant attempts to conceal the confinement by moving the victim to a location not visible to potential witnesses, the confinement is secret. *Franzen*, 622 N.E. 2d at 887. In *Franzen*, the defendant met the victim at a bar parking lot, where he knocked the victim unconscious and dragged her thirty feet into a field behind a fence. He then dragged her an additional 130 feet into the field, where sorghum plants were high enough to conceal them. In fact, a bouncer from the bar was unable to observe the victim from the bar's parking lot. Under these facts, the court held that the defendant's confinement was "secret." *Id*. The court reasoned that the defendant successfully attempted to conceal the victim by dragging her 160 feet into a dark field that was not visible to "anyone who might have wandered out into the parking lot." *Id*.

Like in *Lamkey* and unlike in *Franzen*, Mr. Tate confined Mr. Campbell in a visible location close to a public area. The living room in which Mr. Tate confined Mr. Campbell is visible through a large picture window that runs the length of the living room. Moreover, the living room is close to a public area, being only twenty feet and two steps up from a moderately traveled commercial and residential street. Although the living room is not as close to or as public an area as the vestibule in *Lamkey*, which was only two steps up from a busy street, the picture window is significantly larger than the glass door in *Lamkey*. Therefore, Campbell's living room is arguably as visible as the vestibule in *Lamkey*. In any event, the living room is far removed from the dark field in

Franzen, in which the tall sorghum plants and fence concealed the victim from any potential witness who might have wandered out into the parking lot 160 feet away.

The possibility of witnesses further demonstrates the visibility of the location of Mr. Campbell's confinement. Mr. Campbell's neighbor is able to see figures and movement within Mr. Campbell's living room during the day and is able to see much more clearly into the living room at night. Moreover, like the motorist in *Lamkey*, passersby would have seen Mr. Campbell had they looked in the window, especially after 8:00 p.m., when the light automatically switched on inside the room.

The State may argue that the mere possibility of witnesses to the confinement does not negate secrecy. However, the fact that no one actually looked in Mr. Campbell's window does not undermine the argument that the confinement was not secret. In *Lamkey*, the court held that the confinement was not secret in part because the confinement was "in an area clearly visible to anyone walking or driving down the street." Moreover, in *Franzen*, the court held that the confinement was secret, in part, because the victim was concealed from "anyone who might have wandered out into the parking lot." *Lamkey* and *Franzen* imply that it is the *possibility* of a witness viewing the confinement that is important rather than the happenstance of an actual witness.

Further, like the defendant in *Lamkey* and unlike the defendant in *Franzen*, Mr. Tate did not attempt to move Mr. Campbell to a more concealed location, which would have made the location more secret. Like the *Lamkey* defendant's failure to move the victim to his upstairs apartment, Mr. Tate did not attempt to move Mr. Campbell to an upstairs bedroom, where the home is mainly brick, or to a more concealed room on the first floor. Mr. Tate even failed to close the curtains of the living room window or unplug the automatic light. This conduct contrasts with the defendant's actions in *Franzen*, who twice moved the victim deeper into the sorghum field.

However, confinement also is secret when the defendant confines the victim in a location not visible to the public and successfully attempts to conceal the victim from the knowledge of potential witnesses. *People v. Enoch*, 522 N.E.2d 1124 (Ill. 1988). In *People v. Enoch*, witnesses saw the defendant and the victim walking together toward and within 100 feet of the victim's apartment. Later that night, the victim's boyfriend arrived at her apartment and unsuccessfully tried to determine if the victim was home. He rang the doorbell several times, checked the victim's place of work to see if she was still there, and called her on the telephone. The defendant failed to answer the telephone or doorbell, and the victim's boyfriend assumed she was not at home. Later, the boyfriend looked through the apartment windows, but he could not see the victim inside the bedroom of her apartment. *Id.* at 1134.

Under these facts, the Court held that the defendant's confinement of the victim was secret. *Id.* The bedroom of the victim's apartment was not visible to the public and, by refusing to answer the doorbell or telephone, the defendant acted to conceal the victim further. Moreover, the Court reasoned that the defendant's actions in concealing the victim successfully kept her confinement from the knowledge of any potential witnesses. No one knew the victim was home until after the defendant left her premises. *Id.*

The State will surely compare *Enoch* to the present case, arguing that each defendant confined the victim in the relative privacy of the victim's own home, and that each defendant attempted to further conceal the confinement by refusing to answer the telephone or doorbell. However, *Enoch* is distinguishable. Although both defendants failed to answer the telephone or doorbell, Mr. Tate did not conceal Mr. Campbell from the knowledge of others. First, unlike the basement apartment in *Enoch*, Mr. Tate confined Mr. Campbell in a visible location. Had anyone actually looked through Mr. Campbell's picture window, they would have seen him confined in the living room. Therefore, despite Mr. Tate's failure to answer the doorbell or telephone, the visibility of the location made it possible for a witness to view the confinement. In contrast, the boyfriend in *Enoch* was unable to see her by looking through the apartment windows.

Second, both Mr. Campbell's neighbor and his interior designer actually knew that Mr. Campbell was home. The neighbor saw Mr. Tate and Mr. Campbell on the porch of Mr. Campbell's house. Because they were next to each other and on the front porch, the neighbor believed that "they were going to enter the home." In contrast, witnesses in *Enoch* saw the defendant and the victim together from 100 feet away from the victim's apartment. Because of the distance that remained to the apartment, and because the apartment was in a mixed residential and commercial area with many possible destinations for the two, these witnesses did not know the defendant and the victim were in the victim's apartment.

Although Mr. Tate failed to answer when the interior decorator rang the doorbell or called on the telephone, Ms. Stewart assumed Mr. Campbell was home because Mr. Campbell's car was parked in front of his home. In contrast, in *Enoch*, the victim's boyfriend assumed that the victim was not at home and attempted to locate her elsewhere.

Accordingly, Mr. Tate has a viable defense that the confinement was not secret. He confined Mr. Campbell in a location close to a public area and visible to potential witnesses. Additionally, he did not conceal Mr. Campbell from the knowledge of others.

SAMPLE MEMO C:
ONE-ISSUE OFFICE MEMORANDUM ILLUSTRATING
FORMAT OPTION 3

MEMORANDUM

To: Chief of Felony Prosecutions
From: Assistant Prosecutor
Re: Gerry Arnold case—Residential Burglary Prosecution
Date: August 15, 20XX

QUESTION PRESENTED

Is a detached garage a "living quarters" in which the owners "actually reside" under Illinois' Residential Burglary Statute, when the owners' college-age son uses it several days a week and on weekends as a getaway retreat and sleeps there half the year?

> **The Question Presented**
> 1. Relevant area of law.
> 2. Element of the law that presents the issue.
> 3. Critical facts that frame the issue.

SHORT ANSWER

Yes. A detached garage used as a retreat and seasonal sleeping place is a "living quarters" under the Statute. The owner frequently and regularly uses the garage for residential activities associated with a living quarters. The garage is furnished to reflect that use.

> **The Short Answer:**
> 1. Answers the question.
> 2. Briefly explains the answer.

STATEMENT OF FACTS

On August 10, 20XX, Defendant, Gerry Arnold, burglarized Carl and Rita Stripes' two-car detached garage. The State has charged Arnold under the Residential Burglary Statute. Arnold's attorney has moved to dismiss the charge, contending that the Stripes' garage is not a "dwelling" within which the Stripes "reside," as required by the Statute.

> This ¶ describes the procedural context of the case.

The garage is located approximately thirty feet behind the Stripe home. The Stripes have converted two-thirds of the garage into quarters for the couple's college-age son, Michael Stripe, to use as a getaway. They have walled-off that section of the garage from the section that stores the family car. The converted section of the garage has a window and a locked door.

> The remaining paragraphs tell the factual story of the case as it relates to the issue: whether the Stripes' garage is a dwelling.

Michael spends two to three evenings a week and his free time on weekends in the getaway, writing and listening to music and watching television. In addition, Michael

> Thus, details of Arnold's arrest are not included because they are not relevant to the dwelling issue.

is the lead singer of a band, R.E.N., that plays once a month in clubs around town. The band practices in the garage on Sunday mornings and stores some of their equipment there. During the summer and fall when his parents are in town, Michael sleeps in the garage on a futon in a loft area. When his parents travel to Florida during the winter and spring, Michael sleeps in the house.

The garage is equipped to accommodate Michael's interests. In addition to the futon, the garage contains an expensive sound system, a portable five-inch television, and a mini-refrigerator. The garage has electricity and a space heater, but no running water or heat.

DISCUSSION

Overview paragraph:
1. Ultimate conclusion.

The State can likely prosecute Arnold for residential burglary under Illinois' Residential Burglary Statute (the "Statute"). To prosecute Arnold successfully under the

2. Elements of the rule of law.

Statute, the State must prove that Arnold "knowingly and without authority enter[ed] the *dwelling place* of another." 720 Ill. Comp. Stat. § 5/19-3 (2004) (emphasis added).

3. Dispenses with non-issues.

There is no real dispute that Arnold "knowingly" entered the Stripes' garage or that his entry was "without authority." Whether the garage is a "dwelling place" is more prob-

4. Identifies the issue as defined by statute.

lematic. The Statute defines a dwelling as "a house, apartment, mobile home, trailer, or *other living quarters* in which ... the owners or occupants *actually reside* ...." 720 Ill. Comp. Stat. § 5/2-6(b) (2004) (emphasis added). This memorandum addresses whether the Stripes' garage is a "living quarters" in which Michael Stripe "actually resides," and thus a dwelling.

Thesis paragraph:
1. Legal issue conclusion.

The Stripes' garage is a dwelling because it is a "living quarters" in which Michael Stripe "actually resides." When

2. Relevant factors.

determining whether a structure is a living quarters, courts evaluate the type of activities for which the owners use the structure, as well as the physical evidence of those activities and the frequency of such activities. A structure

3. Synthesized rule statements from cases.

is considered a dwelling when the owners frequently use the structure for activities that occur in a living quarters, and the furnishings reflect that use. *People v. McIntyre*, 578 N.E.2d 314 (Ill. App. Ct. 1991); *People v. Thomas*, 561 N.E.2d 57 (Ill. 1990). Although a structure's attachment to the main residence is also relevant, physical attachment to the primary residence is not necessary. *McIntyre*, 578 N.E.2d at 315. Therefore, a structure used as an extension of the home's living quarters may be a dwelling even though it is not physically connected to the primary residence. Because Michael Stripe frequently and regularly uses the Stripes' garage as a living quarters, it satisfies the statutory definition of "dwelling."

> 4. Brief application of factors to client situation.

A. Type of Use.

The owners must use a structure for activities associated with a living quarters for the structure to be classified as a dwelling. *People v. McIntyre*, 578 N.E.2d 314, 315 (Ill. App. Ct. 1991). In *McIntyre*, the owners used a screened porch for "sitting, eating, and cooking." They ate their meals on the porch in the summer and cooked meals there during the winter. *Id.* The court held that the porch was a "living quarters" under the Statute, reasoning that the owners' use of the porch for "sitting, eating, and cooking" made it "part of the living quarters" of their home. *Id.*

> Rule Explanation—Factor 1:

> Case 1—facts & rationale that relate to "type of use" factor.

In contrast, where a structure is used only for commercial activities, it is not a dwelling. *People v. Thomas*, 561 N.E.2d 57, 58 (Ill. 1990). In *Thomas*, the owner used her portion of the garage of a multi-unit apartment building to store large quantities of perfume for a commercial business. The Court held that the attached garage, "at least in this instance," was not a dwelling because it was not used as a "living quarters." *Id.* at 58.

> Case 2—facts & rationale that relate to "type of use" factor.

However, the Court left open the possibility that a garage could, given the appropriate use as a living quarters, constitute a dwelling under the Statute. The Court reasoned that "an attached garage is not *necessarily* a 'dwelling' within the meaning of the residential burglary statute." *Id.* (emphasis added). That language implies that a garage, appropriately used as a residence or living quarters, could be a dwelling under the Statute. *See also People v. Silva*, 628 N.E.2d 948, 953 (Ill. App. Ct. 1993) (noting that *Thomas* left open the possibility for a garage to be a dwelling under the Statute).

> Case 2 discussion continued. *Note:* A case of secondary importance is used parenthetically to lend further support for the writer's interpretation of Case 2.

Like the owner's use of the porch in *McIntyre*, Michael Stripe used the Stripes' garage for activities commonly as-

> Rule Application—Factor 1
> 1. Thesis for Factor.

2. Client facts that prove the thesis.

3. Comparisons to *McIntyre* and *Thomas* to further support the thesis.

Factor 1(a)—Evidence of Use.

Facts in *McIntyre* case AND application to Stripes' garage. Because this is a minor sub-factor that does not require extensive discussion, the rule explanation & rule application are combined into a single paragraph.

Rule Explanation: Factor 1(b)—Frequency of Use.

Facts in the *McIntyre* and *Thomas* cases that relate to frequency of use.

Rule Application: Factor 1(b)—Frequency of Use.

1. Thesis

2. Client facts that support the thesis.

3. Comparisons to cases that lend further support to the thesis.

sociated with a living quarters. Like the activities of "sitting, eating, and cooking" in *McIntyre*, Michael Stripe's use of the garage for playing and listening to music, watching television, and eating snacks are uses commonly associated with a living quarters. In addition, Michael Stripe's use of the garage as a sleeping quarters during the summer and fall only strengthens the argument that the garage is a dwelling under the Statute. Unlike the *McIntyre* activities of barbecuing, eating, and sitting, which can occur outside of a dwelling, sleeping is an activity uniquely associated with a living quarters. Moreover, Michael Stripe's use of the garage is clearly distinguishable from that in *Thomas*, where the owner used the garage only for storage purposes.

Further, the furnishings in a structure can serve as evidence of its use as a living quarters. In *McIntyre*, the owners furnished their porch with wrought-iron furniture and a barbecue grill that reflected their use of the porch for "sitting, eating, and cooking." 578 N.E.2d at 315. Similarly, Michael Stripe's sound system, small television, mini-refrigerator, and futon reflect that he uses the garage for activities associated with a living quarters.

An occupant must not only use a structure as part of the living quarters of the home, but use it for those purposes on a frequent and regular basis. In *McIntyre*, the owners ate most of their meals on the porch in the summer and cooked meals there four or five times a week in the winter. 578 N.E.2d at 315. In contrast, the owner in *Thomas* presumably used the garage only on those limited occasions on which she delivered perfume to be stored there, or moved the perfume to a location where it would be sold. 561 N.E.2d at 58.

Like the owners' use of the porch in *McIntyre*, the frequency of Michael's use of the garage also reflects its use as a living quarters. Michael spends at least two to three evenings a week and his spare time on weekends in his getaway. Moreover, during the summer and fall, he sleeps there seven nights a week. Michael's regular and frequent use of the garage far exceeds the limited, occasional use of the garage in *Thomas*. In fact, when the garage was burglarized in August, Michael's frequency of use even exceeded that of the owners in *McIntyre*, who only used the porch four to five times a week.

B. Proximity to Primary Residence.

The proximity of the structure to the primary residence is also a relevant factor. In *McIntyre*, for example, when holding that the porch was part of the home's living quarters, the court observed that "the porch is attached and enclosed...." 578 N.E.2d at 314. However, this factor does not seem to be as important as the manner in which the owners use the structure. For example, in *Thomas*, the Court minimized the importance of the garage's physical attachment to the residence. The Court reasoned that "[a] garage, at least in this instance, *whether attached to the various living units or not*, cannot be deemed a residence or living quarters." 561 N.E.2d at 58 (emphasis added). By that statement, the Court implied that the garage's physical attachment to the owner's home was not as important as its use.

Nevertheless, the Defendant may argue that, despite Michael Stripe's frequent use of the garage for activities associated with a living quarters, the garage's physical detachment from the Stripes' home prevents it from being a "living quarters" in which the owners "reside." Under this theory, the Defendant would argue that the garage, standing alone, is not a living quarters in which anyone resides. The garage has no running water, bathroom facilities, or heat. Thus, the garage's status as a dwelling is dependent upon whether it can reasonably be viewed as an extension of the Stripe family's living quarters within the home itself. The Defendant would argue that the fact that the *McIntyre* porch was physically attached to the family's home was essential to the court's holding. Only because it was physically attached to the home could the porch reasonably be viewed as an extension of the family's living quarters. In contrast, the Stripes' garage stands thirty feet away from their residence.

While having some merit, this argument should fail. Although the *McIntyre* court did note that the porch was physically "attached and enclosed," it concluded that it was the owners' "activities" and *use* of the porch that made

---

Rule Explanation: Factor 2 —

Rationale in *McIntyre* & *Thomas* that explains "proximity" factor.

Rule Application: Factor 2 —
1. Thesis for opposing argument #1.
2. Explores the basis of the opposing argument.

3. Writer's conclusion re: validity of opposing argument.
4. Explores McIntyre case to illustrate the writer's point.

the porch "part of the living quarters of the house." 578 N.E.2d at 314. Thus, the court implied that the activities for which the porch was used were more important than the porch's attachment to the home. Moreover, the fact that the porch was separated from the utility room of the owners' home by a door with "three locks" lends less significance to the attached/detached distinction. The presence of three locks implies that the porch area was not an open part of the main residence, but was instead physically separate from the main residence. Like the physically separate porch in *McIntyre*, the Stripes' garage is used as an extension of the Stripe family's living quarters.

2nd opposing argument for Factor 2:
1. Thesis for opposing argument.
2. Explores the basis of the opposing argument.

Defendant might also argue that the legislative history suggests that the legislators did not intend for the Statute to cover structures such as garages. As the court noted in *People v. Silva*, 628 N.E.2d 948 (Ill. App. Ct. 1993), the legislature amended the Statute in 1986 to clarify and narrow the meaning of the term "dwelling." The court quoted the following statement of Senator Sangmeister made during legislative hearings: "It was even brought to our attention by the Illinois Supreme Court in a number of cases that… there should be a better definition to the dwelling house. We are having people prosecuted for residential burglary for breaking into… unoccupied buildings *such as garages*." *Id*. at 951 (emphasis added).

3. Writer's conclusion re: validity of that argument.

4. Arguments that support the conclusion.

This argument lacks merit. The *Silva* court noted that "[t]he residential burglary statute is designed to protect the 'privacy and sanctity of the home,' with a view toward the 'greater danger and potential for serious harm from burglary of a home as opposed to burglary of a business.'" 628 N.E.2d at 951 (quoting *People v. Edgesto*, 611 N.E.2d 49 (Ill. App. Ct. 1993)). Senator Sangmeister's concern that people are being prosecuted for breaking into "unoccupied buildings" is consistent with the general legislative purpose to deter residential burglary because of its potential for serious harm. An occupied garage used as a living quarters invokes the same legislative concerns for the sanctity of the home and the increased risk of harm that results from an invasion of that home. Moreover, the Illinois Supreme Court decided the *Thomas* case only a few years after the amendment. In *Thomas*, the Court suggested that a garage used as a living quarters would be a dwelling under the Statute.

CONCLUSION

The State can likely prosecute Arnold for residential burglary under the Statute, because the Stripes' garage should be deemed a "dwelling" under the Statute. Not only does Michael Stripe use the garage for residential activities, but he uses it frequently and regularly, and the furnishings reflect that use. The mere fact that the garage is not attached to the primary residence does not deprive it of its status as a living quarters. Therefore, as a living quarters, the Stripes' garage is a "dwelling" under the Statute.

Ultimate and legal issue conclusions.

SAMPLE MEMO D:
MULTI-ISSUE OFFICE MEMORANDUM

MEMORANDUM

To: Senior Attorney

From: Junior Attorney

Date: August 15, 20XX

Re: Mark and Allison McLean—Potential Litigation under the Attractive Nuisance Doctrine

QUESTIONS PRESENTED

Do the clients have a valid claim against landowners under Florida's attractive nuisance doctrine, which requires proof that: (a) the landowners could reasonably foresee the presence of trespassing children on their property, (b) the property contained a hidden danger, and (c) the landowners failed to exercise reasonable care to protect the child from injury?

A. Is the presence of trespassing children reasonably foreseeable when the property is located next to an elementary school; a pond on the property contains inner-tubes, ducks, and fish; and the landowners had previously discovered school children trespassing?

B. Is a dock a hidden danger to a six-year-old child when it is covered by moss and algae, provides the only means of access to the pond, and is so deteriorated that it collapsed under the weight of the child?

C. Do landowners fail to exercise reasonable care to protect children from foreseeable injury when they do not lock the gate to the property, repair the dock, or post warning signs of the deteriorating condition of the dock, although they erected a chain link fence around the property and posted a "Do Not Climb Fence" sign on the fence?

SHORT ANSWER

Yes, the clients have a strong claim against the landowners for injuries sustained by their child under the doctrine of attractive nuisance.

A. First, their child's presence on the property was reasonably foreseeable because the landowners' property is both visible and accessible from an area that young children frequent, it contains objects or conditions that attract children, and the landowners had previously discovered school children trespassing on their property.

B. Second, the deteriorating dock was a hidden danger because a six-year-old child is too young to appreciate its dangerous condition.

C. Finally, the landowners failed to exercise reasonable care to protect trespassing children from the danger of the dock because the burden of taking reasonable precautionary measures was slight when compared to the risk of harm to foreseeable child trespassers.

STATEMENT OF FACTS

On Sunday, May 28, 20XX, six-year-old Mikey McLean drowned in a pond on Fred and Thelma Hurts' property when their dock collapsed out from under him. Mikey's parents, Mr. and Ms. McLean, have retained this firm to represent them in potential litigation against the Hurts.

The Hurts' property contains a man-made pond, which they have stocked with fish and ducks. Approximately twenty years ago, they installed a dock that extends about one foot above and fifteen feet over the pond. Because of the rocky shoreline, the dock is the only means of access to the pond. The Hurts' children, and now their grandchildren, fish in the pond, feed the ducks, and play on inner-tubes the Hurts leave in the pond.

Ten years ago the Reed Elementary School was built on property adjacent to the Hurts' property. After the school was built, the Hurts erected an inexpensive chain-link fence around their property. The fence installer attempted to persuade the Hurts to build a privacy fence around their property, informing them that the four foot high chain-link fence would not keep out school children. However, the Hurts declined to purchase the more expensive privacy fence. Instead, they posted a "No Trespassing" sign on the fence.

It became common practice for elementary school students to feed the ducks through the chain-link fence. The Hurts have not objected to this practice. However, when two of Mikey's classmates climbed the fence to feed the ducks that were swimming in the pond, the Hurts told the children that they "should get back to school." Mikey observed this incident. After that incident, some of the older students began to dare each other to climb the fence without getting caught. Apparently to prevent the students from climbing the fence, in May, 20XX, the Hurts removed the "No Trespassing" sign and replaced it with a "Do Not Climb Fence" sign.

On Sunday of Memorial Day weekend, Mikey and two classmates decided to visit the ducks. The Hurts were out of town for the Memorial Day weekend. Due to the warning sign, Mikey and his friends knew that they should not climb the fence. Instead, they entered the property through an unlocked gate. Mikey's two friends ran across the dock and dove into the pond to swim and play on the inner-tubes. Mikey followed them onto the dock. Because he could not swim well, he decided to stay on the dock and toss bread crumbs to the ducks in the pond. While he was standing on the dock, it collapsed out from under him. Mikey fell into ten feet of water and drowned.

On the day of the fatal accident, the Hurts' wooden dock was decaying and rotting. However, the decay was partially hidden by a green shiny coating of moss and algae growing on the dock. The Hurts claim that they had planned to replace the dock, but postponed the repairs until the winter months.

DISCUSSION

The McLeans have a strong negligence claim against the Hurts under Florida's common law doctrine of attractive nuisance. In determining whether a landowner is liable for injuries to a child trespasser under the attractive nuisance doctrine, Florida courts require the plaintiff to prove that: (1) the child's presence on the property was reasonably foreseeable; (2) the condition that injured the child trespasser was a hidden danger, or "trap"; and (3) the landowner failed to exercise reasonable care to protect foreseeable child trespassers from the hidden danger. All three issues merit discussion.

A. <u>Trespassing Children Were Foreseeable.</u>

When evaluating the foreseeability of trespass, courts consider such factors as the property's visibility and accessibility to young children, its attractiveness to children, and the landowners' knowledge of previous trespass. The Hurts should have reasonably foreseen Mikey's presence on their property. The Hurts' pond, ducks, and inner-tubes are conditions both visible and attractive to the young children who attend an elementary school adjacent to their property. Moreover, they had knowledge that young elementary school children had previously trespassed on their property.

It is foreseeable that children will trespass on property when the property is attractive and alluring to children and the landowner has actual knowledge that children have previously trespassed on the property. *Ansin v. Thurston*, 98 So. 2d 87, 88 (Fla. Dist. Ct. App. 1957). In *Ansin*, the defendant's property contained an artificial pond with white sand banks, a floating dock, and a raft. *Id.* at 88. A child drowned in the pond after playing on the raft. The court upheld a jury's finding that the presence of child trespassers was reasonably foreseeable, holding that it was "certain that children would be attracted to such a place...." *Id.* The court reasoned that the pond was both visible and accessible to children, as it was close to well-traveled streets and homes. Moreover, the property was seven blocks from an elementary school. Finally, the owner knew that children had used the pond for swimming. *Id.; see also Allen v. William P. McDonald Corp.*, 42 So. 2d 706, 707 (Fla. 1949) (holding that white sand banks adjacent to a pond were sufficiently alluring and attractive to children to entice them to trespass).

As in *Ansin*, Mikey was a foreseeable child trespasser. Like the pond in *Ansin*, the Hurts' pond, ducks, and fish were appealing lures that attracted children to the Hurts' property. Moreover, like the raft in *Ansin*, the Hurts' inner-tubes are characteristic water toys that invite children to jump into the pond to play. In addition, the pond was visible and accessible to the young children who attended the adjacent elementary school. In fact, its close proximity to a school that requires the presence of children on a daily basis makes trespass even more foreseeable than in *Ansin*, where the property was seven blocks from an elementary school. Finally, like the landowner in *Ansin*, the Hurts knew that children were trespassing on their property. The Hurts actually observed children climbing the fence to feed the ducks. Accordingly, Mikey was a foreseeable child trespasser on the Hurts' property.

B. The Dock Was a Hidden Danger.

The Hurts' dock was a hidden danger. When evaluating whether a condition is a hidden danger, or trap, courts consider the inherent dangerousness of the condition and the age of the injured child. A condition constitutes a hidden danger, or trap, if its dangerous condition would be hidden to a child because of the child's age and immaturity. *Ansin*, 98 So. 2d at 88. In addition, the dangerous condition that injures the child must have a connection with the object that initially attracts the child onto the property, such that the two conditions jointly contribute to the child's injury. *Starling v. Saha*, 451 So. 2d 516, 518–19 (Fla. Dist. Ct. App. 1984). The dangerous condition of the Hurts' dock would be hidden to a six-year-old child, who would lack the maturity and the experience to recognize that the existence of moss and algae on the wooden dock contribute to structural decay. Moreover, the ducks that initially attracted Mikey to trespass acted in concert with the dock and water to contribute jointly to Mikey's death, as Mikey had to walk onto the dock to feed the ducks. Thus, as analyzed in detail below, each relevant factor supports the conclusion that the Hurts' dock was a hidden danger.

1. The Dock Was Inherently Dangerous to a Young Child.

When a dangerous condition is hidden to a child because of the child's age and immaturity, it constitutes a hidden danger, or trap. *Ansin*, 98 So. 2d 87. In *Ansin*, the defendant's pond contained a floating wooden dock that extended into the water about twelve-feet, well over a child's head. A makeshift raft that was "prone to tip" floated in the water at the end of the dock. A nine-year-old child drowned in the pond after playing on the tipsy raft. *Id*. at 88. The court held that the pond, floating dock, and tipsy raft combined to constitute a hidden trap. The court observed that the tipsy raft floated in water of a depth well over the child's head and reasoned that a nine-year-old boy could not be expected to recognize its danger. *Id.; see also Allen*, 42 So. 2d at 707 (holding that a two-and-a-half-year-old child could not be expected to recognize the danger presented by steep sandy banks that led into water ten feet deep).

Like the dock and raft in *Ansin*, the Hurts' dock was a hidden danger, or trap. In fact, the deceptive safety of the Hurts' dock made it inherently more hidden, and therefore dangerous, to a child trespasser than the raft in *Ansin*. A wooden, anchored dock has a seemingly solid foundation. Children simply do not expect that the "ground" might collapse out from under them. It is precisely because of its illusion of safety that Mikey stayed on the dock. Mikey knew that he did not swim well and deliberately stayed out of the water on a seemingly solid foundation. To a child who does not swim well, the dock promised a safety that it did not deliver. In contrast, a child is more likely to foresee the danger that one might fall off of a raft that floats on the water, particularly the "visibly tipsy raft" in *Ansin*. Unlike Mikey, the child in *Ansin* deliberately risked the danger of the water by jumping from a floating dock onto a floating raft. In short, the Hurts' dock was more dangerous than the floating raft in *Ansin* because its danger was more hidden.

Moreover, Mikey was also younger than the child in *Ansin*, making it less likely that he would appreciate the dangerous condition. Mikey was only six years old, three years younger than the nine-year-old child in *Ansin*. A six-year-old child is far less likely to anticipate that a seemingly solid foundation would collapse out from under his weight than a nine-year-old child would be expected to anticipate that he might fall off of a tipsy raft. Moreover, no six-year-old child would possess the experience and the maturity to appreciate that moss and algae were likely to cover structural decay. In fact, to a six-year-old child, the moss and algae covering the Hurts' dock would serve only to hide the dangerous condition of the deteriorating wood. Certainly, Mikey's two classmates, who walked across the dock to jump into the pond, did not appreciate the danger. Having observed his friends walk across the dock, Mikey would be even less likely to appreciate the dock's hidden danger.

2. The Attractive Condition and Hidden Danger Jointly Contributed to Mikey's Injury.

Florida courts also require that the dangerous condition that injures a child have a connection with the object that initially attracts the child onto the property, such that the two conditions jointly contribute to the child's injury. *Starling v. Saha*, 451 So. 2d 516, 518–19 (Fla. Dist. Ct. App. 1984). The Hurts might argue that the requisite connection does not exist in the present case. They would argue that it was the ducks that lured Mikey onto their property, while the combination of the dock and water injured him. To support that argument, the Hurts would rely on older Florida cases that narrowly construe this requirement. *See Johnson v. Bathey*, 376 So. 2d 848 (Fla. 1979) (holding no cause of action when child was not even aware of existence of condition that injured him until after he had trespassed onto the property); *Newby v. West Palm Beach Water Co.*, 47 So. 2d 527 (Fla. 1950) (holding no cause of action when child was lured to reservoir by spray reflecting rainbows in the air, but drowned by falling into the water).

The Hurts' argument should fail. More recent appellate court cases have broadly construed this requirement, narrowly restricting the older cases to their facts. For example, in *Starling*, a child was lured to the defendant's pool by the prospect of swimming. While swimming, the child became caught and held under water by the suction of an underwater hose and drowned. 451 So. 2d at 517. The court held that the plaintiff satisfied the requirement that the condition that lured the child onto the land also acted to injure the child. *Id.* at 518–19. The court reasoned that it would not interpret *Johnson v. Bathey* "so literally that we abolish application of the attractive nuisance doctrine to concealed dangers operating in connection with conditions or other objects on property, which jointly contribute to the child's injury." *Id.* The court pointed out that the combined effect of the hose that held the child under water, and the water in the pond, drowned the child. *Id.* at 518.

In a more recent case, a Florida appellate court stretched *Bathey* and *Newby* even further. In *Mueller v. South Fla. Water Mgmt. Dist.*, a sixteen-year-old boy trespassed onto the defendant's property to ride on the defendant's dirt bike path. 620 So. 2d 789, 790 (Fla. Dist. Ct. App. 1993). While riding his dirt bike, he was injured by a concealed guardrail that stretched across the path. *Id.* Presumably, the child was not aware of the guardrail when he entered the defendant's property. Despite that fact, the court held that the plaintiff satisfied the requirement that the condition that lured the child onto the land also acted to injure the child. *Id.* at 791. *Cf. Bathey*, 376 So. 2d at 849. Following *Starling*, the court reasoned that the steel guardrail was "an integral part of the dirt bike path, the condition which lured [the child] onto the premises." 620 So. 2d at 791.

Under *Starling* and *Mueller*, the Hurts' dock, ducks, and water all combined to lure Mikey onto the Hurts' property and to injure him. Mikey was lured onto the Hurts' property by the prospect of feeding the ducks that swam in the Hurts' pond. In order to gain access to the ducks swimming in the pond, Mikey was compelled to walk over the Hurts' dock. (The dock provided the only access to the water.) When the dock collapsed, Mikey was thrown into the pond and drowned. The combination of the ducks, dock, and water jointly contributed to Mikey's death. Accordingly, the Hurts' dock, combined with the ducks and water, constituted a hidden danger, or trap.

C. The Hurts Failed to Exercise Reasonable Care.

In evaluating whether a landowner has exercised reasonable care to protect trespassing children from hidden dangerous conditions, courts balance the likelihood of child trespassers and the degree of danger posed by the hidden condition against the burden imposed on the landowner to protect child trespassers from harm and the preventive measures the landowner has taken. As the likelihood of child trespassers and resulting harm increases, the burden imposed on a landowner to protect child trespassers from harm also increases. *Howard v. Atlantic Coast R.R. Co.*, 231 F.2d 592, 594 (5th Cir. 1956); *Samson v. O'Hara*, 239 So. 2d 151, 152 (Fla. Dist. Ct. App. 1970). Here, it was easily foreseeable that children would trespass on the Hurts' dock while the Hurts were out of town and that the dangerous condition of the dock would seriously injure a trespassing child. Because the Hurts could have easily prevented Mikey's death by taking such minimal protective measures as locking the gate or posting a sign warning of the dock's condition, they failed to exercise reasonable care to protect Mikey from harm.

When landowners know of a dangerous condition on their property and fail to take minimal measures to protect foreseeable child trespassers from the risk of serious harm, the landowners have failed to exercise reasonable care. In *Samson*, an eighteen-month-old child drowned in a neighbor's swimming pool after being attracted to it by the sound of a hose running into the water. 239 So. 2d at 152. Although the defendants had built an enclosure around the pool, they left open a door in the pool enclosure. While the defendants were not at home, the child wandered through the door and fell into the pool. *Id.* On these facts, the court held that a jury could find that the defendants failed to exercise reasonable care to protect the child from harm. The court reasoned that a jury should weigh the foreseeability of a child trespassing onto the defendants' pool area against the "ease of guarding against injury...." *Id.* Implicit in the court's opinion was the suggestion that a jury could reasonably find that the risk of harm to a child far outweighs the burden of locking a gate.

Like the defendants in *Samson*, the Hurts failed to take even minimal precautionary measures to protect foreseeable child trespassers from a dangerous condition that posed a serious risk of harm. As in *Samson*, the Hurts built a fence around their property. However, as the court implied in *Samson*, by leaving the gate unlocked they negated the protective effect of the fence. The burden of locking the gate instead of merely closing it was small compared to the danger of serious injury. Thus, locking a gate to enclose a swimming and fishing hole is a simple precaution that a reasonable person would have taken under any circumstances. Moreover, the duty to take this simple precaution is enhanced when, as here, the Hurts were out of town for the long holiday weekend. Leaving a gate unlocked over a long holiday weekend was an open invitation for disaster.

Further, when a landowner has knowledge that children trespass on the property, and the degree of danger is great, the landowner exercises reasonable care by repeatedly investigating to determine whether the precautionary measures were effective and by making repeated new efforts to keep child trespassers away. In *Howard*, the defendant railroad covered abandoned wells on its property by closing them with boards and nailing them shut. 231 F.2d at 593. The railroad also posted "No Trespassing" signs on its property. Despite these precautions, an employee of the railroad discovered boys swimming naked in an abandoned well. The employee verbally ordered the boys to leave and then replaced the boards and nailed them shut. When these efforts proved to be ineffective, the defendant cut down the bushes around the well, reasoning that the boys would be deterred from swimming naked without the bushes for cover. *Id.* The defendant's employee then went back to the well to determine whether the latest efforts to deter trespassing had been successful. When the defendant's employee again found boys swimming in the well, he told them they would not be allowed to swim there anymore. The defendant then ordered a bulldozer to fill up the well with dirt. Before the bulldozer could do so, the plaintiff's child drowned in the well. *Id.*

The court held that the well did not present a hidden, unusual danger. *Id*. at 595. However, in dictum, the court indicated that the defendant had exercised reasonable care to keep the child trespassers away. The court reasoned that the defendant had repeatedly and persistently attempted to deter the children from trespassing, and it concluded that a landowner is not required to ensure the success of its efforts. *Id*.

The Hurts' attempts to deter children from trespassing on their property fall far short of the repeated and persistent efforts of the railroad company in *Howard*. The Hurts' efforts to prevent harm to trespassing children consisted of: (1) installing an inexpensive chain link fence the installer warned them would not keep out trespassing children; (2) posting a "No Trespassing" sign and replacing it with a "Do Not Climb Fence" sign; and (3) verbally admonishing previous trespassers to "get back to school." These efforts do not rise to the level of reasonable care, particularly in light of the minimal steps the Hurts could have taken to prevent harm.

The Hurts' precautionary measures were ineffective and not reasonably calculated to prevent harm to trespassing children. As the fence installer warned, the Hurts' four foot chain link fence was not designed to, nor was it effective in, preventing children from entering their property. As the Hurts observed, school children regularly climbed the fence. The Hurts' failure to improve the quality of their fence, or to replace it, contrasts with the railroad company's repeated efforts to board up the abandoned well after discovering trespassers. Even if the Hurts' fence could be considered a safety precaution, their failure to lock the gate while they were out of town for the long holiday weekend wholly negates its effectiveness as a preventive device.

Moreover, the Hurts' written and verbal warnings were also ineffective and meaningless. Their failure to lock the gate while they were out of town renders their "Do Not Climb Fence" sign meaningless as a preventive device. Mikey and his friends understood the literal meaning of the "Do Not Climb Fence" sign and, therefore, looked for an open gate. By entering the property through an unlocked gate, Mikey and his friends did not disobey any written warning posted by the Hurts. Nor did their entry into the property violate any verbal warning. On prior occasions, the Hurts had only warned children not to climb the fence and to "get back to school." Mikey could reasonably have interpreted the verbal warning to "get back to school" in a literal sense rather than as a statement of the Hurts' desire for the children to leave their property. Their vague verbal warnings stand in stark contrast to the railroad company's specific and repeated warnings in *Howard* that the children were not allowed to swim in the well and were not allowed to trespass on the railroad company's property.

Moreover, with minimal expense and inconvenience, the Hurts could easily have protected children from the serious risk of harm posed by the decaying dock and water. First, the Hurts admit that they knew the dock was decaying and needed to be replaced. However, they wanted to wait until winter to make the necessary repairs, presumably out of a desire to use the dock throughout the summer months. By repairing the dock during the summer, the Hurts would not have incurred any additional expenses beyond that which they had already planned to incur. At most, the Hurts would have been inconvenienced by the loss of their dock for part of the summer. When weighing the serious risk of injury posed by the dock against the Hurts' inconvenience, a trier of fact should find that the Hurts had a duty to replace the dock when it needed to be repaired. Even if a trier of fact would find that the Hurts were reasonable in delaying repairs, reasonable precaution required them to post a sign warning that the dock was dangerous. By failing to do so, children were not aware of the dock's hidden danger. Accordingly, the Hurts failed to exercise reasonable care to protect child trespassers from serious injury.

CONCLUSION

The McLeans have a strong claim against the Hurts under the attractive nuisance doctrine. First, Mikey McLean was a foreseeable trespasser on the Hurts' property. Second, the deteriorating dock was a hidden, dangerous trap to a six-year-old child and acted in concert with the water and ducks to harm Mikey. Third, the Hurts failed to exercise reasonable care to prevent injury to a trespassing child.

SAMPLE MEMO E:
SHORT MEMO

This memo addresses whether the Stripes' garage constitutes a "dwelling" under Illinois' Residential Burglary Statute for purposes of prosecuting Gerry Arnold under that Statute. The Statute defines a dwelling place as "a house, apartment, mobile home, trailer, or *other living quarters* in which ... the owners or occupants *actually reside* ...." 720 Ill. Comp. Stat. 5/2-6(b) (2004) (emphasis added). Although the law is not entirely clear, the Stripes' garage is likely a "living quarters" in which Michael Stripe "actually resides." Therefore, there is a strong argument that the Stripes' garage is a dwelling under Illinois' Residential Burglary Statute, and that the State can therefore successfully prosecute Mr. Arnold under that Statute.

A structure is considered a living quarters when the owners frequently use the structure for activities that occur in a living quarters. For example, in *People v. McIntyre*, an enclosed, attached porch was considered a dwelling under the Statute. 578 N.E.2d 314 (Ill. App. Ct. 1991). The *McIntyre* court emphasized that the owners frequently used the attached, screened porch for "sitting, eating, and cooking" at least four or five times a week. *Id*. at 315. The court held that these activities made the attached porch "part of the living quarters of the house." *Id*.

On the other hand, where a structure is attached, but used only for commercial, rather than residential activities, it is not a living quarters under the Statute. *People v. Thomas*, 561 N.E. 2d 57 (Ill. 1990). In *Thomas*, the Court held that the attached garage, "at least in this instance," was not a living quarters because the owner used the garage only to park her car and to store boxes of perfume for her business. *Id*. at 64.

Like the owners of the porch in *McIntyre*, Michael Stripe uses the Stripes' garage more like a living quarters than a typical garage. Like the activities of "sitting, eating, and cooking," Michael Stripe uses the garage as an extension of the living quarters of the Stripes' home. The garage is Michael Stripes' getaway in which he writes and plays music, watches television, and eats light meals. During the summer and fall, he even sleeps in the garage on a futon that has been set up in the loft area of the garage. Like the owners in *McIntyre*, Michael Stripe regularly and frequently uses the garage as part of the living quarters of the house. Michael Stripes' use of the garage as a retreat and part-time sleeping quarters is a far cry from the garage in *Thomas*, in which the owner used the garage only for storage purposes.

Defendant might argue, however, that despite Michael Stripes' frequent use of the garage for activities associated with a living quarters, the garage's physical distance from the Stripes' home distinguishes it from the porch in *McIntyre*, which was attached to the home. Unlike the attached porch in *McIntyre*, the Stripes' garage stands thirty (30) feet away from their home, and has no running water, bathroom facilities, or heat. Thus, the garage's status as a dwelling is dependent upon whether it can reasonably be viewed as an extension of the Stripe family's living quarters within the primary residence itself.

While having some merit, the Defendant's argument should fail. Both the *McIntyre* and *Thomas* courts emphasized the actual activities that occurred within the structures themselves, not the structures' proximity to the homes themselves. Moreover, the legislative purpose underlying the Statute suggests that the legislators were concerned about the increased potential for danger when thieves break into homes. For example, in *People v. Silva*, the court noted that the reason the legislature enacted the residential burglary statute, with more severe penalties than for other burglaries, is because of the "greater danger and potential for serious harm from burglary of a home as opposed to burglary of a business." 628 N.E.2d 948, 951 (Ill. App. Ct. 1993). The burglary of an occupied garage used as a living quarters carries the same potential for increased risk of harm as a burglary of a home.

In conclusion, a strong case can be made that the Stripes' garage is a "living quarters" in which Michael Stripe resides, and is thus a dwelling, for purposes of prosecuting Arnold under the Residential Burglary Statute.

Appendix B

SAMPLE CLIENT LETTERS

SAMPLE CLIENT LETTER A

Charlotte Turley, Esq.
105 S. Central Ave.
St. Louis, MO 63105
January 5, 20XX

Mr. & Mrs. Johnson
234 N. Bemiston
St. Louis, MO 63105

<u>Confidential Attorney/Client Communication</u>

Re: Dispute with Apartment Management Corp.

Dear Mr. & Mrs. Johnson,

It was a pleasure meeting you last week. As you requested, I have analyzed the viability of a legal claim against your landlord to recover for the injuries you suffered when you fell on an icy sidewalk at your apartment complex. This letter summarizes the facts as I understand them and my analysis of Missouri law concerning a landlord's legal duty to keep common walkways free from snow and ice. My research suggests that we could make a viable legal claim that your landlord was negligent under Missouri law. Unfortunately, however, the law is less than clear, and we would face some legal hurdles in recovering damages against your landlord.

Under the facts as I understand them, on December 18, 20XX, Mr. Johnson slipped and fell on an icy patch of the sidewalk that leads to several different apartments at your apartment complex. You advised me that the sidewalk was icy and that the landlord had not shoveled the walkway or placed any salt on the sidewalk. You have discussed the incident with your landlord, and he has denied all responsibility for your accident. Your landlord claims that if the tenants wish to have walkways free from snow and ice, they are "welcome" to shovel the walkways themselves. The landlord insists that he has never agreed to assume that responsibility. However, because the landlord mowed the lawn in the summer, you assumed that he would also shovel the common sidewalks in the winter. I have examined your lease, and it does not address which party is responsible for keeping the common walkways safe from weather hazards.

Mr. Johnson, you have also provided me with medical bills that reflect extensive injuries to your ankle. These injuries unfortunately prevent you from being able to continue your duties as a liquor delivery truck driver. These duties require you to unload, lift, and carry heavy boxes. At present, your medical bills are about $10,000.00. You do not have medical insurance and would like to know whether the law can require your landlord's insurance company to pay your medical bills and compensate you for your lost wages. You estimate your medical damages will be $20,000.00.

Based on these facts, I researched Missouri law and found that, although the law is not entirely clear, we have a viable legal claim against your landlord for negligence. Under the legal theory of "negligence," we would argue that your landlord had a *legal duty* to keep the common premises safe from foreseeable injuries, and that he violated that duty when he failed to keep the walkways free from snow and ice.

When determining whether your landlord violated his legal responsibility to you under the law of "negligence," the court would examine previous court decisions to determine how other courts have interpreted the law of negligence. In similar cases, courts have held that landlords are legally responsible for injuries suffered by their tenants only if the landlord had a "legal duty" to the tenants. Courts have found that landlords have a duty to keep an apartment building's "common" areas safe from permanent hazards. Although the walkway is part of the "common" area, unfortunately, Missouri courts have distinguished cases where the danger in the common areas is caused by a *temporary* weather hazard, such as snow. When the danger is caused by snow, courts have not imposed a duty upon landlords to shovel the snow from common walkways. Courts have justified this rule by noting that the duty to remove snow would "subject the landlord to an unreasonable burden of vigilance and care."

However, a trend in landlord/tenant court decisions does offer some hope. The last reported Missouri opinion that decided the issue of snow removal is more than forty years old. Even in that more than forty-year-old decision, the court noted that the more "modern" rule adopted in other states imposed a duty on landlords to shovel snow from their common walkways. We could argue that more recent Missouri Supreme Court opinions reflect this state's willingness to follow a national trend to protect tenants' rights to a greater degree than they have been protected in the past.

In fact, in more recent years the Missouri Supreme Court has implied that landlords have a broad duty to keep common areas safe from all dangers of which the landlords have "reasonable notice." For example, the Missouri Supreme Court has imposed a "duty" on a landlord to place speed bumps in the parking lot of an apartment building. In that case, a child was injured on the parking lot of the landlord's apartment complex when a speeding bicycle struck her. The Supreme Court affirmed a jury verdict for the child, finding that the landlord should have taken the precaution of installing speed bumps on the parking lot. The Court reasoned that, "as strongly emphasized in recent cases," the landlord owes a duty to its tenants to make common areas of leased property reasonably safe when the landlord has notice of a problem. The Missouri Supreme Court has also found that a landlord had a duty to relocate the fire escape on an apartment building so that criminal intruders could not use the fire escape to break into a tenant's apartment.

Under the broad language and shifts in policy reflected in the more recent Supreme Court opinions, we could argue that the landlord owed you a duty to keep the sidewalk free from ice because the landlord had "reasonable notice" of the danger. The landlord had actual notice that snowy and icy conditions existed, as public and private schools in the City of St. Louis were closed for two days prior to your injury. Given the known snow and ice conditions, the landlord arguably had "reasonable notice" that a tenant might slip and fall on the icy sidewalk. Under this argument, by failing to keep the sidewalk safe, the landlord violated his duty to you under the law. If a court were to adopt this interpretation of the law, the law would permit you to recover damages for injuries you suffered as a result of the landlord's breach of duty.

Unfortunately, these more recent Missouri Supreme Court cases did not address whether the older "temporary hazard" cases involving snowy conditions are still valid law in this state. Despite a policy trend that favors tenants, and broad policy language that favors us, the latest Supreme Court decisions do not explicitly reject any of the older cases that protect landlords from liability for injuries from temporary conditions such as snow. Because the older cases are the only higher-level court cases that address a landlord's responsibility to protect tenants from temporary hazardous conditions, a trial court would probably follow these older cases. More realistically, our best chance to prevail in such a lawsuit would be before a higher court, most likely the Missouri Supreme Court.

Although a lawsuit would present some hurdles that could take a number of years to pursue, you do have several options to consider at this point. We could file a lawsuit against your landlord in which we would claim that he was negligent in failing to keep the common walkways clear from snow and ice. Given the present state of the law in Missouri and your desire to resolve this dispute quickly, we could then push for a quick settlement of your claims. Given the time and expense of such a lawsuit, your landlord may well be willing to settle your claims to avoid what would likely be a lengthy legal proceeding. Moreover, given the possible shift in Missouri law in favor of tenants' rights, the landlord might also be reluctant to take this case to trial and risk setting an unfavorable "precedent" that would impose on the landlord more onerous legal duties in the future. Given these considerations, the landlord may well be willing to negotiate a settlement of your legal claims before your legal case would actually go to trial.

Another option would be for me to contact the landlord's lawyer and pursue the possibility of settling your legal claims informally, without actually filing a lawsuit. This option could save you the expense of filing a lawsuit. At the same time, however, the landlord might be less willing to enter into an out-of-court settlement without a pending lawsuit. Of course, should the landlord fail to respond to our settlement overtures, or fail to offer a reasonable sum of money to reimburse you for the damages you sustained, we could always file a lawsuit at that point.

After you have had an opportunity to think this over, please call and set up an appointment so that we can discuss your legal options in greater detail. As we discussed in our meeting, you have plenty of time to make a decision; however, I want to remind you that there is a five-year statute of limitations in Missouri to file a legal claim. I will wait to hear from you before I take any further action.

Very truly yours,

Charlotte Turley

Charlotte Turley

SAMPLE CLIENT LETTER B

John Burroughs, Esq.
173 Culver Blvd., Suite 205
Ft. Lauderdale, Florida 33301
August 25, 20XX

Mr. & Mrs. McLean
256 Sunrise Lane
Ft. Lauderdale, Florida 33301

<u>Confidential Attorney/Client Communication</u>

Re: Fred & Thelma Hurt—Attractive Nuisance Legal Claim

Dear Mr. & Mrs. McLean,

It was a pleasure to meet you last week, although I am sorry that it was under such sad circumstances. Following our meeting, I researched the law in Florida and confirmed that property owners whose land contains a dangerous condition, such as a pond or pool, are generally legally responsible for any injuries to young children who gain access to the dangerous condition through unlocked gates. From my research, I believe we have a very strong legal claim against the Hurts should you wish to pursue legal action against them.

Before I discuss the law and your legal alternatives, I'd like to review my understanding of the facts so that I can confirm that I have an accurate understanding of what happened. As you may know, the factual background of any legal case is critically important, as lawsuits are often won or lost based on factual nuances. I am uncomfortably aware of how painful it must be to think back to the tragic incident; however, it's important that my understanding is correct. Please let me know if my understanding of the facts is incorrect in any way.

As I understand the facts, on Sunday, May 28, 20XX, your six-year-old son, Mikey, and two of his friends entered the Hurts' property through an unlocked gate. The Hurts' property has a man-made pond and dock that has attracted small children to their property for a number of years. Ten years ago, after an elementary school was built on property adjacent to their property, the Hurts erected a fence around their property. It is your understanding that the fence installer tried to persuade the Hurts to build a privacy fence around their property rather than a four-foot high chain-link fence, because the installer believed that the chain-link fence would not deter school children from entering the Hurts' property. Nonetheless, the Hurts declined to purchase the more expensive privacy fence and elected instead to erect the inexpensive chain-link fence with a "No Trespassing" sign posted on the fence.

Unfortunately, the chain-link fence did not keep young children from entering the Hurts' property. In the past, the Hurts did not object to children feeding the ducks through their chain-link fence. However, when two of Mikey's friends climbed the fence to feed the ducks that were swimming in the pond, the Hurts told the children that they "should get back to school." After that incident, some of the older students began to dare each other to climb the fence without getting caught. Apparently to prevent the students from climbing the fence, the Hurts removed the "No Trespassing" sign and replaced it with a "Do Not Climb Fence" sign.

On May 26th, the Hurts left town for the holiday weekend, leaving the gate unlocked while they were away. On Sunday, May 28th, Mikey and two friends decided to visit the pond and entered the Hurts' property through the unlocked gate. Mikey's friends ran across the dock and dove into the water to swim, but Mikey stayed on the dock to feed the ducks. Unfortunately, the dock was decaying and rotting, but the decay was partially hidden by a moss and algae growing on the dock. While Mikey was standing on the dock, it collapsed from under him, and Mikey was not able to swim to safety. You have learned that the Hurts planned to replace the dock, but had postponed the repairs until the winter months.

Based on these facts, I have researched Florida law. Should you wish to pursue a legal action, I think we have a strong claim against the Hurts under a legal theory called "attractive nuisance." Under this legal theory, landowners are legally responsible for injuries sustained by children when: (1) they have a dangerous condition on their property; (2) they have reason to foresee that children would be attracted to the dangerous condition; and (3) they failed to exercise reasonable precautions to protect trespassing children from the dangerous condition.

Here, the dock and pond constitute a hidden danger to children—particularly children of Mikey's age, who would not be able to appreciate that the moss and algae on the wooden dock might be hiding structural decay. Moreover, the Hurts have implicitly admitted that the dock was dangerous because they planned to replace the dock in its entirety but had postponed the repairs until the winter months.

In addition, the Hurts had reason to foresee that children would enter their property. The dock, pond, and ducks were not only attractive and alluring to children, but the Hurts had actual knowledge that it was common practice for children to enter their property in order to feed the ducks and swim in the pond. During the holiday weekend in particular, it was easily foreseeable that children would enter the Hurts' property while they were out of town.

Finally, the Hurts failed to take reasonable precautions to protect trespassing children from danger. When evaluating whether a landowner has taken "reasonable precautions," courts balance the degree of danger posed by the hidden dangerous condition against the preventive measures the landowner took to prevent injury. As the likelihood of harm increases, the landowner's burden to protect children from that harm also increases. Here, it was easily foreseeable that children would trespass on the Hurts' dock while the Hurts were out of town and that the dangerous condition of the dock could seriously injure a child who entered their property. Moreover, the Hurts could have easily prevented this tragedy by taking such minimal protective measures as locking the gate or posting a sign warning of the dock's dangerous condition. Therefore, we have a strong legal claim that they failed to take reasonable precautions to protect children from harm.

Given the strength of your legal claim, there are a number of options available to you. First, we could file a lawsuit against the Hurts; in my opinion, such a lawsuit would be successful. Although no legal remedy could ever begin to compensate you for the loss you have suffered, this option would likely allow you to recover substantial monetary damages from the Hurts. However, a lawsuit is also time-consuming and would be emotionally painful, as well, given the tremendous loss that you have suffered. On the other hand, a lawsuit has the potential for you to exact justice against the Hurts and, perhaps, to use the legal system to help protect other children from such tragedies in the future.

A second alternative would be to enter into out-of-court settlement negotiations with the Hurts' lawyer. Under this option, I would meet with the Hurts' lawyer and attempt to settle your legal claims out-of-court. An advantage of this option is that you would not be constrained by the legal remedies the law can offer, but could agree to non-legal remedies as well. For example, in addition to a monetary settlement, you could insist that the Hurts replace their fence with a more expensive fence that might help prevent other injuries in the future. You could also insist that the Hurts replace their dock immediately or agree to fill in their pond with dirt to remove the attractive nuisance entirely. Of course, the Hurts would have to agree to this option and to any such terms in order for this alternative to be successful. Nonetheless, if the Hurts were unwilling to enter into an out-of-court settlement agreement, your other legal options would still be preserved.

A third alternative would be to explore alternative dispute resolution processes such as mediation or arbitration. On the spectrum of available options, the option of pursuing alternative dispute resolution ("ADR") falls somewhere between an out-of-court negotiation and a lawsuit itself. Both of these processes would require the agreement of both parties. However, if both parties agree to enter into an ADR process, these processes are generally quicker and less expensive than a formal lawsuit. At the same time, they might bring greater pressure to bear on the Hurts than an informal out-of-court negotiation.

In a mediation proceeding, both parties would select a neutral person to mediate the dispute and to help the parties reach an out-of-court agreement. This can sometimes be a successful way of settling a legal dispute should out-of-court negotiations between the two lawyers prove to be unsuccessful. However, this option would likely take more time than an informal negotiation and would also be more expensive, as both parties are responsible to pay for the mediator's time and expenses.

In terms of legal formality, a legal arbitration proceeding is a step up from mediation, but less formal than a lawsuit. Like mediation, the parties would select a neutral third-party to oversee the process. However, unlike a mediator, who works with both parties to achieve a settlement agreement, an arbitrator assumes the role of a "judge" in the case. In that role, the arbitrator listens to testimony, considers the "evidence," and issues a legal ruling in favor of one party or the other. In that sense, arbitration is like an abbreviated lawsuit; however, an arbitration proceeding would be scheduled much sooner than a trial, and would likely be less expensive as well.

Finally, after thinking all of this over, you might decide that you are not interested in pursuing any legal option at all. You mentioned during our meeting that you weren't entirely sure whether you were willing to put yourselves in the position of having to re-live the trauma of this tragic event. I understand completely if you should decide that this option best serves the needs of your family.

After you have had a chance to think this over, please give me a call to schedule a follow-up meeting so that we can discuss the various alternatives that are available to you. I want to help you make a decision that is best for you under all of the circumstances. As we discussed in our meeting, you have plenty of time to make a decision; however, I wanted to mention again that there is a four-year statute of limitations in Florida to file a legal claim. I look forward to hearing from you.

Best regards,

John

John Burroughs

Appendix C

SAMPLE BRIEFS

(Fact-Centered)

PLAINTIFF'S SAMPLE BRIEF:
SPOUSAL WIRETAP PROBLEM

UNITED STATES DISTRICT COURT
DISTRICT OF NEW HAMPSHIRE

MICHAEL HARRISON,	)	
	)	
Plaintiff,	)	
	)	
vs.	)	No. 05-1097
	)	
KATHRYN HARRISON,	)	
	)	
Defendant.	)	

PLAINTIFF'S MEMORANDUM IN SUPPORT OF
MOTION FOR SUMMARY JUDGMENT

INTRODUCTION

Plaintiff, Mr. Michael Harrison, is entitled to recover compensatory and punitive damages, attorneys' fees, and other reasonable litigation costs for the Defendant's unlawful interception of his telephone calls in violation of Section 2520 of the federal wiretap statute. 18 U.S.C. § 2520. The Supreme Court has long recognized the right to privacy and has included within this right a constitutional right to privacy in wire communications. *Berger v. New York*, 388 U.S. 41 (1967). Thus, the federal wiretap statute expressly and unambiguously prohibits the interception of wire communications except under narrowly proscribed circumstances, such as when "one of the parties to the communication has given prior consent to such interception."18 U.S.C. § 2511(2)(d).

When evaluating whether a party has given consent to the interception of wire communications, the First Circuit Court of Appeals has directed that, "in light of the prophylactic purposes of Title III, implied consent should not be casually inferred." *Williams v. Poulos*, 11 F.3d 271, 281 (1st Cir. 1993). Indeed, implied consent is not constructive consent, but is consent in *fact*. Consent is implied "only in a *rare case* where the court can conclude with assurance 'from surrounding circumstances… that the party *knowingly agreed* to the surveillance.'" *United States v. Lanoue*, 71 F.3d 966, 981 (1st Cir. 1995) (emphasis added). The present controversy is not even close to such a rare case. Here, the uncontroverted testimony reveals that Mr. Harrison was never expressly informed that *any* telephone calls would be monitored, much less that he himself would be a target of the interceptions. Without even the most minimal knowledge that his telephone calls would be intercepted, Mr. Harrison could not, and did not, knowingly agree to the surveillance. Therefore, the Defendant, Ms. Kathryn Harrison, is liable as a matter of law for violating the federal wiretap statute.

STATEMENT OF MATERIAL FACTS

1. Plaintiff, Michael Harrison, and Defendant, Kathryn Harrison, were divorced on February 6, 2021. Four days after the couple became legally separated on November 1, 2020, Defendant began intercepting Mr. Harrison's out-going and in-coming telephone calls. (M. Harrison Dep. 35:5 (Mar. 13, 2021); K. Harrison Dep. 10:15 (Mar. 14, 2021).)

2. Because the couple was in the midst of divorce proceedings, relations were very "strained." (K. Harrison Dep 11:15.)

3. In fact, the Harrisons' marriage had deteriorated to the point that, while still living in the same house, the couple slept in separate bedrooms and "strived to keep contact to a minimum." Additionally, sexual relations between the couple had ceased, and Defendant accused Mr. Harrison of engaging in an extramarital affair. (M. Harrison Dep. 15:9-22.)

4. Mr. Harrison has testified that he "had no idea she was recording my telephone calls, nor would I have ever agreed to such an invasion…." (M. Harrison Dep. 35:5.)

5. In her deposition, Defendant contends that, in early November, 2020, she "told" Mr. Harrison that she would begin intercepting his telephone calls. (K. Harrison Dep. 51:2.)

6. Several weeks earlier, the nanny who had been caring for the couple's nine-year-old son, Dillon, tendered her resignation. When the nanny tendered her resignation, Defendant decided that Dillon had outgrown the need for a full-time nanny and decided to hire a housekeeper, whose responsibilities would also include caring for Dillon. (K. Harrison Dep. 50:11-51:20.)

7. Defendant has testified that she was concerned that the new thirty-year-old housekeeper not misuse her telephone privileges. Defendant states that she

verbally communicated to Mr. Harrison a list of requirements for the new housekeeper, including the requirement that the housekeeper "not make improper use of the telephone." (K. Harrison Dep. 52:4-54:7.)

8. It is this statement that Defendant contends constituted "notice" that Defendant would begin recording all of Mr. Harrison's telephone calls. (K. Harrison Dep. 54:8.)

9. Because relations were strained, Mr. Harrison "vaguely recalls" his former wife making a reference to the housekeeper's use of the telephone, but he did not attend to the details. After Defendant communicated a list of the requirements for the new housekeeper, Mr. Harrison told his former wife to "go ahead and take care of it." (K. Harrison Dep. 55:8; M. Harrison Dep. 36:5.)

10. Defendant then hired the housekeeper on November 3, 2020 and began recording all telephone calls into and out of the couple's home. Calls were taped from November 5, 2020 until December 10, 2020. In total, Defendant recorded fifty-three (53) of Mr. Harrison's telephone calls during this time period. (K. Harrison Dep. 60:2.)

11. Defendant introduced some of these tapes into evidence during the couple's divorce proceedings. (Pl.'s Compl. ¶ 8 (Jan. 5, 2021).)

12. The couple had briefly monitored the home's telephone calls on two previous occasions a number of years earlier. Nine years ago, in 2012, when Defendant was in the process of hiring Dillon's first nanny, Defendant was concerned that the nanny might spend "too much time on the telephone when she should be spending time with Dillon." (K. Harrison Dep. 105:12.)

13. Defendant concedes that one of the reasons the couple decided to monitor the telephone was because of the nanny's relatively young age—she was only nineteen (19) years old at the time. (K. Harrison Dep. 105:14.)

14. Therefore, the couple agreed that, for an "indefinite period of time, all telephone calls into and from the house would be recorded." (K. Harrison Dep. 106:18; M. Harrison Dep. 77:4-77:22.)

15. Seven years later, when the couple hired a new nanny, they were again concerned about her relatively young age—age twenty-one (21). Therefore, they agreed to again record all in-coming and out-going telephone calls for a period of approximately one month until they were confident that they had made a sound decision in hiring the nanny. (K. Harrison Dep. 110:5-111:2; M. Harrison Dep. 78:11-79:15.)

16. At the time of each of these previous instances, there was no marital discord in the couple's marriage, and both husband and wife decided to monitor the telephone calls only after clearly discussing the issue and mutually agreeing to that course of action. (K. Harrison Dep. 112:16-112:25; M. Harrison Dep. 82:11-82:24.)

17. On March 15, 2021, Mr. Harrison filed this civil action, alleging that his wife's actions in recording his telephone calls violate the federal wiretap statute, 18 U.S.C. § 2520. Following discovery, Plaintiff, Mr. Harrison, has filed this motion for summary judgment, contending that he is entitled to damages, attorneys' fees, and other relief as a matter of law because he did not consent to the recording of his telephone calls.

ARGUMENT

Under Rule 56 of the Federal Rules of Civil Procedure, a court "shall" grant a moving party's motion for summary judgment if the evidence proves "there is no genuine dispute as to any material facts." Fed. R. Civ. P. 56(a). In that situation, the moving party is entitled to judgment as a matter of law. *Id.* The purpose of Rule 56 "is to enable the trial court to readily dispose of cases on matters of law" when a trial is unnecessary. *Rohner v. Union Pac. R.R. Co.*, 225 F.2d 272, 274 (10th Cir. 1955). This Brief will prove that a trial is unnecessary in this case, as the evidence unequivocally proves that Defendant violated Section 2520 of the federal wiretap statute.

When evaluating whether a party has given consent to the interception of wire communications, the First Circuit Court of Appeals has directed that, "in light of the prophylactic purposes of Title III, implied consent should not be casually inferred." *Williams v. Poulos*, 11 F.3d 271, 281 (1st Cir. 1993). Indeed, implied consent is not constructive consent, in which one might be held to a standard that he "should have known" his telephone calls would be intercepted. *Campiti v. Walonis*, 611 F.2d 387, 393 (1st Cir. 1979). Instead, consent is implied "only in a *rare case* where the court can conclude with assurance 'from surrounding circumstances... that the party *knowingly agreed* to the surveillance.'" *United States v. Lanoue*, 71 F.3d 966, 981 (1st Cir. 1995) (emphasis added). The First Circuit Court of Appeals has further directed that, when evaluating whether a party has given consent, "the surrounding circumstances must *convincingly* show that the party knew about and consented to the interception...." *Id.* (emphasis added). Thus, consent is implied only when a party has been expressly and unmistakably warned of both the manner and the scope of the interception, and knows that he himself will be the target of monitoring. *Williams*, 11 F.3d at 281; *Griggs-Ryan v. Smith*, 904 F.2d 112, 118 (1st Cir. 1990). An expectation that one's calls *might* be monitored, without unmistakable notice as to the manner and scope of interception, does not rise to the level of consent. *Campiti*, 611 F.2d at 393.

Here, the uncontroverted evidence reveals that not only was Mr. Harrison never informed of the scope and manner of the interceptions, but he was never expressly informed that *any* telephone calls would be monitored. Absent such actual knowledge, Mr. Harrison did not knowingly agree to the interception of his telephone calls by his estranged wife. Because Mr. Harrison did not consent to the interceptions of his telephone calls, Defendant is liable as a matter of law for violating the federal wiretap statute.

Indeed, courts have held that when the target of wiretapping has not been expressly notified of both the manner and the scope of the interception, and has no *actual knowledge* that he himself will be a target of monitoring, implied consent may not be inferred. *Williams*, 11 F.3d 271. In *Williams*, the defendants hired the plaintiff to be the CEO of defendants' financially strained company. During the plaintiff's orientation, defendants informed the new CEO that they were monitoring telephone calls in the office as part of an effort to reduce employee telephone abuse. The defendants expressly told the new CEO that there was a "system in place to deter employee phone abuse by randomly monitoring employee phone calls." *Id*. at 276. However, the new CEO did not know that the defendants were monitoring his own telephone calls, as well. *Id*. Even though the CEO knew about, and consented to, the defendants' random monitoring of employee telephone calls, the court held that the CEO did not impliedly consent to the monitoring of his *own* telephone calls. *Id*. at 282.

The court reasoned that the CEO did not have actual knowledge of the scope of the monitoring. Thus, the fact that the CEO consented to the monitoring of *employee* telephone calls was not sufficient to infer that he consented to the monitoring of his *own* telephone calls. *Id*. In other words, the scope of the CEO's consent was more limited than the scope of the monitoring. Importantly, the court discounted testimony that the CEO had indeed been informed that the scope of the monitoring would also include the recording of his own telephone calls. *Id*. The court considered the surrounding circumstances, reasoning that, "[i]t is difficult to believe that the newly installed CEO and Chairman of the Board would have assented to the intercepting and recording of his conversations by subordinates with whom he was engaged in a power struggle." *Id*. at 282 n.18. By considering the surrounding circumstances, the court essentially concluded that it is unlikely that a person who is feuding with another person would consent to the recording of his own telephone conversations.

Additionally, consent is implied only when the target of a wiretap is expressly and "unmistakably warned" that all calls on a line will be intercepted, and the target voluntarily continues to use the telephone despite the express warning. *Griggs-Ryan*, 904 F.2d at 118. In *Griggs-Ryan*, the plaintiff was a tenant at a campground operated by the defendant, his landlady. Although the tenants did not have individual telephones, they were allowed to use the landlady's telephone. After receiving obscene telephone calls that she suspected were made by the tenant's friend, the landlady "repeatedly informed" the tenant that *all* telephone calls to her home were being recorded. *Id*. at 117. The tenant subsequently received a telephone call at the defendant's home. When the voice appeared to be that of the obscene caller, the landlady listened in on an extension telephone and recorded the call. When she discovered that the parties were engaged in an illegal drug transaction, the landlady gave the tape to the police. *Id*. at 114. In light of such "unmistakable warnings" that were repeated on a "number of occasions," the court held that the tenant impliedly consented to the monitoring of his telephone calls. *Id*. at 118. The court reasoned that the tenant "effectively acquiesced in the interception" when he opted to converse on the landlady's telephone after repeatedly and expressly being told of the monitoring. *Id.*

Like the plaintiff in *Williams* and unlike the plaintiff in *Griggs-Ryan*, Mr. Harrison was not expressly and "unmistakably warned" of either the manner *or* the scope of any interceptions. In fact, Mr. Harrison was not notified that any telephone calls would be recorded *at all*, much less his own. Thus, Mr. Harrison had even less notice than the plaintiff in *Williams*, who was at least notified of the partial scope of the interceptions—that "monitoring" was in place to deter telephone abuse by employees. Here, Defendant's description of her intentions was far more ambiguous than in *Williams*. Defendant testified that she told Mr. Harrison she "was hiring a housekeeper" and that, among a laundry list of other requirements for the new housekeeper, she "wanted to make sure that the housekeeper did not make improper use of the telephone." (Material Fact No. 7.) Expressing a concern that the housekeeper might make "improper use of the telephone" simply does not constitute express, unmistakable notice that the Defendant would be recording all of the home's in-coming and out-going calls. This alleged "notice" was made even more ambiguous by the fact that Defendant's expressed concern about the housekeeper's improper use of the telephone was buried within a long laundry list of other concerns. (Material Fact No. 9.)

In sum, Mr. Harrison was not warned of either the manner or the scope of any such interceptions. Defendant has not contended, nor can she contend, that she ever told Mr. Harrison that her concern for the housekeeper's improper use of the telephone would take the form of recording the housekeeper's telephone calls. (Material Fact No. 7.) Thus, the Defendant did not inform Mr. Harrison of the manner of such monitoring. Nor did Defendant ever tell Mr. Harrison that the scope of the recording would include all of the home's in-coming and out-going calls, including his own. (Material Fact No. 4.) The record is noticeably devoid of any such testimony. Thus, Defendant did not inform Mr. Harrison of the scope of such monitoring. As the *Williams* court noted, without even this minimal knowledge as to the manner and scope of the recordings, consent cannot be inferred from this record.

Moreover, in stark contrast to *Griggs-Ryan*, where there was not even a scintilla of evidence to suggest that the tenant did not understand the landlady's express warnings, here there is an abundance of evidence suggesting not only that Mr. Harrison did not *know* about the interceptions, but that he would never have consented to such an invasion of his privacy. At the time of the interceptions, the couple was in the midst of divorce proceedings and relations were very "strained." (Material Fact No. 4.) In his deposition, Mr. Harrison testified that, while he "vaguely recalls" his former wife saying something about the new housekeeper, he did not attend to the details. (Material Fact No. 9.) Mr. Harrison also testified that "I had no idea she was recording my telephone calls, nor would I have ever agreed to such an invasion...." (Material Fact No. 4.)

Like the beleaguered CEO in *Williams*, the idea that Mr. Harrison would have knowingly assented to the interception and recording of his telephone conversations by his estranged wife strains credibility. At the time of the telephone interceptions, the Harrison's marriage had deteriorated to the point that the Defendant had accused Mr. Harrison of an extramarital affair. (Material Fact No. 3.) Although the couple continued to reside in the same home after a legal separation, they lived in separate bedrooms and all sexual relations had ceased. (Material Fact No. 3.) Indeed, the Defendant began intercepting Mr. Harrison's telephone calls just four days after the couple became legally separated. (Material Fact No. 1.) As the court concluded in *Williams*, it would strain credibility to believe that Mr. Harrison would have knowingly assented to the interception and recording of his conversations by his estranged wife "with whom he was engaged in a power struggle." 11 F.3d at 282 n.18.

Moreover, even when a common practice might give rise to an "expectation" that telephone calls *might* be intercepted, a party does not impliedly consent to such interceptions absent express notice of the scope and manner of the interceptions. *Campiti*, 611 F.2d at 393. In *Campiti*, it was common practice for prison officials to monitor the telephone calls of inmates by listening in on an extension phone. In fact, the prison had a special extension phone system in which an extension phone was "wired directly into the main switchboard," allowing prison officials to monitor both employees' and inmates' telephone calls. *Id*. at 390. The prison contended that prisoners knew about the monitoring and had the expectation that their calls might be monitored. *Id*. When the plaintiff, a prisoner, asked a staff officer to place a telephone call for him, another staff officer monitored the conversation.

Even though it had been common practice for prison officials to monitor calls, the court held that the prisoner did not impliedly consent to the monitoring. In so holding, the court rejected the contention that, based on the prison's past practices, the prisoner "should have known his call would probably be monitored." *Id*. at 393. In essence, the court rejected the notion that a person could impliedly consent to monitoring unless the party was *expressly* notified of the monitoring, and was shown to have *actual knowledge* of the monitoring.

As the court in *Campiti* made clear, the fact that the Harrisons monitored the telephone calls of former nannies several years earlier does not create a presumption that Mr. Harrison consented to the interception of his own telephone calls during an acrimonious divorce. On the two occasions in the distant past in which the couple briefly monitored the home's telephone calls, they did so out of a concern for the relative youthfulness and potential immaturity of their child's nannies, who were only nineteen and twenty-one years old respectively. This concern should not have been present when the Defendant hired a new housekeeper in November 2020. The new housekeeper was not only thirty years old, but their child was also more mature and better able to demand that the housekeeper be available to cater to his needs when necessary. Tape recordings made years earlier simply do not create an expectation that the Defendant, estranged from her husband, would unilaterally decide to again begin recording telephone calls. Because no telephone calls had been intercepted for at least two years, the Harrisons could not be deemed to have engaged in a common practice of intercepting telephone calls. However, as the *Campiti* court made clear, even a "common practice" of intercepting telephone calls does not constitute implied consent, without an express, unmistakable warning that telephone calls would be intercepted.

<u>CONCLUSION</u>

As the First Circuit Court of Appeals has made clear, consent cannot be implied except in the "rare case" in which the surrounding circumstances "*convincingly* show that the party knew about and consented to the interception." *United States v. Lanoue*, 71 F.3d 966, 981 (1st Cir. 1995) (emphasis added). Here, Mr. Harrison was not expressly and "unmistakably warned" that *any* telephone calls would be recorded, much less his own. Moreover, the surrounding circumstances compel the conclusion that not only did Mr. Harrison not consent to the interception of his telephone calls, but that he would never have consented to such interceptions given the acrimony of the divorce proceedings.

Wherefore, the Plaintiff prays that this Court grant the Plaintiff's motion for summary judgment and grant compensatory and punitive damages, attorneys' fees, other reasonable litigation costs, and such other and further relief as this Court deems just and proper.

DEFENDANT'S SAMPLE BRIEF: SPOUSAL WIRETAP PROBLEM

UNITED STATES DISTRICT COURT
DISTRICT OF NEW HAMPSHIRE

MICHAEL HARRISON,	)	
	)	
Plaintiff,	)	
	)	
vs.	)	No. 05-1097
	)	
KATHRYN HARRISON,	)	
	)	
Defendant.	)	

DEFENDANT'S MEMORANDUM IN SUPPORT OF
MOTION FOR SUMMARY JUDGMENT

INTRODUCTION

The federal wiretap statute expressly authorizes the interception of wire communications when "one of the parties to the communication has given prior consent to such interception." 18 U.S.C. § 2511(2)(d). The Statute affords a "safe harbor not only for persons who intercept calls with the explicit consent of a conversant but also from those who do so after receiving *implied* consent." *Griggs-Ryan v. Smith*, 904 F.2d 112, 116 (1st Cir. 1990) (emphasis added). When evaluating whether a party has given consent to the interception of wire communications, the First Circuit Court of Appeals has directed that the consent requirement be "construed broadly." *Id.* The First Circuit has also instructed that consent need not be explicit but, instead, can be "inferred from surrounding circumstances indicating that the [party] knowingly agreed to the surveillance." *Id.* at 116–17. When a party has been notified that calls are being monitored, that party's continuing use of the telephone reflects that he "knowingly agreed to the surveillance" and impliedly consented to the interception. *Id.* at 118. Here, Plaintiff, Mr. Michael Harrison's, continuing use of the telephone following his wife's warning that she intended to monitor the telephone constitutes implied consent. Accordingly, Plaintiff's complaint must be dismissed as a matter of law.

STATEMENT OF FACTS

1. Defendant, Kathryn Harrison, married the Plaintiff, Michael Harrison, on June 16, 2010. The couple has one son, Dillon, who is nine years old. (K. Harrison Dep. 15:5-15:18 (March 14, 2021).)

2. Because both parties have busy professional careers, for the past nine years the couple have hired live-in nannies and housekeepers to help care for Dillon. Since their son's birth, the couple has hired three different caretakers to care for Dillon. (K. Harrison Dep. 18:11-18:14; M. Harrison Dep. 76:17 (March 13, 2021).)

3. When the first nanny was hired to care for Dillon, the couple was concerned about the nanny's potential improper use of the telephone. The couple discussed, and then mutually agreed, to record all incoming and out-going telephone calls for an indefinite period of time so that they could ensure that they had made a sound hiring decision. (K. Harrison Dep. 20:07-20:29; M. Harrison Dep. 75:08-75:28.)

4. The Harrisons followed an identical process when they hired a second nanny seven years later. When the couple hired a third caretaker less than two years later, Mrs. Harrison adopted the same monitoring procedure the couple had used in the past, after discussing the issue with her husband. (K. Harrison Dep. 84:4-85:6.)

5. The couple hired their first nanny shortly after Dillon's birth in 2012. After interviewing the nanny, the couple was concerned that the nanny might spend "too much time on the telephone when she should be spending time with Dillon." (K. Harrison Dep. 25:17.)

6. Therefore, the couple decided that, for an "indefinite period of time, all telephone calls into and from the house would be recorded" with a tape recorder. (K. Harrison Dep. 105:12-106:18; M. Harrison Dep. 77:4-77:22.)

7. In other words, the Harrisons agreed to record the Plaintiff's telephone calls, as well as Mrs. Harrison's telephone calls, along with the nanny's calls. (K. Harrison Dep. 106:12; M. Harrison Dep. 77:20.)

8. In his deposition, Plaintiff stated that he "loves his son," and that his "son's welfare comes first." (M. Harrison Dep. 26:12.)

9. Therefore, the Plaintiff acknowledged that he not only agreed to such monitoring but thought it was a "good idea." (M. Harrison Dep. 77:22.)

10. After the nanny consented to the Harrisons' policy, *all* of the telephone calls going into and out of the home were recorded for a period of approximately one month. (K. Harrison Dep. 91:6.)

11. Just two years ago, when the couple hired a new nanny, they again agreed to record all in-coming and out-going telephone calls for a period of time until they were confident that they had made a sound decision in hiring the nanny. (K. Harrison Dep. 68:9-68:18.)

12. Again, with a tape recorder, the couple recorded *all* in-coming and out-going telephone calls for a period of one month. The recorded telephone

conversations again included all of Plaintiff's telephone calls, as well as all of Mrs. Harrison's telephone calls. (K. Harrison Dep. 110:5-111:2; M. Harrison Dep. 78:11-79:15.)

13. Again, Plaintiff agreed that this was a "good decision." (M. Harrison Dep. 79:18.)

14. In November 2020, when the most recent nanny resigned, the couple agreed to hire a housekeeper whose responsibilities would also include caring for Dillon. (K. Harrison Dep. 50:11-51:20.)

15. When the couple hired the housekeeper, Mrs. Harrison was again concerned that the new housekeeper, who would also care for their son, not misuse her telephone privileges. Therefore, Mrs. Harrison wanted to continue the couple's past practice of recording all telephone calls for a period of "about a month." (K. Harrison Dep. 51:19.)

16. Before doing so, Mrs. Harrison had a discussion with her husband about the new caretaker for the couple's son. During that discussion, Mrs. Harrison verbally communicated to her husband that she "wanted to make sure that the housekeeper did not make improper use of the telephone." (K. Harrison Dep. 52:4-54:7.)

17. In his deposition, Plaintiff conceded that his wife did, indeed, "make a reference to the housekeeper's use of the telephone." (M. Harrison Dep. 34:17.)

18. Although he also claims that he "wasn't interested in the details" of hiring his son's caretaker and "wasn't listening," Plaintiff concedes that, within the same conversation, he told his wife to "go ahead and take care of it." (M. Harrison Dep. 34:22-36:5.)

19. After this discussion, Mrs. Harrison hired the housekeeper and had her sign an agreement consenting to the taping of her telephone conversations. (K. Harrison Dep. 54:19.)

20. As she had in the past, Mrs. Harrison again recorded all telephone calls into and out of the couple's home for approximately one month (from November 5, 2020, when the housekeeper was hired, until December 8, 2020). (K. Harrison Dep. 60:2.)

21. Plaintiff's disinterest in the hiring process of his son's caretaker may have been a symptom of the domestic conflict that had surfaced between the couple. Although the couple became legally separated on November 1, 2020, they continued to reside in the same household through the end of December, 2020. (K. Harrison Dep. 11:22; M. Harrison Dep. 14: 24.)

22. When Mrs. Harrison began listening to the tapes, she discovered that some of her husband's telephone conversations were suggestive of an illicit romantic liaison. Thus, some of these tapes have been used in the couple's divorce proceedings. (K. Harrison Dep. 82:11.)

23. On March 15, 2021, Plaintiff filed this civil action, alleging that his wife's actions in recording his telephone calls violate the federal wiretap statute, 18 U.S.C. § 2511(2)(d). Following discovery, the Defendant, Mrs. Harrison, has filed this motion for summary judgment, contending that this action must be dismissed as a matter of law because the Plaintiff consented to the taping of his telephone conversations.

<u>ARGUMENT</u>

Under Rule 56 of the Federal Rules of Civil Procedure, a court "shall" grant a moving party's motion for summary judgment if the evidence proves "there is no genuine dispute as to any material facts." Fed. R. Civ. P. 56(a). In that situation, the moving party is entitled to judgment as a matter of law. *Id*. The purpose of Rule 56 "is to enable the trial court to readily dispose of cases on matters of law" when a trial is unnecessary. *Rohner v. Union Pac. R.R. Co.*, 225 F.2d 272, 274 (10th Cir. 1955). This Brief will prove that a trial is unnecessary in this case, as the evidence unequivocally proves that Mrs. Harrison did not violate Section 2520 of the federal wiretap statute.

When evaluating whether a party has given consent to the interception of wire communications, the First Circuit Court of Appeals has directed that the consent requirement be "construed broadly." *Griggs-Ryan v. Smith*, 904 F.2d 112, 116 (1st Cir. 1990). Importantly, consent need not be explicit but, instead, can be "inferred from surrounding circumstances indicating that the [party] knowingly agreed to the surveillance." *Id*. at 116-17. Such surrounding circumstances can include the parties' past practices as well as the verbal communication itself. When a party has been notified that all calls are being recorded, his continuing use of the telephone reflects that he "knowingly agreed to the surveillance" and impliedly consented to the interception. *Id*. Here, based on the Harrisons' past practices, as well as Mrs. Harrison's verbal communication of her intention to record all telephone calls, the Plaintiff not only knew that telephone calls would be recorded, but also knew that his own telephone calls would be recorded. Therefore, he impliedly consented to the monitoring.

Courts have consistently held that when a party has been told that all incoming telephone calls would be recorded for an indefinite period of time, that party's continuing use of the telephone constitutes implied consent to the monitoring. *Griggs-Ryan*, 904 F.2d 112. In *Griggs-Ryan*, the plaintiff was a tenant at a campground operated by the defendant, his landlady. The tenants did not have individual telephones, and were therefore allowed to use the landlady's telephone. *Id*. at 114. The defendant informed the tenants that, because she was being plagued by obscene telephone calls, she would record all incoming calls. *Id*. Although it would have been reasonable for a tenant to assume the landlady would stop taping once she realized that a specific call was not obscene, the landlady did not explicitly inform the tenants of this practice. *Id*. at 118. However, it was in fact the landlady's practice to stop taping a call once she realized the call was not obscene or threatening. The plaintiff subsequently received a telephone call at the landlady's home. After notifying the plaintiff that he had a telephone call, the defendant listened in on an extension telephone and recorded the entire call. When she discovered that the parties were engaged in an illegal drug transaction, the landlady gave the tape to the police. *Id*. at 114.

The court held that the plaintiff "effectively acquiesced in the interception" when he opted to converse on the defendant's telephone after being told that all calls would be recorded. *Id*. at 118. Even though the purpose of the monitoring was to screen for obscene callers, the court was not persuaded by the fact that a tenant might reasonably presume the scope of any monitoring would be limited to the initial greeting phase of a telephone call. Instead, the court emphasized that, when the landlady informed the plaintiff that she would record all in-coming calls, she did not expressly limit the scope of the monitoring to the greeting phrase of the telephone call. Absent an express verbal statement limiting the scope of the monitoring, the tenant could not later claim that the landlady's authority was limited to screening for obscene callers. By continuing to receive calls on the defendant's telephone line, the tenant "knowingly agreed to the surveillance." *Id*. Importantly, the court concluded: "His consent, albeit not explicit, was manifest. No more was required." *Id*.

In addition, a party's use of the telephone does not imply consent to monitoring only when he does not have even *minimal knowledge* that the scope of the monitoring would include the recording of his own telephone calls. *Williams v. Poulos*, 11 F.3d 271, 281–82 (1st Cir. 1993). In *Williams*, the defendants installed a surveillance system to monitor office telephone calls as part of an effort to reduce employee telephone abuse. The plaintiff, the new CEO of the company, was told that there was a "system in place to deter *employee* phone abuse by randomly monitoring *employee* phone calls." *Id*. at 276 (emphasis added). However, the court found that the new CEO was *not* told that his own telephone calls would be monitored, nor was he told of the manner in which the monitoring would occur. Moreover, as a new CEO, the plaintiff presumably had no first-hand knowledge of the defendants' past monitoring practices. After the plaintiff was hired, the defendants initially only monitored the telephone lines of employees on a random basis. Later, however, the defendants admitted that they began to specifically target and monitor the CEO's own telephone calls because they were "openly feuding" with him. *Id*. at 276. In other words, although the defendants expressed to the new CEO that they would be monitoring employee telephone calls to deter employee telephone abuse, they actually began recording the new CEO's telephone calls for the purpose of uncovering information pertaining to their feud. *Id*.

Because the expressed scope of the monitoring differed from the *actual* scope of the monitoring, the court held that the CEO did not impliedly consent to the monitoring of his own telephone calls. *Id*. at 282. Although the new CEO was told only that *employee* telephone calls would be monitored, his own calls were later targeted after the parties began feuding. The court reasoned that, without even "minimal knowledge" that he himself would be the target of monitoring, the plaintiff could not have consented to the monitoring. *Id.*

As in *Griggs-Ryan*, Plaintiff in the present case was notified of both the scope and the manner of monitoring. Mrs. Harrison's verbal communication to her husband concerning the monitoring of the telephone must not be viewed in a vacuum, but instead must be construed in light of the couple's past practices. As the *Griggs-Ryan* court instructed, all of the surrounding circumstances must be considered when determining whether consent has been implied. From the time the couple hired their child's first nanny, the couple have engaged in a practice of recording all telephone calls—in-coming and out-going—for a period of approximately one month following the new hire. In each case, the scope of the recording included not just the nanny's calls, but also the Plaintiff's telephone calls and Mrs. Harrison's telephone calls. (Material Fact Nos. 3, 4 &7.) When the Harrisons hired their child's first nanny, both spouses agreed that recording all telephone calls for a period of time was necessary to help them assess whether a new caretaker was someone they trusted and wanted to retain as an employee. (Material Fact No. 3.) Plaintiff has acknowledged that he not only agreed to such monitoring but thought it was a "good idea." (Material Fact No. 9.)

This practice of recording all of the telephone calls into and out of their home continued when the couple hired a new nanny seven years later. (Material Fact No. 4.) Again, the Plaintiff has conceded that he was not only aware of this practice, but thought it was a "good decision." (Material Fact No. 13.) By his own admission, Plaintiff was aware of, and approved, the parties' practice of recording each telephone call going into and out of their home. Thus, in each instance, the Plaintiff's own admissions reveal that he was expressly aware of both the scope of the monitoring (all in-coming and out-going calls) and the manner of the monitoring (recording each telephone call).

It is against this backdrop that Mrs. Harrison's verbal communications to her husband in November 2020 must be construed. In November 2020, when the couple hired a new caretaker for their son, Mrs. Harrison wanted to continue the couple's past practice of recording all telephone calls to ensure that the new caretaker was responsible and someone they wanted to retain. (Material Fact No. 15.) Like the defendant in *Griggs-Ryan*, she verbally communicated her intention to her husband. She told her husband that she wanted "to make sure that the housekeeper did not make improper use of the telephone." (Material Fact No. 15.) In light of their past practices when hiring new caretakers for their son, Plaintiff must have understood that this statement meant his wife would tape-record all incoming and outgoing calls for a period of about one month. Each time in the past when the couple had a concern about a new caretaker's improper use of the telephone, such a concern was not merely a theoretical expression of anxiety, but, rather, meant that there would be a corresponding action—the recording of all incoming and out-going telephone calls for a period of about one month. Thus, Mrs. Harrison's expression of concern could not reasonably have been construed to mean anything other than what it has meant in the past upon a new hiring—that all telephone calls in the family home would be recorded.

The couple's past practices, together with Mrs. Harrison's verbal communications, clearly alerted Plaintiff to both the manner and the scope of the monitoring. The couple had in place only one means of monitoring telephone calls—a tape recorder. They have used the same tape recorder to monitor the household's telephone calls from the time they hired their first nanny nine years ago. (Material Fact Nos. 6 & 12.) Thus, Plaintiff was well aware of the *manner* of monitoring. The Plaintiff was also well aware of the *scope* of the monitoring. Unlike in *Williams*, where the defendants installed an expensive surveillance system that could monitor select telephone calls of randomly selected employees, the Harrisons had only one means of monitoring telephone calls—to record each and every telephone call coming into and going out of the couple's home. Thus, unlike the defendant in *Williams*, who was never told, and did not have even *minimal knowledge* that the scope of any monitoring would include his own telephone calls, Plaintiff was well aware from past practice that his telephone calls would be recorded.

In fact, the Plaintiff had even clearer notice of the scope of monitoring than the plaintiff in *Griggs-Ryan*. In *Griggs-Ryan*, the plaintiff was told that his landlady wanted to monitor telephone calls because she was receiving obscene calls. Under these circumstances, it might have been reasonable for the plaintiff to believe that his landlady would hang up the telephone once she realized the call was for him, and not an obscene call. Thus, he arguably had no actual notice that his landlady would record any of his telephone calls after the few seconds it might take to verify that a caller was not an obscene caller. In contrast, the Plaintiff in the present case was well aware of the scope of the monitoring. He has conceded that he knew and approved of the monitoring in the past, knew that monitoring meant that *all* incoming and outgoing calls would be tape-recorded for an indefinite period of time, and believed that it was a "good idea" and a "good decision." (Material Fact Nos. 9 & 13.) Despite this knowledge, the Plaintiff continued to place calls into and out of the couple's home. His continued use of the telephone, despite his knowledge of the recordings, constitutes implied consent. As the court reasoned in *Griggs-Ryan*, "[h]is consent, albeit not explicit, was manifest. No more was required." 904 F.2d at 118.

Notably, the Plaintiff has not only failed to dispute Mrs. Harrison's testimony, but he verbally communicated to her what reasonably seemed to be express consent to the monitoring. Plaintiff conceded that Mrs. Harrison did indeed "make a reference to the housekeeper's use of the telephone." (Material Fact No. 18.) Within that same conversation, the Plaintiff also conceded that he told his wife to "go ahead and take care of it." (Material Fact No. 18.) Although Plaintiff's continued use of the telephone itself constituted implied consent, the admission that he told his wife to "go ahead and take care of it" comes dangerously close to *express* consent. Thus, this admission is a much stronger indication of consent than in *Griggs-Ryan*, where the tenant never verbally acquiesced at all in the landlady's monitoring of his calls.

Moreover, although relations between the couple were strained as a result of their legal separation, Mrs. Harrison had no reason to construe the Plaintiff's statement to "go ahead and take care of it" to mean anything other than consent to recording all in-coming and out-going telephone calls. Plaintiff loves his son, and has testified that his "son's welfare comes first." (Material Fact No. 8.) Out of love for his son, Plaintiff has readily admitted that, in the past, he believed it was a "good idea" to record all of the home's telephone calls for a period of time following a new hire. (Material Fact Nos. 8 & 9.) Because his son's welfare comes first, Mrs. Harrison had every reason to believe that, like her, the Plaintiff would again think it was a "good idea" to monitor the caretaker's use of the telephone to ensure that their child was in good hands. Under those circumstances, Plaintiff's instruction to "take care of it" can only reasonably be construed as consent to the couple's practice of monitoring telephone calls.

Had the Plaintiff wanted to engage in a different monitoring practice than the couple had used before, he was required to communicate that limitation to his wife. As the court in *Griggs-Ryan* made clear, any uncommunicated expectation to change the scope of the monitoring is ineffectual. Thus, in *Griggs-Ryan*, it was irrelevant that the tenant may have believed the scope of the landlady's monitoring was narrower than it actually was in practice. Similarly, if the Plaintiff had entertained a belief that, due to the couple's legal separation, the monitoring should be narrower in scope so as to exclude his own telephone calls, he was required to communicate this expectation to Mrs. Harrison. In the absence of any request not to engage in the usual practice, it can be inferred from the surrounding circumstances that the Plaintiff agreed to the recording, just as he had in the past.

Finally, the present case is a far cry from *Campiti*, in which the court held that a prisoner did not impliedly consent to monitoring when the prison staff had never, on any occasion, notified the prisoners that their calls would be monitored. *Campiti v. Walonis*, 611 F.2d 387, 393–94 (1st Cir. 1979). In so holding, the court rejected the prison's contention that a mere "expectation" of monitoring would constitute implied consent, without some type of notification. *Id.* As the *Griggs-Ryan* court later observed, in *Campiti* "no general warnings had been given," nor were there any regulations notifying prisoners that their calls might be monitored. *Griggs-Ryan*, 904 F.2d at 118. In fact, the court noted that the prisoner in *Campiti* had every reason to believe that his call would *not* be electronically monitored. From past practice, prisoners knew that calls would be monitored when a corrections officer physically stood near the telephone. *Id.* Prisoners presumably did not know of the electronic monitoring. During the telephone call at issue, the prisoner "elected to speak at a time when no officer was physically present, unaware that his jailers were listening on an extension telephone in another room." *Id.* Thus, not only was the prisoner never informed that his telephone call might be monitored, but the prison's own past practices led the prisoner to believe that his telephone call would in fact *not* be monitored.

In stark contrast to *Campiti*, the Harrisons' express verbal discussions and past practices gave the Plaintiff actual notice that all of his calls would be recorded — not just that they *might* be recorded, but that they *would* be recorded. Unlike *Campiti*, where the prisoner's expectation from past conduct was that the prison would *not* record his telephone call, the couple's past practices led Plaintiff to believe that his calls *would* be recorded. The Harrisons had discussed their concern that new caretakers might abuse the telephone, and they had come to an express agreement as to how to address that concern—by recording all in-coming and out-going telephone calls for a period of about a month. When Mrs. Harrison again repeated her concern that the newly hired caretaker might abuse the telephone, the message was clear—Mrs. Harrison would, once again, record all of the in-coming and out-going telephone calls for a period of about a month. When the Plaintiff told Mrs. Harrison to "go ahead and take care of it," he conveyed his agreement to the recordings. (Material Fact No. 18.) Simply because Plaintiff is now unhappy that several of his telephone conversations suggested marital misconduct does not give him a license to rewrite history and feign ignorance as to the parties' agreement.

CONCLUSION

The facts clearly show that Plaintiff consented to the recording of his telephone calls. The express verbal discussions between the couple, Plaintiff's stated acknowledgements of recordings being a "good idea" within those discussions, and the couple's past practice of recording telephone calls when hiring a new caretaker for their son all demonstrate that Plaintiff consented to the recordings. Thus, there was no violation of the federal wiretap statute.

Wherefore, the Defendant prays that Plaintiff's action be dismissed, with prejudice, and for such other and further relief as this Court may deem just and proper

Appendix D

SAMPLE BRIEFS

(Law-Centered)

SAMPLE BRIEF A:
TITLE VII BRIEF

UNITED STATES DISTRICT COURT
SOUTHERN DISTRICT OF NEW YORK

RACHEL JOHNSON,
    Plaintiff

vs.   No. CV05-2589

EXTERIOR PRODUCTS, INC., and

RONALD CRANE,
    Defendants.

DEFENDANT'S MEMORANDUM IN SUPPORT OF
MOTION TO DISMISS

James Ternian, Esq.
Attorney for Defendant Ronald Crane
57 Grand Blvd.
New City, New York 11234
(501) 123-2345

TABLE OF CONTENTS

TABLE OF AUTHORITIES

INTRODUCTION

Defendant, Ronald Crane, respectfully requests that this Court issue an order dismissing Plaintiff's complaint pursuant to Fed. R. Civ. P. 12(b)(6) for failure to state a claim upon which relief can be granted. Defendant is entitled to an order dismissing Plaintiff's complaint because he cannot provide the relief Plaintiff seeks. Plaintiff seeks from Mr. Crane in his individual capacity compensatory and punitive damages under Title VII and the 1991 Amendments to Title VII. However, those statutes apply only to employers, not to individuals in their individual capacities. Because Plaintiff is suing Mr. Crane in his individual capacity and because Mr. Crane does not qualify as an employer under the statutes, he cannot provide the relief Plaintiff seeks.

The plain language of Title VII defines "employer" so as to provide exclusive employer liability and, therefore, to exclude individuals in their individual capacities. Moreover, the remedies available under Title VII are remedies that only employers, and not individuals in their individual capacities, can provide. When Congress amended Title VII in 1991, it merely strengthened the remedies available to victims of Title VII violations by adding the potential for compensatory and punitive damages; Congress did not expand the class of defendants against whom victims could proceed. Thus, it preserved Title VII's provision of exclusive employer liability. Finally, as intended by Congress, exclusive employer liability sufficiently achieves the dual goals of those statutes: to deter discrimination and to compensate victims of discrimination. Realizing that individuals face deterrents outside of the statutes, Congress excluded them from liability to ensure that employers vigilantly police their workplaces and workforces. Accordingly, Mr. Crane is entitled to an order dismissing Plaintiff's complaint for failure to state a claim upon which relief can be granted.

STATEMENT OF FACTS

Plaintiff, Rachel Johnson, has filed a Complaint seeking from Mr. Crane in his individual capacity compensatory and punitive damages for alleged violations of Title VII. In her Complaint, Plaintiff claims that Mr. Crane made a series of unwanted sexual advances toward her while she worked for him at Exterior Products, Inc. Additionally, Plaintiff claims Defendant threatened to retaliate against her for rejecting his unwanted sexual advances. Finally, Plaintiff claims Defendant, in fact, did retaliate against her by sabotaging her professionally, namely by claiming she had made unwanted sexual advances toward him and by rescheduling a meeting at which Plaintiff was to speak and not informing her, thus ensuring that she missed the meeting, and then firing her.

ARGUMENT

I. THE PLAIN LANGUAGE OF TITLE VII REFLECTS THAT CONGRESS ENVISIONED EXCLUSIVE EMPLOYER LIABILITY FOR VIOLATIONS OF TITLE VII.

Defendant, Mr. Crane, is entitled to an order dismissing Plaintiff's complaint because the plain language of Title VII reflects that Congress envisioned exclusive employer liability for violations of Title VII. First, Title VII defines "employer" so as to provide for exclusive employer liability and, therefore, to exclude individuals in their individual capacities. Second, the remedies available under Title VII are remedies that only employers, and not individuals in their individual capacities, can provide. Therefore, Mr. Crane is not liable to Plaintiff for compensatory or punitive damages under Title VII.

A. *Title VII's Definition of "Employer" Provides for Exclusive Employer Liability for Violations of Title VII.*

When prohibiting employers from discriminating against their employees, Title VII narrowly defines employer as "a person engaged in an industry affecting commerce who has fifteen or more employees... and any agent of such a person...." 42 U.S.C. § 2000e(b). By defining employer as a "person... who has fifteen or more employees... and any agent of such a person," Congress codified its intention to exclude individuals in their individual capacities from liability for violations of Title VII. First, individuals in their individual capacities do not qualify as "person[s]... who ha[ve] fifteen or more employees." Individuals do not have employees, employers do.

Second, interpreting the statutory language to include individuals in their individual capacities would produce an absurd result. The conjunctive term "and" links the term "any agent" to the phrase "person... who has fifteen or more employees." Thus, as an "agent" of an employer, an individual employee's liability would depend on whether the employer employed fifteen or more employees. Individuals who are "agents" of employers with fewer than fifteen employees would be exempt from liability—as an agent of an employer with fewer than fifteen employees, they would fall within the statutory exemption. In contrast, individuals who are "agents" of employers with fifteen or more employees would be liable in their individual capacities. Because their employer would not fall within the exemption, they would similarly not be exempt. Congress could not have intended this result. *Hudson v. Soft Sheen Prods.*, 873 F. Supp. 132, 135 n.2 (N.D. Ill. 1995).

Finally, reading individual liability into the Statute would thwart Congress' goal of shielding small entities with limited resources from the cost of litigating Title VII claims. As federal courts have noted, "Congress' explicit limitation of the definition of 'employer' to 'a person engaged in an industry affecting commerce who has 15 or more employees' suggests an intent to protect those with limited resources from liability." *Haltek v. Village of Park Forest*, 864 F. Supp. 802, 805 (N.D. Ill. 1994). Indeed, "[if] Congress decided to protect small entities with limited resources from liability, it is inconceivable that Congress intended to allow civil liability to run against individual employees." *Miller v. Maxwell's Int'l, Inc.*, 991 F.2d 583, 586 (9th Cir. 1993).

Thus, the "any agent" language merely incorporates respondeat superior liability into the statute and ensures that employers are liable for the discriminatory acts of their employees acting in their official capacities. *See id.* at 586 ("The obvious purpose of this [agent] provision was to incorporate respondeat superior liability into the statute.") (quoting *Padway v. Palches*, 655 F.2d 965, 968 (9th Cir. 1982)). Even the courts that have found individuals liable under Title VII have found them liable only in their official capacities, not in their individual capacities. *See id.* ("Many of the courts that purportedly have found individual liability under that statute actually have held individuals liable in their *official* capacities and not in their individual capacities.").

B. *The Remedies Available Under Title VII Confirm that Congress Intended Exclusive Employer Liability for Violations of Title VII.*

Moreover, the remedies available under Title VII confirm that Congress intended the "any agent" language merely to incorporate respondeat superior liability into the Statute. Title VII originally allowed successful plaintiffs to recover only injunctive relief, reinstatement or hiring, or up to two years of back pay. 42 U.S.C. § 2000e-5(g). These remedies are "'damages [that] an employer, not an individual would generally provide....'" *Hudson v. Soft Sheen Prods.*, 873 F. Supp. 132, 134 (N.D. Ill. 1995) (quoting *Weiss v. Coca-Cola Bottling Co.*, 772 F. Supp. 407, 411 (N.D. Ill. 1991)). For example, "'individual defendants cannot be held liable for back pay.'" *Miller*, 991 F.2d at 585 (quoting *Padway*, 665 F.2d at 968). Had Congress intended individuals to be liable in their individual capacities for violations of Title VII, it would have included in Title VII a remedy that individuals could provide. By failing to do so, Congress indicated its intent to impose exclusive employer liability for violations of Title VII.

II. WITH THE 1991 AMENDMENTS, CONGRESS EXPANDED THE SCOPE OF REMEDIES WHILE PRESERVING THE CLASS OF DEFENDANTS AGAINST WHOM VICTIMS OF TITLE VII VIOLATIONS COULD PROCEED.

The 1991 Amendments to Title VII preserved Title VII's provision of exclusive employer liability. In amending Title VII in 1991, Congress expanded the scope of remedies available to victims of Title VII violations. *See* H. R. Rep. No. 40, 102nd Cong., 1st Sess., pt. 1 (1991) (noting that the purpose of the amendments to Title VII is "to strengthen existing remedies to provide more effective deterrence and ensure compensation commensurate with the harm suffered..."). However, Congress specifically did not expand the class of defendants against whom victims could proceed. Instead, Congress codified this intent by leaving unaltered Title VII's definition of employer, by enacting damages caps based on the number of "employees" a defendant has, and by focusing on *employer* payment of damages and on *employer* deterrence in the legislative history to the 1991 Amendments. Therefore, Mr. Crane is not liable to Plaintiff for compensatory and punitive damages under Title VII.

A. *In the 1991 Amendments, Congress Preserved Title VII's Provision of Exclusive Employer Liability.*

In enacting the 1991 Amendments to Title VII, Congress expanded the scope of remedies available to victims of a Title VII violations. However, Congress did not expand the class of defendants against whom victims could proceed. Instead, Congress left unaltered Title VII's definition of employer and preserved the exclusion of employers with fewer than fifteen employees. *See* 42 U.S.C. § 1981a(b)(3). Had Congress intended to expand the class of defendants to include individuals in their individual capacities, it would have done so explicitly. "Congress must have been aware that the majority of jurisdictions interpreted ... Title VII to exclude individual liability. Congress would not have expected to change the law with silence." *Hudson v. Soft Sheen Prods.*, 873 F. Supp. 132, 136 (N.D. Ill. 1995).

B. Section 1981a's Damage Caps Make Sense Only in the Context of Exclusive Employer Liability.

The elaborate liability scheme of the 1991 Amendments confirms that Congress intended to preserve Title VII's provision of exclusive employer liability. In expanding the scope of remedies available to victims of Title VII violations to include compensatory and punitive damages, Congress also carefully limited the damages to which an employer could be subjected depending upon the number of employees employed by the employer. For example, on the low end, Congress subjected an employer who employs between fourteen and 101 employees to no more than $50,000 in compensatory and punitive damages. 42 U.S.C. § 1981a(b)(3)(A). On the high end, Congress subjected an employer who employs more than 500 employees to no more than $300,000 in compensatory and punitive damages. *Id.* § 1981a(b)(3)(D). Congress' failure to include a damage cap for individuals reflects that they did not contemplate individual liability for compensatory and punitive damages under the Amendments. *See Hudson*, 873 F. Supp. at 135 ("[I]f Congress had envisioned individual liability under Title VII for compensatory and punitive damages, it would have included *individuals* in this litany of limitations....") (quoting *Miller v. Maxwell's Int'l, Inc.*, 991 F.2d 583, 588 n.2 (9th Cir. 1993)).

Moreover, reading individual liability into the Statute would mean that individuals would be subjected either to unlimited liability or to liability that depends upon the size of the employer for whom they work. Neither of these alternatives makes sense. First, subjecting employees to unlimited individual liability is simply inconsistent with Congress' careful efforts to prescribe the parameters of employer liability. "It is unreasonable to think that Congress would protect small entities from the costs associated with litigating discrimination claims and limit the available compensatory and punitive damages based on the size of the ... employer, but subject an individual supervisory employee to unlimited liability." *Haltek v. Village of Park Forest*, 864 F. Supp. 802, 805 (N.D. Ill. 1994). This result would cavalierly subject individuals to the vagaries of juries while protecting employer liability. Such a result would not only be manifestly unfair to individual employees but would thwart Congress' carefully calibrated scheme of damages.

Second, imposing individual liability depending upon the size of the employer for whom the individual works is equally as nonsensical and unfair. Under this scenario, individuals who work for an employer with fewer than fifteen employees would not be subject to liability at all, while individuals who work for employers with fifteen or more employees would be subject to liability. In other words, it would create an incentive for potential violators of Title VII to work for small employers to ensure that they could escape liability. Congress could not have intended this result. *Hudson*, 873 F. Supp. at 135.

Moreover, the damage caps reflect an employer's ability to pay, not an individual's ability to pay. In enacting the damage caps, Congress carefully calibrated the caps to consider an employer's ability to pay and the amount necessary to "punish" the offending employer, i.e., "to make it hurt." Thus, the calibrated damages caps reflect Congress' intention not to bankrupt an employer or punish an employer beyond the amount necessary to "make it hurt." Imposing an employer's damages cap on its individual employees would create unfair results that Congress could not possibly have intended. The calibrated damage caps do not similarly reflect an individual's ability to pay or the amount necessary to "punish" an individual. An individual who works for a large company does not necessarily have the ability to pay up to $300,000 in compensatory and punitive damages for violating Title VII, nor is that amount necessary to punish the individual. In fact, that penalty would easily bankrupt many employees and would thwart the legislative intent to avoid that prospect. Thus, the damages caps make sense only in the context of exclusive employer liability.

C. *The Legislative History to Section 1981a Reflects that Congress Intended Exclusive Employer Liability.*

The legislative history to the 1991 Amendments also confirms that Congress intended only to expand the scope of remedies available, not to expand the class of defendants against whom victims of Title VII violations could proceed. None of the Committee Reports, including the House Reports on the 1991 Amendments and the Senate Reports on the precursor bill to the 1991 Amendments, even mention individual liability. *See Hudson v. Soft Sheen Prods.*, 873 F. Supp. 132, 136 (N.D. Ill. 1995) (detailing the failure of the legislative history to mention individual liability). Instead, the legislative history is replete with references to *employer* compensation and the possibility of *employer* deterrence. For example, Congress focused on the need for employers to compensate wronged employees. The House Reports reflect Congress' intent to prevent "employers who intentionally discriminate [from avoiding] any meaningful liability." H.R. Rep. No. 41, 102nd Cong., 1st Sess., pt. 2, at 4 (1991). The Senate Reports addressed the need to make "employers liable for all losses—economic or otherwise—[that] are incurred as a consequence of prohibited discrimination." *Id*. at 5.

The legislative concern with deterrence also focused on employers, not on individual employees. The Senate Reports noted that employers must provide "punitive damages… in cases of intentional discrimination if the employer acted with 'malice'…."

Id. The reports also observed that employer liability "will serve as a necessary deterrent to future acts of discrimination…." *Id.* Even the suggested mechanisms for deterrence are restricted to mechanisms an employer might implement, not an individual. Congress hoped to "encourage employers to design and implement complaint structures [that] encourage victims to come forward by overcoming fear of retaliation and fear of loss of privacy…. Data suggests that employers do indeed implement measures to interrupt and prevent employment discrimination when they perceive that there is increased liability." *Id.* at 18 (statement of Dr. Klein).

Moreover, the vocal dissenters to the Amendment failed to mention individual liability in their complaints. Had they considered individual liability even a remote possibility, they would have objected.

> [T]he dissenters supplied exhaustive, thoughtful, and even caustic responses to the Amendments. On such issues as the cost of business, number of litigants, and remuneration of lawyers, [Congress] apparently thought of every conceivable negative outcome and shouted it from the rooftops… [H]ad they considered individual liability a conceivable outcome, they would also have considered it a negative one and denounced it in a similar fashion. Yet they never mentioned it.

Hudson, 837 F. Supp. at 138.

III. EXCLUSIVE EMPLOYER LIABILITY ACHIEVES TITLE VII'S GOALS OF COMPENSATION AND DETERRENCE.

Finally, exclusive employer liability sufficiently achieves Title VII's goals. Title VII's two main goals are "to compensate the victims of discrimination… and to deter discrimination in the future." *Hudson v. Soft Sheen Prods.*, 873 F. Supp. 132, 135-36 (N.D. Ill. 1995). Exclusive employer liability achieves those goals because the expansion of remedies in the 1991 Amendments ensures adequate compensation, because the expansion of remedies encourages and ensures that employers will police their workplaces and their workforces, and because individuals already face effective deterrents aside from individual liability.

The 1991 Amendments to Title VII ensure that victims of discrimination will be adequately compensated. In enacting the 1991 Amendments to Title VII, Congress expanded the scope of remedies available to victims of Title VII violations to include compensatory and punitive damages. Congress enacted this expansion out of recognition that Title VII often failed to adequately compensate victims of Title VII violations. *See* H.R. Rep., 102nd Cong., 1st Sess., pt. 1 (1991). By making employers liable for damages, Congress recognized that employers, not individuals, are best able to provide the necessary compensation.

Additionally, restricting liability to employers, as Congress intended, adequately serves the deterrent purpose of the 1991 Amendments. By imposing liability on employers, Congress ensured that employers would police their workplaces and workforces. "A company that risks liability for the discriminatory acts of its agents will police its employees and institute disciplinary measures to deter discriminatory acts." *Haltek v. Village of Park Forest*, 864 F. Supp. 802, 805-06 (N.D. Ill. 1994). No employer would permit its employees to violate Title VII when the employer is liable for the Title VII violation. "An employer that has incurred civil damages because one of its employees believes he can violate Title VII with impunity will quickly correct that employee's erroneous belief." *Miller v. Maxwell's Int'l, Inc.*, 991 F.2d 583, 586 (9th Cir. 1993).

Moreover, individuals face deterrents outside of Title VII that promote the Congressional goal of deterring future discrimination. For example, individuals face both professional and social sanctions in the form of demotion or firing and disapproval. They face "a loss of employment status, defense fees, and social approval." *Hudson*, 873 F. Supp. at 136. In addition, any conduct that violates Title VII also subjects an individual to civil liability for, among other things, assault, battery, and intentional infliction of emotional distress, or criminal liability for criminal sexual assault. Thus, individual liability under Title VII is unnecessary. It would be redundant as a deterrent and would unfairly expose individuals to double or triple punishment.

It may be that imposing individual liability in addition to employer liability would ensure adequate compensation and provide an added deterrent for individual behavior. However, Congress did not provide for individual liability in enacting Title VII and the 1991 Amendments to Title VII. It is not the role of the judiciary to expand the statute in pursuit of "some vague, aspirational broad intent. Congress had lofty goals but provided limited means for reaching those goals. Individual liability was not one of them." *Hudson*, 873 F. Supp. at 136.

For the foregoing reasons, Defendant, Mr. Crane, respectfully requests that this Court grant Defendant's motion to dismiss Plaintiff's complaint for failure to state a claim upon which relief can be granted.

SAMPLE BRIEF B:
FIFTH AMENDMENT BRIEF

UNITED STATES DISTRICT COURT
EASTERN DISTRICT OF MISSOURI

UNITED STATES OF AMERICA	)	
	)	
vs.	)	No. 05-9783
	)	
FRANK BROWNE,	)	
	)	
Defendant.	)	

DEFENDANT'S MEMORANDUM IN SUPPORT OF MOTION TO QUASH THE SUBPOENA OF DEFENDANT'S DIARY

INTRODUCTION

Defendant, Mr. Frank Browne, seeks to quash the Government's subpoena of the personal contents of his diary because its contents are protected by the Fifth Amendment to the United States Constitution. The Supreme Court has long held that the Fifth Amendment protects personal papers as well as oral testimony. *Boyd v. United States*, 116 U.S. 616 (1886). Although business documents do not fall within the privilege, the Supreme Court has carefully preserved *Boyd*'s protection of private, personal papers. *United States v. Doe*, 465 U.S. 605 (1984); *Fisher v. United States*, 425 U.S. 391 (1976). Because the contents of Mr. Browne's diary are private, personal papers subject to the protection of the Fifth Amendment, the Government cannot subpoena their disclosure.

STATEMENT OF FACTS

After charging Mr. Browne with unlawful distribution of marijuana in violation of 21 U.S.C. § 841, the Government served Mr. Browne with a subpoena requesting that he produce certain documents, including his personal diary. (Subpoena of 12/l/10.) Mr. Browne objects on the grounds that the Fifth Amendment protects his diary from compelled disclosure.

Mr. Browne's diary contains his most private daily thoughts and reflections on the vicissitudes of life. Mr. Browne's diary is replete with his personal reflections about his romantic life, chronicling the highs and lows of the intimate relationship he has had with his girlfriend of four years. (*See, e.g.*, Diary at 15.) Following the death of his mother, Mr. Browne used his diary as an outlet to express his innermost feelings of grief and regrets. (Diary at 7, 21.) Mr. Browne poignantly notes that: "I am consumed with grief. I never had the chance to say good-bye. I never had the chance to say I was sorry—for not being the son she wanted me to be, and for a million other things." (Diary at 21.) Mr. Browne also voiced in his diary his feelings about the progress of his psychotherapy, lamenting: "Will this therapy ever end? Sometimes it all seems too hopeless. Every time we peel off a layer of pain, a deeper layer is revealed." (Diary at 4.) Although the diary contains incriminating statements regarding the use of a boat for illegal drug distribution, Mr. Browne also used his diary as an outlet to express his personal despair over his drug addiction. (Diary at 9, 27.) Finally, Mr. Browne expressed private thoughts in his diary that he was not ready to share "with anyone, including Ms. Jones," his psychotherapist. (Diary at 5.)

ARGUMENT

I. THE FIFTH AMENDMENT'S PRIVILEGE AGAINST COMPULSORY SELF-INCRIMINATION PROTECTS PERSONAL PAPERS.

The Fifth Amendment grants a privilege against self-incrimination, stating that: "No person... shall be compelled in any criminal case to be a witness against himself...." U.S. Const. amend. V. This privilege against compulsory self-incrimination derives from the Fifth Amendment's "'respect [for] a private inner sanctum of individual feeling and thought'... that necessarily includes an individual's papers." *Bellis v. United States*, 417 U.S. 85, 91 (1974) (quoting *Murphy v. Waterfront Comm'n of Harbor*, 378 U.S. 52, 55 (1964)). Accordingly, the Supreme Court has long held that the privilege protects personal papers as well as oral testimony. *Boyd v. United States*, 116 U.S. 616 (1886). Although business documents do not fall within that "private inner sanctum," *see United States v. Doe*, 465 U.S. 605 (1984); *Fisher v. United States*, 425 U.S. 391 (1976), the Supreme Court has carefully preserved *Boyd*'s protection of personal papers. Moreover, the courts in this district have recognized that *Boyd* continues to protect personal papers. *See In re Grand Jury Subpoena*, 144 F.R.D. 357 (D. Minn. 1992), *rev'd on other grounds sub nom.; United States v. Spano*, 21 F.3d 326 (8th Cir. 1994).

The privilege against compulsory self-incrimination derives from the Fifth Amendment's "'respect [for] a private inner sanctum of individual feeling and thought'... that necessarily includes an individual's papers." *Bellis*, 417 U.S. at 91. In particular, it recognizes that "compelling self-accusation... would be both cruel and unjust." *Boyd*, 116 U.S. at 629. While the privilege may at times protect the guilty, the Supreme Court has admonished that "the evils of compelling self-disclosure transcends any difficulties... in the detection and prosecution of crime." *United States v. White*, 322 U.S. 694, 698 (1944). These evils include subjecting people to "iniquitous methods of prosecution," *id.*, betraying "the inviolability of the human personality," risking encroachment on the basic liberties of all citizens, and undermining the adversarial system. *Murphy*, 378 U.S. at 55. Accordingly, the Fifth Amendment proscribes invasion into "the privacies of life." *Boyd*, 116 U.S. at 630.

Personal papers are part of "the privacies of life." Failure to protect personal papers would thwart their development, thus inhibiting creativity and suppressing expression. Moreover, failure to protect personal documents would adversely affect the innocent as well as the guilty. *Boyd*, 116 U.S. at 629. Finally, failing to protect personal documents would create an artificial distinction between an individual's oral testimony and writings, even if the two are substantively identical. The Fifth Amendment does not contemplate such an anomalous result.

Accordingly, the Supreme Court has long held that the Fifth Amendment protects personal papers as well as oral testimony. *Boyd*, 116 U.S. at 633. In *Boyd*, the Court equated seizing a person's documents as evidence against him with compelling that person to be a witness against himself: "And we have been unable to perceive that the seizure of a man's private books and papers to be used in evidence against him is substantially different from compelling him to be a witness against himself." *Id*. Additionally, the Court admonished that "any forcible and compulsory extortion of a man's own testimony or of his private papers . . . is within the condemnation of [the Fifth Amendment]," *id*. at 630, and "contrary to the principals of a free government." *Id*. at 635–36.

Since *Boyd*, the Supreme Court has reiterated *Boyd's* protection of personal papers. For example, in *Bellis*, the Supreme Court acknowledged that "[i]t has long been established… that the Fifth Amendment… protects an individual from compelled production of his personal papers." 417 U.S. at 87. And, in *White*, the Supreme Court observed that it is the Fifth Amendment's "historic function [to protect an individual] from compulsory incrimination through his own testimony or personal records." 322 U.S. at 701. In each of these cases, the Supreme Court could not have been clearer; the Fifth Amendment protects individuals from the compelled production of their personal papers.

Although the Supreme Court recently concluded that *Boyd* does not protect *business* documents, it has preserved *Boyd's* protection of personal papers. *See Doe*, 465 U.S. at 610; *Fisher*, 425 U.S. at 403. In *Fisher*, the Court held that the Fifth Amendment does not protect the contents of tax records prepared by the defendant's accountant. 425 U.S. at 393. The Court based this holding on the fact that business documents do not implicate the privacy interests of personal papers: "special problems of privacy [that] might be presented by subpoena of a personal diary are not involved here." *Id*. at 407 n.7. Additionally, the Court preserved *Boyd's* protection of personal papers by emphasizing that "[w]hether the Fifth Amendment would shield the taxpayer from producing his own tax records… is a question not involved here; for the papers demanded here are not his 'private papers.'" *Id*. at 414.

Similarly, *Doe* preserved *Boyd's* protection of personal papers. In *Doe*, the Court held that the Fifth Amendment did not protect the contents of business records in the possession of the owner of a sole proprietorship. 465 U.S. at 617. However, the *Doe*

Court preserved *Boyd*'s protection of personal papers by premising its holding on the corporate nature of the documents. The Court carefully noted that "each of the documents sought here pertained to [the defendant's] business." *Id.* at 610 n.7.

Justice O'Connor's solitary *Doe* concurrence that "the Fifth Amendment provides absolutely no protection for the contents of private papers of any kind," *id.* at 618 (O'Connor, J., concurring), in no way undermines *Doe*'s preservation of *Boyd*'s protection of personal papers. First, no other Justice agreed with her broad statement; thus, it is merely the dicta of a solitary justice. Second, in a powerful partial concurrence, Justice Marshall, joined by Justice Brennan, chided Justice O'Connor and expressly reaffirmed *Boyd*'s protection for personal papers:

> This case presented nothing remotely close to the question that Justice O'Connor eagerly poses and answers.... Were it true that the Court's opinion stands for [that] proposition... I would assuredly dissent.

Id. at 618–19 (Marshall, J., concurring in part and dissenting in part).[1]

Finally, although the Eighth Circuit has not had occasion to address the issue, the courts in this district recognize that *Boyd* continues to protect personal papers. In 1992, the district court could not have been clearer: "An individual may refuse to comply with a subpoena duces tecum seeking personal records by asserting the Fifth Amendment's privilege." *In re Grand Jury Subpoena*, 144 F.R.D. 357, 361 (D. Minn. 1992). Therefore, this Court should follow the Supreme Court and the courts in this district in recognizing that *Boyd* continues to protect personal papers.

II. DEFENDANT'S DIARY IS A PERSONAL PAPER ENTITLED TO FIFTH AMENDMENT PROTECTION FROM COMPELLED DISCLOSURE.

Mr. Browne's diary is the quintessential personal paper entitled to Fifth Amendment protection. Privileged personal papers are those papers in which the defendant has a legitimate expectation of privacy. *Bellis v. United States*, 417 U.S. 85, 87-88 (1974). Because of the deeply personal and private nature of diaries, diaries are "a fortiori" the kind of intimate personal recordings that are protected under the Fifth Amendment. *Fisher v. United States*, 425 U.S. 391, 426 (1976) (Brennan, J., concurring). Moreover, when an individual records his private thoughts and affairs in a diary, it is protected from disclosure by the Fifth Amendment, even if the diary also contains sporadic references to business matters. A personal paper becomes a business record that is not entitled to Fifth Amendment protection only if it is the type of document normally used to record business transactions, and the actual entries in the document list business transactions. *United States v. Mason*, 869 F.2d 414, 416 (8th

---

1. The Court in *Baltimore Dep't of Social Servs. v. Bouknight*, 493 U.S. 549 (1990), also preserved *Boyd*'s protection of personal papers. *Bouknight* did not involve the production of documents of any sort, but instead the production of a child in a noncriminal case. Because *Bouknight* did not involve the privacy interests present in *Boyd*, *Bouknight* is inapt.

Cir. 1989). Here, Mr. Browne's diary recorded his most intimate and private thoughts and reflections on life. Mr. Browne legitimately expected that these intimate recordings would remain private. Therefore, the diary is protected from compelled disclosure by the Fifth Amendment to the United States Constitution.

As the Eighth Circuit recognized in *Mason*, disclosure of certain intimate papers might "break the heart of our sense of privacy." *Id.* The compelled disclosure of documents used to record and list business transactions are not such intimate documents. In *Mason*, the defendants recorded in day-timers the detailed daily business activities of their marijuana operation. The defendants recorded in the day-timers such items as the "rate of growth of the marijuana plants, the expected costs of completing the project, the expenses incurred, and the formula by which profits would be distributed." *Id.* The Eighth Circuit appropriately held that these business journals were more like the business records in *Doe* than personal diaries. A day-timer is the type of document normally used to record business transactions. Moreover, the daily entries recorded actual business transactions. *Id.* at 416.

In contrast to the day-timers in *Mason*, a personal diary is not the type of document used to record business transactions, but is a deeply personal record of one's most intimate reflections. Nor does Mr. Browne use his diary for the purpose of recording business transactions. Instead, Mr. Browne's diary is replete with his personal reflections regarding his relationship with his girlfriend and the joys and the sorrows of their relationship (*see, e.g.*, Diary at 15), his relationship with his mother and his attempts to deal with her death (*see, e.g.*, Diary at 7, 21), the slow progress of his psychotherapy (*see, e.g.*, Diary at 27), and anxiety about his career (*see, e.g.*, Diary at 15.) Additionally, throughout his diary, Mr. Browne refers to feelings of helplessness because of his addiction and to his deep desire for a sense of control over the problem. (*See, e.g.*, Diary at 7, 21, and 28.) Finally, Mr. Browne laments that his innermost feelings are so private that he cannot "share" his life with anyone, including his psychotherapist.

Mr. Browne's sporadic, incriminating references to his potential involvement in drug distribution do not rise to the level of "listing business transactions." In contrast to the day-timers in *Mason*, in which the defendants routinely recorded such business details as profits and expenses, Mr. Browne's incriminating statements lack the type of detail and frequency of detail recorded in business journals. Instead, Mr. Browne's sporadic references to involvement in drug distribution include thoughts that he was "scared" when he took the boat (Diary at 9), and his fear that his girlfriend will discover his activities (Diary at 14). Such entries do not remotely resemble the day-to-day records of the operations and financial condition of a "sophisticated marijuana growing facility," as did the day-timers in *Mason*.

CONCLUSION

A diary is the quintessential personal paper that strikes at the very heart of our sense of privacy. Because Mr. Browne uses his diary for the purpose of recording his most intimate thoughts and feelings, it is protected from compelled disclosure by the Fifth Amendment. Therefore, the Defendant, Mr. Browne, respectfully requests that this Court enter an order quashing the Government's subpoena of Mr. Browne's personal diary.

Appendix E

SAMPLE APPELLATE COURT BRIEF

CRIMINAL WIRETAP PROBLEM

UNITED STATES COURT OF APPEALS
FOR THE TWELFTH CIRCUIT[1]

No. 99-769

UNITED STATES OF AMERICA,

Plaintiff-Appellee,

v.

JAMES HART,

Defendant-Appellant.

BRIEF FOR APPELLANT

---

1. This is a mythical circuit.

TABLE OF CONTENTS

TABLE OF AUTHORITIES

STATEMENT OF JURISDICTION

This Court has jurisdiction over this appeal pursuant to 28 U.S.C. § 1291.

STATEMENT OF THE ISSUES

I. The District Court erred in finding that, as part of the Government's "satisfactory explanation" for its two-month delay in obtaining a judicial seal of wiretap evidence, the Government need not prove that its pre-sealing procedures protected the tapes from any possibility of tampering, which would afford the same level of protection as an immediate judicial seal would have provided.

II. The District Court erred in finding that the Government provided a "satisfactory explanation" for its sealing delay when the Government lost the tapes for two months, only to find the tapes in an open box in an office supply room, and the Government can neither account for the tapes' whereabouts for the two-month period in which they were missing or explain why the box of tapes had been opened.

STATUTE INVOLVED

18 U.S.C. § 2518 (8)(a) provides as follows:

> (8) (a) The contents of any wire, oral, or electronic communication intercepted by any means authorized by this chapter shall, if possible, be recorded on tape or wire or other comparable device. The recording of the contents of any wire, oral, or electronic communication under this subsection shall be done in such way as will protect the recording from editing or other alterations. Immediately upon the expiration of the period of the order, or extensions thereof, such recordings shall be made available to the judge issuing such order and sealed under his directions. Custody of the recordings shall be wherever the judge orders. They shall not be destroyed except upon an order of the issuing or denying judge and in any event shall be kept for ten years. Duplicate recordings may be made for use or disclosure pursuant to the provisions of subsections (1) and (2) of section 2517 of this chapter for investigations. The presence of the seal provided for by this subsection, or a satisfactory explanation for the absence thereof, shall be a prerequisite for the use or disclosure of the contents of any wire, oral, or electronic communication or evidence derived therefrom under subsection (3) of section 2517.

PRELIMINARY STATEMENT

The Defendant, Mr. James Hart, appeals from a conviction under 18 U.S.C. § 371. Before trial, Mr. Hart moved to suppress the Government's sole evidence against him on the ground that the Government failed to comply with the mandatory requirements of the federal wiretap statute. 18 U.S.C. § 2518 (8)(a). The Government had failed to obtain an immediate judicial seal of the wiretap evidence. Mr. Hart alleged that the Government failed to provide a "satisfactory explanation" for its sealing delay, as required by 18 U.S.C. § 2518 (8)(a). The District Court denied that motion and later convicted Mr. Hart of violating 18 U.S.C. § 371. Mr. Hart appeals the lower court's denial of his motion to suppress the wiretap evidence and the conviction based on that evidence. The opinion of the District Court is unreported and appears in the Transcript of Record (R. 22–26).

<u>STATEMENT OF THE CASE</u>

Defendant, Mr. James Hart, is an accountant for many small businesses, including Oak Hill Dry Cleaning. (R. at 5.) Oak Hill Dry Cleaning is owned by individuals the Government believes to be members of the Desperado crime syndicate. On August 11, 2020, the lower court granted authorization to intercept Mr. Hart's home telephone for a period not to exceed thirty (30) days.

On September 6 and 7, the Government obtained the tapes it later used as the sole evidence of Mr. Hart's culpability. (R. at 9.) On September 7, 2020, Agent T. Friday removed the tapes from the surveillance van parked near Mr. Hart's home and took them to the investigating bureau's office. (R. at 10.) Although Agent Friday was aware that the Bureau was moving offices the next day, she dropped the tapes in a plain cardboard box identical to the thousands of cardboard boxes used for the move. (R. at 10.) Agent Friday also testified that she placed a label on the box indicating that the box was to be transported to the courthouse. (R. at 10.) In contrast, the building janitor testified that no label appeared on the box of tapes. (R. at 14.) The Government cannot explain this factual discrepancy. (R. at 15.) Finally, although Agent Friday testified that she sealed the box of tapes (R. at 10.), the building janitor testified that the box of tapes "was open. You could look right in and see what was inside." (R. at 14.)

For more than a month after the Bureau moved offices, Agent Friday never telephoned or appeared at the courthouse to ensure the tapes arrived for sealing. (R. at 11.) Agent Friday never asked the court clerk to confirm whether a judge had sealed the tapes. (R. at 11.) And, despite the fact that Agent Friday had no responsibilities other than this case during this entire time period, Agent Friday did not make a single attempt to locate her only evidence in this case. (R. at 12.)

It was not until October 10, 2020, that Agent Friday finally called the courthouse to inquire whether the tapes had been sealed. (R. at 12.) It was not until then that Agent Friday began searching for the missing tapes. Although Agent Friday testified that she undertook an intensive search of the office building and personally called the movers (R. at 12), nearly a month elapsed before Agent Friday was able to locate the tapes. It was not until November 8, 2020, that Agent Friday finally stumbled upon the missing tapes while looking for party decorations. (R. at 13.) The Government speculates that the tapes sat exposed in an open box in the unlocked office supply room for over two months. (R. at 13.) The exposed tapes sat in the busy supply room amidst note pads, pencils, office supplies, and party decorations, open to the 5,000 occupants of the building who frequent the room for coffee and office supplies. (R. at 14.)

SUMMARY OF ARGUMENT

The evidence obtained by the Government from a wiretap on Mr. Hart's home telephone is inadmissible at trial because the Government failed to comply with the requirements of the wiretap statute. The District Court therefore erred in denying Mr. Hart's motion to suppress the wiretap evidence. The wiretap statute requires the Government to safeguard the tapes by immediately obtaining a judicial seal or by providing a "satisfactory explanation" for its failure to do so. 18 U.S.C. § 2518 (8)(a). In this case, the Government failed to comply with its statutory obligation. After intercepting private telephone conversations from Mr. Hart's home telephone, the Government failed to surrender the tapes immediately to a judge, who could have protected the tapes' integrity with a judicial seal. The Government also failed to provide a "satisfactory explanation" for its failure to seek immediate judicial protection.

A "satisfactory explanation" requires that the Government satisfy two standards. First, a "satisfactory explanation" requires the Government to prove that its pre-sealing procedures protected the tapes from any possibility of tampering. Congress enacted the immediate sealing requirement as an external safeguard to ensure that the integrity of wiretap tapes would remain inviolate.

Therefore, when the Government fails to protect the integrity of the tapes by immediately obtaining the protection of a judicial seal, its alternative explanation must ensure a similar level of protection. With today's modern technology, tapes can easily be altered without detection by even skilled experts. Thus, requiring the Government to prove that its pre-sealing procedures protected the tapes from any possibility of tampering is the only effective means of protecting the integrity of wiretap evidence. Here, the Government wholly failed to provide any level of protection to its sensitive evidence. Instead, the wiretap tapes sat exposed in an open box in a busy, unlocked storage room for over two months. The box sat exposed, available to any one of the 5,000 occupants of the building, or any visitor to the storage room, who might be tempted to tamper with the tapes.

Second, a "satisfactory explanation" requires that the Government act with reasonable diligence to minimize the sealing delay. Again, the Government's conduct falls far short of this standard. The sealing delay was caused by a mistake, a mistake that was not only foreseeable but easily preventable. Although the Government knew that its bureau offices would be moving the following day, Agent Friday failed to take any precautions to ensure that the tapes would be safely delivered to the courthouse for sealing. Instead, she dropped the tapes into a box identical to the thousands of moving boxes used to move office files and supplies. To compound that initial carelessness, Agent Friday delayed over a month before she placed a single telephone call to ensure that the tapes had arrived at the courthouse for sealing. Upon finding the tapes were missing, it took Agent Friday almost another full month to locate the tapes, despite the fact that she ultimately found them in an open box in an office supply room. The Government's lengthy delay in obtaining the protection of a judicial seal violates the mandatory provisions of Title III, 18 U.S.C. § 2518(8)(a).

ARGUMENT

I. AS PART OF ITS "SATISFACTORY EXPLANATION," THE GOVERN-MENT MUST PROVE THAT ITS PRE-SEALING PROCEDURES PRO-TECTED THE WIRETAP TAPES FROM ANY POSSIBILITY OF TAM-PERING.

Title III states in no uncertain terms: "The presence of the seal as provided for by this subsection [an immediate seal], or a satisfactory explanation for the absence thereof, shall be a *prerequisite* for the use or disclosure" of the tapes. 18 U.S.C. § 2518(8) (a) (emphasis added). In this issue of first impression, the plain language of Title III requires that the Government comply with one of two procedures as a "prerequisite" to introducing wiretap tapes into evidence during trial. Concerned with the abuse of electronic surveillance techniques, Congress enacted the first prerequisite, the imme-diate sealing requirement, as an external safeguard to ensure that the integrity of wiretap tapes would remain inviolate. When the Government fails to protect the in-tegrity of the tapes by immediately obtaining a judicial seal, the Government's alter-native satisfactory explanation must ensure a similar level of protection. Whether the Government satisfies the legislative requirement of obtaining an immediate seal, or takes the scenic route to obtain the seal, the Government must prove that its *proce-dures* protected the integrity of the tapes. Without such a safeguard, the statutory protective device of immediate judicial supervision would be rendered meaningless. *United States v. Johnson*, 696 F.2d 115 (D.C. Cir. 1981). Accordingly, the District Court erred in failing to require the Government to prove that its pre-sealing procedures protected the tapes from any possibility of tampering. As a pure question of law, this issue is subject to de novo review.

When Congress enacted Title III, it sought to ensure that the purity of the gathered evidence would remain unsullied. This purpose is clearly reflected in the statutory language itself. Section (8)(a) provides that interceptions of conversations must be accomplished "in such way as will protect the recording from editing or other alter-ations." 18 U.S.C. § 2518(8)(a). The Congressional intent expressed in that language could not be clearer. Congress enacted Title III to protect the integrity of evidence that might be used as evidence in a criminal trial. *See also United States v. Sklaroff*, 506 F.2d 837, 840 (5th Cir. 1975) (noting that the purpose of Section 2518(8)(a) "is to safeguard the recordings from editing or alteration").

The legislative history also reflects this clear and unequivocal Congressional pur-pose. "Preservation of the integrity of tape recordings was unquestionably a funda-mental concern of the drafters of Title III." *United States v. Gigante*, 538 F.2d 502, 505 (2d Cir. 1976). When Congress enacted Title III's detailed restrictions on electronic surveillance, it "intended to ensure 'careful judicial scrutiny throughout' the process of intercepting and utilization of such evidence." *Id.* (quoting *United States v. Marion*, 535 F.2d 697, 698 (2d Cir. 1976)). The Senate Reports noted that, because of the "widespread use and abuse of electronic surveillance techniques," Congress enacted this statute to "safeguard the identity, physical integrity, and contents of the recordings to assure their admissibility in evidence." S. Rep. No. 1097, 90th Cong., 2d Sess. 2193 (1968), *reprinted in* 1968 U.S. Code Cong. & Admin. News 2193.

Maintenance of the integrity of such evidence is an integral part of the Congressional plan to "limit the use of intercept procedures to those situations clearly calling for the employment of this extraordinary investigative device." *United States v. Giordano*, 416 U.S. 505, 527 (1974). Thus, Section 2518 plays a "central role in the statutory scheme." *Id.* at 528. *See also United States v. Chavez*, 416 U.S. 562 (1974); *United States v. Diana*, 605 F.2d 1307, 1312 (4th Cir. 1979) (observing that Section 2518 "is a central or functional safeguard in Title III's scheme to prevent abuses….'") (quoting *United States v. Chun*, 503 F.2d 533, 542 (9th Cir.1974)). "Clearly all of the carefully planned strictures on the conduct of electronic surveillance, e. g., the "minimization" requirement of Section 2518(5), would be unavailing if no reliable records existed of the conversations which were, in fact, overheard." *Gigante*, 538 F.2d at 505.

By requiring the immediate sealing of wiretap evidence, Congress sought to protect the purity of that evidence. After sealing, the records become "confidential court records," and cannot be unsealed without a court order. S. Rep. 1097, 90th Cong., 2d Sess. 2193 (1968), *reprinted in* 1968 U.S. Code Cong. & Ad. News 2193. The statutory requirement of judicial supervision therefore creates a procedural assumption of integrity because the judicial seal ensures the tapes were handled in a manner that precludes any possibility of tampering. *United States v. Johnson*, 696 F.2d 115, 123 (D.C. Cir. 1981). Thus, the immediate sealing requirement serves as an external, procedural safeguard against tampering.

Only procedural safeguards can ensure that the integrity of sensitive wiretap evidence remains inviolate. Procedural safeguards are necessary because tape-recorded evidence is highly vulnerable to tampering and is cost-prohibitive to prove. In fact, with modern technology, it is often impossible to detect. *Id.* at 124. As the court in *Johnson* observed:

> Tapes that are made for use in criminal investigations can be falsified, even by relatively unskilled persons, in ways that are superficially convincing…. Such alterations, moreover, are likely to go undetected because a highly skilled forensic examiner who is an expert in the fields of tape recording, signal analysis, and speech communication, using the best available analysis equipment, can take weeks and even months to establish with reasonable certainty the fact that a tape has been falsified. The advantage, in terms of effort, time and cost is clearly with the forger.

Id.

Congress carefully incorporated external safeguards within the Statute to avoid the costly, time-consuming, and inconclusive expert inquiries that inevitably result from fact-finding expeditions. *Id.* By proving it held the tapes in a manner that ensures their integrity remained inviolate, the Government's satisfactory explanation not only affords the level of protection of an immediate seal but avoids the problems Congress sought to avoid.

Finally, fairness mandates that the Government bear this burden. "Inasmuch as a need for a 'satisfactory explanation' only arises when those in charge of the wiretap operation fail to do their homework and to present the tapes for immediate sealing, any doubts about the integrity of the evidence should be laid at law enforcement's doorstep." *United States v. Mora*, 821 F.2d 860, 868 (1st Cir. 1987). Therefore, the District Court committed reversible error by declining to compel the Government to prove that its procedures safeguarded its evidence from any possibility of tampering.

II. THE GOVERNMENT FAILED TO PROVIDE A "SATISFACTORY EX-PLANATION" FOR ITS TWO-MONTH DELAY IN SEALING THE WIRETAP TAPES.

The Government has failed to provide the statutorily-mandated "satisfactory explanation" in this case. A satisfactory explanation requires both that the Government's pre-filing procedures ensured the tapes' integrity, *United States v. Johnson*, 696 F.2d 115 (D.C. Cir. 1976), and that it acted with reasonable diligence to obtain the required judicial safeguard, *United States v. Gigante*, 538 F.2d 502, 505 (2d Cir. 1976). These standards are necessary to implement the procedural safeguards reflected in Section 2518(8)(a). As the United States Supreme Court cautioned, "Congress intended to require suppression where there is failure to satisfy any of those statutory requirements that directly and substantially implement the congressional intention to limit the use of intercept procedures…." *United States v. Giordano*, 416 U.S. 505, 527 (1974). Here, the Government has not satisfied either prerequisite of a "satisfactory explanation." Therefore, the District Court erred in refusing to suppress the wiretap evidence.

A. *The Government Failed to Store the Tapes in a Manner that Protected Them from Any Possibility of Tampering.*

When the Government fails to obtain an immediate judicial seal, it must store the tapes in a manner that ensures their integrity. Mere governmental knowledge of the tapes' whereabouts does not even begin to rise to the level of protection required. Instead, the Government ensures the tapes' integrity by placing its *own* physical seal on the tapes, *United States v. Diana*, 605 F.2d 1307 (4th Cir. 1979), and by limiting access to the tapes to authorized personnel, either by appointing a custodian to guard the tapes, and/or by placing the tapes in a limited access vault. *United States v. Mora*, 821 F.2d 860, 868 (1st Cir. 1987). Here, the Government failed to take any such precautions to secure the tapes' integrity. In fact, the Government not only has no idea where the tapes were stored during the two-month period in which they were lost, but has no explanation for why the box was found open and without an identifying seal. The Government's failure to secure the tapes' integrity falls far short of the required satisfactory explanation.

Only by instituting procedures that preclude any possibility that the tapes might be compromised can the Government satisfactorily explain its sealing delay. For example, the Government can ensure the integrity of tapes by placing its own seal on the tapes. *United States v. Diana*, 605 F.2d 1307 (4th Cir. 1979). A physical seal, if broken, provides a visual warning that someone has attempted to tamper with the evidence. In *Diana*, the government initialed and affixed seals to each of the envelopes containing wiretap evidence. *Id.* at 1310-11. An FBI agent ensured that each of the envelopes had a piece of Scotch tape over at least one of his initials placed on the back of the envelope. "The purpose of this procedure was that if anyone would attempt to get inside the envelope, not only would they tear the envelope… they [would] break the seal where my initials were…. I felt there was [no] way anyone could break that seal without me seeing it…." *Id.* at 1315–16. Under these facts, the court held that the government's precautions were "satisfactory." *Id.* at 1316. The court reasoned that the government's precautions ensured that the tapes' integrity remained inviolate. Even with these procedures, the court admonished the government "to be more careful in the future," noting that its "opinion should not be read as a license to disregard the sealing requirement." *Id.*

Further, the Government can adequately safeguard the integrity of wiretap tapes by instituting strict security procedures, such as guarding the tapes or locking them within a locked vault. In *United States v. Mora*, the government designated a Massachusetts State Policeman as custodian of the tapes. 821 F.2d 860, 862 (1st Cir. 1987). The trooper placed the tapes in a cardboard box, closed the box, and signed it. He then sealed the box within a plastic bag. The trooper originally kept the bag at a listening post, which was staffed and guarded twenty-four hours a day. After two weeks, he removed the tapes and placed them in a locked vault that was accessible only to limited, authorized personnel. The vault was equipped with an alarm system. Id. Under these facts, the court could not find "any scintilla of evidence" that the tapes could have been tampered with, even after "scour[ing] the record, searching in vain for any intimation that the content of the tapes was compromised." *Id.* at 869. *See also United States v. Johnson*, 696 F.2d 115 (D.C. Cir. 1976) (tapes stored in a locked vault with access limited to authorized personnel).

In stark contrast to the government's strict security measures in *Diana*, *Mora*, and *Johnson*, the Government in the present case took absolutely no precautions to secure the tapes in a manner that ensured their integrity would remain inviolate. Unlike the government precautions in *Diana*, the Government not only failed to secure the individual tapes in protective envelopes, but Agent Friday may have failed to take even the most elementary precaution of sealing the box itself so that casual observers could not gain access to this sensitive evidence. Although Agent Friday testified that she sealed the box (R. at 10.), the building janitor testified the box "was open. You could look right in and see what was inside." (R. at 14.) The Government has not explained this factual discrepancy. If, indeed, Agent Friday never sealed the box itself, then the box containing the Government's sensitive evidence was left open to public view for a period of two months. The entire group of tapes purportedly sat, exposed, in an open box in an unlocked storage room amidst party decorations and office supplies. The tapes sat in that open box for over two months. In vivid contrast to the locked vaults with limited access in *Mora* and *Johnson*, the storage room was unlocked and easily accessible to the 5,000 occupants of the building who had reason to frequent this room for coffee, office supplies, and party decorations.

If, however, Agent Friday did seal and label the box, as she testified, then the fact that it was later found, open and without a label, raises the troubling possibility that the security of the tapes was in fact compromised. In *Diana*, *Mora*, and *Johnson*, because of the government's strict security procedures, after "scouring" the record, the courts found that there was no intimation or "scintilla of evidence" that the tapes could possibly have been compromised. In glaring contrast, the Government in the present case has not and cannot explain why the box of tapes was later found open and without a label. This factual discrepancy raises the ominous possibility that an unidentified individual opened the box and tampered with the tapes. In fact, any one of the 5,000 occupants of the building, or any visitor to the office supply room, could have removed the tapes from their box and tampered with them. Having failed to obtain an immediate judicial seal, the external safeguard against tampering, the Government wholly failed to ensure that the tapes' integrity remained inviolate during its two-month delay. The Government's total failure to explain the tapes' whereabouts during its two-month delay does not rise to the level of a "satisfactory explanation." Accordingly, the District Court erred in refusing to suppress the tapes.

B. *The Government Failed to Act with Reasonable Diligence.*

Even when the Government stores tapes in a manner that protects their integrity, its explanation is not "satisfactory" unless it acts with reasonable diligence to obtain a judicial seal. *United States v. Vazquez*, 605 F.2d 1269 (2d Cir. 1979). Governmental mistake, even innocent mistake, does not constitute reasonable diligence. *United States v. Gigante*, 538 F.2d 502, 505 (2d Cir. 1976). The Government acts with reasonable diligence only when the delay is caused by legitimate law enforcement purposes and the Government diligently acts to minimize the delay in obtaining the judicial seal. Here, the delay was caused by no legitimate law enforcement purpose. Moreover, the Government's initial mistake in losing the tapes in the first place is exacerbated by its failure to minimize the delay. It was the Government's own inattention and neglect that caused the two-month sealing delay. The Government's carelessness and neglect does not rise to the level of reasonable diligence.

Inattention to governmental files does not constitute reasonable diligence. In *Gigante*, the government's only explanation for its delay in obtaining a judicial seal was that the agent in charge of the files left the government's employ. 538 F.2d at 504. The new agent was unaware the tapes had not received a judicial seal until one year later. *Id*. Even though the tapes had been stored in a locked cabinet under agency seal prior to receiving judicial attention, the court held that the government failed to provide a satisfactory explanation for its sealing delay. *Id*. at 505.

The court reasoned that the government's "explanation" for its mistake was "no explanation whatsoever." *Id*. at 504. Mere mistake does not constitute reasonable diligence, even with a change in personnel. In so holding, the court emphasized the importance of the immediate sealing requirement as "an integral part of this statutory scheme." *Id*. at 505. The court cautioned that "[m]aintenance of the integrity of such evidence is part and parcel of the Congressional plan to 'limit the use of intercept procedures to those situations clearly calling for the employment of this extraordinary investigative device.'" *Id*. (citing *United States v. Giordano*, 416 U.S. 505, 527 (1974)).

A government's explanation is "satisfactory" only when the delay is caused by legitimate law enforcement purposes and the government diligently acts to minimize the sealing delay. For example, in *Vazquez*, the government's delay in obtaining a judicial seal was caused by its difficulty in transcribing the tapes. 605 F.2d at 1279. Most of the conversations on the 200 tapes were in Spanish, requiring translation. Even with limited equipment, a limited number of Spanish-speaking agents, and a lack of sufficient personnel to handle the scope of the investigation, the government nevertheless worked to minimize the sealing delay. *Id*. Working around the clock, the government submitted the tapes for sealing after a delay of only one to two weeks. *Id*. at 1274. The court accepted the government's explanation as "satisfactory," noting the government's legitimate law enforcement purposes and its diligence in attempting to produce the tapes as quickly as possible. *Id*. at 1279. The court emphasized that government personnel worked diligently *around the clock* to comply with the Statute (as well as using strict security measures to ensure their integrity). Even then, the court cautioned the government about its one to two week delays:

> However, in law as in life, today's satisfactory explanation may very well be tomorrow's lame excuse. As the federal and state case law in this area grows, the failure to foresee and where possible, prevent sealing delays becomes less justifiable, as law enforcement officials must be expected to learn from their own experiences and those of others.... It is our role to exclude from evidence tapes not sealed in conformance with the law, and we are aware that by faithfully performing this statutory duty we encourage law enforcement officers to perform their duties in an equally rigorous manner.

Id. at 1280.

Tomorrow has arrived. And the Government's "lame excuse" does not even approach the level of rigor and diligence required by the Statute. In vivid contrast to the government's one- to two-week delay in *Vazquez* caused by a legitimate law enforcement purpose, the Government's only explanation for its two-*month* delay in the present case is that it made a "mistake" and lost the box of tapes in the confusion of an office move. As the *Gigante* court aptly noted, the Government's mistake is "no excuse whatsoever." In fact, the Government's lack of diligence far exceeds the level of carelessness in *Gigante*. Unlike the agent in *Gigante*, who left the government's employ, Agent Friday assumed full responsibility for the Government's evidence from the time the Government obtained the tapes to the time she finally stumbled upon them. In fact, this case was Agent Friday's *only* responsibility during that time period.

Agent Friday failed to act with reasonable diligence in losing the tapes in the first place. Agent Friday was well aware that the 5,000 occupants of the building were moving the next day. However, she failed to take the extra precautions required in anticipation of such a move. Notably, Agent Friday failed to place the tapes in a secured, locked, and labeled file cabinet that would survive the move to the new building. Nor did she appoint a custodian to personally transport this sensitive evidence to the courthouse. Instead, she dropped the tapes in a box identical to the thousands of boxes used to move office supplies. And, although Agent Friday testified that she sealed the box (R. at 10.), the box was open when discovered two months later. If the box of tapes was not later opened by an unknown individual, then Agent Friday failed to take even the most elementary precaution of sealing the box itself so that tapes could not be inadvertently tossed out of the box during the chaos of the move (or intentionally removed by any one of thousands of persons who had access to the open box). Finally, if the label Agent Friday testified that she placed on the box was not somehow removed from the box, the only alternative explanation for its absence is that Agent Friday never labeled the box in the first place. Any such failure to label the box would only exacerbate her lack of diligence in tossing the tapes into an open box identical to thousands of moving boxes.

Agent Friday also failed to act with diligence in locating the lost tapes. Despite her knowledge of the office move, Agent Friday waited a full month before taking even the elementary precaution of placing a telephone call to ensure that the government's critical evidence arrived at the courthouse. Not until October 10, 2020, did Agent Friday finally call the courthouse to inquire whether the tapes had been sealed. It was not until after that telephone call that Agent Friday begin searching for the missing tapes, and it was not until nearly a month later when, on November 8, 2020, Agent Friday finally stumbled upon the missing tapes while looking for party decorations. (R. at 12.) The Government speculates that the tapes sat exposed in an open box in the unlocked storage room for over two months. (R. at 12.) This highly sensitive evidence sat, openly exposed, in a busy storage room amidst note pads, pencils, office supplies and party decorations, open to the 5,000 occupants of the building who frequent the room for coffee and office supplies.

CONCLUSION

Because the Government neither acted with reasonable diligence to minimize its two-month sealing delay, nor protected the tapes from any possibility of tampering, Defendant requests that the judgment of the District Court be reversed and remanded with instructions to the District Court to grant Defendant's motion to suppress the wiretap tapes.

Respectfully submitted,

DATED: _____   _____

Attorney for Defendant/Appellant

CERTIFICATE OF SERVICE

I, _____, do hereby certify that I have this date served a true and correct copy of the Appellant's Brief upon counsel for the Appellee by placing a true and correct copy of the Appellant's Brief in the United States mail, with sufficient postage affixed, and addressed as follows:

William Schultz, Esq.
125 Sonoma Blvd.
Crichton, [State]

Dated this _____ day of _____, 20XX.

_____

Attorney for Defendant/Appellant

SAMPLE LETTERS

SAMPLE SETTLEMENT LETTER

CERTIFIED MAIL
RETURN RECEIPT REQUESTED

November 15, 20XX

Ms. Liza Capshaw
2811 Windemere
Ft. Lauderdale, FL

<u>CONFIDENTIAL SETTLEMENT COMMUNICATION</u>

Re: *McLean v. Hurt*

Dear Ms. Capshaw:

I represent Mr. and Mrs. McLean in the lawsuit they have recently filed against your clients in which they seek damages for the death of their young child. They are understandably anxious to seek full recovery under the law following the drowning death of their child in your clients' man-made pond. However, to avoid protracted litigation, my clients are willing to allow me to explore settlement possibilities. My clients have authorized me to make the following offer: they will agree to dismiss this suit if your clients remit payment in the sum of $1,500,000. This offer will remain open until 5:00 p.m. on December 1, 20XX. This letter is intended as a confidential settlement communication pursuant to Rule 408 of the Federal Rules of Evidence and Rule 1-14.1 of the Florida Evidence Code. As such, it will not be admissible in the above proceeding, or any other proceeding, for any purpose.

As you are probably aware, on May 28, 20XX, my clients' young son drowned in the Hurts' pond. Although your clients knew that young children enjoyed feeding the ducks on their pond, they left town for the holiday weekend, leaving the gate to the pond unlocked, and the dock in a state of disrepair. Their actions in leaving this attractive nuisance accessible to young children is even more troublesome in light of the fact that they knew the dock was dangerous and in need of repair. Yet they had delayed the long-needed repairs. Mikey McLean drowned in the Hurts' pond after the dock collapsed under his slight weight.

Under Florida law, the Hurts are liable for Mikey's death under the doctrine of attractive nuisance. For over forty years, a long line of Florida courts have consistently held landowners liable for the injuries sustained by child trespassers when the landowners leave a dangerous condition on their property and have reason to believe that children attracted to the dangerous condition will trespass onto the property. *See, e.g., Ansin v. Thurston*, 98 So. 2d 87 (Fla. Dist. Ct. App. 1957); *Samson v. O'Hara*, 239 So. 2d 151 (Fla. Dist. Ct. App. 1970).

Here, the combination of the Hurts' dilapidated dock, the man-made pond, and the ducks that swam in the pond, was dangerous and yet inviting and attractive to small children. The Hurts both knew the dock was dilapidated and dangerous, and knew that children from the neighboring elementary school trespassed onto their dock to feed the ducks. Yet they left this attractive nuisance open and accessible to children while they left town for the long holiday weekend.

The Hurts' liability under Florida law is clear. If this case is tried, the jury will not be focused on liability, but on the amount of damages to award the parents of their only child—a six-year-old son. After evaluating Florida law, I think you will agree that our $1,500,000 settlement offer is more than reasonable.

Our offer remains open until 5:00 p.m. on December 1, 20XX. If I do not hear from you by then, I will be in touch with you to schedule depositions.

Sincerely,

Beth Manning

Beth Manning

SAMPLE DEMAND LETTER

July 20, 20XX

CERTIFIED MAIL
RETURN RECEIPT REQUESTED

The Bancroft Corporation
c/o Thomas Jones, President
1128 Madison Avenue, Suite 120
New York, New York 2002

Dear Mr. Jones,

This firm represents Suartez and Associates (the "Landlord"). The Bancroft Corporation (the "Tenant"), is in default of its obligations under a Lease Agreement by and between the Landlord and Tenant, dated April 10, 20XX (the "Lease"). Rent is due and owing for the months of June and July 20XX in the amount of Fifteen Thousand Two Hundred Sixty-Five Dollars and Fifty-Eight Cents ($15,265.58) per month, as required under Paragraph 4 of the Lease, together with late charges in the amount of One Thousand Three Hundred Fifty-Six Dollars and Fifty Cents ($1,356.50), required pursuant to paragraph 15(c) of the Lease.

If Tenant does not pay to Landlord the sum of Thirty-One Thousand Eight Hundred Eighty-Seven Dollars and Sixty-Six Cents ($31,887.66) by 5:00 p.m. on July 28, 20XX, the Landlord intends to exercise its rights and remedies under the Lease. These rights and remedies include, but are not limited to, terminating the Lease, instituting suit for recovery of possession of the leased premises, and recovering all damages incurred by the Landlord as a result of this default, including legal fees.

Sincerely,

Joe Litton

Joseph Litton

cc: [client]

INDEX